69291039

MUCKAMORE ABBEY HOSPITAL
LIBRARY *

Identification and Treatment
of Alcohol Dependency

**This book is to be returned on or before
the last date stamped below.**

Identification
Treatment of
Alcohol Dependency

LIBREX

MUCKAMORE ABBEY HOSPITAL LIBRARY *

D1340592

OTHER HEALTH & SOCIAL CARE BOOKS FROM M&K:

The Clinician's Guide to Chronic Disease Management for Long-Term Conditions: A Cognitive–Behavioural Approach
ISBN: 978-1-905539-15-4 • 2008

Pre-Teen and Teenage Pregnancy: A 21st Century Reality
ISBN: 978-1-905539-11-6 • 2007

Inter-Professional Approaches to Young Fathers
ISBN: 978-1-905539-29-1 • 2008

Routine Blood Results Explained (2/e)
ISBN: 978-1-905539-38-3 • 2007

The Management of COPD in Primary and Secondary Care
ISBN: 978-1-905539-28-4 • 2007

Living with Dying: Perspectives on Death, Dying and Living with Loss
ISBN: 978-1-905539-21-5 • Forthcoming 2008

Identification and Treatment of Alcohol Dependency

Edited by

Colin R. Martin RN BSc PhD YCAP CPsychol CSci AFBPsS

Chair in Mental Health, University of the West of Scotland, Ayr, Scotland

01254133

Identification and Treatment of Alcohol Dependency
Edited by Colin R. Martin
ISBN: 978-1-905539-16-1
First published 2008

All rights reserved. No part of this publication may be reproduced, stored in a retrieval system, or transmitted in any form or by any means, electronic, mechanical, photocopying, recording or otherwise, without either the prior permission of the publishers or a licence permitting restricted copying in the United Kingdom issued by the Copyright Licensing Agency, 90 Tottenham Court Road, London, W1T 4LP. Permissions may be sought directly from M&K Publishing, phone: 01768 773030, fax: 01768 781099 or email: publishing@mkupdate.co.uk

Any person who does any unauthorised act in relation to this publication may be liable to criminal prosecution and civil claims for damages.

British Library Catalogue in Publication Data
A catalogue record for this book is available from the British Library

Notice
Clinical practice and medical knowledge constantly evolve. Standard safety precautions must be followed, but, as knowledge is broadened by research, changes in practice, treatment and drug therapy may become necessary or appropriate. Readers must check the most current product information provided by the manufacturer of each drug to be administered and verify the dosages and correct administration, as well as contraindications. It is the responsibility of the practitioner, utilising the experience and knowledge of the patient, to determine dosages and the best treatment for each individual patient. Any brands mentioned in this book are as examples only and are not endorsed by the Publisher. Neither the Publisher nor the author(s) assume any liability for any injury and/or damage to persons or property arising from this publication.

The Publisher
To contact M&K Publishing write to:
M&K Update Ltd · The Old Bakery · St. John's Street
Keswick · Cumbria CA12 5AS
Tel: 01768 773030 · Fax: 01768 781099
publishing@mkupdate.co.uk
www.mkupdate.co.uk

Designed and typeset in 11/13 Candara by S. Maria Hampshire.
Cover and graphics by Luke Kelsey.
Printed in England by Reed's Printers Ltd.

- 7 SEP 2009

Dedication

This book is dedicated to
my wife Dr Caroline Hollins Martin,
my daughter Miss Caragh Brien,
and my mother and father.

Contents

Contents

Part Five: Clients with complex needs

Part Six: Reproductive and developmental concerns

Foreword

For many years the identification and treatment of alcohol dependency have been seen by healthcare professionals as being firmly lodged within the agenda of mental health nurses, psychiatrists and the voluntary sector. As any GP, practice nurse, member of the emergency services or midwife will tell you, this is no longer true.

The misuse of alcohol is causing significant problems for modern society. Alcohol misuse is seen as a primary cause of childhood poverty and child abuse, of teenage antisocial behaviour, unplanned pregnancies, underweight and brain-damaged babies, chronic ill health, premature death, malnutrition, long-term mental health problems and aggressive behaviour. It is linked to obesity, family breakdown and unemployment and it can lead to drug abuse and criminal behaviour patterns. Its misuse affects not only the individual and his or her family but also wider society. And the cost of misuse to the police and NHS social services bill is staggering.

Every day, professionals are faced with patients and clients who are affected in one way or another by alcohol misuse and abuse.

One problem we all face is a lack of information. In order to provide the best support possible we all need to understand every aspect of the complex picture that surrounds those who seek help and support. Many of these people have complex histories, sometimes complicated by misrepresentation. They often forget to take prescribed medication, have abnormal nutritional patterns and are constantly aggressive, even to their best friends. They are damaged physically, psychologically and socially. They may have an underlying pathological condition such as diabetes, asthma or AIDS that is made worse by alcohol, and they may be homeless or poorly housed. Very often, textbooks offer a mere chapter or two on this complex and wide-ranging problem, and fail to address the 'bigger picture'.

Colin Martin has brought together an excellent set of contributors to produce a truly comprehensive text that will ensure all interested professionals can not only update their knowledge but also better understand each other's roles and how best to help patients and clients through shared working to achieve a common goal of better health. This book is not just for people who see themselves as having a primary role in the field, but also for those – teachers, the police and family members – who live daily with its effects.

Professor Dame Betty Kershaw
University of Sheffield, UK

Acknowledgements

I would like to thank all those clinicians and academics who have generously contributed chapters to this book. The insights of these esteemed professionals in the field highlight the myriad of complex interacting factors that contribute to the significant issues surrounding and defining alcohol dependency. I would also like especially to thank two long-term research partners in the alcohol field – Professor Victor Preedy at King's College London and Dr Adrian Bonner at the University of Kent at Canterbury – for their friendship and collaboration over the past decade; our work together has always been a source of great pleasure to me.

I am also very grateful to Professor Dame Betty Kershaw at the University of Sheffield and Professor Cynthia McDougall O.B.E. at the University of York for their support and confidence in my academic work over the years, this book being one of the end-points.

My best friends – Phil Hutchins, Dr Mark Newberry, Dr Suzy Newberry, Julie Robbins and Peter Robbins – have also indirectly contributed to the production of this book by their enduring enthusiasm, interest and support of my work.

Thanks are also due to Mike Roberts at M&K Update for his support for the book and to Maria Hampshire for guiding it smoothly through the publication process.

Finally, I would like to acknowledge and thank the many clients and patients I have had the privilege of working with clinically over the past 20 years in the addictions field.

Colin Martin
October 2008

About the Editor

Professor Colin R. Martin is Chair in Mental Health at the University of the West of Scotland and Adjunct Professor at the Royal Melbourne Institute of Technology (RMIT) University, Melbourne, Australia. Professor Martin is a Chartered Health Psychologist and a Chartered Scientist. Having originally trained in psychiatric nursing, he specialised in the addictions field and, following further training, worked as a community psychiatric nurse and then as an addictions counsellor in the NHS. On completion of his BSc and PhD degrees in psychology, Professor Martin worked in senior management posts in the NHS, followed by academic posts in the UK and the Far East, during which he conducted original research in both addiction and the mental health aspects of chronic disease. He has published many scientific papers in psychology, biology, and medical and nursing journals. Professor Martin is Honorary Consultant Psychologist to The Salvation Army Ethics Committee, UK and Eire Territories and was instrumental in formulating the addictions policy of the Salvation Army (UK and Eire) over recent years to develop high-quality and evidence-based clinical care and services.

Professor Martin was brought up in East London and is currently living in Scotland. He is married to Caroline and has one daughter, Caragh. He is a qualified pilot who enjoys flying, sailing, juggling and horse riding (both traditional and bare-back with a bridle). His remaining ambition is to ride an ostrich.

About the Contributors

Olga B.A. van den AKKER *Department of Psychology, Middlesex University, London; ACU, Birmingham Women's Hospital, Birmingham, UK*
Professor van den Akker is a chartered health psychologist and Professor of Health Psychology. She has published many original research papers in the area of psychology and the psychobiology of fertility.

Susan ATKINSON *Psychology Group, Faculty of Health, Leeds Metropolitan University, Leeds, UK*
Dr Atkinson, formerly a teacher, is a cognitive psychologist specialising in neurocognitive development in children. She is a senior lecturer in psychology.

Jürgen BARTH *Institute of Social & Preventive Medicine (ISPM), Division of Social and Behavioural Health Research, University of Bern, Switzerland*
Dr Barth is a senior researcher and clinical psychologist at the universities of Freiburg in Germany and Bern in Switzerland. He is an active researcher in the area of rehabilitation psychology with many papers on comorbidity of somatic and mental disorders. As an active clinical practitioner he is trained within the sphere of cognitive–behavioural therapy.

Adrian B. BONNER *Centre for Health Services Study, University of Kent, Canterbury, UK*
Dr Bonner is a Reader in Addictive Behaviours. He is also a neuroscientist and an advisor on addiction for the United Nations. He has published many scientific papers on the biochemistry and genetics of alcohol dependency, and authored a number of influential books on addiction and social exclusion.

Thomas CARNWATH *Pierremont Unit, Darlington, UK*
Dr Carnwath is a consultant psychiatrist specialising in addiction. He has published a number of papers in the field of addiction.

Zarrar A. CHOWDARY *Pierremont Unit, Darlington, UK*
Dr Chowdary is a senior registrar specialising in addiction.

Christopher C.H. COOK *Department of Theology & Religion, Durham University, UK*
Professor Chris Cook, a consultant psychiatrist specialising in addiction, is a Professorial Research Fellow in the Department of Theology and Religion at Durham University. He has published extensively in the areas of addiction and spirituality.

W. Miles COX *School of Psychology, Bangor University, Wales, UK*
Professor Cox specialises in the psychology of addictive behaviours. He has published many influential research papers on the psychology of addiction.

Chris DALY *Wentworth House, Bolton Salford & Trafford Mental Health NHS Trust; Manchester Alcohol Service, Withington Hospital, Manchester, UK*
Dr Daly is a consultant psychiatrist specialising in addiction. Wentworth House is an inpatient alcohol detoxification unit specialising in complex withdrawals and dual diagnosis.

Javad S. FADARDI *School of Psychology, University of Wales, Bangor, UK; Department of Psychology, Ferdowsi University of Mashhad, Iran*
Dr Fadardi is a research officer at Bangor University who has published extensively on the psychology of addiction.

Helen FAWKNER *Psychology Group, Faculty of Health, Leeds Metropolitan University, Leeds, UK*
Dr Fawkner is a senior lecturer in psychology and an active researcher in the areas of body image, body dysmorphia and eating control. She has published a number of original research papers in these areas.

Mick P. FLEMING *School of Health, Nursing and Midwifery, University of the West of Scotland, UK*
Mr Fleming is a lecturer in mental health. He is a psychosocial interventions therapist with clinical and research interests in severe mental health problems and addiction issues.

John H. FOSTER *Department of Health and Social Sciences, Middlesex University, London, UK*
Dr Foster is a principal lecturer in mental health who has published many research papers on psychosocial aspects of alcohol dependency.

Jeanette GARWOOD *School of Social Sciences, Leeds Metropolitan University, Leeds, UK*
Dr Garwood is a forensic psychologist specialising in forensic and legal areas and a senior lecturer in criminology.

Colin A. GRAHAM *Accident & Emergency Medicine Chinese University of Hong Kong; Trauma Emergency Centre, Prince of Wales Hospital, Hong Kong SAR*
Professor Graham is an academic emergency medicine specialist who has conducted research and published extensively in this and related areas. He has a clinical interest in management of alcohol abuse and dependency within the emergency department setting.

Kirsten HAIN *Barts and The London, Queen Mary School of Medicine, University of London, London, UK*
Mrs Hain is a graduate in biochemistry and a postgraduate medical student. She has a clinical interest in alcohol dependency.

Katrijn HOUBEN *Department of Clinical Psychological Science, Maastricht University, The Netherlands*
Dr Houben received her PhD (under the supervision of Prof Dr Reinout Wiers) on the assessment of implicit cognitive processes in addiction. She is now a postdoctoral researcher at Maastricht focusing on assessment and training of associative processes and executive functions in addictive behaviours.

Anne LINGFORD-HUGHES *Academic Unit of Psychiatry, University of Bristol, Bristol, UK*
Dr Lingford-Hughes is a consultant psychiatrist specialising in addiction. She is also an active researcher and has published extensively in the area of the neurobiology of addiction.

Colin R. MARTIN *School of Health, Nursing and Midwifery, University of the West of Scotland, UK*
Professor Martin is chair in mental health with a clinical and academic interest in alcohol dependency and has published a number of original papers and book chapters on the topic.

Catherine MUYEBA *Bolton Salford and Trafford Mental Health NHS Trust, Manchester, UK*
Dr Muyeba is a consultant psychiatrist specialising in addiction.

Victor R. PREEDY *Department of Nutrition and Dietetics, King's College London, London, UK*
Professor Preedy is chair of biochemistry and has published extensively in the areas of genetics, molecular biology and nutrition of alcohol abuse and dependency.

Rajkumar RAJENDRAM *Nutritional Sciences Research, School of Life Sciences, King's College London; General Medicine & Intensive Care, John Radcliffe Hospital, Oxford, UK*
Dr Rajendram is a specialist registrar in general medicine and intensive care in the Oxford Deanery who also has an active research programme on alcohol dependency and clinical nutrition.

Matthew REANEY *Applied Health Psychology (AHP) Research, Uxbridge, UK*
Mr Reaney is a Senior Scientist in measuring and evaluating health outcomes.

Tim SCHOENMAKERS *Department of Clinical Psychological Science, Maastricht University, The Netherlands*
Mr Schoenmakers is a research student (under the supervision of Prof Dr Reinout Wiers) who has published a number of original research papers on the changeability of appetitive processes in alcohol and drug use.

Leila Maria SORAVIA *University of Bern, Department of Psychiatry Research, Bern; Psychological Institute, Clinical Psychology and Psychobiology Department, University of Zurich, Switzerland*
Dr Soravia is a clinical psychologist with research interests in cognitive–behavioural therapy, the psychosocial and neurobiological mechanisms of anxiety disorders, and the pathogenesis and treatment of anxiety disorders and personality disorders.

Jane SPEIGHT *Applied Health Psychology (AHP) Research, Uxbridge, UK*
Dr Speight is a chartered health psychologist and the Director of AHP Research. She has published many papers relating to the measurement of psyhcological outemes in various conditions and she has a special interest in quality of life research.

Rajaventhan SRI RAJASKANTHAN *Centre for Gastroenterology, Royal Free Hospital, London, UK*
Dr SriRajaskanthan is a research registrar. His academic and practical fields of interests include alcoholic liver disease, non-alcoholic steatohepatitis (NASH), inflammatory bowel disease, and neuroendocrine tumours. He has published many original research papers in the area of biochemical aspects of alcohol dependency.

Terry THOMAS *School of Social Sciences, Leeds Metropolitan University, Leeds, UK*
Dr Thomas is a Professor of Criminal Justice Studies and a former local authority social worker. He has researched in the areas of offending by people with mental health problems, sexual offending and youth offending.

Carolien THUSH *Department of Clinical Psychological Science, Maastricht University, The Netherlands*
Dr Thush received her PhD (under the supervision of Prof Dr Reinout Wiers) on the assessment of implicit cognitive processes and early intervention in addictive behaviours in adolescents.

Clive TOBUTT *Faculty of Health & Human Sciences, Thames Valley University, London, UK*
Mr Tobutt is a lecturer in mental health with research interests in drug-related deaths and criminal justice integration programmes, and alcohol and drug workplace issues.

Steven TRENOWETH *Faculty of Health & Human Sciences, Thames Valley University, London, UK*
Dr Trenoweth is a lecturer in mental health who has authored a number of books in the area of mental health and has clinical and research interests in alcohol dependency.

Ben WATSON *Academic Unit of Psychiatry, University of Bristol, Bristol, UK*
Dr Watson is a psychiatrist and clinical research fellow in the Psychopharmacology Unit. He trained in psychiatry at the Maudsley Hospital in London and his research interests include the neurobiology of addiction and neuroimaging.

Reinout W. WIERS *Department of Psychology, University of Amsterdam, The Netherlands*
Professor Wiers is professor of developmental psychopathology. His primary interests are the implicit cognitive processes in relation to the development and maintenance of addictive behaviours and applications to interventions. He has published many papers in this area.

Introduction

Colin R. Martin

Alcohol dependency represents an enduring problem for both the individual and wider society. Despite contemporary media coverage on increasingly dangerous levels of drinking in the United Kingdom, the fact remains that excessive alcohol consumption has been a distinguishing feature of western society for generations. Alcohol dependency represents a paradox, since illicit drug use is generally demonised, yet alcohol remains our favourite and accepted drug of choice.

Policy regarding addiction has generally focused on illegal drugs such as heroin, cocaine and amphetamines. This priority is clearly evidenced by the disproportionate amount of health funding allocated to this area compared to alcohol dependency. However, beyond the recent political sound bites regarding excessive and dangerous levels of alcohol consumption, a true distinction between alcohol and illegal drug use is that alcohol production and sales represent a huge fiscal contribution to the government coffers. Therefore, imposing stricter regulation on the sale and consumption of alcohol is unlikely, not least because of the potential reduction of revenue for central government. The majority of people who consume alcohol do so responsibly and non-problematically; however a significant minority experience severe and sometimes life-threatening illnesses and mental health problems as a consequence of their relationship with alcohol, and understanding and addressing these issues is the focus of this book.

Importantly, alcohol abuse and dependence sits within a philosophical cusp with respect to causation; advocates of (a) issues of personal responsibility and (b) disease processes over which the individual has no control are represented in more or less equal measures. However, what cannot be dismissed is that alcohol dependency represents a complex interaction between physiological and psychological processes, couched within the individual and societal milieu.

Consequently, the perception of alcohol dependency as a behavioural disorder in psychological terms is not inconsistent with the clinical presentation of clearly physiological phenomena such as chemical dependence, withdrawal symptoms, and alcohol-related liver disease. Understanding alcohol dependency in a comprehensive way thus requires an appreciation of the complex interplay between these diverse factors to appreciate the *gestalt* that represents the final end-point of clinical presentation in the individual.

This book is arranged in a number of themed parts, which largely represent the key areas in the process of facilitating access to effective clinical management. Part One, *Identification*, therefore, is an important part of the book because it is one of the most difficult and challenging areas for the busy health worker whose primary discipline may not be alcohol or drug abuse.

Part Two then looks at the medical management of alcohol dependence, since once chemical dependence on alcohol is identified, clinical intervention – including pharmacological management – is invariably required. This however, represents not only a vital stage of treatment but also a relatively short period of intervention. The perception that effective treatment starts and stops with a 1-week period of inpatient or community detoxification is highly erroneous. The behavioural issues that bring the alcohol-dependent individual into contact with clinical services will require longer-term psychological intervention; in this respect, detoxification represents just the start of the therapeutic journey for clients. Part Three of the book explores the main psychological approaches to interventions that are aimed at facilitating and promoting long-term positive behavioural change in terms of the individual's relationship with alcohol. Alcohol dependency represents a dynamic environment in terms of clinical research, and important insights into alcohol dependence are emerging on an almost weekly basis.

Part Four explores a number of the salient emerging themes – the role of self-help groups, the abstinence vs controlled-drinking debate, spirituality, and quality of life, among others. Quality of life has become an important primary and secondary outcome in clinical research and clinical trials across the spectrum of possible clinical presentations and this dimension in relation to alcohol dependency is becoming increasingly important. Part Five explores the issue of alcohol dependency with clients who have more complex needs, a theme raised in the chapter on dual diagnosis. Finally, Part Six explores a number of the early life-course issues that are germane to alcohol dependency.

It is hoped that this book will not only provide a handy and evidence-based book for the busy health professional, but will also promote interest and understanding of the complex psychobiosocial synthesis that represents the clinical presentation of alcohol dependency.

Part One

Identification

1

Alcohol dependency—
The extent of the problem

Kirsten Hain and Adrian B. Bonner

"Society has chosen to co-exist with a potentially dangerous and addictive drug."

This statement formed part of the concluding remarks in a landmark report into alcoholism by the Royal College of Psychiatrists in 1979. Alcohol consumption was then – and still is – a major feature of social activity. In the modern era, going to bars and pubs with friends is one of the UK's most popular pastimes and drinking is a significant factor in facilitating social networks. While many people are able to control their intake and usage, there is a significant subset of people for whom alcohol becomes a destructive part of their lives. In 2004, 26 per cent of the UK population aged 16–64 were reported as having an 'alcohol use disorder' (British Medicine Association, 2006). The Royal College of Psychiatrists and current estimates suggest the cost of alcohol misuse to the UK is around £20 billion. In this chapter the extent and impact of alcohol misuse in society will be addressed.

The levels of antisocial behaviour and linked increased levels of 'binge' drinking have been responded to by new legislation which includes the use of antisocial behaviour orders (ASBOs) and 'zero tolerance' strategies adopted by the police. Within Europe, the UK has the highest rates in young people of alcohol use, binge drinking, drunkenness, and use of marijuana and problem drugs (Forensic Science Service, 2000; Hibell *et al.*, 2004). Furthermore the rate of illicit drug use among young adolescents has nearly doubled in the last few years. The UK is among the European countries with the highest rates of problem drug use, having an estimated 266,000 drug-addicted members, a ratio of about 1 in 200 of the population. The highest risk is in young males – over 50 per cent of people presenting for treatment in England, Scotland and Wales are aged below 30, with a male to female ratio of 3 to 1. Lifetime illicit drug use has been estimated at 22 per cent among 13 to 14-year-olds and 42 per cent among 16 to 19-year-olds in the UK.

Alcohol—the neglected strategy

Despite advice from the medical and health-related professions, alcohol misuse was not included in the UK anti-drug strategies launched in 1998 in *Tackling Drugs to Build a Better Britain* (Home Office, 1998; updated in 2002). In view of the extensive ill health, social problems, criminality and costs to society, it seems irrational that effective strategies to reduce alcohol-related harm have been poorly developed by successive UK governments. There are approximately 7 million people in England who drink excessively, and over 1 million experience alcohol dependence. The cost of alcohol-related harm is £20 billion per annum. Drummond (2005) has reported that indices of alcohol-related harm have increased in the past 10 years in the UK, and relate to greater affordability and consumption of alcohol. The greatest increase has been seen in young people – and young women in particular.

Proposals for a 'national alcohol strategy' have been developed by a number of professional groups and non-government agencies such as Alcohol Concern (1999). These proposals include increased taxation on alcohol, restricting availability, restricting the density of outlets, changing the minimum drinking age and blood alcohol limit for driving, as well as the provision of brief interventions and treatment for those affected. However, there are many competing interests driving the development of the UK Government's alcohol policy, not least being the revenue and employment generated by the production and sale of alcohol.

The *Alcohol Harm Reduction Strategy for England* (Prime Minister's Strategy Unit, 2004) emphasises the responsibility of the individual drinker and the alcohol industry. The new Licensing Act of 2003 is unlikely to make a positive impact on alcohol-related harm. On the contrary, there is preliminary evidence that the introduction of 24-hour drinking laws may have trebled alcohol-related admissions to accident and emergency departments in inner city areas at night (Newton *et al.*, 2007).

Drummond (2005) concluded that whole population measures need be considered to reduce alcohol consumption, and that 'positive lessons from tobacco policy need to be translated to the alcohol field'. He also stated that alcohol strategies must 'balance the rights of the majority of the population not to be affected by the misuse of alcohol by a minority, against the freedom of the individual to use alcohol in any way he or she chooses'. Robust evidence is being collected on the links between the price of alcoholic drinks and their consumption, and whether increased consumption is related to affordability. Furthermore, heavy drinkers and under-age drinkers are more affected by the price of alcohol than other drinkers.

This evidence and data relating to the effect of advertising on alcohol consumption is being used to influence the development of the Alcohol (Harm Reduction) Bill currently being debated in Parliament. In this political initiative the Government is being pressured to address the pricing, display, advertising, education and labelling of alcohol. The Bill received a second reading in October 2007; it will be a helpful contribution to health, public order and alcohol-related offences.

The renewed alcohol strategy

The Government's renewed alcohol strategy (*Safe, Sensible, Social: The Next Steps in the National Alcohol Strategy*) was published in June 2007 (Department of Health, 2007) and contains a detailed programme of work to address the health harms, violence and antisocial behaviour associated with alcohol, while ensuring that people are able to enjoy alcohol safely and responsibly.

Mechanisms of alcohol dependence

The term 'addiction' has been applied to a number of activities across society in which we may all participate at one time or another; it is recognised that some people are 'addicted' to shopping, exercise, food, gambling and sex. In the UK, addiction to psychoactive illicit and licit (e.g. caffeine) substances is the most harmful behaviour because these substances affect the central nervous system, causing a change in consciousness or state of mind. To understand the process of 'dependence' specific terminology is used, as in Fig. 1.1.

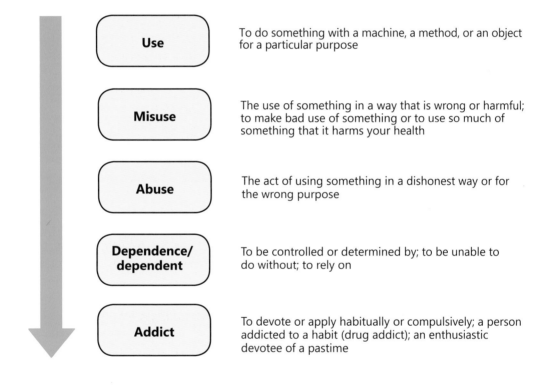

Use — To do something with a machine, a method, or an object for a particular purpose

Misuse — The use of something in a way that is wrong or harmful; to make bad use of something or to use so much of something that it harms your health

Abuse — The act of using something in a dishonest way or for the wrong purpose

Dependence/ dependent — To be controlled or determined by; to be unable to do without; to rely on

Addict — To devote or apply habitually or compulsively; a person addicted to a habit (drug addict); an enthusiastic devotee of a pastime

Figure 1.1 The development of alcohol-related harm (definitions from *Oxford Advanced Learner's Dictionary*, 2007).

These terms indicate a spectrum of use, or participation in an activity or behaviour that develops from a harmless act, leading to maladaptive behaviours with significant and negative consequences to the person and those around them. A person will repeat a behaviour if the consequence of that behaviour is pleasurable or 'rewarding' – this is positive reinforcement. Many natural instincts involving reward, such as obtaining food, water or sex, are thought to act along specific neural pathways. The area of the brain most associated with these 'pleasure pathways' is the limbic system – the VTA, or ventral tegmental area (Bonner, 2006a) which is depicted in Fig. 1.2.

Dopaminergic fibres descend from the VTA, terminating at the nucleus accumbens where dopamine is released; this is the mesolimbic pathway. Commonly abused drugs, such as opiates, amphetamine, cocaine and alcohol, cause dopamine to be released from the nucleus accumbens. When alcohol reaches the brain, a combination of dopamine release and receptor activation results in pleasure and reinforcement, which can lead on to dependency. Dopamine and its actions in the mesolimbic pathway are therefore major factors in the pursuit of pleasurable stimuli. Naturally produced opioid peptides in the brain are associated with high levels of euphoria, and alcohol has also been shown to act at the level of opioid peptides, thus increasing the rewarding affects of alcohol (Bonner, 2006a,b).

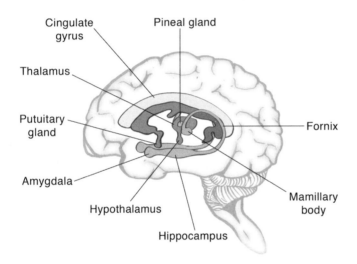

Figure 1.2   Areas of the brain associated with reward, including the limbic system.

Defining alcohol dependence

These are the seven main criteria (Edwards, Marshall and Cook, 2003):

- There is narrowing of the drinking repertoire.
- Alcohol becomes increasingly important in the person's life.
- There is increasing tolerance to alcohol use.
- Withdrawal symptoms are experienced on repeated occasions.
- Drinking is used to avoid withdrawal.
- There is a compulsion to drink.
- After abstinence, reinstatement may occur.

The subsequent diagnostic criteria for alcohol dependence (DSM-IV) were first published in 1994. They are listed in Box 1.1. Biological and environmental factors, including genetic vulnerability, nutrition and nurturing, all contribute towards alcohol dependence. A family history of alcohol misuse has been reported in up to 50 per cent of heavy drinkers. Cloninger (1987) describes two types of transmission in alcoholic people, type 1 and type 2. Type 2 alcoholics (previously type A) had an earlier onset of alcohol disorder than type 1 alcoholics (previously type B). However, this has been contested by Otter, Huber and Bonner (1995) and Windle (2004). Windle reports four subtypes – mild course, polydrug, negative affect, and chronic/ASP (where ASP means 'antisocial personality'). If this statistically robust study is clinically valid, the implications are that Cloninger's two-type typology approach will result in treating the heterogeneous group of alcoholic people (type A, or *non-ASP*) as if they are a homogeneous group.

Box 1.1   **DSM-IV diagnostic criteria for alcohol dependence (Edwards, 1976)**

Alcohol dependence is a maladaptive pattern of alcohol use, leading to clinically significant impairment or distress, as manifested by three or more of the following seven criteria, occurring at any time in the same 12-month period:

1. Tolerance, as defined by either (i) a need for markedly increased amounts of alcohol to achieve intoxication or desired effect, or (ii) markedly diminished effect with continued use of the same amount of alcohol.

2. Withdrawal, as defined by either (i) the characteristic withdrawal syndrome for alcohol, or (ii) alcohol is taken to relieve or avoid withdrawal symptoms.

3. Alcohol is often taken in larger amounts or over a longer period than was intended.

4. There is a persistent desire or there are unsuccessful efforts to cut down or control alcohol use.

5. A great deal of time is spent in activities necessary to obtain alcohol, use alcohol or recover from its effects.

6. Important social, occupational, or recreational activities are given up or reduced because of alcohol use.

7. Alcohol use is continued despite knowledge of having a persistent or recurrent physical or psychological problem that is likely to have been caused or exacerbated by the alcohol (e.g. continued drinking despite recognition that an ulcer was made worse by alcohol consumption).

Windle's analysis indicates that *chronic ASP* problems occur in both men and women, although this subtype is higher in men (48.6 per cent) than in women (27 per cent). *Negative affect* was found to be greater in women (14.6 per cent) than in men (8 per cent). Noble *et al.* (1998) proposed that one subtype of alcoholic may be related to a specific polymorphic type of dopamine (DA) receptor. This is most likely to map on to the *chronic/ASP* subtype, whereas polymorphisms of GABA (gamma-aminobutyric acid) are possibly related to *negative affect* clinical subtypes. The features of type 1 and type 2 alcoholism are summarised in Box 1.2.

Box 1.2 **Features of type 1 and type 2 alcoholism (Cloninger, 1987)**

Type 1 alcoholism

- Mild to severe abuse
- Influenced by genetics and (postnatal) environment
- Later onset (after 25)
- Associated with psychological dependence and guilt

Type 2 alcoholism

- Moderate abuse
- Associated with alcoholic fathers
- Earlier drinking (before age 25)
- Unable to abstain
- Mainly in males
- Associated with aggressive/antisocial behaviour

Environment greatly contributes to drinking patterns: availability of alcohol, life events, culture and attitudes to alcohol can reinforce dependence (Edwards, Marshall and Cook, 2003). Yet not all people who abuse alcohol or other drugs will become dependent. One study followed 8100 male and female alcohol abusers aged 15 to 24 and found that after a 10-year interval only 12–13 per cent had become dependent (Paton and Touquet, 2005). Thus it appears that abuse and dependence represent two separate entities. A discussion of genetic behaviours underlying drink behaviour is beyond the scope of this chapter.

Alcohol use and misuse in the community

The current benchmark for (maximum) daily alcohol consumption in the UK is 4 units per day for men and 3 units per day for women (Alcohol Concern, 2002). Prior to 1995, guidelines for 'sensible drinking' were reflected in a *weekly* figure; however, weekly consumption of alcohol concealed short-term 'binge' drinking which has a stronger correlation with medical and social harm (Office of National Statistics, 2002). These suggested daily units are thought to be a safe level for regular drinking; if the daily amount is exceeded, it is recommended that people refrain from drinking for at least 48 hours to allow the body to recover. Box 1.3 illustrates how alcohol units are quantified.

Box 1.3 **Units of alcohol (Alcohol Concern, 2002)**

One unit of alcohol = 8 g or 10 mL of pure alcohol and is equivalent to:

- Half a pint of normal strength lager (3–3.5%)
- One 175 mL glass of wine (12%)
- One 25 mL measure of spirits

The key findings of the *General Household Survey* 2002 were that:

- 35% of men exceeded daily benchmarks at least once a week compared to 20% of women.
- Men aged 16–24 were more likely to drink in excess.
- Ethnic minorities were less likely to drink and they drank less.
- There was no significant change in the number of men drinking more than 50 units a week or women drinking more than 35 units per week.
- Northern England had the highest rates of exceeding benchmarks (42% in the North East, North West, Yorkshire and Humber *cf.* 36% in other regions and 26% in London).
- Men drank an average of 15.8 units per week and women 6.5 units per week.
- Generally drinking fell in all age groups especially those aged 16–24 between 2000 and the time of the survey (see Table 1.1).

Table 1.1   Males and females aged 16–24 who exceed weekly benchmarks in the years 2000 and 2005 (General Household Survey, 2002b)

Year	Men (%)	Women (%)
2000	41%	27%
2005	27%	24%

Between 1998 and 2002 the GHS appeared to show an increase of heavy drinkers among young females (Alcohol Concern, 2002). The number of females exceeding the daily benchmarks on at least one occasion per week is shown in Table 1.2. However, data from 2003 until 2005 have shown a decrease in heavy drinking in this age group. It is uncertain whether this is a true decline, as a result of better health advice and advertising that have helped to modify drinking behaviour, or whether females are now less inclined to reveal the true amount that they drink (Department of Health, 1995).

Table 1.2   Females aged 16–24 exceeding daily benchmarks at least once a week from 1998 to 2005 (Department of Health, 1995)

Year	Women (%)
1998	24%
2002	28%
2003	23%
2004	24%
2005	22%

Alcohol misuse can be divided into binge drinkers and chronic drinkers. Binge drinkers, primarily represented by the 16–24-year-old group, generally intend to get drunk, usually in large groups on weekend nights. They are often victims of violence or commit violence and are frequently found in hospital emergency departments (Royal College of Psychiatrists, 2001). Chronic/heavy drinkers consume large amounts of alcohol regularly, more than 10 units a day over a long period of time. Chronic drinkers are usually over 30 years of age and two-thirds are men, according to The Cabinet Office (Prime Minister's Strategy Unit, 2004). Table 1.3 illustrates drinking behaviour of men and women in the UK.

Table 1.3 How the UK population drinks (Prime Minister's Strategy Unit, 2004)			
	People drinking at this level (millions)		
Alcohol consumed (units)	*Men*	*Women*	*Total*
Abstainers (0)	1.6	3.1	4.7
Low to moderate drinking (0–14/21 weekly)	12.1	14.2	26.3
Above daily guidelines (4–8/3.6 daily max. in past week)	3.2	2.6	5.8
Binge drinking (8+/6+ daily max. in past week)	4.0	1.9	5.9
Moderate to heavy drinking (14/21–35/50 weekly)	3.9	2.5	6.4
Heavy drinking (35/50 weekly)	1.2	0.6	1.8

In 2005 and 2006, there were in excess of 19,000 diagnoses of alcohol-related cirrhosis episodes in England – an increase of 187 per cent in the last 9 years. The incidence of liver disease in young people is causing concern among health professionals. Increases have been seen in the number of young women who binge drink and, concomitantly, in hospital admissions of females aged under 18, compared to males. Hospital admissions of people with alcohol poisoning have almost doubled during the last 10 years (Gridley, 2007).

The impact of misuse in the UK

More than 9.1 million people in England drink above the recommended levels, with 1.7 million males and 0.6 million females regarded as 'heavy' drinkers, and 900,000 thought to be alcohol-dependent (General Household Survey, 2005; Office of National Statistics, 2005; Royal College of Psychiatrists, 2001). This has many social and economic consequences, most noticeably for the National Health Service and the police. It is difficult to calculate the number of deaths caused each year by alcohol consumption because there are indirect and direct consequences of drinking; estimates range from 5000 to 40,000 deaths per year (Bonner and Waterhouse, 1996). Alcohol is causally related to 60 different medical conditions, to an extent which is linked to the type and volume of consumption (Lelbach, 1976; Rehm, 2003).

There have been significant changes in alcohol consumption and alcohol-related health conditions during the last 50 years (Room, 2006). Alcohol-related hospital admissions are rising by 80,000 per year with 811,000 admissions (6% of all admissions) in 2006 (Department of Health, 2008). There is strong evidence that excess alcohol consumption is related to increased morbidity and mortality (Rajendram and Preedy, 2005), a major component of which is alcoholic liver disease.

Total lifetime alcohol consumption appears to be a determinant of liver damage; 20 per cent of men consuming more than 12 cans of beer a day for 10 years develop liver cirrhosis. In the UK Government's recent alcohol strategy report, some 22,000 deaths per year were associated with alcohol misuse. Around 6000 of these were as a direct result of excessive consumption, namely alcoholic liver cirrhosis and acute intoxication. Recent NHS data (Alcohol Concern, 2002; Department of Health, 1995; Royal College of Psychiatrists, 2001) indicate that:

- 1 out of every 6 people attending accident and emergency departments has some alcohol-related problem (rising to 8 out of 10 at peak times).

- 150,000 hospital admissions every year are related to alcohol.
- Between 1997 and 2000 there was a four-fold increase in deaths from alcoholic cirrhosis in people aged 35–44.
- 21 per cent of psychiatric admissions are alcohol-related.
- More than 30,000 hospital admissions every year are for alcohol dependence.
- Approximately 1000 suicides every year are related to alcohol.
- Approximately 500 people are killed each year due to drink driving.

These shocking figures reveal how alcohol impacts on the NHS alone. It is estimated that alcohol costs the health service around £1.7 billion per year, with £95 million of it going towards specialist treatment (Royal College of Psychiatrists, 2001). It is also evident that alcohol results in premature deaths and chronic illness. In 2000, the peak age of alcohol-related mortality was between 45 and 59; prior to this it had been more than 55 years of age. Alcohol-related illness and premature deaths also cost the UK economy £6.4 billion per year through lost productivity, including 17 million days lost every year due to alcohol use or alcohol-related illness. Crime and antisocial behaviour are also strongly affected by alcohol misuse, with around 50 per cent of all crimes being linked to alcohol misuse, that is, the equivalent of 1.2 million incidents (Alcohol Concern, 2002; Department of Health, 1995; Royal College of Psychiatrists, 2001). A third of all incidents of domestic violence (360,000 cases per year) and more than half of all assailants convicted of rape were found to be under the influence of alcohol. The social consequences of high alcohol intake include an increase in unprotected sex, leading to unplanned births and increases in sexually transmitted diseases. The cost of alcohol-related crime is estimated at £7.3 billion per year (Royal College of Psychiatrists, 2001). Other social consequences of alcohol misuse include its effect on family life. Table 1.4 summarises the social and financial burden of alcohol misuse in the UK.

Table 1.4   Annual cost to the UK from alcohol-related harm (adapted from Prime Minister's Strategy Unit, 2004)

SECTOR	Cost (£ billions)	No. people affected/incidences
Family and social networks	Unknown (unquantifiable)	780,000–1.3 million children affected by parent alcohol problems (including child poverty) 5,000–20,000 street drinkers
Health	£1.4–1.7 to the health service	4,000–4,100 deaths (acute causes) 11,300–17,900 deaths (chronic causes)
Workplace	Up to £6.4 to the economy: • £1.2–1.8 absenteeism • £1.7–2.1 lost working days • £2.3–2.5 due to deaths	11–17 million days lost to sickness 15–20 million days lost to reduced employment
Crime and public disorder	Up to £7.3 including: • £4.7 human costs • £0.5 due to drink-driving • £1.8 to criminal justice system • £3.5 to services (consequential) • £1.7–2.1 to services (anticipatory)	360,000 victims domestic violence 90,000 drunk/disorderly arrests 530 deaths due to drink-drivers

Alcohol use in Europe

Europe is the heaviest drinking region of the world. Approximately 11 litres of pure alcohol are drunk per person per year – that is 2.5 times more than the 'world average' (Anderson and Baumberg, 2006). Table 1.5 shows the number of people in the European Union who drink alcohol at various levels. It shows there are approximately 58 million heavy drinkers in Europe.

Table 1.5	**Number of people in the European Union at different drinking levels**		
	Definition of alcohol consumption		**Number of adults (age 16+)**
	Men	*Women*	**drinking at that level**
Abstaining	0 grams/day	0 grams/day	25 million
Level I	0–40 grams/day	0–20 grams/day	53 million
Level II	40–60 grams/day	20–40 grams/day	36 million
Level III	60+ grams/day	40+ grams/day	22 million

The alcohol-related statistics for Europe (Anderson and Baumberg, 2006) also bear a close resemblance to those of the UK, whereby 50 per cent of violent crimes and 40 per cent of incidences of domestic violence are related to alcohol misuse. In Europe, it is also associated with:

- 2000 of all murders per year (4 out of every 10 murders)
- 17,000 deaths per year (from road-traffic accidents)
- 10,000 suicides (1 out of every 6)
- 45,000 deaths (from liver cirrhosis).

Such data confirm that alcohol abuse is not solely a UK problem, with the cost to the European Union in the region of 125 billion Euros (£85 billion). According to the *Alcohol Harm Reduction Strategy for England* alcohol is an important part of the UK economy, and of society as a whole, with an approximate market value of £30 billion per year providing around a million jobs (Prime Minister's Strategy Unit, 2005). However, as described previously, the cost of alcohol misuse in the UK is also detrimental to the economy and to society. In 2004, the Government launched the National Alcohol Strategy (NAS). It was felt that alcohol misuse needed a higher profile and should be distinguished from other forms of drug misuse. Within the NAS, several core objectives were set, namely:

- To improve targeted education and communication.
- To improve identification and treatment of alcohol problems.
- To improve coordination and enforcement of existing powers against crime and disorder.
- To encourage the industry to continue to promote responsible drinking and to continue to take a role in decreasing alcohol-related harm.

Box 1.4 highlights some of the ways in which each objective is to be tackled. Clearly the objectives in the NAS will require input from a variety of sources, not only the Department of Health but also from the departments of education, culture, media and sport and others (*Alcohol Harm Reduction Strategy for England*; Prime Minister's Strategy Unit, 2005). However, lack of new money and an emphasis on addressing criminal consequences – as opposed to the health and social consequences – of alcohol abuse are major criticisms of the UK Government strategy.

Box 1.4	**Key areas to be addressed in the National Alcohol Strategy (NAS)**

Education and communication
- Make the 'sensible drinking' message understandable
- Improve education at school
- Target those perceived to be at greater risk

Identification and treatment
- Improve training to increase awareness (medical schools, other health professions)
- Provide more help to vulnerable groups (homeless, drug addicts, and young people)
- Ensure early identification
- Develop a 'models of care framework' for alcohol treatment services
- Pilot schemes assessing targeted screening and 'brief intervention' techniques

Alcohol-related crime and disorder
- Increase use of penalty notices (drunk and disorderly)
- Increase the number of community support officers at night
- Approach industry for voluntary contribution to manage alcohol-related disorders
- Victims and perpetrators of violence to receive help from alcohol treatment services

Supply and industry responsibility
- Develop a voluntary social responsibility scheme
- Encourage (voluntary) sensible drinking messages on products
- Ensure advertising is not targeted at under 18s or endorses irresponsible behaviour

New government statistics show that alcohol-related hospital admissions are rising by 80,000 a year, accounting for 6% of all admissions. It now appears that a voluntary code, involving the sale of alcoholic beverages, is not being respected by premises selling alcohol. Work is now underway on development of a mandatory code to help enforce responsible practices. These include the labelling of bottles, staff training, the management and design of outlets, and the prevention of sales of alcohol to those under the legal age. This tightening of control over the alcohol industry will be in parallel with implementation of a Youth Action Plan.

Conclusions

Alcohol misuse is a major health and social problem in the UK, costing some £20 billion to the NHS, criminal justice system and other areas, not to mention the emotional cost to families and friends (*Alcohol Harm Reduction Strategy for England*; Prime Minister's Strategy Unit, 2005). Treating alcohol dependency requires a long-term programme involving detoxification, rehabilitation and maintenance. The time a person spends at each stage depends on how dependent that person is, their support network, motivation and other social and environmental factors. There is often great pressure to relapse or continue drinking; maintaining old drinking friendships, fear of failure, family stresses and job pressures are just some of the obstacles to recovery.

A greater understanding of developmental and family-related influences is required to develop a holistic approach to the biological, psychological and social dimensions of problematic alcohol use. This should include strategies to limit the availability of alcohol, particularly to young people, and influence the drinking culture in the UK, which suffers some of the most severe alcohol-related health and social problems in Europe (Anderson and Baumberg, 2006).

References and further reading

Alcohol Concern (1999). *Proposals for a National Alcohol Strategy for England*. London: Alcohol Concern.

Alcohol Concern (2002). *100% Proof: Research on Action on Alcohol*. London: Alcohol Concern.

Anderson, P. and Baumberg, B. (2006). *Alcohol in Europe*. London: Institute of Alcohol Studies.

Bonner, A. and Waterhouse, J.E. (eds). (1996). *Addictive Behaviour: Molecules to Mankind*. London: Macmillan.

Bonner, A.B. (2006a). Individual functioning. In: *Social Exclusion and the Way Out: An Individual and Community Perspective on Social Dysfunction*. Chichester: John Wiley, pp.19–36.

Bonner, A.B. (2006b). Neurobiological basis of maladaptive behaviour. In: *Social Exclusion and the Way Out: An Individual and Community Perspective on Social Dysfunction*. Chichester: John Wiley, pp. 99–122.

British Medical Association (2006). *Alcohol Misuse*. Available at: http://www.bma.org.uk/ap.nsf/Content/tacklingalcoholmisuse (last accessed August 2008).

Cloninger, C.R. (1987). A systematic method for clinical description and classification of personality variants. A proposal. *Archives of General Psychiatry*, **44**(6), 573–88.

Department of Health (1995). *Sensible Drinking*. London: Department of Health.

Department of Health (2008). *Safe, Sensible, Social – Consultation on Further Action*. London: Department of Health.

Department of Health, Home Office, Department of Education and Skills and the Department of Culture, Media and Sport (2007). *Safe, Sensible, Social: The Next Steps in the National Alcohol Strategy*. London: The Stationery Office.

Drummond, C. (2005). Alcohol and Government Policy. In: Bonner, A.B. (ed.) *Proceedings of the ESBRA Conference 2005*. Canterbury: University of Kent.

Edwards, G. (1976). Alcohol-related problems in the disability perspective. A summary of the consensus of the WHO group of investigators on criteria for identifying and classifying disabilities related to alcohol consumption. *Journal of Studies on Alcohol,* **37**(9), 1360–82.

Edwards, G., Marshall, E. and Cook, C. (2003). *The Treatment of Drinking Problems*. Cambridge: Cambridge University Press.

Forensic Science Service (2000). *Drug Abuse Trends*. London: Forensic Science Service.

General Household Survey (2005). *Smoking and Drinking*. London: Office of National Statistics.

Gridley, S. (2007). *Pricing, Display, Advertising, Education and Labelling*. London: Sandra Gridley.

Hibell, B., Andersson, B., Bjarnason, T., *et al.* (2004). *The ESPAD Report 2003. Alcohol and Other Drug Use Among Students in 35 European Countries*. Swedish Council for Information on Alcohol and Other Drugs (CAN) and the Pompidou Group at the Council of Europe. Stockholm, Sweden.

Home Office (1998). *Tackling Drugs to Build a Better Britain*. London: HMSO.

Home Office. (2002). *Tackling Drugs to Build a Better Britain: Updated National Drug Strategy*. London: HMSO.

Lelbach, W.K. (1976). Epidemiology of alcoholic liver disease. *Progress in Liver Disease*, **5**, 494–15.

McCambridge, J., Strang, J. and Butler, C.C. (2006). Hazardous drinking and the NHS: the costs of pessimism and the benefits of optimism. *British Journal of General Practice*, **56**(525), 247–48.

Newton, A., Jalah, S., Pahal, G.S., van den Berg, E. and Young, C. (2007). Impact of the new UK licensing law on emergency hospital attendances: A cohort study. *Emergency Medicine Journal*, **24**(8), 532–34.

Noble, E.P., Zang, X., Ritchie, T., *et al.* (1998). D_2 dopamine receptor and GABA-a receptor beta-3 subunit genes and alcoholism. *Psychiatry Research*, **81**, 133–47.

Office of National Statistics (2002). Drinking. In: *General Household Survey 2002*. London: Office of National Statistics.

Office of National Statistics (2005). *Smoking* and *Drinking*. London: Office of National Statistics.

Otter, C., Huber, J. and Bonner, A. (1995). Cloninger Tridimensional Personality Questionnaire – Reliability in an English sample. *Personality and Individual Differences*, **18**(4), 471–80.

Oxford Advanced Learner's Dictionary (2007). Oxford: Oxford University Press.

Paton, A. and Touquet, R. (2005). *ABC of Alcohol,* 4th edn. Oxford: Blackwell.

Prime Minister's Strategy Unit (2004). *Alcohol Harm Reduction Strategy for England*. London: The Cabinet Office.

Prime Minister's Strategy Unit (2005). *Alcohol Harm Reduction Strategy for England*. London: The Cabinet Office.

Rajendram, R. and Preedy, V.R. (2005). Effect of alcohol consumption on the gut. *Digestive Diseases*, **23**(3–4), 214–21.

Rehm, J. (2003). Alcohol-related morbidity and mortality. *Alcohol Research and Health*, **27**(1), 39–51.

Room, R. (2006). British livers and British alcohol policy. *Lancet,* **367**(9504), 10–11.

Royal College of Psychiatrists (1979). *Report of a Special Committee of The Royal College of Psychiatrists*. London: Tavistock.

Royal College of Psychiatrists (2001). *Alcohol – Can the NHS Afford it*? London: RCP.

Windle, M. and Scheidt, D.M. (2004). Alcoholic subtypes: are two sufficient? *Addiction,* **99**(12), 1508–19.

2 Assessing alcohol use and misuse in primary care

Steve Trenoweth and Clive Tobutt

A **key health issue for the UK Government is reducing levels of alcohol-related mortality (Cabinet Office, 2004). There has been great concern about the social, economic and health-related costs of alcohol misuse in British society (Department of Health, 1995, 2005a; Department of Health, Home Office, Department of Education and Skills and Department of Culture, Media and Sport, 2007). One study found that over 8 million people in England drink alcohol problematically (Department of Health, 2005a). Furthermore, it is estimated that 20 per cent of hospital inpatient admissions are for alcohol-related problems, and that approximately 20 per cent of all patients visiting their family doctor consume alcohol above the recommended levels of drinking (World Health Organization, 2005; Coulton *et al.*, 2006).**

The effects of consuming alcohol depend on a variety of other factors including age, weight and gender, how quickly it is drunk, how much the individual is used to drinking, whether it is drunk on an empty stomach or accompanying a meal or following a meal, and whether medication or other substances have also been taken. In 2007, the World Health Organization estimated that the trend for standardised liver cirrhosis deaths in the UK population has increased steadily over the last 27 years from 4.5 per 100,000 of the population to 10.88 per 100,000. This is a doubling of the rate and it is *still* rising. In this chapter, we explore how primary care health professionals may facilitate the assessment and identification of those people 'at risk' of alcohol misuse and related physical and psychological harm, in order to develop suitable health promotion strategies and interventions or, in urgent cases, to expedite appropriate referrals to specialist agencies and services.

The challenge for primary care

People with alcohol-related problems present many challenges to primary-care staff and are often heavy consumers of health services (Department of Health, 2005b; Babor *et al.*, 2003). However, the majority of hazardous drinkers are undiagnosed and often present with symptoms or problems that at first seem unconnected to their drinking. For example, Edwards, Marshall and Cook (2003) claim that primary care doctors miss around 25 per cent of drinking problems in their own general practice. This comment has been supported by Aertgeerts *et al.* (2001) whose review of a number of alcohol-related primary care studies estimated that between 1 per cent and 36 per cent of patients with alcohol-related problems, or alcohol dependence, were not correctly detected. Nevertheless, Huntley and Touquet (2004) argue that assessing for alcohol-related problems in primary care settings is difficult, not because of the skill of the general practitioner or nurse, but because the subject is more difficult to raise than in hospital-based settings. An earlier study by Thom and Tellez (1986) reports that it is considered an intrusion to the patients' private life when general practitioners ask patients about their alcohol consumption. This view is also supported by Aria *et al.* (2003) who argue that general practitioners are good at handling alcohol problems like liver cirrhosis and delirium tremens but not early prevention in hazardous drinkers. In addition, Huntley *et al.* (2001) report that emergency-department doctors in hospitals in England do not routinely ask about or document alcohol consumption. Edwards *et al.* (2003) support this view of the hard-pressed clinician with a limited time to assess each patient.

Categories of alcohol use

When undertaking any assessment, it is important to be clear about what is actually being assessed. As such, a distinction needs to be (and often is) drawn between 'hazardous' and 'harmful' drinking, on the one hand, and 'dependence' on the other.

Anderson and Baumberg (2006) argue that the terms that must be used when discussing alcohol consumption are levels or categories of drinking such as 'hazardous drinking', 'harmful drinking', 'intoxication', 'episodic heavy drinking', and 'alcohol dependence'. This is because many imprecise terms are used which are not standardised or are open to interpretation, and these terms include 'moderate drinking', 'sensible drinking' and 'responsible drinking' or 'social drinking', 'excessive drinking', 'alcoholism', 'alcohol abuse' and 'alcohol misuse'.

The consumption of alcohol refers to the alcohol content that is 100 per cent ethanol. Alcoholic drinks vary in their alcohol content depending on whether they are brewed or distilled. Alcohol 'use' is an imprecise term, but in the UK the *Alcohol Strategy* (Department of Health, Home Office, Department of Education and Skills and the Department of Culture, Media and Sport, 2007) persists with the term 'sensible drinking', arguing that it is 'drinking in a way that is unlikely to cause yourself or others significant risk of harm'. However, it must be stated that there are *no* safe levels of drinking because alcohol is both a poison and a drug of dependence (Edwards, 2000).

Alcohol intoxication

'Alcohol intoxication' or 'being drunk' is associated with obvious symptoms and behaviours. It is a short-term condition that can be defined as impairment in both someone's psychological and psychomotor performance. The condition is reversible after a day or so and, depending on how much alcohol was consumed, the person will recover from the effects of the intoxication (Edwards, 2000).

The volume of alcohol drunk will also determine the severity of the intoxication, as will the social setting, social expectations of the person drinking and the social–cultural meaning of 'being drunk', which can alter over time and vary between communities (MacAndrew and Edgerton, 1970).

Hazardous drinking

In 'hazardous' drinking, the individual's pattern of alcohol use is such that they are seen to be at an elevated risk of developing health-related problems, but are currently not experiencing such harm (Department of Health, 2005a; Department of Health *et al.*, 2007). Hazardous drinkers tend to drink at levels over the recommended number of standard alcohol units, either in levels that are harmful to their health or infrequent sessions of episodic heavy drinking (binge drinking). The World Health Organization (Rhem *et al.*, 2003) argues that hazardous drinking for men is the consumption of 60 g or more of alcohol daily or in one drinking occasion, and 40 g or more for women. In England, this relates to 8 or more standard drinks for men and 6 or more standard drinks for women (Department of Health *et al.*, 2007).

Harmful drinking

Babor *et al.* (2003) argue that 'harmful drinking' needs a variety of factors to be taken into consideration. For example, the pattern of drinking and the frequency and quantity of drinking per occasion is such that there is clear evidence of short-term or long-term alcohol-related harm, that may be physical or psychological in nature (World Health Organization, 1992). Harmful drinkers usually drink at levels above those recommended by the UK Government, typically at higher levels than most hazardous drinkers (Department of Health, 2006; Department of Health *et al.* 2007).

Episodic heavy drinking

'Episodic heavy drinking' (where large amounts of alcohol are drunk in a relatively short space of time with the specific objective of getting drunk) among young people is now the focus of the UK Government's new alcohol strategy, *Safe, Sensible, Social* (Department of Health *et al.* 2007). Indeed, the advice since the previous strategy (Prime Minister's Strategy Unit, 2004) regarding the weekly standard alcohol levels has now been amended. Hence, the current advice is now for a *daily* limit of up to 4 standard units for men and up to 3 standard units for women, with two alcohol-free days during any one week (Department of Health *et al.*, 2007). The recommendations for pregnant women are that they should drink no more than 1 or 2 standard units per week (Department of Health *et al.*, 2007). Indeed, in some people with comorbid physical or psychiatric illness (e.g. depression or liver damage), or in the very young and the elderly, even these limits cannot be assumed to be safe.

Alcohol dependence

In 'alcohol dependence' people are not only drinking above the recommended levels but are experiencing symptoms of dependence – characterised by a cluster of behavioural, psychological, and physiological symptoms that may develop after repeated alcohol use (World Health Organization, 1992; American Psychiatric Association, 1994). Typically, such symptoms include persistent drinking, despite harmful and negative health-related consequences, a strong desire or compulsion to consume alcohol (with an associated difficulty in controlling its use), a preoccupation with alcohol, and increased alcohol tolerance (that is, a need for significantly increasing amounts of alcohol to achieve the desired effect) (World Health Organization, 1992;

Babor *et al.,* 2003). Indeed, the 'alcohol dependence syndrome' is a set of medical diagnostic criteria (Edwards and Gross, 1976) that is associated with psychological, biological and social criteria (World Health Organization, 1992). However, there are strict medical criteria for this diagnosis, so for anyone to be diagnosed with 'alcohol dependence' they must demonstrate three of the six criteria outlined in Box 2.1 over a period of 12 months.

Box 2.1	Criteria for alcohol dependence (three criteria must be met in 2 months)

1. Increased tolerance to alcohol
2. Repeated withdrawal symptoms
3. Relief of alcohol withdrawal symptoms
4. Drinking becomes central to daily living
5. Drinking is uncontrollable
6. Reinstatement after abstinence

The term 'alcohol dependence syndrome' replaces the term 'alcoholism', which only focuses on the compulsive behaviour associated with alcohol consumption and the loss of control aspects (Edwards and Gross, 1976). Drinkers who are less severely dependent may still display the features of the dependence syndrome. For example, someone who is less severely dependent on alcohol may experience their alcohol withdrawal symptoms during the day, so they will be 'clock-watching' at work, eager either to drink or consume alcohol secretly to stop the symptoms. However, someone who is more severely alcohol-dependent usually suffers from alcohol withdrawal earlier in the morning, often requiring their first drink on waking, and often vomiting after that first drink but able to keep the second drink down. People in this category may have serious and long-standing physical health disorders or social problems (Edwards *et al.,* 2003).

Health implications of alcohol misuse

There are many implications of alcohol misuse, not only for the individual but also for society, most obviously health-related problems (Department of Health, 1999). Indeed, alcohol-related health and social problems tend to increase with rises in consumption (Alcohol Concern, 2001). However, there is no definitive and direct causal association between alcohol misuse and harm, and it is likely that some people who exceed the recommended levels will not come to harm. If someone experiences harm, then this is most likely to have a multifactorial aetiology for which their alcohol use may be a contributory factor. However, there are increased *risks* (Babor *et al.,* 2001; Cabinet Office, 2004; Department of Health, 2006). Drinking above 50 standard units of alcohol by men per week and 35 units by women is strongly associated with risks of harm to health (Anderson and Baumberg, 2006).

Current levels of alcohol misuse in British society present a significant public health issue costing over £20 billion per year and, at peak times, up to 70 per cent of all admissions to accident and emergency departments are thought to be alcohol-related (Cabinet Office, 2004;

Department of Health, 2005b). Episodic, heavy (binge) drinking can bring additional health risks, such as accidents, alcohol poisoning and vulnerability to sexual assault, while chronic and excessive use of alcohol is particularly linked with development of liver cirrhosis, pancreatitis, cancer, haemorrhagic stroke, premature death and suicide (Babor *et al.*, 2003; Edwards, Marshall and Cook, 2003). Indeed, nearly 5000 cancer deaths each year are thought to be related to alcohol misuse; chronic alcohol misuse is particularly associated with cancers of the oral cavity and pharynx, larynx, oesophagus and liver (Babor *et al.*, 2001). Additionally, alcohol can lead to significant harm to the fetus in pregnant women and, in vulnerable people, the more common medical conditions (like hypertension, gastritis and diabetes) may be attributed to short-term alcohol consumption at lower levels (Anderson and Baumberg, 2006).

The European Commission (2003) reported on mortality-associated alcohol dependence with liver cirrhosis in the European Union, estimating that men aged 45–64 years are the most likely candidates for death from this disease. These deaths represent 4.2 per cent of all male deaths in the European Union, although in younger age groups 6 out of every 10 deaths in those aged under 65 are associated with alcohol dependence. For women, liver cirrhosis as cause of death is lower than that in men (2.1 per cent), although 5 out of every 10 deaths occur before the age of 65. Anderson and Baumberg (2006) report that alcohol-related dependence in any one European member state is from 1 per cent to 5 per cent of the total adult population. For more about the consumption of alcohol in Europe, see Chapter 1. Psychological and psychiatric disorders such as depression (Department of Health, 2005c) can also be aggravated by alcohol use, and there is a need for all healthcare professionals to appreciate the complexity of how alcohol use and misuse may be linked to mental health problems.

The current advice is to *expect* comorbid substance misuse among people with pre-existing severe mental health problems rather than seeing this as unusual (National Treatment Agency, 2002, 2006a,b). People who are 'dual diagnosed' (Department of Health, 2002, 2006), such as those who present with comorbid mental health and alcohol problems, often have complex needs that require comprehensive and specialist assessment and intervention (Cabinet Office, 2004; National Treatment Agency, 2002, 2006a). It is not always clear if the alcohol use is the primary or secondary problem. For example, does the patient's alcohol use lead to their mental health problem? Does he or she use alcohol to cope with psychological or psychiatric symptoms (Sudbury, 2001)? What does seem clear, however, is the link between alcohol dependence and depression (Sudbury, 2001). There are sex differences here also it appears, as male alcohol dependence is a *precursor* to depression, but in women it seems to be a *consequence*. While alcohol misuse declines with age, its use in older age seems to be particularly associated with comorbid mental health problems, and also with concomitant use of prescribed medication that exacerbates symptoms of dementia risk and cognitive decline, and increases the risk of stroke (Christensen, Low and Anstey, 2006). However, it is important to bear in mind the use of alcohol as a form of pain control; as such, there have been calls for appropriate pain assessments to be undertaken alongside alcohol screening in older people (Brennan, Schutte and Moos, 2005).

Models of care

The National Treatment Agency (NTA) has recently outlined an integrated model of care, with four tiers of escalating complexity of assessment and interventions (National Treatment Agency,

2002, 2006a,b). The first tier comprises assessment and interventions in non-substance-misuse specific services (such as primary care and general medical services) and as such are likely to involve a wide range of non-specialist staff (e.g. primary care or general medical staff, social workers, teachers, community pharmacists, probation officers and housing officers).

The so-called 'Tier 1' services target screening and assessment for those drinking in excess of guidelines on 'safe' drinking (Department of Health, 2005a, 2006) providing appropriate and targeted health education advice and information on sensible drinking and also providing simple brief interventions to reduce alcohol-related harm. Crucially, Tier 1 services are well placed to identify those requiring referral for more intensive interventions. Tier 1 services are, therefore, important in providing assessments and services in conjunction with more specialist community and inpatient drug and alcohol treatment services found at Tiers 2 to 4, for example, in community-based or residential substance-misuse services, and treatment and aftercare for those leaving residential or custodial care.

Primary care services provide valuable opportunities to combine Tier 1 assessment and screening and early intervention strategies (Coulton *et al.,* 2006) in line with the *Alcohol Harm Reduction Strategy for England* (Cabinet Office, 2004) and Standard Two of the *National Service Framework for Mental Health*, which requires primary care services to be able to assess the needs of people with mental health problems, and to support their access to appropriate services (Department of Health, 1999).

Thus within primary care services it is possible to make headway in reducing the prevalence of alcohol-related problems by intervening early when people are beginning to use alcohol hazardously, and encouraging them to reduce consumption (Cabinet Office, 2004). Such early interventions form an important part of a continuum of responses to alcohol misuse, ranging from providing health education advice and information and brief interventions through to more complex specialist assessment and treatment.

Indeed, it is hoped that the early identification and treatment of alcohol misuse will not only improve the health of individual people and communities but also save money and reduce levels of repeat consultations in primary care (Babor *et al.,* 2003).

Levels of assessment

The National Treatment Agency (2002, 2006a,b) identifies levels of assessment of increasing complexity, depth and detail that are broadly reflective of the model described above and the skills and specialisms of staff who work within them (Scottish Executive, 2002). There are, of course, general principles of good practice in assessments at all levels, such as the need for assessments to be seen as an ongoing process rather than one-off events, as each person's needs are likely to evolve over time.

There will, therefore, need to be ongoing review and re-assessment, carried out at regular intervals to ensure appropriate care planning and coordination between agencies and services. In line with broader government healthcare policy (Department of Health, 2001) and in order to maximise effective engagement, assessment and subsequent care planning needs to be an inclusive process in which the client and the assessor work in partnership to identify need and to negotiate an appropriate and acceptable plan of care. Finally, assessing risk is an important and integral element in all levels of assessment with the specific aims of identifying whether an individual is likely to pose a risk to themselves or to others as a result of their alcohol use (Department of Health, 2002, 2006).

Level 1 assessment

This first level – the 'screening and referral' assessment – is a possible 'gateway' into a process of care for the person with alcohol misuse problems. Importantly, this process must be seen as a helpful and non-threatening experience. Information gathered at this stage is most likely to be relatively basic, comprising personal and historical data about the client, along with information about their levels and patterns of alcohol use (Department of Health, 2006; Scottish Executive, 2002). Indeed, such initial 'screening' is undertaken to afford the identification of alcohol consumption at a level that is sufficiently high to cause concern; many specially developed screening tools are available for this (see later) (Cabinet Office, 2004). However, as a minimum, the 'screening and referral' assessment needs to include the following (Department of Health, 2006; National Treatment Agency, 2002, 2006a,b):

- identification of a drug or alcohol misuse problem (hazardous, harmful or dependent use)
- identification of related or coexisting problems (e.g. physical, psychological or social)
- identification of immediate risks (e.g. self-harm, harm to physical health, self-neglect, suicide risk, and harm to others, including risks of harm to children and other domestic violence, harm to treatment staff and risks of driving while intoxicated)
- an assessment of the need for, and subsequent urgency of, referral.

Level 2 assessment

While our concern in this chapter is principally to identify assessments appropriate to primary care, most likely to be at Level 1, it is of importance that such professionals understand how their assessments fit into the care pathway of the client with alcohol problems. Hence, the Level 2 'substance misuse triage' assessment is seen as a filtering process that aims to establish the intervention or tier of service that would best suit the client with alcohol misuse problems. Level 2 assessments provide a fuller picture of the alcohol misuse problem and the specialist alcohol intervention that is needed.

Level 3 assessment

Finally, at Level 3, a 'comprehensive substance misuse assessment' may be appropriate when a client has been referred to a specialist agency. This assessment would clarify and cover in detail the nature and extent of drug use, physical and psychological health, risk to self or others, sexual health, personal and social skills, social and economic circumstances, previous treatment episodes and assets and attributes of the individual (National Treatment Agency, 2002; Scottish Executive, 2002).

Assessments in primary care

Primary healthcare professionals should be able to routinely carry out Level 1 assessments to screen for and identify alcohol misuse (National Treatment Agency, 2002, 2006a,b). Here we review various approaches, tools and strategies that may assist primary healthcare staff to assess and screen for alcohol misuse.

There are many tools and instruments to aid in identification of (and intervention for) hazardous and harmful drinkers. Screening instruments are useful because they can be self-administered by adults and are quick and easy to fill in. They can indicate issues or problems, or even dependence. Simple and reliable instruments like the Alcohol Use Disorders Identification Test (AUDIT) (Sanders *et al.,* 1993a,b) and the Fast Alcohol Screening Test (FAST) (Hodgson *et al.,* 2002) can be used to identify hazardous and harmful drinkers and provide an indication of the likely extent and severity of their alcohol-related problems. As these drinkers do not have significant evidence of alcohol dependence, advice and brief interventions are often suitable to meet the needs of both these groups (Department of Health, 2006).

Alcohol Use Disorders Identification Test (AUDIT)

The AUDIT was developed by Sanders *et al.* (1993a,b) to help clinicians in primary care settings to screen and identify problem or harmful drinking among their clients or patients who would need either to stop or reduce their alcohol consumption. The AUDIT consists of ten questions covering three domains: recent alcohol consumption; harmful or hazardous drinking; and dependence symptoms. The tool can be self-administered or administered by the clinician. The ten questions can take less than two minutes (Babor *et al.,* 2001) to complete although it is possible to do them much more quickly (Patton *et al.,* 2004). This instrument is very sensitive and specific for identifying alcohol-related problems such as harmful or hazardous drinking (Piccinelli *et al.,* 1997) and for symptoms of dependence (Conigrave *et al.* 1995a,b). Babor *et al.* (2001) consider that the AUDIT can be used in a variety of settings, including primary care, emergency departments in inpatient hospitals, hospital outpatient departments, and within psychiatry, occupational health, and the criminal justice system as well as by the military. The original study was conducted in Norway, Bulgaria, Kenya, Mexico, Australia and the USA. It appears to be the best screening instrument across countries and populations, and is best at identifying hazardous drinking in both adults and young people (Dawe *et al.,* 2002).

Fast Alcohol Screening Test (FAST)

The FAST was developed by Hodgson *et al.* (2002a) specifically for use within emergency departments and other medical settings where there is a need to rapidly assess alcohol use. The original study was conducted in NHS hospital settings (emergency departments, fracture clinics and dental clinics) and in primary healthcare settings in England and Wales (Hodgson *et al.,* 2002b). The FAST consists of four questions, aimed at identifying hazardous or harmful drinking as well as alcohol-related harm and dependence.

Assessments of 'readiness to change'

It can be important to ascertain someone's 'readiness to change' regarding their use of alcohol. It is helpful to think of 'readiness to change' not as a discrete category, but as a continuum along which a person's decision to change can be located somewhere between 'not ready to change' and 'eager to change'. As such, the person's readiness to change can embrace concepts of the importance they attach to changing their alcohol use (due, for example, to personal concerns for their own health), and also to their perception of their ability to make necessary changes – that is, their self-efficacy (Rollnick, Heather and Bell 1992). This can be assessed directly, for example, by asking: 'On a scale of one to ten, how important is it for you to change your alcohol use, where one is not at all important and ten is extremely important?' (Miller and Rollnick, 2002).

Other useful strategies for exploring 'readiness to change' include open-ended questions that establish the context of alcohol use, such as exploring with the person how, and if, they wish the future to be different from the present. Another useful approach for establishing the context of someone's alcohol use is the 'typical day' scenario (Miller and Rollnick, 2002), a useful technique in which the patient describes a day in their life and their subsequent use of alcohol; the goal is to 'simply follow the patient through a sequence of events focusing on both behaviour and feelings' (Rollnick, Heather, and Bell 1992).

Furthermore, people with substance misuse problems often express ambivalence regarding their addictions, so it can be of considerable importance to establish what sustains the behaviour (i.e. the 'good things' about their alcohol use – from their own perspective) as well as eliciting any concerns that may subsequently influence their behaviour change (i.e. the bad things about their alcohol use). This can be helpful to articulate and identify the 'decisional balance' facing the individual (Rollnick, 1998) and the perceived benefits and costs of their alcohol use.

Clinical assessment

In addition, to direct assessments of alcohol use or misuse, clinical assessments can be useful for ascertaining alcohol-related problems. Primary care professionals should be alerted by such signs and consider that they may be related to the use or misuse of alcohol. For example, falls and injuries might be signs of heavy drinking. Tremors of the hand or tongue, along with excessive and abnormal capillarisation of the facial skin and neck; yellowish blotches on the skin may be further signs of prolonged alcohol use. The condition of the conjunctival tissue should be assessed for the extent of burgundy-coloured capillary engorgement and scleral jaundice (a greenish-yellow tinge in the sclera).

While most clients are accurate about their self-reported consumption, under-reporting of alcohol use sometimes occurs. The use of breathalysers to measure blood alcohol concentration (BAC) can be useful in the screening process. Furthermore, biological markers of alcohol use above safe limits can help confirm the individual's self-reporting as well as clinical observations. BAC is one of four biological markers, although it is not an exact science – the average amount of alcohol expunged from the body is about 15 mg per 100 mL of blood per hour (Edwards *et al.*, 2003). The mean corpuscular volume (MCV) of red blood cells and serum levels of gamma glutamyl transferase (GGT), aspartate aminotransferase (AST) and especially carbohydrate-deficient transferrin (CDT) can indicate recent excessive alcohol consumption (Dawe *et al.*, 2002).

However, it is important to realise that false-positive MCV readings can occur as a result of vitamin B12 or folic acid deficiencies, thyroid or chronic liver disease, or when other drugs are being used (like barbiturates) that induce GGT; of course, hand tremor can result from nervousness, a neurological disorder, or nicotine dependence (Babor *et al.*, 2003; Scottish Intercollegiate Guidelines Network, 2003).

Conclusions

The screening and assessment of alcohol use in primary care has considerable advantages for early and targeted interventions in people with alcohol misuse issues. Identifying patients in primary care who are likely to benefit from brief interventions will also help achieve targets set out in the UK's harm reduction strategy (Coulton *et al.*, 2006; Department of Health *et al.*, 2007). This requires training, resources, and incentives for staff, as appropriate. Primary care professionals may be concerned about the potential time they would spend on incorporating alcohol screening and brief interventions into their consultations. Clear lines of communication between the tiers of treatment intervention are essential to facilitate appropriate and timely referrals (Alcohol Concern, 2002). With integrated care planning, as well as the use of joint inter-agency protocols, this will inevitably improve the standards of care in this field.

References and further reading

Aartgeerts, B., Buntinix, F., Ansoms, S. and Fevery, J. (2001). Screening properties of questionnaires and laboratory tests for the detection of alcohol abuse or dependence in a general practice population. *British Journal of General Practice*, **51**, 206–17.

Alcohol Concern (2001). *Screening Tools for Healthcare Settings*. Available at: http://www.alcoholconcern.org.uk/files/20080527_132528_Screening%20tool%20factsheet.pdf (last accessed October 2008).

Alcohol Concern (2002). *Advice on How to Engage Primary Care Teams in Alcohol Projects*. Available at: http://www.alcoholconcern.org.uk/files/20030910_141423_primary%20care%20and%20alc%20projects%20factsheet.pdf (last accessed October 2008).

American Psychiatric Association (1994). *Diagnostic and Statistical Manual of Mental Disorders (DSMIV)*, 4th edn. Washington, DC: American Psychiatric Association.

Anderson, P. and Baumberg, B. (2006). *Alcohol in Europe. A Public Health Perspective.* A Report for the European Commission. London: Institute of Alcohol Studies.

Aria, M., Kauhanen, J., Larivaara, P. and Rautio, P. (2003). Factors influencing inquiry about patients' alcohol consumption by primary health care physicians: qualitative semi-structured interview study. *Family Practice*, **20**(3), 270–75.

Babor, T., Caetano, R., Casswell, S., *et al.* (2003). *Alcohol: No Ordinary Commodity. Research and Public Policy*. Oxford: Oxford University Press.

Babor, T., Higgins-Biddle, J., Dauser, D., Higgins, P. and Burleson, J. (2005). Alcohol screening and brief intervention in primary care settings: implementation models and predictors. *Journal Studies on Alcohol*, **66**(3), 361–68.

Babor, T., Higgins-Biddle, J., Saunders, J. and Monteiro, M. (2001). *AUDIT: The Alcohol Use Disorders Identification Test Guidelines for Use in Primary Care*, 2nd edn. Geneva: WHO.

Brennan, P., Schutte, K. and Moos, R. (2005). Pain and use of alcohol to manage pain: Prevalence and 3-year outcomes among older problem and nonproblem drinkers. *Addiction*, **100**, 777–86.

Cabinet Office. (2004). *Alcohol Harm-Reduction Strategy for England*. London: The Cabinet Office.

Christensen, H., Low, L. and Anstey, K. (2006). Prevalence, risk factors and treatment for substance abuse In older adults. *Current Opinion in Psychiatry*, **19**, 587–92.

Conigrave, K., Hall, W. and Saunders, J. (1995a). The AUDIT questionnaire: choosing a cut-off score. *Addiction*, **90**, 1349–56.

Conigrave, K., Saunders, J. and Whitfield, J. (1995b). Diagnostic tests for alcohol consumption. *Alcohol and Alcoholism*, **30**, 13–26.

Coulton, S., Drummond, C., James, D., *et al.* (2006). Opportunistic screening for alcohol use disorders in primary care: Comparative study. *British Medical Journal*, **332**, 511–17.

Dawe, S., Loxton, N., Hides, L., Kavanagh, D. and Mattick, R. (2002). *Review of Diagnostic Screening Instruments for Alcohol and other Drug Use and other Psychiatric Disorders*, 2nd edn. Brisbane, Australia: Commonwealth Department of Health Ageing.

Department of Health (1995). *Sensible Drinking: The Report of an Interdepartmental Working Group*. London: The Stationery Office.

Department of Health (1999). *National Service Framework for Mental Health: Modern Standards and Service Models*. Available at: http://www.dh.gov.uk/en/Publicationsandstatistics/Publications/PublicationsPolicyAndGuidance/DH_4009598 (last accessed October 2008).

Department of Health (2001). *The Expert Patient*: A *New Approach to Chronic Disease Management for the 21st Century*. Available at: http://www.dh.gov.uk/en/Publicationsandstatistics/Publications/PublicationsPolicyAndGuidance/DH_4006801 (last accessed October 2008).

Department of Health (2002). *Mental Health Policy Implementation Guide: Dual Diagnosis Good Practice Guide*. Available at: http://www.dh.gov.uk/en/Publicationsandstatistics/Publications/PublicationsPolicyAndGuidance/DH_4009058 (last accessed October 2008).

Department of Health (2005a). *The Alcohol Needs Assessment Research Project* (*ANARP), The 2004 ANARP for England*. Available at: http://www.dh.gov.uk/en/Publicationsandstatistics/Publications/PublicationsPolicyAndGuidance/DH_4122341 (last accessed October 2008).

Department of Health (2005b). *Alcohol Misuse Interventions: Guidance on Developing* a *Local Programme Of Improvement*. Available at: http://www.dh.gov.uk/en/Publicationsandstatistics/Publications/PublicationsPolicyAndGuidance/DH_4123297 (last accessed October 2008).

Department of Health (2006). *Dual Diagnosis in Mental Health Inpatient and Day Hospital Settings*. Available at: http://www.dh.gov.uk/en/Publicationsandstatistics/Publications/PublicationsPolicyAndGuidance/DH_062649 (last accessed October 2008).

Department of Health, Home Office, Department of Education and Skills and the Department of Culture, Media and Sport (2007). *Safe, Sensible, Social: The Next Steps in the National Alcohol Strategy*. London: The Stationery Office.

Edwards, G. (2000). *Alcohol – The World's Favourite Drug*. London: Thomas Dunne.

Edwards, G. and Gross, M. (1976). Alcohol dependence: provisional description of a clinical syndrome. *British Journal of Addiction,* **84**, 850–52.

Edwards, G., Marshall, J. and Cook, C. (2003). *The Treatment of Drinking Problems. A Guide for the Helping Professions*, 4th edn. Cambridge: Cambridge University Press.

European Commission (2003). *Alcohol in the Workplace. A European Comparative Study on Preventative* and *Supporting Measures for Problem Drinkers in their working Environment*. Brussels: European Commission Directorate for Employment and Social Affairs.

Hodgson, R., Alwyn, T., John, B., Thom, B. and Smith, A. (2002a). The FAST alcohol screening test. *Alcohol and Alcoholism*, **37**(1), 61–66.

Hodgson, R., Alwyn, T., John, B., *et al.* (2002b). *Manual for the Fast Alcohol Screening Test* (*FAST), Fast Screening for Alcohol Problems*. London: NHS Health Development Agency; University of Wales College of Medicine.

Huntley, J. and Touquet, R. (2004). Screening for alcohol misuse. *Family Practice*, **21**(2), 222–23.

Huntley, J., Blain, C., Hood, S. and Touquet, R. (2001). Improving detection of alcohol misuse in patients presenting to an accident and emergency department. *Emergency Medicine Journal*, **18**, 99–00.

MacAndrew, C. and Edgerton, R. (1970). *Drunken Comportment*. London: Nelson.

Miller, W.R. and Rollnick, S. (2002). *Motivational Interviewing: Preparing People for Change*, 2nd edn. New York: Guilford Press.

National Treatment Agency for Substance Misuse (NTA) (2002) *Models of Care for the Treatment of Adult Drug Misusers. Part Two: Full Reference Report*. London: National Treatment Agency for Substance Misuse and the Department of Health.

National Treatment Agency for Substance Misuse (2006a). *Models of Care for the Treatment of Adult Drug Misusers: Update 2006*. London: NTA for Substance Misuse; Department of Health.

National Treatment Agency for Substance Misuse (2006b). *Models of Care for Alcohol*. London: NTA for Substance Misuse; Department of Health.

Patton, R., Hilton, C., Crawford, M. and Touquet, R. (2004). The Paddington alcohol test: A short report. *Alcohol and Alcoholism*, **39**(3), 266–68.

Piccinelli, M., Tessari, E., Bortolomamasi, M., *et al.* (1997). Efficacy of the alcohol-use disorders test as a screening tool for hazardous alcohol intake and related disorders in primary care: A validity study. *British Medical Journal*, **314**(7078), 420–24.

Rehm, J., Room, R., Monterio, M., Gmel, G., Jernigan, D. and Frick, U. (2003). Global distribution of average volume of alcohol consumption and patterns of drinking. *European Addiction Research*, **9**(4), 147–56.

Rollnick, S. (1998). Readiness, importance and confidence: critical conditions of change in treatment. In: Miller, W. and Heather, N. (eds). *Treating Addictive Behaviors*, 2nd edn. New York: Plenum Press.

Rollnick, S., Heather, N. and Bell, A. (1992). Negotiating behaviour change in medical settings: The development of brief motivational interviewing. *Journal of Mental Health*, **1**, 25–37.

Sanders, J., Aasland, O., Babor, T., de la Fuente, J. and Grant, M. (1993a). Alcohol consumption and related problems among primary healthcare patients: WHO collaborative project on early detection of persons with harmful alcohol consumption. Part I. *Addiction*, **88**, 349–62.

Sanders, J., Aasland, O., Babor, T., de la Fuente, J. and Grant, M. (1993b). Development of the Alcohol Use Disorders Identification Test (AUDIT). WHO collaborative project on early detection of persons with harmful alcohol consumption. Part II. *Addiction*, **88**, 791–04.

Scottish Executive (2002). *Integrated Care for Drug Users: Assessments. Digest of Tools Used in the Assessment Process and Core Data Sets*. Available at: http://www.drugmisuse.isdscotland.org/eiu/intcare/intcare.htm (last accessed October 2008).

Scottish Intercollegiate Guidelines Network (SIGN) (2003). *The Management of Harmful Drinking* and *Alcohol Dependence in Primary Care*. Available at: http://www.sign.ac.uk/pdf/sign74.pdf (last accessed October 2008).

Sudbury, P. (2001). Alcoholism-affected comorbidity of major depression and genetic and specific environmental risk factors. *Evidence Based Mental Health*, **4**, 30.

Thom, B. and Tellez, C. (1986). A difficult business: detecting and managing alcohol problems in general practice. *British Journal of Addiction*, **81**, 405–18.

World Health Organization (1992). ICD-10: *The ICD-10 Classification of Mental and Behavioural Disorders: Clinical Descriptions and Diagnostic Guidelines*. Geneva: WHO.

World Health Organization (2005). *Global Status Report on Alcohol 2004*. Geneva: WHO.

World Health Organization (2007). *European Health for All Database (HFA-DB)*, WHO Regional Office for Europe. Updated January, 2007. Available at: http://data.euro.who.int/hfadb (last accessed October 2008).

3

Alcohol problems in the emergency department

Colin A. Graham

This chapter considers the ways in which alcohol-affected patients interact with emergency departments, modes of presentation, common medical and psychosocial problems, difficulties faced when dealing with alcohol-addicted people, and the chronic medical issues related to alcohol dependency, as well as screening for alcohol problems in these patients.

Addictions affect all aspects of a person's life, and they impact upon all aspects of health care. Similarly, alcohol has a profound effect on all aspects of acute and emergency health services. The hospital emergency department frequently provides acute-care services to drug or alcohol-addicted people. Its central role as the 'final common pathway' in acute crisis management in the modern health service means that everyone working in health services or addiction care should know what it can provide. The emergency department needs access to specific specialist services to provide high-quality services to addicts in their care. The emergency department also has an emerging and crucial role in identifying people who are addicted to alcohol (Smith *et al.*, 1996) and other drugs (Ryan and Spronken, 2000). For example, emergency physicians, in collaboration with specialists in mental health care and addiction services, have developed the Paddington Alcohol Test (PAT) which is now used in many UK hospitals for screening patients presenting with acute conditions that may be alcohol-related (Smith *et al.*, 1996). Emergency departments provide initial care to anyone who presents, whether they are self-referred, referred by another healthcare professional or brought in by the ambulance service. Clearly, there are limits to the amount and type of care that can be provided and much of this help falls into the realms of crisis management and avoidance.

Alcohol and the emergency department

In a wide variety of guises, alcohol (ethanol) leads to significant numbers of patients presenting to the emergency department with acute or chronic problems. Not all those affected by alcohol will visit the department, and not all those who visit with alcohol-related problems will be addicted to alcohol. However, alcohol addiction increases the chances of someone requiring emergency department services for medical, mental health or social reasons. In the UK, it is estimated that 12 per cent of attendances every year are related to alcohol intoxication. A further 12–27 per cent of attendances relate to alcohol-related chronic problems, including medical illnesses and traumatic conditions (Royal College of Physicians of London, 2001). Other western societies have similar patterns of presentations with respect to alcohol. In the USA between 1992 and 2000, there were around 7.6 million alcohol-related attendances in annually, with a rising trend observed over that same period (McDonald *et al.*, 2004); this amounts to an annual incidence of 28.7 attendances per 1000 of the population. In Australia, around 5 per cent of attendances are alcohol-related, but patients with alcohol, drug and mental health problems are reported to take up to 10 per cent of emergency staff's time (King *et al.*, 2004). In Hong Kong, alcohol is a relatively rare cause of presentation to the emergency department, accounting for just 1–2 per cent of attendances. Only 6.5 per cent of major trauma patients in Hong Kong are alcohol-related (Rainer *et al.*, 2000). In mainland China, alcohol addiction has been reported to be low. It has become increasing significant over the last decade, but the exact figures for alcohol-related attendances are not available (Hao *et al.*, 2004; Wei *et al.*, 1999; Yang, 2002).

In the UK, premises that sell alcohol are licensed for business for a specified number of hours per day. Restriction of licensing hours was trialled in Scotland 10 years ago (Graham *et al.*, 1998) but had no appreciable impact on attendances and assaults presenting to the emergency department. The extension of drinking hours, as a result of the 2003 Licensing Act that allow s24-hour availability of alcohol, may lead to increases in alcohol-related attendances (Goodacre, 2005), but few studies have assessed the impact of these reforms so far. A recent study suggests that there has been an increase in overnight attendances (between 9 PM and 9 AM) in one inner-city hospital since licensing hours were extended, with significant increases in alcohol-related assaults, injuries and hospital admissions (Newton *et al.*, 2007). If this data is confirmed by other research, it will suggest that increasing availability of alcohol in developed societies leads to increased demands on emergency departments and the health service in general.

Modes of presentation to the emergency department

Acute alcohol intoxication

Acute alcohol intoxication leads to initial euphoria followed by a depressed overall mood; neurological effects include general incoordination, ataxia, pupillary dilation, slowing of responses, and slurring of speech. Chronic excessive consumption of alcohol leads to further effects, including tolerance (the requirement for higher doses of alcohol to achieve the same effect), fatty liver, hepatocellular destruction (ultimately leading to hepatic cirrhosis), peripheral neuropathy, cerebral atrophy, malnutrition and vitamin deficiencies. Acute alcohol intoxication can cause significant morbidity, particularly in young people. Ethanol has a direct toxic effect and frequently leads to a decreased conscious level, hypoxia, hypotension, pulmonary aspiration and hypothermia, along with the commonly observed nausea, vomiting and headache.

Children and young people

Occasionally, children under the age of 8 are brought to the emergency department having ingested some alcohol. Most young children cannot tolerate the unusual taste of alcoholic beverages, so severe alcohol intoxication is rare. Acute intoxication should be managed as a medical emergency, as alcohol can cause significant respiratory and cardiovascular depression in children.

As always, the 'ABC' (airway, breathing, circulation) of resuscitation should be applied to all children who are unwell and the airway should be cleared, maintained and protected. Breathing should be supported by a bag–valve–mask device supplemented with high-flow oxygen (10–15 litres per minute) as required. Their circulation should be assessed by checking the presence and quality of their pulse, their capillary refill time (which should be less than 2 seconds) and their blood pressure. If there is evidence of poor perfusion, 10–20 mL/kg of intravenous 0.9 per cent saline should be given and the response assessed. If there is still evidence of poor circulation, medical help from senior emergency staff should be sought urgently; senior paediatric and intensive care opinions should be obtained rapidly to ensure that alternative diagnoses such as sepsis have not been overlooked.

The capillary glucose should be checked early and regularly to exclude hypoglycaemia, which is common. Hypoglycaemia is defined as a blood glucose level of less than 3 mmol/L. If present, it should be treated with a 10–20 per cent dextrose infusion administered intravenously. Take care also to ensure there is no evidence of head injury (see below). Scrupulous attention to these aspects and active observation with repeated assessment will lead to an uneventful recovery.

Careful and tactful enquiries should be made of the parents and other caregivers (especially older siblings and teenage babysitters) about the presence of alcohol in the family home, access to the alcohol, and supervision. If there is any suspicion of neglect or deliberate administration of alcohol to a small child, referral to social services – or, rarely, the police – may be required.

Young people

Young people (defined here as those aged between 12 and 21), often under the legal age for drinking alcohol, are regularly brought to the emergency department under the apparent influence of alcohol by concerned parents or by the police. It is vital to exclude reversible medical conditions such as hypoglycaemia, which can present in an identical way to alcohol intoxication (as described above). It is also important to look for evidence of head injury as far as is possible by conducting a thorough examination. If there is any possibility *whatsoever* of head injury (e.g. a vague history or a small bruise to the face or scalp) then a computed tomography (CT) scan of the head is essential. It is absolutely vital that an altered conscious level is not attributed to alcohol alone until the presence of intracranial pathology has been actively excluded by CT scanning. If a head injury is suspected and the patient is under the influence of alcohol, cervical spine injury should also be suspected, and appropriate spinal immobilisation should be instituted at the earliest opportunity, followed by appropriate imaging.

There have been cases in the UK where young people who appear to be under the influence of alcohol are discharged to police custody, only to deteriorate and die due to their unrecognised severe head injury (Inquiry, 1999). Severe brain injury can occur *without* external signs of head trauma – if there is *any* doubt then extreme caution must be exercised. If reversible causes are excluded and a positive diagnosis of alcohol intoxication is made, the patient can be discharged home in most cases to continue their recovery. It is essential that the patient is at least capable of conducting a coherent conversation and walking steadily before discharge, otherwise the chances of sustaining further injury are unacceptably high. It is advisable to ensure that the patient is clearly improving before discharge, because intracranial pathology such as delayed extradural haematoma or spontaneous intracerebral haemorrhage can confuse the situation occasionally. If the apparently 'drunk' patient fails to improve over several hours, a CT scan of the brain should be strongly considered.

Alcohol intoxication and co-ingestion of illicit drugs is a common mode of presentation. It can occur across all age groups and is seen increasingly among the 'middle class' who abuse cocaine along with alcohol. These patients pose particular problems because the depressant effects of alcohol interact with various effects of the other ingested substance. For example, combinations of alcohol and benzodiazepines or opiates have a synergistic depressant effect on the cardiorespiratory and neurological systems, and intensive supportive care is often necessary, and occasionally management in a critical care unit. Occasionally young people who appear to be intoxicated have actually taken illicit drugs such as MDMA (commonly known as 'ecstasy') or ketamine, with or without alcohol. Similarly, ingestion of alcohol with cocaine combines the depressant effects of alcohol with the stimulant effects of cocaine. This can confuse the clinical picture for ambulance and emergency-department staff. Care must be taken, as far as is reasonable, to identify any potential co-ingestants; if there is any suggestion of this, inpatient admission and observation for 24 hours are recommended as a minimum.

Any patient who is discharged from the emergency department with acute alcohol intoxication must be released into the care of a responsible, and sober, adult. Teenagers who present sometimes do so because alcohol consumption is an accepted part of their normal family life, for them and their parents. It is important to try to identify these cases by directly interviewing family members, if possible. Early proactive intervention can be considered to try to minimise or prevent ongoing problems.

Special circumstances

At certain times of the year, for example during major sporting events or specific festivals (like the Hogmanay celebrations that take place every New Year's Eve in Edinburgh) large numbers of young people ingest alcohol to excess. Many of them end up in the emergency department, with typical symptoms of alcohol intoxication, and are far from their home, often accompanied by equally intoxicated friends. Plans need to be made in advance to look after these vulnerable people, who remain at risk from hypoglycaemia, hypothermia, and occult head injury. Every year in Edinburgh, on Hogmanay night, one ward is converted into an alcohol observation ward, with experienced nurses observing up to 40 patients overnight until they are deemed fit for discharge according to the criteria mentioned earlier (O'Donnell *et al.*, 1998). It is easier to place mattresses directly on the ward floor in these situations, to minimise the risk of patients falling out of bed in an unfamiliar environment. There should be extra supplies of blankets, vomit bowls and tissues to cope with the inevitable effects of acute alcohol excess.

Under these circumstances, concerns about undesirable behaviour may warrant the provision of extra security staff for the emergency department and holding area. However, once again, it must be emphasised that aggressive behaviour can result from occult severe brain injury or hypoglycaemia, so efforts must be made to exclude these before simply labelling the behaviour as 'alcohol-related'. Senior medical staff must be involved in the management of these patients to minimise avoidable morbidity (O'Donnell *et al.*, 1998).

Chronic alcohol abuse

Chronic alcohol abuse is a massive problem in western society today, although the incidence of chronic alcohol abuse is rising in other parts of the world as well (such as China) due to increasing affluence and the increasing adoption of western eating and drinking habits. In particular, there seems to be increasing evidence of 'problem drinking' and a three-fold increase in death rates over the last decade (Information Services Division, 2005). There is a spectrum of presentations of chronic alcohol abuse that starts with 'problem drinking' (drinking excessively or drinking associated with domestic or street violence) and ends with alcoholic liver disease and alcohol-induced medical problems such as those listed in Table 3.1.

The principal medical problems from an emergency-department perspective are those conditions requiring urgent resuscitation, such as massive upper gastrointestinal bleeding. Prompt emergency treatment followed by specialist referral for timely emergency endoscopy is required, but it is not easy to organise in reality. Massive upper gastrointestinal haemorrhage is often associated with coagulopathy secondary to liver disease in the alcoholic patient, which increases bleeding and worsens prognosis. Massive blood loss is also associated with hypothermia, which further worsens coagulopathy, so once bleeding has become massive the probability of a good outcome deteriorates rapidly.

Atrial fibrillation due to chronic alcohol abuse is common, and the relatively new concept of the 'holiday heart' is being seen more frequently with the increasing incidence of binge drinking. Men appear to be particularly at risk (Frost and Vestergaard, 2004). The term 'holiday heart' refers to the sudden onset of paroxysmal atrial fibrillation, usually in response to a sudden large binge of alcohol at the start of a holiday period (Koul *et al.*, 2005). Atrial fibrillation can have significant morbidity, particularly if it results in embolic stroke. It is particularly prevalent during weekends, especially in relatively young people.

The spectrum of alcoholic liver disease is enormous (and is covered comprehensively in Chapter 6). The principal issues from the perspective of an emergency department remain those of acute gastrointestinal bleeding and hepatic encephalopathy secondary to hepatic cirrhosis and portal hypertension. These demand urgent resuscitation, and possible referral to an intensive care unit. Acute and chronic pancreatitis are common and can be confused with alcoholic ketoacidosis (AKA). AKA appears to be increasing in incidence and is undoubtedly under-diagnosed (McGuire *et al.*, 2006). In addition, several studies suggest AKA as a factor in sudden death among alcohol abusers (Kadis *et al.*, 1999; Pounder *et al.*, 1998).

Chronic alcohol intake can lead to deficiencies of thiamine and other vitamins, leading to neuropsychiatric sequelae such as Wernicke's encephalopathy, Korsakoff syndrome and peripheral neuropathies. Current recommendations emphasise the need for intravenous administration of concentrated B vitamins to all acutely unwell people with chronic alcohol abuse.

Alcohol withdrawal syndrome is frequently seen in the emergency department setting, most often during the 24-hour period of observation that is usually required following a minor head injury in the presence of alcohol. It starts between 6 and 12 hours following the last drink, and can involve agitation, sweating, tachycardia and vomiting. It is treated very effectively with oral diazepam at a dose of 10–20 mg per hour until clinical relief is evident. Inexperienced medical and nursing staff are often unprepared for the large doses of diazepam that are needed to effectively treat this condition, but a standard treatment pathway based on the Clinical Institute

Table 3.1	Alcohol-induced medical problems
Acute gastrointestinal haemorrhage	Gastritis Mallory–Weiss tear secondary to vomiting Peptic ulcer disease Oesophageal varices (portal hypertension)
Pancreatitis	Acute pancreatitis Chronic pancreatitis
Alcoholic liver disease	Alcoholic hepatitis Alcohol-induced fatty liver Alcohol-induced cirrhosis Portal hypertension Hepatic encephalopathy
Neurological problems	Peripheral neuropathy Cerebral atrophy Chronic subdural haematoma Acute head injury Alcohol withdrawal syndrome Delirium tremens
Neuropsychiatric sequelae	Wernicke's encephalopathy (thiamine deficiency) Korsakoff syndrome
Cardiovascular problems	Chronic atrial fibrillation 'Holiday heart' – paroxysmal atrial fibrillation Cardiomyopathy
Metabolic problems	Hypoglycaemia Alcoholic ketoacidosis Thiamine deficiency

Withdrawal Assessment for Alcohol (CIWA) scale (Sullivan *et al.*, 1989) has proven to be very useful in many UK emergency departments. It is related to – but is distinct from – delirium tremens, which is a medical emergency with a high mortality. Delirium tremens is covered in detail in Chapter 8.

Trauma

Injuries of all types are more common in people affected by acute or chronic alcohol ingestion. In 2005, a study in Scotland showed that 53 per cent of patients attending the emergency department with an alcohol-related problem had sustained an injury (NHS Quality Improvement Scotland, 2007).

Acute alcohol intoxication

Acute alcohol intoxication releases inhibitory centres in the brain and leads to the adoption of behaviours associated with increased risk. Intoxicated people are therefore more likely to put themselves, and their companions, in high-risk situations. For example, driving is a high-risk behaviour; when alcohol is involved, crashes tend to occur at greater speeds, with more severe injuries, and they result in higher mortality than when no alcohol is involved. Intoxicated pedestrians are more likely to be knocked down by a car than sober pedestrians.

Legislation has an important role in reducing injuries from road traffic crashes with respect to alcohol. The legal limit for alcohol in drivers in the UK is 80 mg/dL of blood, which is rigidly enforced. Despite this, the risk assessment mechanisms and reactions of drivers are markedly impaired at this level, so other countries have adopted lower levels – Australia and Hong Kong have set 50 mg/dL as the limit. The widely publicised UK 'drink-driving' campaign that takes place over the Christmas and New Year festive season undoubtedly saves lives by intercepting drivers who are over the limit. However, reports suggest that a 'hard core' of persistent offenders continues to recklessly drink and drive, often with tragic results.

Chronic alcohol abuse

Chronic alcohol abuse leads to other issues with respect to injury. Those suffering from chronic liver disease often have impaired coagulation and therefore do not mount a normal response to acute haemorrhage. This leads to increased bleeding rates, increased incidences of hypothermia and acidosis, admission to intensive care units and death. The malnutrition commonly seen in chronic alcohol abusers means that these patients often develop wound complications following trauma, and are 'slow healers' who may require a longer time in hospital than their non-alcohol-abusing counterparts with similar injuries. Chronic alcohol abusers are more at risk of specific injuries such as chronic subdural haematoma. This can occur after trivial injuries or even without trauma. A high index of clinical suspicion and a low threshold for CT scanning may help to reduce the morbidity associated with chronic subdural haematoma.

Violence

Intentional violence is a major aspect of alcohol abuse-related trauma, particularly binge drinking and chronic alcohol abuse. Violent crime is more common in people under the influence of alcohol, although it is generally accepted that the presence of alcohol is not a legally mitigating factor in these cases. There is some association between alcohol intake and facial trauma as well as the incidence of penetrating trauma, including stabbings.

In some parts of the UK there is an embedded 'knife culture', such that when someone goes out for a drink they may carry a knife as well (Bleetman *et al.,* 1997; Leyland, 2006). This is a recipe for disaster. Again the victims tend to be young men who are also under the influence of alcohol and carrying a weapon. A policy of 'sensible drinking' and the previously successful knife amnesties may make a difference, but more draconian measures such as using metal detectors to screen for weapons in high risk areas (such as city centres) may prove to be more effective in the long term. In recent years, some police authorities have taken the initiative to set up 'violence-reduction units' but it remains to be seen if these units are effective in the longer term.

Domestic violence, particularly against women, is also strongly associated with alcohol consumption. In the UK, several high-profile media campaigns have been undertaken over the last decade to specifically address this. Alcohol-control agencies and violence-reduction initiatives may be helpful in the short term but the long-term success of such initiatives is again much harder to prove.

Violence often spills over into the emergency department once victims arrive there (James *et al.*, 2006). Some departments in the UK now have their own police officers, and many emergency departments in the USA have full-time armed security staff and airport-style inspections before anyone can access the emergency department, to minimise the risks to staff from weapons. Nursing staff in emergency departments are widely recognised as one of the most likely professional groups to be victims of workplace violence, and patients under the influence of alcohol are frequently implicated. Methods of reducing risk include the use of security staff, de-escalation techniques, the presence of police and, ultimately, the 'banning' of specific patients who persistently and recklessly endanger staff and other patients. This last resort is much easier to suggest than to enforce in reality.

There is no easy answer to these violence issues. They demand a coordinated and multi-disciplinary approach from many different agencies (including the emergency department, the police and justice services, and addiction services and psychiatrists) to formulate locally applicable plans that deal with intoxicated and alcohol-abusing patients. A recent UK study reported on the beneficial effects of a combined emergency medicine and police intervention in a city-centre setting on alcohol-related violence; effects were seen particularly on alcohol-related assaults (Warburton and Shepherd, 2006).

Screening for alcohol problems in the emergency department

Alcohol abuse and addiction leads to serious social effects as well as medical and health issues. A major aspect of treating the effects of alcohol abuse is finding the right method for identifying the presence of a problem, and then intervening appropriately. Various tools have been devised for identification of alcohol problems, such as the AUDIT, which was developed by the World Health Organization for primary care settings, not specifically the emergency department (Babor *et al.*, 1992). The work by Touquet and colleagues in the emergency department of St Mary's Hospital in London led to the development of the Paddington Alcohol Test, or PAT (Smith *et al.*, 1996). This is a short screening questionnaire that can be performed by staff in the emergency department in response to a range of trigger conditions known to be highly associated with alcohol misuse (e.g. falls, collapse, head injury and assault). The PAT questions and notes are shown in Figs 3.1 and 3.2.

Touquet frequently refers to the 'teachable moment' – the one point in time when the alcohol abuser may realise that alcohol is the source of their difficulties (Patton *et al.*, 2005). The 'teachable moment' appears to have a short half-life, around 2 days, and therefore follow-up for any intervention for alcohol problems needs to be given quickly and from the emergency department (Williams *et al.*, 2005). Given that many people present at a time of crisis (when their alcohol habit has brought them to a point of ill health or recent injury) and because the 'teachable moment' is so short, the emergency department seems a logical and appropriate place to identify patients in need of help (Touquet and Brown, 2006; Touquet and Paton, 2006). Indeed, the literature on PAT bears this concept out; between 31 and 46 per cent of those offered an appointment with an alcohol health-worker following an emergency attendance at the emergency department take up the offer and receive a single targeted session of advice and practical help (Patton *et al.*, 2005).

PADDINGTON ALCOHOL TEST (PAT)

Consider PAT for ALL of the TOP 10 reasons for attendance. Circle number(s) below for any specific trigger(s):

1. FALL (incl. trips)	**2. COLLAPSE (incl. fits)**	**3. HEAD INJURY**
4. ASSAULT	**5. ACCIDENT**	**6. UNWELL**
7. NON-SPECIFIC G.I.	**8. CARDIAC (i. chest pain)**	**9. PSYCHIATRIC (incl. DSH/OD) (specify)**
10. REPEAT ATTENDER	**Other (specify):**	

Proceed only after dealing with patient's 'agenda,' i.e. patient's reason for attendance. We routinely ask all patients with (state reason for screening) about their use of alcohol.

QUESTION 1: Do you drink alcohol?

Yes *(go to question 2)*
No *(end)*

QUESTION 2: What is the most you will drink in any one day (standard alcohol units)?

If necessary, please use the following guide to estimate total daily units (standard pub units in brackets; home measures are often three times the amount!)

Alcopops	330 mL (1.5)	☐				
Beer/lager/cider	Pints (2)	☐	Cans (1.5)	☐	1 L bottles (4.5)	☐
Strong beer/lager/cider	Pints (5)	☐	Cans (4)	☐	1 L bottles (10)	☐
Wine	Glasses (1.5)	☐	75 cl bottles (9)	☐		
Fortified wine (sherry, port, martini)	Glasses (1)	☐	75 cl bottles (12)	☐		
Spirits (gin, vodka, whisky, etc.)	Singles (1)	☐	75 cl bottles	☐		

The medically recommended daily limits of alcohol are 4 units/day for a man or 3 units/day for a woman.

QUESTION 3: How often do you drink more than twice the recommended amount?

Never or less than weekly *(go to question 4)*
Every day *(Dependent Drinker; PAT +ve; ? Pabrinex/chlordiazepoxide)*
.... times per week *(Hazardous Drinker; may be PAT +ve)*

QUESTION 4: Do you feel your attendance here is related to alcohol?

Yes *(PAT +ve)*
No

If PAT +ve, give feedback (e.g. 'We advise you that this drinking is harming your health'). If drinking daily, but not excessively, advise about drink-free days.

QUESTION 5: We would like to offer you advice about your alcohol consumption. Would you be willing to see our alcohol nurse specialist?

Yes (*PAT +ve***)**
No

Figure 3.1 Questions from the Paddington Alcohol Test (PAT). With kind permission of Professor Robin Touquet. For further information about the Paddington Alcohol Test (PAT) contact Professor R. Touquet (robin.touquet@st-marys.nhs.uk) or Adrian Brown RMN (ade.brown@nhs.net).

The Paddington Alcohol Test (PAT) is a clinical and therapeutic tool for screening hospital patients for both hazardous and dependent drinking – enabling the giving of initial Brief Advice (BA). The PAT was specifically developed for use by clinicians in a busy emergency department, employing attendance as a 'TEACHABLE MOMENT' (Williams et al., 2005). PAT is non-judgemental, enabling patients to develop insight into their drinking, its cause and effect. Using the PAT, plus referral to AHW (for definitive Brief Intervention) results in lower alcohol consumption and reduces the likelihood of re-attendance (Crawford et al., 2004). It takes only about 30 seconds to complete the PAT.

1. Deal with the patient's reason for attending and their presenting condition first, thereby gaining their confidence so they are in a more receptive frame of mind.

2. If the patient has one of the TOP 10 conditions listed at the top of the PAT, or some other indication of recent consumption of alcohol, then proceed with the PAT questions.

3. Ask Question 1 'We routinely ask all patients with (this condition) if they drink alcohol – do you drink?'. If the answer is 'No' (PAT–ve) then discontinue (providing the clinician agrees with the answer).

4. If the answer is 'Yes' then go to Question 2 'What is the most that patient will drink in one day?' For the United Kingdom: 8 gms absolute alcohol = 10 mL alcohol = 1 unit. Standard Alcohol Units (SAU) = % ABV × volume (in litres) where '% ABV' is 'the percentage of alcohol by volume' as indicated on bottle or can. Please use the guide to help you (and the patient) calculate amounts – drinks vary so much that the use of standard alcohol units is necessary for consistency. It may be less judgemental to focus solely on quantity rather than what they drink.

5. Having estimated the number of units consumed, if this is more than double the recommended daily limits (8 units for men or 6 units for women), then ask Question 3 'How often do you drink more than 8 or 6 units? This helps differentiate the dependent drinker, who will need on-going support, from the hazardous or 'binge' drinker who may only need one session of Brief Intervention. The sooner binge drinking is detected, the more effective is the use of the PAT. The acceptance of an appointment with an Alcohol Liaison Nurse (AHW) demonstrates awareness of a problem and the desire for help.

6. If there is evidence of chronic alcohol misuse, poor diet and confusion, ataxia or ophthalmoplegia, then give intravenous Pabrinex at the earliest opportunity (I & II (×2) in 100 mL 0.9% saline infused over half an hour) (Thompson *et al.*, 2002).

7. Everyone who has said yes to Question 1 should be asked Question 4: 'Do you feel your current attendance is related to alcohol?'. If the answer is 'Yes' then you have started brief advice (BA) by the patient associating drinking with resulting hospital attendance. If they deny any association (but in your clinical judgement have been drinking) you might say 'Would you be in hospital if you had NOT been drinking?'.

8. Ask Question 5. If the answer is 'Yes' then leave the PAT form in the AHW referrals box, with diary for BI. Appointments are at 10 AM the next morning (no limit on numbers). N.B. It is known that the earlier that appointment is offered, the more likely the patient is to attend – please encourage them to take the next available appointment rather than defer it. If PAT + (but AHW 'No') give the patient the *Think About Drink* leaflet and even the AHW appointment card as they may change their mind and return. File the completed PAT form in the patient notes so that it will be scanned in case the patient returns.

9. If PAT +ve, Alcohol Liaison Nurse 'Yes' on discharge computer screen record: A&E clinics → A&E Alcohol Clinic, unless admitted.

10. If patient is PAT –ve, do not write on the form (it is recycled).

Figure 3.2   Notes on how to use the Paddington Alcohol Test (PAT).

There is evidence that a brief intervention by an alcohol health-worker may reduce alcohol intake at 6-month follow-up (Ballesteros *et al.*, 2004), including recent high-quality evidence from a UK-based randomised-controlled trial (Crawford *et al.*, 2004). Furthermore, this approach appears to be both cost effective and clinically effective (Barrett *et al.*, 2006). A 2002 systematic review concluded that screening and brief interventions should be part of routine clinical practice (D'Onofrio and Degutis, 2002). Further research is needed to look at this aspect in other healthcare systems and other geographic and cultural settings.

Another aspect raised by the implementation of the PAT is the apathy and lack of enthusiasm that many emergency department staff have towards the problem of alcohol abuse. Certainly there is a perception among the staff that they have enough to do dealing with the physical and immediate mental health needs of their patients, without involving themselves with treatment of the underlying cause. However, the only long-term solution to alcohol abuse is to deal with the underlying issues, and it has been shown that continuous audit of junior medical staff can improve not only their use of the PAT but also the rate of detection of alcohol abuse in the emergency department (Huntly *et al.*, 2001). One novel method studied recently involved measuring blood alcohol concentrations in the emergency department with encouraging results (Csipke *et al.*, 2007). Further efforts to improve the detection of alcohol abuse in the emergency setting and instituting ways to deal with it through brief targeted intervention are likely to be the way forward.

The interface between the emergency department and alcohol services

The interface between emergency and addiction services has traditionally been a difficult area. Previously, many alcohol management clinics could only accept referrals from a patient's general practitioner; it is not surprising that many patients never returned to see their general practitioner after the index emergency department visit for follow-up, given the short half-life of the 'teachable moment'. In this way, many opportunities for intervention were lost. Evidence suggests that if emergency department staff identify a suitable patient, that patient should be referred to an appropriate agency in a timely and direct manner to take full advantage of the 'teachable moment'. Referral routes have improved significantly over the last decade in the UK, but in some areas of the country (and indeed the rest of the world) progress is not so obvious.

Alcohol health-workers have been employed in some centres in UK emergency departments, with close links to psychiatric and addiction services. Other departments use psychiatric liaison nurse specialists to form a partnership between the emergency department and supporting services for victims of alcohol and drug addiction. Some of these workers have been funded by primary care trusts in the UK, to reflect the fact that traditionally alcohol health-workers were located in the community setting rather than the hospital setting. The emergency department bridges that gap for many patients with alcohol problems and this model seems to be effective. One study has noted that the majority of drug addicts dying suddenly had contact with the emergency department at some point in the past, and suggested that the department might be a good place to identify and provide support to this vulnerable group (Ryan and Spronken, 2000). It is likely that this process also applies to patients who are addicted to alcohol. Future research may help to clarify what further methods of intervention may be useful for these patients.

Conclusions

Patients with alcohol problems, acute and chronic, frequently present to the emergency department with challenging and diverse problems and pathology. A coordinated approach between the emergency department and supporting services may improve the quality of care for these patients, and may reduce avoidable mortality and morbidity. Specific training and audit for staff is important, and interfaces with addiction and alcohol services should be established and enhanced.

Screening for alcohol problems in the emergency department has been shown to be cost effective and a clinically useful way to identify patients with alcohol problems; this practice should be encouraged. Further high-quality research is required to identify optimum methods for screening and intervention for alcohol problems in emergency departments in other healthcare settings and other countries.

References and further reading

Babor, T.F., De la Fuente, J.R., Saunders, J. and Grant, M. (1992). *AUDIT – The Alcohol Use Disorders Identification Test: Guidelines for Use in Primary Health Care*. Geneva: WHO.

Ballesteros, J., Duffy, J.C., Querejeta, I., *et al.* (2004). Efficacy of brief interventions for hazardous drinkers in primary care: systematic review and meta-analysis. *Alcoholism: Clinical and Experimental Research*, **28**, 608–18.

Bleetman, A., Perry, C.H., Crawford, R. and Swann, I.J. (1997). Effect of Strathclyde police initiative 'Operation Blade' on accident and emergency attendances due to assault. *Journal of Accident and Emergency Medicine*, **14**, 153–56.

Csipke, E., Touquet, R., Patel, T., *et al.* (2007). Use of blood alcohol concentration in resuscitation room patients. *Emergency Medicine Journal*, **24**(8), 535–38.

D'Onofrio, G. and Degutis, L.C. (2002). Preventive care in the emergency department: screening and brief intervention for alcohol problems in the emergency department: A systematic review. *Academic Emergency Medicine*, **9**, 627–38.

Frost, L. and Vestergaard, P. (2004). Alcohol and risk of atrial fibrillation or flutter: A cohort study. *Archives of Internal Medicine*, **164**(18), 1993–98.

Goodacre, S. (2005). The 2003 Licensing Act: An act of stupidity? *Emergency Medicine Journal*, **22**, 682.

Graham, C.A., McLeod, L.S. and Steedman, D.J. (1998). Restricting extensions to permitted licensing hours does not influence the numbers of alcohol or assault related attendances at an inner city accident and emergency department. *Journal of Accident and Emergency Medicine*, **15**, 23–25.

Hao, W., Su., Z., Liu, B., *et al.* (2004). Drinking and drinking patterns and health status in the general population of five areas of China. *Alcohol and Alcoholism*, **39**(1), 43–52.

Huntly, J.S., Blain, C., Hood, S. and Touquet, R. (2001). Improving detection of alcohol misuse in patients presenting to an accident and emergency department. *Emergency Medicine Journal*, **18**, 99–104.

Information Services Division NHS National Services Scotland (2005). *Alcohol Statistics Scotland 2005*. ISD Scotland Publications: Edinburgh. http://www.alcoholinformation.isdscotland.org/alcohol_misuse/files/AlcoholStatisticsScotland2005.pdf (last accessed October 2008).

Inquiry Held Under Fatal Accidents and Sudden Deaths Inquiry (Scotland) Act, 1976 for Gordon Scott Niven. 5 March 1999. Sheriff Principal E.F. Bowen. Scottish Court Service.

James, A., Madeley, R. and Dove, A. (2006). Violence and aggression in the emergency department. *Emergency Medicine Journal*, **23**, 431–34.

Kadis, P., Balazic, J. and Ferlan-Marolt, V. (1999). Alcoholic ketoacidosis: A cause of sudden death in chronic alcoholics. *Forensic Science International*, **103**, S53–59.

King, D.L., Kalucy, R.S., de Crespigny, C.F., Stuhlmiller, C.M. and Thomas, L.J. (2004). Mental health and alcohol and other drug training for emergency department workers: one solution to help manage increasing demand. *Emergency Medicine Australasia*, **16**, 155–206.

Koul, P.B., Sussmane, J.B., Cunill-De Sautu, B. and Minarik, M. (2005). Atrial fibrillation associated with alcohol ingestion in adolescence: holiday heart in pediatrics. *Pediatric Emergency Care*, **21**(1), 38–39.

Leyland, A.H. (2006). Homicides involving knives and other sharp objects in Scotland, 1981–003. *Journal of Public Health*, **28**, 145–47.

McDonald, A.J. 3rd, Wang, N. and Camargo, C.A. Jr (2004). US emergency department visits for alcohol-related diseases and injuries between, 1992 and 2000. *Archives of Internal Medicine*, **164**(5), 531–37.

McGuire, L.C., Cruickshank, A.M. and Munro, P.T. (2006). Alcoholic ketoacidosis. *Emergency Medicine Journal*, **23**, 417–20.

Newton, A., Sarker, S.J., Pahal, G.S., van den Bergh, E. and Young, C. (2007). Impact of the new UK licensing law on emergency hospital attendances: A cohort study. *Emergency Medicine Journal*, **24**(8), 532–34.

NHS Quality Improvement Scotland (2006). *Understanding alcohol misuse in Scotland. Harmful drinking 1: The size of the problem*. Edinburgh: Scottish Emergency Department Alcohol Audit (SEDAA) Group. Available at: http://www.nhshealthquality.org/nhsqis/files/Alcohol_size%20of%20prob_web.pdf (last accessed October 2008).

O'Donnell, J.J., Gleeson, A.P. and Smith, H. (1998). Edinburgh's Hogmanay celebrations: beyond a major disaster. *Journal of Accident and Emergency Medicine*, **15**(4), 272–73.

Patton, R., Hilton, C., Crawford, M.J. and Touquet, R. (2004). The Paddington Alcohol Test: A short report. *Alcohol and Alcoholism*, **9** (3), 266–68.

Patton, R., Crawford, M. and Touquet, R. (2005). Hazardous drinkers in the accident and emergency department – who attends an appointment with the alcohol health-worker? *Emergency Medicine Journal*, **22**, 722–23.

Pounder, D.J., Stevenson, R.J. and Taylor, K.K. (1998). Alcoholic ketoacidosis at autopsy. *Journal of Forensic Science*, **43**, 812–16.

Rainer, T.H., Chan, S.Y., Kwok, K., *et al.* (2000). Severe trauma presenting to the resuscitation room of a Hong Kong emergency department. *Hong Kong Journal of Emergency Medicine*, **7**(3), 129–35.

Royal College of Physicians of London (2001). *Alcohol – Can the NHS afford it? Recommendations for a coherent alcohol strategy for hospitals*. Report of a Working Party of the Royal College of Physicians of London, pp. 9–20.

Ryan, J.M. and Spronken, I. (2000). Drug-related deaths in the community: A preventive role for accident and emergency departments. *Journal of Accident and Emergency Medicine*, **17**, 272–73.

Smith, S.G.T., Touquet, R., Wright, S., *et al.* (1996). Detection of alcohol misusing patients in accident and emergency departments: the Paddington alcohol test (PAT). *Journal of Accident and Emergency Medicine*, **13**, 308–12.

Sullivan, J.T., Sykora, K., Schneiderman, J., Naranjo, C.A. and Sellers, E.M. (1989). Assessment of alcohol withdrawal: The revised Clinical Institute Withdrawal Assessment for Alcohol scale (CIWA-Ar). *British Journal of Addiction*, **84**, 1353–57.

Touquet, R. and Brown, A. (2006). Alcohol misuse: Positive response. Alcohol health work for every acute hospital saves money and reduces repeat attendances. *Emergency Medicine Australasia*, **18**, 103–07.

Touquet, R. and Paton, A. (2006). Tackling alcohol misuse at the front line. *British Medical Journal*, **333,** 510–11.

Warburton, A.L. and Shepherd, J.P. (2006). Tackling alcohol-related violence in city centres: effect of emergency medicine and police intervention. *Emergency Medicine Journal*, **23,** 12–17.

Wei, H., Derson, Y., Xiao, S., Li., L. and Zhang, Y. (1999). Alcohol consumption and alcohol-related problems: Chinese experience from six area samples, 1994. *Addiction*, **94**(10), 1467–76.

Williams, S., Brown, A., Patton, R., Crawford, M.J. and Touquet, R. (2005). The half-life of the 'teachable moment' for alcohol misusing patients in the emergency department. *Drug and Alcohol Dependence*, **77**(2), 205–08.

Yang, M.J. (2002). The Chinese drinking problem: A review of the literature and its implication in a cross-cultural study. *Kaohsiung Journal of Medical Science*, **18**(11), 434–50.

4 Dual diagnosis

Anne Lingford-Hughes and Ben Watson

The term 'dual diagnosis' is broad. In its simplest form it refers to a person having two concurrent diagnoses, or in other words one who is suffering from more than one medical condition. For the purposes of this chapter, we will define the term 'dual diagnosis' according to its common medical usage, as the coexistence of a mental disorder and a substance-misuse disorder, with alcohol being the substance we focus on.

Alcohol-misuse disorders

In the UK, the recommended levels of alcohol consumption are up to 14 units per week for women and 21 units per week for men (Royal College of Physicians, 1995). It is also recommended that no more than 2–3 units are consumed in any one day and at least 2 days are alcohol free. Drinking more than this is associated with increased likelihood of harm (physical and mental health, social, forensic) and is termed 'hazardous'.

A 'binge' is defined for women as drinking more than 6 units per day, and for men more than 8 units per day. The term 'alcohol use disorder' incorporates harmful drinking and dependence. When physical or mental health is affected, drinking is defined as 'harmful' in the ICD-10 classification system. 'Dependence' is a 'cluster of physiological, behavioural and cognitive phenomena in which the use of alcohol takes on a much higher priority for a given individual than other behaviours'. For dependence, three or more of the criteria in Box 4.1 (overpage) must be present in the previous year.

The relationship between alcohol and psychiatric disorders

Alcohol is widely available, relatively cheap, and predominantly used as a social lubricant, and for its short-term euphoric effects. In addition, it is frequently used to alleviate symptoms of psychiatric illness. It is common to find symptoms of psychiatric disorders such as depression, anxiety and psychosis in patients misusing alcohol, and these disorders also increase the risk of alcohol misuse itself. Such patients may also be physically unwell and are often the most challenging to engage with and treat, having a prognosis that is frequently poor.

> **Box 4.1 Dependence diagnosed on the basis of three or more of the following criteria in previous year**
>
> 1. A strong desire or compulsion to drink alcohol
> 2. Difficulty in controlling alcohol use
> 3. Withdrawal symptoms
> 4. Tolerance
> 5. Progressive neglect of other activities
> 6. Continued alcohol use in the face of overtly harmful consequences

Anxiety

Alcohol is a fast-acting and effective anxiolytic, which may, for many people, start their journey into dependence. Anxiety is often experienced as a symptom of withdrawal that can fuel more alcohol intake, resulting in a vicious cycle of anxiety and alcohol consumption. The ICD-10 categorises anxiety disorders as phobic (social, simple, agoraphobic), generalised, panic disorder and obsessive–compulsive (World Health Organization, 1992). Panic disorder and generalised anxiety disorder can emerge from periods of alcohol misuse, however, the association with obsessive–compulsive disorder is less robust. Anxiety disorders and alcohol dependence demonstrate a reciprocal causal relationship over time, with anxiety disorders leading to alcohol dependence and vice versa (Kushner *et al.*, 1990). It may be that they share an underlying aetiology involving hypofunction of the GABA (gamma-aminobutyric acid) neurotransmitter system.

Depression

The relationship between alcohol and depression is bi-directional as depression can increase consumption but it can also arise from an alcohol-use disorder. Higher rates of comorbidity have also been reported in women (Merikangas *et al.*, 1996).

Community surveys in the US have revealed that people are two to three times more likely to have a depressive disorder if they have an alcohol disorder (Grant and Harford, 1995; Kessler *et al.*, 1994). UK surveys report a significant association between alcohol misuse and affective disorders (Farrell *et al.*, 2003). An 18-month follow-up period in a UK study showed that hazardous drinking was not associated with depression at follow-up, and vice versa, however, an association with dependence and binge drinking was suggested (Haynes *et al.*, 2005).

Bipolar disorder

Bipolar disorder carries the greatest risk of any axis-one disorder for the co-existence with a drug or alcohol disorder. There is higher risk for those with a type 1 bipolar disorder than a type 2 bipolar disorder, and if alcohol dependence is present then there is an increased risk of mania.

Schizophrenia

There is a strong association between schizophrenia and alcohol misuse. The ECA study (Epidemiologic Catchment Area) reported the prevalence of substance misuse in schizophrenia stands at 47 per cent, with the majority misusing alcohol. There are many theories to explain this comorbidity, in addition to that of self-medication. It has been suggested that people with schizophrenia have risk factors of substance misuse, e.g. poor cognitive, social and vocational function and poverty. Another theory is that of 'comorbid addiction vulnerability', which is underpinned by dysfunction in the reward circuitry. Patients with schizophrenia therefore abuse substances because they find them rewarding and fail to anticipate and respond to the negative consequences. Despite these hypotheses, diagnosis and clinical management in this group of patients remains challenging.

Diagnosis and assessment

Diagnosis

As with all medical assessments, a full history, a physical examination and appropriate investigations are necessary to make a thorough assessment. A common challenge to clinical management of dual diagnosis is simply a failure to identify either the presence of alcohol misuse in those presenting with psychiatric symptoms or the presence of psychiatric disorders in those presenting with alcohol misuse. Patients with unrecognised dual diagnosis can often be dismissed as being 'treatment resistant' or as 'difficult cases'. Many people referred to alcohol services may already be taking psychotropic medication, such as antidepressants, and may even be on their second or third type due to a lack of response. Alcohol consumption often is not recorded in a patient's notes or documented as 'social', therefore it is important to remember to ask about alcohol consumption in any clinical history. There are several screening questionnaires such as the CAGE (an acronym for cut down, annoyed, guilty, and eye-opener; Mayfield *et al.*, 1974) and the AUDIT (see Chapter 2) (Saunders *et al.*, 1993) that can be used to aid recognition.

Psychiatric illness commonly presents with physical rather than psychological symptoms, which further complicates the clinical picture. Many of these symptoms may be caused or exacerbated by alcohol misuse. An enquiry about alcohol consumption should also be raised if a patient is taking medication for common consequences of alcohol misuse, such as gastritis or indigestion. A full physical examination is helpful for making a diagnosis and clinicians should particularly look for the stigmata of alcohol disease.

Once dual diagnosis has been identified, a careful history that tries to establish which came first should be obtained, to help distinguish between substance-*induced* and substance-*related* psychiatric disorders. The history should include the age of onset of the disorders, their chronology, how alcohol use and mood are related, whether there is persistence of psychiatric illness during abstinence, and whether there is a family history of either disorder. In addition, it is important to determine the safety of prescribing medication, with a particular consideration for risk of deliberate self-harm.

In assessing the impact of the alcohol misuse on the patient's psychiatric disorder, and vice versa, it is also important to ask why they are drinking alcohol, what effects they expect to get, and any consequences of its use. When teasing out the contribution of a psychiatric disorder to alcohol misuse (or vice versa) it is important to understand what psychiatric symptoms may be associated with intoxication, withdrawal and dependence. It is also valuable to assess for any symptomatic differences between moderate or heavy alcohol use. A full drug history must form part of the assessment because there are a wide number of drugs in addition to alcohol that a patient may be using, including nicotine and caffeine, and illicit drugs such as cannabis, opiates, cocaine, amphetamines and prescribed medications. The psychiatric disorders associated with alcohol used to combat a previous and existing psychiatric disorder may also be different, for example drinking alcohol to combat depression may then lead to emergence of an anxiety disorder.

Investigations

Urinalysis, breathalyser readings and blood tests are simple investigations that should complement the history and physical examination. A urinary drug screen helps detect misuse of other substances. A breathalyser reading is useful and can shed light on how the patient is presenting; a high alcohol level with withdrawal symptoms suggests high tolerance and dependence, whereas a low alcohol level and intoxication suggests low tolerance. Blood tests can help identify alcohol misuse, and biological markers include liver function tests such as serum gamma glutamyl transferase (GGT) and mean corpuscular volume (MCV). A rise in these markers is often the reason for someone's drinking to come under the spotlight. Blood tests are also important for assessing the impact of alcohol misuse on the body (e.g. liver dysfunction).

Re-assessment

An important principle in the management of dual diagnosis is that of re-assessment. When faced with a complex and challenging clinical problem there is a need to move forward in treatment based on the diagnosis made at any point in time. The clinical picture can change with additional health problems and misuse of other substances, and the management needs to adapt accordingly. Re-assessment is especially important in patients who have undergone detoxification after many years of alcohol dependence. Psychiatric diagnoses may have been made a long time beforehand during comorbid alcohol misuse and may need to be revisited to avoid any unnecessary continuation of psychotropic medication.

Treatment approach

Key to the approach of clinical management of dual diagnosis is an understanding of the complex relationship between alcohol dependency and psychiatric illness, as well as comprehensive assessment of both problems before suggesting therapeutic intervention. Achieving abstinence and then re-assessing the clinical picture after 2–3 weeks of sobriety is the ideal scenario, however, this is often difficult to achieve and, therefore, both disorders need to be treated concurrently. It is important to note that improvements seen in either the mental disorder or alcohol dependence do not necessarily result in progress in the other. While it is common to refer to a patient's psychiatric disorder or alcohol dependence as primary or secondary, this distinction may have limited use clinically. There are problems when labelling something as primary or secondary; if a disorder labelled as primary fails to be successfully managed or treated, then the secondary disorder may be forgotten and the patient discharged. Removing or minimising the contribution of alcohol misuse is an important aim of treatment as it can significantly improve the clinical picture. This has clearly been shown in the case of depressive symptoms, for example (Brown *et al.*, 1988).

An integrated biopsychosocial approach to clinical management, involving both psychosocial and pharmacological interventions, underpins treatment for both psychiatric disorders and alcohol dependency. The details of the current evidence-based guidelines for the separate clinical management of these disorders are beyond the scope of this chapter. There are very few placebo-controlled trials of the treatment of dual diagnosis, resulting in little robust evidence to guide management. Further, very few trials specifically examine the best psychosocial approach for treating comorbid alcohol misuse and psychiatric disorders, or how the approach used for either disorder might work better in the presence of the other. Consequently, there is a greater emphasis in this chapter on the psychopharmacological treatment of comorbidity, for which there is a larger body of evidence.

It is important to note that the same medications can be used to treat different psychiatric diagnoses and other medical conditions, as well as the comorbid alcohol misuse. It should therefore be clear what the medication is being used to treat and what goals are hoped to be achieved; plans must be put in place to review the medication if these goal are not reached.

On reviewing the literature about pharmacological treatment it is clear that there are numerous methodological limitations to the studies that have been done. There is a wide variety of studies, but only a few are randomised-controlled trials – or even trials. Many have only small samples and durations. Despite the urgent need for randomised-controlled trials in this population, there is currently sufficient evidence to support and guide a pharmacological approach.

Safety considerations

Given the potential for hepatic impairment with alcohol misuse, there should be a degree of caution when prescribing for a comorbid patient group. Liver function should be assessed before starting treatment. When there is significant hepatic impairment, the liver can have a reduced capacity to metabolise drugs, as well as a reduced ability to synthesise plasma proteins. Obviously this is a concern in patients who are prescribed psychotropic medication, which can be hepatotoxic, or extensively metabolised in the liver, or highly protein bound. General principles for prescribing in patients with hepatic impairment include choosing a low-risk drug, using as few drugs as possible, and starting with low doses which are then increased slowly. Liver function should be carefully monitored throughout treatment.

Like every treatment, the balance of risks and benefits needs to be considered for all medications in each person. Prescribers are advised to check their national prescribing formulary and seek advice if necessary.

For simplicity and clarity we have approached psychiatric illness in the four broad diagnostic categories of anxiety, depression, bipolar disorder and schizophrenia.

Anxiety

Psychological approaches are commonly applied to treat many forms of anxiety, although pharmacotherapy is frequently used in addition. There is limited knowledge, however, about treating anxiety comorbid with alcohol dependence (Scott *et al.*, 1998). Anxiety symptoms may improve simply with abstinence from alcohol. Anxiety is a feature of alcohol withdrawal and 40 per cent of inpatients undergoing alcohol detoxification had significantly elevated anxiety ratings in the first week; however, in the following week their scores returned to normal (Brown *et al.*, 1991). This emphasises the need for re-assessment once the acute withdrawal period is over. If abstinence is not achieved, it is still desirable to minimise the contribution of alcohol to the mental state. Clearly, if alcohol is being used as an anxiolytic, then relapse after or during alcohol treatment is more likely if the anxiety disorder is not also treated. Generally drinking should be addressed *first*, with treatment of the anxiety disorder still being considered and started sooner rather than later.

Successful treatment of an anxiety disorder can result in improved drinking behaviour even if the patient is still drinking, however, this will have greater impact if drinking is at non-dependent levels.

Psychological interventions form the mainstay of treatment for alcohol dependence and these frequently involve group work. People with anxiety disorders, and in particular social anxiety disorder, often avoid groups as they find them difficult. This obviously hinders treatment in comorbid patients. Individual therapy and anxiety-management groups are strategies used by some services to tackle the problem. One clinical trial addressed the question of whether concurrent treatment was beneficial in this population (Randall *et al.*, 2001a). They randomised comorbid subjects to treatment with cognitive–behavioural therapy (CBT) over 12 weeks for alcohol dependence alone or together with CBT for social anxiety disorder. The results showed that social anxiety and drinking behaviour improved in both groups, but the group that received treatment for both anxiety and alcohol had poorer outcomes in drinking behaviour. This study did not look at whether treatment for alcohol misuse or anxiety should come first.

Another study compared outpatient CBT with 12-step facilitation therapy in subjects with alcoholism and social anxiety disorder. Abstinence was achieved for longer in women with CBT than with 12-step therapy, but the reverse was seen in men (Randall *et al.*, 2000).

There is little evidence regarding pharmacological treatment for patients with anxiety where their alcohol misuse is being addressed, but the British Association for Psychopharmacology guidelines recommend using selective serotonin-reuptake inhibitors (SSRIs) as the first-line pharmacotherapy (Baldwin *et al.* 2005; Lingford-Hughes *et al.*, 2004). There is one study showing paroxetine is superior to placebo in improving anxiety in patients with social phobia and alcohol dependence, but its effects on drinking were less consistent (Randall *et al.*, 2001b). There have been several randomised-controlled trials of buspirone in alcohol dependence comorbid with generalised/non-panic anxiety disorder or high levels of anxiety. Results are mixed and buspirone is not recommended as it has not consistently been shown to improve anxiety or alcohol outcomes.

It is generally not advisable to use benzodiazepines as a treatment for anxiety in comorbid patients. Due to greater 'rewarding' effects, abstinent alcohol-dependent patients may be at greater risk of benzodiazepine abuse (Ciraulo *et al.*, 1997). Those with severe dependence, polysubstance abuse or antisocial personality disorder are most at risk. There is some evidence, however, that for those who are less severely dependent, benzodiazepine prescribing may not result in abuse. In general, their use in this population requires careful consideration; assessment by a specialist addiction service is recommended prior to starting treatment (Ciraulo and Nace, 2000; Ciraulo *et al.*, 1988; Posternak and Mueller, 2001).

Depression

Depressive symptoms improve with abstinence from alcohol in patients with comorbid alcohol misuse and depression (Brown and Schukit, 1988). The first goal should generally be abstinence, or at the very least minimal alcohol consumption. Many patients find this difficult to achieve, therefore a more pragmatic approach of treating them both together is often needed. There should still be an emphasis on treating the alcohol misuse because improvement in depressive symptoms is unlikely with continuing misuse. Once abstinence is achieved, treatment of the depression should not be forgotten because it can help promote the ongoing recovery process. We refer readers to the National Institute for Clinical Excellence guidelines for management of depression (NICE, 2007). There are no trials that specifically explore the best psychosocial approach to treat comorbid alcohol misuse and depression, although there is some evidence to guide the use of antidepressants in this population. Antidepressants are not recommended for the initial treatment of mild depression, but there are several interventions that are also helpful in alcohol misuse, such as exercise, problem solving, and advice on sleep hygiene.

The quality of the trials investigating pharmacotherapy of depression with alcohol misuse is not always optimum. There have, however, been two meta-analyses looking at the treatment of depression in patients with substance dependence, including alcohol misuse (Nunes and Levin, 2004; Torrens *et al.*, 2005). They generally reach the same conclusion, that antidepressants should only be used in those with clear depression as a concurrent therapy to treatment specifically focused on alcohol misuse. A significant effect on substance-misuse outcome was only seen in those studies showing larger improvements in depression. This underlines the importance of antidepressants not being used as a stand-alone treatment. It was also very clear that there was no significant effect of antidepressants in patients without comorbid depression.

Nunes and Levin stated that 'antidepressant medication exerts a modest beneficial effect for patients with combined depressive and substance use disorders'. Interestingly the effect on depression of the antidepressant correlated to placebo response. A lack of beneficial antidepressant effect was found in those studies that had a high placebo rate. A suggested explanation is that those with a lower placebo response rate had waited over a week after stopping alcohol before starting their antidepressants. This period of abstinence may have reduced recruitment of patients whose depressive symptoms were predominantly related to alcohol use and withdrawal. This finding supports the suggestion of many clinical guidelines to start antidepressants 2 to 3 weeks after detoxification.

Studies looking at the effect of tricyclic antidepressants (TCAs) in alcoholism and depression found they seem to have a more robust effect on mood than on drinking. Despite the suggestion that TCAs may be effective, their use is not routinely recommended. Many people use alcohol impulsively when deliberately self-harming or attempting suicide and TCAs have cardiotoxic effects when taken with alcohol in overdose. Both the meta-analyses found that SSRIs did not perform as well as other antidepressants which were mainly tricyclic antidepressants.

There is also evidence to suggest that patients with type 2 alcoholism (i.e. males with positive family history and antisocial and impulsive personality traits) do not respond well to SSRIs and may even do worse in treatment if they are prescribed. However, a randomised-controlled trial showed that fluoxetine appears to be effective in improving drinking behaviour and depression in severely depressed patients (Cornelius *et al.*, 1997). The 'new' antidepressants have not yet been tested in clinical trials; it may be that those with combined serotonergic and noradrenergic activity have greater efficacy in comorbid patients. Mirtazapine has been reported to reduce depressive symptoms and craving in alcohol-dependent depressed patients, however, this was in an 8-week naturalistic study with no comparative group (Yoon *et al.*, 2006). Mirtazapine, but not venlafaxine, has been reported to reduce depressive and anxiety symptoms during alcohol detoxification (Liappas *et al.*, 2005).

In a comorbid population, the initial focus should be on achieving abstinence; while antidepressants may improve mood, they should not be routinely started if a patient is still actively drinking. If abstinence is not possible, then starting antidepressant medication may need to be considered. SSRIs appear to be effective in treating severely depressed patients and are safer than TCAs, however, there is a need for evaluation of the other antidepressants with combined serotonergic and adrenergic activity. If depression persists despite achieving abstinence, then SSRIs are likely to be effective and the guidance for non-comorbid depression should be followed.

Bipolar disorder

Alcohol misuse is common in bipolar disorder, although there remains very little information to guide treatment. There are difficulties with the use of lithium in a comorbid population. Patients are usually advised not to drink alcohol when taking lithium, which can lead to poor compliance in those prioritising their alcohol consumption. Lithium carbonate may also not be effective in bipolar variants such as dysphoric, mixed or rapid-cycling, which are over-represented in bipolar alcohol-dependent patients. In addition, lithium has been shown to be ineffective in decreasing alcohol consumption in depressed alcoholic people (Dorus *et al.*, 1989).

Research involving anticonvulsants, however, appears more optimistic. Trials suggest that valproate may have greater acceptability than lithium because it has fewer side effects (Weiss *et al.*, 1998). Interestingly many of the anticonvulsants show efficacy in treating alcohol dependence alone, e.g. topiramate (Johnson *et al.*, 2007). Because they have mood stabilising properties in addition to this, it has been suggested that anticonvulsants are the treatment of choice in a comorbid population. This hypothesis is currently only theoretical, so a systematic look at these medications is now needed to see whether any particular one does have benefit in treating comorbid patients. There is only one trial of valproate in patients with bipolar disorder and alcohol dependence (Salloum *et al.*, 2005). In this double-blind placebo-controlled study, all patients received treatment as usual, which included lithium carbonate and psychosocial interventions, and were then randomised to receive valproate or placebo. Those who received valproate had fewer heavy-drinking days and improved GGT levels. However, there was no difference between the groups in terms of improvement of manic or depressive symptoms.

Given the lack of evidence, it is not possible to make specific recommendations regarding pharmacological approaches. The evidence currently available points to some advantages of anticonvulsants over lithium in comorbid patients. More knowledge is still needed about the role of different mood stabilisers in improving substance misuse either directly or indirectly, by improving their bipolar illness.

Schizophrenia

There is very limited information to guide clinical management of this group of patients. Most of the research looks at schizophrenia with comorbid substance misuse, rather than comorbid alcohol misuse specifically. However, it seems reasonable to apply this to comorbid alcohol misuse given that second only to nicotine, alcohol is the most commonly abused substance, seen in over a third of patients (Regier *et al.*, 1990). There have been no published randomised-controlled trials of pharmacotherapy for schizophrenia and comorbid substance misuse that use substance misuse as a specific outcome measure.

Antipsychotic medication forms the mainstay of pharmacological treatment in schizophrenia. Typical antipsychotics have been used widely in animal models to increase self-administration of stimulants such as cocaine or amphetamine. Clinical studies suggest that patients with schizophrenia and comorbid substance misuse may be more resistant to typical antipsychotic medication – it may cause more side effects, increase substance misuse and reduce compliance. With the advent and increasing use of atypical antipsychotic medication (i.e. those with lower propensity to cause side effects) it has been suggested that atypical antipsychotics should be used in patients with comorbid substance misuse. There is little information however on atypical antipsychotics in this group of patients. Early case reports and open studies report improvement in substance-misuse disorder when switching from typical to atypical antipsychotics.

There has been a recent review of case notes of patients with schizophrenia and substance-misuse disorder (Petrakis *et al.*, 2006). The addiction severity index was used to assess clinical change. The review reported that those maintained on a typical antipsychotic showed no change in addiction severity index. Those who were maintained on, or switched to, an atypical antipsychotic (such as olanzapine, risperidone or quetiapine) did improve, with a decrease in addiction severity index. But the comparison to those maintained on a typical antipsychotic was not significant. Thus they suggested that atypical antipsychotics (in the absence of other substance-misuse disorder treatment) are not more effective in reducing comorbid substance misuse in schizophrenia. One randomised-controlled trial has reported that patients with first-episode schizophrenia and substance misuse responded to either olanzapine or haloperidol at 12 weeks (Green *et al.*, 2004). This showed that patients who had a substance-misuse disorder responded more poorly to antipsychotics than those who did not. The data also suggested that those with an alcohol-use disorder responded less well to olanzapine than those who did not, and that this difference was not seen with haloperidol. The 2-year data, which was recently published, unfortunately did not report any substance-misuse outcomes.

The majority of published studies looking at antipsychotic medication in this patient population have been about clozapine. There are several case reports, a retrospective survey, naturalistic surveys and trials all suggesting that clozapine reduces substance misuse in patients with schizophrenia. Clozapine is associated with improvements of up to 85 per cent for comorbid patients' use of substances including alcohol, with no patients showing an increase in substance use. A recent report suggests it is also useful for preventing relapse of substance misuse, in addition to just achieving abstinence or significant reductions in use (Brunette *et al.*, 2006).

It is not clear why clozapine may be different to other atypical antipsychotics. It has been hypothesised that its effect is due to clozapine-related improvements in psychosis. This leads to a reduced need to self-medicate psychiatric symptoms, a greater insight into the negative consequences of substance abuse, and improved psychosocial functioning. It may be due to lower levels of side effects, or the fact that it has an antidepressant activity and improves negative symptoms. Some have suggested that clozapine's pharmacology is important because it has a richer receptor-binding profile than many other antipsychotics. It binds relatively more strongly to serotonin receptors than to the dopamine D_2 receptors, which have traditionally been seen as the main site of antipsychotic action.

Given the lack of information, it is hard to draw up specific recommendations for treatment of this population. It has been hypothesised that the differences in response to typical and atypical antipsychotics may be due to differences in dose rather than the type of medication. The suggestion is that observed adverse effects of typical antipsychotics are due to higher equivalent doses being prescribed, but further research is needed to clarify this issue. The currently available evidence suggests that atypical antipsychotics may have a more favourable outcome than typical antipsychotics, although there is no control data to support this (with the exception of clozapine). Therefore, it does not seem unreasonable to use clozapine sooner rather than later when a patient has a difficult-to-manage substance misuse disorder combined with schizophrenia.

Pharmacotherapy for alcohol dependence in a comorbid population

The focus so far has been on the use of pharmacotherapy for psychiatric disorders in a comorbid population. The rationale behind this approach is that diminishing psychiatric symptoms will make the patient more accessible to psychosocial treatment for alcohol misuse, and will also reduce the patient's vulnerability to relapse. More recently, the same rationale has been applied to the use of pharmacotherapy to treat alcohol dependence as an adjunct to psychosocial treatment. The medications used in alcohol dependence alone are disulfiram (Antabuse), naltrexone and acamprosate. Little has been reported about the use of such 'alcohol-targeted' drugs in a comorbid population.

While disulfiram may be an odd choice of treatment for those with comorbid disorder, since it can precipitate anxiety, depression, mania and psychosis, there are a number of reports of it being used successfully in such disorders. The drug works by blocking aldehyde dehydrogenase, a key enzyme involved in the metabolism of alcohol. It also inhibits an enzyme from the same family called dopamine beta-hydroxylase. In preclinical models disulfiram can lead to increased dopamine and reduced norepinephrine (noradrenaline) levels. It is proposed that the alteration in balance of these neurotransmitters affects mood, but how this effect contributes to its clinical efficacy is unclear.

By contrast, naltrexone is a relatively inert drug in that it does not appear to precipitate any mental health problems. A randomised-controlled trial of naltrexone in schizophrenia with alcohol dependence showed that naltrexone led to fewer drinking days, fewer heavy-drinking days and less craving without any worsening of psychosis (Petrakis *et al.*, 2004). It was noted, however, that naltrexone may be more likely to work in patients with better controlled psychiatric symptoms.

A recent randomised-controlled trial compared disulfiram and naltrexone alone and in combination with placebo in a comorbid population, including those with major depression, anxiety or psychosis (Petrakis *et al.*, 2005). At the end of the 12-week study period, disulfiram and naltrexone alone reduced the number of drinking days per week and resulted in more consecutive days of abstinence compared to placebo. Disulfiram and naltrexone were equally efficacious and there were no added benefits from taking both drugs. It is worth noting that a very high rate of abstinence was achieved even with placebo (66 per cent) because this was a highly motivated group of patients. It may be that lower rates of abstinence are associated with a more pronounced medication effect. The rates of side effects reported for either medication were similar to those in non-dual diagnosed populations.

There have been subsequent secondary analyses of this group of patients (Petrakis *et al.*, 2007). Patients with current major depression (55 per cent) were compared to those without. Reductions in depression were reported for all active treatments and placebo, and efficacy of the drugs was found not to be affected by the depression. When the group was split into psychotic and non-psychotic disorders it was notable that those with psychosis who were treated with naltrexone or disulfiram alone or in combination showed significant improvement in the total number of heavy-drinking days. They did not report any more side effects or adverse reactions and there was no change in their psychotic symptoms. Similarly when the subgroup with post-traumatic stress disorder (PTSD) was examined, it was found that either naltrexone or Antabuse improved outcomes in terms of alcohol consumption. PTSD symptoms also improved over time, more so with disulfiram than naltrexone. It was suggested that this is related to a reduction in brain levels of norepinephrine.

Conclusions

The clinical presentation of comorbid psychiatric disorder and alcohol-misuse disorder can be complex and confusing. The need for simplicity and clarity is paramount in the clinical management of dual diagnosis. Assessment should include a thorough history that attempts to decipher the interplay of the alcohol and psychiatric disorder, and the contribution each is making to the mental state. This should be followed by appropriate investigations and regular re-assessment as the clinical picture evolves. Despite the limited evidence on how best to treat this challenging problem, there is sufficient available to provide some guidance. In addition to the use of psychiatric medication and psychological interventions in the therapeutic approach, pharmacotherapy to specifically treat the alcohol-misuse disorder should not be overlooked.

References and further reading

Anderson, I.M., Nutt, D.J. and Deakin, J.F.W. (2000). Evidence-based guidelines for treating depressive disorders with antidepressants: A revision of the 1993 British Association for Psychopharmacology Guidelines. *Journal of Psychopharmacology*, **14**, 3–20.

Baldwin D.S., Anderson, I.M., Nutt, D.J., et al. (2005). Evidence-based guidelines for the pharmacological treatment of anxiety disorders: recommendations from the British Association for Psychopharmacology. *Journal of Psychopharmacology*, **19**(6), 677–96.

Brown, S.A. and Schuckit, M.A. (1988). Changes in depression among abstinent alcoholics. *Journal of Studies on Alcohol,* **49**, 412–17.

Brown, S.A., Irwin, M. and Schuckit, M.A. (1991). Changes in anxiety among abstinent male alcoholics. *Journal of Studies on Alcohol,* **52**, 55–61.

Brunette, M.F., Drake, R.E., Xie, H., McHugo, G.J. and Green, A.I. (2006). Clozapine use and relapses of substance use disorder among patients with co-occurring schizophrenia and substance use disorders. *Schizophrenia Bulletin*, **32**(4), 637–43.

Ciraulo, D.A. and Nace, E.P. (2000). Benzodiazepine treatment of anxiety or insomnia in substance abuse patients. *American Journal of Addiction,* **9**, 276–79.

Ciraulo, D.A., Barnhill, J.G., Ciraulo, A.M., *et al.* (1997). Alterations in pharmacodynamics of anxiolytics in abstinent alcoholic men: subjective responses, abuse liability, and electroencephalographic effects of alprazolam, diazepam, and buspirone. *Journal of Clinical Pharmacology*, **37**, 64–73.

Ciraulo, D., Sands, B. and Shader, R. (1988). Critical review of liability for benzodiazepine abuse among alcoholics. *American Journal of Psychiatry*, **145**, 1501–06.

Cornelius, J., Salloum, I., Ehler, J., *et al.* (1997). Fluoxetine in depressed alcoholics. *Archives of General Psychiatry*, **54**, 700–05.

Dorus, W., Ostrow, D.G., Anton, R., *et al.* (1989). Lithium treatment of depressed and nondepressed alcoholics. *Journal of the American Medical Association*, **262**(12), 1646–52.

Farrell, M., Howes, S., Taylor, C., *et al.* (2003). Substance misuse and psychiatric comorbidity: an overview of the OPCS National Psychiatric Morbidity Survey. *International Review of Psychiatry*, **15**(1/2), 43–49.

Grant, B. and Harford, T.C. (1995). Comorbidity between DSM-IV alcohol-use disorders and major depression: results of a national survey. *Drug and Alcohol Dependence*, **1**, 97–06.

Green, A., Tohen, M., Hamer, R., *et al.* and the HGDH Research Group (2004). First episode schizophrenia-related psychosis and substance use disorders: acute response to olanzapine and haloperidol. *Schizophrenia Research*, **66**(2/3), 125–35.

Haynes, J.C., Farrell, M., Singleton, N., *et al.* (2005). Alcohol consumption as a risk factor for anxiety and depression. Results from the longitudinal follow-up of the National Psychiatric Morbidity Survey. *British Journal of Psychiatry*, **18**, 544–51.

Johnson, B.A., Rosenthal, N., Capece, J.A., *et al.* and the Topiramate for Alcoholism Advisory Board Study Group (2007). Topiramate for treating alcohol dependence: A randomized controlled trial. *Journal of the American Medical Association*, **298**(14), 1641–51.

Kessler, R.C., McGonagle, K.A., Zhao, S., *et al.* (1994). Lifetime and 12-month prevalence of DSM–III–R psychiatric disorders in the United States. *Archives of General Psychiatry*, **51**, 8–19.

Kushner, M.G., Sher, K.J. and Beitman, B.D. (1990). The relation between alcohol problems and anxiety disorders. *American Journal of Psychiatry*, **147**, 685–95.

Liappas, J., Paparrigopoulos, T., Tzavellas, E. and Rabavilas, A. (2005). Mirtazapine and venlafaxine in the management of collateral psychopathology during alcohol detoxification. *Progress in Neuropsychopharmacology and Biological Psychiatry*, **9**, 55– 60.

Lingford-Hughes, A., Potokar, J. and Nutt, D. (2002). Treating anxiety complicated by substance misuse. *Advances in Psychiatric Treatment*, **8**, 107–16.

Lingford-Hughes, A., Welch, S. and Nutt, D. (2004). Evidence based guidelines for the pharmacological management of substance misuse, addiction, and comorbidity: Recommendations from the British Association for Psychopharmacology. *Journal of Psychopharmacology*, **18**, 293–35.

Mayfield, D., McLeod, G. and Hall, P. (1974). The CAGE questionnaire: Validation of a new alcoholism screening instrument. *American Journal of Psychiatry*, **131**, 1121–23.

Merikangas, K.R., Angst, J., Eaton, W., *et al.* (1996). Comorbidity and boundaries of affective disorders with anxiety disorders and substance misuse: Results of an international task force. *British Journal of Psychiatry*, **168**(Suppl.30), 58–67.

National Institute for Health and Clinical Excellence (2007). *Clinical Guideline 23: Depression. Management of depression in primary and secondary care.* Available at: http://www.nice.org.uk/CG023NICEguideline (last accessed October 2008).

Nunes, E. and Levin, F. (2004). Treatment of depression in patients with alcohol or other drug dependence: A meta-analysis. *Journal of the American Medical Association*, **291**, 1887–96.

Petrakis, I.L., Leslie, D., Finney, J.W. and Rosenheck, R.P. (2006). Atypical antipsychotic medication and substance use-related outcomes in the treatment of schizophrenia. *American Journal of Addiction,* **15**(1), 44–49.

Petrakis, I.L., O'Malley, S., Rounsaville, B., Poling, J., *et al.* and the VA Naltrexone Study Collaboration Group. (2004). Naltrexone augmentation of neuroleptic treatment in alcohol abusing patients with schizophrenia. *Psychopharmacology*, *(Berlin)*, **172**(3), 291–97.

Petrakis, I.L., Poling, J., Levinson, C., *et al.* and the VA VISN I MIRECC study group (2005). Naltrexone and disulfiram in patients with alcohol dependence and comorbid psychiatric disorders. *Biological Psychiatry*, **57**, 1128–37.

Petrakis, I.L., Ralevski, E., Nich, C., *et al.* and the VA VISN I MIRECC study group (2007). Naltrexone and disulfiram in patients with alcohol dependence and current depression. *Journal of Clinical Psychopharmacology*, **27**, 160–65.

Posternak, M.A. and Mueller, T.I. (2001). Assessing the risks and benefits of benzodiazepines for anxiety disorders in patients with a history of substance abuse or dependence. *American Journal of Addiction,* **10**, 48–68.

Randall, C.L., Johnson, M.R., Thevos, A.K., *et al.* (2001b). Paroxetine for social anxiety and alcohol use in dual-diagnosed patients. *Depression* and *Anxiety*, **14**, 255–62.

Randall, C.L., Thomas, S.E. and Thevos, A.K. (2000). Gender comparison in alcoholics with concurrent social phobia: implications for alcoholism treatment. *American Journal of Addiction*, **9**, 202–15.

Randall, C.L., Thomas, S.E. and Thevos, A.K. (2001a). Concurrent alcoholism and social anxiety disorder: A first step towards developing effective treatments. *Alcoholism: Clinical and Experimental Research*, **25**, 210–20.

Regier, D.A., Farmer, M.E., Rae, D.S., *et al.* (1990). Comorbidity of mental disorders with alcohol and other drug abuse. Results from the Epidemiologic Catchment Area (ECA) Study. *Journal of the American Medical Association*, **264**, 2511–18.

Royal College of Physicians (1995). *Alcohol and the Heart in Perspective: Sensible Drinking Reaffirmed*. Report of a Joint Working Group of the Royal College of Physicians, the Royal College of Psychiatrists and the Royal College of General Practitioners. London: Royal College of Physicians.

Salloum, I.M., Cornelius, J.R., Daley, D.C., Kirisci, L., Himmelhoch, J.M. and Thase, M.E. (2005). Efficacy of valproate maintenance in patients with bipolar disorder and alcoholism: A double-blind placebo-controlled study. *Archives of General Psychiatry*, **62**(1), 37–45.

Saunders, J.B., Aasland, O.G., Babor, T.F., De la Fuente, J.R. and Grant, M. (1993). Development of the Alcohol Use Disorders Identification Test (AUDIT), WHO collaborative project on early detection of persons with harmful alcohol consumption – II. *Addiction,* **88**, 791–04.

Scott, J., Gilvarry, E. and Farrell, M. (1998). Managing anxiety and depression in alcohol and drug dependence. *Addictive Behaviors*, **23**, 919–31.

Torrens, M., Fonseca, F., Mateu, G. and Farre, M. (2005). Efficacy of antidepressants in substance use disorders with and without comorbid depression. A systematic review and meta-analysis. *Drug and Alcohol Dependence*, **78**, 1–22.

Weiss, R.D., Greenfield, S.F., Najavits, L.M., *et al.* (1998). Medication compliance among patients with bipolar disorder and substance use disorder. *Journal of Clinical Psychiatry*, **59**, 172–74.

World Health Organization (1992). *The ICD-10 Classification of Mental* and *Behavioural Disorders*. Geneva: WHO.

Yoon, S.J., Pae, C.U., Kim, D.D., *et al.* (2006). Mirtazapine for patients with alcohol dependence and comorbid depressive disorders: A multicentre, open label study. *Progress in Neuropsychopharmacology and Biological Psychiatry*, **30**, 1196–201.

5 Biomarkers of alcohol abuse

Rajaventhan SriRajaskanthan and Victor R. Preedy

Health problems related to alcohol abuse are common causes of disease in western countries (Room *et al.,* 2005). Alcohol is the leading risk factor for disease burden in developing countries; however, it is the third largest risk factor for disease burden in developed countries (World Health Organization, 2004). Excessive alcohol consumption has an important effect on individual people and society as a whole, imposing a major financial burden on the UK National Health Service (Maynard and Godfrey, 1994; SriRajaskanthan and Preedy, 2006). In the USA, it is estimated 18 million adults are affected by alcohol abuse, with annual costs to society in excess of $185 billion (Wurst *et al.,* 2005).

Over the last 40 years there has been a marked increase in alcohol consumption on a global scale (World Health Organization, 2004). Within the UK, there has been a recent rise in alcohol consumption over the last few years (see Fig. 5.1). In addition, there has been an increase in alcohol-related morbidity and mortality (Leon and McCambridge, 2006; Prime Minister's Strategy Unit, 2004). Cirrhosis rates in the UK have increased markedly from 1950 to, 2002, the largest increase being seen in women and the 25–44-year-old group (Leon and McCambridge, 2006). The most common cause of cirrhosis in the western world is secondary to alcohol.

The toxic metabolites of alcohol affect nearly every organ of the body; consequently there are at least a hundred medical conditions that can be caused by excessive alcohol consumption (SriRajaskanthan and Preedy, 2007). Most of these conditions are related to chronic excessive alcohol intake. Unfortunately most people who consume excess alcohol are not identified within the community; this is in part due to a lack of sensitive and specific markers of alcohol consumption. Studies have shown that up to 20 per cent of patients attending general practice clinics consume alcohol at excessive levels, although up to 98 per cent of these patients are not identified in the primary care setting (Kaner *et al.,* 1999). The reasons for poor identification of patients with excessive alcohol consumption are numerous; importantly patients often deny an increased intake. There is good evidence that brief interventions for excessive alcohol use, aimed at reducing consumption and subsequent alcohol-related harm and dependence, are both clinically and cost effective (Bertholet *et al.,* 2005; Fleming *et al.,* 2002; Moyer *et al.,* 2002).

Biomarkers are needed for a variety of different clinical scenarios – to identify people with an excessive alcohol consumption; to identify those developing organ damage secondary to alcohol; to determine the actual levels of alcohol in the body at certain times (e.g. after a road traffic accident); to identify people at risk of developing alcohol-dependency disorders. Markers are currently available for some of these clinical situations, while others are only in the experimental stage.

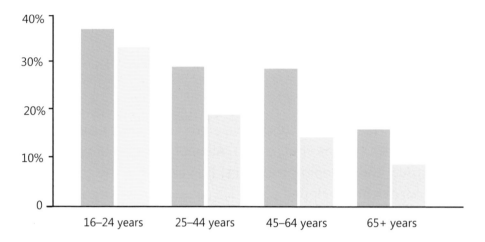

Figure 5.1 Percentage of males (*left-hand columns*) and females (*right-hand columns*) in different age groups drinking above the recommended safe levels (weekly benchmarks) in the UK in 2002–2003. Adapted from Institute of Alcohol Studies (2005).

Alcohol-related disorders, for example alcoholic liver disease, can occur in people without alcohol dependency. Alcoholism itself, by definition, implies both a mental and physical dependence on alcohol. This in turn leads to heavy and often uncontrolled drinking patterns (SriRajaskanthan and Preedy, 2006). However, not all alcoholic people will develop alcoholic liver disease; in fact some studies indicate that only 20 per cent of people consuming excessive amounts of alcohol over a 10-year period develop liver cirrhosis (Preedy and Watson, 2005). So biomarkers that may be specific at identifying people with alcohol-related liver disease may not pick up the large number of alcoholic people in a population without liver disease.

Conversely, people with only a moderately excessive alcohol intake and without any physical or mental dependence on alcohol, may well proceed to develop numerous complications secondary to alcohol. There is strong evidence showing that low to moderate regular alcohol consumption is beneficial in terms of cardiovascular risk and mortality (Fuchs *et al.*, 1995; Marmot *et al.*, 1981; Preedy and Watson, 2005). When analysing alcohol and mortality, there is a U-shaped curve, whereby non-drinkers have a higher mortality than low to moderate drinkers (people whom consume 1–2 units of alcohol a night). However, beyond this level of alcohol intake the mortality rises exponentially. Therefore any biomarkers that are developed to assess alcohol consumption need to be sensitive enough to differentiate low to moderate drinkers from heavy drinkers. This chapter will look at the markers currently in use in clinical practice; these include well-established markers like the mean corpuscular volume (MCV), liver enzymes and serum alcohol. In addition, we will review newer established markers such as carbohydrate-deficient transferrin (CDT), as well as describing the markers that are under evaluation or in experimental stages of development. The role of clinical questionnaires in conjunction with biomarkers will be discussed, as will the use of combined biomarkers in clinical practice.

Alcohol levels

Measurements of alcohol in blood, urine or the breath are useful for identifying acute alcohol levels. Breath analysis is used by the police for testing drivers by the roadside. In addition, it is useful to check if someone has had any recent alcohol intake, hence can be used to check abstinence. The accuracy of alcohol measurement is limited to the time taken for the alcohol to be metabolised to acetaldehyde (see Fig. 5.2). The result obtained from serum alcohol is difficult to interpret unless the time of drinking and volume of alcohol drunk are known. A single value cannot differentiate between acute or chronic abuse (Helander *et al.*, 1996). Even though alcohol levels measured in blood, urine or the breath are useful for identifying acute use, they do not provide any information about the severity of alcohol use (Neumann and Spies, 2003).

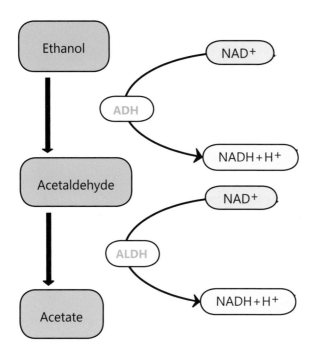

Figure 5.2 The pathway for metabolism of alcohol to acetate via acetaldehyde (ADH, alcohol dehydrogenase; ALDH, acetaldehyde dehydrogenase; NAD, nicotinamide dehydrogenase; NADH reduced nicotinamide dehydrogenase).

Mean corpuscular volume (MCV)

The mean volume of the red blood cell, termed mean corpuscular volume (MCV), has been recognised to increase in individuals after prolonged excessive alcohol intake (Wu *et al.*, 1974). An increased MCV is seen in 34–89 per cent of alcohol abusers (Chick *et al.*, 1981). An increased MCV usually occurs without an associated anaemia and with normal vitamin B12 and folate levels (Sillanaukee *et al.*, 1998). The pathophysiological mechanism through which alcohol leads to macrocytosis has not been fully elucidated, although a direct toxic effect of alcohol on the bone marrow is one possible mechanism.

The life span of a red blood cell is 120 days and, as a result, following abstinence it may take months for the MCV to return to normal. Interestingly patients that drink excessively on an irregular basis do not always develop an elevated MCV (Meerkerk *et al.*, 1999). As mentioned earlier, folate deficiency is not always associated with macrocytosis, but folate levels are decreased in up to 30 per cent of patients which could, in part be due to dietary deficiency (Conigrave *et al.*, 2003; Manari *et al.*, 2003).

MCV as a marker in heavy drinkers has a sensitivity of over 40 per cent, and it is usually more sensitive in women (Morgan *et al.*, 1981). MCV has shown a good correlation with the intensity of drinking, whereby more intense alcohol consumption is associated with a higher MCV (Koivisto *et al.*, 2006). MCV can be used to monitor the long-term drinking patterns of patients. However, following cessation of alcohol, the MCV takes 2–4 months to normalise, and may even rise in the short term immediately after abstinence, possibly because of effects on the bone marrow leading to increased reticulocyte production as the bone marrow recovers (Aithal *et al.*, 1998; Niemela, 2007; SriRajaskanthan and Preedy, 2006). When compared to other traditional markers, MCV has been found to be more sensitive than GGT and CDT in women (Sillanaukee *et al.*, 2000).

MCV is rather limited as a screening tool since it has low sensitivity, often below 50 per cent (Meerkerk *et al.*, 1999). Furthermore, the MCV can be raised in a variety of different pathologies, including deficiencies in vitamin B12 and folate, hypothyroidism, reticulocytosis, liver disease, certain haematological conditions and as a result of medications that alter folate metabolism (e.g. phenytoin).

Serum aminotransferases (AST and ALT)

Serum aminotransferases are intracellular enzymes found within the liver as well as other tissues. Aspartate aminotransferase (AST) is found in the cytosol and mitochondria of hepatocytes, as well as in skeletal muscle, the heart, kidney, brain and pancreas (Pratt and Kaplan, 2000). Alanine aminotransferase (ALT) is found in the cytosol of hepatocytes; the highest concentration is located in the liver, although it is expressed in other tissues. Both enzymes are involved in amino acid metabolism (Conigrave *et al.*, 2003).

AST and ALT are raised in liver damage, rather than alcohol abuse *per se*; they act more as markers of hepatocyte injury than specific markers of alcohol use. However, serum concentrations of AST and ALT are frequently elevated in alcoholic patients (Rosman and Lieber, 1994). Studies have shown around a third of alcohol-dependent people have raised AST (Helander and Tabakoff, 1997; Hietala *et al.*, 2006; Rosman and Lieber, 1994). A ratio of the AST level to the ALT level (AST : ALT) of more than 2 is suggestive of an alcohol aetiology, since most patients with non-alcohol-related disease have ratios of less than 1 (Niemela, 2007).

Aminotransferases are not usually increased by a single episode of excessive drinking (Nemesanszky *et al.*, 1988) although this is what happens with gamma glutamyl transferase (GGT) – another liver enzyme that will be discussed later. As a screening test, aminotransferases are less sensitive than GGT for identifying heavy alcohol consumption (Conigrave *et al.*, 2003).

Gamma glutamyl transferase (GGT)

GGT is found within epithelial cells lining the biliary ductules within the liver. It is also expressed in many other tissues, including the brain, kidney and pancreas, although at lower concentrations. GGT is a membrane-bound glycoprotein enzyme that catalyses the transfer of the gamma glutamyl moiety of glutathione to various peptide acceptors (Sherman *et al.*, 2002). It is a very sensitive indicator of hepatobiliary disease or insult, rather than being specific to alcohol consumption. Currently, GGT is the most commonly used biomarker in problem drinkers (Niemela, 2007). It is usually the first hepatic enzyme to become elevated in patients with alcoholic liver disease. Many studies have shown a clear positive correlation between levels of GGT and alcohol consumption, however, the sensitivity of this marker has been quite varied (Neumann and Spies, 2003). Following cessation of drinking, GGT levels usually return to normal after 5 weeks (Neumann and Spies, 2003; Sharpe, 2001).

In non-heavy drinkers a one-off heavy intake of alcohol will not necessarily lead to an elevated GGT. In people with a history of heavy drinking, resumption of alcohol following a period of abstinence leads to a more rapid rise in GGT (Nemesanszky *et al.*, 1988). Monitoring serum GGT concentrations may also help to distinguish chronic alcoholics with or without liver disease (Rosman and Lieber, 1994). Elevated serum GGT is found in 20 per cent of men and 15 per cent of women who consume approximately 40 g alcohol per day (Sharpe, 2001).

As a screening tool, GGT is found to be elevated in 30–50 per cent of heavy drinkers in the general community (Lof *et al.*, 1994; Nemesanszky *et al.*, 1988). Within the community of people with a raised GGT, between 50 per cent and 72 per cent of the elevated GGT levels can be attributed to alcohol (Neumann and Spies, 2003). GGT lacks sensitivity and specificity for use as a screening tool for heavy alcohol intake, since it is a marker of hepatic injury which is elevated in other causes of hepatitis. In addition, it is often raised in other conditions like renal failure, myocardial infarction and pancreatic disease (Conigrave *et al.*, 2003; Lee *et al.*, 2006). Furthermore, GGT is inducible and thus levels may be falsely elevated by the ingestion of drugs such as phenytoin.

Carbohydrate-deficient transferrin (CDT)

Carbohydrate-deficient transferrin (CDT) was first reported by Stibler and Kjellin (1976), when they described abnormal microheterogeneity of transferrin in the cerebrospinal fluid and serum of patients with alcoholic cerebellar degeneration. Transferrin is a glycoprotein comprised of a single polypeptide chain with two N-linked polysaccharide chains. The polysaccharide chains are branched with terminal sialic acid residues. There are several isoforms of human transferrin with different levels of sialylation. Alterations in the frequency of these isoforms present within the serum forms the basis of the CDT test. In a normal healthy person, the predominant isoform is the tetrasialotransferrin. However, in people with a consistent alcohol intake of over 60–80 g alcohol per day for at least 2 weeks, elevated mono- and disialotransferrin isoforms can be detected.

CDT was the first biomarker to be approved by the Food and Drugs Administration in the USA, for assessment of alcohol-related disease. Numerous studies have looked at the specificity and sensitivity of this marker in different clinical settings. The results have been mixed; many studies show it is an effective tool in screening for excessive alcohol use (Fleming and Mundt, 2004; Koch *et al.*, 2004). Initial studies examining CDT as a marker of excess alcohol use compared heavily-dependent alcoholics against teetotallers (abstainers) or people with a low alcohol intake. Consequently the initial results showed a high sensitivity and specificity for CDT as a marker. However, as further work was done on more heterogeneous populations, the results were not as conclusive (Allen *et al.*, 1994; Meerkerk *et al.*, 1999). Studies have shown that CDT is no better than GGT in assessing heavy alcohol intake accurately. With regards to its sensitivity and specificity the results have been very variable; Helander, Carlsson, and Borg (1996) felt that it was much the same as GGT. Data concerning the correlation between the amount of ethanol consumed and serum CDT are inconsistent (Niemela, 2007). CDT is measured in a number of ways; some of the older techniques, although accurate, are not practical for a standard biochemical lab setting.

Most studies evaluating CDT in clinical settings have used CDTect and %CDT microcolumn immunoassay systems. CDT and GGT have been used alone and in combination in various studies, based on the rationale that they act as independent markers of heavy alcohol consumption and therefore combined use will have a higher diagnostic yield (Chen *et al.*, 2003; Sillanaukee *et al.*, 2000). This increased diagnostic benefit of combined GGT and CDT has been supported by further work in different cohorts of patients; these include studies that followed up alcoholic people with normal GGT activities (Reynaud *et al.*, 1998), that evaluated progress of patients in treatment for alcoholism (Allen *et al.*, 1999), and that assessed alcohol consumption in a general medical clinic (Aithal *et al.*, 1998). Overall CDT is considered to be the more *specific* marker and GGT the more *sensitive* marker of chronic alcohol abuse (see Box 5.1).

Box 5.1 Factors that influence markers of chronic alcohol abuse	
GGT (gamma glutamyl transferase)	Male sex (more likely to show test elevation) People of South Asian, Mexican or Brazilian descent Medications (e.g. phenytoin and NSAIDs)* Obesity Liver and biliary disease
AST (aspartate aminotransferase)	People of South Asian, Mexican or African descent Obesity Liver and biliary diseases Muscle diseases Medications (e.g. NSAIDs, antibiotics)
ALT (alanine aminotransferase)	People of South Asian, African or Mexican descent Obesity Liver and biliary diseases Medications (e.g. NSAIDs, antibiotics)
CDT (carbohydrate-deficient transferrin)	Male sex (more sensitive) Obesity Appears unaffected by chronic liver diseases
MCV (mean corpuscular volume)	Female sex (more sensitive in women) Vitamin B12 or folate deficiency and haemolysis Liver disease Hypothyroidism Medications (e.g. anticonvulsants, oral contraceptives)

NSAIDs, nonsteroidal anti-inflammatory drugs.
* Via induction of microsomal enzymes.

Compared with CDT, GGT produces false-positive results for chronic alcohol abuse in many diseases, such as obstructive liver disease, hepatitis, fatty liver, liver cirrhosis, liver cell carcinoma, liver metastases, cardiac insufficiency, mononucleosis, renal transplant, hyperthyroidism, diabetes mellitus and pancreatitis (see Tietz, 1995). In contrast to CDT, GGT is greatly affected by several medications and drugs of abuse like barbiturates, cephalosporins, anabolic steroids, phenothiazines, oestrogens, oral contraceptives, phenytoin, primidone, and thyrostatic and antirheumatic agents (Tietz, 1995). Finally, neither marker is well validated – either alone or in combination – for identifying moderate to heavy drinkers.

New markers and future markers

Over recent years there have been many advances in developing markers that may help identify people with an excessive alcohol intake, or accurately assess the last time someone consumed alcohol. These markers have been developed initially in a preclinical setting, and are now being evaluated on human and animal models.

5-hydroxytryptophol and 5-hydroxyindoleacetic acid (5-HIAA)

5-Hydroxytryptophol and 5-hydroxyindoleacetic acid (5-HIAA) are both serotonin metabolites. Ethanol consumption leads to a shift in serotonin metabolism, leading to increased formation of 5-hydroxytryptophol and a consequent decrease in 5-HIAA production. The ratio of 5-hydroxytryptophol to 5-HIAA provides a marker which has been validated in a number of studies, including in healthy (Borucki *et al.*, 2005) and alcohol-dependent people (Spies *et al.*, 1999). Collection of urine is needed to assess levels of both compounds and provides evidence of alcohol up to 78.5 hours after ingestion, although sensitivity is limited after 30 hours (Borucki *et al.*, 2005). Further clinical use is possible in forensic medicine to identify people who had recently been drinking alcohol; also it would be a sensitive indicator of relapse after a period of abstinence (Niemela, 2007).

Ethyl glucuronide (EtG)

Ethyl glucuronide (EtG) is a water-soluble product excreted in urine with a half life of 2 hours. It is produced by the metabolism of ethanol by uridine 5'-diphospho-glucuronosyl transferase (UDP glucuronosyl transferase). Only a tiny fraction (approximately <0.1 per cent) of all alcohol consumed is metabolised via this route. Following cessation of regular alcohol consumption, EtG remains in the urine for several days (3–5 days) (Borucki *et al.*, 2005). One study compared EtG with the 5-hydroxytryptophol to 5-HIAA ratio and fatty acid ethyl esters (FAEEs). This study concluded that EtG was superior at identifying recent alcohol consumption in healthy subjects with a sensitivity of 100 per cent for more than 30 hours (Borucki *et al.*, 2005), however it involves technically demanding techniques such as liquid chromatography tandem mass spectrometry.

Sialic acid

Sialic acid is an acetylated derivative of neuraminic acid attached to carbohydrate chains, expressed on glycoproteins and glycolipids and acute-phase reactants. Serum levels of sialic acid are elevated in some heavy drinkers. However, this elevation is not specific to alcohol intake, and is found to be elevated in other diseases including renal failure, diabetes and inflammatory disorders (Bakri *et al.*, 2004). A role for this marker in differentiating between the effects of liver disease and alcohol abuse has been postulated (Niemela, 2007).

Acetaldehyde adducts

There is evidence from both human alcoholic subjects and animal studies that metabolism of alcohol produces an array of reactive products, among which aldehydes are most common. In addition, ethanol metabolism leads to oxidative stress which, in turn, results in lipid peroxidation and generation of aldehydes, including 4-hydroxynonenal and malondialdehyde, as illustrated in Fig. 5.3. These are reactive products that interact with proteins leading to the development of adducted proteins (Worrall *et al.*, 2001). The adducts have been found in the liver of alcoholic patients (Niemela, 2001). In addition to adduct formation secondary to breakdown of ethanol, it has been postulated that in conditions of increased oxidative stress, due to a high-fat diet or folate deficiency, alcohol abuse leads to increased adduct formation (Niemela, 2007). Currently there are no routine applications for measuring these adducts in clinical settings, and further work in this field is needed. A hybrid malondialdehyde–acetaldehyde adduct is formed when there is concomitant malondialdehyde.

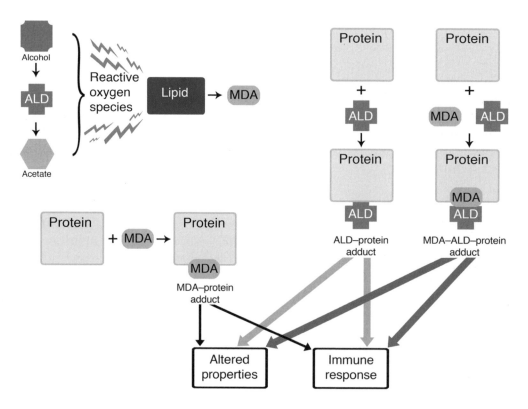

Figure 5.3   The pathway for the formation of protein adducts during alcohol metabolism. Reactive products (mainly aldehydes) are produced, including acetaldehyde (ALD). Oxidative stress (via peroxidation of lipids) leads to production of other aldehydes, like malondialdehyde (MDA). These aldehydes interact with proteins to form various adducts, such as malondialdehyde–acetaldehyde, which have altered properties and have an effect on the immune system.

Clinical questionnaires

The use of clinical questionnaires to aid the diagnosis of alcohol consumption is well established in clinical practice. Numerous questionnaires are available that have been validated in a number of different studies. The CAGE (Mayfield *et al.*, 1974), the AUDIT (Alcohol Use Disorders Identification Test; *see also* Chapter 2) (Allen *et al.*, 1997; Gache *et al.*, 2005) and the MAST (Michigan Alcohol Screening Test; MacKenzie *et al.*, 1996) tools are used to screen for alcohol abuse. Used alone, these questionnaires have variable success in identifying patients at risk of excess alcohol consumption (MacKenzie *et al.*, 1996). When answered truthfully they act as very good screening tools (Bataille *et al.*, 2003; Coulton *et al.*, 2006). However, they can be cumbersome to use in practice.

Different questionnaires are focused at different specific problems; for example, some assess total alcohol consumption, while others focus on issues of dependence (Gache *et al.*, 2005). Importantly some studies have combined the use of these questionnaires together with biochemical markers, and these have shown significantly improved sensitivity and specificity in identifying patients at risk of alcoholism or with increased alcohol consumption (Allen *et al.*, 1998; Bataille *et al.*, 2003).

Conclusions

There is a clear requirement for a method that enables healthcare professionals to accurately identify and screen patients at risk of developing health complications secondary to excessive alcohol intake. To date, there are no perfect markers for routine clinical use, but the use of clinical parameters (including drinking history, examination and biomarkers) does allow for the identification of such patients. Further work may lead to the development of better markers.

References and further reading

Aithal, G.P., Thornes, H., Dwarakanath, A.D. and Tanner, A.R. (1998). Measurement of carbohydrate-deficient transferrin (CDT) in a general medical clinic: Is this test useful in assessing alcohol consumption? *Alcohol and Alcoholism*, **33**(3), 304–09.

Allen, J., Litten, R.Z. and Lee, A. (1998). What you need to know: detecting alcohol problems in general medical practice. *Singapore Medical Journal*, **39**(1), 38–41.

Allen, J.P., Litten, R.Z., Anton, R.F. and Cross, G.M. (1994). Carbohydrate-deficient transferrin as a measure of immoderate drinking: remaining issues. *Alcoholism: Clinical and Experimental Research*, **18**(4), 799–812.

Allen, J.P., Litten, R.Z., Fertig, J.B. and Babor, T. (1997). A review of research on the Alcohol Use Disorders Identification Test (AUDIT). *Alcoholism: Clinical and Experimental Research*, **21**(4), 613–19.

Allen, J.P., Sillamaukee, P. and Anton, R. (1999). Contribution of carbohydrate deficient transferrin to gamma glutamyl transpeptidase in evaluating progress of patients in treatment for alcoholism. *Alcoholism: Clinical and Experimental Research*, **23**(1), 115–20.

Bakri, R.S., Afzali, B., Covic, A., *et al.* (2004). Cardiovascular disease in renal allograft recipients is associated with elevated sialic acid or markers of inflammation. *Clinical Transplantation*, **18**(2), 201–04.

Bataille, V., Ruidavets, J.B., Arveiler, D., *et al.* (2003). Joint use of clinical parameters, biological markers and CAGE questionnaire for the identification of heavy drinkers in a large population-based sample. *Alcohol and Alcoholism*, **38**(2), 121–27.

Bertholet, N., Daeppen, J.B., Wietlisbach, V., Fleming, M. and Burnand, B. (2005). Reduction of alcohol consumption by brief alcohol intervention in primary care: systematic review and meta-analysis. *Archives of Internal Medicine*, **165**(9), 986–95.

Borucki, K., Schreiner, R., Dierkes, J., *et al*. (2005). Detection of recent ethanol intake with new markers: comparison of fatty acid ethyl esters in serum and of ethyl glucuronide and the ratio of 5-hydroxytryptophol to 5-hydroxyindole acetic acid in urine. *Alcoholism: Clinical and Experimental Research*, **29**(5), 781–87.

Chen, J., Conigrave, K.M., Macaskill, P., Whitfield, J.B. and Irwig, L. (2003). Combining carbohydrate-deficient transferrin and gamma-glutamyl transferase to increase diagnostic accuracy for problem drinking. *Alcohol and Alcoholism*, **38**(6), 574–82.

Chick, J., Kreitman, N. and Plant, M. (1981). Mean cell volume and gamma-glutamyl-transpeptidase as markers of drinking in working men. *Lancet*, **1**(8232), 1249–51.

Conigrave, K.M., Davies, P., Haber, P. and Whitfield, J.B. (2003). Traditional markers of excessive alcohol use. *Addiction*, **98**(Suppl.2), 31–43.

Coulton, S., Drummond, C., James, D., *et al*. (2006). Opportunistic screening for alcohol use disorders in primary care: Comparative study. *British Medical Journal*, **332**(7540), 511–17.

Fleming, M. and Mundt, M. (2004). Carbohydrate-deficient transferrin: validity of a new alcohol biomarker in a sample of patients with diabetes and hypertension. *Journal of the American Board of Family Practice*, **17**(4), 247–55.

Fleming, M.F., Mundt, M.P., French, M.T., Manwell, L.B., Stauffacher, E.A. and Barry, K.L. (2002). Brief physician advice for problem drinkers: Long-term efficacy and benefit-cost analysis. *Alcoholism: Clinical and Experimental Research*, **26**(1), 36–43.

Fuchs, C.S., Stampfer, M.J., Colditz, G.A., *et al*. (1995). Alcohol consumption and mortality among women. *New England Journal of Medicine*, **332**(19), 1245–50.

Gache, P., Michaud, P., Landry, U., *et al*. (2005). The Alcohol Use Disorders Identification Test (AUDIT) as a screening tool for excessive drinking in primary care: reliability and validity of a French version. *Alcoholism: Clinical and Experimental Research*, **29**(11), 2001–07.

Helander, A., Beck, O. and Jones, A.W. (1996). Laboratory testing for recent alcohol consumption: comparison of ethanol, methanol, and 5-hydroxytryptophol. *Clinical Chemistry*, **42**(4), 618–24.

Helander, A., Carlsson, A.V. and Borg, S. (1996). Longitudinal comparison of carbohydrate-deficient transferrin and gamma-glutamyl transferase: complementary markers of excessive alcohol consumption. *Alcohol and Alcoholism*, **31**(1), 101–07.

Helander, A. and Tabakoff, B. (1997). Biochemical markers of alcohol use and abuse: experiences from the Pilot Study of the WHO/ISBRA Collaborative Project on state and trait markers of alcohol. International Society for Biomedical Research on Alcoholism. *Alcohol and Alcoholism*, **32**(2), 133–44.

Hietala, J., Koivisto, H., Anttila, P. and Niemela, O. (2006). Comparison of the combined marker GGT-CDT and the conventional laboratory markers of alcohol abuse in heavy drinkers, moderate drinkers and abstainers. *Alcohol and Alcoholism*, **41**(5), 528–33.

Institute of Alcohol Studies (2005). *Excessive and Problem Drinking in Great Britain*. Available at: http://www.ias.org.uk/resources/factsheets/drinkinggb_excessive.pdf (last accessed September 2008)

Kaner, E.F., Heather, N., McAvoy, B.R., Lock, C.A. and Gilvarry, E. (1999). Intervention for excessive alcohol consumption in primary health care: Attitudes and practices of English general practitioners. *Alcohol and Alcoholism*, **34**(4), 559–66.

Koch, H., Meerkerk, G.J., Zaat, J.O., Ham, M.F., Scholten, R.J. and Assendelft, W.J. (2004). Accuracy of carbohydrate-deficient transferrin in the detection of excessive alcohol consumption: a systematic review. *Alcohol and Alcoholism*, **39**(2), 75–85.

Koivisto, H., Hietala, J., Anttila, P., Parkkila, S. and Niemela, O. (2006). Long-term ethanol consumption and macrocytosis: diagnostic and pathogenic implications. *Journal of Laboratory and Clinical Medicine*, **147**(4), 191–96.

Lee, D.H., Silventoinen, K., Hu., G., *et al*. (2006). Serum gamma-glutamyltransferase predicts non-fatal myocardial infarction and fatal coronary heart disease among 28,838 middle-aged men and women. *European Heart Journal*, **27**(18), 2170–76.

Leon, D. A. and McCambridge, J. (2006). Liver cirrhosis mortality rates in Britain from 1950 to 2002: an analysis of routine data. *Lancet*, **367**(9504), 52–56.

Lof, K., Seppa, K., Itala, L., Koivula, T., Turpeinen, U. and Sillanaukee, P. (1994). Carbohydrate-deficient transferrin as an alcohol marker among female heavy drinkers: a population-based study. *Alcoholism: Clinical and Experimental Research*, **18**(4), 889–94.

MacKenzie, D., Langa, A. and Brown, T.M. (1996). Identifying hazardous or harmful alcohol use in medical admissions: a comparison of AUDIT, CAGE and Brief MAST. *Alcohol and Alcoholism*, **31**(6), 591–99.

Manari, A.P., Preedy, V.R. and Peters, T.J. (2003). Nutritional intake of hazardous drinkers and dependent alcoholics in the UK. *Addiction Biology*, **8**(2), 201–10.

Marmot, M.G., Rose, G., Shipley, M.J. and Thomas, B.J. (1981). Alcohol and mortality: a U-shaped curve. *Lancet*, **1**(8220), 580–83.

Mayfield, D., McLeod, G. and Hall, P. (1974). The CAGE questionnaire: validation of a new alcoholism screening instrument. *American Journal of Psychiatry*, **131**(10), 1121–23.

Maynard, A. and Godfrey, C. (1994). Alcohol policy – evaluating the options. *British Medical Bulletin*, **50**(1), 221–30.

Meerkerk, G.J., Njoo, K.H., Bongers, I.M., Trienekens, P. and van Oers, J.A. (1999). Comparing the diagnostic accuracy of carbohydrate-deficient transferrin, gamma-glutamyltransferase, and mean cell volume in a general practice population. *Alcoholism: Clinical and Experimental Research*, **23**(6), 1052–59.

Morgan, M.Y., Camilo, M.E., Luck, W., Sherlock, S. and Hoffbrand, A.V. (1981). Macrocytosis in alcohol-related liver disease: its value for screening. *Clinical and Laboratory Haematology*, **3**(1), 35–44.

Moyer, A., Finney, J.W., Swearingen, C.E. and Vergun, P. (2002). Brief interventions for alcohol problems: a meta-analytic review of controlled investigations in treatment-seeking and non-treatment-seeking populations. *Addiction*, **97**(3), 279–92.

Nemesanszky, E., Lott, J.A. and Arato, M. (1988). Changes in serum enzymes in moderate drinkers after an alcohol challenge. *Clinical Chemistry*, **34**(3), 525–27.

Neumann, T. and Spies, C. (2003). Use of biomarkers for alcohol use disorders in clinical practice. *Addiction*, **98**(Suppl.2), 81–91.

Niemela, O. (2001). Distribution of ethanol-induced protein adducts in vivo: relationship to tissue injury. *Free Radical Biology and Medicine*, **31**(12), 1533–38.

Niemela, O. (2007). Biomarkers in alcoholism. *Clinica Chimica Acta: International Journal of Clinical Chemistry*, **377**(1–2), 39–49.

Pratt, D. S. and Kaplan, M.M. (2000). Evaluation of abnormal liver-enzyme results in asymptomatic patients. *New England Journal of Medicine*, **342**(17), 1266–71.

Preedy, V.R. and Watson, R.R. (2005). *Comprehensive Handbook of Alcohol-Related Pathology*. San Diego: Elsevier.

Prime Minister's Strategy Unit (2004). *Alcohol Harm Reduction Strategy for England*. London: HMSO.

Reynaud, M., Hourcade, F., Planche, F., Albuisson, E., Meunier, M.N. and Planche, R. (1998). Usefulness of carbohydrate-deficient transferrin in alcoholic patients with normal gamma-glutamyl transpeptidase. *Alcoholism: Clinical and Experimental Research*, **22**(3), 615–18.

Room, R., Babor, T. and Rehm, J. (2005). Alcohol and public health. *Lancet*, **365**(9458), 519–30.

Rosman, A. S. and Lieber, C.S. (1994). Diagnostic utility of laboratory tests in alcoholic liver disease. *Clinical Chemistry*, **40**(8), 1641–51.

Sharpe, P.C. (2001). Biochemical detection and monitoring of alcohol abuse and abstinence. *Annals of Clinical Biochemistry*, **38**(6), 652–64.

Sherman, D.I.N., Preedy, V.R. and Watson, R.R. (2002). *Ethanol and the Liver. Mechanisms and Management*, 1st edn. London: Taylor and Francis.

Sillanaukee, P., Aalto, M. and Seppa, K. (1998). Carbohydrate-deficient transferrin and conventional alcohol markers as indicators for brief intervention among heavy drinkers in primary health care. *Alcoholism: Clinical and Experimental Research*, **22**(4), 892–96.

Sillanaukee, P., Massot, N., Jousilahti, P., *et al.* (2000). Dose response of laboratory markers to alcohol consumption in a general population. *American Journal of Epidemiology*, **152**(8), 747–51.

Spies, C.D., Herpell, J., Beck, O., *et al.* (1999). The urinary ratio of 5-hydroxytryptophol to 5-hydroxyindole-3-acetic acid in surgical patients with chronic alcohol misuse. *Alcohol*, **17**(1), 19–27.

SriRajaskanthan, R. and Preedy, V.R. (2006a). Biochemical markers of alcoholism and their clinical effectiveness. *Clinical Effectiveness in Nursing*, **9**, e280–85.

SriRajaskanthan, R. and Preedy, V.R. (2006b). Diagnosis and management of alcoholic liver disease: a review. *Clinical Effectiveness in Nursing*, **9**, e286–94.

SriRajaskanthan, R. and Preedy, V.R. (2007). Alcohol as a toxic agent: not just the liver and brain and not every drinker. *Journal of Nutritional and Environmental Medicine*, **16**, 1–13.

Stibler, H. and Kjellin, K.G. (1976). Isoelectric focusing and electrophoresis of the CSF proteins in tremor of different origins. *Journal of the Neurological Sciences*, **30**(2–3), 269–85.

Tietz, W. (1995). *Clinical Guide to Laboratory Tests*, 3rd edn. Philadelphia: WB Saunders.

World Health Organization (2004). *Global Status Report on Alcohol 2004*. Geneva: World Health Organization.

Worrall, S., Niemela, O., Parkkila, S., Peters, T.J. and Preedy, V.R. (2001). Protein adducts in type I and type II fibre predominant muscles of the ethanol-fed rat: preferential localisation in the sarcolemmal and subsarcolemmal region. *European Journal of Clinical Investigation*, **31**(8), 723–30.

Wu, A., Chanarin, I. and Levi, A.J. (1974). Macrocytosis of chronic alcoholism. *Lancet*, **1**(7862), 829–31.

Wurst, F.M., Alling, C., Aradottir, S., *et al.* (2005). Emerging biomarkers: new directions and clinical applications. *Alcoholism: Clinical and Experimental Research*, **29**(3), 465–73.

Diagnosis and management of alcoholic liver disease

Rajaventhan SriRajaskanthan and Victor R. Preedy

Alcohol has been one of man's favoured beverages for thousands of years. Since the beginning of recorded history, references to alcoholic beverages have been made. Ancient Greek and Egyptian texts record social and health problems pertaining to the use of alcohol, as well as referring to the initial effects of intoxication (Room et al., 2005). Alcohol has been shown to be causally related to over a hundred medical conditions (SriRajaskanthan and Preedy, 2007). Around 4 per cent of the burden of disease and 3.2 per cent of all deaths globally are attributable to alcohol. This makes it the foremost health risk in low-mortality developing countries (World Health Organization, 2006). Alcoholic liver disease is one of the most heavily researched conditions causally related to alcohol. Global alcohol consumption has increased between 1960 and now, but a decrease in consumption is seen in previously heavy consumers of alcohol like France, Italy and Spain. There has been a marked increase in the developing countries and in Eastern Europe (SriRajaskanthan and Preedy, 2006c; World Health Organization, 2004, 2006).

Over the last 30 years, our understanding of the pathological mechanisms of alcoholic liver disease and its clinical management has increased markedly. Within the UK there has been a marked increase in alcohol consumption over the last 40 years (Rehm *et al.*, 2003; Room, 2006) and, more recently, in perceived societal disorder and social disharmony. In the UK alone the total cost of alcohol misuse is estimated at £20 billion a year; this includes a cost of £1.7 billion to the National Health Service (Malone and Friedman, 2005).

Within the UK there has been an 18 per cent rise in deaths from alcohol-related diseases between the years of 2000 and 2004 (Leon and McCambridge, 2006). See Fig. 6.1 (overpage) for alcohol-related deaths in women and men. Fig. 6.2 shows the total number of deaths between 1991 and 2005. Excess alcohol consumption is clearly correlated with increased morbidity and mortality (Rajendram *et al.*, 2006). The aim of this chapter is to provide an overview of alcoholic liver disease, embracing both the pathogenic and clinical aspects. We shall briefly discuss the mechanisms by which alcohol leads to systemic toxicity, and the histological changes that occur to the liver with excessive alcohol use. We will review the management of alcoholic liver disease, alcoholic hepatitis and the systemic complications of liver disease.

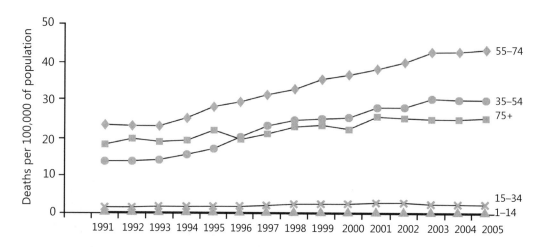

Figure 6.1a   Alcohol-related deaths among boys and men in different age groups between 1991 and 2005. Data derived from UK National Statistics.

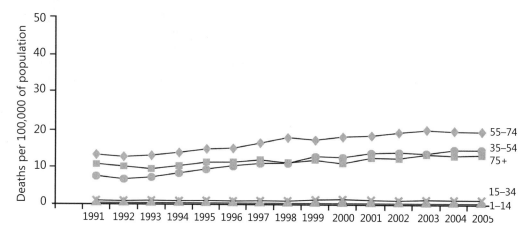

Figure 6.1b   Alcohol-related deaths among girls and women in different age groups between 1991 and 2005. Data derived from UK National Statistics.

Alcohol is the leading cause of cirrhosis in established economies; the relative risk of alcohol is 13 for men and women consuming more than 60 g and 40 g of alcohol daily, respectively (Reuben, 2006). Studies have shown that when a threshold level of 60 g per day (in men) and 20 g per day (in women) is exceeded for a long period of time, it increases the risk of hepatotoxicity (Savolainen *et al.*, 1993). More recently evidence has emerged to support the notion that lifetime consumption of alcohol is an important factor in establishing risk of developing alcoholic liver disease (Preedy and SriRajaskanthan, 2006; Savolainen *et al.*, 1993). However, not all persons that exceed this threshold level will develop alcoholic liver disease; in fact only 20 per cent of men consuming more than 12 cans of beer a day for 10 years developed cirrhosis (Sherman *et al.*, 2002). This is thought to relate to a combination of genetic and environmental factors that alter a person's predisposition to developing alcoholic liver disease.

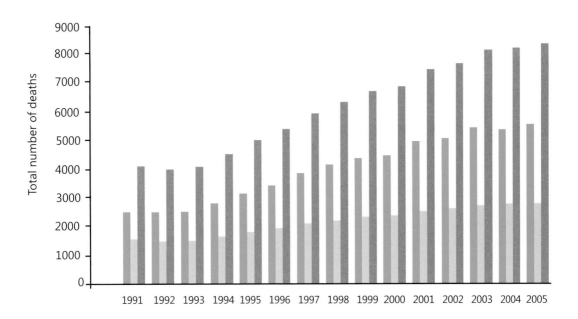

Figure 6.2 Total number of alcohol-related deaths in the UK in the years from 1991 to 2005 in men (*blue*), women (*pale blue*) and both (*grey*). Data derived from World Health Organization, 2004.

Metabolism of alcohol

Systemic metabolism of alcohol to acetaldehyde is almost entirely hepatic and occurs via three pathways:

- alcohol dehydrogenase (ADH)
- the microsomal–ethanol oxidising system (MEOS)
- catalase.

The last is considered to be relatively insignificant. After ingestion of alcohol, blood alcohol concentration peaks and then there is a pseudo-linear decline in blood alcohol levels. Alcohol cannot be stored within the body and hence over 90 per cent is metabolised by the liver. The remainder is excreted unchanged in the urine, sweat and breath (Paton, 2005).

In most people with low and moderate alcohol intakes, nearly all alcohol is metabolised via ADH. However, with heavy intake the MEOS system starts to play a more active role (Sherman *et al.*, 2002). This pathway consists of cytochrome P450-IIE1, which is embedded in the endoplasmic reticular membrane. This enzyme is primarily located in the centrilobular zone of the liver acinus. In novice drinkers it contributes to only a minor part of the total alcohol metabolism, while in established heavy drinkers it accounts for a greater proportion of total alcohol metabolism (Preedy and Watson, 2005). In other words – it is inducible.

The first step in metabolism via the ADH pathway is conversion of alcohol to acetaldehyde via ADH (see Fig. 5.2 in Chapter 5). Acetaldehyde is an extremely toxic substance that, in normal people, is metabolised to acetate by aldehyde dehydrogenase; acetate is relatively inactive (Preedy and Watson, 2005). Acetaldehyde causes a variety of pathogenic reactions, such as deactivation of proteins and increased collage production, which can in turn lead to fibrosis. Activation of Kupffer cells by endotoxins and subsequent inflammatory cascades that involve cytokines, chemokines and adhesion molecules are also important in the pathogenesis of alcoholic liver disease (Lumeng and Crabb, 2001).

Genetic and environmental factors predisposing to alcoholic liver disease

The genes transcribing ADH and acetaldehyde dehydrogenase (ALDH) are very closely corr-elated with development of alcoholism. Genetic susceptibility to alcoholism has been noted in twin, adoption and familial clustering studies. People with high-activity ADH, encoded by the ADH2*2 or ADH3*2 allele, are at reduced risk of alcoholism (Lumeng and Crabb, 2001; SriRajaskanthan and Preedy, 2007). Of the seven human ADH gene loci, the frequency of different alleles depends on ethnic background. ADH2*2 is commonly expressed in Asians, while ADH2*1 is expressed in Caucasians and African–Americans (SriRajaskanthan and Preedy, 2007; Thomasson et al., 1991).

The different ADH genotypes have similar rates of alcohol metabolism (that is, the conversion of alcohol to acetaldehyde). However there is a clear difference in the alcohol drinking behaviour. It has been found that the ADH2*2 allele was found to be substantially more common in the non-alcoholic group than in alcoholics among Chinese people living in Taiwan (Lumeng and Crabb, 2001; Thomasson et al., 1991). Similar findings have been found in studies involving other ethnic groups, for example the Maori people of New Zealand and Spanish people (Borras et al., 2000). Furthermore, studies have shown that ADH2*1 alleles are more prevalent in heavy drinkers than in moderate drinkers (Zintzaras et al., 2006).

The two main ALDH enzymes have different cellular localisation, with ALDH-1 in the cytosol and ALDH-2 in the mitochondria. Alcohol consumption is known to cause facial flushing in oriental races, including Chinese and Japanese people (Higuchi et al., 1994a). This is thought to be related to accumulation of acetaldehyde due to 'deficiency' of active ALDH-2 (in that they have the ALDH2*2 form of the enzyme, which is relatively inactive in comparison to the ALDH2*1 form). The ALDH2*1 form is seen predominantly in Caucasian people and most other races (Harada et al., 1982). There is evidence that ALDH-2 deficiency is linked to reduced frequency and quantity of alcohol consumption and a reduced risk of alcoholism (Higuchi et al., 1994). However, in this group of people, with only mild flushing, drinking heavily increases their risk of developing alcoholic liver disease, due to increased damage induced by high acetaldehyde concentrations (Crabb et al., 2004).

Diagnosis of alcoholic liver disease

The diagnosis of alcoholic liver disease is not always straightforward. Patients are not always reliable or accurate in recording their alcohol intake, including their past history of heavy alcohol use. It has been well documented that medical practitioners are inadequate at identifying at-risk patients. It has been estimated that about 20 per cent of all patients presenting to general practitioners in the UK consume alcohol at excessive levels, yet up to 98 per cent of these are not identified in the general-practice setting (Kaner *et al.*, 1999). Unfortunately, no unequivocal screening tools are currently available, either biochemical or questionnaire-based, for accurately assessing risk in 100 per cent of cases (SriRajaskanthan and Preedy, 2006a).

Furthermore, it has become increasingly clear that there is marked variation between people with respect to the amount of alcohol needed to cause alcoholic liver disease. Different thresholds have been proposed for identifying the amount of alcohol that must be consumed to result in alcoholic liver disease. One study by Lelbach (1976) stated that 80 g per day and 60 g per day for 10–12 years will result in cirrhosis in men and women, respectively, although lower values (40 g and 20 g per day) have been hypothesised (Sherman *et al.*, 2002). The diagnosis can only be made in the absence of other causes of liver disease, so all patients should be tested for viral, autoimmune and hereditary causes of hepatic dysfunction. The diagnosis is based on clinical history, examination, blood tests and abdominal ultrasound. The ultimate diagnosis of alcoholic liver disease can only be confirmed on liver biopsy. Furthermore, there is often a poor correlation between clinical signs and symptoms, biochemical results and histology. As we shall below, there are different histological stages of alcoholic liver disease.

Often patients with advanced disease can present without any symptoms and/or signs. However, there are symptoms that patients may initially present with that can vary in severity. Symptoms may include anorexia, nausea, vomiting, abdominal pain or distension. They can also present with more alarming symptoms, for example haematemesis, decreased consciousness or even coma, or aggression. Clinical examination, again, can be normal in patients with cirrhosis, but they may also present with the classical symptoms of parotid enlargement, hypertension, gout, prominent spider naevi, Dupuytren's contracture, gynaecomastia, a pseudo-cushingoid appearance, testicular atrophy, hair loss and proximal myopathy.

Laboratory features can appear normal even in patients with cirrhosis. Classically they include elevated GGT, macrocytosis, plasma aspartate transaminase levels greater than alanine transaminase (the ratio is 2:1) and hypertriglycerideamia. Even in patients with severe alcoholic hepatitis, the transaminases will rarely rise to more than 400 IU/L. Other markers that may be abnormal are clotting factors, and this is due to poor liver production of proteins. In addition, the full blood count can be revealing in that excessive alcohol intake is associated with a macrocytosis, which is independent of nutritional deficiencies. Thrombocytopenia may also be a feature in patients with hypersplenism secondary to portal hypertension.

As mentioned earlier, the gold standard for confirming the diagnosis of alcoholic liver disease is liver biopsy and histology. However, in cases where the clinical diagnosis is secure, a liver biopsy may not be mandatory (McCullough and O'Connor, 1998). In addition to confirming the diagnosis, liver biopsy would help exclude other causes of cirrhosis, and in patients presenting early with disease it would help predict prognosis.

Histological stages of alcoholic liver disease

There are three main histological stages of liver disease, namely:

- fatty liver
- alcoholic hepatitis, and
- cirrhosis.

Alcoholic fatty liver

Fatty liver is the commonest pathological finding in patients who abuse alcohol. Initially it was considered to be a benign condition. Clinically these patients are often asymptomatic, with normal clinical examinations. However, they may exhibit some upper abdominal discomfort, and 10–28 per cent of patients with fatty liver may exhibit some sign of chronic liver disease (Hislop *et al.*, 1983). Blood tests may well be normal, but patients may have mildly raised alanine transaminase, and gamma-glutamyl transferase (GGT) (SriRajaskanthan and Preedy, 2006a). Fatty liver is due to fat cells accumulating within the liver parenchyma. The excess lipids created by disruption of the metabolic pathways form large droplets within the hepatocytes. Fatty liver is a pathological diagnosis, and is defined as more than 5 per cent of cells containing fat droplets. There is some evidence that a mixed pattern of steatosis with giant mitochondria is more predictive of progression to cirrhosis (Teli *et al.*, 1995). Previously, alcoholic fatty liver was thought to be a benign condition and it was thought that progression to alcoholic hepatitis was necessary before the development of cirrhosis. However, there is now evidence that progression from fatty liver to cirrhosis can occur directly without histologically progressing to alcoholic hepatitis (Reeves *et al.*, 1996; Sherman *et al.*, 2002).

Alcoholic hepatitis

This condition can only be diagnosed accurately from liver biopsy, since the clinical features are variable. On liver biopsy it is characterised by hepatocellular necrosis (most prominent in the centrilobular region of the hepatic acinus), macro- and microvesicular steatosis, leukocytic infiltration, fibrosis and Mallory bodies (Sherlock, 1990; Sherlock and Dooley, 2006). Mallory bodies are intracellular cytoplasmic inclusions that vary in size from small granules to large masses. They are a characteristic (not a specific feature) of alcoholic hepatitis. Other histological features present within the liver in alcoholic hepatitis include apoptotic bodies, cholestasis and infiltration by mononuclear cells. Unsurprisingly, there is no clear association between histological findings and clinical symptoms (French *et al.*, 1993).

Cirrhosis

The word cirrhosis is derived from the Greek term *scirrhus*. It is used to describe the tawny surface of the liver seen in cirrhosis. Fibrosis within the liver eventually culminates in the development of cirrhosis. The formation of scarring that eventually leads to cirrhosis is due to an imbalance between the formation of extracellular matrix and removal by the stellate cells. The extracellular matrix is composed of collagens, glycoproteins and proteoglycans; it provides the normal scaffolding for hepatocytes. In established cirrhotic liver disease, alterations occur in the vasculature of the portal system. There is increased splanchnic arterial flow and correspondingly an increased splanchnic venous inflow to the liver. This increase in flow is mediated by numerous vasodilating agents, for example glucagon, substance P and nitric oxide (Sherman *et al.*, 2002). Within the liver the increased resistance to portal flow which leads to portal hypertension is due to changes in hepatic architecture related directly to fibrosis, as well as release of vasoconstricting and vasodilating agents (e.g. nitric oxide and hydrogen sulphide) from stellate cells (Garcia-Tsao, 2006a).

Management of alcoholic liver disease

This can be divided broadly into management of the direct effects on the liver and management of the systemic complications secondary to cirrhosis and/or alcoholic hepatitis. The most important prognostic factor in patients with alcoholic liver disease is stopping drinking. In patients with fatty liver secondary to alcohol, who do not have any features of alcoholism or alcohol-dependent behaviour, cessation or education with regards to alcohol consumption is often sufficient (Zhang *et al.*, 2005). It is well documented that liver damage is reversible in patients who stop drinking at an early stage of liver disease (Marsano *et al.*, 2003). In patients with fatty liver who show or admit to features of alcohol dependence then a more robust approach is often needed to help them stop drinking. There is evidence that self-help books, repeated consultations with a primary-care physician and referral to professional organisations such as Alcoholics Anonymous are of benefit (Paton, 2005). In people with a physical as well as a mental dependence on alcohol, abrupt cessation can lead to development of withdrawal symptoms. This encompasses a broad range of symptoms from mild nausea to delirium tremens (Ashworth and Gerada, 1997).

Therapies for alcoholic hepatitis

Medical therapy

Corticosteroids can improve the short-term survival of patients with severe alcoholic hepatitis. Over the last 15 years many studies have been performed to assess the potential benefit of steroids in patients with alcoholic hepatitis (SriRajaskanthan and Preedy, 2006b). A recent meta-analysis involving a total of 215 patients showed a higher survival rate of those treated with corticosteroids than those given placebo (Mathurin *et al.*, 2002). The role of corticosteroids is only beneficial in patients with severe alcoholic hepatitis in the absence of sepsis and gastrointestinal haemorrhage. Severe alcoholic hepatitis has traditionally been scored by the Maddrey's discriminant function, in which a score of 32 or more indicates severe hepatitis. Over the last 10 years other scoring systems have also been validated for assessing mortality risk in patients with severe alcoholic hepatitis. The Glasgow Alcoholic Hepatitis score is now commonly used in many clinical settings to aid assessment of patients; a score of 9 or more indicates severe alcoholic liver disease.

Pentoxifylline is a phosphodiesterase inhibitor that suppresses tumour necrosis factor alpha (TNF-α) and downregulates the expression of intercellular adhesion molecule-1 (ICAM-1) in monocytes (Shirin *et al.*, 1999). In alcoholic hepatitis, elevated TNF-α is an indicator of poor outcome (Rongey and Kaplowitz, 2006). A study by Akriviadis *et al.* showed a greater survival benefit at 28 days in patients suffering from severe alcoholic hepatitis and treated with pentoxifylline (Akriviadis *et al.*, 2000). Interestingly the main cause of death in the placebo group, who did not receive pentoxifylline, was hepatorenal syndrome. The protective effect of pentoxifylline against developing hepatorenal syndrome was reported by other groups previously (McHutchinson and Draguesku, 1991).

Infliximab is a chimeric mouse/human antibody that binds to TNF-α and blocks its effects. Trials are still underway to see if there is any benefit in using infliximab rather than steroids. There has been one large trial comparing the two agents, but this trial was stopped early due to the poor outcome in the infliximab group (Naveau *et al.*, 2004). S-adenosyl-methionine (SAM) is a methyl donor and has an important role in metabolism of nucleic acids. Preclinical studies in animals show that administering SAM decreases the amount of liver injury caused by alcohol. However, a recent Cochrane Review (Rambaldi and Gluud, 2006) concluded that there was no benefit in administering SAM to patients with alcoholic liver disease.

Liver transplantation

Even though alcoholic liver disease is the most common cause of cirrhosis in Europe and North America, physicians are still reluctant to consider these people for transplantation. An Austrian study showed that only 5 per cent of patients with end-stage alcoholic liver disease were assessed for liver transplants (O'Grady, 2006). The reasons for this remain complex, but there is a perception that patients with alcoholic liver disease have a self-inflicted disease. However, this is inaccurate. As mentioned earlier, not all alcoholics develop alcoholic liver disease, and not all patients with the disease are alcohol dependent. Coexisting factors such as genetic susceptibility and hepatitis C means that people who drink as much as their peers may develop alcoholic liver disease on a background of moderately heavy drinking. In the UK, around 25 per cent of liver transplantations are in patients with alcoholic liver disease.

Survival rates after liver transplantation are comparable with those for cirrhosis from other aetiologies (Burra and Lucey, 2005). However, there are concerns that following transplantation there is a relapse to previous drinking patterns. Studies have shown a marked variation in the percentage of patients post-transplantation that continue to drink (O'Grady, 2006). In the UK, a minimum period of 6 months' abstinence from alcohol while awaiting a transplant is needed before transplantation is considered. Of course, survival in those who return to alcohol is poorer than those who continue to abstain.

Nutrition

Malnutrition hastens the development and susceptibility to alcoholic liver disease (Marsano and McClain, 1991; Marsano, 2003; Preedy and Watson, 2005), and it is associated with increased mortality in patients with alcoholic liver disease. A study by Mendenhall and colleagues (Mendenhall *et al.*, 1995) found the degree of malnutrition was correlated with severity of liver disease. This occurs due to both deficiencies in macro- and micronutrients (Arteel *et al.*, 2003; Gyamfi and Wan, 2006; Mezey, 1998). Many alcoholic people have diets deficient in calories obtained from fats and proteins, although their overall total caloric intake may be increased. Furthermore, fat absorption is in part regulated by bile salt production, which is altered in alcoholic liver disease (Halsted, 2004).

Macronutrient deficiencies in carbohydrates, fats and proteins are linked to increased development of alcoholic liver disease. Protein deficiency is also associated with pathogenesis of the disease (Roongpisuthipong *et al.*, 2001). Patients with chronic liver disease develop a number of defects in protein metabolism, including decreased production of albumin and clotting factors (Lieber, 2003). There is evidence that increased intake of polyunsaturated fatty acids and vegetable oils is associated with enhanced liver damage, while saturated fats have some protective effects against alcoholic liver disease (Mezey, 1998; Nanji, 2004).

Micronutrient deficiencies have also been shown to accelerate progression of liver disease (Lieber, 2003). Furthermore, each nutritional deficiency can lead to specific disorders and conditions. These can present themselves clinically as an overt condition, subclinically or appear following concomitant pathology or metabolic stress. Vitamin deficiency is also common among alcoholic patients (Manari *et al.*, 2003). In addition to a decreased oral intake of vitamins, there is evidence to suggest that maldigestion and impaired intestinal absorption contribute to the deficiency of vitamins and other micronutrients (Lieber, 2003).

Nutritional support of patients with alcoholic liver disease will need to be tailored and will depend on each patient's current clinical situation. For example, patients with 'fatty liver' and evidence of chronic liver disease often benefit from nutritional assessment because if they stop drinking they can lose up to 80 per cent of their daily calorie intake. Patients presenting with severe alcoholic hepatitis often require much more nutritional support, in the form of nasogastric or enteral feeding. Such support has been shown to reduce mortality and morbidity. The nutritional support needed by cirrhotic patients depends in part on the severity of liver injury. In those with well-compensated disease, a good balanced diet encompassing a variety of foods is sufficient to ensure adequate nutritional status.

Management of portal hypertension

Portal hypertension is a common problem complicating many causes of chronic liver disease. It is not specific to alcoholic liver disease. Interestingly portal hypertension improves on cessation of alcohol consumption. The pathophysiological mechanisms leading to portal hypertension are unclear, but three main hypotheses are widely accepted:

• First, due to altered architecture in the liver as a result of fibrosis there is increased portal pressure, which leads to increased production of lymph. When the rate of lymph production exceeds its removal, ascites may develop (Sherman *et al.*, 2002).

• Second, increased plasma volume due to sodium retention may well lead to cirrhosis. The sodium and water retention is postulated to occur secondary to hepatorenal reflex.

• Third, splanchnic arterial vasodilatation occurs secondary to portal hypertension and may result in increased blood volume in the splanchnic vascular bed. Pooling of blood leads to reduced central arterial blood volume, which causes activation of the renin–angiotensin–aldosterone system (Arroyo and Gines, 1992).

Clinical features of portal hypertension include ascites and varices. Accumulation of ascites is a feature of decompensated alcoholic cirrhosis; furthermore, it can occur in severe alcoholic hepatitis. Other than abstinence from alcohol, which on its own is enough to cause resolution of minimal ascites, other medical therapies are available. Treating ascites improves the patient's quality of life but does not improve mortality (Marsano *et al.*, 2003). Initially diuretics are used to treat ascites, commonly spironolactone plus a loop diuretic such as furosemide.

In resistant ascites, the first-line treatment is a therapeutic paracentesis (Garcia-Tsao, 2006a). The ascites will recur and hence numerous admissions for paracentesis may be required. In cases in which recurrence of ascites is problematic, the use of transjugular intrahepatic portosystemic shunts is considered. Recently, meta-analyses of trials comparing transjugular intrahepatic portosystemic shunts to large-volume paracentesis were evaluated. The results showed that these shunts were good at resolving the recurrence of ascites. However, there was an increased incidence of hepatic encephalopathy (D'Amico *et al.*, 2005).

Spontaneous bacterial peritonitis occurs when the ascitic fluid within the peritoneal cavity becomes infected. The underlying pathophysiological mechanism leading to infection remains unclear; however, translocation of bacteria from the gut into the ascitic fluid is one possible mechanism (SriRajaskanthan and Preedy, 2006b). The diagnosis is confirmed if there is a polymorphonuclear cell count of over 250 cells per mL of ascitic fluid. Treatment is with antibiotics, but there is still a 20 per cent mortality rate with each episode (Marsano *et al.*, 2003).

Development of varices is also a complication of portal hypertension. Portal pressure is defined as the pressure in the portal vein (the normal range is 1–5 mmHg). Development of varices is thought to occur when the pressure is greater than 10–12 mmHg (Feu *et al.*, 1995). Due to this high pressure it is postulated that blood is diverted via collateral vessels. Commonly these vessels are located in the oesophagus and stomach. Varices in the oesophagus and stomach are present in 50 per cent of cirrhotic patients, and each year between 5–20 per cent of them develop varices (Garcia and Sanyal, 2001).

The role of beta-blockers in primary prevention of variceal haemorrhage is well documented. Their role in primary prevention for the development of varices was recently studied in a randomised placebo-controlled trial; the results showed no benefit in reducing development of varices (Garcia-Tsao, 2006b). Other studies looked at the role of combining beta-blockers with endoscopic variceal ligation as primary prophylaxis in patients with varices; they found a decreased variceal haemorrhage rate in patients treated with both modalities versus beta-blockers alone (Jutabha *et al.*, 2005). Specific therapy for control of bleeding in acute variceal haemorrhage involves combining endoscopic variceal ligation with vasoactive drugs such as terlipressin. These vasoactive drugs work by causing mesenteric arterial vasoconstriction and thus reduce portal pressure.

Appropriate management of airway and circulation are also imperative. Some patients will require intubation if their conscious level is diminished, and adequate fluid resuscitation is essential to maintain good perfusion throughout the body. As secondary prophylaxis (i.e. prevention of further variceal haemorrhage after the first episode) a combination of endoscopic variceal ligation and beta-blockers are recommended (Garcia-Tsao, 2006b).

The use of transjugular intrahepatic portosystemic shunts in recurrent variceal haemorrhage should be reserved for patients who have failed medical management involving endoscopic therapy and beta-blockers. There is increased incidence of encephalopathy in patients with transjugular intrahepatic shunts, and no overall mortality benefit.

Hepatic encephalopathy

Hepatic encephalopathy is a neuropsychiatric condition that occurs in patients with advanced alcoholic liver disease. It presents with features of cognitive, psychiatric and motor impairment. The underlying cause remains unclear and is likely to be multifactorial. Portosystemic collaterals which develop in alcoholic liver disease due to portal hypertension often shunt ammonia away from the liver. This is likely to play an important role in the pathogenesis of hepatic encephalopathy (Abou-Assi and Vlahcevic, 2001; Garcia-Tsao, 2006a). Factors such as sepsis, gastrointestinal haemorrhage, spontaneous bacterial peritonitis, constipation and electrolyte disturbance may precipitate an episode of encephalopathy (Butterworth, 2003). Following a transjugular intrahepatic shunt insertion, development of encephalopathy is a frequent event (Garcia-Tsao, 2006b). Management of hepatic encephalopathy involves removing the precipitating factor, if possible. The use of lactulose as the gold-standard treatment is still recommended. However, there have been no randomised-controlled trials (Ferenci, Herneth, and Steindl, 2003). Acarbose is a hypoglycaemic agent that has been found to reduce ammonia levels and improve intellectual function in patients with encephalopathy (Gentile *et al.,* 2005).

Conclusions

Alcoholic liver disease is a growing problem within the UK and there appears to be an increase in cirrhosis rates over the last 40 years (Leon and McCambridge, 2006). The WHO global alcohol report showed that alcohol intake is generally falling in the heaviest consuming countries of the world, like France and Italy, but there has been a marked rise in consumption in Eastern Europe and developing countries throughout the world (World Health Organization, 2004). Although alcohol intake is closely related to development of alcoholic liver disease, other factors play an important role in determining susceptibility. Outcome is still poor for patients with cirrhosis secondary to alcoholic liver disease, and the importance of good nutritional status and abstinence from alcohol is paramount to improving survival.

References and further reading

Abou-Assi, S. and Vlahcevic, Z.R. (2001). Hepatic encephalopathy. Metabolic consequence of cirrhosis often is reversible. *Postgraduate Medicine*, **109**(2), 52–60, 63.

Akriviadis, E., Botla, R., Briggs, W., Han, S., Reynolds, T. and Shakil, O. (2000). Pentoxifylline improves short-term survival in severe acute alcoholic hepatitis: A double-blind, placebo-controlled trial. *Gastroenterology*, **119**(6), 1637–48.

Arroyo, V. and Gines, P. (1992). Arteriolar vasodilation and the pathogenesis of the hyperdynamic circulation and renal sodium and water retention in cirrhosis. *Gastroenterology*, **102**(3), 1077.

Arteel, G., Marsano, L., Mendez, C., Bentley, F. and McClain, C.J. (2003). Advances in alcoholic liver disease. *Best Practice and Research in Clinical Gastroenterology*, **17**(4), 625–47.

Ashworth, M. and Gerada, C. (1997). ABC of mental health. Addiction and dependence-II: Alcohol. *British Medical Journal*, **315**(7104). 358–60.

Borras, E., Coutelle, C., Rosell, A., *et al.* (2000). Genetic polymorphism of alcohol dehydrogenase in Europeans: The ADH2*2 allele decreases the risk for alcoholism and is associated with ADH3*1. *Hepatology*, **31**(4), 984–89.

Burra, P. and Lucey, M.R. (2005). Liver transplantation in alcoholic patients. *Transplant International*, **18**(5), 491–98.

Butterworth, R.F. (2003). Pathogenesis of hepatic encephalopathy: new insights from neuroimaging and molecular studies. *Journal of Hepatology*, **39**(2), 278–85.

Crabb, D.W., Matsumoto, M., Chang, D. and You, M. (2004). Overview of the role of alcohol dehydrogenase and aldehyde dehydrogenase and their variants in the genesis of alcohol-related pathology. *Proceedings of the Nutrition Society*, **63**(1), 49–63.

D'Amico, G., Luca, A., Morabito, A., Miraglia, R. and D'Amico, M. (2005). Uncovered transjugular intrahepatic portosystemic shunt for refractory ascites: A meta-analysis. *Gastroenterology*, **129**(4), 1282–93.

Ferenci, P., Herneth, A. and Steindl, P. (2003). Newer approaches to therapy of hepatic encephalopathy. *Seminars in Liver Disease*, **16**, 329–38.

Feu, F., Garcia-Pagan, J.C., Bosch, J., *et al.* (1995). Relation between portal pressure response to pharmacotherapy and risk of recurrent variceal haemorrhage in patients with cirrhosis. *Lancet,* **346**(8982). 1056–59.

French, S.W., Nash, J., Shitabata, P., *et al.* (1993). Pathology of alcoholic liver disease. *Seminars in Liver Disease*, **13**(2), 154–69.

Garcia, N. Jr, and Sanyal, A.J. (2001). Portal hypertension. *Clinics in Liver Disease*, **5**(2), 509–40.

Garcia-Tsao, G. (2006a). Portal hypertension. *Current Opinion in Gastroenterology*, **22**(3), 254–62.

Garcia-Tsao, G. (2006b). The transjugular intrahepatic portosystemic shunt for the management of cirrhotic refractory ascites. *Nature Clinical Practice Gastroenterology* and *Hepatology*, **3**(7), 380–89.

Gentile, S., Guarino, G., Romano, M., *et al.* (2005). A randomized controlled trial of acarbose in hepatic encephalopathy. *Clinical Gastroenterology and Hepatology*, **3**(2), 184–91.

Gerada, C. and Ashworth, M. (1997). ABC of mental health. Addiction and dependence-I: Illicit drugs. *British Medical Journal*, **315**(7103), 297–00.

Gyamfi, M.A. and Wan, Y.J. (2006). The effect of ethanol, ethanol metabolizing enzyme inhibitors, and vitamin E, on regulating glutathione, glutathione *S*-transferase, and *S*-adenosylmethionine in mouse primary hepatocyte. *Hepatology Research*, **35**(1), 53–61.

Halsted, C.H. (2004). Nutrition and alcoholic liver disease. *Seminars in Liver Disease*, **24**(3), 289–04.

Harada, S., Agarwal, D.P., Goedde, H.W., Tagaki, S. and Ishikawa, B. (1982). Possible protective role against alcoholism for aldehyde dehydrogenase isozyme deficiency in Japan. *Lancet,* **2**(8302), 827.

Higuchi, S., Matsushita, S., Imazeki, H., Kinoshita, T., Takagi, S. and Kono, H. (1994). Aldehyde dehydrogenase genotypes in Japanese alcoholics. *Lancet,* **343**(8899), 741–42.

Hislop, W.S., Bouchier, I.A., Allan, J.G., *et al.* (1983). Alcoholic liver disease in Scotland and northeastern England: presenting features in 510 patients. *Quarterly Journal of Medicine*, **52**(206), 232–43.

Jutabha, R., Jensen, D.M., Martin, P., Savides, T., Han, S.H. and Gornbein, J. (2005). Randomized study comparing banding and propranolol to prevent initial variceal hemorrhage in cirrhotics with high-risk esophageal varices. *Gastroenterology*, **128**(4), 870–81.

Kaner, E.F., Heather, N., McAvoy, B.R., Lock, C.A. and Gilvarry, E. (1999). Intervention for excessive alcohol consumption in primary health care: Attitudes and practices of English general practitioners. *Alcohol and Alcoholism*, **34**(4), 559–66.

Lelbach, W.K. (1976). Epidemiology of alcoholic liver disease. *Progress in Liver Disease*, **5**, 494–515.

Leon, D.A. and McCambridge, J. (2006). Liver cirrhosis mortality rates in Britain from 1950 to 2002: an analysis of routine data. *Lancet,* **367**(9504), 52–56.

Lieber, C.S. (2003). Relationships between nutrition, alcohol use and liver disease. *Alcohol Research and Health*, **27**(3), 220–31.

Lumeng, L. and Crabb, D.W. (2001). Alcoholic liver disease. *Current Opinion in Gastroenterology*, **17**(3), 211–20.

Malone, D. and Friedman, T. (2005). Drunken patients in the general hospital: their care and management. *Postgraduate Medical Journal.*, **81**(953), 161–66.

Manari, A.P., Preedy, V.R. and Peters, T.J. (2003). Nutritional intake of hazardous drinkers and dependent alcoholics in the UK. *Addiction Biology*, **8**, 201–10.

Marsano, L. and McClain, C.J. (1991). Nutrition and alcoholic liver disease. *Journal of Parenteral and Enteral Nutrition*, **15**(3), 337–44.

Marsano, L.S., Mendez, C., Hill, D., Barve, S. and McClain, C.J. (2003). Diagnosis and treatment of alcoholic liver disease and its complications. *Alcohol Research and Health*, **27**(3), 247–56.

Mathurin, P., Mendenhall, C.L., Carithers R.L. Jr, *et al.* (2002). Corticosteroids improve short-term survival in patients with severe alcoholic hepatitis (AH), Individual data analysis of the last three randomized placebo controlled double-blind trials of corticosteroids in severe AH. *Journal of Hepatology*, **36**(4), 480–87.

McCullough, A.J. and O'Connor, J.F. (1998). Alcoholic liver disease: proposed recommendations for the American College of Gastroenterology. *American Journal of Gastroenterology*, **93**(11), 2022–36.

McHutchinson, J.G. and Draguesku, R.B. (1991). Pentoxifylline may prevent renal impairment (hepatorenal syndrome) in severe alcoholic hepatitis. *Hepatology, 14*, 96A.

Mendenhall, C., Roselle, G.A., Gartside, P. and Moritz, T. (1995). Relationship of protein calorie malnutrition to alcoholic liver disease: A re-examination of data from two Veterans Administration cooperative studies. *Alcoholism: Clinical and Experimental Research, 19*(3), 635–41.

Mezey, E. (1998). Dietary fat and alcoholic liver disease. *Hepatology, 28*(4), 901–05.

Nanji, A.A. (2004). Role of different dietary fatty acids in the pathogenesis of experimental alcoholic liver disease. *Alcohol, 34*(1), 21–25.

Naveau, S., Chollet-Martin, S., Dharancy, S., *et al.* (2004). A double-blind randomized controlled trial of infliximab associated with prednisolone in acute alcoholic hepatitis. *Hepatology, 39*(5), 1390–97.

O'Grady, J.G. (2006). Liver transplantation alcohol-related liver disease: (deliberately) stirring a hornet's nest!. *Gut, 55*(11), 1529–31.

Paton, A. (2005). Alcohol in the body. *British Medical Journal, 330*(7482). 85–87.

Preedy, V.R. and SriRajaskanthan, R. (2006). *Alcohol as a toxic and disease-forming agent.* Background document for WHO Global alcohol meeting. Geneva: World Health Organization.

Preedy, V.R. and Watson, R.R. (2005). *Comprehensive Handbook of Alcohol-Related Pathology.* San Diego: Elsevier.

Rajendram, R., Lewison, G. and Preedy, V.R. (2006). Worldwide alcohol-related research and the disease burden. *Alcohol and Alcoholism, 41*, 99–06.

Rambaldi, A. and Gluud, C. (2006). *S*-adenosyl-L-methionine for alcoholic liver diseases. *Cochrane Database of Systematic Reviews,* (2)p CD002235.

Reeves, H.L., Burt, A.D., Wood, S. and Day, C.P. (1996). Hepatic stellate cell activation occurs in the absence of hepatitis in alcoholic liver disease and correlates with the severity of steatosis. *Journal of Hepatology, 25*(5), 677–83.

Rehm, J., Room, R., Monteiro, M., *et al.* (2003). Alcohol as a risk factor for global burden of disease. *European Addiction Research, 9*(4), 157–64.

Reuben, A. (2006). Alcohol and the liver. *Current Opinion in Gastroenterology, 22*, 263–71.

Rongey, C. and Kaplowitz, N. (2006). Current concepts and controversies in the treatment of alcoholic hepatitis. *World Journal of Gastroenterology, 12*(43), 6909–21.

Room, R. (2006). British livers and British alcohol policy. *Lancet, 367*(7), 10–11.

Room, R., Babor, T. and Rehm, J. (2005). Alcohol and public health. *Lancet, 365*(9458), 519–30.

Roongpisuthipong, C., Sobhonslidsuk, A., Nantiruj, K. and Songchitsomboon, S. (2001). Nutritional assessment in various stages of liver cirrhosis. *Nutrition, 17*(9), 761–65.

Savolainen, V.T., Liesto, K., Mannikko, A., Penttila, A. and Karhunen, P.J. (1993). Alcohol consumption and alcoholic liver disease: Evidence of a threshold level of effects of ethanol. *Alcoholism: Clinical and Experimental Research, 17*(5), 1112–17.

Sherlock, S. (1990). Alcoholic hepatitis. *Alcohol and Alcoholism, 25*(2/3), 189–96.

Sherlock, S. and Dooley, J. (2006). *Diseases of the Liver and Biliary System.* Oxford: Blackwell.

Sherman, D.I.N., Preedy, V.R. and Watson, R.R. (2002). *Ethanol and the Liver. Mechanisms and Management,* 1st edn. London: Taylor and Francis.

Shirin, H., Dotan, I., Papa, M., *et al.* (1999). Inhibition of concanavalin-A-induced acute T-cell-dependent hepatic damage in mice by hypothyroidism. *Liver, 19*(3), 206–11.

SriRajaskanthan, R. and Preedy, V.R. (2006a). Intake of beer, wine and spirits. In: Preedy, V.R. and Watson, R.R., eds. *Beer in Health and Disease Prevention.* London: Elsevier.

SriRajaskanthan, R. and Preedy, V.R. (2006b). Biochemical markers of alcoholism and their clinical effectiveness. *Clinical Effectiveness in Nursing, 9*, e280–85.

SriRajaskanthan, R. and Preedy, V.R. (2006c). Diagnosis and management of alcoholic liver disease, a review. *Clinical Effectiveness in Nursing, 9*, e286–94.

SriRajaskanthan, R. and Preedy, V.R. (2007). Alcohol as a toxic agent: not just the liver and brain and not every drinker. *Journal of Nutritional and Environmental Medicine*, **16**, 1–13.

Teli, M.R., Day, C.P., Burt, A.D., Bennett, M.K. and James, O.F.W. (1995). Determinants of progression to cirrhosis or fibrosis in pure alcoholic fatty liver. *Lancet,* **346**(8981). 987–90.

Thomasson, H.R., Edenberg, H.J., Crabb, D.W., *et al.* (1991). Alcohol and aldehyde dehydrogenase genotypes and alcoholism in Chinese men. *American Journal of Human Genetics*, **48**(4), 677–81.

World Health Organization (2004). *Global Status Report on Alcohol 2004*. Geneva: WHO.

World Health Organization (2006). *Public health problems caused by harmful use of alcohol*. Available at: http://www.who.int/nmh/WHA58.26en.pdf (last accessed October 2008).

Zhang, F.K., Zhang, J.Y. and Jia, D.J. (2005). Treatment of patients with alcoholic liver disease. *Hepatobiliary and Pancreatic Disease International*, **4**, 12–17.

Zintzaras, E., Stefanidis, I., Santos, M. and Vidal, F. (2006). Do alcohol-metabolizing enzyme gene polymorphisms increase the risk of alcoholism and alcoholic liver disease? *Hepatology,* **43**(2), 352–61.

Part Two

Medical Interventions

7 Detoxification

Colin R. Martin

Detoxification is the planned withdrawal of alcohol and supplementation during the withdrawal phase with medication that reduces the risks of complications of withdrawal. The context of this chapter is to define detoxification within the realm of a clinically managed intervention and treatment approach. However, bear in mind that many individuals with alcohol dependency will have experienced a proxy of detoxification through lack of access to alcohol. Although the classical medical management of detoxification involves substituting alcohol with a prescribed pharmacological agent, typically a benzodiazepine, there is a relatively convincing rationale for detoxification with alcohol via a tapered-dose route; however, such approaches have yet to enter the mainstream of treatment options.

Detoxification of the individual with a chemical-dependency problem requires a systematic appraisal of the presenting client's level of chemical dependency, a selection of the most appropriate pharmacological intervention, and an appreciation of the optimal setting for the detoxification to take place. Central to the formulation will be an assessment of the client's degree of chemical dependency in order to effectively manage the withdrawal phase with appropriate levels of medication. It should not be underemphasised that alcohol withdrawal can carry life-threatening consequences in the form of delirium tremens and withdrawals seizures (see Chapter 8). Finally, the client should indeed want to detoxify from alcohol if detoxification is to be considered an appropriate *part* of the treatment enterprise geared towards helping someone who is alcohol-dependent.

Why detoxification?

The rationale for detoxification represents a treatment end-point of the interacting factors of alcohol dependence, tolerance and withdrawal. Although alcohol dependence includes both psychological and physiological changes in the individual, detoxification focuses on the physiological aspects of alcohol dependence. Those clients who become chemically dependent on alcohol will have developed tolerance, whereby repeated exposure leads to a need for more of the drug to achieve the same effect. Tolerance (as a physiological concept) specifies that cellular adaptation has taken place in that person's central nervous system (Follesa *et al.*, 2006; Krystal *et al.*, 2003; Tabakoff and Hoffman, 1988). Therefore, when alcohol consumption abruptly ceases, or is significantly reduced, the nervous system experiences a 'rebound effect' manifesting in symptoms of withdrawals. These withdrawal symptoms, sometimes referred to as a withdrawal syndrome, cannot only be distressing for the client but can in some instances be life threatening.

Detoxification is the process of ameliorating such symptoms in a systematic and controlled way, without fostering a secondary dependence on the medication used for detoxification. The severity withdrawal symptoms (see Box 7.1) can vary in degree.

Box 7.1   Symptoms of withdrawal

* Tremors
* Insomnia
* Increased heart rate
* Increased respiration
* Headache
* Nausea
* Vomiting
* Anxiety
* Restlessness
* Withdrawal seizures

In a small minority of people, withdrawal may result in the serious, life-threatening phenomenon of delirium tremens, The main signs and symptoms of delirium tremens are outlined in Box 7.2. Detoxification is therefore an essential component of the therapeutic battery, and it has the potential to be life-saving. It is often the first step in the process of rehabilitation for people who are chronically alcohol dependent.

Box 7.2   The signs and symptoms of delirium tremens

* Clouding of consciousness
* Disorientation in time and place
* Visual hallucinations
* Tactile hallucinations
* Paranoid delusions
* Anxiety
* Fear
* Anger
* Self-harm behaviour

When is detoxification necessary?

Generally speaking, with relatively mild chemical dependency, stopping alcohol consumption is unlikely to result in complications (UK Alcohol Forum, 2001). There are individual differences in the degree of dependency and withdrawal-symptom profile that are independent of the average amount of alcohol routinely consumed. Consequently, recommendations regarding a level of drinking at which to implement pharmacological detoxification are necessarily vague and any protocol should be cautious, with regular and detailed monitoring. There are certain circumstances where pharmacological intervention may not be necessary. These are:

- if there is a relatively modest level of alcohol consumption, of less than 15 units per day in men and 10 units per day in women, plus an absence of recent withdrawal symptoms and recent relief drinking (drinking to prevent withdrawal symptoms)
- when there is an absence of a positive breath-alcohol test and an absence of withdrawal symptoms
- so-called 'binge' drinkers in whom the duration of drinking period is less than 7 days and consumption was not more than 20 units per day.

Clients fitting the above criteria, while not necessarily needing formal detoxification, should be made aware of some of the symptoms they may experience in the first few days of abstinence, in particular anxiety and difficulty sleeping. The same advice should also be given to clients who do require detoxification. Clients who do not fulfil the above criteria – but are chemically dependent on alcohol – should be considered for detoxification.

The appropriate setting

The options for those requiring detoxification generally fall into two setting types: inpatient (hospital) or home (primary care). The actual quality and type of setting may vary in both cases, in circumstances that are often independent of both the health professional and the client. Detoxification in an inpatient setting may take place in a specialist addiction unit, a specialist alcohol unit, an acute admission psychiatric unit, or in a general hospital medical ward. Each setting may be part of national (public) health service provision or provided privately. Peculiarly, in the case of a hospital admission, the alcohol-dependent client may find himself under the care of a specialist addiction psychiatrist, a general psychiatrist, a liver specialist or a gastroenterologist. The issues surrounding provision are surprisingly complex, influenced both by regional and demographic factors, as they are for many areas of health care.

However, with respect to detoxification, the lack of dedicated public-health service provision for intervention in certain parts of the UK creates a situation whereby the public purse funds private care provision. Such arrangements may produce good circumstances for detoxification to take place within pleasant surroundings, but the efficacy of such arrangements in providing comprehensive personalised treatment programmes in which detoxification is part of the therapeutic programme of care, remains questionable.

The circumstances for home detoxification are very complex and influenced by the client's housing circumstances, social milieu and quality of primary-care service provider. There is impressive evidence to suggest that home detoxification is a viable alternative to inpatient detoxification for the majority (approximately 75 per cent) of people (Hayashida *et al.*, 1989). Further, there is compelling evidence that suggests there is no advantage of either setting type over length of time of sobriety following detoxification (Hayashida *et al.*, 1989).

Not surprisingly, most clients would prefer home detoxification (Stockwell *et al.*, 1990). Consequently, there is both a good health-economics case and a good client-centred case to be made for home detoxification in appropriate individuals. Hospitalisation, therefore, should generally be considered for individuals who require supervision and/or who are at risk of major complications of withdrawal during detoxification.

Box 7.3 lists conditions in which patient detoxification is strongly advised, and mentions several important contraindications to home detoxification. The list is by no means exhaustive and the practitioner should always consider the safety of the client. Consequently, if in doubt or if presented with an ambiguous situation, inpatient care represents the most appropriate route to detoxification.

Box 7.3   Signs and symptoms for which inpatient detoxification is advised

- Delirium tremens
- Epilepsy
- Confusion
- Hallucinations
- Poor nutrition
- Self-harm risk
- Lives alone
- History of withdrawal seizures
- Unsuccessful home detoxification
- Difficult-to-control withdrawal symptoms
- Polyabuse issues, multiple chemical dependency or drug abuse
- Home circumstances unsupportive to a goal of abstinence
- Currently experiencing acute physical illness
- Currently experiencing acute mental health problems
- Unwilling to be seen daily

Pharmacological intervention

A number of pharmacological agents have been used to manage alcohol withdrawal symptoms during detoxification. The recommendation of the most efficacious medication for this purpose probably represents a work in progress because several agents have been proposed, and are supported by evidence relating to therapeutic advantage. However, the most common and accepted approaches for detoxification from alcohol revolve around the use of the benzodiazepine family of drugs.

Benzodiazepines

The current medication of choice to control withdrawal symptoms is the benzodiazepine group of drugs (Department of Health, 1999; 2007). The most commonly used are chlordiazepoxide (Librium) and diazepam (Valium). Other benzodiazepines can be used, such as oxazepam.

Benzodiazepines are, of course, drugs of dependence so a tapering approach is used in concert with a short period of detoxification, to avoid the risk of substituting one chemical dependence (alcohol) for another (benzodiazepines). To avoid benzodiazepine dependence, the duration of detoxification should be no longer than 7 days. A client who still experiences significant withdrawal symptoms after 7 days may be co-dependent on another substance of abuse that is unknown to the health professional. However, this is unlikely because simple screening methods are available for detecting drugs of abuse in urine. Stringent sampling procedures must be in place to avoid errors (Levy *et al.*, 2007).

There has been considerable debate regarding the most appropriate benzodiazepine to use in detoxification. One primary focus has been the issue of any therapeutic advantage of long-acting over short-acting benzodiazepines, or vice versa (Mayo-Smith, 1997). No firm conclusions relevant to a treatment recommendation have been made to date. Some strong evidence exists, however, suggesting diazepam is comparatively more associated with abuse and alcohol-related mortality (Serfaty and Masterton, 1993). On balance, chlordiazepoxide probably represents the best option for detoxification, particularly in a home detoxification setting.

Chlomethiazole (CMZ)

Chlomethiazole (formerly chlormethiazole or Hemenevrin) has a long history of use in detoxification. It is very effective at controlling withdrawal symptoms. However, it does have significant potential for addiction (Glatt, 1978) as well as having dangerous and sometimes fatal interactions with alcohol (McInnes, 1987). Hence this medication has fallen out of favour as a detoxification agent of choice. The use of chlomethiazole is contraindicated in home detoxific-ation (Duncan and Taylor, 1996) – in fact, it appears to be rarely used now in inpatient detoxification. Given the established efficacy of benzodiazepines in the control of alcohol withdrawal, there really does seem to be no *prima facie* argument for the preference of chlomethiazole over this family of compounds.

Medication to reduce the risk of withdrawal seizures

Given the significant risk of seizures that may accompany alcohol withdrawal, the use of antiepileptic medication has been hotly debated, both as a primary and as an adjunctive treatment for detoxification (Berglund *et al.*, 2001; Temkin, 2001). However, despite the intuitive optimism that surrounds the use of antiepileptic medications like carbamazepine (Tegretol), the evidence to support use of such medications is not forthcoming either in general detoxification or in specific prevention of withdrawal seizures (Berglund *et al.*, 2001; Temkin, 2001). People with a history of withdrawal seizures should be managed in a specialist inpatient setting and an individualised plan of care devised. This should (a) maintain close observation (b) reduce the risk of a withdrawal seizure and (c) effectively manage a seizure should it occur.

Detoxification procedures

Tapered fixed-dose detoxification

The tapered fixed dose of a benzodiazepine (usually chlordiazepoxide) represents a standard and successful approach to detoxification. The standard tapered-dose regimen begins with 20 mg of chlordiazepoxide four times per day, reducing over the next 5–7 days. Withdrawal symptoms should be monitored regularly and the regimen reviewed systematically in response to the withdrawal symptom profile. A typical tapered regimen is shown in Table 7.1.

Table 7.1	Tapered detoxification regimen with 10-mg chlordiazepoxide tablets (all doses are in mg)			
	8 PM	**12 noon**	**6 PM**	**10 PM**
Day 1	—	30	30	30
Day 2	20	20	20	30
Day 3	20	10	10	20
Day 4	10	10	Omit	20
Day 5	Omit	10	Omit	10

Inpatient detoxification

Inpatient detoxification offers an opportunity to monitor the regimen and modify it, if needed, with prescribed medication should excessive withdrawal symptoms be observed. Careful and routine assessment of withdrawal symptoms is carried out, usually four to six times daily. The choice of inpatient detoxification selects clients who are at higher risk, so related assessments and treatment are conducted where appropriate (e.g. parenteral thiamine for people diagnosed with Wernicke's encephalopathy; neurocognitive investigations for those showing neurological deficits; nutritional support for people who are undernourished). Detoxification may precipitate the onset of Wernicke's encephalopathy, therefore inpatient facilities will have appropriate treatments readily available (see Chapter 10 for treatment of Wernicke–Korsakoff syndrome); these will include the provision of parenteral thiamine, as well as resuscitation facilities in the extremely rare instance of anaphylaxis occurring following parenteral thiamine administration.

Home detoxification

Home detoxification, as highlighted earlier, may suit people who have appropriate support and who are at low risk of complications arising from detoxification. Clients should be monitored by home visit at least once daily during the detoxification. It is also desirable to visit them for at least 2–3 days following detoxification, to check for any residual withdrawal symptoms (extremely unlikely) or a return to drinking (possible), and to assess their mood. These visits also provide an ideal opportunity for the client to discuss future treatment options and allow the health professional to emphasise that detoxification represents the *start* of a therapeutic alliance, rather than the end. It should be pointed out to the client that detoxification is an essential *part* of the treatment enterprise, and not a final treatment in itself. Apart from supporting and facilitating a therapeutic alliance with the client, the role of the health professional beyond that of monitoring includes conveying essential information about what the client should expect during the detoxification procedure. This necessarily includes both advice and directions. The health professional should inform the client of the signs of withdrawal and the rationale for the use of medication to control withdrawal symptoms. Discuss fully with the client any questions (or, indeed, misconceptions) they may have regarding the detoxification. Clients should be advised to drink water, fruit juice or decaffeinated hot drinks because they are likely to feel thirsty. They should record the quantity of fluids they take and be advised not to drink more than 3 litres in any 24-hour period. They should also be told about reducing their caffeine intake to a minimum, drinking no more than three cups of normal coffee or five cups of normal tea per day. Substitution with *additional* decaffeinated coffee or tea is recommended for people who wish to or who normally drink more than the recommended maximums of normal coffee or tea per day.

Explain to the client that they may experience excessive anxiety or agitation in the first few days of detoxification. Basic instruction in techniques to reduce anxiety may be useful; the health professional supervising the detoxification should be familiar with these approaches. The client should be advised that they may have difficulty sleeping during the detoxification and to expect this; also point out that it may be several weeks before a normal sleep pattern is resumed. Regular eating should be encouraged; stress that this is a very important part of their care, even if they experience a poor appetite.

Inform the client of the absolute importance of sticking to the regimen. Also explain that if they experience any drowsiness then they should omit a dose and review the situation with the health professional who is supervising their detoxification at the earliest opportunity. A 24-hour contact number is highly desirable for contacting the health services or primary care in the unlikely event of complications during the detoxification procedure. Clients should be advised not to drive or operate machinery while taking their detoxification medication.

Clients who agree to a home detoxification will have agreed not to drink alcohol. Further, the health professional should emphasise the dangers of drinking 'on top' of the prescribed detoxification medication. A breathalyser should be available for routine checks of alcohol consumption.

Clients who are considered suitable for home detoxification but who might be at risk of developing Wernicke–Korsakoff syndrome (a highly contentious notion among many health professionals – including the author of this chapter) should be treated with parenteral thiamine, in the form of Pabrinex, which should be administered intramuscularly for 3 days (two ampoules on each occasion). Even in the context of home detoxification, Pabrinex is administered where resuscitation facilities are available, such as in a general practice. This does, of course, add an extra complication to the home-detoxification procedure. It should be stressed that a client who is considered at risk of Wernicke–Korsakoff syndrome should be preferentially considered for inpatient detoxification. Indeed, a very convincing and compelling clinical case can be made for malnourished clients at risk of Wernicke–Korsakoff syndrome *not* being treated for alcohol withdrawal in an inpatient setting. This issue may be influenced – if not dictated – by local health-service provision, but the consequences to the client of inappropriate or ineffective treatment for Wernicke–Korsakoff syndrome (which may be an artefact of treatment in the wrong setting) can be either chronically debilitating or fatal.

Oral thiamine supplementation

One of the (supposed) myths about neurocognitive deterioration and neurostructural damage in chronic alcohol dependency concerns the use of oral vitamin supplements, in particular oral thiamine, as an effective treatment for preventing occurrence of such damage. There are currently no published studies revealing the efficacy of such an approach, although oral vitamin supplementation has entered the realm of treatment approaches, albeit in a non-evidence-based manner. Further, for those clients who relapse to heavy or dependent levels of alcohol consumption, absorption of such supplements will inevitably be impaired. However, the lack of evidence does not necessarily signify the lack of a therapeutic benefit; it is just that studies have yet to be conducted to determine any real benefit to clients.

The British National Formulary (BNF) recommends a dose of 200–300 mg of oral thiamine daily for treating severe thiamine deficiency. Clinical guidelines of the Scottish Intercollegiate Guidelines Network (2003) recommend that oral thiamine should be prescribed indefinitely for patients with chronic alcohol abuse or dependency issues in concert with dietary insufficiency. Prophylactic prescription of thiamine (150 mg per day in divided doses) orally for 1 month was recommended by the NHS National Library for Health in 2007, based on the findings of Cook and colleagues (1998).

Conclusions

Detoxification is an essential component of a comprehensive programme of care. It is often the beginning of the treatment journey for the client. However it should not be viewed as a single treatment approach for chronic alcohol dependency. The focus of detoxification is on the safe management of alcohol withdrawal symptoms over a period of no more than 7 days. Various options for detoxification are available that can be tailored to the individual client's clinical presentation and home circumstances. Home detoxification is a valuable and cost-effective treatment route for those who are at low risk of complications during detoxification, have adequate support at home and appropriate clinical support from a primary healthcare provider.

There is good evidence that many clients prefer detoxification in the familiar surroundings of their home. Detoxification at home also may appeal to people who are concerned about the stigma sometimes associated with hospital admission for an alcohol problem. Inpatient detoxification, in contrast, is an alternative approach more suited to clients whose clinical circumstances place them at high risk of complications of alcohol withdrawal, or if they do not have a home environment conducive and supportive to home detoxification.

References and further reading

Berglund, M., Andreasson, S., Franck, J., Fridell, M., Hakanson, I. and Johansson, B. (2001). *Treatment of Alcohol and Drug Abuse: An Evidence-based Review*. Stockholm: The Swedish Council of Technology Assessment in Health Care.

Cook, C.C., Hallwood, P.M. and Thomson, A.D. (1998). B vitamin deficiency and neuropsychiatric syndromes in alcohol misuse. *Alcohol and Alcoholism*, **33**, 317–36.

Department of Health (1999). *Drug Misuse and Dependence: Guidelines on Clinical Management*. London: HMSO.

Department of Health (2007). *Drug Misuse and Dependence: Guidelines on Clinical Management. Update*. London: HMSO.

Duncan, D. and Taylor, D. (1996). Chlomethiazole or chlordiazepoxide in alcohol detoxification. *Psychiatric Bulletin*, **20**, 599–01.

Follesa, P., Biggio, F., Talani, G., *et al*. (2006). Neurosteroids, GABA-A receptors, and ethanol dependence. *Psychopharmacology*, (*Berl*), **186**, 267–80.

Glatt, M.M. (1978). Chlomethiazole addiction. *British Medical Journal*, **2**, 894–95.

Hayashida, M., Alterman, A.J., McLellan, A.T., O'Brien, C.P., Purtill, J.J. and Volpicelli, J.R. (1989). Comparative effectiveness and costs of inpatient and outpatient detoxification of patients with mild-to-moderate alcohol withdrawal syndrome. *New England Journal of Medicine*, **320**, 358–65.

Krystal, J.H., Petrakis, I.L., Mason, G., Trevisan, L. and D'Souza, D.C. (2003). *N*-methyl-D-aspartate glutamate receptors and alcoholism: reward, dependence, treatment, and vulnerability. *Pharmacology and Therapeutics*, **99**, 79–94.

Levy, S., Sherritt, L., Vaughan, B.L., Germak, M. and Knight, J.R. (2007). Results of random drug testing in an adolescent substance abuse program. *Pediatrics*, **119**, e843–48.

Mayo-Smith, M.F. (1997). Pharmacological management of alcohol withdrawal. A meta-analysis and evidence-based practice guideline. American Society of Addiction Medicine Working Group on Pharmacological Management of Alcohol Withdrawal. *Journal of the American Medical Association*, **278**, 144–51.

McInnes, G.T. (1987). Chlomethiazole and alcohol: A lethal cocktail. *British Medical Journal (Clinical Research edn)*, **294**, 592.

NHS National Library for Health (2007). *Introduction to Alcohol Misuse*. Available at: http://www.library.nhs.uk/mentalHealth/viewResource.aspx?resID=79021 (last accessed October 2008).

Ritson, B. and Chick, J. (1986). Comparison of two benzodiazepines in the treatment of alcohol withdrawal: effects on symptoms and cognitive recovery. *Drug and Alcohol Dependence*, **18**, 329–34.

Scottish Intercollegiate Guidelines Network (SIGN). (2003). *The Management of Harmful Drinking and Alcohol Dependence in Primary Care: A National Clinical Guideline*. Edinburgh: Royal College of Physicians.

Serfaty, M. and Masterton, G. (1993). Fatal poisonings attributed to benzodiazepines in Britain during the 1980s. *British Journal of Psychiatry*, **163**, 386–93.

Stockwell, T., Bolt, L., Milner, I., Pugh, P. and Young, I. (1990). Home detoxification for problem drinkers: acceptability to clients, relatives, general practitioners and outcome after 60 days. *British Journal of Addiction,* **85**, 61–70.

Tabakoff, B. and Hoffman, P.L. (1988). Tolerance and the etiology of alcoholism: hypothesis and mechanism. *Alcoholism: Clinical and Experimental Research*, **12**, 184–86.

Temkin, N.R. (2001). Antiepileptogenesis and seizure prevention trials with antiepileptic drugs: meta-analysis of controlled trials. *Epilepsia*, **42**, 515–24.

UK Alcohol Forum (2001). *Guidelines for the Management of Alcohol Problems in Primary Care and General Psychiatry*. London: UK Alcohol Forum.

8 Delirium tremens

Chris Daly and Catherine Muyeba

> *I dreamt a dream the other night, I couldn't sleep a wink*
> *The rats were tryin' to count the sheep and I was off the drink*
> *There were footsteps in the parlour and voices on the stairs*
> *I was climbin' up the walls and movin' round the chairs.*
> *I looked out from under the blanket up at the fireplace*
> *The Pope and John F. Kennedy were starin' in me face*
> *Suddenly it dawned at me I was getting the old D.T.s*
> *When the Child o' Prague began to dance around the mantelpiece.*
>
> **Lyrics from *Delirium Tremens* by Christy Moore**
> **(Reproduced with kind permission of Yellow Furze Music)**

Delirium tremens is the most severe complication of alcohol withdrawal. It is characterised, as in the song above, by hallucinations (classically visual but also auditory, olfactory and tactile), severe tremor and confusion. The patient will often present with agitation, insomnia and delusions and a range of physical symptoms, e.g. tachycardia, hyperthermia, hypertension and tachypnoea. One of the key roles in assisting individuals undertaking alcohol withdrawal is the prevention identification and treatment of delirium tremens. This chapter will review these areas and the evidence-base for treatment.

Alcohol withdrawal—the clinical picture

After acute cessation of alcohol in a dependent individual, the timing of withdrawals is usually as shown in Table 8.1. The client does not need to go through all these stages. Hallucinations are relatively more common occurring in 3–10 per cent of cases, and many will not go on to develop delirium. Seizures occur in 3–15 per cent of those with alcohol dependence undergoing withdrawal, and 30% of these will go on to develop delirium. Seizures are a significant risk factor for the later development of withdrawal delirium (Hall and Zador, 1997). The onset of delirium tremens is usually between 3 and 5 days after cessation of alcohol. It can arise in individuals who are still drinking but at a significantly reduced level of consumption. The onset of confusion may be gradual but usually in the setting of increasingly severe withdrawal phenomena. In some cases, the development of delirium may be the first sign of alcohol problems in people not previously diagnosed as alcohol dependent (Mehta *et al.*, 2004).

Table 8.1	Timing of alcohol withdrawals	
Stage	**Symptom**	**Timing**
I	Tremor	6–36 hours
II	Hallucinations	12–48 hours
III	Seizures	6–48 hours
IV	Delirium tremens	3–5 days

There is evidence of increased mental confusion, changes in consciousness, disorientation in time and place, and vivid hallucinations (Turner *et al.*, 1989; Mattick and Jarvis, 1993). Perceptual disturbances can occur in different modalities, but are commonly visual. The client is often terrified, perplexed or severely agitated, and can be physically aggressive. There is marked tremor and autonomic disturbance evidenced by sweating, fever, and tachycardia, raised blood pressure and dilated pupils. Dehydration is common, and they might be febrile. Significant pyrexia indicates poor prognosis and will require further investigation.

Clinical case vignette 8.1

Urgent request for a home visit to review a 50-year-old man with a 30-year history of daily heavy consumption of up to one and a half litres of vodka a day. G.J. shows increasing physical deterioration and weight loss. He has not been seen outside his flat for three days. On review, G.J. shows significant tremor with coarse shaking of his arms, trunk and head. He presents with severe sweating and tachycardia of 130 beats per minute. He is confused and extremely frightened. He is experiencing vivid visual hallucinations, thrashing out at a swarm of bees, and has barricaded his window to stop the horses coming into his property (he lives on the eighth floor).

The symptoms tend to peak after 4–5 days, and the episode can last from 24–72 hours; however, intermittent periods of confusion, particularly in the evening, may continue for days to weeks. In some people the confusion, agitation and hallucinations persist for several days or weeks. The cause of death in patients with delirium tremens is usually secondary to the clinical manifestations of the condition itself or complications caused by concurrent illnesses such as pneumonia. The complications reflect poor nutrition, immunosuppression, and fluid and electrolyte imbalances. The clinical features of delirium tremens are shown in Box 8.1.

Box 8.1 **Clinical features of delirium tremens (the DTs)**

- Marked tremor
- Severe agitation
- Disorientation and confusion
- Autonomic disturbance (raised pulse and respiratory rate, hypertension)
- Vivid hallucinations

Diagnosis of delirium tremens

There are small differences in the diagnostic criteria for delirium tremens used in the DSM-IV and ICD-10 systems. Both are included in Box 8.2 (overpage) for completeness. The first description of delirium tremens in the literature was in 1813. Pearson (quoted in Erwin *et al.*, 1998) described observations of 'acute brain fever of drunkards'. Sutton named the syndrome delirium tremens in the same year (Erwin *et al.*, 1998). In 1953, Victor and Adams identified alcohol withdrawal as the causative factor for delirium tremens in their review of 266 patients – 12 per cent developed seizures, 18 per cent hallucinations, and 5 per cent delirium tremens (Victor and Adams, 1953). Isbell gave alcohol to ten volunteers with morphine addiction; four took 266–346 mL of 95 per cent alcohol for 7–34 days and six took 383–489 mL of 95 per cent alcohol for 48–87 days. When their alcohol was stopped, they were observed for symptoms of withdrawal (Isbell *et al.*, 1955) (see Fig. 8.1).

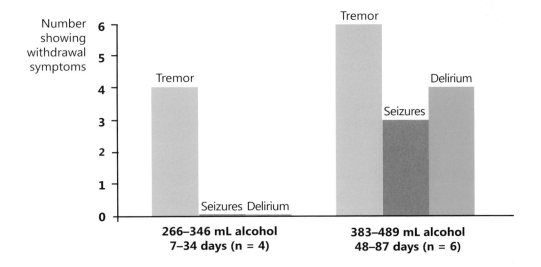

Figure 8.1 Withdrawal symptoms after cessation of alcohol in 10 morphine-addicted volunteers after receiving different quantities of 95% alcohol for different durations as shown. Adapted from Isbell et al. 1955; cited in Kaim *et al.* 1969.

Box 8.2   ICD-10 and DSM-IV diagnostic criteria for delirium tremens

ICD 10 F10.4 Alcohol withdrawal state with delirium

The general criteria for alcohol withdrawal state must be met (F10.3).

The general criteria for delirium must be met (F05).

A. There is clouding of consciousness, that is reduced clarity of awareness of the environment, with reduced ability to focus, sustain or shift attention.

B. Disturbance of cognition is manifest by both (i) impairment of immediate recall and recent memory with relatively intact remote memory; and (ii) disorientation in time, place and person.

C. At least one of the following psychomotor disturbances is present: (i) rapid unpredictable shifts from hypoactivity to hyperactivity; (ii) increased reaction time; (iii) increased or decreased flow of speech; or (iv) enhanced startle reaction.

D. There is disturbance of sleep or of the sleep–wake cycle, as manifested by at least one of the following (i) insomnia, which in severe cases may involve total sleep loss, with or without daytime drowsiness or reversal of the sleep–wake cycle; (ii) nocturnal worsening of symptoms; and (iii) disturbing dreams or nightmares, which may continue on waking as hallucinations or illusions.

E. Symptoms have rapid onset and show fluctuations over the course of the day.

F. There is objective evidence from the history, physical and neurological examination or laboratory test of an underlying cerebral or systemic disease that can be presumed to be responsible for the clinical manifestations in criteria A–D (in this case alcohol withdrawal).

DSM-IV

A. Disturbance of consciousness (i.e. reduced clarity of awareness of the environment), with reduced ability to focus, sustain, or shift attention.

B. A change in cognition (such as a memory deficit or disorientation or a language disturbance) or the development of a perceptual disturbance that is not accounted for by pre-existing, established or developing dementia.

C. The disturbance develops in a short period (usually hours or days) and tends to fluctuate during the day.

D. There is evidence from history, physical examination or laboratory findings that the symptoms in criteria A and B developed during or shortly after a withdrawal syndrome.

Pathophysiology of delirium tremens

Understanding the adaptive processes involved in the development of tolerance to alcohol is essential for understanding withdrawal phenomena. Alcohol is a central nervous system depressant, which acts by increasing activity at the GABA (gamma aminobutyric acid) receptor. GABA is the main inhibitory neurotransmitter. Increasing tolerance is related to reduced susceptibility of GABA-A receptors to alcohol. These receptors require alcohol to stimulate release of GABA; when alcohol is withdrawn there is reduced GABA activity as a result of this homeostatic mechanism and the inhibitory function is greatly reduced. This is shown in Fig. 8.2.

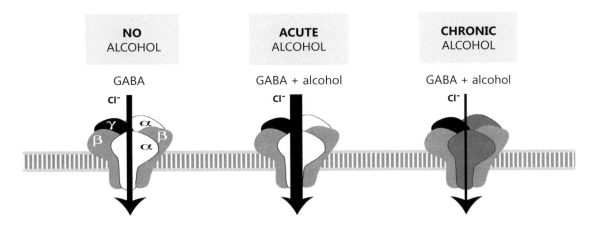

Figure 8.2 The GABA-A receptor (α1–6, β1–3, γ1–3) *before* and *after* chronic and acute alcohol consumption. Increasing tolerance leads to receptor subunit switching. Cl, chloride ions; GABA, gamma aminobutyric acid. Adapted from Mahmoudi *et al.*, 1997.

Acute use of alcohol blocks N-methyl-D-aspartic acid (NMDA) glutamate receptors (this is the main excitatory neurotransmitter). With chronic use of alcohol there is a corresponding upregulation of NMDA glutamate receptor activity (see Fig. 8.3, overpage). Withdrawal can be explained by the removal of alcohol on this adapted system. The GABA system is less responsive to stimulation (including by benzodiazepines) and the glutamate system is overactive, leading to the observation of neuronal hyperactivity. The effect is potentiated by repeated cycles of withdrawal from alcohol (the effect of 'kindling') with the observation of worsening severity of withdrawal symptoms (including the development of seizures and delirium tremens).

Another effect of the reduction of GABA activity is the reduction in inhibition on other neurotransmitter systems. Reduced inhibition of the dopamine system leads to dopamine overactivity and may account for many of the symptoms of delirium tremens. Recent work on brain-derived neurotrophic factor (BDNF), which influences brain dopamine responses, showed that BDNF genetic polymorphisms in a sample of Japanese people are associated with the risk of violence and alcohol withdrawal delirium (Matsushita *et al.*, 2004). In a review of research into genetic predisposition for developing delirium tremens, two replicated studies implicated that the genes related to dopamine transmission, the D_3 receptor and solute-carrier family 6, showed polymorphisms in people with delirium tremens (van Munster *et al.*, 2007). This indicates a variety of possible mechanisms for the inherited risk of developing delirium tremens.

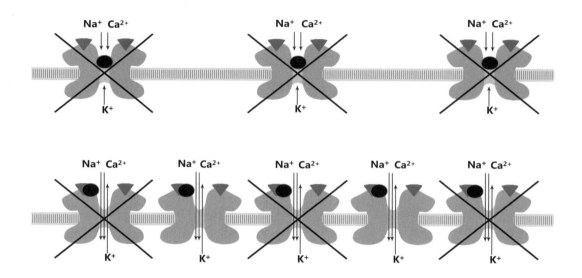

Figure 8.3   Chronic blockade of the NMDA system by alcohol (*upper panel*) leads to upregulation of NMDA receptors (*lower panel*). The passage of sodium (Na), calcium (Ca) and potassium (K) ions is indicated by the arrows. The small black circles represent magnesium ions.

Epidemiology of delirium tremens

In inpatient clinical trials of the treatment of alcohol withdrawal the incidence of delirium tremens in those treated with placebo is 5 per cent (Mayo-Smith *et al.*, 1997). The incidence in treated populations is lower. In a meta-analysis of prospective randomised-controlled trials treatment with benzodiazepines reduced the risk of developing delirium tremens by 4.9 cases per 100 patients (Mayo-Smith *et al.*, 1997). Some populations may be at a more significant risk.

Assessment for delirium tremens

In a comprehensive assessment of an alcohol-dependent patient a detailed history will highlight relevant key points in identifying high-risk patients. This should include the drinking history, which will determine the severity of dependence and how this has evolved over time. It is essential to document the history of previous withdrawals and complications encountered during detoxification, including a history of worsening withdrawal symptoms particularly withdrawal seizures and previous episodes of delirium tremens. It is good practice to measure the severity of alcohol dependence using a standardised rating scale, e.g. the Severity of Alcohol Dependence Questionnaire (SADQ) (Stockwell *et al.*, 1994). The physical complications of alcohol must be enquired about through a systematic review of the respiratory, cardiovascular, gastrointestinal, neuromuscular and central nervous systems, identifying any potential risk factors for delirium tremens. Information about medical problems and prescribed medication should be sought. A detailed account of the patient's social circumstances will provide useful information about their pattern of drinking, homelessness and their nutritional status. A full physical examination including a neurological examination is important at initial contact to provide a baseline assessment. This should be repeated regularly to monitor any changes, with a view to prompt treatment. Key things to look for include tachycardia, pyrexia, raised blood pressure, disorientation, confusion, tremors and agitation. Using a withdrawal assessment scale such as the Clinical Institute Withdrawal Assessment for Alcohol (Revised) (CIWA-Ar) is essential to accurately assess the severity of withdrawal symptoms to trigger prescribing of benzodiazepine medication and to monitor the patient's progress (Sullivan *et al.*, 1989).

Prediction and prevention of delirium tremens

Delirium tremens is a well-recognised complication of alcohol withdrawal and is associated with significant mortality (Chick, 1989). Once established, it is a difficult condition to treat. It is, therefore, important that its development is prevented if possible. In order to reduce the risk, patients who are likely to develop the condition need to be identified early. The 'at-risk' patients can then be managed intensively and treated appropriately to prevent the onset of delirium tremens.

Risk factors

Research has shown that the risk of developing delirium tremens is related to a number of factors (Ferguson *et al.*, 1996; Schuckit *et al.*, 1995; Wetterling *et al.*, 1994). Studies have demonstrated the following factors predispose patients to delirium tremens:

- previous complicated withdrawal syndrome (Wetterling *et al.*, 1994)
- a long history of alcohol misuse (Schuckit *et al.*, 1995)
- a comorbid medical condition (Ferguson *et al.*, 1996; Fiellin *et al.*, 2002; Lee *et al.*, 2005; Palmstierna, 2001)
- elevated systolic blood pressure (Palmstierna, 2001)
- abrupt cessation of intensive drinking
- metabolic abnormalities (Tonnesen, 1982; Jost *et al.*, 1992; Wetterling *et al.*, 1994)
- use of sedative hypnotic drugs (Schuckit *et al.*, 1995)
- older age and male sex (Schuckit *et al.*, 1995)
- brain injury (Lukan *et al.*, 2002).

In a study conducted by Palmstierna and colleagues, five key factors predicted the risk of developing delirium tremens. They are: concurrent infectious disease, tachycardia of more than 120 beats per minute on admission, evidence of alcohol withdrawal symptoms at blood alcohol levels of more than 1 g per litre, a history of epileptic seizures, and/or a history of delirium tremens. These factors were noted to be positive predictors for delirium tremens.

Further studies identified three main factors, alone or in combination, as being closely associated with increased risk of developing delirium tremens. These are elevated systolic blood pressure, a comorbid medical condition, and history of complicated alcohol withdrawal. The patient can be screened for these risk factors by clinicians. The positive predictive factors for development of DTs are shown in the Box 8.3 (overpage).

Box 8.3 **Positive predictive factors for development of DTs (Palmstierna, 2001)**

- Concurrent infectious disease
- Tachycardia >120 beats per minute
- Withdrawals at BAC (blood alcohol concentration) of more than 1 g per litre
- History of epileptic seizures
- History of delirium tremens

The following case vignette illustrates the risk factors for the development of delirium tremens (including previous history of delirium, co-occurring infection, severe withdrawal with high blood alcohol concentration) as well as the 'kindling' effect of worsening delirium with repeated withdrawal.

Clinical case vignette 8.2

A 35-year-old man with previous heroin dependence. Stabilised on methadone for 10 years. Heavy drinking associated ever since. Was drinking 45 units of strong cider per day and had history of multiple previous detoxifications in general medical setting with worsening withdrawal symptomatology (including four previous episodes of delirium tremens and withdrawal seizures). There was associated jaundice, marked peripheral neuropathy, myopathy and weight loss. On admission blood alcohol concentration was 505 mg per 100 mL. Severe tremor and pulse of 108 beats per minute. Patient was commenced on 50 mg chlordiazepoxide three times daily. On day 3 he developed pyrexia, confusion, visual hallucinations, aggression and paranoid delusions and was found to have a chest infection. Delirium tremens was diagnosed. Increased dose of 100 mg chlordiazepoxide three times daily, continued parenteral vitamins, commenced antibiotics and haloperidol. Confusion persisted for 7 days (longer than previous episodes) and severity of delirium and agitation was worse.

Prevention of delirium tremens

Once someone has been identified as being at high risk of developing delirium tremens, they should be started immediately on a higher-dose detoxification regimen (e.g. 50 mg chlordiazepoxide four times daily plus 20 mg as necessary). This should be maintained for 3–5 days unless contraindicated.

There should be regular review of the severity of alcohol withdrawal using a suitable scale such as the CIWA-Ar (Sullivan *et al.*, 1989) on an hourly basis. Doses of benzodiazepines on an as-required basis should be given if the severity of withdrawal is moderate or severe. Some authors believe a loading dose of a long-acting benzodiazepine can avert the onset of delirium tremens in those showing prodromal signs (e.g. with 100 mg chlordiazepoxide). There should be careful monitoring of fluid balance and electrolytes, particularly potassium and magnesium. The patient should be fully physically reviewed on a daily basis for the first 3–5 days. Prophylactic parenteral B vitamins should be administered (e.g. one pair of Pabrinex ampoules per day, intramuscularly or intravenously). The various regimens for prevention of delirium tremens are summarised in Box 8.4.

Box 8.4 **Prevention of delirium tremens**

1. High-dose benzodiazepine chlordiazepoxide 50 mg four times daily
2. Regular monitoring of withdrawal severity with the CIWA-Ar
3. Regular dispensing of benzodiazepine if moderate or severe withdrawals
4. Parenteral B vitamins
5. Fluid balance and electrolyte monitoring

Differential diagnosis of delirium tremens

The clinical presentation of delirium tremens is similar to several medical and psychiatric disorders. Some of these illnesses can occur concurrently and it is important to recognise that many patients will have more than one cause of delirium, and it is important to treat all conditions.

Alcohol withdrawal symptoms can mimic severe anxiety and panic disorder, but patients will not usually be confused. Drug intoxication and withdrawal can present with agitation and confusion and it is important to screen for illicit drugs. This applies to prescribed medication such as anticonvulsants, and therefore, routine blood tests must include serum blood levels of prescribed medication, which are likely to cause delirium. Hypocalcaemia, hypomagnesaemia and hypoglycaemia can present as delirium, but this improves when corrected. Furthermore, infections like meningitis, encephalitis, and other systemic infections can all present with a pattern similar to that of delirium tremens.

There may be other signs of the infection such as fever, neck stiffness, and raised white blood cell count. One of the most important conditions to exclude is Wernicke–Korsakoff syndrome, which often co-occurs. The differential diagnosis is summarised in Box 8.5.

Investigations

Studies have been undertaken to identify clinical routine investigations at admission that can be performed to highlight risk factors for the development of delirium tremens (Wetterling *et al.*, 1994; Schuckit *et al.*, 1995; Ferguson *et al.*, 1996; Palmstierna, 2001; Fiellin *et al.*, 2002). Decreased serum electrolyte concentrations – especially chloride, potassium and magnesium – raised serum levels of alanine aminotransferase (ALT) and gamma glutamyl transferase (GGT), metabolic disturbance and hypoglycaemia indicate a higher risk for development of the condition.

Routine blood tests such as a full blood count with differential, urea and electrolytes, glucose, liver function tests, clotting profile, thyroid function and serum drug screening for anticonvulsants, for example, should be done to guide treatment of the patient with imminent or established delirium tremens (Burns, 2007). Blood cultures may be required if infection is

Box 8.5	Differential diagnosis of delirium tremens (Burns *et al.*, 2007)
Trauma	Head trauma
Vitamin deficiency	Wernicke–Korsakoff syndrome Vitamin B12 deficiency
Metabolic	Hypoglycaemia Diabetic ketoacidosis Encephalopathy (hepatic, hypertensive, uraemia)
Poisoning	Drug intoxication (e.g. heroin, cocaine) Toxic ingestion (e.g. salicylates, anticholinergics) Carbon monoxide
Infection	Meningitis Brain abscess HIV and AIDS
Others	Electrolyte imbalances (hypomagnesaemia, hyponatraemia, hypocalcaemia) Acute liver failure Chronic renal failure Cerebral vascular accidents (embolism, haemorrhage) Thyrotoxicosis

suspected. Urinalysis is also of value to rule out illicit drug intoxication or other withdrawal syndromes (Burns, 2007). Chest x-ray and urine culture and sensitivity are necessary to rule out infection. Imaging studies including chest x-ray, to rule out concomitant pneumonia, are important. A CT scan of the head might be indicated in patients with focal or persistent seizures or recent head injury and where clinical examination indicates neurological deficits (Feussner *et al.*, 1981). An electrocardiogram would show cardiac arrhythmias, a recognised complication of alcohol dependence. The various investigations of DTs are summarised in Box 8.6.

Mortality

In a case series from Boston City Hospital, mortality for delirium tremens was 560 out of 2357 (24 per cent) cases between 1915 and 1936. Current mortality is 2–10 per cent due to earlier recognition and improvements in general health and treatment. Cause of death in this series was delirium tremens in 153, pneumonia in 135, dilatation of the heart in 80 and brain injury in 27. This shows the often multiple pathologies that are implicated and additional risk factors for mortality in those presenting with delirium tremens (Moore *et al.*, 1939). Predictors of mortality were studied by Tavel and colleagues (Tavel *et al.*, 1961). A temperature greater than 104° F was associated with 45 per cent mortality. Seizures in addition to delirium tremens were associated

> **Box 8.6 Investigation of delirium tremens**
>
> - Blood tests:
>   - Full blood count (FBC),
>   - Urea and electrolytes (U&Es)
>   - Magnesium
>   - Liver function tests (LFTs)
>   - Gamma glutamyl transferase (GGT)
>   - Clotting profile
>   - Glucose
> - Thyroid function tests
> - Serum drug screen (e.g. anticonvulsants)
> - Urine drug screen
> - Chest x-ray
> - CT brain scan
> - ECG

with a mortality of 24 per cent. Other risk factors identified were co-occurring liver disease, pneumonia, hypotension and trauma. Overall mortality has improved because of improvements in identification, treatment and general medical care. More recent studies indicate mortality from delirium tremens of between 0 per cent and 1 per cent (Ferguson *et al.*, 1996).

Treatment of established delirium tremens

Supportive care

Supportive and skilled nursing care is central to the safe management of individuals with delirium tremens. The environment should be quiet and well lit with infrequent changes in nursing care at a suitably competent level. Nursing care should be aimed at reassurance and reorientation of the patient and maintaining safety for the patient and others. Environmental aids to orientation include putting patient names on doors, and a calendar and clock can be useful. There should be regular assessment to consider risks, especially of violence and aggression and a deteriorating physical state with regular review of the vital signs. The level of nursing cover may require one-to-one nursing, and criteria for transfer must be considered.

Monitor the patient for signs or symptoms of withdrawal using the CIWA-Ar and symptom-triggered prescribing of benzodiazepines (see later). Ensure adequate hydration. Individuals with delirium tremens may have significant fluid loss (up to 6 litres per day) through pyrexia, tremor and sweating. A fluid balance chart, regular persuasion to drink and/or an intravenous fluid regimen will be required to prevent dehydration and electrolyte disturbance complicating the picture of confusion. There is a need to monitor electrolytes daily, especially potassium and magnesium, and to correct abnormalities as appropriate using oral or (in the case of magnesium sulphate) parenteral supplements. Nutritional status should be assessed often as patients will be significantly malnourished and require dietary supplements.

Pharmacological management

Historically, pharmacological treatments of delirium tremens have ranged from the use of intravenous alcohol (difficult to titrate the effect plus ongoing alcohol-related harm) to the use of morphine, chloral hydrate, insulin therapy and hydrotherapy! With the possible exception of alcohol, these have all been superseded.

As discussed above, the primary role of treatment is to prevent the onset of delirium tremens. If this is unsuccessful or a patient presents in delirium tremens, the evidence base for effective treatment suggests the use of sedative hypnotic drugs as first line. The guidelines published by the American Society of Addiction in 2004 (Mayo-Smith *et al.*, 2004) are an essential reference guide for management and will be widely quoted in the following sections.

The evidence base for the effect on mortality of treatment with benzodiazepines and other sedatives includes no placebo-controlled trials. However, a series of five trials comparing sedative–hypnotic medications with neuroleptic medication indicated that sedative–hypnotic agents were more effective in reducing mortality; the relative risk of mortality in those treated with neuroleptics was 6.6 (CI 1.2–34.7) (Chambers and Schultz, 1965; Friedhoff and Zitrin, 1959; Goldbert *et al.*, 1967; Kaim *et al.*, 1972; Thomas and Freedman, 1964). There did not appear to be any differences in the effectiveness of various sedative–hypnotic medications studied.

Sedative–hypnotic agents were also superior to neuroleptic drugs in reducing the duration of alcohol withdrawal delirium. The time required to control agitation was shorter with intravenous diazepam than other studied sedatives. An alternative is to use intramuscular lorazepam. Some intensive settings have used continuous infusion of shorter-acting sedatives like midazolam, but this has not been compared with intermittent dosing with longer-acting agents in appropriate studies. The dose required to control delirium can vary greatly, with initial dosing to control agitation of between 15 and 200 mg of diazepam top cumulative doses of sedative of greater than 2000 mg of diazepam. In one patient, medication to control delirium included a cocktail of over 12000 mg of diazepam, 121 mg of lorazepam, 3050 mg of chlordiazepoxide and 2025 mg midazolam over an 8-week period (Wolf *et al.*, 1993).

In the majority of settings, long-acting benzodiazepines are the treatment of choice. Most studies have used diazepam, which, with its more rapid onset in action, may be preferred to chlordiazepoxide. There are reported cases of patients who are refractory despite the use of massive doses of long-acting benzodiazepines, in whom barbiturates or propofol were required to control the symptoms of delirium. Although not recommended in the guidelines, there is some evidence of improved control of delirium tremens with chlomethiazole (Athens, 1986).

In reviewing the evidence for the use of neuroleptic agents in delirium tremens the authors of the guidelines state that they are inferior to sedative–hypnotic agents in mortality and duration of delirium, but are still widely used. Neuroleptic medication should not be used without sedative–hypnotic medication to control delirium. The most commonly studied drug is haloperidol. No studies using newer atypical neuroleptics were identified, and these drugs cannot be currently recommended. Other agents used to treat alcohol withdrawal (e.g. beta-adrenergic antagonists, alpha agonists) do not prevent delirium. Studies have supported the use of carbamazepine for treatment of alcohol withdrawal but there is no convincing evidence for its use in the prevention or treatment of delirium tremens. Around 40 per cent of cases of Wernicke–Korsakoff syndrome emerge after delirium tremens. It is therefore essential to treat all cases with parenteral vitamins.

Settings

The most appropriate setting for the management of patients presenting with delirium tremens will depend on locally agreed protocols and the severity of the physical presentation and co-occurring conditions.

General psychiatric inpatients specialist alcohol detoxification facility

The management protocols in these settings should include supportive care (see above). Maintain high-dose oral chlordiazepoxide 50–100 mg three times daily plus PRN (as required) 20 mg every 2–4 hours to produce control of agitation and light sedation. Alternatively, diazepam at a dose of 50 mg three times daily can be used; this has a faster onset of action than chlordiazepoxide. The use of symptom-triggered prescribing – where doses of chlordiazepoxide or diazepam are administered depending on the severity of withdrawal in the moderate or severe range using, for example, the CIWA-Ar scale – can be effective. Continue using the chosen benzodiazepine at the dose required to produce light sedation until the delirium settles. Monitor for signs of benzodiazepine toxicity and over-sedation and titrate the dose accordingly. Give haloperidol 2–5 mg 4–6 hourly or PRN (orally, intramuscularly or intravenously) for control of agitation and psychotic symptoms. Some units use significantly higher doses of haloperidol, up to 480 mg in 24 hours (Wong, 2005) but this is not recommended. All patients should receive parenteral vitamin supplementation with, for example, two pairs of Pabrinex ampoules three times per day for 3–5 days and oral vitamins (thiamine 50 mg four times daily and vitamin B Compound Strong two tablets twice daily, to correct vitamin deficiencies and treat co-occurring Wernicke–Korsakoff syndrome. Monitor the patient on a daily basis for fluid and electrolyte balance, correcting any abnormalities in potassium and magnesium (the latter with magnesium oxide orally or magnesium sulphate intramuscularly). Consider rapid tranquillisation and the use of the Mental Health Act, as appropriate. Carefully consider the criteria for transfer to inpatient medical care, including intercurrent significant physical health pathology such as pneumonia, alcoholic hepatitis, and worsening jaundice or uncontrolled delirium with the above regimen. This is not an exhaustive list and it is essential that the criteria for transfer are carefully agreed with medical colleagues.

General medical settings

The management protocols in general medical settings should include *all of the above* PLUS one dose of diazepam 5 mg intravenously. If this is not effective in reducing agitation, repeat the dose in 5–10 minutes. If the second dose is not effective, give diazepam 10 mg intravenously every 5–10 minutes for a further two doses. If this is still not effective, give diazepam 20 mg intravenously for subsequent doses until sedation is achieved. Thereafter maintain the patient in a lightly somnolent state using diazepam 5–20 mg hourly.

Alternatively give lorazepam 1–40 mg intramuscularly every 30–60 minutes until the patient is calm and lightly sedated. Intramuscular doses should be given hourly thereafter to maintain the level of somnolence. Some authors recommend the use of lorazepam as this can be more easily titrated against withdrawal symptoms and it may be preferred in elderly patients and in those with significant liver pathology.

Intensive care

There should be careful consideration of the criteria for transfer to intensive care settings. In certain cases the symptoms of delirium tremens are refractory despite massive doses of benzodiazepines. Alternative agents whose mechanism of action is different from benzodiazepines may be required due to the reduced susceptibility of GABA receptors (see above). In these cases, phenobarbital, midazolam and propofol have been tried (Coomes and Smith, 1997).

Conclusions

Delirium tremens is the most serious withdrawal phenomenon with a significant morbidity and mortality. The primary goal of detoxification is the prevention of the onset of delirium. Detection of those at risk is paramount, and instigating high-dose benzodiazepines can avert onset in many cases. The condition, if it emerges, is treated with high-dose benzodiazepines. Some cases may prove refractory.

References and further reading

Abraham, E., Shoemaker, W.C. and McCartney, S.F. (1985). Cardiorespiratory patterns in severe delirium tremens. *Archives of Internal Medicine*, **145**, 1057.

Athens, D. (1986). Comparative investigation of chlomethiazole and neuroleptic agents in the treatment of alcoholic delirium. *Acta Psychiatrica Scandinavica*, **73**, 167–70.

Mehta, S.R., Prabhu, H.R.A., Swamy, A.J., Dhaliwal,. D. and Prasad, D. (2004). Delirium tremens. *Medical Journal of the Armed Forces of India*, **60**, 25–27.

Burns, M.J. (2007). *Delirium tremens*. Available at: http://www.emedicine.com/med/topics524.htm (last accessed October 2008).

Chambers, J.F. and Schultz, J.D. (1965). Double-blind study of three drugs in the treatment of acute alcoholic states. *Quarterly Journal of Studies on Alcohol*, **26**, 10–18.

Chick, J. (1989). Delirium tremens. *British Medical Journal*, **298**, 3–4.

Coomes, T.R. and Smith, S.W. (1997). Successful use of propofol in refractory delirium tremens. *Annals of Emergency Medicine*, **30**, 825–28.

Dittmar, G. (1991). Alcohol delirium: update on an old disorder. *Medizinische Klinik*, **86**, 707–12 (in German).

Erwin, W.E., Williams, D.B. and Speir, W.A. (1998). Delirium tremens. *Southern Medical Journal*, **91**, 425–32.

Ferguson, J.A., Suelzer, C.J., Eckert, G.J., Zhou, X.H. and Dittus, R.S. (1996). Risk factors for delirium tremens development. *Journal of General and Internal Medicine*, **11**, 410–14.

Feussner, J.R., Linfors, E.W., Blessing, C.L. and Starmer, C.F. (1981). Computed tomography brain scanning in alcohol withdrawal seizures. *Annals of Internal Medicine*, **94**, 519–22.

Fiellin, D.A., Patrick, G., O'Connor, M.D., *et al.* (2002). Risk for delirium tremens in patients with alcohol withdrawal syndrome. *Substance Abuse*, **23**, 83–93.

Friedhoff, A.J. and Zitrin, A. (1959). A comparison of the effects of paraldehyde and chlorpromazine in delirium tremens. *New York State Journal of Medicine*, **59**, 1106–63.

Goldbert, T.M., Sanz, C.J., Rose, H.D. and Leitschuh, T.H. (1967). Comparative evaluation of treatments of alcohol withdrawal syndromes. *Journal of the American Medical Association*, **201**, 99–02.

Griffin, R.E., Gross, F.A. and Teitelbaum, H.S. (1993). Delirium tremens: A review. *Journal of American Osteopathic Association*, **93**, 929–32.

Guthrie, S.K. (1989). The treatment of alcohol withdrawal. *Pharmacotherapy*, **9**, 131–43.

Hall, W. and Zador, D. (1997). The alcohol withdrawal syndrome. *Lancet*, **349**, 1897–900.

Hersh, D., Kranzler, H., Roger, E., *et al.* (1997). Persistent delirium following cessation of heavy alcohol consumption: diagnostic and treatment implications. *American Journal of Psychiatry*, **154**, 846–51.

Isbell, H., Fraser, H.F., Wikler, A., Belleville, R.E. and Eiserman, A.J. (1955). An experimental study of the etiology of 'rum fits' and delirium tremens. *Quarterly Journal of Studies on Alcohol*, **16**, 1–33.

Jost, A., Hermle, L., Spitzer, M., *et al.* (1992). Clinical and laboratory differentiation of alcohol withdrawal syndrome and alcoholic delirium. *Psychiatrische Praxis*, **19**, 16–22 (in German).

Kaim, S.C., Klett, C.J. and Rothfield, B. (1969). Treatment of alcohol withdrawal states: Comparison of four drugs. *American Journal of Psychiatry*, **125**, 1640–46.

Kaim, S.C. and Klett, C.J. (1972). Treatment of delirium tremens: A comparative evaluation of four drugs. *Quarterly Journal of Studies on Alcohol*, **33**, 1065–72.

Lee, J.H., Jang, M.K., Lee, J.Y., *et al.* (2005). Clinical predictors for delirium tremens in alcohol dependence. *Journal of Gastroenterology and Hepatology*, **20**, 1833–37.

Lukan, J.K., Reed, D.N., Looney, S.W., Spain, D.A. and Blondell, R.D. (2002). Risk factors for delirium tremens in trauma patients. *Journal of Trauma Injury Infection and Critical Care*, **53**, 901–06.

Mahmoudi, M., Kang, M.H., Tillakaratne, N. and Olsen, R.W. (1997). Chronic intermittent ethanol treatment in rats increases GABA (A) receptor alpha-4-subunit expression: possible relevance to alcohol dependence. *Neurochemistry*, **68**, 2485–92.

Mattick, R. and Jarvis, T. (1993). *An outline for the management of alcohol problems: Quality assurance in the treatment of drug dependence project. Monograph No. 20. National Drug Strategy*. Canberra, Australia: Commonwealth Department of Human Services and Health.

Matsushita, S., Kimura, M., Miyakawa, T., *et al.* (2004). Association study of brain-derived neurotrophic factor gene polymorphism and alcoholism. *Alcoholism: Clinical and Experimental Research*, **28**, 1609–12.

Mayo-Smith, M.F., Beecher, L.H., Fischer, T.L., *et al.* (2004). Management of alcohol withdrawal delirium. An evidence-based practice guideline. *Archives of Internal Medicine* **164**, 1405–12.

Mayo-Smith, M.F., Cushman, P.J., Hill, A.J., *et al.* (1997). Pharmacological management of alcohol withdrawal: A meta-analysis and evidence-based practice guideline. *Journal of the American Medical Association*, **278**, 145–51.

Moore, M. and Gray, M.G. (1939). Delirium tremens: A study of cases at Bolton City Hospital. *New England Journal of Medicine*, **220**, 953–56.

Palmstierna, T. (2001). A model of predicting alcohol withdrawal delirium. *Psychiatric Services*, **52**, 820–23.

Schuckit, M.A., Tipp, J.E., Reich, T., *et al.* (1995). The histories of withdrawal convulsions and delirium tremens in 1648 alcohol-dependent subjects. *Addiction*, **90**, 1335–47.

Stockwell, T., Sitharthan, T., McGrath, D. and Lang E. (1994). The measurement of alcohol dependence and impaired control in community samples. *Addiction*, **89**, 167–74.

Sullivan, J.T., Sykora, K., Schneiderman, J., Naranjo, C.A. and Sellers, E.M. (1989). Assessment of alcohol withdrawal: the revised clinical institute withdrawal assessment for alcohol scale (CIWA-Ar). *British Journal of Addiction*, **84**, 1353–57.

Tavel, M.E., Davidson, W. and Batterton, T.D. (1961). A critical analysis of mortality associated with delirium tremens: review of 39 fatalities in a 9-year period. *American Journal of Medical Sciences*, **242**, 18–29.

Thomas, D.W. and Freedman, D.X. (1964). Treatment of the alcohol withdrawal syndrome: comparison of promazine and paraldehyde. *Journal of the American Medical Association*, **188**, 316–18.

Tonnesen, E. (1982). Delirium tremens and hypokalaemia. *Lancet*, **2**(8289). 97.

Turner, R.C., Lichstein, P.R., Peden, J.G. Jr, Busher, J.T and Waivers, L.E. (1989). Alcohol withdrawal syndromes: A review of pathophysiology, clinical presentation, and treatment. *Journal of General Internal Medicine*, **4**, 432–44.

Van Munster, B.C., Korevaar, J.C., de Roolj, S.E., Levi, M. and Zwinderman, A.H. (2007). Genetic polymorphisms related to delirium tremens: A systematic review. *Alcoholism: Clinical and Experimental Research*, **31**, 177–84.

Victor, M. and Adams, R.E. (1953). The effect of alcohol on the nervous system. *Research Publications of the Association for Research on Nervous and Mental Disease*, **32**, 526–73.

Wetterling, T., Kanitz, R.D., Veltrup, C., *et al.* (1994). Clinical predictors of alcohol and withdrawal delirium. *Alcoholism: Clinical and Experimental Research*, **18**(5), 1110–02.

Wetterling, T., Weber, B., Depfenhart, M., *et al.* (2006). Development of a rating scale to predict the severity of alcohol withdrawal syndrome. *Alcohol and Alcoholism*, **41**, 611–15.

Wolf, K.M., Shaugnessy, A.F. and Middleton, D.B. (1993). Prolonged delirium tremens requiring massive doses of medication. *Journal of the American Board of Family Practice*, **6**, 502–04.

Wong, S.-L. (2005). *Treatment of delirium tremens*. Available at: http://www.uspharmacist.com (last accessed October 2008).

9 Pharmacological treatment approaches

Zarrar A. Chowdary and Thomas Carnwath

The treatment of alcohol dependence occurs in two phases: the first phase is detoxification (see Chapter 7). The second is supporting patients in remission, abstinence and rehabilitation. According to the Agency for Healthcare Research and Quality (1999; pp. 1–60) the aims of the second phase include: treating dependence, including craving and loss of control; enhancing abstinence and minimising relapse by the threat of, or the development of, aversive consequences (or both) in response to alcohol consumption; treating any comorbid disorders that increase the likelihood of alcohol use; and treating the consequences of alcohol use, such as protracted abstinence symptoms, cognitive impairment, and liver problems. This chapter focuses on the second phase. It does not address the issue of treating the consequences of alcohol misuse.

Medication should always be viewed as adjunctive to psychosocial intervention. The drugs most commonly used are disulfiram, acamprosate and naltrexone, but many others are being investigated or under development. Disulfiram has been prescribed for over 50 years. It showed very promising results during the initial period, however, increasing experience has revealed high relapse rates and a tendency to poor compliance. Acamprosate is an anti-craving agent, and has shown moderate efficacy in treatment outcomes, with the majority of patients showing better abstinence periods than on placebo. Naltrexone, an opioid antagonist, is associated with a reduced number of drinking days, but again compliance appears to be an issue. Various combinations of these medicines have also been investigated. Serotonergic agents and anticonvulsants have recently shown some promise (Williams, 2005).

Disulfiram (Antabuse)

Disulfiram was introduced in the early part of the 20th century and has been widely used since then. The philosophy behind its use is that it acts as a deterrent. It changes the body's response to alcohol ingestion, making it into an unpleasant experience. It therefore prevents drinking, but also induces an adverse association with the experience of drinking.

Mechanism of action

Normally alcohol is oxidised to acetaldehyde, and then acetaldehyde is converted into acetate by aldehyde dehydrogenase. Disulfiram inhibits the action of this enzyme, and the resulting accumulation of acetaldehyde causes the unpleasant 'disulfiram–ethanol reaction' (or DER). Aldehyde dehydrogenase is found mostly in the liver, but also in the stomach lining, where it may play a major role in alcohol metabolism (Haber *et al.*, 1996).

   Women have less enzyme activity there than men (Frezza *et al.*, 1990) which may partly explain why they are more prone to liver damage. Two genetic variants of this enzyme have been identified, with low and high activity. Most people of Asian background have a variant with low activity, which results in poor tolerance of alcohol consumption, and therefore relatively low rates of dependence (Mizoi *et al.*, 1983). Ball (2004) described this as 'being equipped with in-built disulfiram'.

Evidence

Early clinical studies showed promising results, but the study designs have later been criticised. Fuller *et al.* (1986) conducted a controlled, blinded multicentre trial, which led to the conclusion that disulfiram reduces the frequency of alcohol consumption after relapse; but there was a significant association between adherence to drug regimen and abstinence. Chick *et al.* (1992) performed a trial where the efficacy of supervised disulfiram was compared with vitamin C. The group receiving supervised disulfiram showed reduced weekly consumption, increased days of abstinence and a fall in serum gamma glutamyl transferase (GGT) which is an enzyme that indicates liver damage when released into the blood. Both Hughes and Cook (1997) and Anton *et al.* (2001) reviewed the outcome studies and concluded that disulfiram works best when supervised and when the patient is involved in the therapeutic programme. Close adherence to medication is essential for disulfiram to be effective, and for this reason disulfiram implants were at one stage often used. The above reviews indicated that implants were ineffective, partly because therapeutic levels of medication are not obtained.

Criteria for prescribing disulfiram

Are there particular patients that benefit from disulfiram? Banys (1988) proposes the following selection criteria:

- Patients who can tolerate a treatment relationship.
- Patients who are relapse-prone (but in treatment).
- Patients who have failed with less structured approaches.
- Patients in early abstinence who are in crisis or under severe stress.
- Patients in established recovery for whom individual/group psychotherapy is a relapse risk.
- Patients who specifically request it.

Sereny *et al.* (1986) report that patients likely to benefit are those who continue treatment despite responding poorly. Patients who might do better with unsupervised disulfiram include those who are older (Baekeland *et al.*, 1971; Fuller and Gordis, 1986), more socially stable (Fuller and Gordis, 1986) and higher in motivation (Baekeland *et al.*, 1971). Contraindications include cardiac failure, coronary artery disease, history of stroke, hypertension, psychosis, severe personality disorder, suicide risk, pregnancy and breastfeeding. It should generally be avoided in patients with abnormal liver function. Pregnant women should not be prescribed disulfiram because it has been reported to cause fetal abnormalities. Anyone with a condition that impairs their ability to understand the risks associated with disulfiram should not receive it.

Prescribing and monitoring

Before treatment, measurements should be made of blood pressure, pulse and liver function, and an ECG (electrocardiogram) should be taken, as well as taking a careful history of cardiac problems. Disulfiram is usually initiated with a loading dose of 800 mg as a single dose at bedtime, then on the next 3 days 600 mg, 400 mg and 200 mg, respectively. The usual maintenance dose is 200 mg per day, but this may be increased if patients are able to 'drink over the top'. Patients should be informed of the dangers of consuming alcohol within 7 days of disulfiram, and of possible interactions with vinegar, perfumes, cosmetics, foodstuffs containing alcohol, and other medications. They should inform the pharmacist before purchasing over-the-counter preparations. Treatment is much more likely to be successful if the patient agrees to receive supervised use, by means of tablets dissolved in water, and is actively involved in treatment, for example receiving support from a community worker. Supervision may take place in a special clinic or with the help of a spouse or other concerned relative. Thrice-weekly consumption is possible, and may be helpful in this regard (for example, 400 mg on Monday and Wednesday and 600 mg on Saturday).

Treatment should not be continued for longer than 6 months without careful review. Liver function tests should be monitored because of a small risk of drug-induced hepatitis. Wright *et al.* (1988) reviewed the literature on disulfiram hepatitis, and concluded that most patients with hepatitis developed symptoms within 2 weeks to 2 months of use. He noted that six patients died. He recommended that liver function tests should be obtained before treatment, at 2-week intervals for 2 months and thereafter at 3–6-month intervals. On the other hand, Chick *et al.* (1999) found that the onset of hepatitis is usually very rapid and therefore frequent testing may not detect it. He recommends instead that it is most important to educate patients about the dangers of hepatitis and to advise them to stop treatment immediately if any adverse effects are noted. Saxon *et al.* (1998) looked at disulfiram use in patients with previously abnormal liver tests and concluded that overall it is safe for patients to take disulfiram, provided that liver function is regularly monitored.

The consensus at present is that patients should be educated about the risk of hepatitis, but that also liver function tests should be taken within the first 6 weeks and thereafter at 6-month intervals.

Side effects

Side effects are reported as initial drowsiness and fatigue, nausea and vomiting, halitosis, reduced libido, rarely psychotic reactions (depression, paranoia, schizophrenia and mania), allergic dermatitis, peripheral neuropathy and hepatic cell damage. However, Christensen and colleagues (1984) carried out a double-blind study on the side effects of disulfiram compared with placebo, and found no statistically significant difference.

Poulsen *et al.* (1992) analysed reports to the Danish Committee on Adverse Drug Reactions during 1968–1991. In that period, 154 adverse drug reactions to disulfiram were reported, mostly of hepatic, neurological, dermatological and psychiatric problems, in decreasing order of frequency. Over the 23-year period, 14 deaths were reported in Denmark, which corresponds to a rate of 1 per 25,000 treatment years; the chief cause was liver toxicity. This report does not state explicitly what doses were implicated in the adverse reactions.

Disulfiram-ethanol reaction (DER)

The reaction can occur within 10 minutes of ingesting alcohol and can last for several hours (it may require intensive supportive therapy – oxygen should be available). The typical reaction is characterised by flushing, nausea, vomiting, tachycardia and dyspnoea.

The currently recommended dose of disulfiram carries little risk of a severe DER. Higher doses (up to 3 g per day) were used in the past, and these did lead to severe reactions, and even death on occasions. Toxic side effects such as psychotic reactions and neuropathy also appear to be dose-related. This history may still be having a negative effect on doctors, even today, discouraging them from using what can be a very useful drug. Although lower doses are now used routinely, it should be remembered that some patients may need to have their dose increased. Brewer (1984) reported that doses of 250–500 mg are insufficient to cause DER in some patients.

Drug interactions

Disulfiram interacts with drugs that are metabolised by the cytochrome p450 enzyme system. It may enhance the effects of the following classes of medications: anticoagulants, tricyclic antidepressants, antiepileptics (particularly phenytoin), benzodiazepines and theophylline – thus increasing the risk of toxicity.

Acamprosate (Campral)

Acamprosate (calcium acetyl homotaurinate) has been prescribed for over a decade and has shown moderate efficacy among patients trying to achieve abstinence. Its main effect appears to be as anti-craving agent, but its mode of action has not been fully elucidated. Acamprosate affects multiple receptors in the central nervous system. It possesses GABA-ergic effects in rats and humans (Daoust *et al.*, 1992; Gerra *et al.*, 1992; Gewiss *et al.*, 1991) but it is not a direct GABA agonist (Grant and Woolverton, 1989). It does not bind to the GABA-A receptor or enhance chloride currents in the GABA-A receptor. It is unlikely, then, that the GABA-ergic effects are the only pharmacologic mechanism (Durbin *et al.*, 1996).

A restorative effect is suggested by experiments in rats, where acamprosate reduces the postsynaptic effect of excitatory amino acid transmitters (Zeise *et al.*, 1993), blocking the release of glutamate in the nucleus accumbens induced by alcohol withdrawal (Dahchour *et al.*, 1998). It blocks presynaptic GABA-B receptors and enhances NMD-A receptor activation simultaneously. Thereby it restores glutamatergic neurotransmission in the nucleus accumbens and restores the balance between inhibitory and excitatory neurotransmission, in a central nervous system which has been disrupted by chronic alcohol consumption (Berton *et al.*, 1998). It may also reduce the rewards associated with alcohol. Both acamprosate and homotaurine delay or suppress the ethanol-stimulated increase in the release of dopamine in the nucleus accumbens. This results in a reduction in ethanol intake by interfering with the ability of ethanol to activate the mesolimbic dopamine reward system (Olive *et al.*, 2002).

Evidence

The bulk of the evidence supports the use of acamprosate as an adjunctive treatment for maintaining abstinence from alcohol, with moderate effects (Geerlings *et al.*, 1997; Gual and Lehert, 2001; Poldrugo, 1997; Tempesta *et al.*, 2000; Whitworth *et al.*, 1996). However, there are complicating factors when studying this patient population: these include the varied diagnostic categories, different treatment settings, varied amounts of psychosocial or behavioural intervention, the use of concomitant medications, the presence of comorbid diseases, poly-substance misuse, different social classes and high drop-out and placebo response rates. There are two significant negative studies, the UKMAS study based in England (Chick *et al.*, 2000) and one based in South Korea (Namkoong *et al.*, 2003). The explanations for the negative result in UKMAS may include loss of statistical power due to a high drop-out rate, a high rate of relapse before starting the drug, and a background of less intensive treatment in general. The negative finding in the Korean Study may be explained by the short study period, the variable standard of concomitant psychosocial treatment, and the sample characteristics (i.e. they have a more severe form of alcohol dependence, a lower level of social support, and a short interval between the last drink and the first medication).

Dose and duration

The drug is indicated for patients with established alcohol dependence who are finding it difficult to maintain sobriety. Preferably, treatment should be started as soon as possible after detoxification and maintained for 1 year, regardless of relapse. The usual dose for patients receiving acamprosate is based on body weight. Patients who weigh less than 60 kg should be treated with 666 mg (two tablets) three times daily. Those weighing more than 60 kg should receive 666 mg at breakfast, followed by 333 mg at midday and 333 mg at night.

Contraindications, side effects and interactions

Contraindications include renal and severe hepatic impairment, pregnancy and breast feeding. Reported side effects include diarrhoea, nausea, vomiting, abdominal pain, pruritis, occasionally maculopapular rash, rarely bullous skin reactions and fluctuations in libido. Nonetheless, it has been found to be safe and well tolerated in clinical trials. The most common adverse event reported when compared with placebo was diarrhoea (3–48 per cent versus 2–39 per cent, respectively).

The incidence of this appears to be dose-related (Barrias *et al.*, 1997; Lhuintre *et al.*, 1985). No significant drug interactions have been reported with the combined use of acamprosate with ethanol or with other drugs commonly used during alcohol withdrawal or during the period following alcohol withdrawal (i.e. antidepressants, anxiolytics, neuroleptics, and hypnotics). Additionally, acamprosate and naltrexone, as well as acamprosate and disulfiram, have been administered concomitantly without any clinically significant interactions (Besson *et al.*, 1998; Mason, 2001).

Naltrexone

Naltrexone is an opiate receptor antagonist. It has been licensed in the USA and certain European countries as an adjunct in the treatment of alcohol dependence, but so far not in the UK. It has been used in the USA since 1994.

Mechanism of action

As with acamprosate, it is not fully understood how naltrexone acts, but probably it reduces the reinforcing effects of alcohol. Alcohol may have a stimulant effect on endogenous opioids, particularly in people with a positive family history of alcohol misuse (Gianoulakis, 1996). Naltrexone is an opiate receptor antagonist with a high affinity for μ receptors. It therefore blocks this effect and in this way might reduce the euphoria associated with alcohol intake (King *et al.*, 1997; Volpicelli *et al.*, 1995). However, not all alcohol-dependent subjects experience associated euphoria or an increase in endogenous opioids. Naltrexone may also increase the aversive effects of alcohol, as well as reducing cravings for drink. A functional polymorphism of μ-receptor gene has been associated with the response to naltrexone (Oslin *et al.*, 2003). This may explain variability in response to naltrexone in different clinical trials, but these findings need to be replicated on a larger scale and with a better-selected sample.

Evidence

Most of the clinical trials have been conducted over the last 20 years in the USA. They have shown that naltrexone does have a role in treatment of chronic alcohol dependence. Volpicelli *et al.* (1992) conducted double-blind, placebo-controlled studies, showing that naltrexone (50 mg per day) reduces drinking in alcohol-dependent subjects. The lower alcohol consumption by the naltrexone-treated subjects may have resulted from naltrexone's blockage of the pleasure produced by alcohol (Volpicelli *et al.*, 1995). Volpicelli *et al.* (1997) investigated the role of subjective compliance and found that although the patients on naltrexone did better compared to those on placebo, this moderate effect can be improved with better compliance. Morris *et al.* (2001) conducted a randomised placebo-controlled clinical trial and found similar results. It has been found that naltrexone increases the latency to drink alcohol in social drinkers – that is the time taken to drink again after achieving abstinence (Davidson *et al.*, 1996) – and that this may be partially caused by the anti-craving properties of naltrexone. A similar finding was noted by O'Malley *et al.* (1996).

An Australian study found that naltrexone with adjunctive medical advice is effective in the treatment of alcohol dependence, irrespective of whether it is accompanied by psychosocial interventions (Latt *et al.*, 2002). Recently, however, a German randomised-controlled trial found no significant difference in alcohol consumption between groups receiving naltrexone and placebo except for a reduction in serum levels of the liver enzyme GGT in those taking naltrexone. The authors posed the question whether self-reports of drinking in this trial may have been less reliable than GGT as a measure of recent alcohol consumption (Gastpar *et al.*, 2002).

A UK study showed that naltrexone given over a period of 3 months helped patients reduce their alcohol consumption, reduced their perceptions of craving, and improved their global recovery as assessed by their physician. This was accompanied by a reduction in serum markers of alcohol consumption (Chick *et al.*, 2000). However, these effects only occurred in patients who remained compliant with the treatment.

In a US study there was no significant difference between the two groups, in terms of the number of days to relapse, the percentage of days on which drinking occurred, and the number of drinks per drinking day (Krystal *et al.*, 2001). The study population consisted exclusively of male war veterans with severe alcohol dependence, which might explain the different findings from other studies where the population has typically included both sexes and patients with less severe problems.

Nalmefene

Nalmefene is a more recently developed opioid antagonist. It is pharmacologically superior to naltrexone. It has a better side effect profile, less hepatic toxicity, a longer duration of action, a more potent antagonist action and better bioavailability. It was shown to be effective in preventing relapse among patients with alcohol dependence compared to placebo (Mason *et al.*, 1999). Like naltrexone, it is not yet licensed for treatment of alcohol dependence in the UK.

Dose and monitoring

Nalmefene should be initiated in specialist clinics only. The initial dose is 25 mg and the patient should then be maintained on 50 mg daily. The dose may be divided into three doses on a weekly basis (100 mg on Monday, 100 mg on Wednesday and 150 mg on Friday). It should be used in patients who are interested in taking the medication and are involved in a therapeutic programme. It must be used with caution among patients with hepatic and renal impairments. A liver function test should be performed before initiating treatment and then at regular intervals during treatment. Moderately raised liver enzymes should not prevent the use of naltrexone. Patients must not take any opioid-containing agents for analgesia. They should be advised to take an anti-inflammatory or paracetamol instead. If it is essential to take opioids, naltrexone must be stopped for the duration of treatment.

Contraindications and side effects

In pregnant and breastfeeding patients, naltrexone should be used only if the benefits clearly outweigh the risks. No information is available in terms of the effects on the fetus. It must not be used in patients who are currently dependent on opioids and patients with acute hepatitis or liver failure.

Most patients tolerate a dose of 50 mg per day. Side effects may include nausea, vomiting, abdominal pain, headache, reduced energy, joint and muscle pain, anxiety and nervousness. Less frequent side effects include loss of appetite, diarrhoea, constipation, increased thirst, chest pain, increased sweating and lacrimation, irritability, dizziness, chills, delayed ejaculation, decreased potency, rash, depressed mood and increased energy. Occasionally, liver function abnormalities and reversible idiopathic thrombocytopenia have been reported. Nonetheless, it is generally a safe drug, and is well tolerated.

Comparison of disulfirum, acamprosate and naltrexone

Most trials have looked at the difference of outcome between acamprosate and naltrexone, with very few comparing acamprosate or naltrexone against disulfiram. Rubio *et al.* (2001) compared naltrexone to acamprosate and found that the time to first relapse was similar in both groups, but there was a greater number of abstinence days and less craving for alcohol in the naltrexone group. Another study (Kiefer *et al.*, 2003) compared the efficacy of naltrexone and acamprosate, both singly and together, against placebo. As expected, naltrexone, acamprosate and combined medications were significantly superior to placebo. Combination therapy showed the most effective results in terms of the days to relapse compared to acamprosate and placebo, but they were not significantly different from the naltrexone group. Kiefer and Wiedemann (2004) reviewed published studies on combined acamprosate and naltrexone. They concluded that combination therapy is significantly superior in maintaining abstinence and relapse to heavy drinking compared to monotherapy. Also, combination therapy has so far proved safe and well-tolerated.

In comparing naltrexone to disulfiram, de Sousa and de Sousa (2003) found that disulfiram was superior in terms of relapse prevention and maintaining abstinence, but naltrexone was better at reducing craving. In another study (Beeson *et al.*, 1998) acamprosate was compared with placebo, by itself and in combination with disulfiram. Subject groups were stratified for voluntary use of alcohol. The time to the first drink and the abstinent period were both shorter in the placebo group. Combination of disulfiram with acamprosate enhanced the overall effectiveness and was found to be safe.

It may be premature to generalise these studies in view of variable population selection, methodology and treatment outcomes. However, since a high proportion of dependent patients relapse with monotherapy, there is probably a role for combination therapies in patients who have struggled to achieve sobriety with one agent.

Selective serotonin-reuptake inhibitors (SSRIs)

Evidence for the use of SSRI antidepressants in the treatment of alcohol dependence is so far no more than suggestive. Most of the data available is confounded by the presence or absence of mood or anxiety disorder. Where positive effects are found, it is not clear whether SSRIs are treating the alcohol dependence in addition to the mood symptoms, or whether it is merely that reduction in depression reduces the desire to self-medicate with alcohol (Schuckit *et al.*, 1996). Fluoxetine has been shown to reduce alcohol consumption among patients with alcohol dependence and comorbid depressive symptoms (Cornelius *et al.*, 1995), but did not reduce clinical relapse rates in a sample of severely alcoholic men without other psychiatric disorders (Kabel and Petty, 1996).

Alcohol dependence may be divided into type A (low risk/severity) and type B (high risk/severity) and there is evidence that these subtypes respond differently to SSRI antidepressants. Type B usually yields poorer outcomes (Kranzler *et al.*, 1996). Pettinati *et al.* (2000) confirmed the finding of Kanzler, that alcoholic subtypes respond differentially to serotonergic agents and that type A show more favourable outcomes with sertraline compared to placebo. These findings suggest that it is important to consider subtypes when treating alcohol dependence.

In addition, a gender difference in response to pharmacotherapy for alcohol subtypes has been noted. Type A alcoholic men, but not type A alcoholic women, had consistently better outcomes with sertraline compared to placebo. There were no significant differences in drinking with sertraline compared to placebo in type B alcoholic men or women (Pettinati *et al.*, 2004).

Other medications

Carbamazepine has shown some encouraging results in the treatment of alcohol dependence (Mueller *et al.*, 1997). A more promising anticonvulsant has been topiramate, which in one trial reduced the frequency of craving and alcohol use, as well as serum levels of a frequently used marker of alcohol use, carbohydrate-deficient transferrin (CDT) (Rubio *et al.*, 2004). In another randomised-controlled trial, topiramate was shown to be superior to placebo in dependent patients, not only with regard to better abstinence rates but also in improving quality of life. It was also well tolerated, with few drop-outs (Johnson *et al.*, 2004).

Ondansetron, a selective 5-hydroxytryptamine (HT-3) antagonist, has been shown to be effective in the treatment of early-onset alcoholics (type B), who develop problems before the age of 25 (Johnson *et al.*, 2002). This group differs from those with later onset because they usually have higher serotonergic abnormality, a wider range of antisocial behaviour, and a positive family history of alcohol misuse. In comparison to placebo, the ondansetron group yielded better abstinence rates and was also superior with regard to the amount of alcohol consumed. CDT values were also reduced significantly. These findings further support the theory that there may be a significant interaction between the serotonin system and alcoholic subtypes, and that this is relevant to treatment.

Baclofen is a GABA-B receptor agonist. In a preliminary double-blind placebo-controlled study, patients given baclofen had a higher number of abstinence days and a decrease in craving and alcohol intake compared to those on placebo (Addolorato *et al.*, 2002). None of the patients discontinued baclofen due to side effects in the trial. Again, the study size and sample were both very small and findings lack generalisability at present. Drugs under development include other anti-craving agents and drugs that work more selectively on GABA-ergic systems and cannabinoid receptors. Among the more speculative ventures are substances that provide the positive experiences associated with alcohol without the negative effects, and those that inhibit the process of laying down memory in a manner that also counteracts the development of dependence.

Conclusions

Acamprosate, naltrexone and disulfiram are all effective in treating alcohol dependence, when prescribed alongside standard psychosocial management. The evidence does not support definite guidance as to which medication to use when, but in most cases acamprosate would be the first choice because of its low incidence of side effects and interactions and the greater amount of research support. It may be particularly useful where cravings are a major feature of relapse. Naltrexone may be of particular use where patients are unable to achieve sobriety. Disulfiram should generally only be used in patients who are compliant and willing to take it under supervision, whether in a special clinic or by relatives or friends. Combination therapy may be effective when monotherapy has failed. An SSRI antidepressant can be used where there is significant concomitant depression, and perhaps also in type A male alcoholics. Other medications are best reserved for when standard treatment has failed. The next decade is likely to see the introduction of many further effective medications, as our knowledge increases concerning the mechanisms of dependence and of alcohol-related damage.

References and further reading

Addolorato, G., Caputo, F., Capristo, E., *et al.* (2002). Baclofen efficacy in reducing alcohol craving and intake: A preliminary double-blind randomized controlled study. *Alcohol and Alcoholism*, **5**, 504–08.

Agency for Healthcare Research and Quality (1999). *Evidence Report: Pharmacotherapy for Alcohol Dependence, January 1999. Agency for Health Care Policy and Research Agency Publication No. 99-E004.* Research Triangle Park, NC: Research Triangle Institute.

Anton, R. (2001). Pharmacological approaches to the management of alcoholism. *Journal of Clinical Psychiatry*, **62**(Suppl. 20), 11–17.

Baekeland, F., Lundwall, L., Kissin, B. and Shanahan, T. (1971). The correlates of outcome in disulfiram treatment of alcoholism. *Journal of Nervous and Mental Disease*, **53**, 1–9.

Ball, D. (2004). Genetic approaches to alcohol dependence. *British Journal of Psychiatry*, **185**, 449–51.

Banys, P. (1988). The clinical use of disulfiram (Antabuse). A review. *Journal of Psychoactive Drugs*, **20**, 243–60.

Barrias, J., Chabac, S., Ferreira, L., Fonte, A., Potgieter, A. and Teixeira, S. (1997). Acamprosate: multicentre Portuguese efficacy and tolerance evaluation study. *Portuguese Psiquiatria Clinica*, **18**,149–60.

Berton, F., Francesconi, W., Madamba, S., Zieglgansberger, W. and Siggins, G. (1998). Acamprosate enhances *N*-methyl-D-aspartate receptor–mediated neurotransmission but inhibits presynaptic GABA (B) receptors in nucleus accumbens neurons. *Alcohol: Clinical and Experimental Research*, **22**, 183–91.

Besson, J., Aeby, F., Kasas, A., Lehert, P. and Potgeiter, A. (1998). Combined efficacy of acamprosate and disulfiram in the treatment of alcoholism. A controlled study. *Alcohol: Clinical and Experimental Research*, **22**, 573–79.

Brewer, C. (1984). How effective is the standard dose of disulfiram? A review of the alcohol–disulfiram reaction in practice. *British Journal of Psychiatry*, **144**, 200–02.

British National Formulary (2006). *BNF. Volume 51*. London: Pharmaceutical Press.

Carmen, B., Angeles, M., Ana, M. and Josemaria, A. (2004). Efficacy and safety of naltrexone and acamprosate in the treatment of alcohol dependence. A systematic review. *Addiction*, **99**(7), 811.

Chick, J. (1999). Safety issues concerning the use of disulfiram in treating alcohol dependence. *Drug Safety*, **20**, 427–35.

Chick, J., Anton, R., Checinski, K., *et al.* (2000). A multicentre randomised double-blind placebo-controlled trial of naltrexone in treatment of alcohol dependence or abuse. *Alcohol and Alcoholism*, **35**(6), 587–93.

Chick, J., Gough, K., Wojciech, F., *et al.* (1992). Disulfiram treatment of alcoholism. *British Journal of Psychiatry*, **161**, 84–89.

Chick, J., Howlett, H., Morgan, Y. and Ritson, B. (2000). United Kingdom Multicentre Acamprosate Study (UKMAS) A six-month prospective study of acamprosate versus placebo in preventing relapse after withdrawal from alcohol. *Alcohol and Alcoholism*, **35**, 176–78.

Christensen, K., Ronstad, P. and Vaag, U. (1984). Side effects after disulfiram. Comparison of disulfiram and placebo in a double-blind multicentre study. *Acta Psychiatrica Scandinavica*, **69**, 265–73.

Cornelius, R., Salloum, M., Cornelius, D., *et al.* (1995). Preliminary report: Double blind, placebo-controlled study of fluoxetine in depressed alcoholics. *Psychopharmacological Bulletin*, **31**, 297–03.

Dahchour, A., De Witte, P., Bolo, N., Nedelec, J., Muzet, M. and Durbin, P. (1998). Central effects of acamprosate. Part, 1.

Acamprosate blocks the glutamate increase in the nucleus accumbens microdialysate in ethanol withdrawn rats. *Psychiatry Research*, **82**, 107–14.

Daoust, M., Legrand, E., Gewiss, M., Heidbreder, C., DeWitte, P. and Tran, G. (1992). Acamprosate modulates synaptosomal GABA transmission in chronically alcoholised rats. *Pharmacology Biochemistry and Behaviour*, **41**, 669–74.

Davidson, D., Swift, R. and Fitz, E. (1996). Naltrexone increases the latency to drink alcohol in social drinkers, *Alcoholism: Clinical and Experimental Research*. **20**(4), 732.

Durbin, P., Hulot, T. and Chabac, S. (1996). Pharmacodynamics and pharmacokinetics of acamprosate: an overview. In: Soyka, M. (ed.) *Acamprosate in Relapse Prevention of Alcoholism*. Berlin: Springer-Verlag, pp. 47–64.

Frezza, M., Di Padova, C., Pozzato, G., Terpin, M., Baraona, E. and Lieber, C. (1990). High blood alcohol levels in women: the role of decreased gastric alcohol dehydrogenase activity and first pass metabolism. *New England Journal of Medicine*, **322**, 95–96.

Fuller, R. and Gordis, E. (2004). Does disulfiram have a role in alcoholism treatment today? *Addiction,* **99**(1), 21–24.

Fuller, R., Branchey, L., Brightwell, D., *et al.* (1986). Disulfiram treatment of alcoholism: A Veterans Administration Cooperative Study. *Journal of the American Medical Association*, **256**, 1449–55.

Gastpar, M., Bonnet, U., Boning, J., *et al.* (2002). Lack of efficacy of naltrexone in the prevention of alcohol relapse: Results from a German multicenter study. *Journal of Psychopharmacology*, **22**(6), 592–98.

Geerlings, P., Ansoms, C. and van den Brink, W. (1997). Acamprosate and prevention of relapse in alcoholics. *European Addiction Research*, **3**, 129–37.

Gerra, G., Caccavari, R. and Delsignore, R. (1992). Pituitary responses to Ca-acetyl homotaurinate in normal subjects and alcoholics. *Neuroendocrinology Letters*, **14**, 119–26.

Gewiss, M., Heidbreder, C., Opsomer, L., Durbin, P. and de Witte, P. (1991). Acamprosate and diazepam differentially modulate alcohol-induced behavioural and cortical alterations in rats following chronic inhalation of ethanol vapour. *Alcohol and Alcoholism*, **26**, 129–37.

Gianoulakis, C. (1996). Implications of endogenous opioids and dopamine in alcoholism: human and basic science studies. *Alcohol and Alcoholism*, **31**(Suppl.1), 33–42.

Giovanni, A., Fabio, C., Esmeralda, C., *et al.* (2002). Baclofen efficacy in reducing alcohol craving and intake: A preliminary double-blind randomized controlled study. *Alcohol and Alcoholism*, **37**(5), 504–08.

Grant, K. and Woolverton, W. (1989). Reinforcing and discriminative stimulus effects of Ca-acetyl homotaurine in animals. *Pharmacology Biochemistry and Behaviour*, **32**, 607–11.

Gual, A. and Lehert, P. (2001). Acamprosate during and after acute alcohol withdrawal: A double-blind placebo-controlled study in Spain. *Alcohol and Alcoholism*, **36**, 413–18.

Haber, P., Gentry, R., Mak, K., Mirmiran-Yazdy, S., Greenstein, R. and Lieber, C. (1996). Metabolism of alcohol by human gastric cells, Relation to first pass metabolism. *Gastroenterology*, **111**, 863–70.

Hughes, J. and Cook, C. (1997). The efficacy of disulfiram: A review of outcome studies. *Addiction,* **92**, 381–95.

Johnson, B., Daoud, N. and Akher, F. (2004). Oral topiramate reduces the consequences of drinking and improves the quality of life of alcohol-dependent individual. *Archives of General Psychiatry*, **61**, 905–12.

Johnson, B., Roache, J., Dauod, N., Zanca, N. and Valezquez, M. (2002). Ondansetron reduces the craving of biologically predisposed alcoholics. *Psychopharmacology*, **60**(4), 408–13.

Kabel, D. and Petty, F. (1996). A placebo-controlled, double-blind study of fluoxetine in severe alcohol dependence: Adjunctive pharmacotherapy during and after inpatient treatment. *Alcoholism: Clinical and Experimental Research*, **20**(4), 780.

Kiefer, F. and Wiedemann, K. (2004). Combined therapy: What does acamprosate and naltrexone combination tell us? *Alcohol and Alcoholism*, **39**(6), 542–47.

Kiefer, F., Jahn, H., Tarnaske, T., *et al.* (2003). Comparing and combining naltrexone and acamprosate in relapse prevention of alcoholism. *Archives of General Psychiatry*, **60**, 92–99.

King, A., Volpicelli, J., Frazer, A. and O'Brien, C. (1997). Effect of naltrexone on subjective alcohol response in subjects at high and low risk for future alcohol dependence. *Psychopharmacology*, **129**, 15–22.

Kranzler, H., Burleson, J., Brown, J. and Babor, T. (1996). Fluoxetine treatment seems to reduce the beneficial effects of cognitive–behavioural therapy in type B alcoholics. *Alcoholism: Clinical and Experimental Research*, **20**, 1534–41.

Krystal, J., Cramer, J., Krol, W., Kirk, G. and Rosenheck, R. (2001). Naltrexone in the treatment of alcohol dependence. *New England Journal of Medicine*, **345**, 1734–39.

Latt, N., Jurd, S., Houseman, J. and Wutzke, S. (2002). Naltrexone in alcohol dependence: A randomised-controlled trial of effectiveness in a standard clinical setting. *Medical Journal of Australia*, **176**(11), 530–34.

Lhuintre, J., Daoust, M., Moore, N., Chretien, P., Saligaut, C. and Tran, G. (1985). Ability of calcium *bis* acetyl homotaurine, a GABA agonist, to prevent relapse in weaned alcoholics. *Lancet,* **1**, 1014–16.

Martindale (2002). *The Complete Drug Reference*, 33rd edn. Chicago: Pharmaceutical Press, 653–704.

Mason, B. (2001). Treatment of alcohol-dependent outpatients with acamprosate. *Journal of Clinical Psychiatry*, **62**(Suppl.20), S42–48.

Mason, B., Salvato, F., Williams, L., Ritvo, E. and Cutler, R. (1999). A double blind, placebo-controlled study of oral nalmefene for alcohol dependence. *Archives of General Psychiatry*, **56**, 719–24.

Mizoi, T., Tatsuno, Y., Adachi, J., *et al.* (1983). Alcohol sensitivity related to polymorphism of alcohol metabolizing enzymes in Japanese. *Pharmacology, Biochemistry and Behaviour*, **18**, 127–33.

Morris, P., Hopwood, M., Whelan, G., Gardiner, J. and Drummond, E. (2001). Naltrexone for alcohol dependence: a randomised controlled trial. *Addiction,* **96**(11), 1565.

Mueller, T., Stout, R., Rudden, S., Brown, R., Gordon, A., Solomon, D. and Recupero, P. (1997). A double-blind, placebo-controlled pilot study of carbamazepine for the treatment of alcohol dependence. *Alcoholism: Clinical and Experimental Research*, **21**(1), 86.

Namkoong, K., Lee, B., Lee, P., Choi, M. and Lee, E. (2003). Korean acamprosate clinical trial investigators. Acamprosate in Korean alcohol-dependent patients: A multicentre, randomized, double-blind, placebo-controlled study. *Alcohol and Alcoholism*, **38**, 135–41.

Olive, M., Nannini, M., Ou., C., Koenig, H. and Hodge, C. (2002). Effects of acute acamprosate and homotaurine on ethanol intake and ethanol-stimulated mesolimbic dopamine release. *European Journal of Pharmacology*, **437**, 55–61.

O'Malley, S., Jaffe, A., Rode, S. and Rounsaville, B. (1996). Experience of a 'slip' among alcoholics treated with naltrexone or placebo. *American Journal of Psychiatry*, **153**, 281–83.

Oslin, D., Berritine, W., Kranzler, H., *et al.* (2003). A functional polymorphism of the μ-opioid receptor gene is associated with naltrexone response in alcohol-dependent patients. *Neuropsychopharmacology*, **28**, 1546–52.

Pettinati, H., Dundon, W. and Lipkin, C. (2004). Gender differences in response to sertraline pharmacotherapy in type A alcohol dependence. *American Journal of Addictions*, **13**(3), 236–47.

Pettinati, H., Volpicelli, J., Kranzler, H., Luck, G., Rukstalis, M. and Cnaan, A. (2000). Sertraline treatment for alcohol dependence: Interactive effects of medication and alcoholic subtype. *Alcoholism: Clinical and Experimental Research*, **24**(7), 1041–49.

Poldrugo, F. (1997). Acamprosate treatment in a long-term, community-based alcohol rehabilitation programme. *Addiction,* **92**, 1537–46.

Poulsen, H., Loft, S., Andersen, J. and Andersen, M. (1992). Disulfiram therapy – adverse drug reactions and interactions. *Acta Psychiatrica Scandinavica*, **86**, 59–66.

Rubio, G., Jimenez-Arriero, M., Palomo, T., Manzanares, J. and Ferre, F. (2004). Effects of topiramate in the treatment of alcohol dependence. *Pharmacopsychiatry*, **37**, 37–40.

Rubio, G., Jimenez-Arriero, M., Ponce, G. and Palomo, T. (2001). Naltrexone versus acamprosate: One year follow-up of alcohol dependence treatment. *Alcohol and Alcoholism*, **36**(5), 419–25.

Saxon, A., Sloan, K., Reoux, J. and Haver, V. (1998). Disulfiram use in patients with abnormal liver function test results. *Journal of Clinical Psychiatry*, **59**, 313–16.

Schuckit, M. (1996). Recent development in pharmacology of alcohol dependence. *Journal of Consulting and Clinical Psychology*, **64**, 669–76.

Sereny, G., Sharma, V., Holt, J. and Gordis, E. (1986). Mandatory supervised Antabuse therapy in an outpatient program: A pilot study. *Alcoholism: Clinical and Experimental Research*, **10**, 290–92.

de Sousa, A. and de Sousa, A. (2004). One year pragmatic trial of naltrexone versus disulfiram in the treatment of alcohol dependence. *Alcohol and Alcoholism*, **39**(6), 528–31.

Tempesta, E., Janiri, L., Bignamini, A., Chabac, S. and Potgieter, A. (2000). Acamprosate and relapse prevention in the treatment of alcohol dependence: A placebo-controlled study. *Alcohol and Alcoholism*, **35**, 202–09.

Volpicelli, J., Alterman, A., Hayashida, M. and O'Brien, C. (1992). Naltrexone in the treatment of alcohol dependence. *Archives of General Psychiatry*, **49**, 876–80.

Volpicelli, J., Pettinati, H., McLellan, A. and O'Brien, C. (1997). *BRENDA Manual: Compliance Enhancement Techniques with Pharmacotherapy for Alcohol and Drug Dependence*. Philadelphia: Guilford Press.

Volpicelli, J., Watson, N., King, A., Sherman, C. and O'Brien, C. (1995). Effect of naltrexone on alcohol 'high' in alcoholics. *American Journal of Psychiatry*, **152**, 613–15.

Whitworth, A., Fischer, F., Lesch, O., Nimmerrichter, A., Oberbauer, H. and Platz, T. (1996). Comparison of acamprosate and placebo in long-term treatment of alcohol dependence. *Lancet*, **347**, 1438–42.

Williams, S. (2005). Medications for treating alcohol dependence. *American Family Physician*, **72**, 1775–80.

Wright, C., Vafier, J. and Lake, C. (1988). Disulfiram-induced fulminating hepatitis: guidelines for liver-panel monitoring. *Journal of Clinical Psychiatry*, **49**, 430–34.

Zeise, M., Kasparov, S., Capogna, M. and Zieglgansberger, W. (1993). Acamprosate (calcium-acetyl homotaurinate) decreases postsynaptic potentials in the rat neocortex: possible involvement of excitatory amino acid receptors. *European Journal of Pharmacology*, **231**, 47–52.

10 Wernicke–Korsakoff syndrome

Colin R. Martin and Colin A. Graham

This chapter will explore a drastic consequence of alcohol abuse and dependence that has widespread implications for both clinical care and clinical outcome. The Wernicke–Korsakoff syndrome (WKS), while not exclusively observed in those with problem and dependent drinking, has been recognised as an outcome that can result from excessive alcohol consumption coupled with dietary insufficiency (Harper, 2007; Martin *et al.*, 2003; McKeon *et al.*, 2007; Sher, 2004; Stacey and Sullivan, 2004). The neurocognitive (Heap *et al.*, 2002) and neurostructural (Caulo *et al.*, 2005) consequences of WKS often result in irreversible deficits if the early signs of the syndrome, Wernicke's encephalopathy, are not rapidly diagnosed and treated.

Identification of WKS early enough in the clinical presentation trajectory can result in complete reversal with treatment, so understanding of this surprisingly common consequence of alcohol abuse is crucial (Cook and Thomson, 1997). Post-mortem studies have revealed that around 2 per cent of the general population has lesions associated with Wernicke's encephalopathy (Harper *et al.*, 1986; Victor *et al.*, 1971). However the incidence in alcohol misusers is dramatically higher, at greater than 10 per cent (Cook and Thompson, 1997). WKS represents just one type of alcohol-related damage to the brain; others include stroke (Lofti and Meyer, 1989), hepatic encephalopathy (Butterworth, 1993), Marchiafava–Bignami disease (Victor, 1993, 1994) and central pontine myelinolysis (Nakada and Knight, 1984; Wright *et al.*, 1979). This presents a problem in differentiating retrospectively between WKS and other forms of alcohol-related brain damage, particularly as the symptoms of WKS vary from patient to patient.

Aetiology of brain damage

Thiamine deficiency

The mechanism of brain damage in WKS is through dietary insufficiency of thiamine, otherwise known as vitamin B1 (Cook and Thomson, 1997; Cook *et al.*, 1998; Thomson, 2000). Thiamine is crucial to the structural integrity of blood vessels and capillaries throughout the body, including the brain (Watanabe and Kanabe, 1978). Deficits can lead to leakage of blood from vessels and capillaries, resulting in damage to surrounding tissues. Alcohol can inhibit thiamine uptake from the diet, reduce absorption of thiamine from the gastrointestinal tract, and decrease thiamine uptake at the cellular level (Singleton and Martin, 2001; Thomson, 2000). Any activity associated with excessive alcohol consumption, such as vomiting, may result in further nutritional deficit and decreased levels of available thiamine. It should be remembered that though alcohol is technically classified as a food – since it has calorific value – it has no nutritional value. Substitution of nutritional food by alcohol is not uncommon in people with alcohol dependency (Sgouros *et al.*, 2004), thus exacerbating the risks of thiamine deficiency through a malnourished state. A number of brain regions are damaged by thiamine deficiency, including the cerebellum (Butterworth, 1993), the cerebral cortex (Halliday *et al.*, 1994; Langlais *et al.*, 1996) and the mamillary bodies (Calingasan *et al.*, 1996; Jauhar and Montaldi, 2000; Park *et al.*, 2001).

Retrograde amnesia

Martin and Hewitt (1996) describe features of the amnesic syndrome associated with WKS in detail. However, in fully established WKS the memory loss presents as an anterograde amnesia (patchy retrograde amnesia may also be present). An ironic artefact of this retrograde amnesia, if present, is that the patient may not remember being an excessive drinker! The anterograde amnesia begins at the time irreversible brain damage occurs. The presence of such profound neurocognitive deficits in function invariably means that long-term rehabilitation, institutionalisation or, at least, high-level supported community care are required. A patient experiencing the anterograde amnesia associated with WKS may not recognise the nurse they see every day over several months; on each occasion the nurse will be greeted as a stranger. WKS in individuals with alcohol problems is unique in one important respect; in this group this profound state of brain damage is a consequence of a behavioural problem, whereas in all other examples of the presentation, an underlying pathological disease state is implicated. For example, thiamine deficiency may occur in patients with cancer (Engel *et al.*, 1991), people with acquired immune deficiency syndrome (Alcaide *et al.*, 2003; Kril, 1996) or hyperemesis gravidarum (Yoon *et al.*, 2005) and in renal patients on dialysis (Jagadha *et al.*, 1987; Ueda *et al.*, 2006). Alcohol abuse and dependence is also notable in that this group represents the majority of patients who present with WKS (Harper *et al.*, 1995).

Wernicke's encephalopathy and Korsakoff's psychosis

An important consideration for the health professional is to reflect that WKS in most instances describes two distinct – but related – disease processes, Wernicke's encephalopathy and Korsakoff's psychosis (Feinberg, 1980). Korsakoff's psychosis represents a chronic irreversible condition consequential to non-identified or ineffectively treated Wernicke's encephalopathy. The window during which to treat acute Wernicke's encephalopathy is relatively short but, if treated effectively, it is entirely reversible in many cases. Therefore, anyone presenting with Korsakoff's psychosis will generally have had Wernicke's encephalopathy – but not all those presenting with Wernicke's encephalopathy will develop Korsakoff's psychosis. There are rare exceptions where someone may develop Korsakoff's psychosis without an episode of Wernicke's encephalopathy (Blansjaar and van Dijk, 1992). The problem remains that diagnostic accuracy has been suggested to be low (Torvik, 1991). Therefore, accurate identification of acute

Wernicke's encephalopathy is crucial to prevent the chronic and debilitating presentation of Korsakoff's psychosis.

Presenting symptom profile of Wernicke-Korsakoff syndrome

A great variety of symptoms may accompany this syndrome (Cook, 2000). One particular problem with identification of WKS is that the symptoms often mimic those of alcohol intoxication; consequently, the health professional may just believe the individual to be drunk, rather than in the initial stages of a life-threatening and chronic state of brain damage. The main signs of acute Wernicke's encephalopathy are:

- ophthalmoplegia or nystagmus
- confusion or impaired consciousness
- ataxia.

However, an immediate problem for the health professional is that only a minority of patients (less than 20 per cent) will present with this constellation of signs (Naidoo *et al.*, 1991). This further complicates the process of diagnosis. An important indicator that someone with an alcohol problem may have the initial stages of WKS is that they do not appear to sober up after cessation of alcohol intake. A comprehensive assessment is required since the implications of missing a diagnosis of Wernicke's encephalopathy are far-reaching. Therefore, a diagnosis of Wernicke's encephalopathy cannot be ruled out; it should be considered for any patient with a history of alcohol abuse or dependency presenting with any of the main signs or symptoms, including memory disturbance, hypotension, hypothermia or unconsciousness. The patient who develops full irreversible WKS (Korsakoff's psychosis) will present with a variety of symptoms that may include:

- anterograde amnesia
- loss of spontaneity and initiative
- confabulation.

Clinical features may be present which are of interest in defining the disorder. They also offer an account of the interaction between residual neurocognitive function and cognitive appraisal mechanisms. Confabulation is a particular case in point, describing the process whereby the patient fills the vacuum in memory function as a consequence of anterograde amnesia by providing recollections that are clearly false (Feinberg, 1980; Talland, 1961).

Anterograde amnesia is an amnesic syndrome in which new memories are not formed, which generally dates from the onset of Korsakoff's psychosis; this is a distinguishing feature of the presentation. Events occurring prior to the onset of WKS are usually preserved and recalled. The anterograde amnesia that accompanies WKS is not, contrary to popular perspectives, entirely global. There is a great deal of evidence that patients with WKS are able to learn certain visuoperceptual learning tasks (Fama *et al.*, 2006), for example. It seems clear that the extent to which the anterograde amnesia is global is most notable in relation to autobiographical memory, although the general mechanisms of storage and processing are impaired (Martin and Hewitt, 1996). The presence of a patchy retrograde amnesia, while by no means always present, is often characterised by cognitive distortions; for example, a genuinely recalled true event may be described as occurring very recently, when in fact the event occurred several years previously. Korsakoff's psychosis also often presents with lack of spontaneity (Blansjaar *et al.*, 1987; Talland, 1960; Zubaran *et al.*, 1997). This may be in part consequential of a lack of recall of personal history as events occur or may represent more widespread damage to neural structures involved in the motivational aspects of behaviour. The main Korsakoff's psychosis symptoms of anterograde amnesia, lack of spontaneity and confabulation will generally range from mild to severe.

Patients with WKS who reside in institutions will have an awareness of their surroundings and will be able to learn their way around. This is an interesting and useful phenomenon within the context of anterograde amnesia because it clearly shows that some new information is being assimilated and recalled. Patients will generally be unaware, however, of the passage of time, and in many respects they will appear 'lost in time'. There are number of cognitive deficits (Brand *et al.*, 2003; Cermak *et al.*, 1988; Krabbendam *et al.*, 2000; Parsons, 1998) associated with WKS beyond that of the gross anterograde amnesia.

Confusion and intravenous glucose infusions

Patients who chronically abuse alcohol are often confused, and one of the presenting signs of acute hypoglycaemia is confusion. Frequently patients with confusion are brought to emergency departments by their friends, by prehospital medical services or by the police. Hypoglycaemia is common in chronic alcoholics; they have depleted reserves of hepatic and muscle glycogen and are chronically undernourished, and lack the initiative and desire to consume nutritionally useful food. It is therefore common for patients (alcoholic and otherwise) presenting in a confused state to the emergency department to be given intravenous glucose infusions. Commendable and clinically efficacious as this undoubtedly is for acute hypoglycaemia, this approach may actually precipitate an acute onset of Wernicke's encephalopathy because intravenously administered glucose increases thiamine requirements (Koguchi *et al.*, 2004; Truedsson *et al.*, 2002).

Caution is therefore necessary for any patient presenting with a confused state and a history of alcohol misuse. Parenteral thiamine should be co-administered to chronic alcohol abusers presenting with hypoglycaemia, along with an intravenous glucose infusion (see below).

Treatment of Wernicke-Korsakoff syndrome

The most effective treatment of WKS is by intervention to prevent the transition of Wernicke's encephalopathy to Korsakoff's psychosis. The standard approach is to treat the underlying thiamine deficiency with high-potency thiamine and multivitamins (vitamin B Complex Strong, known commercially as Pabrinex in the UK). Pabrinex contains thiamine, riboflavin (vitamin B2), pyroxidine (vitamin B6) and nicotinamide. The treatment should be administered either intravenously or intramuscularly, but intravenous administration is necessary if hypoglycaemia co-exists, or if there is any possibility that the patient may abscond rapidly from medical care (as frequently occurs in the emergency department).

Two pairs of this high-potency vitamin B complex should be given three times a day over the first 2 days. Each pair should be mixed in 500 mL of intravenous fluid and administered over 30–60 minutes. These intravenous bags become a deep yellow colour after adding the Pabrinex (the so-called 'banana bag') and gloves should be worn when preparing the solution as reconstituted

Pabrinex can stain the fingers and hands. The solution itself has a noxious odour. If a response to the initial doses is observed, one pair of Pabrinex ampoules should be administered once a day for the following 5 days. Anaphylactic reactions to Pabrinex are not uncommon; consequently, facilities must be available to deal effectively, promptly and safely with any life-threatening anaphylaxis that should occur. In particular, intramuscular epinephrine (adrenaline) should be immediately available and should be given in a dose of 0.5 mL of the 1 in 1000 preparation. This is repeated after 5 minutes if there is no or little improvement. There is no evidence to suggest that oral administration of vitamin B complex is an alternative effective treatment to intravenous or intramuscular administration. Thiamine itself is a necessary cofactor, allowing its uptake by the gut, and therefore oral supplementation in the presence of chronic dietary deficiency will be ineffective until the parenteral thiamine has had a chance to take effect. The notion of oral supplementation of thiamine as a prophylactic treatment for Wernicke's encephalopathy or WKS is ill-conceived and may be born out of the clinician's need to offer some treatment rather than none.

Surprisingly, the selection criteria for patients for prophylactic intravenous or intramuscular administration of Pabrinex have no consistent evidence base, although within the context of alcohol dependency it would seem rational to include all patients undergoing detoxification. In areas with a high prevalence of chronic alcohol abuse, many emergency departments and acute admission units routinely administer intravenous Pabrinex to all patients admitted acutely. A further complication is that the recommendations of the Royal College of Physicians (2001) suggest 200 mg of thiamine in concert with 30 mg of vitamin B a day during the detoxification period, for preventing neuropsychiatric complications of thiamine deficiency (i.e. Wernicke's encephalopathy and WKS). Thomson and Marshall (2006a) point out that the kinetic limitations of metabolism of thiamine administered orally may not achieve the desired therapeutic goal, as per those recommendations.

Others have also observed reduced thiamine availability in alcohol misusers (e.g. Todd and Butterworth, 1999a,b). A further issue is compliance with an oral regimen. Local protocols may vary with regard to oral thiamine and vitamin B prescription.

Finally, there remains some concern in terms of the paucity of the evidence base regarding the dose, route, duration and frequency of thiamine treatment for WKS as a consequence of alcohol abuse (Day *et al.*, 2004).

Hidden groups

Given the issue of poor identification of WKS, one issue of relevance to the perpetuation of avoidable brain damage concerns those groups of heavy drinkers who may not routinely come into contact with health professionals. One particular group is the residents of hostels where alcohol consumption, although discouraged, does not mean they forego their right of abode. There are many such hostels, or 'wet houses', that operate along these lines. It is difficult to reach such groups not only in the provision of clinical services and clinical assessment, but also in terms of primary research in order to gauge the incidence and degree of WKS in these populations. The intrinsic problems associated with identification and treatment of WKS may not be any less among the residents of 'dry houses' (hostels where use of alcohol is forbidden and transgression of the 'no alcohol' policy usually results in the loss of accommodation). The

Salvation Army, for example, who are a huge provider of social services in the UK, run a number of hostels populated by people with a history of problematic drinking. The historical roots of the Salvation Army, based as it is on abstinence lines, means that philosophically non-conflicting hostel provision should be in the form of 'dry houses'. Anyone who loses their 'dry house' hostel place due to resuming alcohol consumption may readily disappear off the radar of care providers, including clinical services with a skills base that is sensitive to detecting alcohol-related brain damage generally, and WKS in particular.

The issues associated with identification of thiamine deficiency in relation to alcohol abuse generally and in these vulnerable community-based groups have been highlighted by Thomson and Marshall (2006a,b). These authors emphasise that detoxification treatment of people with possible Wernicke's encephalopathy should be performed on an inpatient basis. The risk assessment for deciding between an inpatient or outpatient detoxification trial should be based on the central cluster of symptoms associated with this disease.

The explicit specification proposed by Thomson and Marshall (2006a) for selecting individuals for inpatient detoxification and for excluding community detoxification is:

- delirium tremens or a history of delirium tremens
- definite or presumptive diagnosis of Wernicke's encephalopathy
- severe alcohol dependence
- severe physical or mental illness
- a history of seizures
- unsuccessful previous attempts at detoxification.

However, Thomson and Marshall (2006a) emphasise that there are still patients at risk of Wernicke's encephalopathy in the community, for example, those who refuse inpatient detoxification, those detoxified in the community due to lack of inpatient detoxification, and those who refuse intravenous or intramuscular thiamine. Many of these patients will be in frequent contact with their local emergency departments, and it is important for any coherent alcohol management strategy to include the emergency department and its staff in their treatment protocols and systems to avoid missing these vulnerable patient groups.

Use of screening questionnaires

The detection of thiamine deficiency by valid and reliable self-report or a questionnaire administered by a health professional may offer a valuable addition to a comprehensive screening battery for use in people with alcohol problems who may be at risk of WKS. Indeed to detect thiamine deficiency, clinical research studies use questionnaires in combination with anthropometric measurements and biochemical assays (Andrande Juguan *et al.*, 1999). However, the questionnaire is often unwieldy in terms of the number of items in the measure, the length of time to administer the measure, the reliance on accurate patient report, and the use of complex scoring algorithms that often necessitate dedicated statistical software.

However, one recent innovation in the detection of thiamine deficiency by questionnaire is the Thiamine Deficiency Questionnaire (TDQ). This was developed by Sgouros and colleagues in(2004). Evaluated against a 'gold standard' of thiamine polyphosphate levels in red blood cells in severely alcohol-dependent individuals, the TDQ was developed primarily for Wernicke's encephalopathy and alcohol-related problems. The questionnaire consists of 16 items, most of which depend on self-report. The brevity and ease of administration of this tool do not impact significantly on its screening accuracy. A subset of 8 items was found to have a positive predictive value for detecting thiamine deficiency of 74 per cent. Two of the items – 'Missed meals due to lack of funds' and 'Co-occurrence of other nutritionally related conditions' – had very high positive predictive values, suggesting these items may function well as a minimal assessment tool, for example for use within invariably busy emergency departments.

Importantly, items about nutrition had greater predictive value than items about alcohol use, indicating the relative importance of nutritional status in thiamine deficiency compared to the amount and pattern of alcohol use. Sgouros *et al.* (2004) advocate further development of the TDQ to improve the validity of the instrument across a broader range of individuals presenting with alcohol-related problems. Nevertheless, the TDQ demonstrates impressively that short, easily administered questionnaires may have an invaluable role in the early detection of thiamine deficiency in alcohol-dependent people. Further research in this area is necessary and highly desirable.

Rehabilitation

The therapeutic goals of rehabilitation in patients with established WKS focus on the memory deficits (Cermak, 1980; Goldstein *et al.*, 1985; Kashima *et al.*, 1999; van der Linden *et al.*, 1994). Some of them will require further support to help with their alcohol problem, although, paradoxically (as mentioned earlier) some may have forgotten they were drinkers, so the alcohol consumption problem is resolved.

Given the range of difficulties that accompany a diagnosis of WKS, and the fact that there is large variation in terms of symptom presentation, individualised patient care is always necessary. There is, however, some positive evidence regarding WKS. It is clear that, over time, new learning can take place (Fama *et al.*, 2006). Consequently, memory training is not a noble but ineffective therapeutic gesture, but an intervention that may facilitate improvements in recall that, in turn, help to develop and facilitate re-learning of skills and activities of daily living and therefore improve quality of life. These approaches may be instrumental in helping the WKS patient to move from an institutional environment to some form of community-based and more independent supported-living accommodation.

One more important point to raise is that WKS, devastating as it is, is distinct from other progressive neurological disorders, in that established Korsakoff's psychosis does not represent an inevitable pathway to more severe impairments in residual neurocognitive capacity over time.

Conclusions

WKS represents a potentially devastating neurological consequence of thiamine deficiency as a consequence of alcohol misuse. There are pressing clinical issues in terms of recognising the early stages of the presentation – acute Wernicke's encephalopathy – when treatment can be effective and so prevent the chronic and debilitating development of Korsakoff's psychosis.

References and further reading

Alcaide, M.L., Jayaweera, D., Espinoza, L. and Kolber, M. (2003). Wernicke's encephalopathy in AIDS: A preventable cause of fatal neurological deficit. *International Journal of Studies on AIDS*, **14**, 712–13.

Andrade Juguan, J., Lukito, W. and Schultink, W. (1999). Thiamine deficiency is prevalent in a selected group of urban Indonesian elderly people. *Journal of Nutrition*, **129**, 366–71.

Blansjaar, B.A. and Van Dijk, J.G. (1992). Korsakoff minus Wernicke syndrome. *Alcohol and Alcoholism*, **27**, 435–37.

Blansjaar, B.A., Horjus, M.C. and Nijhuis, H.G. (1987). Prevalence of the Korsakoff syndrome in the Hague, the Netherlands. *Acta Psychiatrica Scandinavica*, **75**, 604–07.

Brand, M., Fujiwara, E., Kalbe, E., Steingass, H.P., Kessler, J. and Markowitsch, H.J. (2003). Cognitive estimation and affective judgments in alcoholic Korsakoff patients. *Journal of Clinical* and *Experimental Neuropsychology*, **25**, 324–34.

Butterworth, R.F. (1993). Pathophysiology of cerebellar dysfunction in the Wernicke–Korsakoff syndrome. *Canadian Journal of Neurological Sciences*, **20**(Suppl.3), S123–26.

Calingasan, N.Y., Gandy, S.E., Baker, H., *et al.* (1996). Novel neuritic clusters with accumulations of amyloid precursor protein and amyloid precursor-like protein 2 immunoreactivity in brain regions damaged by thiamine deficiency. *American Journal of Pathology*, **149**, 1063–71.

Caulo, M., Van Hecke, J., Toma, L., *et al.* (2005). Functional MRI study of diencephalic amnesia in Wernicke–Korsakoff syndrome. *Brain*, **128**, 1584–94.

Cermak, L.S. (1980). Improving retention in alcoholic Korsakoff patients. *Journal of Studies on Alcohol,* **41**, 159–69.

Cermak, L.S., Bleich, R.P. and Blackford, S.P. (1988). Deficits in the implicit retention of new associations by alcoholic Korsakoff patients. *Brain and Cognition*, **7**, 312–23.

Cook, C.C. (2000). Prevention and treatment of Wernicke–Korsakoff syndrome. *Alcohol and Alcoholism*, **35**, 19–20.

Cook, C.C. and Thomson, A.D. (1997). B-complex vitamins in the prophylaxis and treatment of Wernicke–Korsakoff syndrome. *British Journal of Hospital Medicine*, **57**, 461–65.

Cook, C.C., Hallwood, P.M. and Thomson, A.D. (1998). B vitamin deficiency and neuropsychiatric syndromes in alcohol misuse. *Alcohol and Alcoholism*, **33**, 317–36.

Day, E., Bentham, P., Callaghan, R., Kuruvilla, T. and George, S. (2004). Thiamine for Wernicke–Korsakoff syndrome in people at risk from alcohol abuse. *Cochrane Database of Systematic Reviews*, CD004033.

Engel, P.A., Grunnet, M. and Jacobs, B. (1991). Wernicke–Korsakoff syndrome complicating T-cell lymphoma: Unusual or unrecognised? *Southern Medical Journal*, **84**, 253–56.

Fama, R., Pfefferbaum, A. and Sullivan, E.V. (2006). Visuoperceptual learning in alcoholic Korsakoff syndrome. *Alcoholism: Clinical and Experimental Research*, **30**, 680–87.

Feinberg, J.F. (1980). The Wernicke–Korsakoff syndrome. *American Family Physician*, **22**, 129–33.

Goldstein, G., Ryan, C., Turner, S.M., Kanagy, M., Barry, K. and Kelly, L. (1985). Three methods of memory training for severely amnesic patients. *Behavior Modification*, **9**, 357–74.

Halliday, G., Cullen, K. and Harding, A. (1994). Neuropathological correlates of memory dysfunction in the Wernicke–Korsakoff syndrome. *Alcohol and Alcoholism*, **2**, 245–51.

Harper, C. (2007). The neurotoxicity of alcohol. *Human and Experimental Toxicology*, **26**, 251–57.

Harper, C., Fornes, P., Duyckaerts, C., Lecomte, D. and Hauw, J.J. (1995). An international perspective on the prevalence of the Wernicke–Korsakoff syndrome. *Metabolic Brain Disease*, **10**, 17–24.

Harper, C.G., Giles, M. and Finlay-Jones, R. (1986). Clinical signs in the Wernicke–Korsakoff complex: A retrospective analysis of 131 cases diagnosed at necropsy. *Journal of Neurology, Neurosurgery and Psychiatry*, **49**, 341–45.

Heap, L.C., Pratt, O.E., Ward, R.J., *et al.* (2002). Individual susceptibility to Wernicke–Korsakoff syndrome and alcoholism-induced cognitive deficit: impaired thiamine utilization found in alcoholics and alcohol abusers. *Psychiatric Genetics*, **12**, 217–24.

Jagadha, V., Deck, J.H., Halliday, W.C. and Smyth, H.S. (1987). Wernicke's encephalopathy in patients on peritoneal dialysis or hemodialysis. *Annals of Neurology*, **21**, 78–84.

Jauhar, P. and Montaldi, D. (2000). Wernicke–Korsakoff syndrome and the use of brain imaging. *Alcohol and Alcoholism Supplement*, **35**, 21–23.

Kashima, H., Kato, M., Yoshimasu, H. and Muramatsu, T. (1999). Current trends in cognitive rehabilitation for memory disorders. *Keio Journal of Medicine*, **48**, 79–86.

Koguchi, K., Nakatsuji, Y., Abe, K. and Sakoda, S. (2004). Wernicke's encephalopathy after glucose infusion. *Neurology*, **62**, 512.

Krabbendam, L., Visser, P.J., Derix, M.M., *et al.* (2000). Normal cognitive performance in patients with chronic alcoholism in contrast to patients with Korsakoff syndrome. *Journal of Neuropsychiatry and Clinical Neurosciences*, **12**, 44–50.

Kril, J.J. (1996). Neuropathology of thiamine deficiency disorders. *Metabolic Brain Disease*, **11**, 9–17.

Langlais, P.J., Zhang, S.X. and Savage, L.M. (1996). Neuropathology of thiamine deficiency: An update on the comparative analysis of human disorders and experimental models. *Metabolic Brain Disease*, **11**, 19–37.

Lotfi, J. and Meyer, J.S. (1989). Cerebral hemodynamic and metabolic effects of chronic alcoholism. *Cerebrovascular and Brain Metabolism Reviews*, **1**, 2–25.

Martin, C.R. and Hewitt, G. (1996). Alcohol, memory and cognition. In: A. Bonner and J. Waterhouse (eds). *Addictive Behaviour: Molecules to Mankind*. Basingstoke: Macmillan).

Martin, P.R., Singleton, C.K. and Hiller-Sturmhofel, S. (2003). The role of thiamine deficiency in alcoholic brain disease. *Alcohol Research and Health*, **27**, 134–42.

McKeon, A., Frye, M.A. and Delanty, N. (2007). The alcohol withdrawal syndrome. *Journal of Neurology, Neurosurgery and Psychiatry*. DOI: doi:10.1136/jnnp.2007.128322. Available online at: http://jnnp.bmj.com/cgi/content/abstract/jnnp.2007.128322v1 (last accessed September 2008).

Mimura, M., Komatsu, S., Kato, M., Yashimasu, H., Wakamatsu, N. and Kashima, H. (1998). Memory for subject performed tasks in patients with Korsakoff syndrome. *Cortex*, **34**, 297–03.

Naidoo, D.P., Bramdev, A. and Cooper, K. (1991). Wernicke's encephalopathy and alcohol-related disease. *Postgraduate Medical Journal*, **67**, 978–81.

Nakada, T. and Knight, R.T. (1984). Alcohol and the central nervous system. *Medicine Clinics of North America*, **68**, 121–31.

Park, S.H., Kim, M., Na., D.L. and Jeon, B.S. (2001). Magnetic resonance reflects the pathological evolution of Wernicke encephalopathy. *Journal of Neuroimaging*, **11**, 406–11.

Parsons, O.A. (1998). Neurocognitive deficits in alcoholics and social drinkers: A continuum? *Alcoholism: Clinical and Experimental Research*, **22**, 954–61.

Royal College of Physicians (2001). *Alcohol – can the NHS afford it? Recommendations for a coherent alcohol strategy for hospitals*. London: Royal College of Physicians.

Sgouros, X., Baines, M., Bloor, R.N., Mcauley, R., Ogundipe, L.O. and Willmott, S. (2004). Evaluation of a clinical screening instrument to identify states of thiamine deficiency in inpatients with severe alcohol dependence syndrome. *Alcohol and Alcoholism*, **39**, 227–32.

Sher, L. (2004). Wernicke–Korsakoff syndrome and alcohol-induced persistent dementia. *Australian and New Zealand Journal of Psychiatry*, **38**, 976–77.

Singleton, C.K. and Martin, P.R. (2001). Molecular mechanisms of thiamine utilization. *Current Molecular Medicine*, **1**, 197–207.

Stacey, P.S. and Sullivan, K.A. (2004). Preliminary investigation of thiamine and alcohol intake in clinical and healthy samples. *Psychological Reports*, **94**, 845–48.

Talland, G.A. (1960). Psychological studies of Korsakoff's psychosis (V), Spontaneity and activity rate. *Journal of Nervous and Mental Disease*, **130**, 16–25.

Talland, G.A. (1961). Confabulation in the Wernicke–Korsakoff syndrome. *Journal of Nervous and Mental Disease*, **132**, 361–81.

Thomson, A.D. (2000). Mechanisms of vitamin deficiency in chronic alcohol misusers and the development of the Wernicke–Korsakoff syndrome. *Alcohol and Alcoholism*, **35**(Suppl.), 2–7.

Thomson, A.D. and Marshall, E.J. (2006a). The treatment of patients at risk of developing Wernicke's encephalopathy in the community. *Alcohol and Alcoholism*, **41**, 159–67.

Thomson, A.D. and Marshall, E.J. (2006b). The natural history and pathophysiology of Wernicke's encephalopathy and Korsakoff's psychosis. *Alcohol and Alcoholism*, **41**, 151–58.

Todd, K. and Butterworth, R.F. (1999a). Mechanisms of selective neuronal cell death due to thiamine deficiency. *Annals of the New York Academy of Sciences*, **893**, 404–11.

Todd, K.G. and Butterworth, R.F. (1999b). Early microglial response in experimental thiamine deficiency: An immunohistochemical analysis. *Glia*, **25**, 190–98.

Torvik, A. (1991). Wernicke's encephalopathy – prevalence and clinical spectrum. *Alcohol and Alcoholism*, **1**(Suppl.), 381–84.

Truedsson, M., Ohlsson, B. and Sjoberg, K. (2002). Wernicke's encephalopathy presenting with severe dysphagia: A case report. *Alcohol and Alcoholism*, **37**, 295–96.

Ueda, K., Takada, D., Mii, A., *et al.* (2006). Severe thiamine deficiency resulted in Wernicke's encephalopathy in a chronic dialysis patient. *Clinical and Experimental Nephrology*, **10**, 290–93.

van der Linden, M., Meulemans, T. and Lorrain, D. (1994). Acquisition of new concepts by two amnesic patients. *Cortex*, **30**, 305–17.

Victor, M. (1993). Persistent altered mentation due to ethanol. *Neurologic Clinics*, **11**, 639–61.

Victor, M. (1994). Alcoholic dementia. *Canadian Journal of Neurological Sciences*, **21**, 88–99.

Victor, M., Adams, R.D. and Collins, G.H. (1971). The Wernicke–Korsakoff syndrome. A clinical and pathological study of 245 patients, 82 with post-mortem examinations. *Contemporary Neurology Series*, **7**, 1–06.

Watanabe, I. and Kanabe, S. (1978). Early edematous lesion of pyrithiamine induced acute thiamine deficient encephalopathy in the mouse. *Journal of Neuropathology and Experimental Neurology*, **37**, 401–13.

Wright, D.G., Laureno, R. and Victor, M. (1979). Pontine and extrapontine myelinolysis. *Brain*, **102**, 361–85.

Yoon, C.K., Chang, M.H. and Lee, D.C. (2005). Wernicke–Korsakoff syndrome associated with hyperemesis gravidarum. *Korean Journal of Ophthalmology*, **19**, 239–42.

Zubaran, C., Fernandes, J.G. and Rodnight, R. (1997). Wernicke–Korsakoff syndrome. *Postgraduate Medical Journal*, **73**, 27–31.

11 Morbid jealousy

Colin R. Martin

The constellation of psychiatric phenomena and physical disease states that surround the primary diagnosis of alcohol dependency is vast. However, most of these clinical presentations are extremely well researched, and treatment protocols and strategies are clearly defined and generally evaluated to inform evidenced-based practice. However, there remains one psychiatric presentation comorbid with alcohol dependency that remains elusive in terms of a dearth of clinical case material in the literature and a general lack of research into the condition. This is the psychiatric condition known as 'morbid jealousy', particularly within the sphere of alcohol dependency; it is sometimes also known as the 'Othello syndrome' after the extreme and irrational jealousy demonstrated by the character of Othello in William Shakespeare's classic play. Morbid jealousy as a syndrome is not exclusive to alcohol dependency, but its occurrence comorbidly with or without alcohol dependence can lead to extreme forensic behaviour, including murder (Goldney, 1977).

What is morbid jealousy?

Clues for understanding the concept of morbid jealousy can be found within the more familiar definition of jealousy – a common, although often uncomfortable, non-psychopathological emotional state. Jealousy is a normal emotion that describes the feeling of inner discomfort and resentment felt by one person toward another, often perceived to be a rival. Jealousy may even be considered an adaptive and appropriate emotion because it provides an evolutionary protective mechanism to the propagation of the individual's genes by exclusive access to a partner within the context of a sexual relationship.

Morbid jealousy represents a psychopathological departure from this normative state, with several distinctive elements of differentiation from jealousy *per se*. First, morbid jealousy is usually bound up with the perception of a rival within a sexual context. Second, the belief in that rivalry is invariably an error. Third, the morbidly jealous person will go to great lengths to eliminate the threat of rivalry. Fourth, the individual experiencing morbid jealousy will often experience extreme, irrational and intrusive thoughts and feelings. Finally, the morbidly jealous person will exhibit extreme, inappropriate and socially unacceptable behaviour in response to the perception of infidelity.

The partner of the morbidly jealous individual could indeed be unfaithful; the presentation of morbid jealousy is defined by incorrect evidence for infidelity accompanied by socially unacceptable and extreme behaviour. The morbidly jealous person will seek confirmation of their partner's unfaithfulness from unconnected events, chance encounters and illusory correlation between events and circumstances. Evidence that supports the faithfulness of their partner is refuted and dismissed, even when such evidence is incontrovertible. It should be noted that morbid jealousy is a complex phenomenon, and untangling morbid jealousy from *normal* jealousy remains an area of fertile research (Maggini et al., 2006).

Reflecting on such a notion of morbid jealousy, readers may consider that they have encountered not just clients or patients but friends and colleagues with such disturbing cognitive and behavioural phenomena. However, this is generally not the case since the behavioural end-points of the morbidly jealous person can lead to forensic consequences. Further, although a clear epidemiology of morbid jealousy has yet to be established, what has been observed is that there is an increased incidence within certain psychiatric populations, including those with a primary diagnosis of alcohol dependency (Michael et al., 1995).

Gender differences have been speculated on in the prevalence and behavioural outcome of morbid jealousy, and have been couched within speculative theoretical accounts of explanation (Freeman, 1990; Harris, 2003; Sagarin, 2005). However, despite the attraction of gender-related differences when formulating psychological and evolutionary accounts of morbid jealousy, evidence to support fundamental differences between the sexes within this domain of mental health remains equivocal (Harris, 2003; Sagarin, 2005).

Morbid jealousy and alcohol dependence

It has long been recognised that there is a raised incidence of morbid jealousy in people presenting with alcohol abuse and alcohol dependency. One surprising finding regarding the incidence of morbid jealousy in those with alcohol problems concerns the very high levels observed. Michael et al. (1995) found more than 30 per cent of men recruited to their study from alcohol treatment units have the characteristic features of morbid jealousy. An aetiological model of the relationship of alcohol to morbid jealousy is not currently clear, with disputes in the literature as to whether morbid jealousy is secondary to alcohol abuse or not (Cobb, 1979; Michael et al., 1995). The picture of comorbid psychopathology that accompanies a diagnosis of alcohol dependence also complicates the deduction of a consistent and coherent aetiological pathway.

Some authors have attempted to give descriptive explanatory accounts of the relationship of alcohol dependence (and other drugs of abuse) to the presentation of morbid jealousy (Kingham and Gordon, 2004); but these accounts are lacking because of the dearth of available research on any unique association of alcohol dependence to morbid jealousy, and the ever-present confounding factor of comorbidity. However, observed case material within the alcohol abuse arena does provide the basis for future research endeavours to unpack this both interesting and disturbing presentation, with workable hypotheses that may be invaluable for elucidating a viable aetiological pathway.

Distinguishing features of morbid jealousy

An architecture of morbid jealousy comprising four critical features has been described by Mullen (1990):

- First, there is an underlying mental disorder that emerges before or with the morbid jealousy.

- Second – and perhaps more contentiously (in the sense that neither a comprehensive epidemiology or a clear aetiological course of morbid jealousy has yet to be demonstrated) – the salient characteristics of the primary psychiatric disorder co-exist with the morbid jealousy.

- Third, a synchrony in the course of the morbid jealousy to the underlying psychiatric disorder is anticipated.

- Fourth, the experience of jealousy has no basis in reality in terms of evidence of unfaithfulness available to the individual.

Mullen's (1990) description of the four features of morbid jealousy is valuable for understanding the observation of such a presentation within the context of an underlying mental health diagnosis. However, as highlighted earlier, this area of psychological experience is under-researched and it is extremely difficult to determine the incidence of jealousy behaviour which may be indistinguishable from that associated with morbid jealousy, but without the presence of an underlying and co-existing psychiatric diagnosis. It is therefore not unreasonable to assume that alternative and clinically valuable descriptions of morbid jealousy may emerge in the future.

Clinical case vignette 11.1

D.P. is a 50-year-old man with over a 30 year history of alcohol abuse and alcohol dependence. The characteristics of morbid jealousy following comprehensive retrospective history-taking appear to have been present for many years. The presentation of morbid jealousy in terms of negative behavioural outcomes and, in particular, violence towards his partner, are most severe when he is intoxicated. However, during episodes of heavy (but not chemically dependent) drinking, the spectre of morbid jealousy remains. D.P. believes his wife has been having sexual intercourse with several men over many years and that she is chronically unfaithful to him. The behavioural manifestation of his delusion is to check his wife's urine for signs of semen and infection. He follows his wife to the toilet when she needs to urinate and orders her to urinate into a 'chamber pot'. Then he checks the contents for 'signs of betrayal'. His wife is understandably distressed by such behaviour but also indulges him in his unreasonable demands through fear of physical violence.

Summing up so far, morbid jealousy is associated with an underlying psychiatric diagnosis. A pressing feature of the presentation is the unhealthy focus on the notion of a partner's unfaithfulness. Preoccupation with partner infidelity is an overarching theme of presentation within morbid jealousy and it is usually expressed within three main forms of psychopathology, none of which is mutually exclusive, so they may co-exist. They are: 'obsessions', 'delusions' and the notion of 'overvalued ideas'.

Obsessions

The role of obsessions within a model of morbid jealousy is controversial because there is recognition by the patient or client that their concerns over their partner's faithfulness are, without evidential basis, indeed irrational. However, such insights do little to ameliorate the intrusive thoughts experienced by the individual, neither do such insights reduce the amount of embarrassment felt by entertaining such thoughts. However, accompanying such obsessions may be a strong compulsive component that can lead to undesirable behaviour like stalking or inappropriate checking of the partner's behaviour, or even limiting their personal freedom. Consistent with the contemporary formulation of obsessive–compulsive disorders, anxiety has a pivotal role in the expression of obsessional morbid jealousy. In this regard, the presence of obsessions within the context of morbid jealousy may be considered as demonstrating a more neurotic rather than psychotic (though nonetheless debilitating) morbid jealousy state.

Clinical case vignette 11.2

P.H. is a 37-year-old man with 20+ years' history of alcohol abuse/alcohol dependence. He has also been diagnosed with major depression and has received inpatient treatment for his depressive disorder. He has received antidepressant medication over a number of years including selective serotonin-reuptake inhibitors (SSRIs) and the older class of tricyclic antidepressants. He stops taking his antidepressant medication when he begins a heavy drinking period. He experiences intrusive and disturbing thoughts concerning the infidelity of his partner. P.H. also knows that these thoughts concerning his partner are groundless from an evidential point of view, and he feels great distress and guilt entertaining such thoughts. However, the preoccupation with such thoughts has expressed itself through aberrant and inappropriate behaviour, including violence to his partner and stalking her both at work and on the very rare occasions she 'gets a late pass' and goes out for the evening with friends. P.H.'s concerns are so great that his partner is virtually confined to the house, except for going to work (and even then he phones her at work regularly to check on what she is doing, who she has been talking to and when she will be leaving). P.H. will invariably be waiting for her outside the office building where she works as a secretary in order to pick her up and take her home. Sometimes P.H. will also enter his partner's place of employment without invitation to check on her.

Delusions

A dominant delusional infrastructure has been observed within the context of morbid jealousy. The focus of the delusional context is the unfaithfulness of the partner. The delusional context can be quite bizarre, beyond that of a delusion of partner infidelity. It may include various delusions that the partner is carrying out activities to cause the morbidly jealous individual physical harm. Alternatively, a delusional structure may be in place whereby the individual believes the partner has been having many lovers and contracted a sexually transmitted disease. A morbidly jealous male with alcohol dependency, for example, may believe their partner has drugged them to make them impotent. This delusion is interesting since, in the event of actual impotence secondary to the pharmacological effects of alcohol, the delusion is about being drugged, probably in order that the partner can engage in sexual proclivities with many other men. Note that there is no evidence of a relationship between sexual dysfunction and morbid jealousy (Shrestha *et al.*, 1985).

Morbid jealousy with high levels of delusional content has been observed across many psychiatric presentations, including schizophrenia (Alimkhanov, 1980), depression (Munro, 1988) and neuropsychiatric disorders (Hassanyeh *et al.*, 1991) including acquired paranoid disorders following traumatic head injury (Achte *et al.*, 1991) and, of course, it is not unknown in alcohol dependency (Michael *et al.*, 1995). Given issues of dual diagnosis generally, and comorbidity of depression with alcohol dependency in particular, it is not surprising to see a delusional component to an observation of morbid jealousy in someone with a primary diagnosis of alcoholism.

Overvalued ideas

The notion of 'overvalued ideas' has found some support as a distinct form of morbid jealousy. To understand how overvalued ideas relate to morbid jealousy it is important to gain some sense of what an overvalued idea is: an overvalued idea is an ostensibly reasonable concept or idea that is elaborated upon by the morbidly jealous individual to a point whereby the conceptualisation now lies outside the realms of fact, and becomes fantasy. Overvalued ideas are not uncommon in people with personality disorders (Cobb, 1979; de Leon *et al.*, 1989; McKenna, 1984). Given that personality disorders are often comorbid with alcohol dependency, the occurrence of overvalued ideas within the context of morbid jealousy can be anticipated. Undesirable behaviour associated with a form of morbid jealousy strongly linked to overvalued ideas could include partner restriction and stalking.

Identification

The constellation of diverse presentations associated with morbid jealousy may confuse the diagnostic picture of this distressing syndrome. However, as in any good clinical practice in relation to the identification of psychiatric phenomena, competent and comprehensive history-taking is key. Corroborative evidence from the individual's partner is also extremely desirable to formulate a picture of the form, or interaction of forms, of morbid jealousy expressed. The healthcare professional suspecting an issue of morbid jealousy within an alcohol-dependent person should refer the client for a formal psychiatric assessment and risk evaluation. Special attention should be given to any specific evidence of violent behaviour that may be indicative of morbid jealousy; again, formal history-taking should illuminate any past occurrences. It should be borne in mind that no screening instrument is currently available for the detection of morbid jealousy. Consequently, critical appraisal of the current and past behaviour of the client through interview may provide the only clues that morbid jealousy is a contemporary issue of clinical concern.

Obviously, additional recorded evidence that becomes available to the health professional, such as a forensic history, which includes violence (in particular, violence to a partner) gives valuable insights into this possibility. During the course of identification and confirmation of the presence of morbid jealousy, the health professional should consider issues of self-harm, potential or actual violence to the partner, potential or actual violence to others and child-protection issues (the nature of morbid jealousy means that the partner is not only at risk, but also the perceived rival). This will obviously entail multidisciplinary and indeed multiagency team work, particularly in relation to child protection.

Therapeutic interventions

Following confirmation of morbid jealousy, intervention aimed at the primary mental health diagnosis is of paramount importance. The occurrence of morbid jealousy within the alcohol-dependent individual would therefore table a range of possible interventions discussed in depth in other chapters within this book. These approaches can be condensed into two main dimensions of the therapeutic armamentarium – those that are either pharmacological or psychological in approach, or a combination of such approaches.

Contextually appropriate treatment approaches are critical. An alcohol-dependent person, for example, who presents with the delusional form of morbid jealousy, may also have dual diagnosis with a psychotic disorder, thus pharmacological management for both presentations may be required, such as detoxification (see Chapter 7) and antipsychotic medication (see Chapter 9). Ideally, in such cases, further assessment of the presence and content of morbid jealousy following detoxification is desirable before commencing any treatment with antipsychotic medication, since the delusional architecture may ameliorate further treatment exclusively for the alcohol dependence. The use of selective serotonin-reuptake inhibitors (SSRIs) may be useful if the form of morbid jealousy is principally obsessional (Lane, 1990; Stein et al., 1994). Cardinal symptoms of depression are not required to be present for the use of SSRIs to be effective, but it should be noted that clinically relevant depression is often comorbid with a primary diagnosis of alcohol dependence (Martin and Bonner, 2000; Soyka and Roesner, 2006). Psychological approaches to therapy, particularly cognitive–behavioural therapy (CBT), can be effective in the treatment of morbid jealousy, especially when the form of presentation is principally obsessional (Bishay et al., 1989; Dolan and Bishay, 1996). However, consistent with pharmacological approaches to treatment, psychological intervention focused on alcohol dependency may facilitate the remission of morbid jealousy phenomena without targeted intervention. Consequently, in the absence of significant risk of harm to either the individual or significant others, psychological treatment of the alcohol dependency should be the principle focus, and any residual morbid jealousy should be treated with CBT.

Alternative types of psychological intervention have been found to impact on the expression and severity of morbid jealousy. Psychodynamic psychotherapy (Seeman, 1979) and couple therapy (Cobb, 1979) may have a role to play in the treatment battery, as may individual counselling. A rider to the use of effective couple therapy concerns possible complexities in the couple's relationship, which may reveal that both partners invest in some circumstances in perpetuating a state of morbid jealousy (Turbott, 1981). A co-dependency may be manifest when the partner wishes to be actively and pathologically desired or cuckolded. Illuminating the possibility of psychopathology within the partner may offer some insight into resistance to (or compliance with) the treatment or a lack of treatment efficacy in a subset of alcohol-dependent individuals presenting with morbid jealousy. Thus, couple therapy may offer an appropriate therapeutic setting to explore this possibility.

In an impressive case report, Blore (1997) revealed that eye movement desensitisation and reprocessing (EMDR) therapy demonstrated impressive efficacy in a PTSD case with co-presenting morbid jealousy. EMDR is a modern psychological intervention often used in the treatment of post-traumatic stress disorder (PTSD). Note that EMDR remains a controversial treatment in terms of modus operandi; the underlying mechanism of therapeutic action may be psychophysiological in contrast to psychological.

Irrespective of the approach to treatment, it is important to focus on the underlying condition co-presenting with morbid jealousy, in particular alcohol dependency. However, given the significant and diverse comorbidity associated with alcohol dependency, expertise in the treatment of mood disorders and personality disorder may inevitably play a vital role in the successful treatment of morbid jealousy in the alcohol-dependent individual.

Conclusions

Morbid jealousy is a complex phenomenon that is relatively common in people presenting with alcohol dependency. Detection of the syndrome is vitally important because of the consequences for the client concerned, for their partner, their children and their perceived rival (should the client act on erroneous beliefs about sexual unfaithfulness). Acting on such beliefs can have severe forensic consequences. Although violence to the partner is not unknown in individuals with alcohol dependency, a morbidly jealous individual's reaction to their beliefs can be extreme and life-threatening. Understanding the key features of how morbid jealousy presents is crucial to health professionals working with people who are alcohol dependent, in order to facilitate identification, referral and treatment of this disturbing psychiatric condition which may accompany alcohol dependency.

References and further reading

Achte, K., Jarho, L., Kyykka, T., *et al.* (1991). Paranoid disorders following war brain damage. Preliminary report. *Psychopathology,* **24**, 309–15.

Alimkhanov, Zh.A. (1980). Delusional psychopathology of the paranoid stage of paranoid schizophrenia. *Zhurnal Nevropatologii Psikhiatrii Imeni S.S. Korsakova*, **80**, 577–80.

Bishay, N.R., Petersen, N. and Tarrier, N. (1989). An uncontrolled study of cognitive therapy for morbid jealousy. *British Journal of Psychiatry*, **154**, 386–89.

Blore, D.C. (1997). Use of EMDR to treat morbid jealousy: A case study. *British Journal of Nursing*, **6**, 984–88.

Cobb, J. (1979). Morbid jealousy. *British Journal of Hospital Medicine*, **21**, 511–18.

Cobb, J.P. and Marks, I.M. (1979). Morbid jealousy featuring as obsessive–compulsive neurosis: treatment by behavioral psychotherapy. *British Journal of Psychiatry*, **134**, 301–05.

de Leon, J., Bott, A. and Simpson, G.M. (1989). Dysmorphophobia: body dysmorphic disorder or delusional disorder, somatic subtype? *Comprehensive Psychiatry*, **30**, 457–72.

Dolan, M. and Bishay, N. (1996). The effectiveness of cognitive therapy in the treatment of non-psychotic morbid jealousy. *British Journal of Psychiatry*, **168**, 588–93.

Freeman, T. (1990). Psychoanalytical aspects of morbid jealousy in women. *British Journal of Psychiatry*, **156**, 68–72.

Goldney, R.D. (1977). Family murder followed by suicide. *Forensic Science*, **9**, 219–28.

Harris, C.R. (2003). A review of sex differences in sexual jealousy, including self-report data, psychophysiological responses, interpersonal violence, and morbid jealousy. *Personality and Social Psychology Review*, **7**, 102–28.

Hassanyeh, F., Murray, R.B. and Rodgers, H. (1991). Adrenocortical suppression presenting with agitated depression, morbid jealousy, and a dementia-like state. *British Journal of Psychiatry*, **159**, 870–72.

Kingham, M. and Gordon, H. (2004). Aspects of morbid jealousy. *Advances in Psychiatric Treatment*, **10**, 207–15.

Lane, R.D. (1990). Successful fluoxetine treatment of pathologic jealousy. *Journal of Clinical Psychiatry*, **51**, 345–46.

Maggini, C., Lundgren, E. and Leuci, E. (2006). Jealous love and morbid jealousy. *Acta Biomedica : Atenei Parmensis*, **77**, 137–46.

McKenna, P.J. (1984). Disorders with overvalued ideas. *British Journal of Psychiatry*, **145**, 579–85.

Martin, C.R. and Bonner, A.B. (2000). A pilot investigation of the effect of tryptophan manipulation on the affective state of male chronic alcoholics. *Alcohol and Alcoholism*, **35**, 49–51.

Michael, A., Mirza, S., Mirza, K.A., *et al.* (1995). Morbid jealousy in alcoholism. *British Journal of Psychiatry*, **167**, 668–72.

Mullen, P.E. (1990). Morbid jealousy and the delusion of infidelity. In: R.B. Bluglass and P. Bowden (eds). *Principles and Practice of Forensic Psychiatry*. London: Churchill Livingstone, pp. 823–34.

Mullen, P.E. (1991). Jealousy: the pathology of passion. *British Journal of Psychiatry*, **158**, 593–401.

Munro, A. (1988). Delusional (paranoid) disorders: etiologic and taxonomic considerations. II. A possible relationship between delusional and affective disorders. *Canadian Journal of Psychiatry*, **33**, 175–78.

Sagarin, B.J. (2005). Reconsidering evolved sex differences in jealousy: comment on Harris (2003). *Personality and Social Psychology Review*, **9**, 62–75.

Seeman, M. (1979). Pathological jealousy. *Psychiatry*, **42**, 351–61.

Shrestha, K., Rees, D.W., Rix, K.J., *et al.* (1985). Sexual jealousy in alcoholics. *Acta Psychiatrica Scandinavica*, **72**, 283–90.

Soyka, M. and Roesner, S. (2006). New pharmacological approaches for the treatment of alcoholism. *Expert Opinion on Pharmacotherapy*, **7**, 2341–53.

Stein, D.J., Hollander, E. and Josephson, S.C. (1994). Serotonin reuptake blockers for the treatment of obsessional jealousy. *Journal of Clinical Psychiatry*, **55**, 30–33.

Turbott, J. (1981). Morbid jealousy – an unusual presentation with the reciprocal appearance of psychopathology in either spouse. *Australian and New Zealand Journal of Psychiatry*, **15**, 164–67.

■ Part Three ■
Psychological Interventions

12 Psychological perspectives on alcohol dependency

Colin R. Martin

This chapter will explore psychological perspectives on the nature of alcohol dependency and alcohol abuse. Importantly, psychological theories provide a contextual background on which applied psychotherapeutic approaches to treatment are based. It should be considered that irrespective of the medical aspects of treatment received by a severely alcohol-dependent individual, the plan of both care and aftercare should include a psychological component, either as a formal relapse prevention strategy, or as an engagement strategy that incorporates a variety of interactional skills designed to facilitate the client in addressing their alcohol issues. There are a variety of psychological theories which have explored the realm of alcohol problems, some of which are geared specifically towards chemical dependency, while others have focused on more general dimensions of psychological functioning and examined differences between those with, and those without, an alcohol problem (Otter and Martin, 1996).

Psychological theories of alcohol abuse and alcohol dependence represent theories of addiction generally, where the particular type of substance of abuse is not necessarily the most salient aspect of the presenting problem. Consequently, for the most part, a psychological theory of addiction will represent the same fundamental model for alcohol abuse/dependence as, for example, heroin dependence. Psychological theories of addiction fall into three main groups: 'behaviourist', 'cognitive' and 'personality'. Inevitably, there is some overlap between the theories and this makes perfect sense in terms of therapeutic approaches, for example, cognitive–behavioural therapy (or CBT) will necessarily have foundations in both behaviourist and cognitive accounts of alcohol/addiction problems.

Behaviourist theories

Behaviourist accounts of alcohol abuse/dependence very much avoid intra-psychic processes and intra-psychic conflict in the development, maintenance and chronicity of a significant alcohol problem. The focus of behavioural theories is on *observed* behaviour and, in the case of alcohol problems, observed *abnormal* behaviour. Enduring behaviourist accounts of alcohol abuse and dependence have traditionally focused on conditioning processes, gravitating towards two distinct mechanisms – *classical conditioning* and *operant conditioning*.

Classical and operant conditioning perspectives

A common core of both these approaches is that of instrumental behaviour, whereby the alcohol abuse behaviour is maintained by the consequences of the alcohol abuse and the individual being instrumental in securing the consequences. These perspectives are particularly useful for understanding some of the complex social consequences of alcohol abuse/dependence in addition to the development of the initial alcohol problem. A good example of this in the classical conditioning idiom is the case of the alcohol-dependent person who returns from the pub and becomes irritable and possibly aggressive with his or her partner. On leaving the pub after a heavy drinking session, the individual's blood alcohol level will start to reduce, and this reduction of the blood alcohol concentration is an unconditioned stimulus. The unconditioned response to the reduction in blood alcohol may be irritability and discomfort. With repeated exposure, the unconditioned stimulus promotes a conditioned stimulus of returning home which *then* becomes associated with a conditioned response of irritability and discomfort. In the absence of the original unconditioned stimulus, returning home becomes an uncomfortable and deleterious experience.

Ultimately, this conditioning process results in a craving for alcohol and this becomes a conditioned behaviour interpreted by the individual as an irresistible desire for alcohol. There is some impressive evidence on the role of conditioning processes in alcohol-related difficulties (Glautier and Drummond, 1994), and this perspective is supported by comparative studies (Cole *et al.*, 1999); however, the relationship between the formation of the conditioned responses is somewhat more sophisticated than the traditional and simple classical conditioning model, often indicating a role for poor underlying inhibitory mechanisms (Finn *et al.*, 1994, 2001). Further, the physiological aspects of conditioned responses in relation to alcohol show important individual differences and family incongruences that indicate complex and possibly exotic underlying mechanisms (Newlin, 1987).

A further development of classical conditioning approaches has been the evolution of cue exposure theory. Cue exposure theory emphasises the role of cues in the development and maintenance of problem alcohol/addiction behaviour. The model predicts that a cue that was present when alcohol was imbibed will be likely to facilitate a conditioned response. This phenomenon is known as *cue reactivity* and has been used to explain the phenomena of cravings in addictions (Heather and Greeley, 1990). One problem with the notion of cue reactivity in relation to alcohol dependency is that there is considerable variability in cue reactivity among people with significant alcohol problems (Bradizza *et al.*, 1999). It has been suggested that a mediating factor known as 'private self-consciousness' (PSC) may be related to the variability in cue reactivity; consequently the use of cue reactivity therapy may preferentially benefit a subgroup of alcohol-dependent people – those with high levels of PSC (Bradizza *et al.*, 1999).

Clearly the concept of PSC represents a significant departure from a purely behaviourist explanation for the development and maintenance of problem drinking, as PSC represents a higher-order cognitive construct. The complexity of a coherent cue exposure model of alcohol dependency is exacerbated by individual differences and may also limit both the appropriateness and efficacy of therapeutic interventions based on cue exposure. Chiang *et al.* (2005) found one subgroup of alcohol-dependent people exposed to cue exposure (who had increased cravings) experienced significant increases in anxiety and insecurity as well as stronger beliefs in the positive effects of consuming alcohol.

Operant conditioning models of alcohol abuse/dependence focus on the role of reinforcers of alcohol-related behaviour. Based on the Skinnerian tradition, behaviour is maintained or extinguished depending on the consequences of the behaviour. Importantly, reinforcers can be positive or negative and can also comprise both punishments and rewards. The notion of positive punishments may seem at first counter-intuitive but the positivity–negativity axis should be considered in terms of the contextual outcome. Consider the case of the heavy drinking session on the night before and the consequential severe 'hangover'. The hangover, although a punishment, represents a positive punishment because of the presence of it. Alternatively, someone experiencing temporary alcohol-related impotence, the infamous 'brewer's droop', will have encountered a negative punishment due to the loss of their capacity to engage in sexual intercourse. It might be anticipated that punishments reduce a behaviour and rewards increase a behaviour.

Another example is of a reinforcement schedule that exacerbates a problematic drinking pattern. A person who has been drinking heavily in the evenings begins to experience withdrawal symptoms from alcohol the following morning. However, these withdrawal symptoms are unpleasant and might constitute a positive punishment in the same way as the hangover. However, he or she may decide to take a drink in the morning to ameliorate the symptoms of withdrawal – the classic 'hair of the dog'. Such *relief* drinking therefore becomes a reinforced response because its effect is to reduce discomfort by (effectively) increasing alcohol consumption in a conventionally inappropriate way. Relief drinking is an example of negative reinforcement.

The mechanisms of reward and punishment are directly related to the relationship between a behaviour and its associated consequences. The operant conditioning model provides a useful explanatory account of the seemingly paradoxical behaviour often observed in people with profound alcohol-related difficulties. This is because the model reveals that excessive alcohol consumption may be positively reinforced by the enjoyable effects following initial depression of the central nervous system associated with alcohol dependence. Further, a person experiencing low mood may have their drinking negatively reinforced by the temporary removal of that low mood by drinking, even though such a strategy may lead to a more severe problem than low mood, namely alcohol dependence.

Operant conditioning models have real-world appeal and help to make sense of the seemingly self-destructive and socially corrosive behaviours observed in problem drinkers; the evidence base has furnished some support for such models (Chiang *et al.*, 2001). However, a purely operant conditioning model has limitations (George and Marlatt, 1983) and may be perceived as a component mechanism among others that may promote problematic drinking behaviour.

This perspective, of course, is related to the integration of behaviourist observations synthesised with cognitive processes, consistent with cognitive–behavioural approaches to treatment discussed in great detail in the relevant chapters on treatment in this volume.

Cue exposure theory

Cue exposure theory has, as mentioned previously, emerged out of the classical conditioning perspectives of addiction. The main rubric of this approach, borrowing much as it does from behaviourism, is that environmental cues have a significant influence on both the development and maintenance of the problem behaviour. A principle tenet underlying this approach is that a cue that was present when alcohol was taken is more likely to promote a cued response; this is a phenomenon known as *cue reactivity* (Cooney *et al.*, 1997). Within the general area of the addictions, the cue exposure model has been useful for explaining seemingly counter-intuitive phenomena observed in addictive behaviours, particularly cravings where someone who has been abstinent for a significant period of time then experiences cravings for alcohol.

The explanation, according to the cue exposure perspective, is that the cravings have been cued by a stimulus that was previously associated with alcohol consumption (Heather and Greeley, 1990). The cue itself could be innocuous, for example, the lighting of a cigarette or entering an environment associated with alcohol consumption. There could be many such cues and the individual may experience a broad variety of cues that give rise to feelings of discomfort in relation to controlling their problem drinking behaviour. The influence of some cues may be below conscious awareness, yet they may still influence behavioural responses; therefore, raising awareness of such mechanisms may be valuable for clients in linking cue-related phenomena such as cravings. There is good evidence in support of the cue exposure perspective (Chiang *et al.*, 2005; Fox *et al.*, 2007; Greeley *et al.*, 1993) but it is still not clear whether cue exposure represents a distinct theoretical departure to behaviourist perspectives or it is merely a part of (or an extension of) conditioning approaches – the concept of cue exposure is surprisingly complex, involving both behavioural and cognitive constructs and neurological states (e.g. Bradizza *et al.*, 1999; Lingford-Hughes *et al.*, 2006).

The fact remains that therapeutic strategies based on cue exposure have shown great promise (Drummond and Glautier, 1994; Loeber *et al.*, 2006; Staiger *et al.*, 1999).

Cognitive accounts

Distinguishing between behaviourist theories and cognitive theories is not clearcut as a number of cognitive approaches have emerged from behavioural approaches and, as we saw earlier in the chapter, behavioural perspectives have developed that clearly incorporate a significant cognitive component (e.g. cue exposure theory). There are, however, a number of cognitive approaches that seek to explain problematic drinking behaviour and, unsurprisingly, some of these have emerged from behaviourist approaches and incorporate elements from these historical psychological roots. A very good example of this psychological melting pot is 'social learning theory'.

Social learning theory

Social learning theory represents an interactionist account of behaviour that has been useful for explaining normative function as well as abnormal and undesirable states, including pathological or problematic drinking. The social learning model was developed by Albert Bandura (1977) and has been a highly influential and enduring theory of human behaviour and behavioural development. It is an interactional theory that incorporates the behaviourist conditioning principles within a model that emphasises the role of cognitive processes. Novel and established experiences facilitate the development of cognitive architecture within the individual that mediates behavioural outcome. This notion represents a departure from purely behaviourist accounts because the cognitive processes are implicit to the development of forethought and decision-making based on cognitive appraisal of a presenting situation. In this sense, the individual can develop a behavioural style not only from their own personal experience but also from what they observe in others, in a process known as modelling.

The capacity to do this has been linked with the development of abnormal behaviour, including problematic drinking, because in addition to the conditioned aspects of behaviour, problem behaviours like excessive drinking may have been modelled by the individual – for example if the individual was brought up in an environment that was permissive to excessive drinking. This person then develops an internal 'template' of behavioural appropriateness that represents a complex cognitive structure. His or her own behaviour is compared against this internal established template and inconsistencies are corrected by amendment of behaviour. The internal template is likely to have been established through modelling, so it is likely that where inconsistencies arise the behaviour will change rather than the template. Consequently, a model is presented where seemingly destructive behaviour such as problematic drinking remains stable, modelled as appropriate in the earlier social environment, and the behavioural reactions to inconsistencies are more likely to be for the individual to remove themselves from circumstances that are not permissive to drinking. In this sense the inconsistencies are corrected by removal from normative or socially appropriate behaviour. The model itself is largely self-regulatory and the process described is termed self-regulation.

The social learning approach is useful for understanding problem drinking behaviour because not only is the explanation evidence based, but it also offers possibilities for behavioural change, for example by modelling of more appropriate behaviour. The degree of self-efficacy (belief in their ability to perform a task to a satisfactory outcome) may be reduced in someone with problem drinking behaviour (Maisto *et al.*, 2000); he or she may use avoidance strategies to avoid conflict that may accompany attempts to address a task they feel unconfident about succeeding in, such as reducing alcohol consumption. Therapeutic approaches within this model include modelling appropriate behaviour, teaching recognition of risk situations and factors for problematic drinking, developing more adaptive coping and problem-solving strategies, and increasing self-efficacy to successfully facilitate the individual coming up with their own solutions to problems. There is good evidence in support of social learning with respect to problem drinking (Akers *et al.*, 1979; Annis, 1991; Evans and Dunn, 1995; Jackson and Oei, 1978; Maisto *et al.*, 2000; Moos and Moos, 2007).

Modification and development of the theory is desirable, however, in order to clarify the relationship between cognitions and behaviour in relation to addiction (Bradizza *et al.*, 1994).

Opponent process theory

Motivational needs clearly play a role in the development and maintenance of goal-directed behaviour. Attempting to explain behaviour beyond the basic physiological needs of homeostasis, Solomon (1980) developed a theory that has some appeal in explaining problem drinking behaviour. It is called the *opponent process theory*. Consistent with the theories already discussed, it is a general theory with applicability to addiction. An important feature of the theory relates to the regulation of affective (emotional) states; these are envisioned within the model as largely automated mechanisms. A key philosophical underpinning of the model is that any experience of stimuli is accompanied by an affective response or – more accurately – an affective *contrast*, as the response will have a (positive or negative) valence. For example, with alcohol a problem drinker early in his or her drinking career may experience a *positive* affective contrast on consumption of alcohol and a *negative* affective response during the descending part of the blood-alcohol curve.

Further down the path of the drinking career, the process of 'affective habituation' may be anticipated. Affective habituation describes the process whereby repeated exposure reduces the positive affective experience of drinking. In many respects (although described within a cognitive model) this process mirrors that of the physiological concept of developing tolerance to alcohol.

A third process within the model (the process of 'affective withdrawal') describes the mechanism by which the affective contrast reaches such a great magnitude that the initial positive effect experienced accompanying drinking is replaced by negative affective experiences, again a model consistent with neuroadaptation as well as cognitive and motivational models.

There are still many unanswered questions in relation to this model in the maintenance of addictive behaviour. The opponent process model is of theoretical interest, but compared to all other models there is limited evidence in support of its application to the area of problem drinking (Gauvin *et al.*, 1993; Newlin, 1985; Shipley, 1982). While it is nominally a cognitive and psychological model, the notion of opponent process mechanisms invariably implies the importance and relevance of underlying physiological substrates.

Problem behaviour theory

Jessor and Jessor (1977) developed this theory principally to explain the development of problem behaviours in adolescence. Therefore, the theory attempts to provide a framework for explaining a constellation of behavioural maladies that may arise. In this respect, problem behaviour theory neither represents a general theory of behaviour nor a theory of addiction, although it has application in this area. The theory is nominally cognitive but (consistent with social learning theory) it is an interactionist theory that combines significant components from personality, environmental and behavioural systems. A focus of the interaction in the system is that each component may have a particular (though infrequently described) propensity for a problem behaviour, the model having been applied to problem drinking, often within the context of adolescent behaviour (Hays *et al.*, 1987; Jessor, 1987). The degree to which each system (personality, environmental and behavioural) interacts produces a 'likelihood', known as a 'proneness', to engage in problem drinking behaviour. The system is dynamic in nature which means that the interactions and therefore levels of proneness will vary across time and across situations. Historically, there has been a good deal of support for problem behaviour theory, particularly because a good percentage of variance in observed problem drinking behaviour has been accounted for by this model (Donovan *et al.*, 1999). However, there is some conjecture that fundamental modification of the theory is desirable (Basen-Engquist *et al.*, 1996; Sadava, 1985).

Expectancy theory has one of the longest heritages in terms of a general theory of behaviour that has been applied the development of problem drinking behaviour. The expectancy theory has its roots in the seminal work of Tolman (1932). In many respects it represents a precursor to social learning theory. Indeed, this model shares many elements of social learning theory, even if different terms may be used to describe similar processes within each model. The focus of the model is the relationship between experience, the formation of beliefs and the formation of specific beliefs that influence behaviour.

One particular belief system is related to 'outcome expectancy'. Outcome expectancy describes the internal cognitive representation that there is a significant and predictive relationship between a behaviour and consequential behavioural outcomes. Therefore such a representation may specify (if drinking occurs) that certain physiological, psychological and affective outcomes will occur. There is good evidence for the face value of expectancy theory; for example, if people believe they are drinking alcohol at a party then they are likely to behave in a way that is consistent with the amount of alcohol they believe they have ingested, even if no alcohol was taken. In this example it is the *belief* that mediates the behaviour, rather than the pharmacological properties of alcohol itself since none has been imbibed.

Expectancy theory is useful for explaining fears and anxieties that people experience in relation to withdrawal of any substance of abuse, including alcohol. It also explains behaviour that would prevent such experiences, such as continued drinking. There is good evidence to support the role of expectancy in problem drinking behaviour and its role in treatment efficacy, but often these observations are reported in relation to social learning aspects of drinking behaviour (Solomon and Annis, 1990) rather than expectancy theory *per se*.

The role of affective state as a mediatory mechanism between expectancies and drinking behaviour also has support (Stein *et al.,* 2000). Here, a clear and important role of mood in the regulation of such behaviour is indicated. Expectancies are an important consideration for therapy because they influence behaviour, however discussion of such expectancies may occur within the context of a number of different psychological models of problem drinking that go beyond expectancy theory.

Personality perspectives

The role of personality in the development of problem drinking behaviour has been of interest to psychologists for many decades. One particular pursuit has been to identify a unique set of personality characteristics that represent an 'addiction signature'. This notion has been summed up by the suggestion of an 'addictive personality'. It is surprising, given the appeal of personality types in psychology, that evidence supporting the premise of an addictive personality is elusive. This may be because problem drinking *specifically* and addictive behaviour *generally* are complex behaviours and the goal of identifying a single personality type to explain problem substance use is likely to be reductionist, particularly considering that alcohol abuse and dependency represent a complex psychobiology (Martin and Bonner, 2005).

Notwithstanding the deficits in understanding addiction from a single unitary personality model, attempts have been made to explain addiction in these terms, notably through Eysenck's (Eysenck and Eysenck, 1985) classic personality formulation based on dimensional traits of introversion–extroversion, neuroticism and psychoticism applied to addiction (Eysenck, 1997). However, irrespective of the appeal, replicability and stability of Eysenck's personality traits, there are problems determining and isolating a unique combination of trait characteristics that are specific to addiction.

Other formulations of personality have been related to alcohol dependency, notably the work of Cloninger (Cloninger, 1987; Cloninger *et al.*, 1988) and Lesch (Lesch *et al.*, 1988, 1990; Lesch and Walter, 1996). Cloninger's work is important because it highlights the relationship between a small number of distinct personality traits, such as reward dependence, novelty seeking and harm avoidance, and their links with underlying neurotransmitter systems. Thus it is one of the first psychobiological models of alcohol dependence subtypes that truly links psychology with biology in a robust and evidenced way. The two subtypes (type I and type II) proposed by Cloninger are differentiated by age of onset and symptom clusters (Cloninger, 1987; Cloninger *et al.*, 1988). A flaw in Cloninger's model, however, is that the personality traits that map onto the underlying neurochemical substrates should be consistent and stable; however Otter *et al.* (1995) and Stewart *et al.* (2004) pointed out that the personality characteristics associated with Cloninger's model are not reproducible in certain contexts. Therefore any formulation of an alcohol dependency model based on such attributes is difficult if the fundamental trait characteristics are not stable. Moreover, associations speculated about within the model have not been supported in several investigations (Penick *et al.*, 1990; Reulbach *et al.*, 2007; Sullivan *et al.*, 1998; Zaninelli *et al.*, 1992).

Cloninger's model as it applies to alcohol dependency has nonetheless been extremely influential and aggressively researched. It has provided many insights into the complex relations between personality traits and the clinical presentation of alcohol dependence (Lin *et al.*, 2007; Parsian *et al.*, 2000; Tupala *et al.*, 2003, 2004; van de Bree *et al.*, 1998; Yoshino *et al.*, 1994). The influential work of Otto Lesch (Lesch *et al.*, 1988, 1990; Lesch and Walter, 1996) in the field of alcohol dependency has led to the development of a novel typology of alcohol dependency that has many impressive and proven clinical attributes (Reulbach *et al.*, 2007). This is discussed in depth in Chapter 21 which focuses on the psychobiological model of alcohol dependence proposed by Martin and Bonner (2005).

Single trait theories

Single trait theories of personality speculate that a dominant personality characteristic represents an enduring individual differences variable, which is salient for differentiating between distinct groups of people. Consequently, the role of such traits has been explored in relation to alcohol dependency to determine whether anyone presenting with problem drinking behaviour differs in orientation or levels of such trait dimensions. Anxiety and depression are of interest in psychopathology generally, but they also satisfy the criteria of trait characteristics as they represent continuums which are relatively stable and enduring and also demonstrate known group differences. There is incontrovertible evidence that people with alcohol-related problems also often present with significant comorbid anxiety and depression (Burns and Teesson, 2002; Burns *et al.*, 2005; Cornelius *et al.*, 2003; Driessen *et al.*, 2001; Evren *et al.*, 2006; Kushner *et al.*, 2005; Madden, 1993).

The role of anxiety and depression in the presentation of alcohol dependence is explored in detail elsewhere in this book – dual diagnosis in Chapter 4 and the psychobiological model of alcohol dependency in Chapter 21. However, it is important to point out with respect to reading those chapters that anxiety and depression do satisfy the main criteria for personality traits, although they are often not operationalised within the context of single trait theories of personality.

A number of other traits have been noted to differ between people presenting with alcohol-related problems and people without this presentation. Much attention has been given to differences relating to self-esteem as a trait variable. Self-esteem, the perceived self-worth of an individual, is often lower in people with alcohol problems (DeSimone *et al.*, 1994; Nyamathi *et al.*, 1998; Walitzer and Sher, 1996) and in people with poorer outcomes following treatment for alcohol dependency (Shaw *et al.*, 1997). Consequently, strategies that enhance self-esteem have value in the therapeutic process and represents a legitimate treatment goal (Byers *et al.*, 1990).

Locus of control (Rotter, 1966) is a generalised expectancy regarding the personal perception of control over life-events. It has also been associated with the clinical presentation of alcohol problems (Farid *et al.*, 1998; Hirsch *et al.*, 1997; Johnson *et al.*, 1991; Koski-Jannes, 1994; Martin and Otter, 1996; Mills and Taricone, 1991). However, findings in this area are sometimes equivocal (Marchiori *et al.*, 1999; Schuckit *et al.*, 1994). It is not uncommon for people presenting with alcohol-related problems to have an external locus of control orientation (Canton *et al.*, 1988), although this directionality has been challenged (Dean and Edwards, 1990). Also, because the concept is linked with self-efficacy (and indeed self-esteem) promotion of a more internal locus of control orientation through the medium of the therapeutic alliance continues to be useful in treatment (Canton *et al.*, 1988). This perspective resonates with evidence that external locus of control is associated with relapse following treatment (Johnson *et al.*, 1991). The concept is recognised as important in the recovery process and attempts have been made to measure elements of it that may be particularly relevant to alcohol dependency (Hirsch *et al.*, 1997; Li *et al.*, 2000; Murray *et al.*, 2006).

Conclusions

A number of psychological models of varying complexity have been proposed to explain the development and maintenance of problematic drinking behaviour and alcohol dependence. Evidence to support each theoretical perspective is often convincing, although it should be recognised that there is some overlap between theoretical perspectives – in some instances different theoretical approaches may be describing similar psychological mechanisms of dependence. It is, of course, contingent on those professionals offering treatment to be aware of the contribution of various psychological models of alcohol dependence and their valuable insights into treatment approaches with this group.

This theme is developed further throughout the book, where the focus is on applied psychological interventions such as cognitive–behavioural therapy. The weight of evidence suggests that there is an important role of psychological processes in the development and maintenance of alcohol problems; in addition, the psychological contribution is extremely important for a comprehensive and integrated psychobiological model of alcohol dependence.

References and further reading

Akers, R.L., Krohn, M.D., Lanza-Kaduce, L. and Radosevich, M. (1979). Social learning and deviant behavior: A specific test of a general theory. *American Sociological Review*, **44**, 636–55.

Annis, H.M. (1991). A cognitive–social learning approach to relapse: Pharmacotherapy and relapse prevention counselling. *Alcohol and Alcoholism*, **1**(Suppl.), 527–30.

Bandura, A. (1977). *Social Learning Theory*. New York: Prentice Hall.

Basen-Engquist, K., Edmundson, E.W. and Parcel, G.S. (1996). Structure of health risk behavior among high school students. *Journal of Consulting and Clinical Psychology*, **64**, 764–75.

Bradizza, C.M., Gulliver, S.B., Stasiewicz, P.R., Torrisi, R., Rohsenow, D.J. and Monti, P.M. (1999). Alcohol cue reactivity and private self-consciousness among male alcoholics. *Addictive Behaviours*, **24**, 543–49.

Bradizza, C.M., Stasiewicz, P.R. and Maisto, S.A. (1994). A conditioning reinterpretation of cognitive events in alcohol and drug cue exposure. *Journal of Behavior Therapy and Experimental Psychiatry*, **25**, 15–22.

Burns, L. and Teesson, M. (2002). Alcohol use disorders comorbid with anxiety, depression and drug use disorders. Findings from the Australian national survey of mental health and well being. *Drug and Alcohol Dependence*, **68**, 299–07.

Burns, L., Teesson, M. and O'Neill, K. (2005). The impact of comorbid anxiety and depression on alcohol treatment outcomes. *Addiction*, **100**, 787–96.

Byers, P.H., Raven, L.M., Hill, J.D. and Robyak, J.E. (1990). Enhancing the self-esteem of inpatient alcoholics. *Issues in Mental Health Nursing*, **11**, 337–46.

Canton, G., Giannini, L., Magni, G., Bertinaria, A., Cibin, M. and Gallimberti, L. (1988). Locus of control, life events and treatment outcome in alcohol-dependent patients. *Acta Psychiatrica Scandinavica*, **78**, 18–23.

Chiang, S.S., Schuetz, C. and Soyka, M. (2005). Effects of cue exposure on the subjective perception of alcohol dependents with different types of cue reactivity. *Journal of Neural Transmission*, **112**, 1275–78.

Chiang, S.S., Schuetz, C.G. and Soyka, M. (2001). Role of aggressivity on reactivity and craving before and after cue exposure in recently detoxified alcoholics: Results from an experimental study. *European Addiction Research*, **7**, 184–92.

Cloninger, C.R. (1987). Neurogenetic adaptive mechanisms in alcoholism. *Science,* **236**, 410–16.

Cloninger, C.R., Sigvardsson, S., Gilligan, S.B., von Knorring, A.L., Reich, T. and Bohman, M. (1988). Genetic heterogeneity and the classification of alcoholism. *Advances in Alcohol and Substance Abuse*, **7**, 3–16.

Cole, J.C., Littleton, J.M. and Little, H.J. (1999). Effects of repeated ethanol administration in the plus maze; a simple model for conditioned abstinence behaviour. *Psychopharmacology (Berl.)*, **142**, 270–79.

Cooney, N.L., Litt, M.D., Morse, P.A., Bauer, L.O. and Gaupp, L. (1997). Alcohol cue reactivity, negative-mood reactivity, and relapse in treated alcoholic men. *Journal of Abnormal Psychology*, **106**, 243–50.

Cornelius, J.R., Bukstein, O., Salloum, I. and Clark, D. (2003). Alcohol and psychiatric comorbidity. *Recent Developments in Alcoholism*, **16**, 361–74.

Dean, P.R. and Edwards, T.A. (1990). Health locus of control beliefs and alcohol-related factors that may influence treatment outcomes. *Journal of Substance Abuse Treatment*, **7**, 167–72.

DeSimone, A., Murray, P. and Lester, D. (1994). Alcohol use, self-esteem, depression, and suicidality in high school students. *Adolescence*, **29**, 939–42.

Donovan, J.E., Jessor, R. and Costa, F.M. (1999). Adolescent problem drinking: Stability of psychosocial and behavioral correlates across a generation. *Journal of Studies on Alcohol,* **60**, 352–61.

Driessen, M., Meier, S., Hill, A., Wetterling, T., Lange, W. and Junghanns, K. (2001). The course of anxiety, depression and drinking behaviours after completed detoxification in alcoholics with and without comorbid anxiety and depressive disorders. *Alcohol and Alcoholism*, **36**, 249–55.

Drummond, D.C. and Glautier, S. (1994). A controlled trial of cue exposure treatment in alcohol dependence. *Journal of Consulting and Clinical Psychology*, **62**, 809–17.

Evans, D.M. and Dunn, N.J. (1995). Alcohol expectancies, coping responses and self-efficacy judgments: A replication and extension of Copper, *et al.*'s 1988 study in a college sample. *Journal of Studies on Alcohol,* **56**, 186–93.

Evren, C., Can, S., Evren, B., Saatcioglu, O. and Cakmak, D. (2006). Lifetime posttraumatic stress disorder in Turkish alcohol-dependent inpatients: Relationship with depression, anxiety and erectile dysfunction. *Psychiatry and Clinical Neuroscience*, **60**, 77–84.

Eysenck, H.J., and Eysenck, M.W. (1985). *Personality and Individual Differences: A Natural Science Approach*. New York: Plenum.

Eysenck, H.J. (1997). Addiction, personality and motivation. *Human Psychopharmacology*, **12**(Suppl.2), S79–87.

Farid, B., Clark, M. and Williams, R. (1998). Health locus of control in problem drinkers with and without liver disease. *Alcohol and Alcoholism*, **33**, 184–87.

Finn, P.R., Justus, A.N., Mazas, C., Rorick, L. and Steinmetz, J.E. (2001). Constraint, alcoholism, and electrodermal response in aversive classical conditioning and mismatch novelty paradigms. *Integrative Physiological and Behavioral Science*, **36**, 154–67.

Finn, P.R., Kessler, D.N. and Hussong, A.M. (1994). Risk for alcoholism and classical conditioning to signals for punishment: Evidence for a weak behavioral inhibition system? *Journal of Abnormal Psychology*, **103**, 293–01.

Fox, H.C., Bergquist, K.L., Hong, K.I. and Sinha, R. (2007). Stress-induced and alcohol cue-induced craving in recently abstinent alcohol-dependent individuals. *Alcoholism: Clinical and Experimental Research*, **31**, 395–03.

Gauvin, D.V., Cheng, E.Y. and Holloway, F.A. (1993). Recent developments in alcoholism: Biobehavioral correlates. *Recent Developments in Alcoholism*, **11**, 281–04.

George, W.H. and Marlatt, G.A. (1983). Alcoholism. The evolution of a behavioral perspective. *Recent Developments in Alcoholism*, **1**, 105–38.

Glautier, S. and Drummond, D.C. (1994). A conditioning approach to the analysis and treatment of drinking problems. *British Medical Bulletin*, **50**, 186–99.

Greeley, J.D., Swift, W., Prescott, J. and Heather, N. (1993). Reactivity to alcohol-related cues in heavy and light drinkers. *Journal of Studies on Alcohol*, **54**, 359–68.

Hays, R.D., Stacy, A.W. and Dimatteo, M.R. (1987). Problem behavior theory and adolescent alcohol use. *Addictive Behaviours*, **12**, 189–93.

Heather, N. and Greeley, J.D. (1990). Cue exposure in the treatment of drug dependence: The potential of a new method for preventing relapse. *Drug and Alcohol Review*, **9**, 155–68.

Hirsch, L.S., McCrady, B.S. and Epstein, E.E. (1997). The drinking-related locus of control scale: The factor structure with treatment-seeking outpatients. *Journal of Studies on Alcohol*, **58**, 162–66.

Jackson, P. and Oei, T.P. (1978). Social skills training and cognitive restructuring with alcoholics. *Drug and Alcohol Dependence*, **3**, 369–74.

Jessor, R. (1987). Problem-behavior theory, psychosocial development, and adolescent problem drinking. *British Journal of Addiction*, **82**, 331–42.

Jessor, R. and Jessor, S.L. (1977). *Problem Behavior and Psychosocial Development: A Longitudinal Study of Youth*. New York: Academic Press.

Johnson, E.E., Nora, R.M., Tan, B. and Bustos, N. (1991). Comparison of two locus of control scales in predicting relapse in an alcoholic population. *Perceptual and Motor Skills*, **72**, 43–50.

Koski-Jannes, A. (1994). Drinking-related locus of control as a predictor of drinking after treatment. *Addictive Behaviours*, **19**, 491–95.

Kushner, M.G., Abrams, K., Thuras, P., Hanson, K.L., Brekke, M. and Sletten, S. (2005). Follow-up study of anxiety disorder and alcohol dependence in comorbid alcoholism treatment patients. *Alcoholism: Clinical and Experimental Research*, **29**, 1432–43.

Lesch, O.M., Dietzel, M., Musalek, M., Walter, H. and Zeiler, K. (1988). The course of alcoholism. Long-term prognosis in different types. *Forensic Science International*, **36**, 121–38.

Lesch, O.M., Kefer, J., Lentner, S., *et al.* (1990). Diagnosis of chronic alcoholism – classificatory problems. *Psychopathology*, **23**, 88–96.

Lesch, O.M. and Walter, H. (1996). Subtypes of alcoholism and their role in therapy. *Alcohol and Alcoholism*, **31**(Suppl.1), 63–67.

Li, E.C., Feifer, C. and Strohm, M. (2000). A pilot study: Locus of control and spiritual beliefs in Alcoholics Anonymous and SMART recovery members. *Addictive Behaviours*, **25**, 633–40.

Lin, S.C., Wu., P.L., Ko., H.C., *et al.* (2007). Specific personality traits and dopamine, serotonin genes in anxiety–depressive alcoholism among Han Chinese in Taiwan. *Progress in Neuropsychopharmacology and Biological Psychiatry*, **31**, 1526–34.

Lingford-Hughes, A.R., Daglish, M.R., Stevenson, B.J., *et al.* (2006). Imaging alcohol cue exposure in alcohol dependence using a pet 15O-H$_2$O paradigm: Results from a pilot study. *Addiction Biology*, **11**, 107–15.

Loeber, S., Croissant, B., Heinz, A., Mann, K. and Flor, H. (2006). Cue exposure in the treatment of alcohol dependence: Effects on drinking outcome, craving and self-efficacy. *British Journal of Clinical Psychology*, **45**, 515–29.

Madden, J.S. (1993). Alcohol and depression. *British Journal of Hospital Medicine*, **50**, 261–64.

Maisto, S.A., Connors, G.J. and Zywiak, W.H. (2000). Alcohol treatment, changes in coping skills, self-efficacy, and levels of alcohol use and related problems 1 year following treatment initiation. *Psychology of Addictive Behaviors*, **14**, 257–66.

Marchiori, E., Loschi, S., Marconi, P.L., Mioni, D. and Pavan, L. (1999). Dependence, locus of control, parental bonding, and personality disorders: A study in alcoholics and controls. *Alcohol and Alcoholism*, **34**, 396–01.

Martin, C.R. and Bonner, A.B. (2005). Towards an integrated clinical psychobiology of alcoholism. *Current Psychiatry Reviews*, **1**, 303–12.

Martin, C.R. and Otter, C.R. (1996). Locus of control and addictive behaviour. In: A.B. Bonner and J. Waterhouse (eds). *Addictive Behaviour: Molecules to Mankind*. Basingstoke: Macmillan, pp. 121–34.

Mills, J.K. and Taricone, P.F. (1991). Interpersonal dependency and locus of control as personality correlates among adult male alcoholics undergoing residential treatment. *Psychological Reports*, **68**, 1107–12.

Moos, R.H. and Moos, B.S. (2007). Protective resources and long-term recovery from alcohol use disorders. *Drug and Alcohol Dependence*, **86**, 46–54.

Murray, T.S., Goggin, K. and Malcarne, V.L. (2006). Development and validation of the alcohol-related God locus of control scale. *Addictive Behaviours*, **31**, 553–58.

Newlin, D.B. (1985). Offspring of alcoholics have enhanced antagonistic placebo response. *Journal of Studies on Alcohol*, **46**, 490–94.

Newlin, D.B. (1987). Alcohol expectancy and conditioning in sons of alcoholics. *Advances in Alcohol and Substance Abuse*, **6**, 33–57.

Nyamathi, A., Keenan, C. and Bayley, L. (1998). Differences in personal, cognitive, psychological, and social factors associated with drug and alcohol use and non-use by homeless women. *Research in Nursing and Health*, **21**, 525–32.

Otter, C.R., Huber, J. and Bonner, A.B. (1995). Cloninger tridimensional personality questionnaire-reliability in an English sample. *Personality and Individual Differences*, **18**, 471–80.

Otter, C.R. and Martin, C.R. (1996). Personality and addictive behaviours. In: A.B. Bonner and J. Waterhouse (eds). *Addictive Behaviour: Molecules to Mankind*. Basingstoke: Macmillan, pp. 87–120.

Parsian, A., Cloninger, C.R. and Zhang, Z.H. (2000). Functional variant in the *drd2* receptor promoter region and subtypes of alcoholism. *American Journal of Medical Genetics*, **96**, 407–11.

Penick, E.C., Powell, B.J., Nickel, E.J., Read, M.R., Gabrielli, W.F. and Liskow, B.I. (1990). Examination of Cloninger's type I and type II alcoholism with a sample of men alcoholics in treatment. *Alcoholism: Clinical and Experimental Research*, **14**, 623–29.

Reulbach, U., Biermann, T., Bleich, S., Hillemacher, T., Kornhuber, J. and Sperling, W. (2007). Alcoholism and homicide with respect to the classification systems of Lesch and Cloninger. *Alcohol and Alcoholism*, **42**, 103–07.

Rotter, J.B. (1966). Generalized expectancies for internal versus external control of reinforcement. *Psychological Monographs*, **80**, 1–28.

Sadava, S.W. (1985). Problem behavior theory and consumption and consequences of alcohol use. *Journal of Studies on Alcohol*, **46**, 392–97.

Schuckit, M.A., Klein, J., Twitchell, G. and Smith, T. (1994). Personality test scores as predictors of alcoholism almost a decade later. *American Journal of Psychiatry*, **151**, 1038–42.

Shaw, G.K., Waller, S., Latham, C.J., Dunn, G. and Thomson, A.D. (1997). Alcoholism: A long-term follow-up study of participants in an alcohol treatment programme. *Alcohol and Alcoholism*, **32**, 527–35.

Shipley, TE. Jr (1982). Alcohol withdrawal and its treatment: some conjectures in the context of the opponent-process theory. *Journal of Studies on Alcohol,* **43**, 548–69.

Solomon, K.E. and Annis, H.M. (1990). Outcome and efficacy expectancy in the prediction of post-treatment drinking behaviour. *British Journal of Addiction,* **85**, 659–65.

Solomon, R.L. (1980). The opponent process theory of acquired motivation: The affective dynamics of addiction *American Psychologist*, **35**, 691–12.

Staiger, P.K., Greeley, J.D. and Wallace, S.D. (1999). Alcohol exposure therapy: Generalisation and changes in responsivity. *Drug and Alcohol Dependence*, **57**, 29–40.

Stein, K.D., Goldman, M.S. and del Boca, F.K. (2000). The influence of alcohol expectancy priming and mood manipulation on subsequent alcohol consumption. *Journal of Abnormal Psychology*, **109**, 106–15.

Stewart, M.E., Ebmeier, K.P. and Deary, I.J. (2004). The structure of Cloninger's tridimensional personality questionnaire in a British sample. *Personality and Individual Differences*, **36**, 1403–18.

Sullivan, P.F., Fifield, W.J., Kennedy, M.A., Mulder, R.T., Sellman, J.D. and Joyce, P.R. (1998). No association between novelty seeking and the type 4 dopamine receptor gene (*drd4*) in two New Zealand samples. *American Journal of Psychiatry*, **155**, 98–101.

Tolman, E.G. (1932). *Purposive Behavior in Animals* and *Man*. New York: Appleton Century Crofts.

Tupala, E., Hall, H., Bergstrom, K., *et al.* (2003). Dopamine D_2 receptors and transporters in type 1 and 2 alcoholics measured with human whole hemisphere autoradiography. *Human Brain Mapping*, **20**, 91–02.

Tupala, E., Hall, H., Halonen, P. and Tiihonen, J. (2004). Cortical dopamine D_2 receptors in type 1 and 2 alcoholics measured with human whole hemisphere autoradiography. *Synapse*, **54**, 129–37.

van den Bree, M.B.M., Johnson, E.O., Neale, M.C., *et al.* (1998). Genetic analysis of diagnostic systems of alcoholism in males. *Biological Psychiatry*, **43**, 139–45.

Walitzer, K.S. and Sher, K.J. (1996). A prospective study of self-esteem and alcohol use disorders in early adulthood: Evidence for gender differences. *Alcoholism: Clinical and Experimental Research*, **20**, 1118–24.

Yoshino, A., Kato, M., Takeuchi, M., Ono, Y. and Kitamura, T. (1994). Examination of the tridimensional personality hypothesis of alcoholism using empirically multivariate typology. *Alcoholism: Clinical and Experimental Research*, **18**, 1121–24.

Zaninelli, R.M., Porjesz, B. and Begleiter, H. (1992). The tridimensional personality questionnaire in males at high and low risk for alcoholism. *Alcoholism: Clinical and Experimental Research*, **16**, 68–70.

13 Motivational interviewing

Mick P. Fleming and Colin R. Martin

Motivational interviewing is a non-directive/partly directive therapeutic approach that works towards changing addictive behaviours. It has been used successfully in the treatment of alcohol dependence (Vasiliaki *et al.*, 2006). As a therapeutic approach, motivational interviewing focuses on eliciting and resolving the thinking, emotions, learning and decision-making or internal factors that influence addictive behaviours. There are other psychosocial interventions for alcohol use. Cognitive–behavioural integrated treatment (C-BIT) has been developed in the UK and is based on the principles of cognitive–behavioural therapy (Graham *et al.*, 2003). The aim of C-BIT is to identify and reconstruct the key cognitions that maintain addictive behaviour. It is designed predominantly for people with comorbid substance use and serious mental health problems. At the time of writing there is limited evidence of efficacious outcomes of this intervention and it is not well established; there is limited use outside of the main geographical area of development.

A motivational model of addictive behaviour

The architects of motivational interviewing are Miller and Rollnick (2002). They base their approach on a motivational model of addictive behaviour. In defining this motivational model, Miller (1996) emphasises the role of psychosocial factors that underpin addictive behaviours, the lack of volitional capacity to regulate the addictive behaviour despite the obvious risks to the person from undertaking the particular addictive behaviour. Underpinning this definition is the central role of social learning theory. The processes of classical and operant conditioning explain the reinforcement or rewards required to ensure that the addictive behaviour persists, despite the harmful risks.

This is not to say that other factors such as the influence of the addictive substance on the body also influence the motivation of the person towards the addictive behaviour. It is an integration of these 'biopsychosocial' factors; for example, a person experiencing unpleasant tremors because of their body's reactions after heavy drinking may appraise this experience as the need for more alcohol because in their previous experiences this has cured the problem.

The person weighs up the pros, such as 'Drinking more alcohol will give me relief from these unpleasant experiences', against the cons of the behaviour, such as 'Drinking more alcohol may result in damage to my body'; the pros are likely to outweigh the cons. After drinking more alcohol and experiencing the reduction of the unpleasant tremors, this may further confirm their decision and appraisal that drinking more alcohol has helped, despite the health risks of organ damage, dehydration and safety. The relief from the unpleasant tremors provides the behavioural reinforcement. In the same situation in the future, that person may well weigh up the pros and cons of drinking more alcohol when they have unpleasant tremors and be motivated to use the same strategy. In such an example, the motivation to continue the behaviour outweighs the motivation to discontinue the behaviour.

What is motivational interviewing?

Motivational interviewing is a style of counselling that is partly based on Carl Rogers' (1951) concept of person-centred counselling approaches. However, many of the factors that motivate addictive behaviours are very personal, internal and potentially more difficult to access, so a more directive approach is integrated into the technique. Exploring and resolving ambivalence and resistance to changing addictive behaviour are central to the process.

Motivational interviewing integrates a series of underlying philosophical and guiding principles, together with a series of directive and non-directive therapeutic techniques or skills. Miller and Rollnick (2002) suggest the rationale for this is that if there are some overarching principles that are both philosophical and guiding for the therapist, then these principles will bind the techniques together.

This would ensure that the spirit, fidelity and context of motivational interviewing is clearly understood by therapists using the approach. Miller and Rollnick have found that since their approach was first introduced in 1991, many people used and tested out techniques that they called motivational interviewing which, in fact, 'bore little resemblance to our understanding of the method' (Miller and Rollnick, 2002; page 33).

Underlying principles of motivational interviewing

Philosophical principles

Motivational interviewing has a central focus on the internal factors that motivate addictive behaviour. Rather than prescribing solutions, their purpose is to identify the client's own resources to effect a change (Van Horn and Bux, 2001). To be effective this focus requires a therapeutic working alliance between the client and the therapist. This partnership, or collaboration, is essential for both parties within the alliance. For the client, such collaboration ensures they do not become a passive recipient of motivational interviewing. This would seriously reduce the efficacy of the approach because it is the client who needs to explore and then alter his or her ambivalence towards changing addictive behaviour. In order to undertake this process, the client requires to be treated as autonomous and must accept personal responsibility for their addictive behaviour and develop the motivation to change that behaviour (Rubak *et al.*, 2005). To create an effective working alliance, the therapist must not only respect the client's autonomy but should also use his or her therapeutic skills and techniques to maintain the collaborative nature of the working alliance, by not overtly directing, telling or advising their client. Within the working alliance, interaction can be guided by the principle of evocation. Information should be elicited from the client rather than being forced. Again this dictates the level and type of questioning skills required by the therapist. The principles of collaboration, autonomy and evocation set the parameters and foundations for the skills and techniques used by the therapist in motivational interviewing. In strict terms, they are also guiding.

Guiding principles

These principles are part of the 'spirit' of motivational interviewing. They set the parameters for the development of the therapeutic alliance and provide a framework within which therapists can utilise the specific skills and techniques of motivational interviewing. They are more closely related to the practice of motivational interviewing than the more general philosophical principles mentioned above. There are four of these guiding principles:

- expression of empathy
- developing discrepancy
- rolling with resistance
- supporting self-efficacy.

Expression of empathy

Understanding of the client's perceptions, thoughts and feelings through their own internal frame of reference, without judging or having any preconceptions, is an important part of the change process. Acceptance of the client as a person and their ambivalence to changing their addictive behaviour as part of the continuum of normal human behaviour not only 'normalises' the behaviour but also encourages self-exploration and overcomes defensiveness.

Expressions of empathy or 'seeing the world through someone else's eyes' requires the use of active listening, in the form of reflective listening (Rogers, 1951). Effectively reflecting back what has been heard from clients in a session not only allows the therapist to check for understanding, but also implies that they are listening to the client's emotional expression, and that this emotional expression is accepted, validated and respected.

On another level, reflective listening also implies that it is the client who is the expert on themselves. It is more likely to lead to an exploration of what strategies and skills the client has tried in the past to change the addictive behaviour, what has worked, and what has led to a relapse.

Developing discrepancy

Whereas expressions of empathy are related to non-directive approaches, developing discrepancy is related to a more directive approach within motivational interviewing. Developing discrepancy is a way of finding a lever to get beyond ambivalence, to change. It refers to the discrepancy that exists between what a client would see as their goals and values and their addictive behaviour (Miller *et al.*, 1992). The role of the therapist is to amplify or increase the discrepancy by thorough clarification of the client's goals (Miller and Rollnick, 2002). A distinction is also made between the *amount* of behaviour change required by the client and the *importance* of the change. This called 'behavioural gap' is defined as the amount of behavioural change required by the client to achieve the behaviour that they have defined as desirable. Developing discrepancy is linked to helping the client identify the importance for that change. Their rationale for this distinction is that the amount of behaviour change required may seem overwhelming and even de-motivate the client. Identifying the importance for the change would not de-motivate the client.

Rolling with resistance

The relationship between the client and therapist may, through the nature of ambivalence, become too adversarial (with the therapist and client arguing and challenging and taking opposite views) and this is likely to entrench ambivalence to change. 'Rolling with resistance' requires a reframing of resistance through the use of open-ended questions that are designed to draw the client's attention to new information, or through the giving of information. In this way, the therapist acknowledges respect, prevents entrenchment, and enhances momentum to change. Collaboration within the therapeutic alliance is an essential prerequisite for this principle.

Supporting self-efficacy

A core aspect of social–cognitive theory, self-efficacy refers to the conviction a person holds regarding their ability to achieve goals and their beliefs about their ability to produce designated levels of performance that exercise influence over events affecting their lives (Bandura, 1994). If a client is not confident that they can achieve successful change, then they will remain ambivalent and not be motivated to change addictive behaviour. Supporting self-efficacy involves identifying any previous attempts at change that the client has made, and which skills were most efficacious. Enhancing levels of confidence requires the application and testing out of these and other skills to changing the present addictive behaviour.

Techniques and skills of motivational interviewing

There are two phases to motivational interviewing. The skills within each phase are described separately in the discussion that follows.

Phase I: Building internal motivation for change

Within motivational interviewing, readiness for change in the client is seen as a product of the interpersonal relationship. This measurement scale is a consonant–dissonant continuum as shown below.

Consonant   **Dissonant**

This continuum, or scale, is a measurement of the nature of the congruence between the client and therapist in terms of aspirations, outcomes and aims, etc., within the working alliance at any given time. This scale should be used by the therapist to judge the nature of the alliance to ensure it is based on congruence or a mutual understanding of their aspirations, outcomes and aims. This congruence, in turn, enhances collaboration and empathic understanding.

In order to fully explore and resolve the client's level of ambivalence to change an important first step is to identify the client's readiness for change. Two important concepts are identified by Miller and Rollnick (2002) – importance of changing behaviour, and confidence to change behaviour. Identifying the level of these two concepts forms the basis of what Miller and Rollnick call the 'client profiles'.

There are other reliable methods for identifying readiness for change, such as the trans-theoretical model of change (Prochaska *et al.*, 1992) which is discussed later in this chapter. This model shares many similar characteristics with motivational interviewing and can easily be used concurrently to aid the efficacy of the motivational interviewing techniques and improve outcomes. Measurement of importance and confidence for change into high or low categories provides four client profiles (Miller and Rollnick, 2002; page 54):

- low importance–low confidence
- low importance–high confidence
- high importance–high confidence
- high importance–low confidence.

Each of these profiles implies individualised client goals for motivational interviewing interventions. For example, clients with low importance/low confidence require help to explore and resolve their ambivalence and help to improve confidence and self-efficacy. Clients with high importance/low confidence need help with improving confidence and self-efficacy.

Change talk is seen as being a reliable indicator of the level of internal motivation to change within the client. It is the opposite of 'resistance to change'. Eliciting 'change talk' draws the client's attention to their internal resources for change and focuses attention on the positive aspects of changing addictive behaviour; it is the main aim in phase I for resolving the client's ambivalence to change. The key approach is eliciting, or drawing out, change talk. The role of the therapist is to guide the client's focus towards change talk, rather than to tell or advise the client about change talk – this would be meaningless to the client and not result in them identifying their own ambivalent thoughts, feelings and resistance, or encouraging them to use their internal resources to overcome these barriers. The therapeutic or counselling skills that can be used for eliciting change talk are not specific to motivational interviewing, but they are effective in providing a structured and guiding strategy.

Agenda-setting allows the therapist and client to structure their sessions. It provides a focus to the therapeutic work if the focus is lost within the session; because an agenda has been set, either the therapist or the client can recommend returning to the agenda. By setting an agenda, it is possible to evaluate the session, either by checking to see if the agenda has been adhered to or whether all the items on the agenda been discussed in enough detail. The philosophical principles of motivational interviewing dictate that the agenda is set collaboratively between the client and the therapist, which gives the client a chance to be offered choices and encourages further collaboration. There is room for both parties to identify priorities for the session and empathic understanding is enhanced.

Elicitation and evocation of change talk determines the style of questioning used within motivational interviewing. Closed, multilayered and assumptive questions will all reduce the amount of information given in the client's answers and narrow and inhibit exploration of ambivalence and change talk. These processes are illustrated in Fig. 13.1.

A *socratic style* of questioning is non-judgemental. It uses open-ended questions that encourage the client to give more information when answering. If asked correctly, socratic questioning encourages the client to investigate and explore internal thoughts and feelings that are outside their normal range of attention, without imposing too much direction (Padesky, 1993). Through the use of socratic questioning the client can be encouraged and guided into exploring the pros and cons of the addictive behaviour or changing behaviour. Examples of socratic questions are:

- How confident would you feel about giving up drinking alcohol?
- What strategies have you used in the past to reduce or give up drinking alcohol?
- You have mentioned some concerns about continuing to drink as much as you do. What are your main worries about continuing to drink as much?
- Could you give me an example of the strategies you have tried in the past?
- Could you expand upon that?

In order to help condition the client further in the process of elicitation of change talk, the therapist needs to provide him or her with reinforcement. This is done through verbal statements of affirmation which can include positive feedback to the client, contingent on and linked to positive behaviour; for example, exploration or attempts to identify ambivalence or change talk.

Summarising is another skill identified by Miller and Rollnick that provides reinforcement for the client to help elicit change talk from them. Summary statements are provided by the therapist to the client that sum up the therapist's interpretation of what has been said by the client over a period of time within the session. It allows the therapist to demonstrate that they have been listening and also to check that they have fully understood what the client has been telling them. If the therapist is skilled they can also demonstrate an empathic and non-judgemental acceptance of the client.

Once change talk has been elicited from the client, the therapist must respond to the change talk in a way that increases the discrepancy between the client's goals and their addictive behaviour. This will increase motivation to change. In order to encourage the client to elaborate on their change talk, the therapist needs to develop the skills to reflect, summarise and affirm change talk. The therapeutic questioning, reflective listening and summarising skills are all essential in the process of encouraging elaboration of change talk.

Resistance is at the opposite end of the spectrum to change talk. It is seen as the normal product of the interpersonal relationship between therapist and client, rather than the product of the client or his or her addictive behaviour. If it persists, however, it is associated with disengagement from treatment and poorer outcomes with regard to changing addictive behaviour. Miller and Rollnick are quite clear that it is the therapist's responsibility to respond and work with the resistance, to prevent it from increasing. The skills for responding to resistance are variations on reflective responses or reframing skills. The latter involves validating what the client has said and offering a new interpretation or explanation. The components of phase I are summarised in Fig. 13.1.

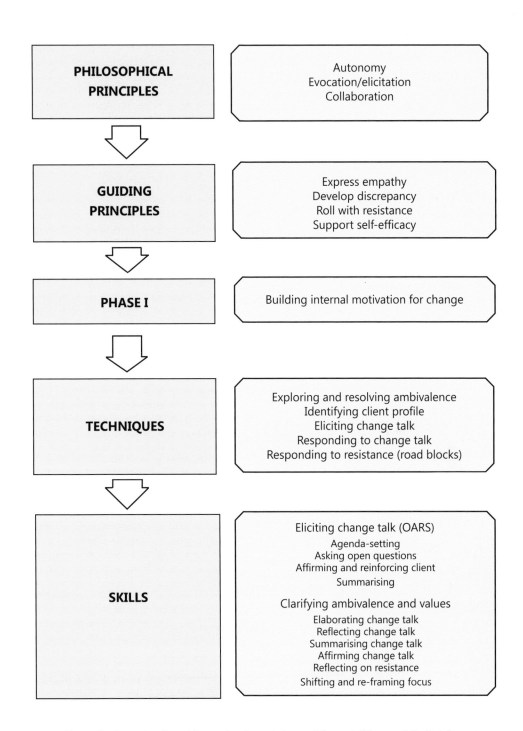

Figure 13.1 Phase I of motivational interviewing. Adapted from Miller and Rollnick, 2002.

Phase II: Strengthening commitment to change

The components of phase II are illustrated in Fig. 13.2. The skills and techniques used in this phase are bound by the same philosophical and guiding principles. Within the process of motivational interviewing there will come a point when the discrepancy between the client's goals and addictive behaviour is at a level that becomes too uncomfortable to maintain. The client's ambivalence to change is lessened, and their confidence and views about the need for change will increase. The therapist needs to recognise the client's readiness for change.

The signs of readiness for change are individualised, varying from client to client. Some common behavioural signs are decreased resistance, increased change talk or the client beginning to try change strategies (Miller and Rollnick, 2002). When this point is reached, the goals of the working alliance change from exploration and resolution of ambivalence to supporting the client's commitment to change. This is achieved through the collaborative development of a structured plan for changing addictive behaviour.

The first part of this process is to summarise the client's present level of ambivalence, motivation, and thoughts about the importance for change and intentions. The rationale for this recapitulation is that together the client and therapist can check the readiness for change, and restate and reiterate the main points and themes explored up to that point. Within this process the skills of asking open questions are bound by the principles of collaboration and evocation of information. Advice that aids the protection and safety of the client can also be offered, but again this is bound by the philosophical principles noted in phase I.

The change plan is the product of the working alliance and should be developed collaboratively between the client and the therapist. Identifying, setting and prioritising goals confirms the discrepancy for the client and helps motivation by itself. The role of the therapist is to help the client set their own meaningful, realistic and achievable goals. The skills of reflective listening, summarising, paraphrasing and clarification are an important aid to helping the client to identify specific goals. The goals must be meaningful because they need to be discrepant with the client's addictive behaviour. They need to be realistic to the client, so that he or she can identify the personal significance for their life and addictive behaviour. Their confidence and self-esteem may be fragile if the goals they set are unrealistic and remain unachieved; indeed the client may interpret this as another failure, leading to increased ambivalence and reduced confidence and motivation. A measurement, or gauge, of the client's confidence towards achieving that particular goal may be helpful in determining achievability of the goal being set. Goals should be specific and based on behaviour change, but clients may link their goals to wider life events and trends, so the therapist may expect some goals to be global.

Specific goals are more objective and therefore more measurable; when exploring positive attempts towards progress of goal achievement, the use of objective measurement, positively framed, will increase motivation. Once goals have been set, the role of the therapist is to help the client identify and plan change or goal-achievement strategies. Miller and Rollnick call this 'considering change options'. Techniques include brainstorming of ideas to generate potential goal-achievement strategies. The therapist can then assist the client to examine the advantages and disadvantages of each potential change strategy by exploring the merits or drawbacks of the potential solutions. The client should be encouraged to identify their assets and strengths that will help in goal achievement. These can be internal resources that the client has, perhaps some skills or knowledge that can be employed to effectively change the addictive behaviour.

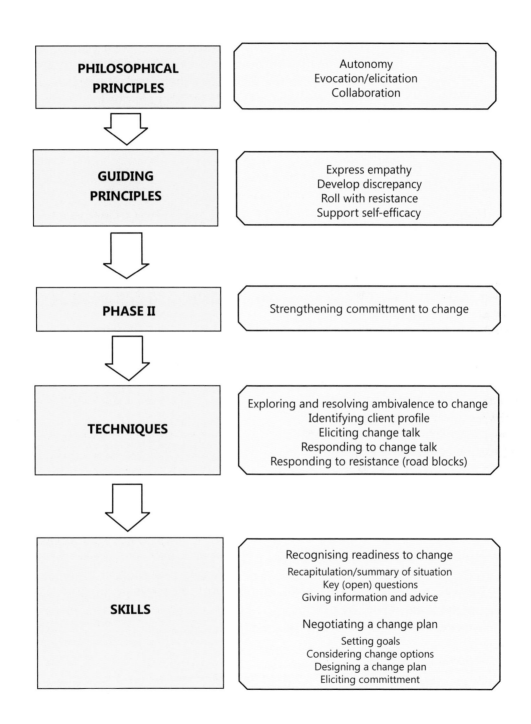

Figure 13.2 Phase II of motivational interviewing. Adapted from Miller and Rollnick, 2002.

Successful strategies used in the past by the client or significant other people or confidants that can support the client in achieving their goal. The plan should also include potential obstacles to change, as well as plans to overcome these obstacles. In this way the client is able to design their own individualised 'change plan'. The change-plan strategy may need to be modified with other solutions to make it more appropriate.

Finally, the therapist should summarise the plan. Once the summary has been made, the client needs to indicate his or her commitment to it. If the client is not fully committed, the therapist should help him or her to explore their continued ambivalence and help to resolve the cause. Once the client has given commitment, the plan can be put into action.

The trans-theoretical model

The trans-theoretical model (Prochaska and DiClemente, 1983) views change as a process that occurs over time – not as a linear or single event. It focuses on internal factors such as cognition, emotions and behaviour that influence decision-making and behaviour change. As the name suggests, it cuts across theoretical boundaries and integrates key constructs and principles from other theories, such as self efficacy and the decisional balance between pros and cons. The two key elements of the trans-theoretical model are the 'stages of change' and the 'processes of change'.

There are five stages of change through which clients will pass as they change their addictive behaviour. Each stage is a discrete category, and each is supported by data from a series of outcome measures of its characteristics stages (Prochaska *et al.,* 1992). Each stage has its own unique and defining characteristics. The five stages are:

- the precontemplation stage
- the contemplation stage
- the preparation stage
- the action stage
- the maintenance stage.

Precontemplation stage

Clients in this stage may wish for change but have no intention of changing their addictive behaviour in the next 6 months. They are likely to be unaware of (or not have information about) the risks of their addictive behaviour, and are more likely to avoid talking about or attending to their addictive behaviour. They would appear to the therapist as unmotivated, and may present for help because of the pressure from friends and family who do see the risks of their addictive behaviour.

Contemplation stage

In this stage, clients are aware that they have a problem with their addictive behaviour and are seriously thinking about changing that behaviour in the next 6 months. There may be no commitment to planning for change. Prochaska, DiClemente and Norcross (1992) describe this stage as 'Knowing where you want to go, but are not quite ready yet'. It is at this stage that clients may use a cost–benefit analysis of the pros and cons of changing their addictive behaviour. Often clients may find the balance in favour of *not* changing and can remain in the contemplation stage for up to 2 years (DiClemente and Prochaska, 1985).

Preparation stage

Clients in this stage have an intention to change in the next month; they have made the decision to change their addictive behaviour and may have engaged in some small behaviour change already, such as remaining abstinent for a few days or reducing their drinking. These clients are yet to take definitive action for change, although they may have made tentative plans for change, perhaps thinking about what help is required to change, or what action is needed to help change their behaviour.

Action stage

This is the stage where clients have taken explicit action to change or modify their behaviour in the last 6 months. Measurable behaviour change or actions such as total abstinence or a clear reduction in the number of drinks per day must have occurred for the client, and the behaviours, to be classed as being in the action stage.

Maintenance stage

Once action has resulted in behaviour change, the client works at preventing relapse back to engaging in the addictive behaviour. During this stage the client works at maintaining and stabilising the changes made. Not practising the addictive behaviour and engaging in a behaviour that is incompatible with the addictive behaviour for more than 6 months would classify the client and behaviour as being in the maintenance stage.

Research within a variety of client groups examining addictive behaviour does confirm the robustness of these change stages (Prochaska *et al.*, 1992). Progress through the stages of change, from precontemplation to maintenance, is desirable but may take more than one attempt. The patterns of change can be described as 'spiral' (Prochaska *et al.*, 1992), whereby clients relapse or recycle through the stages. Relapse can mean regression back to the precontemplation stage, but this is not the normal pattern (Prochaska and DiClemente, 1986). The majority of clients learn from their lapses or failed attempts to change behaviour, and they recycle back to the contemplation or preparation stages and consider a plan for change or action. The implication is that clients gradually move towards changing addictive behaviours once they have begun to move through the stages of change.

The processes of change are activities that explain how clients progress through the stages of change. The processes are at a further level of abstraction from therapeutic models. They are cross-theoretical, and encompass a wide range of multiple techniques, skills and interventions. Principal component analysis was used to analyse between 250 and 400 different therapeutic models and 130 techniques used by self-changers (Prochaska *et al.*, 1992). Ten change processes have the strongest empirical support, as shown in Box 13.1 (overpage).

The experiential processes are useful for progress through the early stages; and behavioural processes are useful for progress through the later stages of the change process (Velicer *et al.*, 1998).

Box 13.1 **Processes of change with the strongest empirical support out of therapeutic models and techniques used by self-changers**

EXPERIENTIAL processes of change

1. Consciousness raising (increasing awareness about the addictive behaviour)
2. Dramatic relief (experiencing emotional arousal)
3. Environmental re-evaluation (how the addictive behaviour affects physical environment)
4. Social liberation (eliciting alternate to addictive behaviour in group setting)
5. Self re-evaluation (exploring how a person feels about themselves in terms of the addictive behaviour)

BEHAVIOURAL processes of change

6. Stimulus control (developing techniques for avoiding or negating the effects of stimuli that elicit addictive behaviour)
7. Helping relationship (trusting and confiding in a person about the addictive behaviour)
8. Counter-conditioning (substituting alternative behaviours for the addictive behaviour)
9. Reinforcement management (rewards received contingent on changing the addictive behaviour)
10. Self liberation (developing belief in the ability to change a behaviour)

Motivational interviewing techniques and the trans-theoretical model

Different clients will be in one of the different stages of change. This means that if the techniques of motivational interviewing are matched to the stage of change that the client is in (see Fig. 13.3), then this congruence would improve monitoring of progress through the stages of change and outcomes. If there is no congruence between the stages of change and the motivational interviewing technique, the technique will not be individualised to the needs of specific clients, and outcomes will be poorer or clients may drop out of treatment. It is clearly possible to integrate the stages of change with the techniques within motivational interviewing. This enables a therapist to identify the stage of change that a client is at and offer the most salient motivational interviewing technique to help progress through to the next stage of change. If this process is accurate and speeds up the progress of client through to the action stage, it may improve action-orientated outcomes.

The efficacy of motivational interviewing

Dunn, Deroo and Rivara (2001) conducted a systematic review of brief interventions which correspond to the definition of motivational interviewing. They found that in 10 out of 15 studies where brief motivational interviewing was used with substance abuse, there were significant behavioural effects (ranging between 0.30 and 0.95) on abstinence, reduced consumption of the abusive substance, and on the number of drinking days per week. The size of these effects were of the same magnitude as those for other brief interventions for substance use. In the same review, mixed results were found when data was analysed for effects over time, with significant effects being reported from 3 months in one study to 12 and 24 months in another. This trend is illustrated in another study included within the review – that by Bien, Miller and

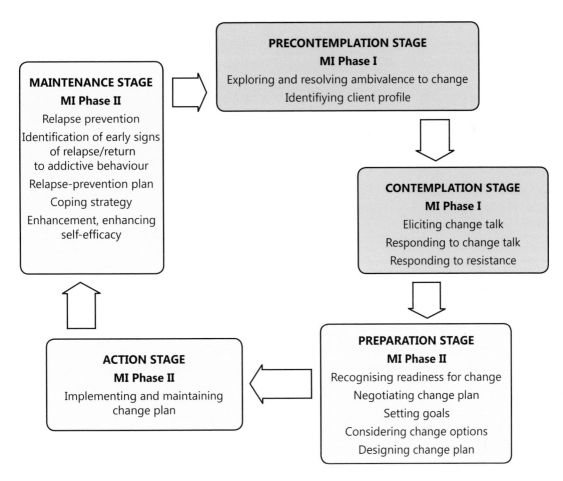

Figure 13.3 Stages of the trans-theoretical model of change and the appropriate motivational interviewing (MI) techniques for each stage.

Boroughs (1993). They randomly allocated 32 outpatients on a substance abuse programme into either a treatment group that received standard outpatient treatment plus two additional hours of assessment and one hour of motivational interviewing, or a control group that received the same additional assessment and a 'placebo' interview. Based on measures of total standard drinks, peak blood alcohol levels and percentage days of abstinence, the treatment group showed superior clinical outcome at 3 months. However, these superior clinical outcomes were no longer significant when measured at 6 months.

This finding was validated by Vasilaki, Hosier and Cox (2006) who analysed the data from 22 studies comparing motivational interviewing with no treatment. In this meta-analysis, the aggregate effect size was 0.18 (95 per cent; confidence interval 0.07–0.29) but was larger, with a value of 0.60 (95 per cent; confidence interval 0.36–0.83), when further analysis examined a follow-up period of 3 months or less. The authors offer a note of caution because the analysis was *post hoc* and therefore the results should be considered as hypothesis generating. The trend appears to be that the positive effects of motivational interviewing are reduced over time, although positive outcomes do not disappear completely and drinking does not return to baseline measures. Dunn and colleagues (2001) also found variations in the amount of time required to deliver efficacious motivational interviewing when they subdivided the studies in their review into groups by study design type (Table 13.1).

Table 13.1   Time required to deliver efficacious motivational interviewing (MI) to clients under different study designs

Study design type	Comparison group	Mean time to deliver
Motivational interviewing	None	104 minutes
Motivational interviewing	Control	98 minutes
Motivational interviewing with treatment as usual	Treatment as usual	190 minutes

Vasilaka *et al.* (2006) compared the time required to deliver efficacious motivational interviewing with other therapeutic interventions. The average duration of motivational interviewing was 53 minutes versus 90 minutes for cognitive–behavioural therapy, skills-based counselling and directive confrontational counselling – making motivational interviewing more cost-effective than other psychosocial alcohol treatments. This finding was central to both the MATCH and UKATT trials discussed below.

Dunn *et al.* (2001) also analysed studies that found motivational interviewing to be more effective among clients with mild to moderate alcohol dependence than clients with mild or severe alcohol dependence and those with no prior alcohol treatment. Results from the analysis by Vasilaki *et al.* (2006) found that the effects of motivational interviewing compared to control groups were more significant when people with more severe problems were excluded (95 per cent confidence interval 0.36–0.44). This led them to conclude that brief motivational interviewing is more efficacious than no treatment in reducing alcohol consumption among hazardous drinkers at less than 3 months. The same analysis concluded that across all studies, designs and all categories of populations, motivational interviewing is an effective treatment for heavy or abusive and low-dependence drinkers.

Dunn, Deroo and Rivara (2001) found evidence for the efficacy of motivational interviewing when sessions of motivational interviewing were integrated as an enhancement to more intensive treatments for substance use. A useful example of this is seen in the study undertaken by Barrowclough *et al.* (2001). Although the sample size was relatively small, 36 clients with a history of comorbid substance use and serious mental health problems were given five sessions of motivational interviewing, along with cognitive–behavioural therapy and family interventions; they were compared to a group receiving usual treatment. Outcomes at 12 months showed an improvement in psychotic symptoms and an increase in days abstinent from drugs and alcohol. Interestingly there was limited, or no convincing, evidence indicating whether the guiding principles (such as increasing self-efficacy or empathic understanding) were important mechanisms for change within the process of motivational interviewing as found in the Dunn, Deroo and Rivara review. Similar conclusions have been drawn from the findings of another rigorous meta-analysis (Vasilaki *et al.*, 2006). This analysis examined studies that referred fidelity to the techniques and principles of motivational interviewing; it found that where measures of fidelity to motivational studies had been developed, 95 per cent of therapist behaviours were consistent with the principles of motivational interviewing. Other studies in this analysis indicated some of the techniques and principles (expressing empathy, rolling with resistance and avoiding argumentation) were used more than the other principles of motivational interviewing. Overall, the effectiveness and use of the main elements of motivational interviewing have been understudied.

MATCH and UKATT trials

The UKATT (UK Alcohol Treatment Trial, 2005a) was the first major multicentre randomised-controlled trial of psychosocial alcohol treatments in the UK. The trial used blind assessments and tested two treatments. The study design and rationale were based on the findings of the Project MATCH study in the USA (Matching Alcoholism Treatments to Client Heterogeneity, 1997, 1998). This particular study had tested three different manualised alcohol treatments in a sample of 1726 participants across nine different sites. Participants were randomly assigned to either one of: cognitive–behavioural skills therapy; 12-step facilitation therapy; or motivational enhancement therapy. The motivational enhancement therapy was closely based on Miller and Rollnick's motivational interviewing manual (1991). The first two treatments consisted of twelve sessions, while the motivational enhancement comprised four sessions over 12 weeks and was considered to be a brief therapy. The results showed that each of the treatments provided equal, but substantial, improvements in drinking status at 1 year and 3 years follow-up. One of the conclusions drawn from these results was that a less intensive and less costly treatment such as motivational enhancement therapy produced very similar results to other more intensive and expensive treatments and it was therefore more cost effective (UKATT, 2001).

The UKATT trial compared the efficacy of manualised social-behaviour network therapy and motivational enhancement therapy in three sites across the UK with 742 participants who had alcohol problems and who would normally have received an offer of treatment for alcohol problems. The social-behaviour network therapy consisted of eight 50-minute sessions delivered over 8–12 weeks. The motivational enhancement therapy consisted of three 50-minute sessions delivered over 8–12 weeks. The study results confirmed the efficacy of both treatments with regard to substantial reductions in alcohol consumption, dependence and problems, with improvements in mental-health-related quality of life (UKATT, 2005a). Only one significant difference was found between the two treatment groups, which was that at 3 months the physical health of the social-behaviour network group was better than the motivational enhancement group. Non-significant differences were found for outcomes relating to drinks per day and the number of days abstinent, although they were in favour of the motivational enhancement group (UKATT, 2005a). The findings from the study confirmed that a brief form of motivational interviewing was as effective as more intensive psychosocial treatments. Cost analysis from the trial showed that both treatments proved to be cost-effective. The average cost of social behaviour and network therapy was £221 compared to a cost of £129 for motivational enhancement therapy. When comparing costs of treatment with costs within health, social and criminal justice services for the groups, both treatments provided a five-fold saving. Both treatments had similar cost effectiveness (UKATT, 2005b).

Conclusions

Motivational interviewing is a complex intervention which is made up of a range of psychosocial strategies underpinned by a number of psychological models. Clinicians using motivational interviewing are required to use a diverse number of skills from person-centred counselling through to goal setting and cognitive restructuring. Evidence suggests it is cost effective when compared to other psychosocial strategies. Nearly all the trials of motivational interviewing have understandably focused on reductions in harmful drinking behaviours and it can produce positive behavioural change in terms of reduced drinking in the short term for people with mild to moderate drinking problems. Some of the benefits fall away after three months but do not disappear completely.

One of the underlying principles of motivational interviewing is the motivational model of addictive behaviour; however clinical trials have not measured this. In future, clinical trials should focus on the effects of motivational interviewing on specific intrinsic and extrinsic motivational behaviours as these remain unknown. Another important focus for clinical trials is to identify which elements of motivational interviewing are the most efficacious and which have limited effect. An understanding of these would provide a full review and adaptation of motivational interviewing in order to increase its efficacy.

References and further reading

Bandura, A. (1994). Self-efficacy. In: V.S. Ramachaudran (ed.) *Encyclopedia of Human Behavior*, 4th edn. New York: Academic Press, pp. 71–81.

Barrowclough, C., Haddock, G., Tarrier, N., *et al.* (2001). Randomized controlled trial of motivational interviewing, cognitive–behavior therapy, and family intervention for patients with comorbid schizophrenia and substance use disorders. *American Journal of Psychiatry* **158**(10), 1706–13.

Bien, TH. Miller, W.H. and Boroughs, J.M. (1993). Motivational interviewing with alcohol outpatients. *Behavioural and Cognitive Psychotherapy*, **21**, 347–56.

DiClemente, C.C. and Prochaska, J.O. (1985). Processes and stages of change: Coping and competence in smoking behaviour change. In: S. Shifman and T.A. Wills (eds). *Coping and Substance Abuse*. San Diego: Academic Press.

Dunn, C., Deroo.L. and Rivara, F.P. (2001). The use of brief interventions adapted from motivational interviewing across behavioral domains: A systematic review. *Addiction*, **96**, 1725–42.

Graham, H.L. Copello, Birchwood, M. and Mueser, K. (eds) (2003). *Substance Misuse in Psychosis: Approaches to Treatment and Service Delivery*. Chichester: John Wiley.

Matching Alcoholism Treatments to Client Heterogeneity (1997). Project MATCH: Post-treatment drinking outcomes. *Journal of Studies on Alcohol*, **58**, 7–29.

Matching Alcoholism Treatments to Client Heterogeneity (1998). Project MATCH: Three-year drinking outcomes. *Alcoholism: Clinical and Experimental Research*, **22**, 1300–11.

Miller, W.R. (1996). Motivational interviewing: research, practice and puzzles. *Addictive Behaviors*, **21**, 835–42.

Miller, W.R. and Rollnick, S. (1991). *Motivational Interviewing: Preparing People to Change Addictive Behavior*. New York: Guilford Press.

Miller, W.R. and Rollnick, S. (2002). *Motivational Interviewing: Preparing People for Change*, 2nd edn. New York: Guilford Press.

Miller, W.R., Zweben, A., DiClemente, C.C. and Rychtarik, R.G. (1992). *Motivational Enhancement Therapy Manual*: A *Clinical Research Guide for Therapists Treating Individuals with Alcohol Abuse* and *Dependence*. Rockville, MD: National Institute on Alcohol Abuse and Alcoholism.

Padesky, C. (1993). *Socratic questioning: changing minds or guiding discovery?* Keynote address delivered at the European Congress of Behavioural and Cognitive Therapies. London, 24 September 1993.

Prochaska, J.O. and DiClemente, C.C. (1983). Stages and processes of self-change of smoking: towards an integrative model of change. *Journal of Consulting and Clinical Psychology*, **51**, 390–95.

Prochaska, J.O. and DiClemente, C.C. (1986). Towards a comprehensive model of change. In: W.R. Miller and N. Heather (eds). *Treating Addictive Behaviours: Processes of Change*. New York: Plenum Press.

Prochaska, J.O., DiClemente, C.C. and Norcross, J.C. (1992). In search of how people change: applications to addictive behaviors. *American Psychologist*, **47**(9), 1102–14.

Rogers, C.R. (1951). *Client-Centred Therapy*. Boston: Houghton-Mifflin.

Rubak, S., Sanboek, A., Lauritzen, T. and Christensen, B. (2005). Motivational interviewing: A systematic review and meta-analysis. *British Journal of General Practice*, **55**, 305–12.

UK Alcohol Treatment Trial (2001). UKATT: Hypothesis, design and methods. *Alcohol and Alcoholism*, **36**(1), 11–21.

UK Alcohol Treatment Trial (2005a). Effectiveness of treatment for alcohol problems: findings of the randomised UK Alcohol Treatment Trial (UKATT). *British Medical Journal* **331**, 541–44.

UK Alcohol Treatment Trial (2005b). Cost effectiveness of treatment for alcohol problems: findings of the randomised UK Alcohol Treatment Trial (UKATT). *British Medical Journal*, **331**, 544–48.

Van Horn, D.H. and Bux, D.A. (2001). A pilot test of motivational interviewing groups for dually diagnosed inpatients. *Journal of Substance Abuse Treatment*, **20**, 191–95.

Vasilaki, E.I., Hosier, S.G. and Cox, W. (2006). The efficacy of motivational interviewing as a brief intervention for excessive drinking: A meta-analytic review. *Alcohol and Alcoholism*, **41**(3), 328–35.

Velicer, W.F., Prochaska, J.O., Fava, J.L., Norman, G.J. and Redding, C.A. (1998). Smoking cessation and stress management: Applications of the transtheoretical model of behaviour change. *Homeostasis*, **38**, 216–33.

14 Cognitive–behavioural therapy

Leila Maria Soravia and Jürgen Barth

Cognitive–behavioural therapy (CBT) is based on the idea that feelings and behaviours are related to a person's thoughts (cognitions) that can be influenced by people him or herself. Cognitions can be changed during psychotherapeutic interventions and specific strategies achieved by psychotherapy may help patients to deal better with critical situations. Therefore, if someone experiences unwanted feelings and behaviours, it is important to identify cognitions that are related to these feelings or behaviours. Individuals can learn how to change these cognitions with more adaptive thoughts that are related to those feelings or behaviours and to learn how to change this thinking by more adaptive thoughts which will lead to more desirable responses (National Association of Cognitive–Behavioural Therapists, 2006). Besides this cognitive approach, CBT is also based on behavioural therapeutic concepts. The cognitive–behavioural model incorporates two major types of learning that have been identified in experimental research – learning by association and learning by consequences.

In learning by association, also called 'Pavlovian' or 'classical conditioning', stimuli that are originally neutral can become triggers for a certain behaviour. In patients with alcohol dependence, situations of alcohol use or cravings result from repeated association of those stimuli with alcohol consumption (Kadden *et al.*, 2003). Triggers can be external to the individual (e.g. settings, locations or people, the sight or smell of a glass of wine) or they can be internal stimuli (e.g. thoughts, emotions, physiological changes). Associations of these stimuli are developed if they occur in close proximity to one another several times. The repeated co-incidence of these situations leads to stronger associations between previously neutral stimuli (e.g. location or emotions) and behaviour (e.g. alcohol use).

The second principle is called 'operant conditioning'. It describes learning by consequences. Within this concept the desire of drinking is strengthened by the consequences (e.g. of being euphoric or feeling more comfortable in social situations) that follow the use of alcohol; therefore drinking is likely to be repeated in the future. The consequences can be differentiated into positive reinforcement (e.g. achieving a positive state like euphoria by the use of alcohol) and negative reinforcement (e.g. reducing an unpleasant state like anxiety).

The cognitive therapeutic approach explains psychiatric disorders, including alcohol dependence, as a maladaptive learning process (Longabaugh and Morgenstern, 1999). Thus the central goal of psychotherapeutic approaches using the CBT model is to develop techniques that are appropriate to change maladaptive cognitions and replace maladaptive behaviour with more adaptive responses to situational triggers.

Principles of cognitive–behavioural psychotherapy for alcohol dependence

From the perspective of cognitive–behavioural psychotherapy, alcohol dependence is a learned behaviour, acquired by experience. Alcohol enables desired physical or psychological states like good feelings or reduced tension. Therefore, on repeated occasions, it may become the preferred way of achieving these states, particularly in the absence of other ways to do so. According to this perspective, the primary task of the treatment is to:

i) to identify the specific needs that alcohol is being used to meet, and
ii) develop skills that provide alternative ways of meeting those needs (Kadden, 2002; Kadden *et al.*, 2003).

The goal of CBT is to help the person recognise critical situations, avoid particular situations, and cope with problematic situations. That is, to *recognise* situations in which they are most likely to drink, to *avoid* these circumstances when appropriate, and to *cope* more effectively with emotional states that may lead to their alcohol abuse. CBT also addresses other life areas that are related to drinking and relapse (Longabaugh and Morgenstern, 1999). Patients often cannot change their living conditions, but they can change how they think about them, and therefore change how they feel and behave. For example, if a person often gets angry because his boss criticises him often, and if anger is a trigger for his drinking, then this trigger will be in the focus of CBT. Circumstances that arouse the patient's anger will be assessed, and any associated thoughts and behavioural processes that occur between the onset of the anger and the patient's drinking will be analysed. The consequences that follow the patient's drinking will also be discussed. The cognitive approach in treatment of alcohol dependence attempts to reduce excessive emotional reactions and self-defeating behaviour by modifying maladaptive beliefs that underlie these reactions. Within functional analysis, identification of the cognition is clear. One approach to changing cognition is the so-called 'socratic dialogue'; this guides the patient by a series of questions to more adaptive thoughts about the future and him or herself. CBT is a structured, goal-oriented educational psychotherapeutic approach. It focuses on actual problems. There are important features of CBT that make it an attractive option for psychotherapy in alcohol abuse, as described in Box 14.1.

Components of cognitive–behavioural therapy

An important precondition for a successful therapy outcome is the patient's motivation to change his problematic behaviour and to join actively in the therapy process. Motivational interviewing (see Chapter 13) and Marlatt's cost–benefit analysis (Marlatt, 1978) are two tools

Box 14.1	**Why CBT is suitable for psychotherapy in alcohol abuse**

1. It is a time-limited, short-term approach that is well suited to the resource capacities of most clinical programmes.

2. It is one of the best evaluated psychotherapeutic approaches for the treatment of substance abuse and has a strong level of empirical support.

3. It is highly structured, so it is feasible for beginners of psychotherapy to perform and it gives patients a feeling of control.

4. It is goal-oriented, therefore the therapy process is clear for the patient and the psychotherapist.

5. It focuses on the immediate concerns of the patient that led him or her to seek treatment.

6. It is a flexible, individualised approach that can be adapted to a wide range of patients as well as a variety of settings (inpatient, outpatient, group, individual).

7. It can be added to other treatments patients receive, such as pharmacotherapy or self-help groups.

that clarify the patient's motivation for therapy. The cost–benefit analysis evaluates from the patient's perspective advantages and disadvantages of alcohol abstinence: are the costs of therapy (e.g. financial expense, time and effort, negative changes) in an adequate relation to the benefits of the therapy (both short-term and long-term)? It is important to point out and make clients realise that psychotherapy cannot solve all of their problems and it might bring up new problems they are not thinking of at present (e.g. the fact that non-drinkers belong to a minority in society). Visualising the advantages and disadvantages of abstinence using a cross-table (like shown that in Box 14.2) helps clients to make better decisions regarding the use of a therapeutic intervention. Furthermore, their personal motives, fears and concerns provide valuable topics for discussion in group therapies (Lindenmeyer, 1999).

Box 14.2	**Advantages/disadvantages analysis for the decision of abstinence in the initial phase of treatment**

	Short-term	**Long-term**
Pros of abstinence		
Cons of abstinence		

According to the guidelines of the National Institute on Drug Abuse (NIDA), the National Institute on Alcohol Abuse and Alcoholism of the National Institutes of Health (NIAAA) and the National Association of Cognitive–Behavioural Therapists (NACBT) the treatment of alcohol-dependent patients includes two main components: functional analysis and skills training.

Functional analysis

Functional analysis helps to identify triggers of drinking behaviour and to select skills areas for training (Kadden, 2002). It identifies situational antecedents of a patient's alcohol use, and the relationship of the drinking behaviour to the consequences. The psychotherapist and the patient identify the patient's thoughts, feelings and circumstances before drinking. This is elaborated for the drinking situations before treatment and for each instance of drinking during treatment. In the initial phase of the treatment, functional analysis helps the psychotherapist and the patient to identify high-risk situations that lead to alcohol drinking. Another aspect of this analysis is to provide insight into the reasons behind his or her drinking of alcohol, e.g. lack of coping with interpersonal difficulties, seeking risks or euphoria which otherwise might not be available in normal life (McCrady, 2001). In later treatment phases, functional analysis of relapses helps to identify critical situations, emotional states or thoughts which the patient still has difficulties to cope with. Some measures and strategies for functional analysis are described below.

Self-report questionnaires

These help to identify antecedents to drinking or drinking urges and to record them throughout the treatment. Evaluation of the questionnaires and discussion of events associated with drinking urges helps the clinician to develop a better understanding of drinking antecedents and consequences, and enables him to track progress through treatment in terms of quantity and frequency of drinking, as well as frequency and intensity of urges to drink.

Analysis of one drinking day

The episodes of one 'typical' drinking day should be in chronological order. The situational context, the concrete drinking behaviour and the immediate effect of alcohol must be recorded for each drinking episode. In terms of the immediate effect of alcohol, the patient is asked to differentiate between two main effects of alcohol abuse: first, it is possible that patients want to achieve positive feelings (e.g. in the form of positive ambience or exuberance) by drinking alcohol; second, alcohol can be used to reduce an uncomfortable state (e.g. being anxious or feeling depressed).

Life curve

The patient is asked to draw the daily amount of alcohol consumption throughout his or her life. Of particular interest are the 'reversal points' – the phases of abstinence or relapses. The client can add detail to the life curve as homework or with the therapist.

Therapy diary

The goal of the diary is to achieve better awareness of risky situations, mood changes, thoughts, demand for alcohol use, conflicts and relapses. The quality of the data depends on the event being recorded as soon as possible. It is important that the feeling corresponding with each event is reported.

Situational analysis

The patient should analyse different situational characteristics (places, times, other people, behaviour of others, the smell of alcohol) and internal states (thoughts, feelings, physiological reactions) which may work as triggers and enhance the probability of drinking alcohol.

Skills training

There is empirical evidence for insufficiently developed social skills in patients with alcoholism (Monti *et al.*, 2002). This might be due to some disadvantage in socialisation that inhibited the development of such skills, or the social skills may have been 'lost' over time because of substance abuse. The lack of social competencies (especially lack of the ability to communicate) is a risk factor for relapse, which again cannot be adequately accomplished because of the lack of skills. Psychotherapy aims, on one hand, to develop specific skills for imminent relapse situations and, on the other hand, to develop unspecific skills that indirectly reduce risky situations.

The coping-skills training approach does not attempt to reduce the impact of triggers (like the 'cue exposure' approach), rather it accepts triggers as given and seeks to train alternative responses to them, so that the person will have several ways of coping with the occurrence of a trigger situation, in place of drinking (Kadden, 2002; Kadden *et al.*, 2003). Having sufficient practice of these alternative new coping skills enhances the probability of using them when a trigger situation arises, instead of drinking.

It is important for clients to be active participants in the skills-training process. The more passive the client is, the less likely he or she is to be motivated to practice skills. Clients who engage in treatment, and begin the process of skills acquisition and cognitive restructuring, become increasingly able to accept responsibility for changing their usual behaviour. To enhance the clients' involvement and participation in this process, the selection of skills taught should match their needs, based on functional analysis. CBT uses teaching tools like role play, homework, modelling and behavioural rehearsal (Kadden *et al.*, 2003; Longabaugh and Morgenstern, 1999).

There are a number of coping-skills training manuals available. The manual by Monti *et al.* (2002) provides session-by-session explanations and practice methods for 25 skills related to problem areas common among dependent clients. The overview of these skills is organised into two broad categories: intrapersonal skills (e.g. managing thoughts and cravings for use, anger management, negative thinking, decision-making, problem-solving) and interpersonal skills (e.g. refusing requests, handling criticism, intimate relationships, general social skills). The interpersonal skill 'drink refusal' is described below.

Drink refusal

Abstinent alcoholics are fairly commonly confronted with offers to use alcohol in social situations and are even pressurised to drink along with others. Knowing how to cope with such offers to use alcohol is an important skill for the majority of dependent clients. They are taught to say 'no' convincingly – without giving a double message – or to suggest some alternative activity that does not involve alcohol, or to change to a different topic of conversation. If the other person persists, they are taught to ask him or her not to offer alcohol any more. The aim of practising this skill should be that the person is able to respond quickly and convincingly when these situations arise. Such situations are practiced best in role play and later in homework exercises.

Role play

Role play is an effective way of exercising a new behaviour in situations associated with alcohol (e.g. a bar or restaurant). Role play lasts approximately 5 minutes during which new behaviour can be taught. If there are any difficulties during role play, it can be interrupted and specific suggestions for improvement can be provided. During subsequent role play these suggestions can be incorporated into the new behaviour.

Role play with 'significant others' (a partner or spouse) focuses on interpersonal skills-training topics in which the patient has the opportunity to actively practise better communication and new behaviours in a more adaptive fashion (Kadden *et al.*, 2003). Role play can be carried out with the therapist or with a 'significant other' and should focus on basic skills like giving and receiving compliments or criticism, assertiveness and non-verbal behaviour. The benefit of this technique is that the patient can be coached directly on how to give or receive something like criticism in a more adaptive way. The goal of role play is to reduce misunderstanding and improve communication, which enhances the maintenance of sobriety.

Homework

Homework (practice exercises) is a powerful adjunct to treatment, because real-life situations can be utilised for practice, enhancing the probability that these behaviours will be repeated in similar situations. The psychotherapist should take care that homework is well prepared. It is advisable to motivate patients to practise any behaviour that has come up in role play. After doing their homework, clients should record facts concerning the setting, their behaviour, the response they evoked, and an evaluation of the adequacy of their performance. Successes and difficulties with the homework are discussed in the next psychotherapy session.

Cue exposure

There is evidence that regular alcohol use establishes cues for further consumption of alcohol (Drummond *et al.*, 1990; Niaura *et al.*, 1988). The intensity of the response is positively related to the subject's degree of dependence (Drummond and Glautier, 1994). These conditioned processes are the rationale for cue exposure therapy as a treatment in alcohol dependence. Repeated exposure to cues (such as a smell) without alcohol use will lead to extinction of conditioned responses, thus reducing the likelihood of relapse to drug-taking behaviour (Drummond *et al.*, 1990; Kavanagh *et al.*, 2006).

Before sessions using cue exposure, patients are told that a reason commonly given for relapse is difficulty in resisting temptation to drink in situations where alcohol is available. The cue exposure therefore is an opportunity to gain confidence in remaining abstinent in these situations. In these sessions, the patient might be exposed to a glass of wine and then asked to hold it, look at it and sniff it. It is recommended that these exposures last for at least 3 minutes and are repeated several times, with a short break between each exposure. The patient is then asked to report any difficulties and thoughts that came to mind as he or she resists having that drink. Additionally, patients rate their self-efficacy to remain abstinent and their mood. Several studies demonstrate the effectiveness of cue exposure, but not as a stand-alone treatment (Monti *et al.*, 1993).

Selecting the treatment setting and modalities

Information from the assessment of drinking habits, problem areas, and motivation is used to make an initial decision about the appropriate setting for treatment. The research literature provides little information to guide clinical decision-making about the level of care appropriate for an individual client (McCrady, 2001). CBT is a flexible and individualised approach and it can be adapted to a wide range of settings like inpatient treatment, partial hospital, day treatment or outpatient treatment. Clients receive between 12 and 16 sessions of 1–1.5 hours' duration. Individual therapies can elaborate very specific individual thoughts and include specific psychosocial conditions (e.g. problems with a partner, work absenteeism) into treatment. Group therapies can encourage patients to learn from the other patients' progress, in the sense of modelling, and to be more motivated for treatment. Mostly a mixture of treatment modalities is used to address specific objectives.

Additional treatment accompanying CBT

There is empirical evidence that self-help groups are most commonly sought sources of help for alcohol-related problems, and particularly for relapse prevention. Therefore, patients are strongly recommended to attend self-help groups in addition to their regular treatments during the recovery process. Alcoholics Anonymous (AA) is the most commonly utilised self-help group. It offers a specific approach to recovery, rooted in the view that alcoholism is a physical, emotional, and spiritual disease with no cure – but is a disease that can be arrested. Recovery is viewed as a lifelong process that involves working on the '12 steps' and abstaining from the use of alcohol. (For a detailed description of Alcoholics Anonymous see McCrady and Irvine, 1989, and Chapter 16 in this book.) Alternative self-help groups have developed in the last few years. The self-help approach called SMART (Self-Management and Recovery Training) is based on cognitive–behavioural principles, and offers several steps to recovery, emphasising awareness of irrational beliefs, self-perceptions and expectancies as core to successful change. In contrast to Alcoholics Anonymous, SMART suggests abstinence as a preferred drinking goal, but emphasises personal choice. An important issue in the treatment of patients with alcohol dependence is the comorbidity with other mental disorders. Especially for depressed patients, cognitive–behavioural therapy provides a good opportunity for addressing thoughts that reflect a depressed mood and alcohol use.

Effectiveness of CBT

CBT interventions for alcohol dependence have a success rate of 40–70 per cent after 1 year and have been demonstrated to be effective in reducing drinking in randomised clinical trials and reviews (Finney and Monahan, 1996; Finney *et al.*, 2003; Holder *et al.*, 1991; Longabaugh *et al.*, 2005; Longabaugh and Morgenstern, 1999; Miller *et al.*, 1995; Roth and Fonagy, 1996). Social skills training emerged in all reviews as an important ingredient, with the best evidence for treatment of alcohol dependence. Therefore, social skills training, which includes identification of specific problem situations, the use of instruction, modelling, cue exposure, role play and behavioural rehearsal, has become the standard of treatment for alcohol dependence. Further, it appears either as primary technique or as a component in intervention conditions in almost all clinical trials with alcohol-dependent populations.

The attempt to identify mechanisms of action inherent to CBT that contribute to its effectiveness, indicate that better coping skills generally are associated with better drinking outcomes, but no conclusions can be drawn regarding the active ingredients of CBT (Longabaugh and Morgenstern, 1999). Therefore, researchers do not yet know how the treatment works to improve drinking outcome. The inability to identify specific mechanisms through which CBT works, suggests a need for more focused analysis of CBT's effectiveness. Morgenstern and Longabough (2000) examined ten studies to identify these mechanisms. In summary, CBT treatment was demonstrated to increase coping behaviour more than comparison treatments, but this increase was either not tested or was found to be unrelated to abstinence. Based on these results, Litt *et al.* (2003) and others pointed out that the efficacy of CBT may be unspecific to the interventions provided, but may be due to the extent patients were encouraged for a change in self-efficacy.

Future studies should therefore pay attention to these non-specific treatment effects, which are very powerful in each kind of psychotherapy. Self-efficacy, readiness to change, general treatment involvement, and the therapeutic alliance are important issues to understand the effectiveness of psychotherapeutic interventions in alcohol dependence.

Cognitive–behavioural psychotherapy is an approach aimed at improving the patients' cognitive and behavioural skills for changing their drinking behaviour. 'CBT assumes that the patient already is motivated to stop or reduce drinking and that he or she only needs to acquire the skills to do so' (Longabaugh and Morgenstern, 1999, p. 82). This assumption may not always be adequate, especially for patients with a long history of substance abuse. In this case, the incorporation of motivational interviewing (see Chapter 13) into CBT is important for enhancing initial motivation. CBT also has limitations when the cognitive functioning of severe alcoholics is already impaired. Advice and highly structured interventions of longer duration are more adequate in this group of patients.

Conclusions

CBT is one of the most effective intervention strategies for the treatment of alcoholism. It uses cognitive (e.g. socratic dialogue) and behavioural (e.g. skills training) approaches. CBT works best when combined with other strategies, such as participation in support groups and pharmaceutical treatment (National Institute of Drug Abuse, 2005) as part of a multimodal approach.

References and further reading

Burtscheidt, W. (2001). *Integrative Verhaltenstherapie bei Alkoholabhängigkeit. Ein Therapiemanual*. Berlin: Springer.

Drummond, D. and Glautier, S. (1994). A controlled trial of cue exposure treatment in alcohol dependence. *Journal of Consulting Clinical Psychology*, **62** (4), 809–17.

Drummond, D.C., Cooper, T. and Glautier, S.P. (1990). Conditioned learning in alcohol dependence: Implications for cue exposure treatment. *British Journal of Addiction,* **85**, 725–43.

Finney, J.W. and Monahan, S.C. (1996). The cost-effectiveness of treatment for alcoholism: A second approximation. *Journal of Studies on Alcohol,* **5**, 229–43.

Finney, J.W., Moyer, A. and Swearingen, C.E. (2003). Outcome variables and their assessment in alcohol treatment studies: 1968–98. *Alcoholism: Clinical and Experimental Research,* **27** (10), 1671–79.

Holder, H., Longabaugh, R., Miller, W.R. and Rubonis, A.V. (1991). The cost effectiveness of treatment for alcoholism: A first approximation. *Journal of Studies on Alcohol,* **52**, 517–40.

Kadden, R., Carroll, K., Donovan, D., *et al.* (2003). *Cognitive–Behavioral Coping Skills Therapy Manual*: A *Clinical Research Guide for Therapists Treating Individuals with Alcohol Abuse* and *Dependence*. Rockville: National Institute on Alcohol Abuse and Alcoholism.

Kadden, R.M. (1999). Cognitive–behavior therapy. In: P.J. Ott and R.E. Tarter (eds). *Sourcebook on Substance Abuse: Etiology*, *Epidemiology*, *Assessment*, and *Treatment*. Boston: Allyn and Bacon.

Kavanagh, D.J., Sitharthan, G., Young, R.M., *et al.* (2006). Addition of cue exposure to cognitive–behaviour therapy for alcohol misuse: A randomized trial with dysphoric drinkers. *Addiction,* **101** (8), 1106–16.

Lindenmeyer, J. (1999). *Alkoholabhängigkeit*, 6. Gottingen: Hogrefe.

Litt, M.D., Cooney, N.L., Kabela, E. and Kadden, R.M. (2003). Coping skills and treatment outcomes in cognitive–behavioral and interactional group therapy for alcoholism. *Journal of Consulting Clinical Psychology*, **71**, 118–28.

Longabaugh, R. and Morgenstern, J. (1999). Cognitive–behavioral coping-skills therapy for alcohol dependence. *Alcohol Research and Health*, **23** (2), 78–85.

Longabaugh, R., Donovan, D.M., Karno, M.P., McCrady, B.S., Morgenstern, J. and Tonigan, J.S. (2005). Active Ingredients: How and Why Evidence-Based Alcohol Behavioral Treatment Interventions Work. *Alcoholism: Clinical and Experimental Research*, **29** (2), 235–47.

Marlatt, G.A. (1978). Craving for alcohol, loss of control and relapse: a cognitive–behavioral analysis. In: P.E. Nathan, G.A. Marlatt and T. Loberg (eds). *Alcoholism: New Directions in Behavioral Research and Treatment*, New York: Plenum.

McCrady, B.S. (2001). Alcohol use disorders. In: D.H. Barlow (ed.) *Clinical Handbook of Psychological Disorders*, 3rd edn. New York: Guilford Press, pp. 376–33.

McCrady, B.S., and Irvine, S. (1989). Self-help groups. In: R.K. Hester and W.R. Miller (eds.). *Handbook of Alcoholism Treatment Approaches: Effective Alternatives*. New York: Pergamon, pp. 153–69.

Miller, W.R., Brown, J.M., Simpson, T.L., *et al.* (1995). What works? A methodological analysis of the alcohol treatment outcome literature. In: R.K. Hester and W.R. Miller (eds). *Handbook of Alcoholism Treatment Approaches: Effective Alternatives*, 2nd edn. New Jersey: Allyn and Bacon.

Monti, P.M., Abrams, D.B., Kadden, R.M. and Cooney, N.L. (1989). *Treating Alcohol Dependence*. New York: Guilford Press.

Monti, P.M., Abrams, D.B., Kadden, R.M. and Cooney, N.L. (2002). *Treating Alcohol Dependence*: A *Coping Skills Training Guide*. New York: Guilford Press.

Monti, P.M., Rohsenow, D.J., Rubonis, A.V., *et al.* (1993). Alcohol cue reactivity: Effects of detoxification and extended exposure. *Journal of Studies on Alcohol,* **54**, 235–45.

Morgenstern, J. and Longabaugh, R. (2000). Cognitive–behavioral treatment for alcohol dependence: A review of evidence for its hypothesized mechanisms of action. *Addiction,* **95** (10), 1475–90.

National Association of Cognitive-Behavioral Therapists (2006). *What is Cognitive Behavior Therapy?* Available at: http://nacbt.org/whatiscbt.htm (last accessed August 2008).

National Institute of Drug Abuse (2005). *Cognitive–Behavioral Therapy: An Overview*. Available at: http://www.nida.nih.gov/ (last accessed August 2008).

Niaura, R.S., Rohsenow, D.J., Binkoff, J.A., Monti, P.M., Pedraza, M. and Abrams, D.B. (1988). The relevance of cue reactivity to understanding alcohol and smoking relapse. *Journal of Abnormal Psychology*, **97**, 133–52.

Project MATCH Research Group (1997). Matching alcoholism treatments to client heterogeneity: Project MATCH posttreatment drinking outcomes. *Journal of Studies on Alcohol,* **58** (1), 7–29.

Roth, A. and Fonagy, P. (1996). *What Works for Whom*: A *Critical Review of Psychotherapy Research*. New York: Guilford Press.

15 Can problematic alcohol use be trained away?

*Reinout W. Wiers, Tim Schoenmakers,
Katrijn Houben, Carolien Thush,
Javad S. Fadardi and W. Miles Cox*

New behavioural treatments aimed at changing and moderating implicit cognitive processes in alcohol abuse

In this chapter a general theoretical framework is first outlined in which alcoholism is viewed as the result of a disturbed balance between largely automatic appetitive processes and more controlled regulatory processes that can inhibit the appetitive impulse to use alcohol. Different interventions from this perspective are then introduced, both the more traditional cognitive–behavioural therapies and new interventions directly aimed at changing the automatic appetitive processes involved. We argue that this approach has the potential to generate a new class of behavioural interventions that can be summarised as varieties of 'training' or 're-training', and which are fundamentally different from and potentially complementary to currently used interventions, sometimes summarised as 'pills' (medication) and 'talking' (psychosocial interventions). Our argument is not that 'training' will make other interventions superfluous, but that they may develop into a helpful third general class of interventions.

A theoretical framework

Until recently, psychological models of alcoholism and other addictive behaviours were rooted in rational decision theory (*cf.* Wiers and Stacy, 2006a,b; West, 2006). The underlying idea was that people, addicted or not, weigh the pros and cons of different behavioural options and then make a rational decision. According to this view, as long as the (short-term) expected benefits outweigh the (long-term) expected harm, people will continue their alcohol and drug use. Recently, it has been proposed that implicit or relatively automatic processes may provide essential clues to understanding addiction (Wiers and Stacy, 2006a,b; Wiers *et al.*, 2007a). The central notion is that behaviour is partly governed by relatively automatic processes that often exert their influence outside conscious control. Note, however, that people can become aware of the *outcomes* of these processes (see Gawronski *et al.*, 2006); the term 'implicit' refers to the idea that the underlying processes are triggered and are, in some cases, executed outside conscious control. The growing focus on these processes does not imply that explicit or deliberate processes are unimportant, but rather that implicit processes must be acknowledged if alcoholism or other addictive behaviours are to be understood and treated.

In many recently formulated dual-process models of addictive behaviours, the general picture is that there are at least two semi-independent systems: a fast associative *impulsive* system, which includes automatic appraisal of stimuli in terms of their emotional and motivational significance, and a slower *reflective* system, which includes controlled processes related to conscious deliberations, emotion regulation and expected outcomes (there are many examples in Wiers and Stacy, 2006; for a general framework of impulsive versus reflective processes see Strack and Deutsch, 2004). Different neural structures underlie these processes (Bechara *et al.*, 2006; Berridge, 2001; Yin and Knowlton, 2006). Implicit cognitive processes have been shown to be important in the understanding of various addictive behaviours, with most research on alcohol abuse (see Cox *et al.*, 2002; 2006; Palfai and Ostafin, 2003; Stacy, 1997; Wiers *et al.*, 2002, 2005; for reviews see Cox *et al.*, 2006; Wiers *et al.*, 2006b, 2007a), but other addictions have been investigated as well (see Ames *et al.*, 2006 for a review).

Implicit processes are assessed with implicit or indirect measures. These measures are implicit in the sense that they capture to-be-measured constructs in a way that is relatively beyond the respondent's intentional control. Hence, instead of asking an alcohol abuser for the reasons behind his or her alcohol abuse, the investigator tries to assess the implicit cognitive motivational processes by registering fast spontaneous reactions to alcohol-related stimuli. As such, these measures may uniquely capture processes that are important in real-life behaviours, including addictions (De Houwer, 2006).

At least three different implicit cognitive processes can be distinguished. First, attentional processes indicate that alcohol abusers show an attentional bias for alcohol-related stimuli (Cox *et al.*, 2006; Franken, 2003). The most commonly used tasks to assess an attentional bias for alcohol-related stimuli include the alcohol Stroop test (see Cox *et al.*, 2006 for a review) and the visual probe task (e.g. Townsend and Duka, 2001). As discussed later, both tests have recently been adapted as re-training versions, to influence alcohol-related attentional bias; these tests and their re-training versions are explained below. The second class of implicit cognitive processes includes automatic memory associations and automatic evaluations. The idea is that once an alcohol-related cue is detected by an alcohol-abuser, this automatically triggers alcohol-related associations that are mostly affective in nature. Heavy drinkers have relatively strong associations of positive arousal when they encounter alcohol cues (Houben and Wiers, 2006; De Houwer *et al.*, 2004; Wiers *et al.*, 2002). There is also some evidence for negative alcohol associations (see Wiers *et al.*, 2006b) and for associations representing negative reinforcement (i.e. negative mood is automatically associated with alcohol use in problem drinkers with psychiatric distress; Zack *et al.*, 1999), but the role of these associations in terms of determining drinking is less clear and warrants further research (Wiers *et al.*, 2006b). Automatic or implicit memory associations can be assessed with spontaneous memory tests using paper and pencil (Stacy, 1997; Stacy *et al.*, 2006) and with a variety of reaction-time paradigms, including the frequently used Implicit Association Test (IAT; Greenwald *et al.*, 1998) and different versions of this test (see Houben *et al.*, 2006 for a review). One way to influence automatic evaluative associations is through *evaluative conditioning*, as discussed below. The third class of implicit cognitive processes includes *automatic action tendencies*. There are two basic motivational orientations, namely *approach* and *avoidance*. Generally, positive evaluations trigger approach tendencies and negative associations trigger avoidance tendencies. Different reaction-time tests have been developed to assess approach and avoidance tendencies and again variations of these tests have recently been used to influence these automatic action tendencies (Wiers *et al.*, 2007b). These tests, as well as their re-training versions, are briefly introduced later in this chapter.

The implicit processes sketched out above can be summarised as follows: when a heavy drinker (or alcohol abuser) encounters an alcohol-related stimulus, it will grab his or her attention, triggering positive and arousing associations, and triggering approach action tendencies. Wiers *et al.* (2007a) hypothesised that after repeated alcohol use, all these appetitive processes will get stronger as a result of neural sensitisation (Robinson and Berridge, 2003). Theoretically, one would expect these different processes to be correlated but, thus far, the size of correlations among tests of attentional bias, memory associations and automatic action tendencies has been surprisingly small. One possible explanation is that not all these processes are related to neural sensitisation, or that neural sensitisation is less important in the later stages of addiction (in which habit formation has been proposed as an alternative mechanism) (Everitt and Robbins, 2005). Another possible explanation of this lack of correlation may be measurement error (*cf.* Cunningham *et al.*, 2001). A third possibility is that in heavy drinkers, these different processes only synchronise after alcohol consumption has initiated. In line with the latter idea, it was found recently attentional bias and approach action tendencies were significantly more correlated in heavy drinkers under the acute influence of alcohol than after a placebo drink (Schoenmakers *et al.*, 2008). Together, these processes will generate an impulse to drink, which will result in drinking – unless the impulse to drink is resisted (see Fig. 15.1). In fact, this 'impulse' can include a whole chain of largely automatic behaviours, that call each other in turn, until the act of drinking occurs (i.e. walking to the fridge, fetching a beer, finding the bottle opener, opening the bottle, and so on; *cf.* Tiffany, 1990).

This capacity to regulate emotional and motivational impulses can be labelled 'emotion regulation' or, more specifically, 'impulse control' (there are other more indirect – and sometimes more efficient – ways to self-regulate emotional impulses). Impulse control critically depends on the ability and motivation to regulate impulses. Ability to regulate impulses is an aspect of executive functions.

People differ in their executive functions and this is important in relation to the development of alcohol abuse. First, poor executive functions are related to vulnerability for alcohol abuse (e.g. Peterson *et al.*, 1992; Sher, 1991). Second, there is increasing evidence that alcohol abuse, especially during adolescence, disturbs the development of executive functions (see the reviews by Dahl and Spear, 2004; Wiers *et al.*, 2007a). Motivation to regulate impulses is an important target in current cognitive–behavioural and motivational interventions. For example, the counselor links the problems that a problem-drinker experiences to the alcohol abuse and, together with the client, makes an explicit analysis of long-term benefits of prolonged alcohol abuse versus stopping (or in milder cases moderating drinking).

Fig. 15.1 overpage shows the theoretical framework discussed (adapted from Wiers *et al.*, 2007a). It includes a number of treatment possibilities from this perspective. In general, when both implicit and explicit cognitive processes influence addictive behaviours, both classes of processes can be targeted in interventions. In the following discussion, interventions that target explicit cognitive processes are introduced first, followed by interventions that target implicit cognitive processes.

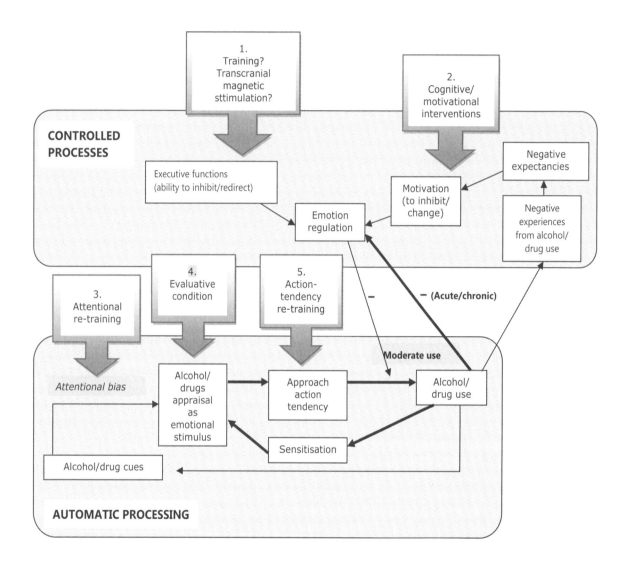

Figure 15.1   Theoretical framework for targeting implicit and explicit cognitive processes in addictive behaviours (adapted from Wiers *et al.*, 2007a).

Moderation of addictive impulses?

Several dual-process models predict that both more reflective explicit and more impulsive implicit cognitive processes influence behaviour (Fazio and Towles-Schwen, 1999; Kahneman, 2003; Strack and Deutsch, 2004). Moreover, an additional assumption of several dual-process models is that the influence of implicit processes on subsequent behaviour is moderated by explicit processes, if motivation and the opportunity to do so are high (Fazio and Towles-Schwen, 1999; Kahneman, 2003; Strack and Deutsch, 2004). Indeed, neurobiological addiction research has shown that the prefrontal cortex and associated areas are not only involved in more reflective decision-making, but also in the moderation of impulses (Bechara, 2005; Kalivas and Volkow, 2005). Dual-process models of addiction specifically predict that the influence of implicit appetitive cognitions on subsequent addictive behaviour might be dependent on moderators such as the level of executive functioning and motivation (e.g. Stacy *et al.*, 2004; Wiers *et al.*, 2007a).

Executive functions

Executive functions can be described as a set of cognitive skills which are relevant to goal-directed behaviours that involve different abilities such as shifting, updating and inhibition (Miyake *et al.*, 2000). Working-memory capacity has been proposed as a central construct that possibly binds these different, but related, executive functions (Kane and Engle, 2002). The relationship between executive functions and alcohol use has been shown to be bidirectional. Poorer executive functioning can be regarded a risk factor for developing addictive behaviours such as drinking alcohol (Peterson *et al.*, 1992; Tapert *et al.*, 2002). Additionally, alcohol abuse has been shown to have negative consequences for the maturation of brain regions (De Bellis *et al.*, 2000), and cause impaired neuropsychological functioning (Brown *et al.*, 2000) and altered processing in executive functioning tasks (Tapert *et al.*, 2004). Prior research has suggested that the influence of implicit automatic processes is indeed moderated by executive control (Feldman-Barrett *et al.*, 2004; Payne, 2005). This has also been proposed more specifically for addictive behaviours (Stacy *et al.*, 2004; Wiers *et al.*, 2007a). However, it should be noted that Fadardi and Cox (2006) showed alcohol attentional bias is not an artefact of poor executive control; the bias still occurs after executive control has been controlled.

Grenard *et al.* (in press) and Thush *et al.* (in press) both evaluated the interaction between working-memory capacity and implicit cognitive processes among at-risk young people and found evidence that implicit alcohol-related associations were stronger predictors of alcohol use among those with lower working-memory capacity than among those with higher working-memory capacity. In a related series of studies, Hofmann *et al.* (in press) showed similar patterns of results for other impulsive behaviours – candy eating, sexual interest and aggression – which were all predicted by the combination of strong associative processes (related to the behaviour of interest) and relatively weak executive control processes.

Finn and Hall (2004) proposed two mechanisms that may be responsible for the moderating influence of executive functioning on the implicit processes–behaviour relationship. First, low activating capacity of working memory makes it difficult to shift attention away from highly activated stimuli to stimuli that are less salient. Second, short-term positive associations with behaviour tend to be highly activated (salient), whereas the long-term negative associations with behaviour are usually weakly activated. Consequently, in high-risk situations (such as being at a party where alcohol is available) the individual needs to be able to switch to less salient goals – such as the intention not to drink large amounts of alcohol, or other information such as the negative consequences of alcohol (mis)use – and attend to this information, while distracting salient information in the current high-risk situation is automatically activated (e.g. the urge to feel intoxicated or to 'give in' to peer pressure). This relationship between executive functioning and behaviour suggests that people who are less able to actively manage less salient but adaptive goals when faced with distracting information are more likely to let their behaviour be guided by distracting salient information that is triggered in the current situation (Stacy *et al.*, 2004; Wiers *et al.*, 2007a).

The clinical implication would be that intervention programs will benefit from behavioural interventions that strengthen frontal inhibitory and executive control. In the development of an addiction especially frontal lobe circuits that are involved in self-regulation and inhibition become damaged, so it makes sense to design interventions in which these functions are specifically trained and strengthened again (Volkow *et al.*, 2004). Indeed, research has shown that executive functions and the associated brain regions are not fixed processes or structures but are characterised by their plasticity and can be modified through feedback and training (Erickson *et al.*, 2007). Although some promising results have been reported with this approach for children with ADHD (attention-deficit hyperactivity disorder) (Klingberg *et al.*, 2005), we do not yet know of applications of this approach to alcohol abuse or other types of addictive behaviours.

On a related note, there is preliminary evidence that a direct stimulation of cortical brain centres involved in the control of appetitive functions through transcranial magnetic stimulation (TMS) may have beneficial effects in reducing craving for cocaine in cocaine-addicted people (Camprodon *et al.*, 2007). Future research has to indicate whether training and/or direct stimulation of executive control functions are effective in restoring executive control in different clinical and non-clinical populations of different ages. Additionally, it has to be investigated in a clinical setting whether these training methods actually have a moderating effect on the influence of implicit cognitive processes on subsequent drinking behaviour.

Motivation

Even if someone has a high level of executive functions, one still needs to be motivated or have a goal in mind to which to apply this executive control (Feldman-Barrett *et al.*, 2004; Klinger and Cox, 2004; Wiers *et al.*, 2007a). Thus the concept of executive functioning does not replace the importance of motivation and goals, just as the concept of motivation does not replace the importance of the capacity to restrain oneself (Towles-Schwen and Fazio, 2006). Indeed, prior research has shown that the influence of implicit processes on behaviour increases when motivation to not act on these salient automatic associations is low (Olson and Fazio, 2004).

The clinical implication would be that interventions can be improved by adding a motivation-enhancement aspect (*cf.* Cox and Klinger, 2004). In fact, interventions that consist of brief motivational interviewing or feedback (Miller and Rollnick, 2002) consistently yield greater support for their efficacy in reducing hazardous drinking in adults compared with educational or information-only interventions (Larimer and Cronce, 2002). However, although brief motivational feedback has been proven to be effective in reducing hazardous drinking in (young) adult populations, this strategy might be less effective in some (at-risk) adolescent populations (for a review see Grenard *et al.*, 2006). This reduced effectiveness in at-risk adolescents might be explained by the differential response to alcohol in adolescents and (young) adults. During adolescence it is not so much the negative sedative effects but rather the positive arousal effects of drinking alcohol that are experienced (National Institute on Alcohol Abuse and Alcoholism, 2005). Therefore, these adolescents might feel they do not have sufficient reason for changing their drinking behaviour (Thush *et al.*, 2007). However, although mixed results are found for the effectiveness of brief motivational interventions in this population, these interventions might still be among the most promising approaches, especially in difficult, at-risk, non-treatment-seeking populations (Moyer *et al.*, 2002).

Recently a first study investigated wether a motivational intervention had a moderating influence on the relationship between implicit cognitive processes and subsequent drinking behaviour. Although the motivational interviewing was well received, no such effect was found (Thush *et al.*, in press).

Attentional re-training using modified visual probe tasks

Attentional bias can be directly manipulated by a procedure called attentional re-training. On one hand this procedure can be used to assess the causal role of attentional bias in cognitive disorders: for example, MacLeod and colleagues (2002) increased attentional bias for negative words and found an increase in stress reactions in a behavioral test, thus demonstrating the causal role of attentional bias in behaviour. On the other hand, attentional re-training has been studied in a clinically relevant way, to decrease attentional bias in people suffering from cognitive disorders. Evidence for the usefulness of clinical re-training is scarce; only some authors have referred to clinical re-training in anxiety (De Jong *et al.*, 2006; Mathews and MacLeod, 2002). In alcohol use, there are now a small number of papers reporting studies on causality and clinical relevance of attentional re-training in heavy social drinkers.

The type of re-training discussed in this part of the chapter is a modification of an attentional bias measure, the visual probe task. The 'measurement version' of this task consists of a number of trials in which an alcohol-related picture and a neutral picture are presented side-by-side on a computer screen for 500 milliseconds. Subsequently, a visual probe (for example, an arrow) replaces one of the pictures. Participants are to classify the arrow as pointing up or down by pressing a response button as quickly as possible. Problem drinkers are overall faster to respond to arrows that replace alcohol-related pictures than to arrows that replace neutral pictures. This finding has been interpreted as attentional bias for alcohol-related stimuli. Their attention is captured by the alcohol picture, therefore it is relatively easy to react to an arrow replacing an alcohol picture (because attention was there already), and relatively difficult to react to an arrow replacing the other picture (because attention has to be switched to the other location). In measurement versions of this test, probes replace pictures from both categories equally often.

In a 're-training' version of this task, it was found that in most (e.g. 90 per cent) or all of the trials, probes replace pictures from only one category. Participants are thereby trained to attend to one category and to avoid the other. Thus, in clinically relevant alcohol re-training, individuals are trained towards neutral images and away from alcohol-related images. This is achieved by letting the probe replace the non-alcohol picture in most (or all) trials. In order to investigate the causal role of attentional bias, both training to attend to alcohol (clinically undesirable!) and training to avoid alcohol-related pictures can be used to assess effects on craving for alcohol and drinking behaviour.

Field and Eastwood (2005) assessed the causal role of attentional bias in relation to craving and drinking using attention training. They trained one group to attend to alcohol-related pictures and one group away from alcohol-related pictures. Subsequently, participants rated their urge to drink and performed a bogus taste test: they rated the taste of an alcoholic drink after which the researchers measured the amount of alcohol they had consumed. In the post-training tests, the group who had been trained to attend to alcohol pictures showed a stronger attentional bias for alcohol, craved more for drinking alcohol, and drank more alcohol during the taste test than the group who had been trained to avoid the alcohol pictures. Noteworthy was that most of the change took place in the clinically undesirable 'attend-alcohol' condition.

Schoenmakers et al. (2007) conducted a study to test the effects of a clinically relevant attentional re-training. They trained one group away from alcohol-related images and compared the results with a no-training control group, who performed an extended visual probe task in which half the probes replaced alcohol pictures and half replaced neutral pictures. Attentional bias decreased in the avoid-alcohol group, but there were no congruent effects on craving and behaviour. In another recent study with an attend-alcohol group, an avoid-alcohol group and a no-training control group, there were no group differences in drinking behaviour, and craving only increased in the attend-alcohol group for participants who were aware of the experimental contingencies during the training (Field et al., 2007).

Effects of the clinical re-training have only been found with the same stimuli from the re-training within the visual probe task; Schoenmakers and colleagues did not find a significant generalisation towards new stimuli, and Field et al. (2007) even reported an unexpected increase in attentional bias for new stimuli. These findings were disappointing, since problem drinkers should ultimately learn to avoid new alcohol stimuli and not only those exemplars used during the re-training. Generalisation towards other measures of attentional bias (the flicker paradigm, and alcohol Stroop task) has been studied, but not been found (Field et al. 2007; Schoenmakers et al. 2007). Such an effect would rule out the alternative explanation that re-training effects are merely task-specific learning effects, because the re-training and measurement versions of the visual probe post-test are very similar (but see the discussion in Field et al., 2007). In addition, different measures of attentional bias measure different aspects of attention, such as early engagement or maintenance of attention. Generalisation towards other measures would therefore indicate that re-training affects multiple aspects of the attention system.

Differential effects on craving, behaviour and generalisation in the reported studies suggest that (in heavy drinkers) training to attend to alcohol is easier than training to avoid alcohol. Increasing the amount of training sessions has been suggested to increase the power of clinically relevant re-training varieties. Furthermore, it is possible that the limited findings in clinical re-training may result from the use of too few different stimuli, so that the training only relates to specific pictures and not the full alcohol category (Schoenmakers et al., 2007a). However, it should be noted that in one study generalisation was found in an attend-alcohol group but not in an avoid-alcohol group using the same number of stimuli (Field et al., 2007).

Other unaddressed issues in the re-training studies discussed so far are types of drinker and motivation to change. All reported studies have been conducted with heavy social drinkers. The effect on alcoholic patients might differ since their attentional bias differs from that of social drinkers (Noel et al., 2006; Stormarck, 1997). Further, researchers have suggested that motivation for someone to change their drinking behaviour plays an important role in the effectiveness of re-training (Wiers et al., 2006a). Participants in the above studies were all unaware of the purpose of the experiments, at least at the time of recruitment, thus motivation did not play a role. Fadardi and Cox (see below) discuss training in which motivation is a key element. Alcoholic people are generally motivated to change and thus may be affected differently by an attentional re-training if the purpose of the training is explained to them. Recently attentional re-training of the visual probe type was tested in a first clinical trial in 37 alcoholics in treatment, who were randomly assigned to either repeated attentional re-training (AR; with new stimuli in each session and motivational feedback on training results) or to placebo training (Schoenmakers *et al.*, 2008). The training was effective, and increased their ability to disengage from alcohol-related cues, measured 3–4 days after the last training session. This effect was generalised to stimuli that were not used in the training sessions. There were preliminary indications of clinically relevant outcomes: after the intervention, in the clinic with the shortest regular treatment programme, AR subjects in the re-training group were discharged sooner than control subjects. And among the few patients who lapsed or relapsed after finishing the intervention, the time to lapse or relapse was longer in the AR re-training condition. Of course, because of the limited sample size these results should be regarded as promising preliminary results – with the emphasis on *promising*.

In summary, studies using attentional re-training with the modified visual task have had effects mainly after increasing attentional bias in social drinkers; they demonstrate that attentional bias has causal effects on craving and drinking. Studies on clinically relevant re-training varieties, however, have shown weak effects in heavy drinkers. However, more promising results have recently been obtained in a first clinical study using a repeated re-training procedure.

Attentional control training program

As discussed earlier, one way to study alcohol-related attentional bias is based on interference. The alcohol Stroop test is one of the most widely used measures of alcohol users' and abusers' attentional bias for alcohol-related stimuli. The test is a modified version of one of the tasks that Stroop (1935) developed for his doctoral thesis. Stroop used two cards with coloured stimuli, and the participants' task was to name the colour of each stimulus on each card. The first card comprised coloured squares; they were used to establish a baseline for individual participant's general performance on colour naming. The second card comprised a series of words naming different colours but each word was printed in a colour that was incongruent with the colour the word referred to, thus the word *red* might be printed in blue ink. Stroop's experiment has been widely used for research, although many researchers have changed the baseline stimuli from coloured squares to coloured symbols (like a string of 'X's), or to *colour congruent* words (e.g. the word *red* is printed in red). The participant's task on the Stroop test is to ignore the meaning of the stimulus and respond to the actual colour of the stimulus – as quickly and accurately as possible. Participants find it more difficult to respond to colour-incongruent stimuli than to colour-congruent ones; thus their reaction times to the former are longer than to the latter. On the classic Stroop test, 'interference' scores are calculated as the mean reaction time to colour-incongruent stimuli *minus* the mean reaction time to colour congruent ones; the size of the interference is considered to be an index of general cognitive flexibility and inhibitory control. In the alcohol version of the Stroop test, two categories of words are used – alcohol-related and alcohol-unrelated. The two categories are matched on various linguistics dimensions (e.g.

frequency of words, number of letters, number of syllables) so that they differ only with respect to their alcohol-relatedness. The words are printed in different colours (usually red, yellow, blue, or green) and the participant must ignore the meaning of the words and respond as quickly and accurately as possible to the colour in which each word appears. Unlike the classic Stroop test, reaction times on an alcohol Stroop are not affected by a conflict between the meaning of the words and the colour in which they appear. Rather, participants' speed in responding to the font colour of the stimuli might suffer from their distraction by the alcohol-relatedness of the stimuli. Unlike the classic Stroop test, these reaction times are not affected by conflict between the meaning of the words and their colour – the distraction results from the alcohol-relatedness of the stimulus.

Alcohol attentional bias is then calculated as the mean reaction time to alcohol-related words *minus* the mean reaction time to alcohol-unrelated words. On the alcohol Stroop test, alcohol abusers and other heavy drinkers show greater attentional bias for the alcohol stimuli than social drinkers (for a review see Cox *et al.*, 2006). When a third category of words is included that relates to the individual person's goals and concerns (apart from their goal of drinking alcohol), alcohol abusers show greater attentional bias for alcohol-related words than for those related to their personal goals (Cox *et al.*, 2000). This suggests that drinking alcohol is an alcohol abuser's most compelling goal.

Fadardi and Cox (2006) developed the Alcohol Attention Control Training Program (AACTP) as a technique to help excessive drinkers overcome their automatic distraction for alcohol-related stimuli, which contributes to their inability to moderate their drinking, especially in high-risk situations (Stasiewicz *et al.*, 1997). The AACTP is designed to neutralise the cognitive processes involved in the automatic chain of drink-related behaviours, by helping excessive drinkers gain more control over their distraction for alcohol-related stimuli. Theoretically, the AACTP was developed to (a) correct the uncontrollability with which excessive drinkers are distracted by alcohol instead of attending to other kinds of stimuli, and (b) increase drinkers' efficiency and speed in diverting their attention away from alcohol when they want to do so.

The AACTP is based on goal setting, immediate feedback, and monitoring participants' progresses through progressive levels of difficulty. At the most difficult level, the participant sees on a computer screen pairs of alcohol and non-alcohol containers (bottles or cans), each of which is surrounded by a narrow, coloured outline. The participant's task is to ignore the alcohol bottle (or can) in each pair and to respond as quickly as possible to the surrounding colour of the non-alcohol bottle (or can). Recently, Fadardi and Cox (2007) evaluated the AACTP with social drinkers, heavy drinkers, and abusive drinkers. Baseline measures were made of each participant's alcohol consumption and attentional bias for alcohol-related and other concern-related stimuli. They underwent other measures including the Readiness to Change Questionnaire (Heather *et al.*, 1993), the Positive Affect and Negative Affect Schedule (Watson *et al.*, 1988) and the Situational Confidence Questionnaire (Annis and Graham, 1988). At the end of AACTP training, participants were re-administered the tests completed at baseline. The abusive drinkers also received a post-training assessment after 3 months. The results were as follows:

• First, both the excessive and the abusive drinkers showed a significantly larger attentional bias for alcohol-related stimuli than the social drinkers. The degree of alcohol-related distraction was positively correlated with the amount of alcohol that participants habitually consumed.

• Second, the excessive drinkers who were trained with the AACTP for two sessions showed a significant reduction in their alcohol-specific distractibility from the pre-training to the post-training assessment. That is, on the post-test their alcohol attentional bias had decreased, but their concern-related attentional bias remained unchanged. These results support the applicability of the AACTP with a non-clinical sample.

• Third, during the initial 1-month waiting period there were no significant reductions in the alcohol abusers' attentional bias for alcohol-related stimuli, their alcohol consumption, or any of the other measures (e.g. readiness to change, situational confidence). However, comparing the pre-training to the post-training assessment, alcohol abusers showed a significant reduction in alcohol attentional bias and alcohol consumption, but increases in their readiness to change, situational confidence, and positive affect. All these improvements were maintained at the 3-month follow-up assessment.

To summarise, the research showed that (a) excessive drinkers can be trained to gain more control over their attentional bias for alcohol, (b) the reductions in alcohol-attentional bias are accompanied by reductions in alcohol consumption, and (c) these reductions are associated with improvements in a variety of other areas of functioning related to drinking. These results are likely to have an impact on how scientists (theoretically) view the initiation and maintenance of abusive drinking. The results are also likely to affect the actual delivery of service, inasmuch as the AACTP – as a tried-and-tested training programme – can be used to improve the effectiveness of treatment for alcohol-related problems.

Changing implicit attitudes through evaluative conditioning

As explained in the introduction, it has been demonstrated that explicit alcohol-related cognitions, as well as implicit associations between alcohol and positive arousal, are important predictors of drinking behaviour (Houben and Wiers, 2006; Wiers *et al.*, 2002). In addition, recent research findings also suggest that implicit associations between alcohol and valence, or implicit attitudes towards alcohol, play a role in drinking behaviour. More specifically, it was demonstrated that participants more easily paired alcohol with positive stimuli than with negative stimuli in the Implicit Association Test as they consumed more alcohol (Houben and Wiers, 2007). Hence, these results suggest that stronger implicit positive attitudes towards alcohol are related to an increase in alcohol consumption (see also De Jong *et al.*, 2007; Payne *et al.* 2008). Therefore, one intervention strategy for reducing drinking could target implicit attitudes towards alcohol.

Gawronski and Bodenhausen (2006) recently proposed the APE-model (Associative and Propositional processes in Evaluation) that specifies under which conditions changes are expected in implicit attitudes. Specifically, they advocate that a direct change in implicit attitudes can be expected when the associative structure is changed, for instance by introducing new associations through evaluative conditioning. Evaluative conditioning refers to changes in the 'liking' of a certain attitude, object or stimulus (the conditioned stimulus, or CS) as a result of repeatedly and consistently pairing that stimulus with other objects or stimuli that have a strong negative or positive affective value (the unconditioned stimuli, or US). Specifically, the underlying idea of evaluative conditioning is that pairings of the CS with a valenced US will cause the attitude towards the CS to change in the direction of the US that it was paired with. Further, it has also been suggested that attitudes develop through processes akin to evaluative conditioning (De Houwer *et al.*, 2001). Consequently, evaluative conditioning might prove to be a straightforward approach for changing implicit attitudes.

While a lot of research has been devoted to examining whether evaluative conditioning can induce attitudes towards novel attitude objects, it has only recently been used to change existing attitudes. Baccus and colleagues (2004), for instance, were able to enhance implicit self-esteem using an evaluative-conditioning procedure. Baccus *et al.* repeatedly exposed participants in the experimental group to consistent pairings of self-relevant words (CS; for example, the participant's own name) with smiling faces (positive US). In contrast, words that were not self-relevant were always paired with either neutral or frowning faces.

For participants in the control group, self-relevant words and non-self-relevant words were randomly paired with smiling, neutral or frowning faces. Importantly, participants in the experimental group showed elevated levels of implicit self-esteem, as indexed by performance on the IAT, as well as lower levels of aggression relative to participants in the control group.

Another example of using evaluative conditioning to change implicit attitudes is found in a recent study by Olson and Fazio (2006). Participants were exposed to pairings of white people with negative stimuli as well as pairings of black people with positive stimuli, interspersed within a stream of 'filler' items. Afterwards, implicit racial attitudes were indexed using an evaluative priming measure. Importantly, Olson and Fazio demonstrated that their evaluative-conditioning procedure reduced prejudice against black people in the conditioning condition relative to a control condition of participants who were not exposed to the critical CS–US pairings.

In light of these promising results, Houben *et al.* (2008) explored whether an evaluative conditioning paradigm, similar to the procedure used by Olson and Fazio (2006), could be used to change implicit and explicit attitudes towards beer in male students. They also examined whether changes in implicit and/or explicit attitudes towards beer induced by evaluative conditioning would produce corresponding changes in their drinking behaviour. Subjects in the experimental group were exposed to an evaluative conditioning procedure during which beer-related pictures (CS) were consistently paired with negative words and pictures (US). Similar to Olson and Fazio's procedure, these critical pairings of beer with negative stimuli were interspersed among a stream of filler items. In contrast, participants in the control group were not exposed to these critical CS–US pairings. Participants in both the experimental group and the control group were told they were performing a vigilance task and were instructed to press a button whenever a pre-specified target was presented. Afterwards, all participants took part in an alleged second study, in which both explicit and implicit attitudes towards beer were measured as well as their drinking behaviour. Results did not yield an effect of the evaluative conditioning procedure with respect to implicit attitudes towards beer, which were assessed using the Affect Misattribution Procedure (AMP; Payne *et al.*, 2005). However, the results did show that students in the experimental group reported significantly less negative explicit attitudes towards beer compared to participants in the control group. Importantly, in a bogus taste test, students in the experimental group drank significantly less beer than those in the control group.

Although results of evaluative conditioning in changing implicit attitudes are less clearcut in alcohol research compared to other areas of research, it seems premature to conclude that such an approach cannot be used to change implicit alcohol-related attitudes. It should be noted that Houben *et al.* (2008) might have been unable to demonstrate changes in implicit attitudes towards beer following an evaluative conditioning procedure due to the implicit measure they used as an index of implicit attitudes towards beer. Specifically, whereas Baccus *et al.* (2004) as well as Olson and Fazio (2006) used well-validated measures of implicit attitudes (such as affective priming and the IAT) Houben and colleagues used a relatively new implicit measure, that may not be as sensitive to implicit attitudes as other established measures. Currently a replication study is being performed.

In conclusion, evaluative conditioning appears to be promising for changing implicit attitudes. Future research will have to establish whether, and under what conditions, evaluative conditioning can be successfully used to change implicit attitudes towards alcohol as well as drinking behaviour.

Assessing and changing automatic action tendencies

Different tests have been used in past years to assess relatively automatic action tendencies. First, a variation of the IAT (Greenwald *et al.*, 1998) has been used (Palfai and Ostafin, 2003; Ostafin and Palfai, 2006). In a standard IAT, the attribute categories are 'positive' or 'pleasant' versus 'negative' or 'unpleasant'. In this motivational variety of the IAT, attribute categories are words related to 'approach' versus 'avoidance', which are combined with alcohol words or a contrast category (an irrelevant contrast 'electricity' in one study, 'water' in the other). The extent to which participants were faster at categorising 'alcohol' and 'approach' together than 'alcohol' and 'avoid' was related to binge-drinking and to cue-induced craving.

De Houwer developed a different test to assess 'approach' versus 'avoidance' motivation – the Stimulus Response Compatibility (SRC) task. This task has been successfully applied to alcohol studies (e.g. Field *et al.*, 2005). Subjects have to move a little matchstick figure (manikin) either towards or away from alcohol pictures, using the arrow keys on the keyboard. High-craving social drinkers were found to be faster 'approaching' than 'avoiding' alcohol pictures. Note that this test is not very implicit, because subjects are instructed in one block of trials to approach the alcohol pictures (move the figure towards them) and to avoid the other pictures, while in the other block they are instructed to avoid the alcohol pictures (move the figure away from them). A more indirect approach–avoidance test has been developed to assess automatic approach action tendencies for alcohol. In this test, subjects react to a feature of the stimulus that is unrelated to the meaning of the stimulus (*cf.* De Houwer, 2003a,b). Subjects reacted to the format of a picture (landscape or portrait, *cf.* Huijding and De Jong, 2005) and these reactions involved an arm movement that moved a joystick away from or towards their body. The rationale behind joystick tasks is that arm flexion (pulling) generates more positive evaluations than extension (pushing). Following the pioneering work of Solarz in the 1960s, Chen and Bargh (1999) demonstrated that positive stimuli trigger 'approach' (pull) movements and negative words trigger 'avoid' (push) movements. The novel aspect of the Approach Avoidance Task (the AAT; Rinck and Becker, 2007) is that the stimulus on the computer screen changes in size as a result of the joystick's movement, increasing with 'pull' and decreasing with 'push' movements. This 'zooming feature' generates a sensation of 'approach' and 'avoidance'. Without this feature, subjects may interpret the movements the opposite way – extending the arm in response to a picture of a beer can be interpreted as a movement away from the body, or as approaching the beer. The zooming feature unambiguously ties in the pull and push movements with approach and avoidance.

The new feature added was to let the participant react to an irrelevant feature of the picture (its format) and to investigate whether heavy and light drinkers have different reaction times when approaching or avoiding the alcohol pictures. Note that this is a truly indirect test, because the instruction is to push or pull the joystick depending on the picture's format (i.e. landscape or portrait) and differences in pushing versus pulling can be assessed for different types of pictures (alcohol pictures, soft drinks, general positive and negative pictures). Heavy drinkers were found to be faster when pulling the alcohol pictures than when pushing them, while light drinkers show the reverse. In addition, heavy drinkers with a genetic variation assumed to be related to the rewarding effects of alcohol – that is, the presence of a G allele in the μ-opioid receptor (*OPRM* gene) as described in van den Wildenberg *et al.* (2007) – showed a particularly strong difference in pulling versus pushing the alcohol pictures (Wiers *et al.*, 2007b). This suggests that heavy drinkers develop strong automatic action tendencies to approach alcohol once they are confronted with stimuli that refer to alcohol. As these implicit action tendencies are related to a genetic variation associated with the rewarding effects of alcohol, these automatic action tendencies may constitute a so-called endophenotype, or biological marker, between a genotype and the distal and heterogeneous phenotype (alcoholism). It should be noted that a recent meta-analysis did not find the same gene to be related to alcoholism (Arias *et al.*, 2006) but a strong appetitive reaction to alcoholism may still be a relevant phenotype in a specific route to alcoholism (early-onset, male alcoholism, *cf.* Barr *et al.*, 2007; Gianoulakis *et al.*, 1996; Van den Wildenberg *et al.*, 2007).

The next question was whether these action tendencies could be re-trained, in a similar way to that described above for alcohol-related attentional bias. In a second study, these automatic action tendencies were re-trained in an implicit learning paradigm, much like the attention training using the visual probe. After an initial test period, in which pictures of alcohol and soft drinks were pushed and pulled equally often, the task changed into a training version. Half of the participants (push-alcohol condition) now pushed the alcohol pictures in most of the cases (90 per cent) and pulled the soft-drink pictures in most of the cases (90 per cent); the other half pulled the alcohol pictures 90 per cent of the time and pushed the soft-drink pictures half of the time.

These results are promising. Participants were successfully trained to push alcohol away (outside awareness), as evident from a post-test with the same test. The effect was generalised to new pictures of alcohol and to a different implicit test of alcohol motivation using words, the IAT (Palfai and Ostafin, 2003). Hence these generalisation effects were stronger than for attentional re-training with a similar set up, described above. In a subsequent taste test, the heavy drinkers who had been successfully trained to push away the alcohol pictures, drank about half as much as heavy drinkers who were successfully trained to pull the alcohol pictures.

Multiple-session versions of this training programme have been developed and are now compared with respect to their effects. One comparison is of a version in which the participants are made aware of the goal of the training (to push the alcohol pictures away) and the implicit learning version, in which they keep the same instruction (to push landscape pictures away, but to pull portrait pictures) and implicitly learn to push alcohol away.

Another important question is to what extent re-training of action tendencies can be used in a clinical setting and whether it results in positive treatment outcomes. Preliminary results from an ongoing first clinical study are promising: after repeated re-training of alcohol action tendencies, patients showed automatic alcohol-avoidance associations (when instructed to push alcohol away *and* without this instruction), both on new pictures in the test used for the re-training (the AAT) and in a different test using words (the IAT). In addition, craving was reduced in the experimental groups, as compared with the control groups (Wiers *et al.*, 2008).

Train away addiction?

In this chapter, a general theoretical framework was first outlined in which addictive behaviours were viewed as the result of an imbalance between largely implicit or automatic appetitive processes and more controlled regulatory processes. We believe this general perspective may provide a useful new perspective for treatment of alcoholism and other addictions. From this perspective, the essential aim of treatment is to restore the balance between these classes of processes – in other words, to decrease the influence of the largely automatic appetitive processes once they are triggered and to increase the influence of regulatory processes over the impulse to engage in the addictive behaviour. Most conventional psychosocial treatments are aimed at increasing control over impulses, either by increasing motivation to refrain from drinking or by teaching and practising ways to avoid or deal with temptations. There is some disagreement about the extent to which current psychosocial treatments can be called successful (Cutler and Fishbain, 2005), but few clinicians or researchers in this area disagree that there is ample room for improvement.

A large part of this chapter was devoted to new strategies developed over the past few years that aim to directly reduce the influence of appetitive impulses over addictive behaviours. We distinguish between three appetitive subprocesses: attentional bias, memory associations and automatic action tendencies. Each of these sub-processes has been targeted by recent re-training studies, often using variations of the same tests used to measure the process, but changed in such a way that the underlying process is not only assessed but also influenced. In all three areas, initial positive findings have been reported; they can be viewed as a 'proof of principle' that these processes can be influenced.

However, these first findings have some limitations, such as generalisation to new stimuli (in the attentional re-training programmes using variations of the visual probe test). Interestingly, in most of the work presented here these effects occur outside the awareness of the majority of participants. We do not yet know whether this is important or whether the effects will be larger, equal or smaller in size when participants are made aware of the purpose of the training.

In a clinical setting, it may be more appropriate to inform patients of the goal of the training, as is currently already done in the AACTP. This may increase motivation to change and the feeling that one can positively influence the outcome of treatment. In general, these training procedures have a very positive motivational message: you can actively work on beating your addiction. In this way, interventions aimed at implicit processes may strengthen explicit processes (and vice versa). It should be noted that at present we have little knowledge of stability of these effects or about their clinical usefulness, although first results from the clinically relevant re-training procedures (repeated attentional re-training with the visual probe test, the AACTP, and the repeated action-tendency re-training) are definitely promising.

We believe there are good reasons to further test clinically relevant varieties of different re-training procedures. Of course there are many other questions to be answered. Issues to be addressed include application in different addictions and combinations of re-training procedures that target different sub-processes (for example, can evaluative conditioning, attentional re-training and re-training of action tendencies enhance each other?) as well as combinations with other interventions. Another interesting possibility – one that we are presently working on – is whether re-training will work over the internet.

From the present theoretical standpoint, a second class of training procedures can aim to increase the regulatory or control processes, either by behavioural training (as has been done in some externalising problem behaviours in children) or by directly stimulating the relevant brain areas through transcranial magnetic stimulation. These approaches are also in their first stage, but are definitely worth further exploration.

One other general approach should be mentioned: rather than re-training automatic processes that lead to addiction, it may be possible to train and automatise alternative behaviours. In other words, let the automatic processes work in favour of alternative, rather than addictive, behaviours. A very simple and straightforward way of doing this is by forming implementation intentions. Implementation intentions have been successful aids in many other health behaviours but have rarely been applied to addictive behaviours (Prestwich *et al.*, 2006).

Implementation intentions consist of a specifically described situation, followed by an action plan. For example, if someone realises that they often drink too much after a hard day's work, they could form the following implementation intention: 'When I am tired after work, I go jogging. Of course it will help if I already have good sport shoes ready waiting for me, rather than a bottle of Scotch'. This example points to a general idea (not entirely new to the field of treatment, but perhaps helpful if more explicit), whereby in general it is a good strategy to use controlled processes in advance to steer anticipated automatic processes in the right direction. It is easier to decide beforehand not to drink when driving than it is to decide when taking orders. There is even preliminary evidence that some self-regulating processes can be automatised (Palfai, 2006).

Conclusions

To conclude, although it may be beneficial to explore different ways for preventing future automatic processes that lead to renewed addictive behaviours, we believe (given the omnipresence of alcohol-related stimuli) it is also important to directly target those automatic processes. Therefore, the emerging general perspective is that addictive behaviours can be viewed as an imbalance between relatively automatic appetitive processes and relatively controlled processes that may serve to inhibit or control these impulses. This knowledge may contribute to further research on the treatment of alcoholism and other addictive behaviours, both by providing a new perspective on existing treatments and through development of entirely new treatments.

References and further reading

Ames, S.L., Franken, I.H.A. and Coronges, K. (2006). Implicit cognition and drugs of abuse. In: R.W. Wiers and A.W. Stacy (eds). *Handbook of Implicit Cognition and Addiction*. Thousand Oaks, CA: Sage, pp. 363–78.

Annis, H.M. and Graham, J.M. (1988). *Situational Confidence Questionnaire: User's Guide*. Toronto: Addiction Research Foundation.

Arias, A., Feinn, R. and Kranzler, H.R. (2006). Association of an *Asn40Asp* (*A118G*) polymorphism in the mu-opioid receptor gene with substance dependence: A meta-analysis. *Drug and Alcohol Dependence*, **83**, 262–68.

Baccus, J.R., Baldwin, M.W. and Packer, D.J. (2004). Increasing implicit self-esteem through classical conditioning. *Psychological Science*, **15**, 498–02.

Barr C.S., Schwandt, M., Lindell S.G., *et al.* (2007). Association of a functional polymorphism in the mu-opioid receptor gene with alcohol response and consumption in male rhesus macaques. *Archives of General Psychiatry*, **64**, 369–76.

Bechara, A. (2005). Decision making, impulse control and loss of willpower to resist drugs: A neurocognitive perspective. *Nature Neuroscience*, **8**, 1459–63.

Bechara, A., Noel, X. and Crone, E.A. (2006). Loss of willpower: abnormal neural mechanisms of impulse control and decision making in addiction. In: R.W. Wiers and A.W. Stacy (eds). *Handbook of Implicit Cognition and Addiction*. Thousand Oaks, CA: Sage, pp. 215–32.

Berridge, K.C. (2001). Reward learning: Reinforcement, incentives, and expectations. In: D.L. Medin (ed.) *The Psychology of Learning and Motivation: Advances in Research and Theory*, *40*. San Diego: Academic Press, pp. 223–78.

Brown, S.A., Tapert, S.F., Granholm, E. and Dellis, D.C. (2000). Neurocognitive functioning of adolescents: Effects of protracted alcohol use. *Alcoholism: Clinical and Experimental Research*, **24**, 164–71.

Camprodon, J.A., Martinez-Raga, J., Alonso-Alonso, M., Shih, M. and Pascual-Leone, A. (2007). One session of high frequency repetitive transcranial magnetic stimulation (rTMS) to the right prefrontal cortex transiently reduces cocaine craving. *Drug and Alcohol Dependence*, **86**, 91–94.

Chen, M. and Bargh, J.A. (1999). Consequences of automatic evaluation: Immediate behavioral predispositions to approach or avoid the stimulus. *Personality and Social Psychology Bulletin*, **25**, 215–24.

Cox, W.M. and Klinger, E., (eds). (2004). *Handbook of Motivational Counseling: Concepts, Approaches, and Assessment*. Chichester: Wiley.

Cox, W.M., Blount, J.P. and Rozak, A.M. (2000). Alcohol abusers' and nonabusers' distraction by alcohol and concern-related stimuli. *American Journal of Drug and Alcohol Abuse*, **26**, 489–95.

Cox, W.M., Fadardi, J.S. and Pothos, E.M. (2006). The addiction Stroop test: Theoretical considerations and procedural recommendations, *Psychological Bulletin*, **132**, 443–76.

Cox, W.M., Hogan, L.M., Kristian, M.R. and Race, J.H. (2002). Alcohol attentional bias as a predictor of alcohol abusers' treatment outcome. *Drug and Alcohol Dependence*, **68**, 237–43.

Cunningham, W.A., Preacher, K.J. and Banaji, M.R. (2001). Implicit attitude measures: Consistency, stability and convergent validity. *Psychological Science*, **12**, 163–70.

Cutler R.B. and Fishbain, D.A. (2005). Are alcoholism treatments effective? The Project MATCH data. *BMC Public Health*, **5**, 75–85.

Dahl, R.E. and Spear, L.P (eds). (2004). Adolescent brain development: Vulnerabilities and opportunities, Vol. 1021 New York: Annals of the New York Academy of Sciences.

De Bellis, M.D., Clark, D.B., Beers, S.R., *et al.* (2000). Hippocampal volume in adolescent-onset alcohol use disorders. *American Journal of Psychiatry*, **157**, 737–44.

De Houwer, J. (2003a). A structural analysis of indirect measures of attitudes. In: J. Musch and K.C. Klauer (eds). *The Psychology of Evaluation. Affective Processes in Cognition and Emotion*. Mahwah, NJ: Erlbaum, pp. 219–44.

De Houwer, J. (2003b). The extrinsic affective Simon task. *Experimental Psychology*, **50**, 77–85.

De Houwer, J. (2006). What are implicit measures and why are we using them? In R.W. Wiers and A.W. Stacy (eds). *Handbook of Implicit Cognition* and *Addiction*. Thousand Oaks, CA: Sage, pp. 11–28.

De Houwer, J., Crombez, G., Koster, E. H.W. and De Beul, N. (2004). Implicit alcohol-related cognitions in clinical samples of heavy drinkers. *Journal of Behaviour Therapy and Experimental Psychiatry*, **35**, 275–86.

De Houwer, J., Thomas, S. and Baeyens, F. (2001). Associative learning of likes and dislikes: A review of 25 years of research on human evaluative conditioning. *Psychological Bulletin*, **127**, 853–69.

De Jong, P., Kindt, M. and Roefs, A. (2006). Changing implicit cognition: Findings from experimental psychopathology. In: R.W. Wiers and A.W. Stacy (eds). *Handbook of Implicit Cognition and Addiction*. Thousand Oaks, CA: Sage, pp. 425–37.

De Jong, P.J., Wiers, R.W., Van de Braak, M. and Huijding, J. (2007). Using the extrinsic affective Simon test as a measure of implicit attitudes towards alcohol: relationship with drinking behavior and alcohol problems. *Addictive Behaviors*, **32**, 881–87.

Erickson, K.I., Colcombe, S.J., Wadhwa, R., *et al.* (2007). Training-induced functional activation in dual task processing: An fMRI study. *Cerebral Cortex*, **17**, 192–204.

Everitt, B.J. and Robbins, T.W. (2005). Neural systems of reinforcement for drug addiction: from actions to habits to compulsion. *Nature Neuroscience*, **8**, 1481–89.

Fadardi, J.S. and Cox, W.M. (2006). *Alcohol Attention Control Training Program (AACTP)*, Version 2.

Fadardi, J.S. and Cox, W.M. (2006). Alcohol attentional bias: drinking salience or cognitive impairment? *Psychopharmacology*, **185**, 169–78.

Fadardi, J.S. and Cox, W.M. (2007). *Reversing the Sequence: Overcoming Alcohol-Attentional Bias Reduces Drinking*. Bangor: University of Wales (Unpublished software.)

Fazio, R.H. and Towles-Schwen, T. (1999). The MODE model of attitude–behaviour processes. In: S. Chaiken, Y. Trope (eds). *Dual Process Theories in Social Psychology*. New York: Guilford, pp. 97–116.

Feldman-Barrett, L.F., Tugade, M.M. and Engle, R.W. (2004). Individual differences in working memory capacity and dual-process theories of the mind. *Psychological Bulletin*, **130**, 553–73.

Field, M. and Eastwood, B. (2005). Experimental manipulation of attentional bias increases the motivation to drink alcohol. *Psychopharmacology*, **183**, 350–57.

Field, M., Duka, T., Eastwood, B., Child, R., Santarcangelo, M. and Gayton, M. (2007). Experimental manipulation of attentional biases in heavy drinkers: do the effects generalize? *Psychopharmacology*, **192** (4), 593–608.

Finn, P.R. and Hall, J. (2004). Cognitive ability and risk for alcoholism: Short-term memory capacity and intelligence moderate personality risk for alcohol problems. *Journal of Abnormal Psychology*, **113**, 569–81.

Franken, I.H.A. (2003). Drug craving and addiction: integrating psychological and neuropsychopharmacological approaches. *Progress in Neuropsychopharmacology and Biological Psychiatry*, **27**, 563–79.

Gawronski, B. and Bodenhausen, G.V. (2006). Associative and propositional processes in evaluation: An integrative review of implicit and explicit attitude change. *Psychological Bulletin*, **132**, 692–31.

Gawronski, B., Hofmann, W. and Wilbur, C.J. (2006). Are 'implicit' attitudes unconscious? *Consciousness and Cognition*, **15**, 485–99.

Gianoulakis, C., Krishnan, B. and Thavundayil, J. (1996). Enhanced sensitivity of pituitary endorphin to ethanol in subjects at high risk of alcoholism. *Archives of General Psychiatry*, **53**, 250–57.

Greenwald, A.G., McGhee, D.E. and Schwartz, J.L.K. (1998). Measuring individual differences in implicit cognition: the Implicit Association Test. *Journal of Personality and Social Psychology*, **74**, 1464–80.

Grenard, J.L., Ames, S.L., Pentz, M.A. and Sussman, S. (2006). Motivational interviewing with adolescents and young adults for drug-related problems. *International Journal of Adolescent Medical Health*, **18**, 53–67.

Grenard, J.L., Ames, S.L., Wiers, R.W., Thush, C., Stacy, A.W. and Sussman, S. (2007). Brief intervention for substance use among at-risk adolescents: A pilot study. *Journal of Adolescent Health*, **40**, 188–91.

Grenard, J.L., Ames, S.L., Wiers, R.W., Thush, C., Sussman, S. and Stacy, A.W. (in press). Working memory moderates the predictive effects of drug-related associations on substance use. *Psychology of Addictive Behaviours*.

Heather, N., Rollnick, S. and Bell, A. (1993). Predictive validity of the Readiness to Change Questionnaire. *Addiction*, **88**, 1667–77.

Hofmann, W., Gschwendner, T., Friese, M., Wiers, R.W. and Schmitt, M. (in press). Working memory capacity and self-regulatory behavior: Towards an individual differences perspective on behavior determination by automatic versus controlled processes. *Journal of Personality and Social Psychology*.

Houben, K., Schoenmakers, T. and Wiers, R.W. (2008). Evaluative conditioning changes beer drinking behaviour and positive explicit attitudes. (Manuscript in preparation.)

Houben, K. and Wiers, R.W. (2006). Assessing implicit alcohol associations with the implicit association test: fact or artefact? *Addictive Behaviours*, **31**, 1346–62.

Houben, K. and Wiers, R.W. (2007). Are drinkers implicitly positive about drinking alcohol? Personalizing the Alcohol-IAT to reduce negative extrapersonal contamination. *Alcohol and Alcoholism*, **42**, 301–07.

Houben, K., Wiers, R.W. and Roefs, A. (2006). Reaction time measures of substance-related associations. In: R.W. Wiers and A.W. Stacy (eds). *Handbook of Implicit Cognition and Addiction*. Thousand Oaks, CA: Sage, pp. 91–104.

Huijding, J. and De Jong, P.J. (2005). A pictorial version of the Extrinsic Affective Simon Task: sensitivity to generally affective and phobia-relevant stimuli in high and low spider-fearful individuals. *Experimental Psychology*, **52**, 289–95.

Kahneman, D. (2003). A perspective on judgment and choice. *American Psychologist*, **58**, 697–20.

Kalivas, P.W. and Volkow, N.D. (2005). The neural basis of addiction: A pathology of motivation and choice. *American Journal of Psychiatry*, **162**, 1403–13.

Kane, M.J. and Engle, R.W. (2002). The role of prefrontal cortex in working-memory capacity, executive attention, and general fluid intelligence: An individual-differences perspective. *Psychonomic Bulletin and Review*, **9**, 637–71.

Klingberg, T., Fernell, E. Olesen, P.J., *et al.* (2005). Computerized training of working memory in children with ADHD – a randomized clinical trial. *Journal of the Academy of Child and Adolescent Psychiatry*, **44**, 177–86.

Klinger, E. and Cox, W.M. (2004). Motivation and the theory of current concerns. In: W.M. Cox and E. Klinger (eds). *Handbook of Motivational Counseling: Concepts, Approaches and Assessment*. Chichester: Wiley, pp. 3–27.

Larimer, M.E. and Cronce, J.M. (2002). Identification, prevention and treatment: A review of individual-focused strategies to reduce problematic alcohol consumption by college students. *Journal of Studies on Alcohol,* **14**, (Suppl.1), 148–63.

MacLeod, C., Rutherford, E., Campbell, L., Ebsworthy, G.H. and Holker, L. (2002). Selective attention and emotional vulnerability: Assessing the causal basis of their association through the experimental manipulation of attentional bias. *Journal of Abnormal Psychology*, **111**, 107–23.

Mathews, A. and MacLeod, C. (2002). Induced processing biases have causal effects on anxiety. *Cognition and Emotion*, **16**, 331–54.

Miller, W.R. and Rollnick, S. (2002). *Motivational Interviewing: Preparing People to Change Addictive Behaviours*, 2nd edn. Guilford: New York.

Miyake, A., Friedman, N.P., Emerson, M.J., Witzki, A.H., Howerter, A. and Wager, T.D. (2000). The unity and diversity of executive functions and their contributions to complex 'frontal lobe' tasks: A latent variable analysis. *Cognitive Psychology*, **41**, 49–100.

Moyer, A., Finney, J., Swearingen, C. and Vergun, P. (2002). Brief interventions for alcohol problems: A meta-analytic review of controlled investigations in treatment-seeking and non-treatment-seeking populations. *Addiction,* **97**, 279–92.

National Institute on Alcohol Abuse and Alcoholism (NIAAA). (2005). The effects of alcohol on physiological processes and biological development. *Alcohol Research and Health*, **28**, 125–31.

Noel, X., Colmant, M., van der Linden, M., *et al.* (2006). Time course of attention for alcohol cues in abstinent alcoholic patients: The role of initial orienting. *Alcoholism: Clinical and Experimental Research*, **30**, 1871–77.

Olson, M.A. and Fazio, R.H. (2004). Trait interferences as a function of automatically activated racial attitudes and motivation to control prejudiced reactions. *Basic and Applied Social Psychology*, **26**, 1–11.

Olson, M.A. and Fazio, R.H. (2006). Reducing automatically-activated racial prejudice through implicit evaluative conditioning. *Personality and Social Psychology Bulletin*, **32**, 421–33.

Ostafin, B.D. and Palfai, T.P. (2006). Compelled to consume: The Implicit Association Test and automatic alcohol motivation. *Psychology of Addictive Behaviors*, **20**, 322–27.

Palfai, T.P. (2006). Automatic processes in the self-regulation of addictive behaviours. In: R.W. Wiers and A.W. Stacy (eds). *Handbook of Implicit Cognition and Addiction,* Thousand Oaks, CA: Sage, pp. 411–24.

Palfai, T.P. and Ostafin, B.D. (2003). Alcohol-related motivational tendencies in hazardous drinkers: Assessing implicit response tendencies using the modified IAT. *Behaviour Research and Therapy*, **41**, 1149–62.

Payne, B.K. (2005). Conceptualizing control in social cognition: How executive functioning modulates the expression of automatic stereotyping. *Journal of Personality* and *Social Psychology*, **89**, 488–03.

Payne, B.K., Cheng, C.M., Govorun, O. and Stewart, B.D. (2005). An inkblot for attitudes: Affect misattribution as implicit measurement. *Journal of Personality* and *Social Psychology*, **89**, 277–93.

Peterson, J.B., Finn, P.R. and Pihl, R.O. (1992). Cognitive dysfunction and the inherited predisposition to alcoholism. *Journal of Studies on Alcohol,* **53**, 154–60.

Payne, B.K., Govorun, O. and Arbuckle, N.L. (2008). Automatic attitudes and alcohol: Does implicit liking predict drinking? *Cognition and Emotion*, **22**, 238–71.

Prestwich, A., Conner, M. and Lawton, R.J. (2006). Implementation intentions: can they be used to prevent and treat addiction? In: R.W. Wiers and A.W. Stacy (eds). *Handbook of Implicit Cognition and Addiction*. Thousand Oaks CA: Sage, pp. 455–69.

Rinck, M. and Becker, E.S. (2007). Approach and avoidance in fear of spiders. *Journal of Behaviour Therapy and Experimental Psychiatry*, **38**, 105–20.

Robinson, T.E. and Berridge, K.C. (2003). Addiction. *Annual Review of Psychology*, **54**, 25–53.

Schoenmakers, T., Lux, I., Goertz, A., van Kerkhof, D., de Bruin, M. and Wiers, R.W. (in press). A randomized clinical trial to measure effects of attentional re-training in alcohol dependent patients.

Schoenmakers, T., Wiers, R.W. and Field, M. (2008). Effects of a low dose of alcohol on cognitive biases and craving in heavy drinkers. *Psychopharmacology*, **197**, 169–78.

Schoenmakers, T., Wiers, R.W., Jones, B.T., Bruce, G. and Jansen, A.T.M. (2007a). Attentional retraining decreases attentional bias in heavy drinkers without generalization. *Addiction*, **102**, 399–405.

Sher, K.J. (1991). *Children of Alcoholics: A Critical Appraisal of Theory and Research*. Chicago: University of Chicago Press.

Stacy, A.W. (1997). Memory activation and expectancy as prospective predictors of alcohol and marihuana use. *Journal of Abnormal Psychology*, **106**, 61–73.

Stacy, A.W., Ames, S.L. and Grenard, J. (2006). Word association tests of associative memory and implicit processes: theoretical and assessment issues. In: R.W. Wiers and A.W. Stacy (eds). *Handbook of Implicit Cognition and Addiction*. Thousand Oaks, CA: Sage, pp. 75–90.

Stacy, A.W., Ames, S.L. and Knowlton, B.J. (2004). Neurologically plausible distinctions in cognition relevant to drug use etiology and prevention. *Substance Use and Misuse*, **39**, 1571–23.

Stasiewicz, P.R., Gulliver, S.B., Bradizza, C.M., Rohsenow, D.J., Torrisi, R. and Monti, P.M. (1997). Exposure to negative emotional cues and alcohol cue reactivity with alcoholics: A preliminary investigation. *Behaviour Research and Therapy*, **35**, 1143–49.

Stormark, K.M., Field, N.P., Hugdahl, K. and Horowitz, M. (1997). Selective processing of visual alcohol cues in abstinent alcoholics: An approach-avoidance conflict? *Addictive Behaviours*, **22**, 509–19.

Strack, F. and Deutsch, R. (2004). Reflective and impulsive determinants of social behaviour. *Personality and Social Psychology Review* **3**, 220–47.

Stroop, J.R. (1935). Studies of interference in serial verbal reaction. *Journal of Experimental Psychology*, **18**, 643–62.

Tapert, S.F., Baratta, B.S., Abrantes, B.A. and Brown, S.A. (2002). Attention dysfunction predicts substance involvement in community youths. *Journal of the American Academy of Child and Adolescent Psychiatry*, **41**, 680–86.

Tapert, S.F., Schweinsburg, A.D., Barlett, V.C., *et al.* (2004). Blood oxygen level dependent response and spatial working memory in adolescents with alcohol use disorders. *Alcohol: Clinical and Experimental Research*, **28**, 1577–86.

Thush, C., Wiers, R.W., Ames, S.L., Grenard, J.L., Sussman, S. and Stacy, A.W. (2008). Interactions between implicit and explicit cognition and working memory capacity in the prediction of alcohol use in at-risk adolescents. *Drug and Alcohol Dependence*, **94**, 116–24.

Thush, C., Wiers, R.W., Moerbeek, M., *et al.* (in press). The influence of motivational interviewing on explicit and implicit alcohol-related cognition and alcohol use in at-risk adolescents. *Journal of Psychology of Addictive Behaviours*.

Thush, C., Wiers, R.W., Theunissen, N., *et al.* (2007). A randomized clinical trial of a targeted intervention to moderate alcohol use and alcohol-related problems in at-risk adolescents. *Pharmacology Biochemistry and Behavior*, **86**, 368–76.

Tiffany, S.T. (1990). A cognitive model of drug urges and drug-use behavior: Role of automatic and nonautomatic processes. *Psychological Review*, **97**, 147–68.

Towles-Schwen, T. and Fazio, R.H. (2006). Automatically activated racial attitudes as predictors of the success of interracial roommate relationships. *Journal of Experimental Social Psychology*, **42**, 698–705.

Townsend J.M. and Duka, T. (2001). Attentional bias associated with alcohol cues: Differences between heavy and occasional social drinkers. *Psychopharmacology*, **157**, 67–74.

van den Wildenberg, E., Wiers, R.W., Janssen, R.G.J., *et al.* (2007). A functional polymorphism of the mu-opioid receptor gene (*OPRM1*) influences cue-induced craving for alcohol in male heavy drinkers. *Alcoholism: Clinical and Experimental Research*, **31**, 1–10.

Volkow, N., Fowler, J. and Wang, G. (2004). The addicted human brain viewed in the light of imaging studies: Brain circuits and treatment strategies. *Neuropharmacology*, **47**, 3–13.

Watson D., Clark, L.A. and Tellegen, A. (1988). Development and validation of brief measures of positive and negative affect: The PANAS scales. *Journal of Personality* and *Social Psychology*, **54**, 1063–70.

West, R. (2006). *Theory of Addiction*. Oxford: Blackwell.

Wiers R.W., Van de Luitgaarden, J., Van den Wildenberg, E. and Smulders, F.T.Y. (2005). Challenging implicit and explicit alcohol-related cognitions in young heavy drinkers. *Addiction,* **100**, 806–19.

Wiers, R.W. and Stacy, A.W (eds). (2006a). *Handbook of Implicit Cognition and Addiction*. Thousand Oaks, CA: Sage.

Wiers, R.W. and Stacy, A.W. (2006b). Implicit cognition and addiction. *Current Directions in Psychological Science*, **15**, 292–96.

Wiers, R.W., Bartholow, B.D., van den Wildenberg, E., *et al.* (2007a). Automatic and controlled processes and the development of addictive behaviours in adolescents: A review and a model. *Pharmacology Biochemistry and Behavior*, **86**, 263–83.

Wiers, R.W., Cox, W.M., Field, M., *et al.* (2006a). The search for new ways to change implicit alcohol-related cognitions in heavy drinkers. *Alcoholism: Clinical and Experimental Research*, **30**, 320–31.

Wiers, R.W., Hesse, C., Rinck, M., Schuck, K., Becker, E. & Lindenmeyer, J. (2008). Re-training the automatic tendency to approach alcohol in alcohol dependent patients. (Manuscript in preparation).

Wiers, R.W., Houben, K., Smulders, F.T.Y., *et al.* (2006b). To drink or not to drink: the role of automatic and controlled cognitive processes in the etiology of alcohol-related problems. In: R.W. Wiers and A.W. Stacy (eds). *Handbook of Implicit Cognition and Addiction*. Thousand Oaks, CA: Sage, pp. 339–61.

Wiers, R.W., Rinck, M., Kordts, R., *et al.* (2007b). Train addictive impulses away! Assessing and retraining automatic tendencies to drink. (Submitted for publication.)

Wiers, R.W., van Woerden, N., Smulders, F.T.Y. and De Jong, P.J. (2002). Implicit and explicit alcohol-related cognitions in heavy and light drinkers. *Journal of Abnormal Psychology*, **111**, 648–58.

Yin, H.R. and Knowlton, B.J. (2006). Addiction and learning in the brain. In: R.W. Wiers and A.W. Stacy (eds). *Handbook of Implicit Cognition and Addiction*. Thousand Oaks, CA: Sage, pp. 185–99.

Zack, M., Toneatto, T. and MacLeod, C.M. (1999). Implicit activation of alcohol concepts by negative affective cues distinguishes between problem drinkers with high and low psychiatric distress. *Journal of Abnormal Psychology*, **108**, 518–31.

■ Part Four ■

Contemporary Issues in Identification and Treatment

16 The role and value of Alcoholics Anonymous

Colin R. Martin

This chapter will explore an established and effective route of support for many people with problem drinking behaviour and a history of alcohol dependency. The self-help groups of the worldwide organisation 'Alcoholics Anonymous' have been an influential and valuable resource for many people in both facilitating and supporting abstinence. Alcoholics Anonymous is a surprisingly effective and acceptable approach to changing problematic drinking behaviour. Moreover, it may be perceived as paradoxical: while the organisation maintains that the group is not a therapy, there can be little doubt from the research conducted on attendees' drinking behaviour that Alcoholics Anonymous does represent an efficacious – and consequently therapeutic – intervention. Alcoholics Anonymous has many advocates for its success, not least the patronage accorded to the organisation by a number of people in the public eye including politicians and film stars. However, the approach of Alcoholics Anonymous is by no means a niche approach; the salient aspects of the approach are often incorporated as crucial elements within a therapeutic programme of care, irrespective of whether the care provider is statutory or private.

This collaboration with traditional services may take many forms, for example the 'stepped' philosophy of Alcoholics Anonymous may be incorporated into the treatment programme (such as in the case of high-profile centres like the Betty Ford Center); alternatively, Alcoholics Anonymous may be highlighted as a source of support during a group therapy programme for alcohol-dependent people. This may take the form of a dedicated session from a member during the programme. It is also not unusual for them to hold a group meeting within an alcohol or addiction treatment unit on a regular, often weekly, basis. This chapter will evaluate the evidence for the use of Alcoholics Anonymous as an option to support anyone with an alcohol dependency problem, whether as an adjunct to established clinical services or as a sole provider of 'intervention'.

A brief history of Alcoholics Anonymous

Alcoholics Anonymous is an international organisation. In the UK alone more than 3000 groups regularly meet. It originated in the USA in the mid 1930s and came about through the meeting of two problem drinkers, a stockbroker and a doctor. Central to their approach was recognising alcoholism as a disease and realising that recovery may be maintained by working with other 'alcoholics' or experiencing 'fellowship' with them. The influence of the founding members had a profound impact on those experiencing alcohol dependency and seeking sobriety and with increasing numbers of 'alcoholics' achieving sobriety, the organisation increased in size, with many groups set up in the USA and Canada, and then internationally. Today Alcoholics Anonymous is a global institution, which has undoubtedly been instrumental in the recovery and continued sobriety of countless people with alcohol problems.

Alcoholics Anonymous group meetings

Group meetings are classified into two types, closed and open. Anonymity, as mentioned in the name of the organisation, is central to the tradition of the movement. *Closed* meetings are reserved only for 'alcoholics'. *Open* meetings, in contrast, are effectively open to anyone, but they are generally attended by 'alcoholics', family members and people wishing to help someone with an alcohol problem.

The 12 steps of Alcoholics Anonymous

The programme is based on discrete 'steps' that describe a process of recovery and a recognition of each person's relationship with alcohol. A central to tenet to the approach is the underlying assumption that a recovered drinker, who has achieved and maintained sobriety by engagement with the 12-step programme, has a unique ability to help facilitate recovery of another person with a drinking problem. In this way, the recovered drinker can act as a 'sponsor' to the uncontrolled drinker. The 12 steps of the programme are based on the experiences of the early members of the organisation. They describe in many ways the common characteristics that bind the fellowship. They are listed in Box 16.1. The spiritual dimension of the organisation permeates throughout these 12 steps. Lay appraisal of the 12 steps suggests that acknowledging such issues is as useful a personal 'code of conduct' as any other for living one's life – irrespective of the presence of an alcohol problem. It is no surprise, therefore, that Alcoholics Anonymous, its underlying philosophy, and the 12 steps, have undoubted appeal to many people experiencing drinking problems. Alcoholics Anonymous describes itself as a fellowship of men and women who come together to share their experience, strength and hope in order to tackle a common problem of alcohol dependency. The only criterion for membership is the expressed desire to stop drinking. Unusually for an organisation with a formal membership, no fees or yearly dues are required. The focus of the organisation is on achieving and maintaining sobriety.

A quintessential characteristic of its underlying philosophy is that 'alcoholism' represents a disease and that the only 'cure' is complete abstinence. In this respect, no mechanisms is in place to support a controlled-drinking approach or other perspectives on the nature of alcohol dependency, such as psychological or sociological models. Further, 'recovered alcoholics' are considered 'in remission' because relapse can occur at any time due to the insidious nature of the disease of 'alcoholism'. Having said that, the resolute focus on the disease-entity of alcohol dependency provides a particularly strong focus on the pursuit and maintenance of abstinence, and recognition of relapse as a common and often-to-be-expected phenomenon.

Box 16.1	The 12 Steps of the Alcoholics Anonymous programme
Step 1	Powerlessness over alcohol
Step 2	Belief in a greater power to aid restoration
Step 3	Turning to God
Step 4	Performing a moral inventory
Step 5	Acknowledging the nature of committed wrongs
Step 6	Defects of character
Step 7	Shortcomings
Step 8/9	Reparation
Step 10	Admitting wrongs
Step 11	Prayer and meditation
Step 12	Spiritual awakening

Classically, Alcoholics Anonymous's approach to achievement and maintaining abstinence, as often quoted within the organisation, is 'one day at a time'. It has long been established that for many people with alcohol dependency, the seeking out of non-medical and non-traditional services for support is a realistic and valuable option (Imber *et al.*, 1976). The seeking of alternative or non-medical help should be considered against evidence that, even within the realm of traditional approaches, the type, intensity and duration of intervention may make little difference to outcome (Edwards *et al.*, 1977).

Furthermore, for many years the needs of people with alcohol dependency were arguably not effectively met by the statutory services (Moore, 1977) therefore it is rational to assume that alternatives would appeal to those motivated to change their problem drinking behaviour.

Evidence for the efficacy of Alcoholics Anonymous

An important question to consider (and fundamentally, a simple one) is: Does Alcoholics Anonymous work? There is incontrovertible evidence for the efficacy of Alcoholics Anonymous and Alcoholics Anonymous-based approaches in facilitating improved outcomes (Cross *et al.*, 1990; Emrick, 1987; Elal-Lawrence *et al.*, 1986; Morgenstern *et al.*, 1997; Smith, 1985; Thurstin *et al.*, 1987). However, such conclusions are based on the premise that goals are essentially abstinence-based, since controlled drinking does not represent a legitimate endpoint within the philosophy of Alcoholics Anonymous. Consequently, it might not be suitable for problem drinkers whose goals are not primarily abstinence, but controlled drinking (Emrick, 1987).

Against its apparent success, more complex factors come into play and these must be considered in any evaluation of the efficacy of the approach. Evidence from people in recovery has indicated that involvement with Alcoholics Anonymous played only a minor role and that the major influences on their behaviour change were the social pressures and the negative consequences of excessive drinking (Nordstrum and Berglund, 1986). However, to be fair to Alcoholics Anonymous, traditional treatment was perceived to be important although having a minor role compared to the dominant social milieu (Nordstrum and Berglund, 1986).

Given the apparent success of Alcoholics Anonymous, the approach has come under scrutiny in terms of attempts to explain the seemingly therapeutic effects of a philosophy that maintains it is not a therapy. One area that has been pursued is to consider the possibility of discrete differences between people with a history of problem drinking who attend Alcoholics Anonymous and those that do not. Interestingly, such investigations have been elusive in revealing tacit and consistent differences between groups (Thurstin *et al.*, 1986). However, one interesting observation is between those who do well in Alcoholics Anonymous and those who do not, in terms of drinking behaviour. Thurstin and colleagues (1986) found that those attendees who do well tended to have lower levels of anxiety and depression and were more socially integrated than those who did less well. This however, should not be surprising because it has been established that anxiety and depression are comorbid in alcohol dependency (Burns and Teesson, 2002; Cornelius *et al.*, 2003; Gratzer *et al.*, 2004; Grothues *et al.*, 2005; Thase *et al.*, 2001) and that the observations of Thurstin *et al.* (1986) may easily be ascribed to the problem-drinking population rather than specifically to Alcoholics Anonymous.

One challenging consideration about its effectiveness must be whether it is a therapy or not, as an understanding of the processes involved may be extremely valuable for incorporating the successful dimensions of Alcoholics Anonymous into more mainstream and statutory forms of care delivery. Khantizian and Mack (1994), though not explicitly describing Alcoholics Anonymous as a psychotherapy, do suggest that its approach has many elements in common with group psychotherapy treatment and they suggest that clinicians should be aware of these underlying dynamic processes in order to appreciate and understand the success of Alcoholics Anonymous. This is important because the therapeutic advantage offered by Alcoholics Anonymous, which is undeniable, may highlight shortcomings in the provision of appropriate and evidence-based after care that should be offered to alcohol-dependent people following initial intervention for their problem, such as an inpatient or community detoxification. Gossop and colleagues (2003) found in a 6-month follow-up study significant and positive advantages in drinking outcomes in Alcoholics Anonymous attenders compared to non-attenders. However, they also emphasised that its role is an important one in light of the often inadequate provision of appropriate after-care services. It would be scandalous, of course, if Alcoholics Anonymous filled a vacuum due to inadequate aftercare service provision, since it does not consider itself a treatment or therapy. However, as aftercare services evolve, it is important for them to learn from the successful components of the Alcoholics Anonymous programme and how such elements may be usefully incorporated into mainstream services. This assertion is not however uncontroversial, even within the realm of statutory inpatient provision (Harris *et al.*, 2003).

Conclusions

In summary, there is a considerable body of evidence, which is constantly accruing, which suggests that membership of Alcoholics Anonymous may be of considerable benefit to some people presenting with alcohol dependency. Importantly, Alcoholics Anonymous represents a philosophy that encapsulates concrete beliefs about the nature of alcohol dependency which may restrict its attractiveness to a particular 'niche' group of people, for example those seeking the pursuit of abstinence and a belief in the disease model of 'alcoholism'. In contrast, people who wish to pursue a controlled-drinking lifestyle may find that Alcoholics Anonymous is not appropriate for them. However, it is important for anyone experiencing chronic alcohol dependency to recognise that Alcoholics Anonymous may work for many people – this fact is useful not only for providing an alternative to traditional treatment approaches, but also for because it gives useful insights into the important components of an alliance that influences fundamental drinking behaviour change.

A question that should be considered with respect to Alcoholics Anonymous in the context of evidence-based practice is: How does this approach work? Alcoholics Anonymous claims that it is not a therapy in the traditional sense, yet the benefit it affords to so many people would clearly be viewed as therapeutic in a clinical perspective. In terms of ethical practice, clinicians may perceive it as a dilemma to advocate an approach that has benefited many people if they do not embrace and believe in the disease model themselves.

There can be little doubt, irrespective of the aetiological perspectives of individual clinicians, that Alcoholics Anonymous is a valuable and important part of recovery and clinicians should at least make someone seeking help for alcohol dependency problems aware of the full variety of support that is available to them, including Alcoholics Anonymous.

References and further reading

Burns, L. and Teesson, M. (2002). Alcohol use disorders comorbid with anxiety, depression and drug use disorders. Findings from the Australian national survey of mental health and well being. *Drug and Alcohol Dependence*, **68**, 299–307.

Cornelius, J.R., Bukstein, O., Salloum, I. and Clark, D. (2003). Alcohol and psychiatric comorbidity. *Recent Developments in Alcoholism*, **16**, 361–74.

Cross, G.M., Morgan, C.W., Mooney, A.J., Martin, C.A. and Rafter, J.A. (1990). Alcoholism treatment: A ten-year follow-up study. *Alcoholism: Clinical and Experimental Research*, **14**, 169–73.

Elal-Lawrence, G., Slade, P.D. and Dewey, M.E. (1986). Predictors of outcome type in treated problem drinkers. *Journal of Studies on Alcohol*, **47**, 41–47.

Edwards, G., Orford, J., Egert, S., *et al.* (1977). Alcoholism: A controlled trial of 'treatment' and 'advice'. *Journal of Studies on Alcohol*, **38**, 1004–31.

Emrick, C.D. (1987). Alcoholics Anonymous: Affiliation processes and effectiveness as treatment. *Alcoholism: Clinical and Experimental Research*, **11**, 416–23.

Gossop, M., Harris, J., Best, D., *et al.* (2003). Is attendance at Alcoholics Anonymous meetings after inpatient treatment related to improved outcomes? A 6-month follow-up study. *Alcohol and Alcoholism*, **38**, 421–26.

Gratzer, D., Levitan, R.D., Sheldon, T., Toneatto, T., Rector, N.A. and Goering, P. (2004). Lifetime rates of alcoholism in adults with anxiety, depression, or comorbid depression/anxiety: A community survey of Ontario. *Journal of Affective Disorders*, **79**, 209–15.

Grothues, J., Bischof, G., Reinhardt, S., *et al.* (2005). Intention to change drinking behaviour in general practice patients with problematic drinking and comorbid depression or anxiety. *Alcohol and Alcoholism*, **40**, 394–400.

Harris, J., Best, D., Gossop, M., *et al.* (2003). Prior Alcoholics Anonymous (AA) affiliation and the acceptability of the 12 steps to patients entering UK statutory addiction treatment. *Journal of Studies on Alcohol*, **64**, 257–61.

Imber, S., Schultz, E., Funderburk, F., Allen, R. and Flamer, R. (1976). The fate of the untreated alcoholic. Toward a natural history of the disorder. *Journal of Nervous and Mental Disease*, **162**, 238–47.

Khantzian, E.J. and Mack, J.E. (1994). How AA works and why it's important for clinicians to understand. *Journal of Substance Abuse Treatment*, **11**, 77–92.

Moore, R.A. (1977). Ten years of inpatient programs for alcoholic patients. *American Journal of Psychiatry*, **134**, 542–45.

Morgenstern, J., Labouvie, E., McCrady, B.S., Kahler, C.W. and Frey, R.M. (1997). Affiliation with Alcoholics Anonymous after treatment: A study of its therapeutic effects and mechanisms of action. *Journal of Consulting and Clinical Psychology*, **65**, 768–77.

Nordstrum, G. and Berglund, M. (1986). Successful adjustment in alcoholism. Relationships between causes of improvement, personality, and social factors. *Journal of Nervous and Mental Disease*, **174**, 664–68.

Smith, D.I. (1985). Evaluation of a residential AA programme for women. *Alcohol and Alcoholism*, **20**, 315–27.

Thase, M.E., Salloum, I.M. and Cornelius, J.D. (2001). Comorbid alcoholism and depression: Treatment issues. *Journal of Clinical Psychiatry*, **62**(Suppl.20), 32–41.

Thurstin, A.H., Alfano, A.M. and Nerviano, V.J. (1987). The efficacy of AA attendance for aftercare of inpatient alcoholics: Some follow-up data. *International Journal of Addiction,* **22**, 1083–90.

Thurstin, A.H., Alfano, A.M. and Sherer, M. (1986). Pretreatment MMPI profiles of AA members and non-members. *Journal of Studies on Alcohol,* **47** (6), 468–71.

17 Controlled drinking in chronic alcohol dependency
A therapeutic option?

Colin R. Martin

This chapter will explore one possible treatment option and treatment goal that was once considered impossible in people presenting with a long-term history of heavy drinking or chronic alcohol dependency. The evidence to support such a treatment option has important ramifications not only for client or patient choice, but also because it raises significant questions about the conceptualisation and contextual framing of alcohol dependency as a disease entity treated within a medical model.

The enigma of controlled drinking

Certainly one of the most controversial and challenging therapeutic notions over the past 20 years has been the possibility of a treatment goal of non-problematic controlled drinking. This possibility has often been ridiculed as an impossibility for people with a history of chronic alcohol dependency, from a number of aetiological and diagnostic perspectives. Firstly, for groups such as Alcoholics Anonymous and for clinicians who work within a disease model, the notion that a previously addicted person can become 'unaddicted' seems diametrically opposed to the only treatment goal – of abstinence. Another challenge to achieving controlled drinking status comes from the range of clinical services which, while not working within a disease model, view abstinence as the most desirable clinical outcome. The final challenge to the controlled drinking approach involves a circular argument, particularly pertinent to those driven by a disease model; that is, that if controlled drinking can be achieved by an individual then that person could not have been an 'alcoholic' in the first place.

So far there seems to be a compelling, if not entirely convincing, rationale against a therapeutic protocol for controlled drinking. However, it is important to also consider what a controlled drinking clinical pathway could add to the therapeutic armamentarium. Firstly, for many people with a history of chronic alcohol dependency, the promotion of a single treatment goal of abstinence may be an anathema. Consequently they may find it extremely difficult to both commit and adhere to a treatment plan that offers a seemingly miserable existence. Paradoxically, a treatment goal of abstinence could indeed be a prelude to relapse if abstinence is the clinical endpoint in the treatment process, yet this same endpoint is unacceptable to the client. Controlled drinking therefore brings an additional and alternative treatment endpoint to the clinical battery, which may be attractive to some people with a history of chronic alcohol dependency. Moreover, controlled drinking allows an alternative treatment endpoint to be evaluated by both the client and the clinician in order to determine not only the possibility of achieving controlled drinking status, but also to demonstrate to those for whom controlled drinking is unachievable, that they (the client) have attained the evidence themselves that abstinence is the only realistic treatment outcome. Despite the rhetoric both for and against controlled drinking, a balanced perspective can only be achieved by critically evaluating the clinical evidence for the efficacy or otherwise of this contentious and provocative treatment option.

Can alcohol-dependent people achieve controlled drinking status?

A watershed in the development of alternative treatment approaches to chronic alcohol dependency was achieved with the publication in 1981 of Heather and Robertson's classic book entitled *Controlled Drinking*. This text revealed for the first time tantalising evidence gathered from a number of research studies that former chemically dependent drinkers had returned to a controlled drinking style. The evidence presented in the book, and the underlying premise that people who are alcohol-dependent can return to a social and non-problematic drinking style, was initially greeted with scepticism by health professionals and those encountering difficulties with uncontrolled and excessive drinking.

Over 20 years has passed since Heather and Robertson's groundbreaking text of 1981. A number of studies have been conducted since then to explore the possible therapeutic advantage of a controlled-drinking treatment. Therefore, it is time to review the strength of the evidence that supports or refutes this possibility. Bear in mind that controlled drinking as an alternative to abstinence had been suggested for some time before the publication of *Controlled Drinking* (for example the work of Cohen *et al.*, 1971, Bigelow *et al.*, 1972 and Lloyd and Salzberg, 1975).

The first major study reporting controlled drinking in a meaningfully large though modest clinical group (20 chemically dependent drinkers) was that of Sobell and Sobell (1973a,b). These investigators gave an impressive account of controlled drinking by a significant number of the participants following a behavioural therapy intervention. This widely cited study was central to the debate on controlled drinking as a therapy option and an important clinical prelude to Heather and Robertson's book on the subject (1981). Some years after this study was completed, an exhaustive follow-up investigation of the original participants was conducted by Pendery *et al.* (1982). An important aspect of this was careful re-examination of the evidence originally presented and additional detailed interviews with the study participants. It was shocking to find that only 1 (5 per cent) of the original clinical cohort had managed to establish a controlled drinking pattern. Further, most of them had been re-admitted due to drink-related problems within 1 year of the original study. Even more startling, four of the participants had died from alcohol-related causes. Interestingly, the single participant who achieved controlled drinking was also the only one who, following review, did not appear to satisfy the criteria for chemical dependency on alcohol.

A further important and potentially damning observation for a controlled drinking alternative to abstinence was that a large minority of the cohort achieved a positive outcome by eventually rejecting controlled drinking as an option and became abstinent. Given that the central tenet of the original study was a behavioural programme aimed at training controlled drinking, the findings of the follow-up paints a picture of failure of this approach.

The findings of Pendery *et al.* (1982) also offer vital clues about a possible mediator in outcome success with the controlled-drinking approach. It is illuminating that these researchers highlighted an important clinical characteristic of the one participant who appeared to be successful in the use of a controlled drinking strategy – the absence of chemical dependency on alcohol. This reveals that subgroup heterogeneity may be an important contributor to a controlled-drinking treatment option. Note that the issue of subgroup heterogeneity is quite complex because sophisticated relationships have been observed in people who are likely to engage in or benefit from a controlled-drinking approach.

Cannon *et al.* (1977) observed that in terms of treatment engagement, people with more severe alcohol-related problems and more extensive social problems (compared to those with less severe alcohol and social problems) were more likely to volunteer for a controlled-drinking programme than an abstinence-based programme. Contrasting this observation with those of Pendery *et al.* it seems that participants who might wish to choose controlled-drinking treatment are also less likely to benefit from it.

A further early pre-treatment study (Pachman *et al.*, 1978) showed that participants who chose controlled drinking as their drinking goal had significantly shorter temporal histories of alcohol abuse and were more highly educated than those whose goal was abstinence. Reviewing these early studies indicates the salience of subgroup categories in both the uptake and outcome of a controlled-drinking treatment option. This is also supported by the work of Peele (1987) who noted considerable variation in the success of controlled-drinking programmes and highlighted that cultural factors may also play an important role in the outcome of a controlled-drinking treatment.

Encouraging findings have been obtained for controlled-drinking approaches. Some of the more impressive research describes case studies followed up for a significant period of time. Before proceeding further it should be noted that case study material, is often viewed (possibly unfairly) as a relatively weak level of evidence compared to randomised controlled trials, which benefit from a control group and a large number of participants. However, one aspect of case studies that is invaluable with respect to the controlled-drinking debate is that observations of one person or a small number of people are carried out longitudinally over an extended time, offering an opportunity to explore the relationship between a controlled-drinking intervention and outcome over several years, so presenting a more naturalistic account of changes over the life-course of a problem drinker following intervention. Booth (1990) reported the case of a 10-year follow-up of a severely dependent problem drinker whose initial treatment goal had been controlled drinking. Despite the severity of his dependence, he managed to obtain his goal of controlled drinking for this long time, an outcome verified by a range of sources. Levy (1990) noted in his study of individualised care for alcohol dependency that among the case material studied, controlled drinking was a more desirable outcome than abstinence for many people.

Sitharthan and Kavanagh (1991) emphasised the role of psychological domains in the success of controlled-drinking interventions. Their study was unusual in that it was conducted in a general hospital setting rather than a psychiatric or primary care setting. However, they identified that drinking status as a marker of controlled drinking success at 6-month follow-up was significantly predicted by patient self-efficacy. The study highlighted that in considering a controlled drinking strategy for chemically dependent drinkers, attending to key psychological domains (such as self-efficacy) is critical to success of the intervention.

A very interesting study was carried out by Makanjoula (1992) on controlled-drinking interventions following admission to an inpatient detoxification service. A pressing feature of the study concerns the treatment setting. Consistent with many inpatient detoxification units, the overall treatment philosophy is to achieve abstinence. Out of a total of 235 people attending the unit and recruited to the study, barely 10 per cent (27 patients) chose a controlled-drinking treatment over abstinence-based approaches. A stark finding was that of these 27, only 9 were able to maintain controlled drinking over a 12-week period. However, these findings need to be viewed in the context of the performance of the majority of participants who chose abstinence. At 2-year follow-up, the performance of the controlled-drinking subgroup was virtually indistinguishable from the abstinence group in achieving goals. Treatment outcome was generally quite poor but this was the same for both the controlled-drinking and abstinence groups. The findings suggest that to criticise controlled drinking as an ineffective treatment is only realistic if abstinence-focused treatments are significantly more successful. These results certainly support that position, and even highlight the importance of a controlled drinking option for some people.

Rosenberg (1993) observed that a constellation of clinical, psychological and individual belief characteristics are associated with the success of a controlled-drinking intervention. It was also noted that no single characteristic was consistently predictive. This is a salient finding as it may reflect methodological differences between studies, for example differences in sample size, clinical cohorts, evaluative outcome measures and associated criteria. However, one consistent trend observed across studies is the lower level of severity of dependence and the fact that a belief that controlled drinking is possible is associated with success at achieving that status. The belief of someone in the ability to control drinking has been linked to post-treatment drinking behaviour (MacKenzie *et al.*, 1994).

Therapeutic considerations

Based on the above evidence, the therapeutic advantage of a controlled-drinking option has long been considered in the treatment battery (Dawe and Richmond, 1997). However, the specific beliefs of clinicians as well as clients may impact on the salience and relevance with which a controlled drinking option is highlighted as a goal within an individualised treatment programme.

Moyer and Finney (2002) conducted a meta-analysis examining the outcomes of people involved in randomised controlled trials who received no treatment, perhaps being randomised to a placebo group or to a waiting list. A surprising observation was that 21 per cent of these untreated problem drinkers became abstinent. In addition, there was a substantial reduction in alcohol consumption compared to baseline. Enrolment on a clinical trial (or simply pre-treatment assessment) may have an inherent effect on health behaviour which is above and beyond that of the intervention (Epstein *et al.*, 2005), but the observation that some people make significant 'therapeutic gains' in terms of their drinking behaviour without specialist intervention or support should not be ignored. Such observations, although challenging for the disease concept of alcohol dependency, serve not only as considerable evidence for the usefulness and appropriateness of a controlled-drinking therapy, but also provide valuable insight into the possibilities of engaging the client in a therapeutic alliance to achieve a broad range of therapeutic goals. Consequently, controlled drinking should be considered a *bona fide* goal for some clients who seek help with problem drinking. However, it should be emphasised that controlled drinking is just one approach of several, so each person's circumstances need to be carefully and systematically appraised to determine the viability of this approach within an individualised care programme.

Conclusions

Controlled drinking is a viable therapeutic approach for some people with alcohol dependency, and it offers an alternative to abstinence-focused approaches. There is considerable evidence for the efficacy of controlled drinking as an intervention in some clients and it can be argued that controlled drinking should be on the agenda for discussion with most clients in order hat they are informed of the full range of treatment options. However controlled drinking, as both a phenomenon and a treatment approach, raises many challenges for the traditional disease model of alcohol dependency. Consequently, this approach might be valuable, but it is likely to remain controversial for some time yet. Further clinical evaluation in this area is both desirable and necessary.

References and further reading

Bigelow, G., Cohen, M., Liebson, I. and Faillace, L.A. (1972). Abstinence or moderation? Choice by alcoholics. *Behavior Research and Therapy*, **10**, 209–14.

Booth, P.G. (1990). Maintained controlled drinking following severe alcohol dependence – a case study. *British Journal of Addiction*, **85**, 315–22; discussion 323–28.

Cannon, D.S., Baker, T.B. and Ward, N.O. (1977). Characteristics of volunteers for a controlled drinking training program. *Journal of Studies on Alcohol*, **38**, 1799–803.

Cohen, M., Liebson, I.A., Faillace, L.A. and Speers, W. (1971). Alcoholism: Controlled drinking and incentives for abstinence. *Psychological Reports*, **28**, 575–80.

Dawe, S. and Richmond, R. (1997). Controlled drinking as a treatment goal in Australian alcohol treatment agencies. *Journal of Substance Abuse and Treatment*, **14**, 81–86.

Epstein, E.E., Drapkin, M.L., Yusko, D.A., Cook, S.M., McCrady, B.S. and Jensen, N.K. (2005). Is alcohol assessment therapeutic? Pretreatment change in drinking among alcohol-dependent women. *Journal of Studies on Alcohol*, **66**, 369–78.

Heather, N. and Robertson, I. (1981). *Controlled Drinking*. London: Methuen.

Levy, M.S. (1990). Individualized care for the treatment of alcoholism. *Journal of Substance Abuse and Treatment*, **7**, 245–54.

Lloyd, R.W. Jr, and Salzberg, H.C. (1975). Controlled social drinking: An alternative to abstinence as a treatment goal for some alcohol abusers. *Psychological Bulletin*, **82**, 815–42.

MacKenzie, A., Funderburk, F.R. and Allen, R.P. (1994). Controlled drinking and abstinence in alcoholic men: Beliefs influence actions. *International Journal of Addiction*, **29**, 1377–92.

Makanjoula, J.D. (1992). Controlled drinking by chronic drunkenness offenders – a British experience. *West African Journal of Medicine*, **11**, 39–47.

Moyer, A. and Finney, J.W. (2002). Outcomes for untreated individuals involved in randomized trials of alcohol treatment.

Journal of Substance Abuse and Treatment, **23**, 247–52.

Pachman, J.S., Foy, D.W. and van Erd, M. (1978). Goal choice of alcoholics: A comparison of those who choose total abstinence versus those who choose responsible, controlled drinking. *Journal of Clinical Psychology*, **34**, 781–83.

Peele, S. (1987). Why do controlled drinking outcomes vary by investigator, by country and by era? Cultural conceptions of release and remission in alcoholism. *Drug and Alcohol Dependence*, **20**, 173–201.

Pendery, M.L., Maltzman, I.M. and West, L.J. (1982). Controlled drinking by alcoholics? New findings and a re-evaluation of a major affirmative study. *Science*, **217** (4555), 169–75.

Rosenberg, H. (1993). Prediction of controlled drinking by alcoholics and problem drinkers. *Psychological Bulletin*, **113**, 129–39.

Sitharthan, T. and Kavanagh, D.J. (1991). Role of self-efficacy in predicting outcomes from a programme for controlled drinking. *Drug and Alcohol Dependence*, **27**, 87–94.

Sobell, M.B. and Sobell, L.C. (1973a). Individualized behavior therapy for alcoholics. *Behavior Therapy*, 4, 49–72.

Sobell, M.B. and Sobell, L.C. (1973b). Alcoholics treated by individualized behavior therapy: One year treatment outcome. *Behaviour Research and Therapy*, **11**, 599–618.

Sobell, M.B. and Sobell, L.C. (1995). Controlled drinking after 25 years: How important was the great debate? *Addiction*, **90**, 1149–53; Discussion 1157–77.

18 Understanding and assessing the impact of alcoholism on quality of life

Matthew Reaney and Jane Speight

Most people are familiar with the term 'quality of life' (or QoL) and intuitively have some understanding of what it involves. In theoretical terms, there are almost as many definitions of quality of life as there are authors that have written about it. There is no universally accepted definition of quality of life (Foster, 2006) and where clear definitions have been lacking, health researchers have often misused the term to refer to a variety of patient-reported outcomes, such as treatment satisfaction, health status and emotional well-being (Edelman *et al.*, 2002; Tankova *et al.*, 2001; Taylor *et al.*, 1994).

Understanding quality of life

There are two reasons why researchers have been prone to label any and all aspects of patient-reported outcomes (PROs) as quality of life. First, quality of life is recognised as an important outcome in its own right, and the term 'quality of life' has become a buzzword in healthcare research. Most major clinical trials in recent years have needed to include some measure of quality of life, but few have really considered what constitutes that quality of life; the measures they have used have been developed from a variety of narrow conceptualisations of health-related quality of life (HR-QoL) or, in many cases, have no conceptual framework at all (Longabaugh *et al.*, 1994). Second, in the absence of a universally agreed definition of quality of life, the measurement of all psychological outcomes (e.g. satisfaction and well-being) comes under this broad heading. Each of these outcomes may be important for quality of life, but they are not quality of life *per se*.

Some would argue that human needs (health, mobility, shelter and food) are the foundations for quality of life and that the degree to which these needs are satisfied is what defines quality of life (Hornquist, 1982):

> *Proponents of the needs-based approach postulate that life gains its quality from the ability and capacity of the individual to satisfy their needs... Quality of life is high when most human needs are fulfilled and low when few needs are being satisfied.*
> (McKenna and Doward, 2004, p.S2)

This definition is flawed however. It will be clear to most people in the western world that having one's basic needs satisfied does not necessarily lead to contentment. Calman's (1984) 'expectations model' (also known as Calman's Gap) suggests that quality of life is a measure of the difference between an individual's hopes and/or expectations and that individual's present experience, that is the difference between perceived and attained goals. This definition has inherently more appeal than the needs-based approach because it is concerned with an assessment of what someone wants from his or her life rather than what is needed in his or her life. Similarly, others argue that 'quality of life is of the highest importance and acts as the driving force behind all actions' (Leplege and Hunt, 1997, p. 47). Despite conceptual inconsistencies, there is a general consensus that quality of life has three inherent characteristics, as described in Box 18.1.

Box 18.1   The three inherent characteristics of quality of life

1. **Subjective**: Each person rates their own quality of life from their unique perspective based on their own feelings, experiences and priorities.

2. **Multidimensional**: If each person thinks about different aspects of their life when attempting to evaluate their own quality of life, this suggests that quality of life has several dimensions, for example physical, social and psychological (Testa and Simonson, 1996).

3. **Dynamic**: Each person's assessment of their own quality of life will change over time, depending on his or her priorities, experiences and circumstances at the given time (Carr *et al.*, 2001).

If quality of life is a subjective, multidimensional, dynamic construct of the difference between perceived and attained goals, then there is a case for adopting the principle that people should decide the extent to which their quality of life is satisfactory, based on their own criteria for what constitutes good quality of life for them personally. If this is accepted, then quality of life needs to be defined as 'what the patient says it is' (Joyce, 1994, p.47) rather than 'what the researcher decides to measure'. Indeed, it has been argued:

> Quality of life is such a subjective evaluation and so specific to the individual ... that there is no substitute for asking [individuals] ... what is important to them, how good these things are in their life and how the elements of their life affect each other and their overall quality of life.
>
> (Walker and Bradley, 2002, p. 144)

Consistent with this approach, it has been found that clinician and patient ratings of the patient's quality of life are rarely well-matched (Foster *et al.*, 2002; Walker and Bradley, 2002). Furthermore, QoL data generally show a moderate correlation (at best) with objective or biomedical outcomes. For example, someone on blood-thinning medication may have good biomedical outcomes (such as no incidence of bleeding) and functional status, leading the clinician to assume that they also have a good quality of life. Clinicians' ratings of their patients' QoL are generally based on health-related outcomes, the aspects of the patient's life with which the clinician is familiar and potentially able to influence. Improvement in quality of life quality of life is, however, not an automatic result of improved clinical status (Malet *et al.*, 2006). Patients see beyond health status, considering aspects of their life such as vitality, social functioning, emotional well-being, and sexual functioning (Foster *et al.*, 2002; Foster, 2006) as well as the demands and side effects of any treatment. Despite good biomedical outcomes, therefore, the patient on blood-thinning medication may report his or her quality of life to be impaired due to the limitations placed on personal and leisure activities by the risk of bleeding. Understanding how the condition and its treatment can affect the individual's quality of life (in ways that are important for them personally) is crucial for maintaining adherence to treatment (Smith and Larson, 2003) and for developing new treatments that may be more acceptable to patients in the long term. Equipped with the results of studies in which the patient's perspective has been assessed, clinicians are better able to understand how medical conditions and their treatments affect outcomes that are important to patients. Resources can then be directed towards treatments and services that would be most valued by patients.

Understanding alcoholism

Alcoholism is the popular term for two disorders: alcohol abuse and alcohol dependence. The American Psychiatric Association's *Diagnostic and Statistical Manual IV* (DSM-IV) (APA, 1994) defines alcohol abuse (DSM code 305.00) as a maladaptive pattern of alcohol use leading to clinically significant impairment or distress. Abuse is commonly diagnosed in people who have recently begun consuming excessive quantities of alcohol. Over time that abuse may progress to dependence, although some alcohol abusers never develop dependence. The DSM-IV defines alcohol dependence (DSM code 303.90) as a maladaptive pattern of alcohol use, leading to clinically significant impairment or distress, as manifested by three or more of the following seven criteria: tolerance, withdrawal, persistent desire, unsuccessful efforts to control alcohol use, time spent in activities necessary to obtain or use alcohol, reduction in social, occupational, or recreational activities, and the consumption of alcohol in larger amounts or over a longer period than was intended. Refer to Chapter 1 for a full discussion of the DSM-IV criteria for alcohol abuse and dependence. The WHO's *International Classification of Diseases 10* (ICD-10) (World Health Organization, 1994) similarly defines alcohol dependence by focusing on an inter-related cluster of psychological symptoms (such as craving), physiological signs (such as tolerance and withdrawal) and behavioural indicators (such as the use of alcohol to relieve withdrawal discomfort). However, the ICD-10 does not define 'alcohol abuse', preferring the concept of 'harmful use' of alcohol. This category was created to minimise the under-reporting of health problems related to alcohol and other drug use. Harmful use (as defined by the WHO) implies alcohol use that causes either physical or mental damage in the absence of dependence.

Alcoholism screening and diagnosis

Despite the focus of the APA and WHO on objective 'measurable' indicators of alcoholism, the individual's subjective perceptions about the nature of his or her relationship with alcohol (and the extent to which he or she perceives there to be a problem) can be more important than objective outcomes. Alcoholism research is inherently subjective, relying on someone to self-report something about which they may be in denial. Indeed, family members are often the first to notice the problems and to seek professional help. People in the early stages of alcoholism may experience only subtle biomedical or health-related changes (Burge and Schneider, 1999) so subjective perceptions of the psychological and social, as well as physical, impacts of alcohol problems are fundamental to diagnosis and treatment. Although the accuracy of a patient's report may be difficult to determine, self-reports of alcohol use from clinical and non-clinical samples are generally valid (Sobell and Sobell, 2003) and reliable (Peters *et al.*, 2003) although often poorly correlated with clinician ratings (Foster *et al.*, 2002).

The basic issue when evaluating the success of any pharmacological or psychological treatment intervention is whether a behavioural change has occurred. As with any 'medical' condition, the assessment of efficacy of an intervention in alcoholism frequently involves a clinical evaluation that focuses on improvements in biomedical signs and symptoms. The primary outcome is a reduction or cessation of alcohol consumption and its associated symptoms. No single treatment approach is effective for all persons with alcohol problems and the concept of individually-tailored treatment is important. Project MATCH is the largest randomised controlled treatment trial ever conducted in alcoholism (recruiting 1800 alcohol-dependent participants) (Cutler and Fishbain, 2005; http://www.pmatch.org). The addition of psychological data to objective biomedical data provides an opportunity to capture the extent and complexity of the multiple facets of alcoholism, as well as the benefits and costs that may result from treatment (Foster *et al.*, 1999). The benefits of evaluation from the patient's perspective has recently been acknowledged by European and American drug regulatory agencies, which now call for the inclusion of such assessment in clinical trials of pharmacological therapies (European Medicines Agency, 2005; Food and Drug Administration, 2006). It is generally accepted as important that a full assessment should go beyond diagnostic classification to provide a more extensive picture, including other areas of life functioning, such as an individual's drinking parameters, the expectancies that accompany and potentially maintain alcohol use, and the biopsychosocial aspects of the individual's life that are affected by drinking (Donovan, 1988). Among the many screening and diagnostic measures for the assessment of alcoholism, Maisto *et al.* (2002) produced a list of 18 validated alcohol-specific self-report measures in the English language, suitable for diagnostic purposes (see Box 18.2). (Validation refers to procedures, including statistical tests, to determine the extent to which a measure assesses what it is intended to assess.) None of these tools includes an assessment of the impact of alcoholism on quality of life, despite widespread acknowledgement that a major determinant and consequence of drinking behaviour at initial assessment and follow-up is an individual's general quality of life (Longabaugh *et al.*, 1994). Further, research has indicated that quality of life is an essential indicator in the multifactorial pathology for both the diagnostic and the therapeutic stages of alcoholism (Malet *et al.*, 2006), providing a broader context for evaluating the effects of intervention than data on consumption alone (Smith and Larson, 2003).

The impact of alcoholism on QoL

Although quality of life is a contentious term, it is generally accepted that it encompasses physical, social and psychological dimensions (Testa and Simonson, 1996). Clearly, alcoholism (defined as incorporating alcohol abuse and alcohol dependence) has the potential to impact on all three dimensions of quality of life in both the short and long term. Alcoholism has been shown to be detrimental to physical or health-related functioning, with effects that include distorted vision, hearing and coordination (Jamison, 1999); vitamin deficiencies (Gloria *et al.*, 1997);

Box 18.2   Alcohol-specific patient-reported measures used for diagnosis (from Maisto *et al.*, 2003)

- Alcohol Craving Questionnaire (ACQNOW)
- Alcohol Dependence Scale (ADS)
- Clinical Institute Withdrawal Assessment (CIWA-AD)
- Composite International Diagnostic Interview (CIDI core) *Version 2.1*
- Diagnostic Interview Schedule for DSM-IV (DIS-IV) Alcohol Module
- Drinker Inventory of Consequences (DrInC)
- Drinking Problems Index (DPI)
- Ethanol Dependence Syndrome (EDS) Scale
- Impaired Control Scale (ICS)
- Personal Experience Inventory for Adults (PEI-A)
- Psychiatric Research Interview for Substance and Mental Disorders (PRISM) (formerly known as the Structured Clinical Interview for DSM-III-R, Alcohol/Drug Version (SCID-A/D))
- Semi-Structured Assessment for the Genetics of Alcoholism (SSAGA-II)
- Severity of Alcohol Dependence Questionnaire (SADQ)
- Short Alcohol Dependence Data (SADD)
- Substance Abuse Module (SAM) *Version 4.1*
- Substance Dependence Severity Scale (SDSS)
- Substance Use Disorders Diagnostic Schedule (SUDDS-IV)
- Temptation and Restraint Inventory (TRI)

sexual impotence (Lemere and Smith, 1973); digestive system disorders including ulcers, inflammation of the pancreas, gastrointestinal problems, and cirrhotic liver damage (Burge and Schneider, 1999; Jamison, 1999); central and peripheral nervous system damage (Heaton *et al.*, 2000; Yokoyama *et al.*, 1991); and cardiovascular disease (Burge and Schneider, 1999).

Similarly, alcohol abuse and dependence have been shown to have numerous psychological effects. These include memory loss (Mann *et al.*, 1999); a reduction of inhibitions (Ehikhamenor and Agwubike, 2004); altered perceptions and emotions and impaired thinking and judgement (Jamison, 1999); impaired memory and sensory–motor coordination (Mann *et al.*, 1999); changes in mood and behaviour including anxiety and depression (Burge and Schneider, 1999); increases in aggression and violence (Bushman and Cooper, 1990) including child abuse; and uninhibited sexual behaviour or a lack of interest in it (Peugh and Belenko, 2001). In addition, alcoholism has detrimental social effects such as impaired social, marital and family relationships, scholastic, job-related, legal, and financial problems (Burge and Schneider, 1999), and inconsistency in parenting behaviour, creating an unpredictable and unstable family environment which can undermine a child's mental and emotional growth (Windle, 1996).

Despite the acknowledged impact of alcoholism on the quality of life of the person and their family, it has rarely been assessed formally in either clinical practice or research (Spitzer *et al.*, 1995). The WHO working group (1994; in Anderson, 1996) recognises the importance of QoL measurements in public health policy, and more recently the French Alcology Society (1999; cited in Malet *et al.*, 2006) consensus conference has indicated that recovery of a good quality of life should be a primary treatment goal. Furthermore, the SFA emphasises both the lack of research and the absence of a specific measurement tool (Malet *et al.*, 2006).

In 1999, Foster *et al.* reported a review of the Medline/BIDS database using the search terms 'QoL' and 'alcoholics', noting only 35 publications published between 1982 and 1997. Eleven of these were excluded because they described the results of medical or quasi-medical procedures or were otherwise irrelevant. Malet *et al.* (2006) replicated the search from 1998 to 2004, identifying only three additional papers, while a search from 2005 to 2006 identified a further two papers of interest in English – one on the treatment of the complications of alcoholic liver disease (Bergheim *et al.*, 2005) and one review of alcoholism and quality of life literature (Donovan *et al.*, 2005). However, our recent adaptation of this search strategy to include additional relevant terms resulted in identification of over 1500 papers. The Medline database was searched over 1982 to 2006 using the terms 'quality of life' OR 'QoL' OR 'HRQoL' and 'alcohol*' where * represents a truncated term.

While most of these may be irrelevant, only briefly mentioning the impact of alcoholism on quality of life in a summary or conclusion, the exercise highlighted the limitations of previous literature reviews that have used the term 'alcoholics' (rather than 'alcohol*' where * represents a truncated term) and 'QoL' only. Rambaldi and Gluud (2005) recently conducted a systematic Cochrane review to assess the beneficial and harmful effects of colchicine (an anti-inflammatory and antifibrotic drug) in patients with alcoholic or non-alcoholic fibrosis or cirrhosis. The authors identified 29 publications describing 15 clinical trials among patients with alcoholic fibrosis, alcoholic hepatitis or alcoholic cirrhosis, as well as patients with viral induced or cryptogenic fibrosis or cirrhosis (a total of 1714). None of these trials examined quality of life as an outcome.

Where such research has been conducted in alcoholism, evidence suggests that the quality of life of participants is reduced compared with that of a normative healthy population (Donovan *et al.*, 2005; Foster *et al.*, 2002; Van Dijk *et al.*, 2004). Furthermore, it is often worse than that observed in many serious somatic or psychiatric disorders (Morgan *et al.*, 2004), and more impaired for women than for men (Foster, Peters and Marshall, 1999). However, the utility of quality of life studies depends on appropriate selection and interpretation of measures. For data to be meaningful there should be evidence that the instrument used has satisfactory psychometric properties, whereby it displays validity, reliability, repeatability, sensitivity and responsiveness; see Fayers and Machin (2000) for more about each term. Very few quality of life measures used in alcoholism research meet these criteria – particularly with respect to validity – and as such the 'quality of life' trends detailed in this paragraph may be referring to health status or functioning rather than quality of life.

Assessing the impact of alcoholism on quality of life

Quality of life can be measured using generic or condition-specific self-report measures. Generic measures assess concepts representing basic human values, which are relevant to everyone's functional status and well-being (which are not age-, disease- or treatment-specific). They enable assessment and comparison across various conditions (Malet *et al.*, 2006) but are rarely sufficiently sensitive to the benefits of condition-specific interventions or treatments. Evaluation of such interventions generally requires condition-specific measures.

Use of generic measures in alcoholism

Various generic instruments have been used to assess issues of relevance to QoL in alcoholism research (see Tables 18.1, 18.2 and 18.3 on the following pages). Among the most widely used are the EQ-5D (EuroQol Group, 1990), the Nottingham Health Profile (NHP; Hunt *et al.*, 1981), the Short Form-36 (SF-36; Ware and Sherbourne, 1992) and WHO-QoL-BREF (WHOQoL Group, 1998). The WHO-QoL-BREF is the only instrument that can be considered as a generic measure of QoL; the others measure health status, in other words they measure the quality of health rather than the quality of life. The SF-36 and EQ-5D in particular have been used most widely but have been frequently misinterpreted.

The Short Form-36 (SF-36)

The SF-36 (Ware and Sherbourne, 1992) is a multipurpose generic health survey. The 36 items are grouped into eight dimensions relating to quality of health, from which two components (physical health and mental health) can be computed. The eight dimensions are:

- physical functioning (PH)
- bodily pain (BP)
- mental health (MH)
- energy/vitality (VT)
- general health perception (GH)
- role limitations due to physical problems (RP)
- role limitations due to emotional problems (RE)
- social functioning (SF).

In 1996, a second version of the SF-36 (SF-36v2) was introduced to improve on the original version (Ware *et al.*, 2000), although the overall scale structure remains the same. The SF-36 been extensively translated and validated, with normative data available for many conditions as well as for the general population in the USA. Due to the fact that it is a well-validated generic instrument, virtually all HR-QoL studies in alcoholism now include the SF-36 despite the lack of clarity regarding its psychometric properties (validity, reliability and sensitivity) in this population. Several studies have shown good psychometric properties for the SF-36 in alcohol-dependent populations (Daeppen, 1998; McKenna *et al.*, 1996; Patience *et al.*, 1997) but recently Foster (2006) has indicated that no studies have demonstrated test–retest reliability (a statistical test in which scores on a well-designed instrument would remain stable as long as the respondent's symptoms remained stable).

Despite its widespread misinterpretation as a measure of quality of life, the SF-36 measures health status (Fayers and Machin, 2000) using a set of generic items originally generated from various physical and role functioning, well-being and health perception measures. The eight dimensions represent the most frequently measured concepts in widely used health surveys and those most affected by disease and treatment (Ware *et al.*, 1993). It includes many items (including self-care and mobility), therefore, that are largely irrelevant to understanding the impact of alcoholism on quality of life. Perhaps more importantly, it is not based specifically on alcoholism, so it excludes many more pertinent and potentially important issues, such as sleep, working life and social isolation, which are common to alcoholism and are likely to be important for quality of life (Foster, 2006). It is therefore unlikely that the SF-36 would be sensitive to differences between treatment groups (Morgan *et al.*, 2004). Babor and colleagues (2006) reported no difference in health status using the SF-12 (a short version of the SF-36) at 3-month and 12-month follow-up in a pre–post quasi-experimental evaluation of 1329 participants, despite observing a statistically significant decrease in drinking behaviour. They suggested that either the SF-12 was not sensitive to the benefits of the intervention or else that the benefits were not apparent in the time frame. The former is the most likely explanation as health status will become an issue only when alcohol begins to cause health problems, far beyond the point at which it may have impacted on quality of life. Other researchers have found the SF-20 to be insensitive (Donovan *et al.*, 2005).

The EQ-5D

The EQ-5D (EuroQoL Group, 1990) is a brief generic measure of health status that provides a simple descriptive profile and a single index value which can be used in the clinical and economic evaluation of healthcare and population health surveys. The descriptive profile consists of five single-item dimensions (i.e. mobility, self-care, usual activity, pain/discomfort, and anxiety/depression) each rated on three levels (no problem; some problem; extreme problem). Respondents indicate the level that best describes their current functioning on each dimension. The five dimensions can be converted into a summary index with a maximum score of one, indicating best health state (using a table of scores available from the EuroQoL Group). The descriptive profile is followed by a single question (How good or bad is your health today?) which is rated on a visual analogue scale (EQ-VAS) ranging from 0 (worst imaginable health state) to 100 (best imaginable health state).

Despite its intended purpose as a measure of health status (EuroQoL Group, 1990) the EQ-5D has been misinterpreted as a measure of quality of life in numerous conditions including two recent studies in alcoholism (Foster, Peters and Kind, 2002; Gunther *et al.*, 2007). In 52 alcohol-dependent outpatients (mean age 48 years), EQ-VAS scores were highly negatively correlated with alcohol consumption, meaning that a low score on the EQ-VAS was associated with high levels of alcohol consumption (Foster *et al.*, 2002). Furthermore, usual activity and anxiety/ depression were the most impaired EQ-5D domains (with 77 per cent and 73 per cent, respectively, reporting some problems or extreme problems) and self-care was the least impaired (no respondents reported an extreme problem) (Foster *et al.*, 2002). This is consistent with criticisms of the SF-3, namely that self-care items such as bathing and dressing oneself are largely irrelevant to understanding the impact of alcoholism on quality of life. However, it must be noted that Foster *et al.* used a small sample (insufficient to detect significant changes in alcohol consumption following intervention) of relatively uneducated people (46 per cent had no formal qualifications) despite known associations between educational attainment and EQ-5D index scores.

Foster and colleagues also administered the 5-item sleep subscale of the NHP (Hunt *et al.*, 1981) to identify the extent of sleep disturbance in people with alcoholism. Over 30 per cent of participants responded positively to all five items, with the majority of participants indicating at least one problem associated with sleep: 75 per cent reported waking in the early hours of the morning; 69 per cent reported sleeping badly at night; 52 per cent reported taking a long time to get to sleep; and 50 per cent reported lying awake at night. Sleep problems are clearly an important domain in alcoholism, and have recently been demonstrated to predict relapse at 3 months (see Foster, 2006).

Table 18.1		Generic health status measures used in alcohol research	

Name	Items	Reference	Key features
15D	15	Sintonen & Pekurinen, 1993	Self-administered instrument to be used in adults aged over 16 years. Can be used to obtain a set of utility or preference weights
EQ-5D	5	The EuroQoL Group, 1990	Provides simple descriptive profile of self-care, mobility, usual activity, pain, anxiety/depression. Gives single index value
General Health Questionnaire (GHQ-12)	12, 20 28, 30 or 60	Goldberg & Williams, 1988	Self-administered screening measure for detecting forms of psychiatric illness
Medical Outcomes Study Short-Form (SF-12, SF-20, SF-36)	12, 20 or 36	Ware & Sherbourne, 1992 (originally)	Items grouped into 8 dimensions: physical functioning (PH), bodily pain (BP), mental health (MH), energy/vitality (VT), general health perception (GH), physical role limitations (RP), emotional role limitations (RE) and social functioning (SF)
Nottingham Health Profile (NHP)	45	Hunt *et al.*, 1981	Based on lay perceptions of health status following interviews with lay people about the effects of illness on behaviour. Two parts, measuring: subjective health status (38 items) and effects of health on daily life (7 items)
Quality of Well-Being Scale (QWB)	27	Anderson, Bush & Berry, 1986	Preference-based measure administered by the interviewer. Measures well-being based on social preferences that society associates with a person's level of functioning (e.g. mobility, physical activity, social activity) and rating of symptomatic complaints that might inhibit function. Combines morbidity and mortality in single index score
Health Utilities Index Mark 3 (HUI-3)	45	Feeny *et al.*, 1995	Measures eight attributes (vision, hearing, speech, ambulation, dexterity, emotion, cognition, pain)

Table 18.2 **Generic quality of life (QoL) measures used in alcohol research**

Name	Items	Reference	Key features
Life Situation Survey (LSS)	20	Chubon, 1995	Used in the general population as well as populations with chronic illnesses or disabilities
Schedule of Evaluation of Individual Quality of Life (SEIQoL)	—	McGee *et al.*, 1991	Developed to assess QoL from the individual's perspective. Interview is conducted. Respondents nominate five aspects of life most important for their QoL, rate them for quality, and indicate their relative importance to each other
WHOQoL-BREF	26	WHOQoL Group, 1998	Includes two items to assess overall QoL and general health and one item for each of 24 facets of QoL. Items grouped into four broad domains (physical, psychological, social relationships and environment)
Quality of Life Enjoyment and Satisfaction Questionnaire (Q-LES-Q)	16, 93	Endicott *et al.*, 1993	Has eight summary scales. Assesses degree of enjoyment and satisfaction experienced in various aspects of daily functioning. Developed and validated for depression. Includes single items that rate overall life satisfaction and satisfaction with any medications that are taken. Also available in short form
Quality of Life Index	68	Ferrans & Powers, 1992	Composed of four subscales in two parts: part one measures satisfaction with various domains of life; part two measures the importance of the same domains to the participant
Quality of Life Inventory	32	Frisch *et al.*, 1992	Weighted measure. Considers satisfaction with 16 areas of life and the perceived importance of these areas to overall well-being. Produces overall score plus a profile of problems and strengths in all 16 areas. Used in treatment planning and outcome assessment
Satisfaction with Life Scale	5	Diener *et al.*, 1985	Assesses life satisfaction using five domains of life. Requires respondents to use their own criteria and weigh these domains themselves

Table 18.3	Generic measures of health-related quality of life used in alcohol research			

Name	Items	Reference	Key features
Multidimensional Index of Life Quality (MILQ)	35	Avis *et al.*, 1996	Patient-informed questionnaire covering satisfaction with nine domains of a person's life. Designed for use in cardiovascular disease
Treatment Outcome Profile (TOP)	27	Holcomb *et al.*, 1998	Self-report measure. Designed to assess changes in quality of life, symptomatology, level of functioning and satisfaction with services

Gunther *et al.* (2007) examined the psychometric properties of the EQ-5D for valuing HR-QoL in 103 alcohol-dependant people in Germany (mean age 49 years). They found that respondents understood and/or accepted the EQ-5D (response rate of greater than 98 per cent), but over a quarter of them (27.6 per cent) reported no problems in any of the dimensions. This phenomenon is known as a 'ceiling effect' and suggests that the EQ-5D is unsuitable for the evaluation of an intervention because those respondents who were 'at ceiling' at baseline would be unable to report any improvement at follow-up. Consistent with the results published by Foster, Peters and Kind (2002) the most affected dimensions were 'usual activities' and 'anxiety/depression' (28.7 per cent and 49.0 per cent reported extreme or moderate problems, respectively).

In addition to the EQ-5D, Gunther and colleagues (2007) used the WHO-QoL-BREF as a comparison 'QoL' measure. The WHO-QoL-BREF (WHO QoL Group, 1998) assesses generic quality of life, and – unlike the EQ-5D and SF-36 – it is not restricted to health-related domains. It has a 2-week recall period and consists of 26 items (each rated on a 5-point scale) from which four domains can be calculated: physical health, mental health, social relationships and environment. Hypothesised relationships between EQ-5D and WHO-QoL-BREF scales were not wholly identified, perhaps because:

> ... the WHO-QoL-BREF domain 'physical', which consists of seven facets ranging from 'mobility', 'pain/discomfort' and 'sleep and rest' to 'dependence on medicinal substances and medical aids' and 'work capacity', may not describe exactly the same underlying construct as the single item of the EQ-5D dimension 'mobility'.
>
> (Gunther *et al.*, 2007, p. 263)

Similarly, Gunther *et al.* (2007) concluded that psychological well-being in alcohol-dependent people is likely to be detected by the EQ-5D only if they specifically experience anxiety and/ or depression; other aspects of their psychological well-being (e.g. stress, energy, positive well-being) will remain undetected. These observations indicate that the EQ-5D is unlikely to be sensitive to the changes in alcoholism severity and/or the benefits of alcohol-related interventions. Studies using the EQ-5D and SF-36 highlight the difficulties inherent in (a) using generic instruments (as each assesses differing constructs), and (b) drawing comparisons and conclusions based on multiple studies employing different measures. Furthermore, and perhaps most importantly, generic instruments are of limited value unless they are to be used for drawing comparisons between various medical conditions and populations.

In summary, neither the SF-36 nor the EQ-5D are sufficient to capture the full impact of alcoholism on quality of life due to the inclusion of many irrelevant domains and the exclusion of many more that are likely to be of greater importance. Foster *et al.* (2002) demonstrated the relevance of sleep as a domain and yet it is not included in either the SF-36 or the EQ-5D. Likewise, neither cognitive function, social isolation, nor the dynamics of environmental support – which have been identified as important determinants of outcomes in this population – are captured by either instrument (Morgan *et al.*, 2004). It is increasingly recognised that when considering an individual disease, a condition-specific measure is preferable (Foster, 2006) providing optimal measurement in term of relevance, specificity and sensitivity.

Use of alcoholism-specific measures

Condition-specific quality of life scales do not allow comparison between conditions (e.g. alcoholism and illicit drug dependence) but have the advantage of providing relevant and, generally, highly sensitive measurement of issues of importance in the given condition. Following their literature review of quality of life in alcoholism, Foster and colleagues (1999) concluded that an alcoholism-specific quality of life measure was needed. However, despite their recommendation and the limitations of using generic measures such as the SF-36 and EQ-5D in alcoholism research, only one alcohol-specific measure has been developed.

Data from the New European Alcoholism Treatment (NEAT) trial, an open multicentre prospective study, were used to develop the AlQoL-9 (Malet *et al.*, 2006), a scale that Malet and colleagues claim epitomises quality of life in alcohol-dependence. It has reportedly 'excellent informative qualities, and is sensitive to most of the factors known to be involved in the quality of life of alcohol-dependent persons' (Malet *et al.*, 2006, p. 186). However, the AlQoL-9 was developed by reducing the 36 items of the French version of the SF-36 to those nine items particularly pertinent to alcoholism. The number of resulting dimensions was found to be quite stable at reporting role, mental, and physical dimensions (as shown in Box 18.3).

The methodology used by Malet and colleagues for adapting the SF-36 into a shorter questionnaire more specific to alcoholism is comprehensive. However, the authors consider the AlQoL-9 to be a scale characteristic of alcohol-dependence-related quality of life, despite the fact that the SF-36 (from which it is derived) is a measure of generic health status and they did not add any alcohol-specific items to the scale. Malet *et al.* (2006) validated the French AlQoL-9 among samples of 104 inpatients and 114 outpatients (mean ages 44 and 48, respectively) seeking treatment, who met the DSM-IV criteria for alcohol dependence. The AlQoL-9 was completed by the patients on the day they were admitted to hospital or at consultation, and again by inpatients 48–72 hours after hospitalisation. The validity of the instrument was satisfactory, with principal components analysis demonstrating that the nine items could be summed to form a single score, theoretically ranging from 9 (lowest HR-QoL) to 41 (optimum HR-QoL). Internal consistency reliability was high (Cronbach's alpha-coefficient of 0.85 in outpatients and 0.71 in inpatients). Test–retest reliability was also considered acceptable (correlations for each of the nine items exceeded 0.5). However, the retest was conducted 48–72 hours following the first administration, despite a 1-month recall period, which would suggest that correlations should have been much closer to 1.0. As 12 per cent of patients presenting with major signs of withdrawal were deemed unfit to complete the questionnaire a second time, this test–retest reliability statistic may be somewhat misleading.

At this time, the AlQoL-9 has not been validated in a larger sample or for use in the English language. Despite adequate psychometric properties, the AlQoL-9 (developed directly from the SF-36) shares the disadvantages of other generic measures in alcoholism research, namely the exclusion of potentially more relevant alcohol-specific domains. Research has shown that at least two very important constructs are not captured by the SF-36; they are 'sleep' and 'social isolation' (Foster, 2006). Although the SF-36 measures the construct of social functioning, it does not adequately assess social isolation. Indeed, the relationship between the SF-36 'social functioning' and NHP 'social isolation' subscales is only moderate (Foster *et al.*, 2004), indicating that they are measuring separate constructs. Thus the AlQoL-9 presents the same limitations as the SF-36 with the only advantage being that highly irrelevant items have been excluded, resulting in a shorter, more relevant measure of health status. In a personal communication, Dr Malet (2006) has suggested that a single item from the sleep subscale of the NHP profile ('I sleep badly at night') could be added to the AlQoL-9 to improve its validity.

Box 18.3   **The items of the Al-QoL 9 (Malet *et al.* 2006)**

- o   Does your health now limit you in climbing several flights of stairs? [1]
- o   How much bodily pain have you had during the past 4 weeks? [2]
- o   In general would you say your health is excellent / ... / poor? [3]
- o   During the past 4 weeks, have you had difficulty in performing the work or other activities as a result of your physical health (for example, it took extra effort)? [4]
- o   How much of the time during the past 4 weeks have you been a very nervous person? [5]
- o   How much of the time during the past 4 weeks have you felt downhearted and blue? [5]
- o   During the past 4 weeks, have you accomplished less than you would like with your work or other regular daily activities as a result of any emotional problems (such as feeling depressed or anxious)? [6]
- o   How much of the time during the past 4 weeks did you feel worn out? [7]
- o   During the past 4 weeks, to what extent have your physical health or emotional problems interfered with your normal social activities with family, friends, neighbours or groups? [8]

Items derived from: [1]SF-36 physical functioning (PH) dimension; [2]SF-36 bodily pain (BP) dimension; [3]SF-36 general health perception (GH) dimension; [4]SF-36 physical role limitations (RP) dimension; [5]SF-36 mental health (MH) dimension; [6]SF-36 emotional role limitations (RE) dimension; [7]SF-36 energy/vitality (VT) dimension; [8]SF-36 social functioning (SF) dimension.

The need for a new measure of quality of life in alcoholism

While generic health status measures have not been specifically developed for people with alcoholism, many are, nevertheless, of use in this population, with the proviso that they are interpreted carefully as measures of quality of health rather than quality of life. The SF-36 includes many domains relevant to alcoholism, but excludes many that, potentially, would be of greater relevance. For example, domains such as 'physical functioning' (e.g. bathing and dressing oneself) will be of less relevance to people with alcoholism than domains such as 'sleep' and 'social isolation', which are not included in most generic measures (excepting the NHP) or the AIQoL-9. The administration of numerous measures to ensure inclusion of all relevant QoL domains is onerous and burdensome for the participant (as well as for the researcher/clinician). However, the inability of any single questionnaire to address all these domains has led Foster (2006) to propose the administration of the five NHP sleep items to supplement the SF-36 in clinical assessment.

The application of the WHO-QoL-BREF (a measure of generic QoL) in alcoholism shows promise because it correlates well with the physical and mental health components of the SF-36 and also measures environmental and social aspects of quality of life. However, to date its only application has been a single alcoholism study with 32 participants. To reiterate the conclusion of Foster and colleagues (1999), there remains a need for an alcoholism-specific QoL measure (informed by interviews with people with alcohol dependence) that focuses on the domains that are most important and salient to people with such problems.

Research has identified numerous facets of quality of life that are affected by alcoholism, including self-esteem, autonomy, stress, work, social isolation, pain, sleep and affective state (Foster *et al.*, 2002), domestic and marital functioning, harmony at home, peace of mind, reputation, self-respect, and religion (Foster *et al.*, 1999). Acknowledging that no single measure is currently sufficient to assess all domains of importance, researchers have administered several generic measures simultaneously; for example Foster, Peters and Kind (2002) used the EQ-5D to measure 'quality of life' but supplemented this with the NHP to assess sleep, and the Hospital Anxiety and Depression Scale (HADS) to assess anxiety and depression.

Furthermore, research has considered only the alcohol abuser's perspective. It has been widely observed that the person with the alcohol problem often does not realise, or may not be ready to acknowledge, that a problem exists. Some objective indicators (such as loss of a job) or biomedical signs of excessive alcohol consumption (such as broken capillaries on the face, trembling hands, and chronic diarrhoea) may be evidence of a problem, but family members are often the first to experience the negative effects (which are more often psychological and/ or social than physical) and seek professional help. It is, therefore, important to realise that alcoholism not only impairs the quality of life of the person who misuses alcohol, but also the quality of life of those who are closest to them, such as family, friends, and colleagues, as well as impacting on society as a whole (Longabaugh *et al.*, 1994). Research by the National Association for Children of Alcoholics (NACOA; see http://www.nacoa.org.uk/) indicates that there are at least 920,000 children and young people (under the age of 18) in the UK living in a home where one or both parents have a problem with alcohol. However, their perspective, and the impact of alcoholism on their quality of life has rarely been systematically assessed.

Conclusions

Health can be measured objectively or subjectively, with most alcoholism research traditionally relying on the former, incorporating data on alcohol consumption (Foster *et al.*, 2000). Due, in part, to a poor association between clinician and patient ratings, and the increasing significance placed on understanding health issues from the patient's perspective, it is becoming more commonplace to assess the patient's subjective experience of his or her symptoms (as well as any treatment) and the impact of these on his or her quality of life (Acquadro *et al.*, 2003). Quality of life is a subjective, multidimensional (encompassing physical, social and psychological components) and dynamic construct. Alcoholism is also (by its nature) subjective, relying on the individual person (or their family members) to self-report problems. Despite the many screening and diagnostic measures for the assessment of alcoholism and the widely acknowledged detrimental effects of alcoholism on quality of life, there are no measures of the impact of alcoholism on that quality of life (Foster *et al.*, 2002; Morgan *et al.*, 2004). Foster *et al.* (1999) identified only 35 studies measuring quality of life in alcoholism, and none of these used alcoholism-specific measures.

Due to a lack of a consensus regarding what constitutes quality of life, generic health status measures (like the SF-36 and EQ-5D) have often been misinterpreted as measures of quality of life. The results of such studies are of great relevance and provide important insights into the problems that alcoholism can induce but, due to misinterpretation of data, the conclusions from most of these studies must be treated with caution. In addition to the lack of conceptual clarity, generic measures include many items that are largely irrelevant to understanding the impact of alcoholism on quality of life. They also exclude highly relevant domains such as the impact on sleep, social life and family life as well as cognitive function and the dynamics of environmental support, domains which are likely to be of greater relevance and contribute to a more valid and sensitive measure of the impact of alcoholism on quality of life. Furthermore, as health status is likely to be impaired only when alcoholism begins to cause health problems (and far beyond the point at which it may have affected someone's quality of life and that of their family), many of the studies that have used generic measures of health status may have under-reported the full impact of alcoholism on quality of life.

An attempt has been made to design an alcohol-specific measure that claims to epitomise health-related quality of life for people with alcohol-dependence. Despite the use of rigorous statistical methods and demonstration of adequate psychometric properties, the AlQoL-9 is limited by its derivation from the SF-36. It shares the disadvantages inherent in other generic measures (as discussed above). Despite these limitations, it is the only measure that has been developed specifically for use in alcoholism, and the brief nine-item AlQoL-9 is likely to be more useful in clinical practice and research for evaluating treatment efficacy than other previously used (as well as longer) generic measures. In certain circumstances, the WHO-QoL-BREF may also be a useful tool, incorporating social and environmental domains (Foster, 2006), though further work is needed to demonstrate its utility in this population.

Much remains to be learned about the full impact of alcoholism on quality of life (Donovan *et al.*, 2005), as defined earlier in this chapter. In various studies, researchers have identified numerous domains that are affected by alcoholism, including self-esteem, autonomy, social environment, religion, and sleep (Foster *et al.*, 1999; 2002), but they have not yet constructed a single scale that includes all the most important and salient domains to people who abuse or are dependent on alcohol. In addition, no notable research has been conducted on the impact of alcoholism on the quality of life of friends, family and colleagues of the person abusing alcohol. Individuals need to be given the opportunity to determine the extent to which their own quality of life is impaired by alcoholism, based on their own criteria for what constitutes a good quality of life for them personally (Joyce, 1994). Only then will we be able to assess the full impact of alcoholism (and its treatment) on quality of life.

References and further reading

Acquadro, C., Berzon, R., Dubois, D., *et al.* (2003). PRO Harmonization Group: Incorporating the patient's perspective into drug development and communication: an ad hoc task force report of the Patient-Reported Outcomes (PRO) Harmonization Group meeting at the Food and Drug Administration. *Value in Health*, **6**, 522–31.

American Psychiatric Association (1994). *DSM-IV: Diagnostic and Statistical Manual of Mental Disorders*, 4th edn. Washington DC: American Psychiatric Association.

Anderson, P. (1996). WHO working group on population levels of alcohol consumption. *Addiction,* **91**(2), 275–84.

Anderson, J.P., Bush, J.W. and Berry, C.C. (1986). Classifying functions for health outcome and quality of life evaluation. *Medical Care*, **24**, 454–69.

Avis, N.E., Smith, K.W., Hambleton, R.K., Feldman, H.A., Selwyn, A. and Jacobs, A. (1996). Development of the multidimensional index of life quality. *Medical Care*, **34**, 1102–20.

Babor, T.F., Higgins-Biddle, J.C., Dauser., D., Burleson, J.A., Zarkin, G.A. and Bray, J. (2006). Brief interventions for at-risk drinking: patient outcomes and cost-effectiveness in managed care organizations. *Alcohol and Alcoholism*, **41**, 624–31.

Bergheim, I., McClain, C.J. and Arteel, G.E. (2005). Treatment of alcoholic liver disease. *Digestive Diseases*, **23**(3/4), 275–84.

Bradley, C. (1996). Measuring quality of life. *The Diabetes Annual*, **10**, 207–24.

Burge, S.K. and Schneider, F.D. (1999). Alcohol-related problems: recognition and intervention. *American Family Physician*, **59**(2), 361–70.

Bushman, B.J. and Cooper, H.M. (1990). Effects of alcohol on human aggression: an integrative research review. *Psychological Bulletin*, **107**(3), 341–54.

Calman, K.C. (1984). Quality of life in cancer patients: a hypothesis. *Journal of Medical Ethics*, **10**, 124–27.

Carr, A.J., Gibson, B. and Robinson, P.G. (2001). Is quality of life determined by expectations or experience? *British Medical Journal*, **322**, 1240–43.

Chubon, R.A. (1995). *Manual for the Life Situation Survey*. Columbia: Columbia School of Medicine.

Cutler, R.B. and Fishbain, D.A. (2005). Are alcoholism treatments effective? The Project MATCH data. *BMC Public Health* Available at: http://www.biomedcentral.com/1471-2458/5/75 (last accessed August 2008).

Daeppen, J.B., Krieg, M.A., Burnand, B. and Yersin, B. (1998). MOS-SF-36 in evaluating health-related quality of life in alcohol-dependent patients. *American Journal of Drug and Alcohol Abuse*, **24**, 685–94.

Diener, E., Emmons, R.A., Larsen, R.J. and Griffin, S. (1985). The Satisfaction with Life Scale. *Journal of Personality Assessment*, **49**, 71–75.

Donovan, D.M. (1988). Assessment of addictive behaviours: Implications of an emerging biopsychosocial model. In: D.M. Donovan and G.A. Marlatt (eds). *Assessment of Addictive Behaviours*. New York: Guilford, pp. 3–48.

Donovan, D., Mattson, M.E., Cisler, R.A., Longabaugh, R. and Zweben, A. (2005). Quality of life as an outcome measure in alcoholism treatment research. *Journal of Studies on Alcohol*, **15**(Suppl.), 119–39.

Edelman, D., Olsen, M.K., Dudley, T.K., Harris, A.C. and Oddone, E.Z. (2002). Impact of diabetes screening on quality of life. *Diabetes Care*, **25**, 1022–26.

Ehikhamenor, E. and Agwubike, E.O. (2004). The need for blood alcohol concentration (BAC) legislation in Nigeria. *Tropical Journal of Pharmaceutical Research*, **3**(1), 319–27.

Endicott, J., Nee, J., Harrison, W. and Blumenthal, R. (1993). Quality of Life Enjoyment and Satisfaction Questionnaire: A New Measure. *Psychopharmacology Bulletin*, **29**(2), 321–26.

European Medicines Agency (EMEA) (2005). Reflection paper on the regulatory guidance for the use of health-related quality of life (HRQL) measures in the evaluation of medicinal products. Available at: http://www.emea.europa.eu/pdfs/human/ewp/13939104en.pdf (last accessed August 2008).

EuroQoL Group (1990). A new facility for the measurement of health-related quality of life. *Health Policy*, **16**, 199–208.

Fayers, P.M. and Machin, D. (2000). *Quality of Life: Assessment, Analysis and Interpretation*. New York: John Wiley.

Feeny, D., Furlong, W., Boyle, B. and Torrance, G.W. (1995). Multi-attribute health status classification systems: Health Utilities Index. *Pharmaco Economics*, **7**(6), 490–502.

Ferrans, E. and Powers, M. (1992). Psychometric assessment of the quality of life index. *Research in Nursing and Health*, **251**, 29–38.

Food and Drug Administration (FDA). (2006). Guidance for industry: patient-reported outcome measures: use in medicinal product development to support labelling claims: draft guidance. *Health and Quality of Life Outcomes*, **4**, 79.

Foster, J.H. (2006). Quality of life measurement and alcoholism: Another arm to nursing practice? *Clinical Effectiveness in Nursing*, **9**(3), e295–301.

Foster, J.H., Marshall, E.J. and Peters, T.J. (2004). Comparison of two quality of life measures in a sample of 240 alcohol-dependent research participants. *Alcoholism: Clinical and Experimental Research*, **28**(8), 46A.

Foster, J.H., Peters, T.J. and Kind, P. (2002). Quality of life, sleep, mood and alcohol consumption: a complex interaction. *Addiction Biology*, **7**, 55–65.

Foster, J.H., Peters, T.J. and Marshall, E.J. (2000). Quality of life measures and outcomes in alcohol-dependent men and women. *Alcohol*, **22**, 45–52.

Foster, J.H., Powell, J.E., Marshall, E.J. and Peters, T.J. (1999). Quality of life in alcohol-dependent subjects – a review. *Quality of Life Research*, **8**, 255–61.

French Alcohology Society (Agence Nationale d'Accréditation et d'Evaluation en Santé) (1999) Consensus conference in alcohology: objectives, indications and modalities for detoxification the alcohol dependent patient. *Alcoologie et Addictologie*, **23**, 109–388.

Frisch, M.B., Cornell, J., Villanueva, M. and Retzlaff, P.J. (1992). Clinical validation of the Quality of Life Inventory: a measure of life satisfaction for use in treatment planning and outcome assessment. *Psychological Assessment*, **4**, 92–101.

Gloria, L., Cravo, M., Camilo, M.E., *et al.* (1997). Nutritional deficiencies in chronic alcoholics: relation to dietary intake and alcohol consumption. *The American Journal of Gastroenterology*, **92**(3), 485–89.

Goldberg, D. and Williams, P. (1988). A *User's Guide to the General Health Questionnaire*. Windsor: NFER Nelson.

Gunther, O., Roick, C., Angermeyer, M.C. and Konig, H.H. (2007). The EQ-5D in alcohol-dependent patients: Relationships among health-related quality of life, psychopathology and social functioning. *Drug and Alcohol Dependence*, **86**(2/3), 253–64.

Heaton, M.B., Mitchell, J.J. and Paiva, M. (2000). Amelioration of ethanol-induced neurotoxicity in the neonatal rat central nervous system by antioxidant therapy. Alcohol effects on the fetus, brain, liver, and other organ systems. *Alcoholism: Clinical and Experimental Research*, **24**(4), 512–18.

Holcomb, W.R., Beitman, B.D., Hemme, C.A., Josylin, A. and Prindiville, S. (1998). Use of a new outcome scale to determine best practices. *Psychiatric Services*, **49**(5), 583–95.

Hornquist, J.O. (1982). The concept of quality of life. *Scandinavian Journal of Social Medicine*, **10**, 57–61.

Hunt, SM., McKenna, S.P., McEwan, J., Williams, J. and Papp, E. (1981). The Nottingham Health Profile: Subjective health status and medical consultations. *Social Science and Medicine*, **15**(A), 221–29.

Jamison, J.R. (1999). *The wellness contract: an experiential learning format for preparing students as primary contact health professionals.* Presented at the HERDSA Annual International Conference, Melbourne, 12–15 July 1999.

Joyce, C.R.B. (1994). Requirements for the assessment of individual quality of life. In: C. Bradley (ed.) *Quality of Life Following Renal Failure: Psychosocial Challenges Accompanying High Technology Medicine*. Chur, Switzerland: Harwood Academic, pp. 43–54.

Lemere, F. and Smith, J.W. (1973). Alcohol-induced sexual impotence. *American Journal of Psychiatry*, **130**, 212–13.

Leplege, A. and Hunt, S. (1997). The problem of quality of life in medicine. *The Journal of the American Medical Association*, **278**(1), 47–50.

Longabaugh, R., Mattson, R., Connors, G. and Cooney, N. (1994). Quality of life as an outcome variable in alcoholism treatment research. *Journal of Studies on Alcohol,* **55**(Suppl.), 119–29.

Maisto, S.M., McKay, J.R. and Tiffany, S.T. (2003). Diagnosis. In: J.P. Allen and V.B. Wilson (eds). *Assessing Alcohol Problems. A Guide for Clinicians and Researchers*, 2nd edn. US Department of Health and Human Services, Public Health Service National Institutes of Health. NIH Publication No. 03–3745.

Malet, L., Llorca, P.M., Beringuier, B., Lehert, P. and Falissard, B. (2006). AlQoL-9 for measuring quality of life in alcohol dependence. *Alcohol and Alcoholism*, **41**, 181–87.

Mann, K., Gunther, A., Stetter, F. and Ackermann,K. (1999). Rapid recovery from cognitive deficits in abstinent alcoholics: a controlled test–retest study. *Alcohol and Alcoholism*, **34**(4), 567–74.

McGee, H.M., O'Boyle, C.A., Hickey, A., O'Malley, K. and Joyce, C.R. (1991). Assessing the quality of life of the individual: the SEIQoL with a healthy gastroenterology unit population. *Psychological Medicine*, **21** (3), 749–59.

McKenna, M., Chick, J., Buxton, M., Howlett, H., Patience, D. and Ritson, B. (1996). The SECCAT survey: I. The costs and consequences of alcoholism. *Alcohol and Alcoholism*, **31**, 565–76.

McKenna, S.P. and Doward, L.C. (2004). The needs-based approach to quality of life assessment. *Value in Health*, **7**(Suppl.1), S1–3.

Morgan, M.Y., Landron, F. and Lehert, P. (2004). Improvement in quality of life after treatment for alcohol dependence with acamprosate and psychosocial support. *Alcoholism: Clinical and Experimental Research*, **28**, 64–77.

Patience, D., Buxton, D., Chick, J., Howlett, H., McKenna, M. and Ritson, B. (1997). The SECCAT survey: II. The alcohol-related problems questionnaire as a proxy for resource costs and quality of life in alcoholism treatment. *Alcohol and Alcoholism*, **32**, 79–84.

Peters, T.J., Millward, L.M. and Foster, J. (2003). Quality of life in alcohol misuse: comparison of men and women. *Archives of Women's Mental Health*, **6**, 239–43.

Peugh, J. and Belenko, S. (2001). Alcohol, drugs and sexual function: a review. *Journal of Psychoactive Drugs*, **33**(3), 223–32.

Rambaldi, A. and Gluud, C. (2005) *Colchicine for alcoholic and non-alcoholic liver fibrosis and cirrhosis*. Cochrane Database Systematic Review. 2005 April 18; (2):CD002148. Update of Cochrane Database Systematic Review 2001; (3):CD002148.w.

Sintonen, H. and Pekurinen, M. (1993). A fifteen-dimensional measure of health-related quality of life (15D) and its applications. In: S.R. Walker and R.M. Rosser (eds). *Quality of Life Assessment: Key Issues in the 1990s*. Dordrecht: Kluwer Academic, pp. 185–95.

Smith, K.W. and Larson M.J. (2003). Quality of life assessments by adult substance abusers receiving publicly funded treatment in Massachusetts. *The American Journal of Drug and Alcohol Abuse*, **29**, 323–35.

Sobell, L.C. and Sobell, M.B. (2003). Assessment of drinking behaviour. Alcohol consumption measures. In: J.P Allen and V.B. Wilson (eds). *Assessing Alcohol Problems. A Guide for Clinicians and Researchers*, 2nd edn. US Department of Health and Human Services, Public Health Service National Institutes of Health. NIH Publication No. 03–3745.

Spitzer, R.L., Kroenke, K., Linzer, M., *et al.* (1995). Health-related quality of life in primary care patients with mental disorders. *The Journal of the American Medical Association*, **274**, 1511–17.

Tankova, T., Dakovska, G. and Koev, D. (2001). Education of diabetic patients – a 1-year experience. *Patient Education and Counseling*, **43**, 139–45.

Taylor, R., Foster, B., Kyne-Grzebalski, D. and Vanderpump, M. (1994). Insulin regimens for the non-insulin dependent: impact on diurnal metabolic state and quality of life. *Diabetic Medicine*, **11**, 551–57.

Testa, M.A. and Simonson, D.C. (1996). Assessment of quality of life outcomes. *New England Journal of Medicine,* **334**(13), 835–40.

Van Dijk, A.P., Toet, J. and Verdurmen, J.E. (2004). The relationship between health-related quality of life and two measures of alcohol consumption. *Journal of Studies on Alcohol,* **65**, 241–49.

Walker, J. and Bradley, C. (2002). Assessing the quality of life of adolescents with diabetes: Using the SEIQoL, DQoL, patient and diabetes specialist nurse ratings. *Practical Diabetes International*, **19**(5), 141–44.

Ware, J.E. and Sherbourne, C.D. (1992). The MOS 36-Item Short-Form Health Survey (SF-36). I. Conceptual framework and item selection. *Medical Care*, **30**(6), 473–83.

Ware, J.E., Kosinski, M. and Dewey, J.E. (2000). *How to Score Version Two of the SF-36 Health Survey*. Lincoln, RI: Quality Metric.

Ware, J.E., Snow, K.K., Kosinski, M. and Gandek, B. (1993). *SF-36 Health Survey Manual and Interpretation Guide*. Boston, MA: New England Medical Center and The Health Institute.

Windle, M. (1996). Effect of parental drinking on adolescents. *Alcohol Health and Research World*, **20**(3), 18–22.

World Health Organization (1994). *International Classification of Diseases 10 (ICD-10)*. Available at: http://www.who.int/classifications/apps/icd/icd10online/ (last accessed August 2008).

World Health Organization (1998). Development of the World Health Organization WHO-QoL-BREF quality of life assessment. *Psychological Medicine*, **28**, 551–58.

Yokoyama, A., Takagi, T., Ishii, H., *et al.* (1991). Impaired autonomic nervous system in alcoholics assessed by heart rate variation. *Alcoholism: Clinical and Experimental Research*, **15**(5), 761–65.

19 Sleep, quality of life and alcohol misuse

John H. Foster

The adverse effects of alcohol on sleep are well documented in the literature. This chapter will first consider the components of one night in a 'normal' individual. It will then go on to discuss four types of sleep disturbance linked to drinking alcohol. These are insomnia, sleep apnoea, grinding of the teeth (sleep bruxism) and restless legs syndrome. All of these have an impact on the quality of life (QoL) of alcohol misusers. Most notably they are linked to worsening affect. QoL is an increasingly important scientific endeavour that seeks to privilege the subjective views of the patient or client and it is now often used when considering treatment outcomes. The subjective assessment of sleep as measured by the Nottingham Health Profile (NHP) has been shown to predict relapse to heavy drinking at 3 months (Foster *et al.*, 1998). The literature concerning self-rating of sleep and some of the measurement tools will also be discussed. The 'gold standard' for measurement of quality of life is the Short Form-36 (SF-36) which is routinely used in quality of life studies with alcohol misusers. Unfortunately it has no measurement of sleep, which is a huge omission in this area. The chapter will conclude by providing recommendations for the integration of sleep and QoL studies in alcohol misusers.

This chapter will take the following format. Initially normal sleep will be described, thereafter it will examine the impact of continuing heavy drinking on an individual's sleeping pattern. The costs in terms of mortality and morbidity will then be briefly considered. Alcohol has been implicated in a number of sleep-related conditions that also have a direct impact on a person's quality of life, such as insomnia, sleep apnoea and restless legs syndrome; each of these will be discussed in turn. The rest of the chapter focuses on how sleep has been measured subjectively in QoL studies and presents a number of recommendations for future research and practice.

Effects of disturbed sleep in the general population

An American Gallup Poll found that insomnia affects over 60 million people in the US alone annually and in the same survey half of the subjects reported it as a serious concern (Wake Up America, 1994). Studies have shown that the prevalence of sleep disturbance is higher in women than in men (Kales *et al.*, 1976). A review of the socioeconomic costs of insomnia (Chilcott and Shapiro, 1996) found that among the direct costs were the increased likelihood of physiological illness, psychiatric disturbance and consequently a greater number of days lost to employers due to sickness. However their most disturbing finding was that insomnia was associated with higher mortality rates. One 9-year study showed a 70 per cent higher mortality rate in men who slept less than 6 hours, compared to those whose slept for more than 6 hours (Wingard and Berkman, 1983).

A normal night's sleep

An average adult sleeps 7.5 to 8 hours every night. In that time the person progresses through two states of sleep during which there are varied amounts of electrical brain activity. These are known as slow-wave sleep (SWS) and rapid eye movement sleep (REM). The majority of sleep is deep and restful and takes the form of SWS. In contrast, REM sleep is less restful, occurs episodically, and takes up about 25 per cent of the sleeping time of young adults. REM episodes occur at about 90-minute intervals and last 5 to 30 minutes. In addition there are 'transitional periods of light sleep' that occur throughout the night (Guyton, 1992).

The stages of a normal night's sleep

There are five recurring cyclical stages in a normal (healthy) night's sleep – four non-REM stages and one REM stage. A sixth 'waking' stage is sometimes included. On this occasion 'waking' means the process of falling asleep. Dreaming occurs during the REM stage. More information on this can be found at: http://www.sleepdisorderchannel.com/stages/index.shtml.

Waking: This can be regarded as pre-sleep and is often referred to as 'relaxed wakefulness' whereby the body is preparing for sleep. When someone falls asleep their muscles are tense and there are erratic eye movements. As waking sleep progresses, the body starts to slow down, the muscles relax and eye movement is in the form of a slow roll.

Sleep stage 1: This equates to drowsiness. Polysomnographic readings show a 50 per cent reduction in activity between this stage and 'waking'. The eyes are now closed, but if the person is aroused they may feel they have not slept. Typically this stage lasts 5–10 minutes.

Sleep stage 2: This is a period of light sleep. If monitored by polysomnographic readings it is marked by peaks and valleys that are also positive and negative waves. These waves are related to spontaneous periods of muscle toning (positive) and muscle relaxation (negative). Two other noteworthy physiological changes also occur: the temperature of the body decreases and the heart rate becomes slower. The body is now preparing to enter deep sleep.

Sleep stages 3 and 4: There are two stages of deep sleep, of which stage 4 is the more intense. The deep sleep stages are also known as slow-wave (SWS) or delta sleep. If monitored through a polysomnograph the waves are slow and high with a steady rhythm.

All the above stages form non-REM (NREM) sleep and last between 90 and 120 minutes. Each stage lasts between 5 and 15 minutes. In fact, stage 2 and 3 'repeat backwards' before the body goes into REM sleep. Figure 19.1 illustrates the temporal order of the sleep stages.

REM sleep: The main characteristics of REM sleep are rapid eye movements, accompanied by an increased and erratic heart rate and respiration. The face, fingers and legs may also twitch. REM sleep is important because it is marked by intense dreaming, in which there is a high level of 'cerebral activity'. However, in parallel to this, there is a degree of paralysis in the muscles of the chin and neck. Therefore REM sleep is a mixture of intense brain activity and muscle relaxation – consequently it is often referred to as 'paradoxical' sleep. The first period of REM lasts 10 minutes. Each subsequent REM stage lengthens, and the final one lasts for 1 hour.

The sleep cycle

The stages repeat themselves as shown in Fig. 19.1. The first cycle lasts about 100 minutes. Each subsequent one is longer as the REM period lengthens; in an average night's sleep we undergo five sleep cycles. Some people suffer from sleep disorders that affect the quality, length and period of sleep onset. Among the factors that affect the sleep cycle are stress, psychological conditions such as depression, antidepressant medications and, of course, alcohol. In the next section we will consider some of the impacts of alcohol on the sleep pattern.

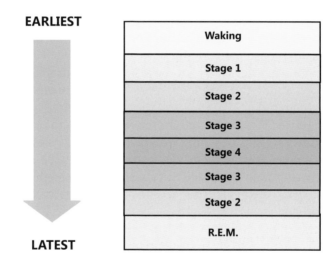

Figure 19.1 The chronological order of the cyclical stages of sleep.

Effects of alcohol on sleep

In addition to the sleep stages described above the product of a night's sleep is a series of chemical reactions controlled by the nerve cells in the lower brainstem. These chemicals are serotonin (linked to sleep onset and the regulation of SWS) and norepinephrine (which regulates REM sleep and encourages arousal). To date the precise mechanisms are not clear (Shepherd, 1994), but it is evident that alcohol has an impact on this chemical balance. Initially alcohol taken at bedtime has a paradoxical stimulating effect. It is, however, a sedative and not surprisingly the initial effect is to decrease the time required to get to sleep. Often alcohol is consumed in the belief that it will aid sleep (Brower, 2001), however it is more likely to lead to sleep disturbance particularly in the latter part of the sleep period (Landholt *et al.*, 1996).

During the latter sleep period a person who has drunk alcohol may sleep in a fitful manner, awakening from their dreams and finding it difficult to return to sleep. When drinking alcohol in an attempt to get to sleep continues over time these disturbances will increase (Vitiello, 1997). The cumulative effect of this pattern will lead to increasing daytime fatigue and sleepiness. According to Vitiello, a healthy normal subject aged 20 years will have a typical sleep latency of 10 minutes or less, 95 per cent sleep efficiency (percentage of time spent asleep as compared with time in bed), few episodes of night-time wakening, and a smooth progression through the sleep stages. The consequences of chronic drinking include reduced latency, diminished efficiency and a disrupted sleep pattern.

Before dealing with the two main sleep morbidities – sleep-disordered breathing (sleep apnoea) and insomnia – two conditions which have been connected with alcohol will be briefly considered.

Restless legs syndrome

A recent contemporary review of this syndrome has been published (Ryan and Slevin, 2006). The syndrome was first described in the 17th century and it was 'further characterised' in 1945. It is a common disorder, with UK data suggesting it affects 15 per cent of the adult population. For more about the condition see: http://www.nhsdirect.nhs.uk/articles/article. aspx?articleId=502&sectionId=5.

The symptoms reported include an urge to move about, with uncomfortable sensations and pains which worsen when lying or sitting down. These make sleep difficult and can result in drowsiness during the day. Restless legs syndrome is connected to iron deficiency and there may be a familial link, although the precise mechanisms involved are unclear. People who are particularly susceptible to restless legs syndrome have conditions that are associated with iron deficiency such as pregnancy, renal failure and anaemia. There have been no systematic trials to examine the efficacy of non-pharmacological therapies in the syndrome but the avoidance of alcohol, nicotine and caffeine is likely to result in an improvement in symptoms.

Sleep bruxism

Sleep bruxism is a condition likely to be encountered by dentists as it involves a constellation of symptoms including teeth grinding while asleep. A general population study in people aged over 15 years (Ohayon and Guilleminault, 2001) used 4972 samples from the UK, 4115 from Germany and 3970 from Italy. This found a 8.2 per cent prevalence rate of teeth grinding during sleep. The equivalent figure for an ICSD (International Classification of Sleep Disorders) sleep bruxism diagnosis was 4.4 per cent.

Table 19.1 shows the conditions associated with sleep bruxism and accompanying odds ratios found in Ohayon study. Heavy alcohol drinking had the highest odds ratio for the risk of sleep bruxism alongside sleep apnoea (which will be described in the next section). The practical consequences of sleep bruxism include muscular discomfort on awakening, tooth grinding, which may require dental intervention.

Table 19.1 **Risk of reporting sleep bruxism (adapted from Ohayon and Guilleminault, 2001)**

Condition associated with sleep bruxism	Odds ratio	95% confidence interval	P value
Sleep apnoea syndrome	1.8	1.2–2.6	< 0.01
Loud snorers	1.4	1.1–1.8	< 0.01
Moderate daytime sleepiness	1.3	1.1–1.6	< 0.01
Heavy alcohol drinkers (3 glasses per day 10 g = 1 glass)	1.8	1.8–2.4	< 0.001
Caffeine drinkers (more than 6 cups per day)	1.4	1.2–1.8	< 0.001
Moderate smokers (10–20 cigarettes per day)	1.3	1.1–1.5	< 0.01
Highly stressed	1.3	1.1–1.6	< 0.001
Anxiety	1.3	1.0–1.6	< 0.05

Sleep-disordered breathing/sleep apnoea

Sleep-disordered breathing (SDB) manifests itself as a 'recurrent obstruction of the upper airway resulting in episodic asphyxia and interruptions to the normal sleep pattern' (Fleetham, 1997). It varies in severity and can be seen as running on a continuum from chronic snoring to severe obstructive sleep apnoea (a disorder of the pharynx, located at the back of the mouth). It is estimated that 2–4 per cent of Americans in the general population suffer from obstructive sleep apnoea (OSA) (Strollo and Rogers, 1996). This results in interrupted breathing (apnoea) that causes the person to wake. They then resume breathing and return to sleep. This can occur hundreds of times during the night and clearly reduces sleeping time and leads to daytime sleepiness. The clinical consequences of untreated sleep apnoea are increased morbidity and mortality, most notably from heart circulatory diseases and accidents caused by tiredness (especially road traffic accidents). Over time there is a marked effect on the person's quality of life and working capacity (Laitinen *et al.*, 2003).

Young *et al.* (1993) found that 2 per cent of women and 4 per cent of men in a community-based study had both daytime sleepiness and an index of five or more episodes of apnoea hourly. Therefore it is as prevalent as asthma and diabetes (Philipson, 1993). Despite this, it often goes undiagnosed, so Fleetham recommends that doctors should routinely ask patients about their own and their 'bed-partners' snoring, interruption of breathing and daytime sleepiness. The factors most implicated in the development of OSA and other SDB disorders are smoking, middle-age, male sex, post-menopause in women, obesity and alcohol. The Finnish guidelines for prevention and treatment of OSA (Laitinen *et al.*, 2003) specifically focus on preventing this condition by the use of general population interventions aimed at weight loss and reducing the consumption of cigarettes and alcohol.

People with alcoholism are at increased risk of OSA especially if they snore (Aldritch *et al.*, 1993). However it has also been found that 'moderate to high' doses of alcohol are associated with a narrowing of the air passage, even in people who do not otherwise exhibit symptoms of OSA (Dawson *et al.*, 1993; Mittler *et al.*, 1988). As a result of alcohol's depressing effects, periods of existing OSA are exacerbated (Dawson *et al.*, 1993).

As previously mentioned, one of the main areas of impairment as a result of OSA is driving. For those people with pre-existing OSA drinking two or more drinks (1 drink is 0.5 oz of ethyl alcohol) per day there is a five-fold risk of being involved in a fatigue-related road traffic accident compared to minimal or non-drinkers with OSA. Finally a combination of alcohol, OSA and snoring increases an individual's risk of heart attack, arrhythmia, stroke and sudden death (Dawson *et al.*, 1993).

Alcohol and insomnia

Of even greater importance to alcohol-dependent people is the paradoxical link between alcohol and insomnia. As mentioned above, alcohol is a sedative and yet if heavy drinking continues the end result is increased sleep disturbance and insomnia. This has a major impact on the quality of life. There are two key papers in this area, by Crum *et al.* (2004) and Brower (2001). Both will be covered in some depth, but before considering them, the evidence concerning insomnia will be briefly outlined. The prevalence of insomnia is high – Breslau *et al.* (1996) found that nearly 25 per cent of their sample reported insomnia at some point in their lifetime. Yet it is rare for an individual to seek professional help for insomnia (Ancoli-Israel and Roth, 1999). General population data have shown that insomnia increases the risk of alcohol abuse, irrespective of baseline psychiatric disorders at 12 months (Weissmann *et al.*, 1997; Ford and Kamerow, 1989) and the link between alcohol and mood disorders (notably anxiety and depression) has been well documented (Kessler *et al.*, 1997; Kushner *et al.*, 2000; Grant and Harford, 1995). Of equal importance is the finding that insomnia and other forms of sleep disturbance can last for many months after detoxification and self-reported sleep scores predict relapse at 3 months following detoxification in a UK treatment sample (Foster *et al.*, 1998; Foster and Peters, 1999).

The Crum paper (Crum *et al.*, 2004) considered sleep disturbance in general, but this is the most appropriate point to discuss such an important work. Crum and colleagues sought to extend the evidence base by examining the interaction between sleep disturbance, alcohol disorders and anxiety/depression and worry over a follow-up period of more than 12 years (median 12.6 years). A total of 1537 participants from the general population who were felt to be 'at risk of developing an alcohol-related problem' (with no prior alcohol-related pathology) were interviewed from the Epidemiologic Catchment Area (ECA) cohort (Eaton and Kessler, 1985). Sleep disturbance was assessed in two ways, using the sleep items in the National Mental Health Diagnostic Interview Schedule (DIS) (Robins *et al.*, 1981) and the question 'Have you been losing sleep because of worry?' (over the past few weeks) taken from the General Health Questionnaire-20 (GHQ-20) (Goldberg and Blackwell, 1970). Alcohol-related problems were assessed with reference to DSM-III-R criteria.

The authors found that sleep disturbance because of worry was associated with the development of problem drinking. After controlling for age factors, gender, ethnicity, level of education, marital status and age of first intoxication, the odds ratio for alcohol problems and worry was 2.05 (1.26–3.35 95% CI; $p = 0.004$). Variables relating to current or past psychiatric history or substance use and use of medical or mental health services were then entered into the regression. The impact on the results was minimal, with an odds ratio of 2.32 (1.31–4.09 95% CI; $p = 0.004$). In contrast, similar analyses relating to anxiety and dysphoria did not produce significant findings. A subsequent analysis was conducted that stratified people with lifetime anxiety or dysphoria at baseline using a similar regression methodology. The odds ratio for problem drinking people with baseline anxiety was 3.82 (1.56–9.38 95% CI; $p = 0.003$); for those without baseline anxiety sleep disturbance did not predict alcohol problems (odds ratio 1.83; 0.86–3.88 95% CI; $p = 0.012$). Similar trends were evident for dysphoria: with dysphoria odds ratio was 2.71 (1.25–5.91 95% CI; $p = 0.003$) and without dysphoria odds ratio was 1.42 (0.57–3.53 95% CI; $p = 0.45$). The relationship between sleep disturbance because of worry and baseline lifetime anxiety/dysphoria was also assessed. In both cases, there was an increased risk of alcohol problems where sleep disturbance was present. Overall these findings point to an important synergistic link between mood disorder, sleep disturbance and alcohol. Sleep disturbance in combination with a mood disorder is more likely to result in the use of alcohol than the presence of a mood disorder alone.

The importance of drinking as a consequence of worry opens up the possibility that alcohol is used as a form of self-medication. This interaction has been explored in greater depth by Brower *et al.* (2001). That study recruited 172 American people receiving treatment for alcohol dependence. They were followed up for a mean of 5 months following baseline assessment when relapse status was ascertained. Any consumption of alcohol in the follow-up period was deemed to constitute a relapse. Measures of self-reported sleep, severity of the alcohol problem, depression and polysomnographic measures were collected. Polysomnography findings are not reported here because the focus of this chapter is on the measurement of self-reported sleep disturbance, and data for the first night's sleep only were reported, which may not be typical of sleep over a longer period. There are a number of medical and psychiatric conditions that influence sleep and people with these were excluded from the study, i.e. current depression, history of psychosis or bipolar disorder, borderline personality disorder, heart disease, severe liver disease, epileptic conditions (not associated with alcohol withdrawal), degenerative central nervous system disease, cerebrovascular disease or recent loss of consciousness due to a head trauma. A past history of anxiety or depression did not exclude anyone from the study. People taking prescribed medications that were judged to affect sleep were also excluded from the study. Sleep disturbance was assessed by the Sleep Disorders Questionnaire – a 175-item instrument measuring subjective sleep quality and complaints relating to nocturnal breathing, leg movements, daytime sleepiness and 'psychiatric distress' during the past 6 months (Douglass *et al.*, 1994). Each item was rated on a Likert scale, from 1 (never/strongly disagree) to 5 (always/ agree strongly). These items were distilled into eight items as a measure of 'insomnia' and one of 'self-medication' (Brower *et al.*, 2001); they are shown in Box 19.1. An individual was positive for insomnia if they scored 4 or 5 in response to any of the insomnia items shown in Box 19.1 and if they scored 4 or 5 on the self-medication item.

Box 19.1	Sleep disorder questionnaire variables used by Brower *et al.* (2001) to measure insomnia and self-medication
Insomnia	I get too little sleep at night
	I often have a poor night's sleep
	I have trouble getting to sleep at night
	I wake up often during the night
	I have been unable to sleep at all for several days
	I feel that my sleep is abnormal
	I feel that I have insomnia
	I have a problem with my sleep
Self-medication	I often use alcohol in order to get to sleep

Over 60 per cent met the criteria of insomnia during the past 6 months and were more likely to report using alcohol to get to sleep than those who were not classified as having insomnia. Only 74 (43 per cent) of the sample were followed up and of these 36 (49 per cent) relapsed. Insomnia total scores were the only significant predictors of relapse at 5 months following a logistic regression. Therefore the relationship was stable even after controlling for severity of dependence and depression scores. Self-medication did not predict relapse. Only 6 per cent of the sample responded positively to the item 'I feel that I have insomnia'. The equivalent response to 'I have been unable to sleep at all for several days' was 4 per cent, suggesting that this sample did not view themselves as having insomnia. The authors suggest that this may be because such a label was seen as stigmatising. In contrast, the other items were endorsed by 18–32 per cent of the sample. Future research might profitably assess what this group regards as symptoms of insomnia. The small sample and disappointing follow-up rate limits the conclusions that can be drawn from what is nonetheless an important study.

Further work has been conducted on the components of self-reported sleep disturbance (Foster and Peters, 1999). In previous work, Foster *et al.* (1998) found that self-reports of sleep as assessed by the NHP (Hunt *et al.*, 1980) subscore was the most significant predictor of relapse at 3 months in a group of 60 socially disadvantaged alcohol-dependent individuals (n = 39 (65%) males). These participants were recruited from an inner-city UK treatment centre and the capture rate was 58 (97 per cent). Every 10 points on the NHP scale (range 0–100) increased the chances of relapse by 1.4. The study by Foster and Peters re-worked the data in terms of the number of times NHP items were positively endorsed by each individual; the results are shown in Table 19.2.

The most significant predictor of 3 months relapse was 'It takes me a long time to get to sleep' – as endorsed by 69 per cent of those who relapsed at 3 months. The NHP sleep variable 'I'm waking in the early hours of the morning' produced a difference between the relapsers and non-relapsers (of $p = 0.018$) although after applying a Bonferonni correction this was deemed as not significant. At 12 weeks, two NHP subscores were associated with a poor outcome; these were 'I sleep badly at night' ($p < 0.001$) and 'It takes me a long time to get to sleep' ($p = 0.008$).

This work has been extended by applying the NHP to 240 people followed up at 12 months from six different UK alcohol treatment settings (Foster, 2007). A full description of the treatment settings is provided in Foster (2004). On this occasion, NHP sleep was not a significant predictor at either 3, 6 or 12 months. However for this study two additional measures were added – the SF-36 (Ware *et al.*, 1993) and the Jarman Index (Jarman, 1983). Despite the fact that sleep did not predict relapse, 85 per cent of the sample had a baseline NHP sleep score above that of general population norms (Hunt *et al.*, 1994). The Jarman Index is a score derived by a given UK administrative area (population around 20,000) which is based on eight census variables. These are: elderly persons living alone; children or infants under 5 years of age; one-parent families; unskilled persons (social class V); unemployed persons; overcrowded accommodation; number of persons changing address within 1 year; and people from ethnic minorities. The composite score is called an 'underprivileged area score'.

The findings of Foster (2007) confirm that the prevalence of disturbed sleep in this population is high but suggests that area-based deprivation is a far more important factor in the outcomes of this group (including quality of life, as the Jarman Index was the most significant predictor of relapse at all three time points.

Foster and Peters (1999) also found that depression scores measured by the Beck Depression Inventory (Beck *et al.*, 1960) were significantly correlated with the NHP sleep subscale scores

Table 19.2   Individual Nottingham Health Profile (NHP) sleep variable responses at (A) baseline and (B) 12 weeks follow-up

(A) AT BASELINE	Total sample (60)		Relapse (36)		Non-relapse (22)		P value
	Yes	No	Yes	No	Yes	No	
I lie awake at night	20 (34%)	40 (66%)	14 (39%)	22 (61%)	5 (23%)	17 (77%)	0.203
I have tablets to help me sleep	8 (13%)	52 (87%)	6 (17%)	30 (83%)	2 (9%)	20 (91%)	0.417
I sleep badly at night	30 (50%)	30 (50%)	22 (61%)	14 (39%)	6 (27%)	16 (73%)	0.012
It takes me a long time to get to sleep	34 (57%)	26 (43%)	25 (69%)	11 (31%)	7 (32%)	15 (68%)	0.005
I'm waking in the early hours of the morning	37 (62%)	23 (38%)	26 (72%)	10 (28%)	9 (41)	13 (59%)	0.005
(B) AT 12 WEEKS FOLLOW-UP	Total sample (58)		Relapse (36)		Non-relapse (22)		P value
	Yes	No	Yes	No	Yes	No	
I lie awake at night	20 (34%)	38 (66%)	17 (47%)	19 (53%)	3 (13%)	19 (87%)	0.203
I have tablets to help me sleep	9 (16%)	49 (84%)	8 (22%)	28 (78%)	1 (4%)	21 (96%)	0.133
I sleep badly at night	25 (43%)	33 (57%)	22 (61%)	14 (39%)	3 (13%)	19 (87%)	0.001
It takes me a long time to get to sleep	26 (45%)	32 (55%)	21 (58%)	15 (42%)	5 (23%)	17 (77%)	0.008
I'm waking in the early hours of the morning	28 (48%)	30 (52%)	23 (64%)	13 (36%)	7 (32%)	15 (68%)	0.017

These differences were tested by a two-tailed Chi-squared test by means of a 2 × 2 contingency table; if any of the cells had less than five members, a two-tailed Fishers exact test was used. Two subjects were lost to follow-up; no assumptions have been made as to their relapse status, therefore they are not presented in the follow-up analyses. A Bonferonni correction has been applied as follows to control for a type I error (0.05/number of variables, i.e. 0.05/5; $p = 0.01$). Taken from Foster and Peters (1999).

(correlation 0.55; $p < 0.001$). Note that depression was not being measured because 10 alcohol-free days are required before the depressant effects of alcohol following detoxification are no longer present. Approximately 85 per cent of all alcohol-dependent people's depression scores return to normal levels within 10 days without further intervention (Davidson, 1995). In the Foster and Peters study, participants were assessed after 4 alcohol-free days, so we cannot conclude that clinical depression was being measured. However the findings build on the work of Crum *et al.* (2004) and have been extended further by using the Hospital Anxiety and Depression Scale (HADS) (Zigmond and Snaith, 1983), the NHP sleep subscale, and quality of life as measured by the EQ-5D (EuroQol) (Brooks and the EuroQoL Group, 1996). These were applied to an outpatient sample of 54 moderately dependent alcoholic people who were currently drinking, followed up at 3 months (Foster *et al.*, 2002).

In that study, the two most endorsed NHP sleep subscores at baseline were once again 'I'm waking in the early hours of the morning' (waking early; 75 per cent) and 'I sleep badly at night' (badly; 69 per cent) (see Table 19.3). However other than 'I take tablets to help me sleep' (take tablets; 30 per cent) all items were endorsed by half or more than half of the sample – confirming the importance of sleep in this group. The study was also able to provide some additional pointers regarding the link between self-reported sleep disturbance and affect. 'Depression caseness' as measured by the HADS was predicted by two NHP sleep subscores – 'badly', (depression caseness B = 2.39, SE 0.85; df 1, p = 0.005) and 'awake' (B = 0.31; SE = 0.11; df = 1; p = 0.004). There were 24 (89 per cent) 'badly' and 20 (74 per cent) 'awake' 'cases' who were also HADS 'depression' 'cases'. There was not a similar relationship between any NHP sleep subscores and 'anxiety caseness'. At 3-month follow-up returning to 'sensible drinking' or abstinence was associated with a diminution in alcohol consumption, but not with a statistically significant improvement in health-related quality of life, sleep or affective status. These results suggest a greater link between depression and disturbed sleep than anxiety, but it must be noted that the sample size was small, the follow-up period was short and these were current drinkers. A further problem may relate to the HADS, specifically whether it measures depression and anxiety caseness. A recent review of the evidence (Martin, 2005) found that the HADS measures three constructs – anhedonia, negative affectivity and autonomic arousal, rather than depression and anxiety.

Table 19.3 **Prevalence of positive responses to each NHP (Nottingham Health Profile) sleep variable (adapted from Foster *et al.*, 2002)**

Positive responses		Number (percentage)	
I'm waking in the early hours of the morning	Waking Early	39	75%
I sleep badly at night	Badly	36	69%
It takes me a long time to get to sleep	Long Time	27	52%
I lie awake at night	Lie Awake	26	50%
I take tablets to help me sleep	Take Tablets	15	30%

The HADS and EQ-5D were used by Cohn *et al.* (2003) to examine the relationship between sleep and affect. On this occasion sleep, as measured by the Pittsburgh Sleep Quality Index (Buysse *et al.*, 1989) had greater links to HADS anxiety rather than depression. The Pittsburgh Sleep Quality Index, or PSQI will be described in greater depth in later in this chapter.

A group of 57 alcohol-dependent people resident in a non-statutory sector rehabilitation unit were followed up after 12 weeks. At baseline there was not a significant correlation between PSQI and depression scores as measured by the HADS. At baseline assessment the participants were 14 days alcohol-free, so many of the depression symptoms which accompany alcohol consumption had disappeared. This is the most likely explanation for the non-significant relationship between PSQI and HADS depression scores. Forty per cent of the sample were followed up at 12 months. Quality of life, as measured by EQ-5D, and depression scores improved significantly. However at this point participants were still experiencing difficulties with sleep and anxiety. These findings suggest that further investigations are required to tease out the interaction between depression, anxiety and disturbed sleeping patterns.

Measures of self-reported sleep

The chapter will now consider some of the tools used to measure disturbed sleep and point to some of the problems with the QoL measures most commonly used in research studies. Recent work (Conroy *et al.*, 2006) has confirmed the importance of self-assessment of sleep. In this study, 18 subjective assessments of sleep were compared with polysomnographic readings; drinking outcomes were then compared during two 6-week periods. Most people tended to overestimate the length of time they took to get to sleep and underestimated waking time after sleep onset. Subjective sleep measures were better predictors of future drinking than polysomnographic readings. In short, this recent study (albeit in only a small sample) provides further evidence of the clinical utility of self-reported sleep measures.

The rest of this chapter will consider some of the measures of self-reported sleep that have been used in research studies and will describe how they have been applied. It will conclude by briefly discussing how sleep measures have been integrated into generic quality of life measures and provide some recommendations for future quality of life studies.

Pittsburgh Sleep Quality Index (PSQI)

One widely used measure of self-reported sleep is the Pittsburgh Sleep Quality Index (PSQI) (Buysse *et al.*, 1989). This questionnaire yields a total sleep disturbance score and also has seven discrete subscores as follows: sleep quality, sleep latency, sleep duration, habitual sleep efficiency, sleep disturbances, use of sleep medication, and daytime dysfunction. A total score of 6 or above is indicative of poor sleep.

The PSQI was applied to a control group and a sample of alcohol-dependent people undergoing detoxification who had been alcohol free for 4 or 5 days (Foster and Peters, 1999). The alcohol-dependent group had significantly poorer PSQI total scores than the controls. There was no difference in PSQI scores across mild, moderate and severe dependency (Potamianos *et al.*, 1984) as measured by the Severity of Alcohol Dependence Questionnaire (SADQ) (Stockwell *et al.*, 1979). However, it too confirmed a significant relationship between self-reported sleep and depression scores as measured by the Beck Depression Inventory (BDI; Beck *et al.*, 1961) in alcohol-dependent people.

A US study has used the PSQI (Currie *et al.*, 2003) as well as a series of other measures with a group of alcohol-dependent men and women. There were two comparison groups; those with short-term (less than 12 months) and long-term (more than 12 months) abstinence. Both of these groups had PSQI scores indicating that their sleep disturbances continued for many months after stopping drinking. The main problems experienced were getting to sleep rather than staying asleep. On this occasion dependency was measured by the 25-item Alcohol Dependence Scale (Skinner and Horn, 1984). Once more there was no difference in PSQI scores across levels of dependency. There was a significant correlation between total PSQI and BDI scores ($r = 0.32$; $p < 0.05$) but it was not as strong as that in Foster and Peters study ($r = 0.68$; $p < 0.001$). The most likely explanation for the difference is that the Currie study excluded subjects who had current major depression; in contrast, Foster and Peters made no attempt to do so.

The other study in this area in which the PSQI has been used is that of Cohn *et al.* (2003). Their findings were discussed previously.

Nottingham Health Profile (NHP)

Later there will be some discussion about generic versus condition-specific quality of life measures. One of the main generic measures that has been used in quality of life studies is the NHP (Hunt *et al.*, 1986). This was devised at Nottingham University in the UK and is based on lay-persons' perceptions of health status. The six subscales are emotional reactions, energy, pain, physical abilities, sleep and social isolation.

An account of the NHP's development is contained in Hunt *et al.* (1980) and the latest published handbook is by Hunt *et al.* (1994). The usual method of scoring depends on weighting of the five individual items. The weights are calculated from the results of a community sample of 1200 people, approximately equal numbers of men and women, aged 18–74, who were representative of patient and non-patient populations. The sample was asked to assess the relative seriousness of each item in comparison to others within the same group (McKenna *et al.*, 1981). An individual can be scored 0–100 on the sleep subscore (higher scores indicate greater health problems). Table 19.4 shows the weightings for each sleep item resulting from the McKenna study.

Table 19.4 **Weightings for each NHP (Nottingham Health Profile) sleep variable (from McKenna *et al.*, 1981)**

Variable	NHP weighting
I'm waking in the early hours of the morning (Waking Early)	12.57
I sleep badly at night (Badly)	21.70
It takes me a long time to get to sleep (Long Time)	16.10
I lie awake at night (Lie Awake)	27.26
I take tablets to help me sleep (Take Tablets)	22.37

To date the NHP sleep subscale has only been applied to alcohol-dependent people by the Foster research group in published studies (Foster *et al.*, 1998; Foster and Peters 1999; Foster *et al.*, 2002). The findings of all these studies have been previously discussed under 'alcohol and insomnia'. They confirmed one of the major limitations with the NHP is when the initially derived weightings are used to score it, many zero scores are produced. This means that any subtle changes in poor health status cannot be detected. Some research has been devoted to determining whether there is a better way to score the NHP sleep subscale. Hunt *et al.* (1986), the designers of the NHP, state that 'it would be meaningless to simply add up the number of affirmative responses out of the 38 possible' ones. The implication of this statement is that there is no meaningful total score for the NHP and that each subscore can stand alone. Kind and Carr-Hill (1987) criticise the methodology employed to derive the weights for each NHP item (McKenna *et al.*, 1981) because they were divided into their subsections *a priori*, but in reality there is a substantial overlap between the items.

For example 'I sleep badly at night' (NHP sleep), 'I'm tired all the time' (NHP energy) and 'Things are getting me down' (NHP emotional reactions) may have been measuring parts of the same construct. However if there is an NHP subscore that can stand alone it is the sleep subscore (Kind and Carr-Hill, 1987). In their study of 1700 people of the five most endorsed NHP items, three came from the NHP sleep subscale. Further work by Kind (1982) compared the weightings of NHP items with a simplified scoring method in the NHP sleep subscore only and recommended that each response is scored either as 0 or 1 according to whether it is positive or negative. Therefore the possible range of scores would be 0–5. Another possibility suggested in that study was to treat each positive response to individual NHP sleep items as being a 'sleep case'. These methodologies were used by Foster *et al.* (2002) and Foster and Peters (1999) respectively.

Sleep Disorders Questionnaire (SDQ)

This is another self-reported measure of sleep status and was used by Brower *et al.* (2001). It has been described in 'alcohol and insomnia' (Box 19.1 shows its components).

Sleep and commonly used generic measures of QoL

The study of quality of life is based on the premise that the subjective views of the participant are paramount. It is a multidimensional construct and most authors agree that it must have at least three core domains – physical, psychological and social (Shumaker and Berzon, 1995). Other terms that could be included under the heading of QoL include social functioning, emotional well-being, role functioning, cognitive functioning, sleep problems, sexual functioning, vitality/energy, pain, life satisfaction, body image and general perceptions of health (Leidy *et al.*, 1999).

In essence, quality of life measures can be divided into two categories: generic and condition-specific. The main advantage of generic questionnaires is that they allow comparisons to be made across disease states, although they may not be able to detect the subtleties of various diseases (i.e. sensitivity is lost) (Patrick and Deyo, 1989). Condition-specific or disease-specific questionnaires are more sensitive to the impact of the disease, however they are limited for comparison purposes. On balance a condition-specific measure is preferable. A condition-specific measure for alcohol-dependent people (the Al-QoL-9) has been developed (Malet *et al.*, 2006) but this has a major limitation in its current form, as will shortly be described.

To date, with the exception of the Malet study, alcohol-related QoL studies have used generic measures. Specifically how these relate to the measurement of sleep will be discussed later. The gold standard of QoL and health-related QoL (HR-QoL) is the SF-36 (Ware *et al.*, 1993). This is now the measure of choice in virtually all alcohol-related quality of life studies. Unfortunately it contains no measure of sleep, which this chapter has shown to be a serious omission when studying alcohol-dependent or alcohol-misusing people. The Al-QoL-9 was formed by distilling items down from the SF-36, so it too has no sleep subscore. The EuroQoL (or EQ-5D) has been used by Foster *et al.* (2002) and Cohn *et al.* (2003), but it also has no measure of sleep. One of the generic measures that shows some promise is the WHO-QoL (World Health Organization WHO-QoL Group, 1995). This was designed under the umbrella of the World Health Organization to assess quality of life from a cross-cultural perspective using both quantitative and qualitative methods. There were 14 field centres from Australia, Croatia, India, France, Israel, Japan, The Netherlands, Panama, Russia, Spain, the UK, the USA and Zimbabwe.

So far only one study has been published that has applied the WHO-QoL to people who are alcohol-dependent (da Silva Lima *et al.*, 2005). This is a small-scale Brazilian study in only 32 people that showed the WHO-QoL-BREF was able to differentiate levels of dependency and had convergent validity with the SF-36. The authors concluded that the WHO-QoL 'proved to be satisfactory for evaluating quality of life in this sample'. Furthermore, the WHO-QoL has one item relating to sleep, namely 'How satisfied are you with your sleep?', which is scored on a scale of 1 to 5 (very dissatisfied to very satisfied).

In time this may prove to be a better measure of quality of life than the SF-36, although with such a small study few conclusions can be drawn. The final generic measure of quality of life used in this area has already been discussed – the Nottingham Health Profile. Since its propensity to produce 0 scores has been discovered it has largely been superseded by the SF-36, but it does have a sleep subscore, unlike all the other generic quality of life measures currently being used.

Conclusions

The author of this chapter believes that the current trend for incorporating the SF-36 into all alcohol-related quality of life studies should be open to question. At the very least it should be supplemented with a measure of self-reported sleep. The way forward could be to use the WHO-QoL as the measure of choice, with a view to garnering more information related to its psychometric properties. One particularly useful area of study would be to establish the level of association between the WHO-QoL-BREF sleep item and the PSQI, SDQ and NHP (scored as per Kind, 1982). This would establish whether it would be acceptable to use the WHO-QoL-BREF without a sleep measure. In the meantime more work should be conducted to determine which measure of self-reported sleep provides the most comprehensive data coverage and without creating interviewee fatigue. At present it is not possible to determine which is the best measure to use.

To conclude, here are two pleas for researchers in this field. First, more resources need to be targeted to investigating self-reported sleep in alcohol-dependent and misusing people. Second, a measure of self-reported sleep needs to be used when conducting quality of life studies in people with alcohol problems.

References and further reading

Aldritch, M., Shipley, J., Tandon, R., Kroll, P. and Brower K. (1993). Sleep-disordered breathing in alcoholics: Association with age. *Alcoholism: Clinical and Experimental Research*, **17**, 1179–83.

Ancoli-Israel, S. and Roth, T. (1999). Characteristics of insomnia in the United States: results of the 1991 National Sleep Foundation Survey I. *Sleep*, **22**(Suppl.2), S347–53.

Beck, A., Mendelson, M. and Mock, J. (1961). Inventory for measuring depression. *Archives of General Psychiatry*, **4**, 561–71.

Breslau, N., Roth, T., Rosenthal, I. and Andreski, P. (1996). Sleep disturbance and psychiatric disorders: a longitudinal epidemiological study of young adults. *Biological Psychiatry*, **39**, 411–18.

Brooks, R. and the EuroQoL Group (1996). EuroQoL: the state of play. *Health Policy*, **37**, 53–72.

Brower, K., Aldrich, M., Robinson, E., Zucker, R. and Greden, J. (2001). Insomnia, self-medication and relapse to alcoholism. *American Journal of Psychiatry*, **158**, 399–404.

Brower, K. (2001). Alcohol's effect on sleep in alcoholics. *Alcohol Research and Health*, **25**, 110–25.

Buysse, D., Reynolds, C., Monk, T., Berman, S. and Kupfer, D. (1989). The Pittsburgh Sleep Quality Index: A new instrument for psychiatry practice and research. *Psychiatry Research*, **28**, 193–210.

Chilcott, L. and Shapiro, C. (1996). The socio-economic impact of insomnia. An overview. *PharmacoEconomics*, **10**(Suppl.), 1–14.

Cohn, T., Foster, J.H. and Peters, T.J. (2003). Sequential studies of sleep disturbance and quality of life in abstaining alcoholics. *Addiction Biology*, **8**, 455–62.

Conroy, D., Arnedt, J., Brower, K., *et al.* (2006). Perception of sleep in recovering alcohol-dependent patients with insomnia: Relationship with future drinking. *Alcoholism: Clinical and Experimental Research*, **30**, 1992–99.

Crum, R., Storr, C., Ya-Fen Chan, M. and Ford, D. (2004). Sleep disturbance and risk for alcohol-related problems. *American Journal of Psychiatry*, **161**, 1197–1203.

Currie, S., Clark, S., Rimac, S. and Malhotra, S. (2003). Comprehensive assessment of insomnia in recovering alcoholics using daily sleep diaries and ambulatory monitoring. *Alcohol: Clinical and Experimental Research*, **27**, 1262–69.

da Silva Lima, A., Fleck, M., Pechansky, F., de Boni, R. and Sukop, P. (2005). Psychometric properties of the WHO quality of life instrument (WHO-QoL-BREF) in alcoholic males – a pilot study. *Quality of Life Research*, **14**, 473–78.

Davidson, K. (1995). Diagnosis of depression in alcohol dependence: Changes in prevalence with drinking status. *British Journal of Psychiatry*, **166**, 199–204.

Dawson, A., Bigby, B., Poceat, S. and Mitler, M. (1993). Effect of bedtime ethanol on total inspiratory resistance and respiratory drive in non-snoring men. *Alcoholism: Clinical and Experimental Research*, **17**, 256–62.

Douglass, A., Bornstein, R., Nino-Murcia, G., *et al.* (1994). The Sleep Disorders Questionnaire. I: Creation and multivariate structure of SDQ. *Sleep*, **17**, 160–67.

Eaton, W. and Kessler, L. (1985). *Epidemiologic Field Methods in Psychiatry: The NIMH Epidemiologic Catchment Area Program.* New York: Academic Press.

Fleetham, J.A. (1997). A wake up call for sleep-disordered breathing. *British Medical Journal*, **314**, 839.

Ford, D. and Kamerow, D. (1989). Epidemiological study of sleep disturbances and psychiatric disorders: an opportunity for prevention? *Journal of the American Medical Association*, **262**, 1479–84.

Foster, J.H. and Peters, T.J. (1999). Sleep as a quality of life indicator and predictor of relapse in alcohol dependents. *Alcoholism: Clinical and Experimental Research*, **23**, 1044–51.

Foster, J.H., Marshall. E.J. and Peters, T.J. (1998). Predictors of relapse to heavy drinking in alcohol dependent subjects following alcohol detoxification – the role of quality of life measures, ethnicity, social class, cigarettes and drug use. *Addiction Biology*, **3**, 333–43.

Foster, J.H., Peters, T.J. and Kind, P. (2002). Quality of life, sleep, mood and alcohol consumption: a complex interaction. *Addiction Biology*, **7**, 55–65.

Foster, J.H. (2004). Conducting research in different alcohol centres: achieving a follow-up rate of 93%. *Drugs: Education Prevention and Policy*, **11**, 263–74.

Foster, J.H. (2007). *Quality of Life in Alcoholics: A Longitudinal Study.* New York: Nova Science.

Goldberg, D. and Blackwell, B. (1970). Psychiatric illness in general practice: a detailed study using a new method of case identification. *British Journal of Medicine*, **1**, 439–43.

Grant, B. and Harford, T. (1995). Comorbidity between DSM-IV alcohol use disorders and major depression: results of a national survey. *Drug and Alcohol Dependence*, **39**, 197–206.

Guyton, A. (1992). *Human Physiology and Mechanisms of Disease*, 5th edn. Philadelphia: WB Saunders.

Hunt, S., McEwen, J. and McKenna, S. (1986). *Measuring Health Status*. London: Croom Helm.

Hunt, S., McKenna, S. and McEwen, J. (1994). *The Nottingham Health Profile User's Manual*. Manchester: Galen Research.

Hunt, S., Sonja, M., McKenna, S., McEwen, J., Backett, E. and Papp, E. (1980). A quantitative approach to perceived health status: a validation study. *Journal of Epidemiology and Community Health*, **34**, 281–86.

Jarman, B. (1983). Identification of underprivileged areas. *British Medical Journal*, **286**, 1705–09.

Kales, A., Caldwell, A., Preston, T., *et al.* (1976). Personality patterns in insomnia. Theoretical implications. *Archives of General Psychiatry*, **33**, 1128–34.

Kessler, R., Crum, R., Warner, L., Nelson, C., Schulenberg, J. and Anthony, J. (1997). Lifetime co-occurrence of DSM-III-R alcohol abuse and dependence with other psychiatric disorders in the National Comorbidity Survey. *Archives of General Psychiatry*, **54**, 313–21.

Kind, P. and Carr-Hill, R. (1987). The Nottingham Health Profile: A useful tool for epidemiologists? *Social Science and Medicine*, **25**, 905–10.

Kind, P. (1982). A comparison of two models for scaling health indicators. *International Journal of Epidemiology*, **11**, 271–75.

Kushner, M., Abrams, K. and Borchardt, C. (2000). The relationship between anxiety disorders and alcohol use disorders: a review of major perspectives and findings. *Clinical Psychology Review*, **20**, 149–71.

Laitinen, L., Anttalainen, U., Pietinalhoo, A., Hamalainen, P. and Koskela, K. (2003) Sleep apnoea: Finnish guidelines for prevention and treatment 2002–2012. *Respiratory Medicine*, **97**, 337–65.

Landholt, H., Roth, C., Dijk, D. and Borbely, A. (1996). Late-afternoon ethanol intake effects nocturnal sleep and the sleep of middle-aged men. *Journal of Clinical Psychopharmacology*, **16**, 428–36.

Leidy, N., Revicki, D. and Geneste, B. (1999). Recommendations for evaluating the validity of quality of life claims for labelling and promotion. *Value in Health*, **2**, 113–27.

Malet, L., Lorca, P., Beringuer, B., Lehert, P. and Falissard, B. (2006). AlQoL-9 for measuring quality of life in alcohol dependents. *Alcohol and Alcoholism*, **41**, 181–87.

Martin, C. (2005). What does the Hospital Anxiety and Depression Scale (HADS) really measure in liaison psychiatry settings. *Current Psychiatry Review*, **1**, 69–73.

McKenna, S., Hunt, S. and McEwen, J. (1981). Weighting the seriousness of perceived health problems using Thurstone's method of paired comparisons. *International Journal of Epidemiology*, **10**, 93–97.

Mittler, M., Dawson, A., Henricksen, S., Sobers, M. and Bloom, F. (1988). Bedtime ethanol increases resistance and respiratory drive in upper airways and produces sleep apnoeas in asymptomatic snorers. *Alcoholism: Clinical and Experimental Research*, **12**, 801–05.

Ohayon, M. and Guilleminault, C. (2001). Risk factors for sleep bruxism in the general population. *Chest*, **119**, 53–61.

Patrick, D. and Deyo, R. (1989). Generic and disease-specific measures in assessing health status and quality of life. *Medical Care*, **27**(Suppl.), S217–32.

Philipson, E. (1993). Sleep apnoea – a major public health problem. *New England Journal of Medicine*, **328**, 1271–73.

Potamianos, G., Gorman, D., Duffy, S. and Peters, T. (1984). The use of the severity of alcohol dependence questionnaire (SADQ) on a sample of problem drinkers presenting at a district general hospital. *Alcohol*, **1**, 441–45.

Robins, L., Heltzer, J., Croughan, J. and Ratcliff, K. (1981). The National Institute of Mental Health Diagnostic Interview Schedule: its history, characteristics and validity. *Archives of General Psychiatry*, **38**, 381–89.

Ryan, M. and Slevin, J. (2006). Restless legs syndrome. *American Journal of Health System Pharmacy*, **63**, 1599–1612.

Shepherd, G. (1994). *Neurobiology*, 3rd edn. New York: Oxford University Press.

Shumaker, S. and Berzon, R. (eds) (1995). *The International Assessment of HR-QoL, Theory, Translation, Measurement and Analysis*. Oxford: Rapid Communications.

Skinner, H. and Horn, J. (1984). *Alcohol Dependence Scale (ADS) User's Guide*. Toronto: Addiction Research Foundation.

Stockwell, T., Hodgson, R., Edwards, G., Taylor, C. and Rankin, H. (1979). The development of a questionnaire to measure the severity of alcohol dependence. *British Journal of Addiction*, **74**, 79–87.

Strollo, P. and Rogers, R. (1996). Obstructive sleep apnoea. *New England Journal of Medicine*, **334**, 99–104.

Vitiello, M. (1997). Sleep, alcohol and alcohol abuse. *Addiction Biology*, **2**, 151–159.

Wake Up America (1994). *A national sleep alert, Vol., 2. Working group reports. Report of the national commission on sleep disorders research*. Washington DC: National Institutes of Health, US Government Printing Office.

Ware, J., Snow, K., Kosinski, M. and Gandek, B. (1993). *SF-36 Health Survey: A Manual and Interpretation Guide*. Boston: The Health Institute New England Medical Centre.

Weissmann, M., Greenwald, S., Nino-Murcia, G. and Dement, W. (1997). The morbidity of insomnia uncomplicated by psychiatric disorders. *General Hospital Psychiatry*, **19**, 245–50.

World Health Organization Quality of Life Assessment (WHOQoL) Group (1995). Position Paper from The World Health Organisation. *Social Science and Medicine*, **41**, 1403–09.

Wingard, D. and Berkman L. (1983). Mortality risk associated with sleeping patterns among adults. *Sleep*, **6**, 102–07.

Young, T., Palta, M., Dempsey, J., Skatrud, J., Weber, S. and Badr, S. (1993). The occurrence of sleep-disordered breathing among middle-aged adults. *New England Journal of Medicine*, **328**, 1230–35.

Zigmond, A. and Snaith R. (1983). The Hospital Anxiety and Depression Scale. *Acta Psychiatrica Scandinavica*, **67**, 361–70.

20 Nutrition in chronic alcoholism

Pathophysiological and clinical aspects

Rajkumar Rajendram and Victor R. Preedy

Ethanol is one of the most commonly used recreational drugs in the world. The chemical structure of the molecule is shown below in Fig. 20.1. The word 'alcohol' is synonymous with 'ethanol', and 'drinking' usually describes consumption of alcoholic beverages. In the UK, alcohol is a staple part of most people's diet – nearly 40 million adults 'drink'. The market for alcoholic drinks is worth more than £30 billion per year (Prime Minister's Strategy Unit, 2003). Although most people drink sensibly, the quantity of alcohol consumed varies significantly between individuals. Many people enjoy the pleasant, psychopharmacological, mood-altering effects of drinking alcohol, which is why it is so often misused; in the UK around 30 per cent of men and 20 per cent of women drink more than the recommended amounts (Prime Minister's Strategy Unit, 2003). Unfortunately, ethanol is profoundly toxic. Excessive consumption can cause dependency and induce pathological changes in most, if not all, organs. The annual cost of the effects of alcohol misuse in the UK has been estimated at a staggering £20 billion (Prime Minister's Strategy Unit, 2003). The cost of treating alcohol-induced disease is estimated at £1.7 billion per year.

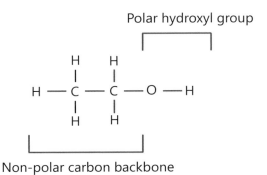

Figure 20.1 The chemical structure of ethanol C_2H_5OH. Ethanol is soluble in water due to its polar hydroxyl (OH) group. The non-polar C_2H_5 group enables ethanol to dissolve lipids and thereby disrupt biological membranes. Adapted from Rajendram *et al.*, 2005.

Ethanol and nutrition

Heavy drinkers often replace a substantial proportion of nutrient-derived calories with alcohol. Consumption of alcohol can therefore have significant effects on their nutrition, and some alcohol-induced diseases result from, or are exacerbated by, the effect of ethanol consumption on the nutritional status of drinkers.

Nutritional value of alcoholic beverages

Alcoholic drinks include low-ethanol-content beverages produced by fermentation of products containing sugar or starch and highly concentrated drinks (spirits) produced by distillation of low-ethanol-content beverages. The concentration of ethanol in alcoholic beverages is usually specified as a percentage of alcohol by volume (ABV), the percentage of alcohol by weight (ABW) or as 'proof'. 'Proof' roughly corresponds in a 2 to 1 ratio to ABV so, for example, 60 per cent proof is equivalent to 30 per cent ABV. The various types of alcoholic beverage differ significantly in their ethanol concentrations. Low-strength beers, for example, usually contain 3–4 per cent ABW, while classic Russian vodka contains 40 per cent ABV (approximately 80 per cent proof, or 32 per cent ABW). Table 20.1 demonstrates the variability in alcohol content of different brands of selected alcoholic beverages.

Table 20.1 **Alcohol content of selected beverages (adapted from Rajendram *et al.*, 2005)**

Beverage	g/dL (ABW)	mmol/L
Low-strength beers	3–4	0.65–0.87
High-strength beers	8–9	1.74–1.96
Wine	7–14	1.52–3.04
Brandy	35–45	7.61–9.78
Vodka	35–50	7.61–10.87
Gin	35–50	7.61–10.87

Besides ethanol, alcoholic beverages predominantly contain water and carbohydrates. Ethanol has a calorific energy value of 7.1 kcal/g (29 kJ/g) which is more than that of carbohydrate (4.1 kcal/g; 16.7 kJ/g). The content of other nutrients (proteins, vitamins and minerals) is usually small. Table 20.2 gives the macronutrient content of various alcoholic beverages.

In the UK, a unit of alcohol (standard alcoholic drink) contains 8 g of ethanol. However, the amount of ethanol in a unit varies worldwide, so to avoid confusion all references to units of alcohol in this chapter are based on the UK definition. Table 20.3 outlines the average amount of ethanol in units in some alcoholic beverages. The unit system is a convenient way of quantifying consumption of ethanol and it offers a suitable means for giving practical guidance. However, there are several problems with it. For example, the ethanol content of various brands of alcoholic beverage varies considerably (the alcohol content of beers and ales is 0.5–9.0 per cent and a pint may contain 2–5 units) and the amount of alcohol consumed in homes bears little relation to standard measures.

The Department of Health and several of the medical Royal Colleges have recommended sensible limits for alcohol intake. These are shown in Table 20.4, in addition to the energy

Table 20.2 **Macronutrient content of 100 mL of various alcoholic beverages and orange juice (for comparison) (data derived from USDA National Nutrient Database for Standard Reference, Release 19, 2006)**

Nutrient content	Light beer	Regular beer	Table wine	Rice wine (saki)	Spirits* (100% proof)	Coffee liqueur (3%)	Orange juice (raw)
Water (g)	94.88	91.96	86.58	78.4	57.50	31	88.3
Ethanol (g)	3.1	3.9	10.4	16.1	42.5	21.7	0
Protein (g)	0.24	1.81	0.07	0.5	0	0.1	0.7
Fat (g)	0	0.46	0	0	0	0.30	0.2
Carbohydrate (g)	1.64	0	2.72	5.0	0	46.8	10.4
Fibre (g)	0	0.16	0	0	0	0	0.2
Total sugars (g)	0.09	3.55	0.79	0	0	46.43	8.4
Energy (kcal)	29.0	43.0	84.0	134	295	336	45

* Spirits are distilled alcoholic beverages such as gin, rum, whisky and vodka.

provided by ingesting these amounts of ethanol. Light-to-moderate drinkers consuming 1 or 2 units per day obtain 56–112 kcal per day from ethanol alone. The value of the unit system is further reduced by variations in ethanol concentrations in each type of alcoholic beverage. For example, the dose of ethanol from a pint of beer varies significantly between brews (see Table 20.5). Similarly, the carbohydrate content varies between types of beverage, and also within each type. For example, distilled spirits whisky, cognac and vodka contain no sugar or carbohydrate; wines contain approximately 1 gram of sugar per decilitre (g/dL); regular beer contains about 3.5 g/L and light beer contains only 0.1 g/dL; and coffee liqueurs contain around 46 g/dL (US Department of Agriculture, 2006; Table 20.2). Regular beer contains approximately 40 kcal/100 mL and a 500 mL can contains approximately 200 kcal. These calories do not always have the same biological value as calories derived from other nutrients (see below for more details).

Table 20.3 **The unit system of ethanol content of alcoholic beverages (adapted from Rajendram *et al.*, 2005)**

Beverage containing ethanol		Units of ethanol
Beer	Half pint (284 mL)	1
	Pint (568mL)	2
Cider	Pint (568mL)	2
Wine	Single glass (125 mL)	1
	Bottle (750 mL)	6
Spirits	Single measure e.g. whisky, gin, vodka	1
	Bottle (750 mL) e.g. vodka	36

Table 20.4 **Energy intake from ethanol found in the recommended maximum intakes of the Department of Health (daily) and the Royal Colleges (weekly). Adapted from Royal College of Physicians, Royal College of Psychiatrists, Royal College of General Practitioners (1995) and Department of Health (1995)**

| | Maximum intakes for women | | Maximum intakes for men | |
	Weekly	Daily	Weekly	Daily
Harmful	35 units* 1984 kcal	1–2 units** 56–112 kcal	50 units 2840 kcal	***
Hazardous	15–35 units 864–1984 kcal	3 units 168 kcal	22–50 units 1248–2840 kcal	4 units 224 kcal
Low risk	0–14 units 0–792 kcal	2–3 units 112–168 kcal	0–21 units 0–1192 kcal	3–4 units 168–224 kcal

*In the UK, 1 unit of alcohol contains 8 g ethanol (1 g of ethanol has calorific content of 7.1 kcal).

**Alcohol consumption has beneficial effects which balance the harmful effects. It is therefore difficult to state that consumption of less than 4 units of alcohol is harmful to men.

*** When pregnant or about to become pregnant, consumption of even small amounts of alcohol (more than 1–2 units of alcohol once or twice per week) may be harmful to the fetus.

Utilisation of calories derived from ethanol

The estimated energy requirement of active adult men is around 2800 kcal per day (11.7 mJ per day) and that of active adult women is approximately 2400 kcal per day (10 mJ per day) (figures according to US Department of Health and Human Services and US Department of Agriculture, 2005). Light-to-moderate drinkers consuming 1–2 units per day obtain 56–112 kcal per day from ethanol alone. Regular drinkers who do not misuse alcohol are often overweight due to added calories from alcohol consumption. This 'alcohol addiction' usually leads to truncal obesity (Tremblay *et al.*, 1995). Someone drinking 35 units of alcohol per week would obtain nearly 2000 kcal/week from ethanol alone. As a result of the high-energy content of alcoholic beverages or because of associated socioeconomic factors and medical disorders, heavy drinkers often replace a substantial proportion of nutrient-derived calories with alcohol. This 'alcohol substitution' may result in primary malnutrition and weight loss (Suter, 2001).

Gruchow *et al.* (1985) found that the total energy intake of male drinkers with an average ethanol intake of 56 g per day was 16 per cent greater than that of non-drinkers. However, the body mass indices of drinkers and non-drinkers were almost identical (BMI scores of about 26). Scores for physical activity were also identical. Higher ethanol intakes result in loss of lean tissue and decline in body weights (Duane and Peters, 1988). The data implies that some of the energy in alcoholic beverages was 'lost' or 'wasted' and was not available to the body for producing or maintaining body mass. Several mechanisms have been suggested for this (Feinman and Lieber, 1998). Some energy may be used during the metabolism of ethanol by the hepatic microsomal ethanol-oxidizing system (MEOS) which is energetically inefficient, prompting generation of heat rather than adenosine triphosphate (ATP). Ethanol may damage hepatocyte mitochondria and cause loss of energy during lipid metabolism by inadequate coupling to ATP production. However, many of these theories are based on studies performed *in vitro* and whether these effects occur *in vivo* is uncertain.

We suggest that as a result of alcohol-induced inhibition of protein synthesis (see below) intracellular protein deposition and the associated cellular cytoplasmic contents are reduced. Loss of tissue protein therefore results in loss of water, minerals and electrolytes (Preedy and Peters, 1992). This hypothesis is supported by the observation that when ethanol provides 30 per cent, 40 per cent or 60 per cent of the total calories it does not enhance thermal energy losses, but increases nitrogen excretion with associated mineral losses (Reinus *et al.*, 1989). In addition, subjects on alcohol feeding regimens increase their urinary excretion of total nitrogen, uric acid and urea and lose weight, in comparison to those on isocaloric control regimens (Atwater and Benedict, 1902; Bunout *et al.*, 1987; McDonald and Margen, 1976).

Table 20.5 **The variability in alcohol content of different beers (percentage alcohol by volume, ABV) (data derived from the Oxford Bottled Beer Database, 2007)**

Beer	Brewery	ABV
O'Doul's Amber NA	Anheuser-Busch	0.5%
Clausthaler	Clausthaler	0.9%
Draught Guinness	Guinness	4.1%
Budweiser Bud Light	Anheuser-Busch	4.2%
Export	Heineken	5.0%
Foster's Lager	Carlton & United Breweries	5.0%
Stella Artois	In Bev	5.2%
Budweiser Bud Ice	Anheuser-Busch	5.5%
Foreign Extra Stout	Guinness	7.5%
Carls Porter	Carlsberg	7.8%
Grand Reserve 1997	Chimay	9%
Gold Label Barley Wine	Whitbread	10%

Interaction between ethanol and nutrition in alcohol-induced disease

'Alcohol substitution' may result in primary malnutrition (Suter, 2001). Secondary malnutrition may result from either maldigestion or malabsorption of nutrients caused by gastrointestinal complications associated with alcoholism, involving especially the pancreas and the small intestine. These effects include malabsorption of thiamine and folate as well as maldigestion and malabsorption secondary to alcohol-induced pancreatic insufficiency and intestinal lactase deficiency (Perlow *et al.*, 1977). For example, villus atrophy is a distinguishing feature of alcohol misuse (Rajendram and Preedy, 2005). Alcohol also promotes nutrient degradation or impaired activation.

Alcoholic liver disease (ALD) was previously thought to be entirely nutritional in aetiology. This concept was based largely on studies in which rats were given ethanol in drinking water (Best *et al.*, 1949). It was found that ALD did not develop unless the diet was deficient in proteins, methionine or choline, and deficiency alone could induce ALD. However, rats dislike alcohol so when administered in drinking water, ethanol consumption usually does not exceed more than 10–25 per cent of the total energy intake of the animal. The resulting blood ethanol concentrations were low (Lieber *et al.*, 1965) so administering alcohol to rodents in drinking water is not a suitable model for human disease.

The aversion to alcohol is overcome when ethanol is incorporated into a totally liquid diet (Lieber *et al.*, 1963, 1965). In order to eat or drink, the animals have no choice but to consume alcohol with the diet. With this technique, the quantity of ethanol consumed increased to 36 per cent of the total energy, an amount relevant to alcohol intake in humans. These studies demonstrated that despite nutritionally adequate diets, isoenergetic replacement of carbohydrates by ethanol consistently induced a five-fold to ten-fold increase in hepatic triglycerides (Lieber *et al.*, 1963, 1965). Isoenergetic replacement of carbohydrate by fat instead of ethanol did not induce steatosis (Lieber *et al.*, 1965). Using this liquid diet technique, alcohol was also shown to be capable of producing cirrhosis in non-human primates, even when the diet was adequate (Lieber and DeCarli, 1974). In addition, the hepatotoxicity of ethanol was established by controlled clinical studies which showed that, even in the absence of dietary deficiencies, alcohol can produce fatty liver and ultrastructural lesions in humans (Lieber *et al.*, 1963, 1965).

Some dietary deficiencies exacerbate the effects of alcohol – in rats a combination of ethanol and a diet deficient in both protein and lipotropic factors induces more hepatic steatosis than either factor alone (Lieber *et al.*, 1969). Protein deficiency reduces secretion of lipoprotein. This exacerbates the lipid accumulation that results from the hepatic metabolism of ethanol. However, the effect of protein deficiency in human adults remains unclear. In children, protein deficiency leads to hepatic steatosis – a manifestation of kwashiorkor – but this does not progress to cirrhosis. In adolescent baboons, protein restriction to 7 per cent of total energy did not significantly affect the liver (even after 19 months). Significant steatosis was observed only when the protein intake was reduced to 4 per cent of total energy (Lieber *et al.*, 1972). However, an excess of protein (25 per cent of total energy, or 2.5 times the recommended amount) did not prevent alcohol-induced accumulation of fat in humans (Lieber and Rubin, 1968).

The nutritional state of alcohol misusers

Many alcoholic people are malnourished. Most of these do not consume a balanced diet and alcohol misuse may interfere with the absorption, utilisation and degradation of ingested nutrients. Alcoholics admitted to hospital with medical complications of alcohol misuse (e.g. severe intoxication or withdrawal) are often severely malnourished. Those who carry on drinking usually continue to lose weight, while abstinence may induce weight gain (World *et al.*, 1984a,b). Their dietary protein intake is usually inadequate (Patek *et al.*, 1975) so they often have signs of protein malnutrition (Iber, 1971; Mendenhall *et al.*, 1985). Anthropomorphic measurements in alcoholic people are often indicative of impaired nutrition; their height-to-weight ratio is low (Morgan, 1981), their muscle mass as estimated by the creatinine–height index is reduced (Mendenhall *et al.*, 1985; Morgan, 1981) and their triceps skinfolds are thin (Mendenhall *et al.*, 1985; Morgan, 1981). However it is important to note that these measurements can be confounded by alcoholic myopathy or chronic alcohol-induced muscle disease (AIMD), which can occur in the absence of malnutrition (Preedy *et al.*, 2003) and can markedly reduce mid-arm circumference (Martin *et al.*, 1985), body mass index and urinary creatinine excretion (Preedy and Emery, 2002).

Most alcohol misusers are less malnourished than those requiring admission to hospital. Some alcoholic people are not malnourished at all. Those with moderate alcohol intake and even those admitted to the hospital for alcohol rehabilitation rather than for medical complications often differ little nutritionally from controls matched for socioeconomic status and health history (Lieber, 2000). Differences in nutritional status between alcohol misusers must reflect, at least partly, total calorific intake, the proportion of total calories obtained from ethanol, differences in dietary intake in general and socioeconomic status. Approximately 50 per cent of all alcohol misusers are deficient in one or more nutrients.

One study found that women drinking one or more one drink per day weighed on average 2.3 kg less than non-drinkers. Their weight, and that of their male counterparts, was more stable over 10 years than that of non-drinkers, whose weight rose (Liu et al., 1994). However, other studies found that alcohol intake, especially when accompanied by high fat intake and sedentary behaviour (Armellini et al., 1993) is associated with truncal obesity, particularly in women (Tremblay et al., 1995).

Moderate alcohol ingestion (16 per cent of total calories as ethanol; approximately 320 kcal in a 2000 kcal diet) is associated with slightly increased total energy intake (Gruchow et al., 1985). Although ethanol has a high calorific energy content, chronic consumption does not result in the expected gain in body weight (Lieber, 1991a). This energy deficit may be partly due to mitochondrial damage and the resulting poor coupling of lipid oxidation with energy production, as well as to microsomal pathways which oxidise ethanol without conserving energy. This 'wasting' of energy may explain why this group with higher total caloric intake do not gain weight despite lower levels of physical activity than teetotallers. When ethanol represents between 16 per cent and 23 per cent of dietary energy intake substitution of ethanol for carbohydrate may occur (Hillers and Massey, 1985). When over 30 per cent of total calories are derived from alcohol, protein and fat intake are significantly reduced. Intake of vitamins A and C and thiamine may fall below recommended dietary allowances (Gruchow et al., 1985). Calcium, iron and fibre intake are also reduced (Hillers and Massey, 1985). The impact of the subtle nutritional alterations produced by ethanol on the pathogenesis of alcohol-induced disease is uncertain.

The mechanisms underlying the dietary changes are unclear. Socioeconomic factors may be important but intake is at least partly impaired by depressed consciousness and reduced appetite during intoxication, hangover and the effects of ethanol on the gastrointestinal tract.

Alcohol and the gastrointestinal tract

The effects of ethanol on the gastrointestinal tract have been reviewed recently (Rajendram and Preedy, 2005) but are summarised here.

Effects of ethanol on digestion and absorption

The major functions of the small intestine – digestion, absorption and secretion – are performed by the brush border membrane (BBM) and depend on the structural integrity of the intestine *in vivo*. Peristalsis gradually propels chyme through the intestine. It requires coordinated smooth muscle function. The physiological regulation of the gastrointestinal tract is complex, involving neural and hormonal impulses as well as factors secreted by the local immune system. The microcirculation supplies essential nutrients. Ethanol-induced gastrointestinal injury results from the interaction of several toxic effects on each of these functional elements (Beck, 1996; Bode and Bode, 2003; Rajendram and Preedy, 2006; Thompson *et al.*, 1996).

Effects of ethanol on small intestinal morphology

Acute administration of alcohol causes haemorrhagic erosions of the epithelium at the tips of villi, villus core contraction and compaction, compression of lacteals, separation of the epithelium from the basal lamina of the villus core, and formation of sub-epithelial blisters which ultimately cause rupture of the epithelium (Bode and Bode, 2003; Thompson *et al.*, 1996). The extent of these morphological changes depends on the concentration, duration of ethanol exposure, species-dependent sensitivity of the mucosa to injury in animal studies, and the nutritional status of the subject (Beck, 1996; Bode and Bode, 2003; Ergerer *et al.*, 2005).

Importantly, recovery is rapid, even during continuous exposure to ethanol. Recovery probably represents re-attachment of healthy epithelial cells to the normal basal lamina (Beck, 1996). Regeneration could occur by rapid migration of viable epithelial cells originating from cells adjacent to the exfoliated ones. A similar mechanism of regeneration has been reported in the small intestine during mucosal injury from other agents (Beck, 1996). However, chronic ethanol exposure does not necessarily produce the florid haemorrhagic changes seen with acute ingestion.

The toxic effects of ethanol on small intestinal morphology can impair the function of the gastrointestinal tract and thereby reduce the absorption of nutrients (Rajendram and Preedy, 2005). The contractile elements of the seromuscular layer are also affected by ethanol, which can also impair gut motility (Rajendram *et al.*, 2003; Rajendram and Preedy, 2006).

Ethanol and intestinal absorption

Absorption of nutrients from the lumen of the gastrointestinal tract occurs in three stages:
*   Stage 1: Transport across the BBM.
*   Stage 2: Passage across the enterocyte.
*   Stage 3: Transport out of the enterocyte across the basolateral membrane.

Each stage of nutrient absorption may be active or passive (diffusion) and different mechanisms are involved for each nutrient. Ethanol reduces the effective surface area available for absorption and inhibits each of these processes. However, there is considerable functional reserve within the small intestine. Therefore a partial inhibition of nutrient absorption in the proximal small intestine may be compensated by greater uptake in the distal small intestine.

Effects of ethanol on the absorption of macronutrients

The absorption of carbohydrates, proteins and lipids has been studied in alcoholic people without confounding disorders such as ALD or pancreatic insufficiency (Pfeiffer *et al.*, 1992). Duodenal absorption was lower in alcoholic people than age-matched controls. However, there was no difference in jejunal absorption. This may reflect the greater alcohol-induced injury in the duodenum (Pfeiffer *et al.*, 1992). Measurement of the absorption of the monosaccharide β-xylose is used clinically to detect malabsorption. Xylose malabsorption occurs in alcoholic people without ALD (Thompson *et al.*, 1996). Although chronic ethanol misuse does not seem to affect absorption of glucose (Beck and Dinda, 1981), acute alcohol inhibits the transport of glucose *in vivo* (Seitz and Homann, 2001). Ethanol concentrations over 2 per cent ABV also inhibit absorption of amino acids, lipids, vitamins and trace elements (Seitz and Suter, 2002). However this inhibition does not appear to be sustained by chronic ethanol administration which did not affect the absorption of L-leucine in rats fed a nutritious diet (Martines *et al.*, 1989).

Effects of ethanol on the absorption of micronutrients

Ethanol inhibits the active transport of low concentrations of folate; however, there is no effect on passive absorption at higher concentrations. The folate deficiency associated with alcohol misuse is primarily due to malnutrition (Halsted and Keen, 1990; Seitz and Suter, 2002). For example, in a UK study all alcoholic people assessed had folate intakes below the recommended nutritional intake (Manari *et al.*, 2003).

Chronic alcohol consumption reduces absorption of vitamin B12. This is probably due to malabsorption in the terminal ileum (Lindenbaum, 1980). However, few alcoholic people have clinical evidence of B12 deficiency (Lindenbaum, 1980; Halsted and Keen, 1990). This may reflect the large body stores of the vitamin. Acute alcohol ingestion reduces thiamine absorption in healthy volunteers and in alcoholic people (Seitz and Suter, 2002). Alcohol inhibits the sodium-dependent active transport of thiamine to the intestinal mucosa. However, at higher concentrations of thiamine, absorption is due to passive diffusion and is not affected by ethanol. Absorption of thiamine recovers within weeks of abstinence (Seitz and Suter, 2002).

Alcohol does not directly affect the absorption of vitamins A, D, E and K. However, cholestasis due to alcoholic hepatitis and cirrhosis, pancreatitis and maldigestion can induce deficiencies of these fat-soluble vitamins (Bode and Bode, 2003; Thompson *et al.*, 1996). Calcium absorption is reduced if hepatic activation of vitamin D is impaired by ALD. Furthermore, deficiency may result from reduced dietary intake in alcohol misusers (Manari *et al.*, 2003).

Iron stores are often increased in alcoholic people (Duane *et al.*, 1992). However, the effects of alcohol on iron absorption remain unclear. An increase in the non-carrier-mediated paracellular absorption of iron may contribute to the iron overload in alcoholic people (Duane *et al.*, 1992). This is particularly relevant for alcoholic beverages rich in iron such as Guinness.

Following absorption, some nutrients are metabolised within the gastrointestinal tract. Ethanol affects this in several ways.

Effects of ethanol on intestinal metabolism

Alcohol affects the metabolism of carbohydrates and lipids in the small intestinal mucosa. Chronic alcohol intake damages the tips of the villi where disaccharidases such as lactase and sucrase are located. The reduction of the activities of these enzymes may exacerbate lactose intolerance (Bode and Bode, 2003; Ergerer *et al.*, 2005). However, as villi regenerate rapidly, the activities of lactase and sucrase are normal within weeks of abstinence. Intestinal triglyceride and cholesterol synthesis are enhanced by acute and chronic alcohol administration (Ergerer *et al.*, 2005). The activities of enzymes responsible for fatty acid esterification are also increased. Alcohol increases the secretion of triglycerides, cholesterol and phospholipids and transport proteins into lymph as well as lymphatic flow (Ergerer *et al.*, 2005). These effects of ethanol may contribute to the development of hepatic steatosis (Ergerer *et al.*, 2005).

Alcohol misuse also affects the metabolism of nutrients by other organs. Therefore, even if alcoholics ingest sufficient proteins, fats, vitamins and minerals, deficiencies may still occur if those nutrients absorbed from the gastrointestinal tract are not broken down, activated or utilised appropriately. Serum levels of vitamin A, for example, are maintained by mobilisation of hepatic stores. Therefore ALD is associated with reduction in hepatic vitamin A, even when injury is only moderate (Leo and Lieber, 1982).

Effect of alcohol on nutrient activation

Pyridoxine
Pyridoxal-5-phosphate (PLP) is the activated form of vitamin B6. Low PLP was reported in over 50 per cent of alcoholics without haematological findings or abnormal liver function tests (Fonda *et al.*, 1989; Lumeng, 1978). This may represent inadequate intake of B6, but increased destruction and reduced formation may also contribute. Chronic ethanol feeding reduced hepatic content of PLP by decreasing net synthesis from pyridoxine (Lumeng *et al.*, 1984, Parker *et al.*, 1979). In the presence of acetaldehyde PLP is more rapidly destroyed in erythrocytes. Acetaldehyde may displace protein-bound PLP, increasing the exposure of PLP to hydrolysis by intracellular phosphatases (Lumeng, 1978; Lumeng and Li, 1974).

Methionine and SAMe
Methionine deficiency has been described in alcohol misusers. However, in some patients with ALD circulating methionine levels are normal (Iob *et al.*, 1967), while in others levels are high (Fischer *et al.*, 1974; Montanari *et al.*, 1988). Moreover, clearance of plasma methionine is delayed after systemic administration to patients with liver damage (Kinsell *et al.*, 1947). Similarly, after oral loading the blood clearance of methionine is slowed (Horowitz *et al.*, 1981). Because about half the methionine is metabolised by the liver, these observations suggest impaired hepatic metabolism of methionine in patients with ALD. Methionine must be activated to *S*-adenosylmethionine (SAMe) by methionine adenosyltransferase (SAMe synthetase) to perform most of its functions as a methyl donor. The activity of SAMe synthetase, the enzyme which activates methionine, is reduced in liver cirrhosis (Duce *et al.*, 1988). Various mechanisms of inactivation of SAMe synthetase have been reviewed elsewhere (Lu, 1998). Long-term alcohol intake has been associated with enhanced methionine utilisation and depletion (Finkelstein *et al.*, 1974). As a consequence, depletion and reduced availability of SAMe could be expected. Indeed, long-term ethanol consumption by non-human primates is associated with a significant depletion of hepatic SAMe (Lieber *et al.*, 1990).

SAMe is used in transmethylation reactions required for nucleic acid and protein synthesis. Methylation is also important for cell membrane functions including membrane fluidity, transport of metabolites and signal transmission across membranes (Hirata *et al.*, 1978, Hirata and Axelrod, 1980). Therefore, depletion of SAMe may promote the membrane injury that has been documented in ALD (Yamada *et al.*, 1985). SAMe is also required for the synthesis of polyamines and is a source of cysteine for glutathione. Therefore, SAMe deficiency induces several adverse effects, including inadequate cysteine and glutathione production. The effects of SAMe deficiency are exacerbated by associated folate, vitamin B6 or B12 deficiencies. The consequences of SAMe deficiency can be prevented by oral administration of SAMe. Blood levels of SAMe increased after oral administration in humans (Bornbardieri *et al.*, 1983). It has been claimed that the liver does not take up SAMe from the bloodstream (Hoffinan *et al.*, 1980), but results in baboons (Lieber *et al.*, 1990) clearly show hepatic uptake of exogenous SAMe.

Ethanol and metabolism of macronutrients

Effects on lipids and carbohydrate metabolism

In alcohol misusers metabolism of lipids and carbohydrates is impaired by an excess of reducing equivalents (e.g. NADH – reduced nicotinamide adenine dinucleotide). The oxidation of triglycerides is affected, 'trapping' fat in hepatocytes and increasing peripheral triglyceride levels (Muller *et al.*, 1992). Insulin resistance is common in alcoholics with liver cirrhosis. This impairs glucose uptake into muscle cells, reducing glycogen production and thereby energy stores. In 15–37 per cent of all alcoholics with cirrhosis, insulin-dependent diabetes develops as an indicator of poor prognosis (Bianchi *et al.*, 1994; Selberg *et al.*, 1993). However, paradoxically, moderate alcohol intake is associated with a reduced incidence of type 2 diabetes mellitus (Carlsson *et al.*, 2003).

Effects on protein metabolism

The effects of ethanol on protein metabolism are particularly important as the prognosis of alcohol misusers with inadequate dietary protein intake is poor (Kondrup and Muller, 1997). In the steady state, the rate of tissue protein synthesis equals the rate of protein degradation. For a fall in protein content to occur, the rate of breakdown must exceed the rate of synthesis (Preedy *et al.*, 1999). As investigation of protein breakdown is difficult *in vivo,* most studies have focused on protein synthesis. Protein synthesis is often measured as a fractional rate. The fractional rate of protein synthesis (k_s) is defined as the percentage of the pool of tissue protein renewed each day (per cent per day). The majority of the clinical studies on protein metabolism have been performed on subjects with ALD, particularly cirrhosis. Although cirrhosis which occurs in 15–20 per cent of alcohol misusers is less common than AIMD (40–60 per cent), patients present with cirrhosis far more often than with AIMD. The diets of alcoholic people are often deficient in one or more nutrients. However, in animal studies, pair-feeding can be controlled so that differences in nutritional intake can be excluded (Preedy *et al.*, 1999). Such animal studies have provided important data on the effects of ethanol on protein metabolism.

Effects on skeletal muscle protein metabolism

AIMD is characterised by proximal weakness, falls and difficulties in gait. Affected people lose up to 30 per cent of their muscle mass. Approximately half to two-thirds of all chronic alcoholics are affected. The rate of skeletal muscle protein synthesis in chronic alcoholics (more than 100 g per day; more than 10 years) is approximately 40 per cent lower than controls (Pacy *et al.*, 1991). Skeletal muscle weights and protein contents are reduced in ethanol treated rats (Preedy *et al.*, 1994a,b). Acute ethanol administration (75 mmol/kg body weight) profoundly reduces k_s in the type II muscle fibre-predominant plantaris (Preedy and Peters, 1988). In the type I fibre-predominant soleus, k_s falls by 22 per cent. The principal fractions of skeletal muscle – the cytoplasmic, myofibrillar, and stromal fraction – are affected equally in the gastrocnemius in response to acute ethanol, that is falls in k_s of approximately 30 per cent are observed (Preedy and Peters, 1988).

Effects on hepatic protein metabolism

Plasma albumin concentration is often reduced in severe liver disease, probably as a result of reduced synthesis or secretion into the circulation (Lieber, 1991b, 1996). Cirrhosis, characterised by hepatic collagen accumulation, develops in 15–20 per cent of all chronic alcoholics. Cirrhosis has been associated with increased protein breakdown, but some studies suggest that it is unaltered (McCullough *et al.*, 1991, 1993). These differences may be entirely due to technical differences between the studies, such as continued drinking during prescribed abstinence. Data derived from animal models of the effects of ethanol on liver protein synthesis appear contradictory, perhaps because of methodological differences. Although administration of ethanol for up to 2 weeks has no effect on hepatic protein synthesis, feeding ethanol for more than 2 weeks reduces liver protein synthesis (Donohue *et al.*, 1989; Smith-Kielland *et al.*, 1983).

Ethanol and protein metabolism in the gastrointestinal tract

Both acute and chronic ethanol administration inhibit protein synthesis in the small intestine (Marway *et al.*, 1996; Rajendram *et al.*, 2003; Rajendram and Preedy, 2005). However, protein synthesis in the colon is relatively unaffected (Marway *et al.*, 1996; Rajendram and Preedy, 2005). Therefore ethanol selectively affects different parts of the gastrointestinal tract. The mechanism of the ethanol-induced effects on protein synthesis remains unclear. Attention has focused on the role of free radicals and oxidative stress (Marway *et al.*, 1996; Rajendram and Preedy, 2006), for example the role of nitric oxide (NO) has been investigated. Administration of NO synthase inhibitors reduced k_s in the jejunum and skeletal muscle in control animals and also increased the sensitivity of jejunal protein synthesis to acute ethanol *in vivo* (Rajendram *et al.*, 2003; see Fig. 20.2). This suggests that overproduction of NO is not involved in the effects of ethanol on protein synthesis in the jejunum or skeletal muscle (Rajendram *et al.*, 2003). More research is required into the mechanisms underlying the effects of ethanol on protein synthesis.

Nutritional therapy in alcoholism

The uptake and metabolism of a wide array of nutrients, including vitamins and trace elements, are affected by alcohol misuse. The resulting deficiencies may induce disease or exacerbate alcohol-induced pathologies. In some cases nutritional supplementation can prevent the development of significant morbidity and mortality.

People consuming over 30 per cent of total calories as alcohol usually ingest less than the recommended daily amounts of carbohydrate, protein, fat, vitamins A, B (especially thiamine) and C, and minerals such as calcium and iron (see above). Although it is sensible to recommend

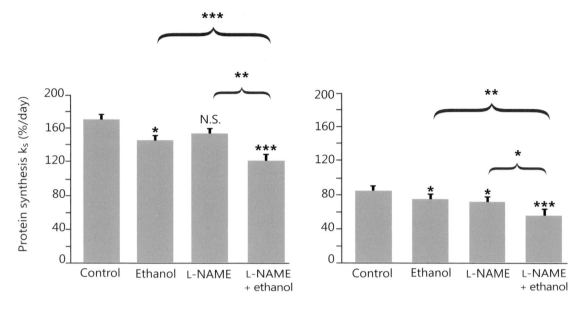

Figure 20.2   Effect of ethanol and a nitric oxide synthase inhibitor (L-NAME; L-omega-nitro-L-arginine methyl ester) on jejunal mucosal (left) and seromuscular (right) protein synthesis *in vivo*. Male Wistar rats were injected intra-peritoneally with saline (0.15 mol/L) as a control, or ethanol alone (75 mmol/kg body weight), L-NAME alone (25 mg/kg), or L-NAME plus ethanol (25 mg/kg plus 75 mol/kg body weight). Rats were killed 3 hours later. All data are mean +/– SEM of five to ten observations. Differences between means were assessed using pooled analysis of variance (NS, $p > 0.05$, *$p > 0.05$, **$p > 0.01$, ***$p > 0.001$). Adapted from Rajendram *et al.*, 2003.

a balanced diet comparable to that of non-alcoholics to prevent deficiency syndromes, this approach does not prevent the direct toxicity of ethanol. Several aspects of alcohol-induced disease improve or resolve with abstinence. Therefore the most beneficial nutritional intervention is inducing and maintaining abstinence in alcohol misusers. Complications from thiamine deficiency are uncommon but are serious and easily treatable. Therefore, thiamine deficiency should be presumed and intravenous thiamine should be given prophylactically to all patients treated for alcohol withdrawal until it can be taken orally.

Alcohol-induced Wernicke–Korsakoff syndrome (WKS) results from thiamine deficiency. This nutritional emergency demands immediate parenteral supplementation of high-dose thiamine. However, there is insufficient evidence from randomised controlled clinical trials to guide clinicians in the dose, frequency, route or duration of thiamine treatment for prophylaxis against or treatment of Wernicke–Korsakoff syndrome due to alcohol abuse (Day *et al.*, 2004). Thiamine should ideally be administered to alcoholic or chronically malnourished patients before intravenous dextrose solutions to avoid precipitation of the syndrome. However in hypoglycaemic patients glucose administration should not be withheld while awaiting thiamine (Marinella, 1998). Riboflavin and pyridoxine should be routinely administered at the dosages usually contained in standard multivitamin preparations (Lieber, 2000). Care should be taken when supplementing pyridoxine because excess pyridoxine can cause a neuropathy characterised by ataxia and burning pain in the feet, beginning approximately 1 month to 3 years following supplementation. Although this usually occurs at very high supplementation doses, complications have been reported with doses as low as 50 mg per day. Adequate folic acid replacement can be accomplished with the usual hospital diet (Lieber, 2000). Additional replacement is optional unless deficiency is severe. Retinol replacement should only be given to patients whose abstinence from alcohol is assured and deficiency has been documented (Lieber, 2000). Zinc replacement is indicated if night blindness is unresponsive to retinol replacement. Magnesium replacement is recommended for symptomatic patients with low serum magnesium (Lieber, 2000). Although uncommon, confirmed iron deficiency in alcohol misusers can be corrected easily with oral supplementation. Treatment of acute pancreatitis may require oral feeding to be witheld for prolonged periods. During this time total parenteral nutrition must be given (Lieber, 2000). Chronic pancreatic exocrine insufficiency is treated by dietary manipulation (including decreases in fat), with oral pancreatic enzymes at mealtime. The nutritional management of acute and chronic ALD should aim to reverse malnutrition and replenish protein without inducing hepatic encephalopathy (Lieber, 2000). It is important to note that ethanol-induced disease affects nutritional requirements, i.e. nutritional requirements are increased.

Supplementation of the essential amino acid methionine has been considered in the treatment of ALD, but excess methionine has significant side effects (Finkelstein and Martin, 1986). Activation of methionine to SAMe is impaired in ALD. Oral administration of SAMe (1.2 g per day) for 6 months significantly increased hepatic glutathione in patients with ALD and non-alcoholic liver disease (Vendemiale *et al.*, 1989). Impressive results were achieved in a recent long-term, multicentre, randomised, double-blind, placebo-controlled, clinical trial involving patients with alcoholic cirrhosis. SAMe significantly improved survival or delayed liver transplantation (Mato *et al.*, 1999). Therefore, SAMe should be replaced in the presence of significant ALD. Similarly, because of impaired activity of phosphatidylethanolamine methyltransferase, supplementation with phosphatidylcholine, possibly as dilinoleoylphosphatidylcholine (DLPC), may be useful (Lieber, 2000).

Future developments

Investigation of the relation between ethanol and nutrition has traditionally been hypothesis-driven. Importantly, it has been elucidated that some processes are unaffected by acute or chronic alcohol exposure. While hypothesis-driven research is very important, the application of holistic – or 'omic' – technologies could rapidly highlight significant pathways, processes or products (Rajendram and Preedy, 2005). In particular, genomics, proteomics and metabolomics could identify thousands of molecular and cellular targets involved in the interaction between ethanol, the nutritional status of alcohol misusers and alcohol-induced disease. For example in a recent study we found that a single bolus of ethanol affects the expression of over 500 genes (M. Avro; unpublished data).

Conclusions

The relationship between alcohol intake, nutritional status and alcohol-induced disease is complex. The calorific value of alcohol is high and can induce primary malnutrition in alcoholic people by displacement of other nutrients from the diet. Secondary malnutrition may result from the toxic effects of ethanol on the gastrointestinal tract. The ethanol-induced reduction of dietary intake, maldigestion and malabsorption often results in deficiency of one or more nutrients in alcohol misusers. However, the effects of ethanol on nutrient metabolism affect even those alcoholics who are not malnourished, resulting for example in impaired protein synthesis. Therefore while it is sensible to encourage alcohol misusers to intake balanced diets to prevent deficiency syndromes, the most important nutritional intervention is encouraging and maintaining abstinence.

References and further reading

Armellini, F., Zamboni, M., Frigo, L., *et al.* (1993). Alcohol consumption, smoking habits and body fat distribution in Italian men and women aged 20–60 years. *European Journal of Clinical Nutrition*, **47**, 52–60.

Atwater, W.D. and Benedict, F.G. (1902). An experimental inquiry regarding the nutritive value of alcohol. *Memoirs National Academy of Sciences*, **8**, 235.

Beck, I.T. and Dinda, P.K. (1981). Acute exposure of small intestine to ethanol: effects on morphology and function. *Digestive Diseases and Sciences*, **26**, 817–38.

Beck, T. (1996). Small bowel injury by ethanol. In: V.R. Preedy and R.R. Watson (eds). *Alcohol and the Gastrointestinal Tract*. Boca Raton: CRC Press, pp. 163–202.

Best, C.H., Hartroft, W.S., Lucas, C.C. and Ridout, J.H. (1949). Liver damage produced by feeding alcohol or sugar and its prevention by choline. *British Medical Journal*, **2**, 1001–06.

Bianchi, G., Marchesini, G., Zoli, M., *et al.* (1994). Prognostic significance of diabetes in patients with cirrhosis. *Hepatology*, **20**, 119–25.

Bode, C. and Bode, J.C. (2003). Effect of alcohol consumption on the gut. Best practice and research. *Clinical Gastroenterology*, **17**, 575–92.

Bornbardieri, G., Pappalardo, G., Bernardi, L., Barra, D., Di Palma, A. and Castrini, G. (1983). Intestinal absorption of S-adenosyl-L-methionine in humans. *International Journal of Clinical Pharmacology, Therapy and Toxicology*, **21**, 186–88.

Bovet, P., Larue, D., Fayol, V., *et al.* (1998). Blood thiamine status and determinants in the population of Seychelles (Indian Ocean). *Journal of Epidemiology and Community Health*, **52**, 148–57.

Bunout, D., Petermann, M., Ugarte, G., Barrera, G. and Iturriaga, H. (1987). Nitrogen economy in alcoholic patients without liver disease. *Metabolism: Clinical and Experimental*, **36**, 651–53.

Caballeria, J., Frezza, M., Hernadez-Munoz, R., *et al.* (1989). Gastric origin of the first pass metabolism of ethanol in humans: effect of gastrectomy. *Gastroenterology*, **97**, 1205–09.

Carlsson, S., Hammar, N., Grill, V. and Kaprio, J. (2003). Alcohol consumption and the incidence of type, 2 diabetes: a 20-year follow-up of the Finnish twin cohort study. *Diabetes Care*, **10**, 2785–90.

Chung, J., Liu, C., Smith, D.E., *et al.* (2001). Restoration of retinoic acid concentration suppresses ethanol-enhanced *c-Jun* expression and hepatocyte proliferation in rat liver. *Carcinogenesis*, **22**, 1213–19.

Day, E., Bentham, P., Callaghan, R., Kuruvilla, T. and George, S. (2004). Thiamine for Wernicke–Korsakoff syndrome in people at risk from alcohol abuse. Cochrane Database of Systematic Reviews, CD004033.

Department of Health (1995). *Sensible Drinking*. London: Department of Health.

Donohue, T.M. Jr, Zetterman, R.K. and Tuma, D.J. (1989). Effect of chronic ethanol administration on protein catabolism in rat liver. *Alcoholism: Clinical and Experimental Research*, **13**, 49–57.

Duane, P. and Peters, T.J. (1988). Nutritional status in alcoholics with or without skeletal muscle myopathy. *Alcohol and Alcoholism*, **23**, 271–77.

Duane, P., Raja, K.B., Simpson, R.J. and Peters, T.J. (1992). Intestinal iron absorption in chronic alcoholics. *Alcohol and Alcoholism*, **27**, 539–544.

Duce, A.M., Ortiz, P., Cabrero, C. and Mato, J.M. (1988). *S*-adenosyl-L-methionine synthetase and phospholipid methyltransferase are inhibited in human cirrhosis. *Hepatology*, **8**, 65–68.

Ergerer, G., Stikel, F. and Seitz, H.K. (2005). Alcohol and the gastrointestinal tract. In: V.R. Preedy and R.R. Watson (eds). *Reviews in Food and Nutrition Toxicity*, Vol., 2. London: Taylor and Francis, pp. 559–72.

Feinman, L. and Lieber, C.S. (1998). Nutrition and diet in alcoholism. In: M.E. Shils, J.A. Olson, M. Shike and A.C. Ross (eds), *Modern Nutrition in Health and Disease*, 9th edn. Baltimore: Williams and Wilkins, pp. 1523–42.

Fernandez, O., Carreras, O. and Murillo, M.L. (1998). Intestinal absorbtion and enterohepatic circulation of folic acid: effect of ethanol. *Digestion*, **59**, 130–33.

Finkelstein, J.D. and Martin, J.J. (1986). Methionine metabolism in mammals. Adaptation to methionine excess. *Journal of Biological Chemistry*, **261**, 1582–87.

Finkelstein, J.D., Cello, F.P. and Kyle, W.E. (1974). Ethanol-induced changes in methionine metabolism in rat liver. *Biochemical and Biophysical Research Communications*, **61**, 475–81.

Fischer, J.E., Yoshimura, N., Aguirre, A., *et al.* (1974). Plasma amino acids in patients with hepatic encephalopathy. *American Journal of Surgery*, **127**, 40–47.

Fonda, M.L., Brown, S.G. and Pendleton, M.W. (1989). Concentration of vitamin B6 and activities of enzymes of B6 metabolism in the blood of alcoholic and nonalcoholic men. *Alcoholism: Clinical and Experimental Research*, **3**, 804–09.

Giulidori, P. and Stramentinoli, G. (1984). A radioenzymatic method for *S*-adenosyl-L-methionine determination in biological fluids. *Analytical Biochemistry*, **137**, 217–20.

Gloria, L., Cravo, M., Camilo, M.E., *et al.* (1997). Nutritional deficiencies in chronic alcoholics: relation to dietary intake and alcohol consumption. *American Journal of Gastroenterology*, **92**, 485–89.

Gruchow, H.W., Sobociaski, K.A. and Barboriak, J.J. (1985). Alcohol, nutrient intake, and hypertension in US adults. *Journal of the American Medical Association*, **253**, 1567–70.

Gruchow, H.W., Sobocinski, K.A., Barboriak, J.J. and Scheller, J.G. (1985). Alcohol consumption, nutrient intake and relative body weight among US adults. *American Journal of Clinical Nutrition*, **42**, 289–95.

Halsted, C.H. and Keen, C.L. (1990). Alcoholism and micronutrient metabolism and deficiencies. *European Journal of Gastroenterology and Hepatology*, **6**, 399–405.

Hidiroglu, N., Camilo, M.E., Beckenhauer, H.C., *et al.* (1994). Effect of chronic alcohol ingestion on hepatic folate distribution in the rat. *Biochemical Pharmacology*, **47**, 1561–66.

Hillers, V.N. and Massey, L.K. (1985). Interrelationships of moderate and high alcohol consumption with diet and health status. *American Journal of Clinical Nutrition* **41**, 356–62.

Hirata, F. and Axelrod, J. (1980). Phospholipid methylation and biological signal transmission. *Science*, **209**, 1082–90.

Hirata, F., Viveros, O.H., Diliberto, E.J. Jr and Axelrod, J. (1978). Identification and properties of two methyltransferases in conversion of phosphatidylethanolamine to phosphatidylcholine. *Proceedings of the National Academy of Sciences of the United States of America*, **75**, 1718–21.

Hoffinan, D.R., Marion, D.W., Cornatzer, W.E. and Duerra, J.A. (1980). *S*-adenosylmethionine and *S*-adenosyl homocysteine metabolism in isolated rat liver. *Journal of Biological Chemistry*, **255**, 10822–27.

Horowitz, J.H., Rypins, E.B., Henderson, J.M., *et al.* (1981). Evidence for impairment of trans-sulfuration pathway in cirrhosis. *Gastroenterology*, **81**, 668–75.

Iber, F.L. (1971). In alcoholism, the liver sets the pace. *Nutrition Today*, **6**, 2–9.

Iob, V., Coon, W.W. and Sloan, W. (1967). Free amino acids in liver, plasma and muscle of patients with cirrhosis of the liver. *Journal of Surgical Research*, **7**, 41–43.

Kinsell, L., Harper, H.A., Barton, H.C., Michaels, G.D. and Weiss, H.A. (1947). Rate of disappearance from plasma of intravenously administered methionine in patients with liver damage. *Science*, **106**, 589–94.

Kondrup, J. and Muller, M.J. (1997). Energy and protein requirements of patients with chronic liver disease. *Journal of Hepatology*, **27**, 239–47.

Leo, M.A. and Lieber, C.S. (1982). Hepatic vitamin A depletion in alcoholic liver injury. *New England Journal of Medicine*, **307**, 597–601.

Leo, M.A. and Lieber, C.S. (1999). Alcohol, vitamin A and beta-carotene: adverse interactions including hepatotoxicity and carcinogenesis. *American Journal of Clinical Nutrition*, **69**, 1071–85.

Lieber, C.S. (1991a). Perspectives: Do alcohol calories count? *American Journal of Clinical Nutrition*, **54**, 976–82.

Lieber, C.S. (1991b). Hepatic, metabolic and toxic effects of ethanol: 1991 update. *Alcoholism: Clinical and Experimental Research*, **15**, 573–92.

Lieber, C.S. (1992). *Medical and Nutritional Complications of Alcoholism: Mechanisms and Management*. New York: Plenum.

Lieber, C.S. (1996). The metabolism of alcohol and its implication to the pathogenesis of disease. In: V.R. Preedy and R.R. Watson (eds). *Alcohol and the Gastrointestinal Tract*. Boca Raton: CRC Press, pp. 19–39.

Lieber, C.S. (2000). Alcohol: its metabolism and interaction with nutrients. *Annual Review of Nutrition*, **20**, 395–430.

Lieber, C.S. and DeCarli, L.M. (1974). An experimental model of alcohol feeding and liver injury in the baboon. *Journal of Medical Primatology*, **3**, 153–63.

Lieber, C.S. and Rubin, E. (1968). Alcoholic fatty liver in men on a high-protein and low-fat diet. *American Journal of Medicine*, **44**, 200–06.

Lieber, C.S., Casini, A., DeCarli, L.M., *et al.* (1990). *S*-adenosyl-L-methionine attenuates alcohol-induced liver injury in the baboon. *Hepatology,* **11**, 165–72.

Lieber, C.S., DeCarli. L.M., Gang, H., Walker, G. and Rubin, E. (1972). Hepatic effects of long term ethanol consumption in primates. In: E.I. Goldsmith and J. Moor-Jankowski (eds). *Medical Primatology*, 3rd edn. Basel: Karger, pp. 270–78.

Lieber, C.S., Jones, D.P. and DeCarli, L.M. (1965). Effects of prolonged ethanol intake: production of fatty liver despite adequate diets. *Journal of Clinical Investigation*, **44**, 1009–21.

Lieber, C.S., Jones, D.P., Mendelson, J. and DeCarli, L.M. (1963). Fatty liver, hyperlipemia and hyperuricemia produced by prolonged alcohol consumption, despite adequate dietary intake. *Transactions of the Association of American Physicians*, **76**, 289–300.

Lieber, C.S., Spritz, N. and DeCarli, L.M. (1969). Fatty liver produced by dietary deficiencies: its pathogenesis and potentiation by ethanol. *Journal of Lipid Research*, **10**, 283–87.

Lindenbaum, J. (1980). Folate and vitamin B12 deficiencies in alcoholism. *Seminars in Hepatology*, **17**, 119–29.

Liu, C., Russell, R.M., Seitz, H.K., *et al.* (2001). Ethanol enhances retinoic acid metabolism into polar metabolites in rat liver via induction of cytochrome P4502E1. *Gastroenterology*, **120**, 179–89.

Liu, S., Serdula, M.K., Williamson, D.F, Mokdad, A.H. and Byers, T. (1994). A prospective study of alcohol intake and change in body weight among US adults. *American Journal of Epidemiology*, **140**, 912–20.

Lu, S.C. (1998). Methionine adenosyltransferase and liver disease: It's all about SAM. *Gastroenterology*, **114**, 403–07.

Lumeng, L.J. (1978). The role of acetaldehyde in mediating the deleterious effect of ethanol on pyridoxal 5'-phosphate metabolism. *Journal of Clinical Investigation*, **62**, 286–93.

Lumeng, L. and Li., T.-K. (1974). Vitamin, B6 metabolism in chronic alcohol abuse. *Journal of Clinical Investigation*, **53**, 693–704.

Lumeng, L., Schenker, S., Li., T.-K., Brashear, R.E. and Compton, M.C. (1984). Clearance and metabolisms of plasma pyridoxal 5' phosphate in the dog. *Journal of Laboratory and Clinical Medicine*, **103**, 59–64.

Manari, A.P., Preedy, V.R. and Peters, T.J. (2003). Nutritional intake of hazardous drinkers and dependent alcoholics in the UK. *Addiction Biology*, **8**, 201–10.

Marinella, M.A. (1998). Thiamine before glucose to prevent Wernicke's encephalopathy: examining the conventional wisdom. *Journal of the American Medical Association*, **279**, 583–84.

Martin, F., Ward, K., Slavin, G., Levi, J. and Peters, T.J. (1985). Alcoholic skeletal myopathy, a clinical and pathological study. *Quarterly Journal of Medicine*, **55**, 233–51.

Martines, D., Morris, A.I. and Billington, D. (1989). The effect of chronic ethanol intake on leucine absorption from the rat small intestine. *Alcohol and Alcoholism*, **24**, 525–31.

Marway, J.S., Bonner, A., Preedy, V.R. and Peters, T.J. (1996). Protein synthesis in the gastrointestinal tract and its modification by ethanol. In: V.R. Preedy and R.R. Watson (eds). *Alcohol and the Gastrointestinal Tract*. Boca Raton: CRC Press, pp. 255–72.

Mato, J.M., Camara, J., Fernandez de Paz, J., *et al.* (1999). *S*-adenosylmethionine in alcoholic liver cirrhosis: a randomized, placebo-controlled, double-blind, multicentre clinical trial. *Journal of Hepatology*, **30**, 1081–89.

McCullough, A.J. and Tavill, A.S. (1991). Disordered energy and protein metabolism in liver disease. *Seminars in Liver Disease*, **11**, 265–77.

McCullough, A.J. (1993). Stable isotopes and urinary nitrogen in the assessment of protein oxidation in cirrhosis. *Italian Journal of Gastroenterology*, **25**, 342–51.

McDonald, J.M.T. and Margen, S. (1976). Wine versus ethanol in human nutrition. Nitrogen and calorie balance. *American Journal of Clinical Nutrition*, **29**, 1093–1103.

Mendenhall, C., Bongiovanni, G., Goldberg, S., *et al.* (1985). VA Cooperative Study on Alcoholic Hepatitis. III. Changes in protein-calorie malnutrition associated with 30 days of hospitalization with and without enteral nutritional therapy. *Journal of Parenteral and Enteral Nutrition*, **9**, 590–96.

Mezey, E. (1985). Effect of ethanol on intestinal morphology, metabolism, and function. In: H.K. Seitz and B. Kommerell (eds). *Alcohol Related Diseases in Gastroenterology*. New York: Springer, pp. 342–60.

Montanari, A., Simoni, I., Vallisa, D., *et al.* (1988). Free amino acids in plasma and skeletal muscle of patients with liver cirrhosis. *Hepatology*, **8**, 1034–39.

Morgan, M.Y. (1981). Enteral nutrition in chronic liver disease. *Acta Chirurgica Scandinavica*, **507**, 81–90.

Muller, M.J., Lautz, H.U., Plogmann, B., Burger, M., Korber, J. and Schmidt, F.W. (1992). Energy expenditure and substrate oxidation in patients with cirrhosis: the impact of cause, clinical staging and nutritional state. *Hepatology*, **12**, 782–94.

Niebergall-Roth, E., Harder, H. and Singer, M.V. (1998). A review: acute and chronic effects of ethanol and alcoholic beverages on the pancreatic exocrine secretion *in vivo* and in vitro. *Alcoholism: Clinical and Experimental Research*, **22**, 1570–83.

Oxford Bottled Beer database (2007). http://www.bottledbeer.co.uk/index.html (last accessed August 2008).

Pacy, P.J., Preedy, V.R., Peters, T.J., Read, M. and Halliday, D. (1991). The effect of chronic alcohol ingestion on whole body and muscle protein synthesis – a stable isotope study. *Alcohol and Alcoholism*, **26**, 505–13.

Parker, T.H., Marshall, J.P., Roberts, R.K., *et al.* (1979). Effect of acute alcohol ingestion on plasma pyridoxal 5'-phosphate. *American Journal of Clinical Nutrition*, **32**, 1246–52.

Patek, A.J., Toth, E.G., Saunders, M.E., Castro, G.A.M. and Engel, J.J. (1975). Alcohol and dietary factors in cirrhosis. *Archives of Internal Medicine*, **135**, 1053–57.

Perlow, W., Baraona, E. and Lieber, C.S. (1977). Symptomatic intestinal disaccharidase deficiency in alcoholics. *Gastroenterology*, **72**, 680–84.

Pfeiffer, A., Schmidt, T., Vidon, N., Pehl, C. and Kaess, H. (1992). Absorption of a nutrient solution in chronic alcoholics without nutrient deficiencies and liver cirrhosis. *Scandinavian Journal of Gastroenterology*, **27**, 1023–30.

Pirola, R.C. and Lieber, C.S. (1972). The energy cost of the metabolism of drugs including ethanol. *Pharmacology*, **7**, 185–96.

Preedy, V.R. and Emery, P.W. (2002). Alcoholic myopathy. Your legs go before your liver. *The Biochemist*, **24**, 11–14.

Preedy, V.R. and Peters, T.J. (1988). Acute effects of ethanol on protein synthesis in different muscles and muscle protein fractions of the rat. *Clinical Science*, **74**, 461–66.

Preedy, V.R. and Peters, T.J. (1992). Protein metabolism in alcoholism. In: R.R. Watson and B. Watzl (eds). *Nutrition and Alcohol*. Boca Raton: CRC Press, pp. 143–89.

Preedy, V.R., Ohlendieck, K., Adachi, J., *et al.* (2003). The importance of alcohol-induced muscle disease. *Journal of Muscle Research and Cell Motility*, **24**, 55–63.

Preedy, V.R., Peters, T.J., Patel, V.B. and Miell, J.P. (1994a). Chronic alcoholic myopathy: transcription and translational alterations. *FASEB Journal*, **8**, 1146–51.

Preedy, V.R., Reilly, M.E., Patel, V.B., Richardson, P.J. and Peters, T.J. (1999). Protein metabolism in alcoholism: Effects on specific tissues and the whole body. *Nutrition*, **15**, 604–08.

Preedy, V.R., Salisbury, J.R. and Peters, T.J. (1994b). Alcoholic muscle disease: features and mechanisms. *Journal of Pathology*, **173**, 309–15.

Prime Minister's Strategy Unit (2003). *Alcohol misuse: How much does it cost?* Annexe to the Strategy Unit Alcohol Harm Reduction project Interim Analytical Report. London: The Cabinet Office.

Rajendram, R. and Preedy, V.R. (2005). The effect of alcohol consumption on the gut. *Digestive Diseases*, **23**, 214–21.

Rajendram, R., Hunter, R., Preedy, V.R. and Peters, T.J. (2005). Alcohol absorption, metabolism and physiological effects. In: Ed. B. Caballero, L. Allen, and A. Prentice (eds). *Encyclopaedia of Human Nutrition*, 2nd edn. Oxford: Elsevier Academic Press, pp. 48–57.

Rajendram, R., Marway, J.S., Mantle, D., Peters, T.J. and Preedy, V.R. (2003). Skeletal muscle and jejunal protein synthesis in normal and ethanol-treated rats: the effect of the nitric oxide synthase inhibitors, L-omega-nitro-L-arginine methyl ester and *N* (G)-nitro-L-arginine *in vivo*. *Metabolism: Clinical and Experimental*, **52**, 397–401.

Reinus, J.F., Heymsfield, S.B., Wiskind, R., Casper, K. and Galambos, J.T. (1989). Ethanol: relative fuel value and metabolic effects *in vivo*. *Metabolism: Clinical and Experimental*, **38**, 125–35.

Royal College of Physicians (1995). *Alcohol and the heart in perspective: Sensible drinking reaffirmed*. Report of a Joint Working Group of the Royal College of Physicians, the Royal College of Psychiatrists and the Royal College of General Practitioners. London: Royal College of Physicians.

Russell, R.M., Rosenberg, I.H., Wilson, P.D., *et al.* (1983). Increased urinary excretion and prolonged turnover time of folic acid during ethanol ingestion. *American Journal of Clinical Nutrition*, **38**, 64–70.

Seitz, H.K. (2000). Alcohol and retinoid metabolism. *Gut,* **47**, 748–05.

Seitz, H.K. and Homann, N. (2001). Effect of alcohol on the orogastrointestinal tract, the pancreas and the liver. In: N. Heather, T.J. Peters and T. Stockwell (eds). *International Handbook of Alcohol Dependence and Problems*. Chichester: Wiley, pp. 149–67.

Seitz, H.K. and Suter, P.M. (2002). Ethanol toxicity and nutritional status. In: F.M. Kotsouis and M. Mackey (eds). *Nutritional Toxicology*, 2nd edn. London: Taylor and Francis, pp. 122–54.

Selberg, O., Burchert, W., van den Hoff, J., *et al.* (1993). Insulin resistance in liver cirrhosis. Positron tomography scan analysis of skeletal muscle glucose metabolism. *Journal of Clinical Investigation*, **91**, 1897–902.

Smith-Kielland, A., Blom, G.P., Svenden, L., Bessesen, A. and Morland, J. (1983). A study of hepatic protein synthesis, three subcellular enzymes, and liver morphology in chronically ethanol fed rats. *Acta Pharmacologica et Toxicologica*, **53**, 113–20.

Stickel, F., Schuppan, D., Hahn, E.G. and Seitz, H.K. (2002). Co-carcinogenic effects of alcohol in hepatocarcinogenesis. *Gut,* **51**, 132–39.

Suter, P.M. (2001). Alcohol, its role in health and nutrition. In: B.A. Bowman and R.M. Russell (eds). *Present Knowledge in Nutrition*, 3rd edn. Washington, DC: International Life Science Institute Press, pp. 497–507.

Thompson, A.D., Heap, L.C. and Ward, R.J. (1996). Alcohol induced malabsorption in the gastrointestinal tract. In: V.R. Preedy and R.R. Watson (eds). *Alcohol and the Gastrointestinal Tract*. Boca Raton: CRC Press, pp. 203–218.

Tremblay, A., Buemann, B., Theriault, G. and Bouchard, C. (1995). Body fatness in active individuals reporting low lipid and alcohol intake. *European Journal of Clinical Nutrition*, **49**, 824–31.

US Department of Agriculture. (2006). *National Nutrient Database for Standard Reference Release 19*. Available at: http://www.nal.usda.gov/fnic/foodcomp/search/ (last accessed August 2008).

US Department of Health and Human Services and US Department of Agriculture. (2005). *Dietary Guidelines for Americans 2005*. Washington DC: US Government Printing Office.

Vendemiale, G., Altomare, E., Trizio, T., *et al.* (1989). Effect of oral *S*-adenosyl-L-methionine on hepatic glutathione in patients with liver disease. *Scandinavian Journal of Gastroenterology*, **24**, 407–15.

Westerfeld, W.W. and Schulman, M.P. (1959). Metabolism and caloric value of alcohol. *Journal of the American Medical Association*, **170**, 197–203.

World, M.J., Ryle, P.R., Jones, D., Shaw, G.K. and Thomson, A.D. (1984a). Differential effect of chronic alcohol intake and poor nutrition on body weight and fat stores. *Alcohol and Alcoholism*, **19**, 281–90.

World, M.J., Ryle, P.R., Pratt, O.E. and Thompson, A.D. (1984b). Alcohol and body weight. *Alcohol and Alcoholism*, **19**, 1–6.

Yamada, S., Mak, K.M. and Lieber, C.S. (1985). Chronic ethanol consumption alters rat liver plasma membranes and potentiates release of alkaline phosphatase. *Gastroenterology*, **88**, 1799–806.

21

A psychological model of alcohol dependency

Colin R. Martin

The issues of alcohol dependency and alcohol abuse produce a myriad of clinical, social, intrapersonal and interpersonal concerns. The knowledge base regarding the understanding of alcohol dependency as a diagnostic entity and the provision of evidence-based treatment approaches has to be viewed within the context of current understanding about this unique, dynamic and complex clinical presentation. Despite the personal, social, forensic and economic costs of alcohol misuse, there is surprisingly little coherency in theoretical attempts to integrate the various and diffuse facets associated with problematic drinking into a predictive and integrated model. A possible explanation for this current state of affairs may be related to the discipline-specific theories that have emerged in the literature. Put simply, there would appear to be an (understandable) bias for psychologists to develop psychological models, psychiatrists to develop psychiatric models, sociologists to develop social models and biologists to develop biological models, with little evidence of cross-disciplinary synthesis. However, integrated explanatory accounts of alcohol misuse are highly desirable given the extent of the problem (Beich *et al.*, 2003; Hasin and Grant, 2004; World Health Organization, 2004) and the often poor outcome associated with current treatment approaches (Emmen *et al.*, 2004; Kane *et al.*, 2004; Roozen *et al.*, 2004).

A fundamental problem in the current treatment approaches to alcohol dependency and abuse is the observation that therapeutic models are generally discipline specific and inconsistent with each other (Hirsh *et al.*, 1997; Koski-Jannes, 1994; Long *et al.*, 1998; Williams *et al.*, 1998). This undesirable state of affairs is largely a consequence of a reductionist approach to attempting to explain what is a complex phenomenon (Bohman *et al.*, 1984, 1987; Bucholz *et al.*, 1994; Devor *et al.*, 1993). Alcohol dependency thus represents an interaction of psychological, biological and social factors (Heath *et al.*, 1997; Johnson *et al.*, 2000; Nakahara *et al.*, 2002, 2003; Reich, 1988). As a result of differing and diverse philosophies underlying varied treatment approaches (with little consensus on the most appropriate treatment initiative against a background of generally poor prognosis) a compelling argument can be made for an integrative approach to the management of alcohol dependency that combines the best elements of the evidence base irrespective of underlying discipline. Attempting to do just that, Martin and Bonner (2005) developed an integrated psychobiological model of alcohol dependency that incorporated physiological aspects of presentation with psychological and psychiatric factors in order to synthesise a contextually appropriate and evidence-based theoretical model of the disorder. A particularly pleasing aspect of Martin and Bonner's (2005) innovative model was that treatment approaches were circumscribed by the underlying theoretical basis of the model. Further, Martin and Bonner (2005) also described a sophisticated methodological approach by which their model could be evaluated in relation to patient/client assessment and treatment outcome. This chapter will outline this contemporary and innovative approach to understanding alcohol dependency in detail.

Martin and Bonner's (2005) model

Fundamental to the model is the integration of psychological and biological factors. Martin and Bonner (2005) acknowledged that social factors have an important role to play in the presentation of alcohol dependency (Blomgren *et al.*, 2004; Morgan *et al.*, 2004), however they cautiously excluded such social factors from the model under the rubric that effective treatment may change the individual's own ability and self-efficacy to positively influence their own social world, a perspective consistent with a psychobiological model of explanation and intervention. Martin and Bonner's (2005) model of alcohol dependency offers economy in the explanation of presentation through the description of a minimum set of salient and interacting domains that account for the presentation.

Anxiety and depression

Key comorbid psychological symptoms associated with alcohol dependency are anxiety and depression (Allan, 1995; Brown *et al.*, 1995; Schade *et al.*, 2004; Zimmerman *et al.*, 2003). Depression is the most common psychiatric comorbid presentation associated with alcohol dependency (Merikangas *et al.*, 1998). Clinically significant comorbid anxiety is also common in alcohol dependency (Penick *et al.*, 1994). Importantly, assessment of anxiety and depression within people presenting with alcohol dependency is lacking, even within the context of specialist clinical services. Martin and Bonner (2005) suggested that this may be because the relationship of anxiety and depression to alcohol dependency is presently poorly understood (Schuckit, 1983).

The onset of comorbid depression in relation to alcohol dependency is critical in unpacking these complex relationships. Martin and Bonner (2005) point out that in the presentation of depression being secondary to alcohol dependency, depressive symptomatology often ameliorates without the need of interventions targeted at depression. This would suggest a biological explanation of depressive symptoms as a consequence of disturbance in the tryptophan precursor in the serotonergic pathway (Martin and Bonner, 2000). Alcohol dependence secondary to a primary depression may, however, produce a different outcome, with detoxification and pharmacological management of alcohol dependency having little impact on the severity of depressive symptoms. Martin and Bonner (2005) suggest that within this type of presentation the depression is not affected by pharmacological management of the alcohol dependence because different underlying mechanisms of presentation are involved compared to clients presenting with primary alcohol dependence/secondary depression. Martin and Bonner (2005) suggest that investigation of subtypes within the clinical group may reveal important treatment and prognostic information. Martin and Bonner (2005) specifically suggest that the use of Lesch typology (Lesch *et al.*, 1988, 1990) may be pivotal in assessing the relevance of co-occurring depressive disorder.

All four of Lesch's subtypes may be identified by comprehensive and skilled history-taking, however it is the type 3 classification that is of particular relevance in relation to the prominence of depressive symptomatology. The type 3 classification describes a stable and chronic depressive syndrome that endures after detoxification and persists even during extensive periods of abstinence (Lesch *et al.*, 1988; Kiefer and Barocka, 1999). The type 3 classification appears to be influenced strongly by social context, so providing some persuasive evidence for the need to incorporate social aspects of the patient's experience within a therapeutic package of support and care. Martin and Bonner (2005) suggest that the relevance of subtype heterogeneity within the overarching clinical presentation of alcohol dependency is key to understanding and developing further a psychobiological model of alcohol dependency and alcohol abuse.

The genetic contribution to alcohol dependence

An important area of research contributing to our understanding of the presentation and course of alcohol dependence is genetics (Fehr *et al.*, 2000). There is incontrovertible evidence for a genetic contribution to the development and manifestation of an alcohol-dependence state with estimates of 40–60 per cent related to inheritance (Merikangas, 1990). However, despite some strong indications of candidate genes as possible 'genes for alcoholism', such as the dopamine D$_2$ receptor (DRD$_2$) *TaqI* A polymorphism (Arinami *et al.*, 1993; Blum *et al.*, 1990; Cloninger, 1991; Lawford *et al.*, 1997), the evidence supporting such assertions remains equivocal (Lee *et al.*, 1999; Matsushita *et al.*, 2001; Sander *et al.*, 1999). Indeed several genes may be involved and these may act as an interaction or as additive contributors. Either way, the complete sequencing of a comprehensive and replicable pathway or 'fingerprint' for alcohol dependency is not likely to be found in the immediate future. There is, however, a good deal of support for the notion of complex psychobiological relationships between alcohol dependence and personality, which may be mediated, at least in part, by genetic factors. Cloninger has outlined an influential bio–psycho–social theory of personality with a key genetic contribution that has been associated with alcohol dependency (Cloninger *et al.*, 1981, 1988a,b; Cloninger and Reich, 1983). However, the strength of Cloninger's model also appears to be a weakness, in that it has been difficult to establish reliable relationships between the personality traits and underlying genes suggested as related within this influential model (Bowirrat and Oscar-Berman, 2004; Wiesbeck *et al.*, 2004).

Moreover, the term 'heritable' may not be the exclusive preserve of genetics; inter-generational transmission of alcohol dependency by definition will include the social, behavioural and, indeed, the learned components of dependency which will interact with underlying biological substrates (Cheng *et al.*, 2004). A family history of alcohol dependency is a significant risk factor for development of this disorder (Trim and Chassin, 2004), but evidence that the risk is determined exclusively by genetic factors has not been forthcoming (Prescott *et al.*, 2004). The implications for the clinician are that family history-positive status represents a risk factor for dependency, but also provides an opportunity to explore which are the salient aspects of the positive history that may have contributed to the clinical presentation – factors that could include social learning and modeling of permissive alcohol behaviour or family violence, and so on. Importantly, the fundamental genetic contribution remains occluded. So, in developing a psychobiological model for contemporary evaluation, the key risk factor that can be identified is a family history of alcoholism, rather than a specific gene for alcohol dependency.

Neurochemistry

A further focus of Martin and Bonner's (2005) model is an appreciation of the role of neurochemistry in all areas of alcohol dependency. One of the main foci in this area is the role of the neurotransmitter serotonin (5-hydroxytryptamine; 5-HT) in the onset of the disorder; it is a tryptophan metabolite that is also implicated in the occurrence of comorbid characteristics associated with alcohol dependency including anxiety and depression (Martin and Bonner, 2000). Martin and Bonner (2005) discuss in some detail the role of this neurotransmitter in various aspects of alcohol dependency, including withdrawal symptom manifestation (Martin and Bonner, 2000), neurocognitive impairment (Bonner *et al.*, 2004), and dysfunction in tryptophan metabolism as a consequence of liver disease resulting in tryptophan and 5-HT depletion (Martin and Bonner, 2000). Martin and Bonner (2005) suggest that full appreciation of the mechanisms of tryptophan metabolism and the impact of alcohol on connected substrates may raise the possibility of nutritional supplementation and tryptophan manipulation in order to positively impact on a variety of phenomena associated with alcohol dependency, including mood disturbance, withdrawal symptom severity and neurocognitive sequelae. Martin and Bonner (2005) emphasise the need to consider the nutritional status of clients presenting with alcohol dependency as an integral part of a comprehensive assessment for treatment. The role of the most quantitatively significant metabolic pathway in tryptophan metabolism – the kynurenine pathway to brain damage – is also emphasised in Martin and Bonner's (2005) model.

Development

Martin and Bonner (2005) maintain that the interaction between biological and psychological factors is especially relevant in people with disadvantaged socioeconomic lifestyles or experience of alcohol dependency. A constellation of deficits is noted in alcohol dependency representing a gestalt of psychological, biological and social impoverishment and an overall increase in mortality and morbidity. Various mechanisms of underlying deficit formation have been proposed including increased apoptosis (Freund, 1994), free radical damage (Gonthier *et al.*, 1991), protein synthesis impairment (Bonner *et al.*, 1996) and deoxyribonucleic acid (DNA) damage (Mansouri *et al.*, 2001; Renis *et al.*, 1996) effects on protein formation via derangements of RNA metabolism. Martin and Bonner (2005) point out that both the development and maintenance of the neuronal integrity of the central nervous system are dependent on the biochemical synchrony of the brain throughout development. Consequently, acute neuronal catastrophic events or the insidious effects of deprivation during childhood may lead to a relatively more vulnerable neurological infrastructure, particularly to the challenges of later alcohol consumption on neuronal substrates. Fetal alcohol syndrome and fetal alcohol spectrum disorder are discussed in Chapter 27 and provide an insight into one particular aspect of this complex set of interactions.

Gender

Gender differences have been noted in alcohol dependency (Barr *et al.*, 2004; Gratzer *et al.*, 2004; Pettinati *et al.*, 2004), a striking observation being a significantly higher incidence rate in men compared to women (Wu and Ringwalt, 2004). Differentiation between biological and psychosocial processes has been observed within the context of gender. There seems to be a more significant genetic contribution to alcohol dependency in men (Heath *et al.*, 1997), but in women psychological factors, particularly affect, and the social milieu appear to have a more significant impact on the occurrence of alcohol dependency (van den Bree *et al.*, 1998). Gender is consequently an important factor within the psychobiological model proposed by Martin and Bonner (2005) and is viewed within the model as a unique source of variance within the context of aetiology.

Personality

There is little doubt that personality characteristics impact on an individual's vulnerability to the development of alcohol dependency; in this respect such characteristics may meaningfully represent risk factors (Cloninger *et al.*, 1981; Godsall *et al.*, 2004; Martin and Otter, 1996). Certain personality characteristics appear to have more significance than others, and, not unexpectedly, one of the more important categories concerns personality disorder, in particular, antisocial personality disorder (ASPD) (Bauer, 1997; Compton *et al.*, 2000; Fu *et al.*, 2002; Hesselbrock and Hesselbrock, 1994; Miranda *et al.*, 2003; Schuckit *et al.*, 1995; Tomasson and Vaglum, 2000; Verheul *et al.*, 1998; Waldstein *et al.*, 1996).

Traumatic head injury and frontal lobe dysfunction have been implicated in the development of ASPD (Malloy *et al.*, 1990; Raine *et al.*, 1994; Vollm *et al.*, 2004) and brain injury is a salient factor within the psychobiological model proposed by Martin and Bonner (2005).

Taking the above components and synthesising them into a coherent and evaluable model, the relationship between these factors is shown in Fig. 21.1 (overpage). Martin and Bonner (2005) proposed a methodology to evaluate the model based on structural equation modeling approaches to data. Using this approach the model can be both evaluated and modified in relation to data. Moreover, within their proposed methodology, the relative contribution of each factor to alcohol dependency and treatment outcome can be determined.

Conclusions

Martin and Bonner's (2005) psychobiological model of alcohol dependency offers much in the way of synthesis and integration across disciplines for understanding what undoubtedly represents a complex clinical presentation. The psychobiological model acknowledges and emphasises that alcohol dependency is multifactorial and that there is a pressing need to develop and improve treatment approaches. These goals can only realistically be met by developing coherent and integrative aetiological models which can be evaluated in a robust and evidence-based manner. The psychobiological model of alcohol dependency proposed by Martin and Bonner (2005) offers a clinically relevant and useful platform on which to pursue research in this complex area of psychopathology.

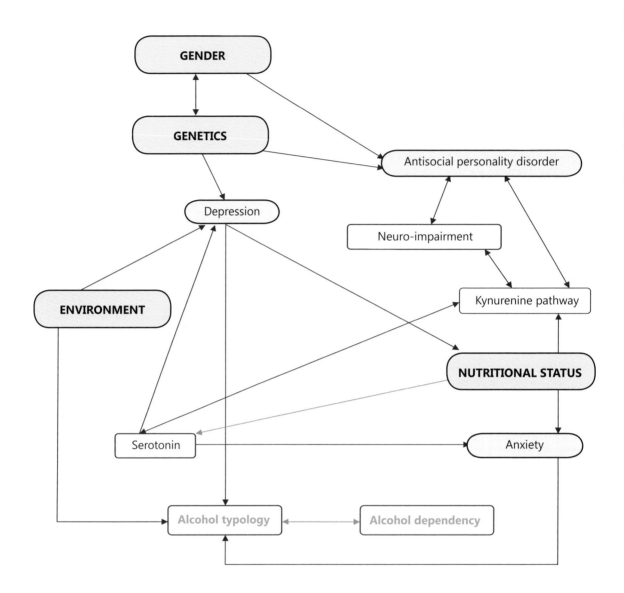

Figure 21.1 A model of alcohol dependency. The arrowheads show the direction of causation.

References and further reading

Allan, C.A. (1995). Alcohol problems and anxiety disorders – a critical review. *Alcohol and Alcoholism*, **30**(2), 145–51.

Arinami, T., Itokawa, M., Komiyama, T., *et al.* (1993). Association between severity of alcoholism and the A1 allele of the dopamine D₂ receptor gene TaqI A RFLP in Japanese. *Biological Psychiatry*, **33**(2), 108–14.

Barr, C.S., Newman, T.K., Lindell, S., *et al.* (2004). Early experience and sex interact to influence limbic–hypothalamic–pituitary–adrenal axis function after acute alcohol administration in rhesus macaques (*Macaca mulatta*). *Alcoholism: Clinical* and *Experimental Research*, **28**(7), 1114–19.

Bauer, L.O. (1997). Frontal P300 decrements, childhood conduct disorder, family history, and the prediction of relapse among abstinent cocaine abusers. *Drug and Alcohol Dependence*, **44**, 1–10.

Beich, A., Thorsen, T. and Rollnick, S. (2003). Screening in brief intervention trials targeting excessive drinkers in general practice: systematic review and meta-analysis. *British Medical Journal*, **327**(7414), 536–42.

Blomgren, J., Martikainen, P., Makela, P. and Valkonen, T. (2004). The effects of regional characteristics on alcohol-related mortality – a register-based multilevel analysis of 1.1 million men. *Social Science and Medicine*, **58**(12), 2523–35.

Blum, K., Noble, E.P., Sheridan, P.J., *et al.* (1990). Allelic association of human dopamine D_2 receptor gene in alcoholism. *Journal of the American Medical Association*, **263**(15), 2055–60.

Bohman, M., Cloninger, C.R., von Knorring, A. L. and Sigvardsson, S. (1984). An adoption study of somatoform disorders. III. Cross-fostering analysis and genetic relationship to alcoholism and criminality. *Archives of General Psychiatry*, **41**(9), 872–78.

Bohman, M., Sigvardsson, S., Cloninger, R. and von Knorring, A.L. (1987). Alcoholism: lessons from population, family and adoption studies. *Alcohol and Alcoholism*, **1**(Suppl.), 55–60.

Bonner, A.B., Martin, C.R. and Hayes, B. (2004). A nutritional approach to enhancing neurocognition in abstinent alcohol abusers. *Alcoholism: Clinical and Experimental Research*, **28**, 52A.

Bonner, A.B., Marway, J.S., Swann, M. and Preedy, V.R. (1996). Brain nucleic acid composition and fractional rates of protein synthesis in response to chronic ethanol feeding: comparison with skeletal muscle. *Alcohol,* **13**(6), 581–87.

Bowirrat, A. and Oscar-Berman, M. (2005). Relationship between dopaminergic neurotransmission, alcoholism, and reward deficiency syndrome. *American Journal of Medical Genetics. Part B. Neuropsychiatric Genetics*, **132**(1), 29–37.

Brown, S.A., Inaba, R.K., Gillin, J.C., Schuckit, M.A., Stewart, M. A. and Irwin, M.R. (1995). Alcoholism and affective disorder: clinical course of depressive symptoms. *American Journal of Psychiatry*, **152**(1), 45–52.

Bucholz, K.K., Cadoret, R., Cloninger, C.R., *et al.* (1994). A new, semi-structured psychiatric interview for use in genetic linkage studies: a report on the reliability of the SSAGA. *Journal of Studies on Alcohol,* **55**(2), 149–58.

Cheng, A.T., Gau, S.F., Chen, T.H., Chang, J.C. and Chang, Y.T. (2004). A 4-year longitudinal study on risk factors for alcoholism. *Archives of General Psychiatry*, **61**(2), 184–91.

Cloninger, C.R. (1991). D_2 dopamine receptor gene is associated but not linked with alcoholism. *Journal of the American Medical Association*, **266**(13), 1833–34.

Cloninger, C.R., Bohman, M. and Sigvardsson, S. (1981). Inheritance of alcohol abuse. Cross-fostering analysis of adopted men. *Archives of General Psychiatry*, **38**(8), 861–68.

Cloninger, C. R. and Reich, T. (1983). Genetic heterogeneity in alcoholism and sociopathy. Research publications. *Association for Research in Nervous and Mental Disease*, **60**, 145–66.

Cloninger, C.R., Sigvardsson, S. and Bohman, M. (1988a). Childhood personality predicts alcohol abuse in young adults. *Alcoholism: Clinical and Experimental Research*, **12**(4), 494–505.

Cloninger, C.R., Sigvardsson, S., Gilligan, S.B., von Knorring, A.L., Reich, T. and Bohman, M. (1988b). Genetic heterogeneity and the classification of alcoholism. *Advances in Alcohol and Substance Abuse*, **7**(3–4), 3–16.

Compton, W.M., Cottler, L.B., Ben Abdallah, A., Phelps, D.L., Spitznagel, E. L. and Horton, J.C. (2000). Substance dependence and other psychiatric disorders among drug dependent subjects: race and gender correlates. *American Journal of Addiction,* **9**(2), 113–25.

Devor, E.J., Cloninger, C.R., Hoffman, P. L. and Tabakoff, B. (1993). Association of monoamine oxidase (MAO) activity with alcoholism and alcoholic subtypes. *American Journal of Medical Genetics*, **48**(4), 209–13.

Emmen, M.J., Schippers, G.M., Bleijenberg, G. and Wollersheim, H. (2004). Effectiveness of opportunistic brief interventions for problem drinking in a general hospital setting: systematic review. *British Medical Journal*, **328**(7435), 318.

Fehr, C., Grintschuk, N., Szegedi, A., *et al.* (2000). The HTR1B 861G>C receptor polymorphism among patients suffering from alcoholism, major depression, anxiety disorders and narcolepsy. *Psychiatry Research*, **97**(1), 1–10.

Freund, G. (1994). Apoptosis and gene expression: perspectives on alcohol-induced brain damage. *Alcohol,* **11**(5), 385–87.

Fu, Q., Heath, A.C., Bucholz, K.K., *et al.* (2002). Shared genetic risk of major depression, alcohol dependence, and marijuana dependence: contribution of antisocial personality disorder in men. *Archives of General Psychiatry*, **59**(12), 1125–32.

Godsall, R.E., Jurkovic, G.J., Emshoff, J., Anderson, L. and Stanwyck, D. (2004). Why some kids do well in bad situations: relation of parental alcohol misuse and parentification to children's self-concept. *Substance Use and Misuse*, **39**(5), 789–809.

Gonthier, B., Jeunet, A. and Barret, L. (1991). Electron spin resonance study of free radicals produced from ethanol and acetaldehyde after exposure to a Fenton system or to brain and liver microsomes. *Alcohol,* **8**(5), 369–75.

Gratzer, D., Levitan, R.D., Sheldon, T., Toneatto, T., Rector, N. A. and Goering, P. (2004). Lifetime rates of alcoholism in adults with anxiety, depression, or comorbid depression/anxiety: a community survey of Ontario. *Journal of Affective Disorders*, **79**(1–3), 209–15.

Hasin, D. S. and Grant, B.F. (2004). The co-occurrence of DSM-IV alcohol abuse in DSM-IV alcohol dependence: results of the National Epidemiologic Survey on Alcohol and Related Conditions on heterogeneity that differ by population subgroup. *Archives of General Psychiatry*, **61**(9), 891–96.

Heath, A.C., Bucholz, K.K., Madden, P.A., *et al.* (1997). Genetic and environmental contributions to alcohol dependence risk in a national twin sample: consistency of findings in women and men. *Psychological Medicine*, **27** (6), 1381–96.

Hesselbrock, V. M. and Hesselbrock, M.N. (1994). Alcoholism and subtypes of antisocial personality disorder. *Alcohol and Alcoholism,* **2(Suppl.**), 479–84.

Hirsch, L.S., McCrady, B. S. and Epstein, E.E. (1997). The Drinking-Related Locus of Control Scale: the factor structure with treatment-seeking outpatients. *Journal of Studies on Alcohol,* **58**(2), 162–66.

Johnson, B.A., Roache, J.D., Javors, M.A., *et al.* (2000). Ondansetron for reduction of drinking among biologically predisposed alcoholic patients: A randomized controlled trial. *Journal of the American Medical Association*, **284**(8), 963–71.

Kane, R.L., Wall, M., Potthoff, S., Stromberg, K., Dai, Y. and Meyer, Z.J. (2004). The effect of alcoholism treatment on medical care use. *Medical Care*, **42**(4), 395–402.

Kiefer, F. and Barocka, A. (1999). Secondary depression in weaned alcoholics: implications of Lesch's typology of chronic alcoholism. *Alcohol and Alcoholism*, **34**, 916–17.

Koski-Jannes, A. (1994). Drinking-related locus of control as a predictor of drinking after treatment. *Addictive Behaviors*, **19**(5), 491–95.

Lawford, B.R., Young, R.M., Rowell, J.A., *et al.* (1997). Association of the D₂ dopamine receptor A1 allele with alcoholism: medical severity of alcoholism and type of controls. *Biological Psychiatry*, **41**(4), 386–93.

Lee, J.F., Lu, R.B., Ko, H.C., *et al.* (1999). No association between DRD₂ locus and alcoholism after controlling the ADH and ALDH genotypes in Chinese Han population. *Alcoholism: Clinical and Experimental Research*, **23** (4), 592–99.

Lesch, O.M., Dietzel, M., Musalek, M., Walter, H. and Zeiler, K. (1988). The course of alcoholism. Long-term prognosis in different types. *Forensic Science International*, **36**(1–2), 121–38.

Lesch, O.M., Kefer, J., Lentner, S., *et al.* (1990). Diagnosis of chronic alcoholism—classificatory problems. *Psychopathology,* **23**(2), 88–96.

Long, C.G., Hollin, C.R. and Williams, M.J. (1998). Self-efficacy, outcome expectations, and fantasies as predictors of alcoholics' post-treatment drinking. *Substance Use and Misuse*, **33**(12), 2383–2402.

Malloy, P., Noel, N., Longabaugh, R. and Beattie, M. (1990). Determinants of neuropsychological impairment in antisocial substance abusers. *Addictive Behaviors*, **15**(5), 431–38.

Mansouri, A., Demeilliers, C., Amsellem, S., Pessayre, D. and Fromenty, B. (2001). Acute ethanol administration oxidatively damages and depletes mitochondrial DNA in mouse liver, brain, heart, and skeletal muscles: protective effects of antioxidants. *Journal of Pharmacology and Experimental Therapeutics*, **298**(2), 737–43.

Martin, C.R. and Bonner, A.B. (2000). A pilot investigation of the effect of tryptophan manipulation on the affective state of male chronic alcoholics. *Alcohol and Alcoholism*, **35**(1), 49–51.

Martin, C.R. and Bonner, A.B. (2005). Towards an integrated clinical psychobiology of alcoholism. *Current Psychiatry Reviews*, **1**, 303–12.

Martin, C.R. and Otter, C.R. (1996). Locus of control and addictive behaviour. In: A. Bonner and J. Waterhouse (eds). *Addictive Behaviour: Molecules to Mankind*. Basingstoke: Macmillan, pp. 121–34.

Matsushita, S., Muramatsu, T., Murayama, M., Nakane, J. and Higuchi, S. (2001). Alcoholism, ALDH2*2 allele and the A1 allele of the dopamine D_2 receptor gene: an association study. *Psychiatry Research*, **104**(1), 19–26.

Merikangas, K.R. (1990). The genetic epidemiology of alcoholism. *Psychological Medicine*, **20**(1), 11–22.

Merikangas, K.R., Stevens, D.E., Fenton, B., *et al.* (1998). Comorbidity and familial aggregation of alcoholism and anxiety disorders. *Psychological Medicine*, **28**(4), 773–88.

Miranda, R. Jr, Meyerson, L.A., Myers, R.R. and Lovallo, W.R. (2003). Altered affective modulation of the startle reflex in alcoholics with antisocial personality disorder. *Alcoholism: Clinical and Experimental Research*, **27**(12), 1901–11.

Morgan, M.Y., Landron, F. and Lehert, P. (2004). Improvement in quality of life after treatment for alcohol dependence with acamprosate and psychosocial support. *Alcoholism: Clinical and Experimental Research*, **28**(1), 64–77.

Nakahara, T., Hashimoto, K., Hirano, M., Koll, M., Martin, C. R. and Preedy, V.R. (2003). Acute and chronic effects of alcohol exposure on skeletal muscle c-myc, p53, and Bcl-2 mRNA expression. *American Journal of Physiology. Endocrinology and Metabolism,* **285**(6), E1273–81.

Nakahara, T., Hirano, M., Uchimura, *H., et al.* (2002). Chronic alcohol feeding and its influence on *c-Fos* and *heat shock protein-70* gene expression in different brain regions of male and female rats. *Metabolism,* **51**(12), 1562–68.

Otter, C.R. and Martin, C.R. (1996). Personality and addictive behaviour. In: Bonner, A. and Waterhouse, J. (eds). *Molecules to Mankind: Perspectives on the Nature of Addiction*. Basingstoke: Macmillan, pp. 87–120.

Penick, E.C., Powell, B.J., Nickel, E.J., *et al.* (1994). Comorbidity of lifetime psychiatric disorder among male alcoholic patients. *Alcoholism: Clinical and Experimental Research*, **18**(6), 1289–93.

Pettinati, H.M., Dundon, W. and Lipkin, C. (2004). Gender differences in response to sertraline pharmacotherapy in type A alcohol dependence. *American Journal of Addiction,* **13**(3), 236–47.

Prescott, C.A., Cross, R.J., Kuhn, J.W., Horn, J. L. and Kendler, K.S. (2004). Is risk for alcoholism mediated by individual differences in drinking motivations? *Alcoholism: Clinical and Experimental Research*, **28**(1), 29–39.

Raine, A., Buchsbaum, M.S., Stanley, J., Lottenberg, S., Abel, L. and Stoddard, J. (1994). Selective reductions in prefrontal glucose metabolism in murderers. *Biological Psychiatry*, **36**(6), 365–73.

Reich, T. (1988). Biological-marker studies in alcoholism. *New England Journal of Medicine*, **318**(3), 180–82.

Renis, M., Calabrese, V., Russo, A., Calderone, A., Barcellona, M.L. and Rizza, V. (1996). Nuclear DNA strand breaks during ethanol-induced oxidative stress in rat brain. *FEBS Letters*, **390**(2), 153–56.

Roozen, H.G., Boulogne, J.J., van Tulder, M.W., van den Brink, W., De Jong, C. A. and Kerkhof, A.J. (2004). A systematic review of the effectiveness of the community reinforcement approach in alcohol, cocaine and opioid addiction. *Drug and Alcohol Dependence*, **74**(1), 1–13.

Sander, T., Ladehoff, M., Samochowiec, J., Finckh, U., Rommelspacher, H. and Schmidt, L.G. (1999). Lack of an allelic association between polymorphisms of the dopamine D_2 receptor gene and alcohol dependence in the German population. *Alcoholism: Clinical and Experimental Research*, **23**(4), 578–81.

Schade, A., Marquenie, L.A., Van Balkom, A.J., *et al.* (2004). Alcohol-dependent patients with comorbid phobic disorders: a comparison between comorbid patients, pure alcohol-dependent and pure phobic patients. *Alcohol and Alcoholism*, **39**(3), 241–46.

Schuckit, M. (1983). Alcoholic patients with secondary depression. *American Journal of Psychiatry*, **140**(6), 711–14.

Schuckit, M.A., Tipp, J.E., Smith, T.L., *et al.* (1995). An evaluation of type A and B alcoholics. *Addiction,* **90**(9), 1189–1203.

Tomasson, K. and Vaglum, P. (2000). Antisocial addicts: the importance of additional axis I disorders for the 28-month outcome. *European Psychiatry*, **15**(8), 443–49.

Trim, R.S. and Chassin, L. (2004). Drinking restraint, alcohol consumption and alcohol dependence among children of alcoholics. *Journal of Studies on Alcohol,* **65**(1), 122–25.

van den Bree, M.B., Johnson, E.O., Neale, M.C., Svikis, D.S., McGue, M. and Pickens, R.W. (1998). Genetic analysis of diagnostic systems of alcoholism in males. *Biological Psychiatry*, **43**(2), 139–45.

Verheul, R., van den Brink, W. and Koeter, M.W. (1998). Temporal stability of diagnostic criteria for antisocial personality disorder in male alcohol dependent patients. *Journal of Personality Disorders*, **12**(4), 316–31.

Vollm, B., Richardson, P., Stirling, J., *et al.* (2004). Neurobiological substrates of antisocial and borderline personality disorder: preliminary results of a functional fMRI study. *Criminal Behaviour and Mental Health*, **14**(1), 39–54.

Waldstein, S.R., Malloy, P.F., Stout, R. and Longabaugh, R. (1996). Predictors of neuropsychological impairment in alcoholics: antisocial versus non-antisocial subtypes. *Addictive Behaviors*, **21**(1), 21–27.

Wiesbeck, G.A., Weijers, H.G., Wodarz, N., *et al.* (2004). Serotonin transporter gene polymorphism and personality traits in primary alcohol dependence. *World Journal of Biological Psychiatry*, **5**(1), 45–48.

Williams, R.J., Connor, J. P. and Ricciardelli, L.A. (1998). Self-efficacy for refusal mediated by outcome expectancies in the prediction of alcohol-dependence amongst young adults. *Journal of Drug Education*, **28**(4), 347–59.

World Health Organization (2004). *Global Status Report on Alcohol*. Geneva: WHO.

Wu, L.T. and Ringwalt, C.L. (2004). Alcohol dependence and use of treatment services among women in the community. *American Journal of Psychiatry*, **161**(10), 1790–97.

Zimmermann, P., Wittchen, H.U., Hofler, M., Pfister, H., Kessler, R.C. and Lieb, R. (2003). Primary anxiety disorders and the development of subsequent alcohol use disorders: a 4-year community study of adolescents and young adults. *Psychological Medicine*, **33**(7), 1211–22.

22 Spirituality and alcohol dependence

Christopher C.H. Cook

Why should there be a chapter on spirituality in a book on the identification and treatment of alcohol dependence? There is no mention of spirituality in either the DSM-IV (American Psychiatric Association, 1994) or ICD-10 (World Health Organization, 1992) criteria for alcohol dependence, and neither is spirituality to be found in any of the major screening questionnaires used to identify cases of alcohol dependence. Further, it might be argued, many treatment programmes for people with alcohol dependence do not include any explicitly spiritual intervention in their therapeutic regimen. Perhaps the real reason for surprise, however, is that since the 'Enlightenment', science and religion have conducted their discourse in different seminar rooms and in different publications. (The 'Enlightenment' refers here to the intellectual movement that began in the 17th century, which emphasised reason as the basis for belief and thus excluded the authority of sacred texts and religious traditions; see Honderich, 1995, pp. 236–37.) It has not been at all usual, at least not until very recently, to find material on subjects such as faith, religion or spirituality in scientific publications, and this is despite the publication of William James' seminal work on the psychology of religion over a century ago (James, 1985; originally published in 1902). Science focuses objectively on reason and evidence, spirituality and religion (at least, so it is argued) on the subjective, intangible and unprovable.

While spirituality is not explicitly mentioned in either DSM-IV or ICD-10, it is increasingly being argued that addiction – alcohol dependence included – is in fact a spiritual disorder, or at least that there is a spiritual dimension to it (e.g. May, 2000). While screening questionnaires do not currently include items on spirituality, the scientific assessment of spirituality by questionnaire or interview is an increasing concern of research in the addictions (Cook, 2004; Miller, 1998). Furthermore, addiction treatment programmes can, and do, incorporate spirituality into their therapeutic work (Jackson and Cook, 2005; Ringwald, 2002). Perhaps most importantly, the history of the so-called '12-Step' mutual help movement, based on the pioneering work of the founders of Alcoholics Anonymous (AA), has had a deep impact on addictions treatment worldwide and cannot be ignored in any serious analysis of the identification and treatment of alcohol dependence. While faith-based treatment and rehabilitation programmes have also been very important on the international treatment scene, it is probably Alcoholics Anonymous that has done most to put spirituality on the addictions treatment agenda. However, spirituality and religion have become an increasing concern in all areas of healthcare research in recent years (Koenig, 2005). The Spirituality Interest Group of the Royal College of Psychiatrists in the UK has grown to be one of the most popular groups within that College (Powell and Cook, 2006), and service users are increasingly demanding adequate attention to their spiritual, as well as their psychological, social and physical needs (Mental Health Foundation, 2002). For all of these reasons, and whatever conclusions might be reached by a particular reader or author about the merits or demerits of spirituality as a clinical and research variable, a book on the identification and treatment of alcohol dependence might now be considered incomplete without at least some attention being devoted to this subject. However, one of the major criticisms of work in this field has been that it is impossible to define spirituality scientifically, and/or that it is in fact a multidimensional concept which fragments into different components when subjected to careful analysis. We must therefore begin by giving attention to the *definition* of spirituality.

Definition of spirituality

There is no doubt that definitions and descriptions of spirituality, even within the addictions literature, vary widely. It is commonly defined as distinct from religion, usually on the basis of experience. For example, Berenson (1990, p. 59) states that: 'Spirituality, as opposed to religion, connotes a direct, personal experience of the sacred unmediated by particular belief systems prescribed by dogma or by hierarchical structures of priests, ministers, rabbis, or gurus'. Others come to the contrary conclusion (Mercadante, 1996, p. 13) thus: 'Spirituality by definition is supported or formed by conceptual and religious structure'. Commonly, reference is made to personal relationships, and especially to relationships with some kind of transcendent order, or God (Dollard, 1983, p. 7): 'Spirituality... is concerned with our ability, through our attitudes and actions, to relate to others, to ourselves, and to God as we understand Him'. However, a variety of concepts are in fact brought into play by different authors. In a systematic review of these definitions and descriptions (Cook, 2004), thirteen such conceptual components of spirituality have been identified, as listed in Box 22.1.

Box 22.1 **Thirteen conceptual components of spirituality (Cook, 2004)**
• Relatedness
• Transcendence
• Humanity
• Core/force/soul
• Meaning/purpose
• Authenticity/truth
• Values
• Non-materiality
• (Non) religiousness
• Wholeness
• Self-knowledge
• Creativity
• Consciousness

In practice, relatedness and transcendence are the most commonly identified concepts. However, even if multidimensional assessment of spirituality as a variable might be warranted, it is not clear that the thirteen concepts are unrelated to each other. Therefore, a definition has been proposed by Cook (2004, pp. 548–49) as shown below.

A definition of spirituality (Cook, 2004)

Spirituality is a distinctive, potentially creative and universal dimension of human experience arising both within the inner subjective awareness of people and within communities, social groups and traditions. It may be experienced as relationship with that which is intimately 'inner', immanent and personal, within the self and others, and/or as relationship with that which is wholly 'other', transcendent and beyond the self. It is experienced as being of fundamental or ultimate importance and is thus concerned with matters of meaning and purpose in life, truth and values.

Numerous research instruments are currently available for the measurement of spirituality as a dependent or independent variable in addictions research (Cook, 2004; Hill and Hood 1999; Morgan, 2002). Obviously, the underlying concepts that inform the design of an instrument will influence its suitability for use in any particular research methodology. At least one validated measure is available which offers a multidimensional approach (Fetzer Institute and National Institute on Aging Working Group, 1999).

The history of spirituality

Spirituality is a relatively recent concept (Cook, 2004, pp. 539–40). Furthermore, it was only following the publication of the seminal works on drunkenness by Rush in 1785 (Rush, 1943) and Trotter in 1804 (Trotter, 1988) that the subject of alcohol dependence (as we now refer to it) became a focus of medical interest. Up until this time, at least in Christian Europe, alcohol consumption was a concern of theology and morality, but not of scientific interest (Cook, 2006). For a century or more it remained a subject of both religious and scientific concern but, as the Enlightenment increasingly relegated matters of religious concern to the private domain, and as secular discourse increasingly excluded theology, the focus changed. During the 20th century, alcohol dependence came to be regarded in medical and scientific circles as a bio-psycho-social syndrome (Edwards and Gross, 1976).

Of course, in other parts of the world, things might have been seen differently. For example, in contrast to Christianity, Islam has consistently proscribed the consumption of alcohol for centuries, largely on the basis of what we might now call concerns of spirituality: in particular the adverse effects of alcohol on social relationships and prayer (Cook, 2006, pp. 11–12). Buddhism, on the other hand, understands the suffering associated with addiction within the broader context of human suffering, and spiritual resources within that faith tradition are increasingly being explicitly applied in the treatment of alcohol dependence (Alexander 1997; Bien and Bien, 2002). In different parts of the world today, Christian (Moos, Mehren and Moos, 1978), Islamic (Abdel-Mawgood *et al.*, 1995), Buddhist (Barrett, 1997) and Native American (Garrett and Carroll,

2000) treatment programmes for alcohol dependence and/or other chemical dependencies incorporate spirituality into their therapy, each according to their own faith tradition. However, the emergence during the 20th century of spirituality as a significant concern in the treatment of alcohol dependence has been particularly related to the history of Alcoholics Anonymous and its spiritual – but not religious – approach to recovery.

Alcoholics Anonymous dates its origins from 10 June 1935, the day Dr Bob Smith, its cofounder, had his last drink (Alcoholics Anonymous, 1976, pp. 171–81). The origins of the society were very much concerned with the mutual help given by one alcoholic to another. However, in a classic account of the history of Alcoholics Anonymous, Ernest Kurtz notes that its roots were in both religion and medicine (Kurtz, 1991, p. 33). On the one hand, the religious roots may be traced to the involvement of its founders in the Oxford Group, an evangelical Christian movement of that time, the personal religious experiences of its founders, and the seminal work of William James, *The Varieties of Religious Experience*. On the other hand, they may be identified in the medical influences of Dr Carl Jung and Dr William Silkworth, not to mention that one of the cofounders was himself a surgeon. According to Kurtz, the core idea of Alcoholics Anonymous was concerned with the hopelessness of the condition and the sense of deflation that arose from this. From this 'rock bottom' position, the founders experienced a kind of conversion: from alcoholism to sobriety, and from destructive self-centredness to creative and human interaction with others (Kurtz, 1991, pp. 33–34).

That Alcoholics Anonymous came to identify itself as 'spiritual rather than religious' doubtless has much to do with the effects of Enlightenment rationalism, already referred to above, and also with the emphasis on personal experience rather than dogmatic religion (Kurtz, 1991, p. 175). Within the pages of *The Varieties of Religious Experience*, which was highly influential on the founders of Alcoholics Anonymous, are examples of how religious conversion can be associated with conversion from alcoholism to sobriety (James, 1985, pp. 201–03). William James emphasised throughout this book the common experiential components of religion; clearly he was no admirer of dogmatic tradition. Thus Alcoholics Anonymous inherited a very slightly ambivalent approach to religion. On the one hand there was a positive sense that religious experience could be a vehicle for recovery from alcoholism, and a largely positive experience of this within the specific tradition of the Oxford Group. On the other hand there was an implication that no particular religious tradition offered more than any other and that the institutional and doctrinal aspects of religion were at least not important, and possibly unhelpful.

Carl Jung also emphasised the need for a 'vital spiritual experience' as a pathway to recovery from severe alcoholism (Alcoholics Anonymous, 1976, pp. 26–27). It was this which formed the basis for his dictum, expressed many years later in a letter to Bill Wilson (the other cofounder of Alcoholics Anonymous), *spiritus contra spiritum*. Jeff Sandoz, a contemporary counsellor and retreat director, pointed out that this dictum can be interpreted both ways (Sandoz, 2004, pp. 44–45). That is, that alcohol (*spiritum*) can be detrimental to spirituality (*spiritus*) but spirituality can also act against alcohol dependence – to bring sobriety and healthy relationships with God and others.

It is this spirituality which has been affirmed within Alcoholics Anonymous, and it has been affirmed in such a way as to ensure that the organisation remains accessible to people from all religious traditions and none. Indeed, although objections that Alcoholics Anonymous is 'too religious' are not infrequently encountered among those who make excuses for not attending its meetings, its members include many agnostics, and even atheists, as well as practising members of all the world's major faith traditions. Alcoholics Anonymous has been influential in the alcohol treatment field if only because of the large number of groups and members that it has accumulated worldwide. Arguably, it has done as much as any of the world's major faith traditions in terms of establishing the importance of a connection between addiction (especially alcohol addiction) and spirituality. However, Alcoholics Anonymous's concept of spirituality, which must now be understood as an almost completely secular spirituality, has flourished in a world in which interest in spirituality generally has been on the increase (Sheldrake, 2005, pp. 7–12). The spirituality of this age is very different to that of the world's historical faith traditions. It is pluralist, syncretistic, and blended with various strands of psychology and psychotherapy. However, it is clearly this interest in spirituality that has fuelled increasing numbers of scientific and medical publications on spirituality and healthcare (Cook, 2004).

Spirituality in clinical practice and recovery

What form might spiritual interventions, or spiritual components of treatment programmes, for alcohol dependence take? There are many possible answers to this question, which are as varied as answers to the broader question of what form any interventions for alcohol dependence might take. Some specific examples will be considered here. However, it is first important to note that some (perhaps many) people recover without any formal treatment, or even without any involvement in a mutual help group.

In his classic longitudinal study of the natural history of alcoholism, George Vaillant (Vaillant, 1983, pp. 190–91) found that religious involvement and Alcoholics Anonymous were sometimes reported as 'non-treatment' factors associated with finding a pathway to abstinence. In the case of 21 men achieving 'secure abstinence', 19 per cent mentioned the former, and 38 per cent the latter. However, at least five men in this study recognised 'mystical belief, prayer, and meditation' as being a 'substitute dependency'. Perhaps, then, spiritual and religious behaviours are in some way related – psychologically or otherwise – to the behaviours that are encountered in alcohol dependence? It has long been suggested that alcoholism is in fact a misguided search for God. In other words, spiritual and religious concerns lay at the heart of the psychodynamics of addiction. William James suggested that alcohol had the power to 'stimulate the mystical faculties of human nature' (James, 1985, p. 387), although he was not unaware that this was achieved at a cost:

> Sobriety diminishes, discriminates, and says no; drunkenness expands, unites, and says yes. It is in fact the great exciter of the Yes function in man. It brings its votary from the chill periphery of things to the radiant core. It makes him for the moment one with truth. Not through mere perversity do men run after it. To the poor and the unlettered it stands in the place of symphony concerts and of literature; and it is part of the deeper mystery and tragedy of life that whiffs and gleams of something that we immediately recognise as excellent should be vouchsafed to so many of us only in the fleeting earlier phases of what in its totality is so degrading a poisoning.

More recently, and in more contemporary psychological language, Jeff Sandoz has argued that alcoholic intoxication induces a god-like euphoria in which illusions of power are associated with tranquillisation of dysphoria (Sandoz, 2004, pp. 36–37). If such intuitions are correct, then one might expect that the replacement of the pathological spirituality of the alcohol dependent state with a more healthy spirituality – whether that of Alcoholics Anonymous, or a religious tradition, or of some other kind – might be therapeutic. Such an objective might form the central focus of treatment, as for example in Alcoholics Anonymous, or else it might form only one component of an overall treatment programme, as for example based on the principles of relapse prevention (Moss et al., 2007). But what form might therapy orientated towards such an objective take? Three examples of spiritually oriented therapy will be considered here: the mutual help programme of Alcoholics Anonymous, an explicitly Christian approach to working with alcohol-dependent people, and a spirituality group as a part of a comprehensive treatment programme provided within a secular medical healthcare setting.

Alcoholics Anonymous

The central principles of the programme (Alcoholics Anonymous, 1977) came to be written down as '12 Steps' which the founding members took in the course of their own recovery. These are listed in Box 22.2.

Box 22.2	The 12 Steps of Alcoholics Anonymous
Step 1	Admitted we were powerless over alcohol – that our lives had become unmanageable.
Step 2	Came to believe that a Power greater than ourselves could restore us to sanity.
Step 3	Made a decision to turn our will and our lives over to the care of God as we understood Him.
Step 4	Made a searching and fearless moral inventory of ourselves.
Step 5	Admitted to God, to ourselves and to another human being the exact nature of our wrongs.
Step 6	Were entirely ready to have God remove all these defects of character.
Step 7	Humbly asked Him to remove our shortcomings.
Step 8	Made a list of all persons we had harmed, and became willing to make amends to them all.
Step 9	Made direct amends to such people wherever possible, except when to do so would injure them or others.
Step 10	Continued to take personal inventory, and when we were wrong, promptly admitted it.
Step 11	Sought through prayer and meditation to improve our conscious contact with God as we understood Him praying only for knowledge of His will for us and the power to carry that out.
Step 12	Having had a spiritual awakening as the result of these steps we tried to carry this message to alcoholic people and to practice these principles in all our affairs.

The first three steps are concerned with a recognition that the alcoholic cannot help him or herself and that they therefore need to turn to a 'higher power', which in step 3 is explicitly referred to as God. This recognition of the need for a higher power – which may be conceived of in very non-theological terms as well as in traditional religious formulations – is fundamental to the spirituality of Alcoholics Anonymous. Steps 4 to 10 clearly reveal the Christian origins of the organisation, for they are very much concerned with confession and repentance. However, the language is of 'moral inventory', 'wrongs', 'defects' and 'shortcomings' rather than sin, and repentance is to be evidenced by a willingness to be changed, and a readiness to 'make amends'. Absolution and forgiveness are not in evidence; the importance of a desire to change and of taking of responsibility for one's own part in a recovery which God alone can bring about is the focus of concern. Steps 11 and 12 anchor the ongoing life of the recovered alcoholic in spiritual practices of prayer, meditation and reaching out to others. However, no specification is made as to what constitutes prayer or meditation. The emphasis here is on submission to God and concern for others. While Alcoholics Anonymous has become associated with a disease model of alcoholism, in fact the 12 Steps do not refer to this, but rather focus on the spiritual process of recovery. It is this process that is central, and all other matters are made subsidiary to it. Similarly, when the 12 Step philosophy is adopted by professional treatment programmes (Cook, 1988a,b) it is the spirituality of the process of recovery that is generally distinctive. The spirituality of Alcoholics Anonymous is therefore very much concerned with a re-evaluation of relationships: with self, others and God. It is expressed in non-theological language and in such a way that it neither requires acceptance of nor conflicts with the doctrines and practices of traditional religion, be that Christianity or any other faith. When it comes to God, the emphasis is on a person's own understanding of God – and therefore remains completely open to varied doctrinal possibilities while also emphasising personal experience, willingness to change, and concern for others. The spiritual transformations experienced in Alcoholics Anonymous may be sudden or gradual, although the model set in their 'Big Book' is much more of the former than the latter (Forcehimes, 2004).

Explicitly religious programmes for recovery

In contrast, explicitly religious programmes for recovery from alcohol dependence place somewhat different emphases. It would be misleading to over-generalise. Harold Koenig, in his book on faith and mental health has classified faith-based organisations that deliver mental health services into five different kinds (Koenig, 2005, pp. 161–240) and, even within a single faith tradition such as Christianity, there can be widely varying theological understandings of the nature of addictive disorders (Cook, 2006, pp. 18–19). What, then, can be said?

Koenig (Koenig, 2005, pp. 134–39) has suggested that religion has a positive part to play in mental health treatment generally, for ten reasons. These would also appear to offer a helpful framework for the present specific purpose of considering the way in which the spirituality of explicitly religious responses to alcohol dependence might be beneficial. They could be applied to religious programmes from any of the world's faith traditions. They are listed in Box 22.3 and are followed in each case by quotations from the text of Cecilia Mariz's study of pentecostalism and alcoholism among the Brazilian poor (Mariz, 1991), which provide an example of how they find expression in one particular Christian tradition's understanding of, and response to, the problem of alcoholism.

Box 22.3 **Ten reasons for the positive role of religion in mental health (Koenig, 2005) as exemplified in Mariz's study of pentecostalism and alcoholism in Brazil (Mariz, 1991)**

1. Religion promotes a positive world view

'In the Pentecostal church, the action of the Holy Spirit and the gifts of the Spirit offer a positive experience through the creation of an alternative reality without the destructive consequences associated with the abuse of alcohol. The profound sense of total wellbeing produced by conversion in the Pentecostal church helps the alcoholic to achieve initial sobriety and the supports ongoing recovery' (Mariz, 1991, p. 81).

2. Religion helps to make sense of difficult situations

'Addiction to alcohol is the work of the devil as are all other physical and psychological diseases, family conflicts, all sinful behaviour' (Mariz, 1991, p. 78).

3. Religion gives purpose and meaning

'The Pentecostal member, under the influence of the Holy Spirit, experiences a profound religious experience which creates a new province of meaning' (Mariz, 1991, p. 80).

4. Religion discourages maladaptive coping

'In the Pentecostal view, drinking alcohol is morally wrong – a sin; irrespective of the amount, the consumption of alcohol is completely condemned ... Drinking alcohol is not condoned as a legitimate way to celebrate or relax ...' (Mariz, 1991, p. 79).

5. Religion enhances social support

'The recovering alcoholic Pentecostals do not face the temptation of drinking because their fellow church members are neither allowed or encouraged to drink ... The struggle for sobriety ... is a collective struggle, a struggle which involves the entire church community' (Mariz, 1991, p. 79).

6. Religion promotes 'other-directedness'

'Both the devil and the alcohol are outside enemies, the external combat against the devil and against alcohol is a collective struggle in which all the religious community is engaged. The struggle for sobriety is not an individual or personal problem ...' (Mariz, 1991, p. 79).

7. Religion helps to release the need for control

'The devil is stronger than any individual and no one can resist his wiles without the support of God' (Mariz, 1991, p. 78).

8. Religion provides and encourages forgiveness

Surprisingly, forgiveness is not explicitly mentioned by Mariz, but it is clearly central to Pentecostal Christian doctrine, and Mariz notes that the concept of alcoholism encountered here 'places responsibility for recovery on the alcoholics but it does not attack their self-esteem or intensify their guilt' (Mariz, 1991, pp. 78–79).

9. Religion encourages thankfulness

Although thankfulness is also not explicitly mentioned, it is implicitly clear that there is much to be thankful for; see (1) above, for example.

10. Religion provides hope

'The Pentecostal church holds much hope for the poor in Brazil ...' (Mariz, 1991, p. 81).

A similar exercise could be conducted in respect of responses to alcohol dependence offered in other Christian traditions, and other world faiths. Similarly, one could identify under most (if not all) of the ten headings benefits of the 'not religious' but spiritual programme of Alcoholics Anonymous. However, while the latter shares with many explicitly religious approaches the recognition of the unmanageability of life without God, and therefore the need to turn to God for help, it differs in its refusal to address wider issues beyond the process of recovery and it embraces a diversity of personal experiences and doctrinal understandings among recovering alcoholics, rather than focusing on the shared experience and understanding of a single faith tradition. At risk of over-simplifying things, one might argue that Alcoholics Anonymous affirms a common understanding of the spirituality of recovery from addiction, while accepting the diversity of religious views. The explicitly religious approach, in contrast, affirms a common understanding of religious faith, within which the diversity of all other things is understood (including spirituality and recovery from addiction).

Spirituality in the medical healthcare setting

Both the 12-Step programme and the explicitly religious approach to recovery can be offered within medical healthcare settings. However, many medical programmes for people recovering from alcohol dependence do not espouse either a 12-step or religious philosophy. What spiritual interventions may be offered in such settings? It might be argued that no specific intervention of this kind is necessary. Outcomes from purely psychological or medical interventions compare well with the 12-step or religious approaches (Humphreys and Gifford, 2006; Project MATCH Research Group 1997, 1998) and chaplains and other religious leaders are available to those who wish to explore spiritual and religious aspects of their treatment. However, against this, it may be argued that integration of spiritual aspects of treatment with the psychological, social and medical aspects might have advantages and appears to be something that many service users appreciate. Many clergy and religious leaders are not well informed about alcohol dependence and many service users feel ashamed to approach them about their struggles in this area. Similarly, medical staff may have negative attitudes towards 12-step programmes (Day *et al.*, 2005) and antagonistic professional attitudes towards involvement in mutual help groups or faith communities are unlikely to benefit service users.

As an example of the kind of intervention that might be offered in a National Health Service programme in the UK, Jackson and Cook (2005) have provided an account of the introduction of a spirituality group into a community programme for people with drinking problems. The group, very simply, provided a space within which to explore what spirituality meant to its members, and any other relevant matters that arose from this, and was facilitated by two staff members. This had various advantages, including the following:

- It offered the possibility of re-framing struggles with drinking in terms of personal (spiritual) growth.
- It encouraged discussion in a non-defensive manner.
- It allowed discussion of issues which were not being dealt with elsewhere in treatment.
- It was complementary to other (medical, psychological and social) treatments in which service users were engaged.

Various themes emerged during the life of this group, including those of a transcendent dimension to life (or lack of it), drinking-related experiences, relationships, meaning and purpose, and (throughout) personal and shared understandings of what spirituality was all about.

Outcome research

Outcome research related specifically to the treatment of alcohol dependence is only now beginning to address spirituality as an independent or dependent variable and it would appear that this is likely to be an area of growth over coming years. Humphreys and Gifford (2006) identify only three outcome studies of spiritually oriented addiction treatment programmes with longitudinal design, comparison groups, high follow-up rates and reliable/valid measures. Of these, two are studies of alcoholism treatment, and one included treatment of both alcohol and other forms of substance misuse:

1. Taking first the study of the treatment of mixed forms of substance dependence, Humphreys and Moos (2001) studied 1774 addicted veterans treated either in a 12-step orientated programme, or else in a cognitive–behavioural orientated programme. The 12-step programmes focused on the first four steps of Alcoholics Anonymous (as above). Patients in the 12-step group showed higher rates of abstinence at follow-up at 1 year after treatment (45.7 per cent versus 36.2 per cent).

2. The largest randomised controlled trial of alcohol treatments ever conducted, known as Project MATCH, compared the efficacy of 12-step facilitation (TSF) with cognitive–behavioural and motivational enhancement therapy (Project MATCH Research Group, 1997). TSF aimed to encourage involvement in Alcoholics Anonymous and the working of the 12 steps. Outcomes between groups were comparable, with TSF clients faring as well as those in other groups, and with benefits maintained at 3-year follow-up (Project MATCH Research Group, 1998). In fact, outpatients low in psychiatric severity fared rather better in TSF.

3. Rudolf Moos and his colleagues (Moos *et al.*, 1978) studied a Salvation Army treatment programme, a half-way house and a hospital-based programme in the treatment of 'skid row' alcoholics. The spiritual components of the Salvation Army programme included attendance at Alcoholics Anonymous meetings as well as more specifically Christian counselling and services. Alcohol consumption decreased (by 57 per cent) and employment increased (by 55 per cent) in all three treatment modalities.

Various other studies suggest that spirituality may be associated with good outcome. Taking first the research on 12-step programmes, Carroll (1993) found that attendance and practice of step 11 were both correlated with purpose in life and with length of sobriety among members. White *et al.* (White *et al.*, 2001) studied people in recovery from alcohol and other drug problems who were recruited from a variety of treatment settings. They found that their measures of spirituality (the Spiritual Health Inventory, the Surrender Scale, and the Life Orientation Test) predicted both self-perception of the quality of recovery and also the number of steps of the 12-step programme completed. Poage *et al.* (Poage *et al.*, 2004) studied recovering alcoholics attending Alcoholics Anonymous and found that length of sobriety was significantly associated with their measure of spirituality (the Spirituality Assessment Scale). Kubicek and his colleagues (Kubicek *et al.*, 2002) studied 13 subjects with 6 years or more of continuous sobriety, finding that the two most commonly reported factors that helped to maintain long-term recovery (both among members and people who remitted spontaneously) were willingness to accept help from supportive people and acceptance of help from God or a 'higher power'. Zemore and Kaskutas (2004) found in 194 recovering alcoholics that longer sobriety predicted, among other things, higher levels of spirituality as measured by the Daily Spiritual Experiences scale.

However, the findings of different studies are not consistent. Brown and Peterson (1991) undertook a preliminary study of their instrument for assessing progress in recovery. They showed no correlation between spirituality and length of sobriety in two samples of subjects attending 12-step groups. Rush (2000) found no correlation between length of sobriety and spirituality as measured by the Spiritual Orientation Inventory in a study of 125 women members of Alcoholics Anonymous, although spirituality was associated both with attendance and religious involvement. Furthermore, Borman and Dixon (1998) found that spirituality measured using the Spiritual Well-Being Scale increased during treatment in people attending non-12-step outpatient programmes, as well as in those attending 12-step outpatient programmes.

Less research has been conducted on explicitly religious programmes for people with alcohol dependence. Roland and Kaskutas (2002) found that subjects reporting high attendance as well as high church attendance were more likely to report sobriety over the preceding 30 days after 1 year of treatment than those with high church attendance alone. Torres Stone and her colleagues (Stone *et al.*, 2006) studied 980 Native Americans and found that participation in traditional spirituality had a significant positive effect on alcohol cessation. (In this study, alcohol inpatient treatment did not show a significant effect on alcohol cessation, but the authors speculate that treatment settings may nonetheless have provided an environment within which traditional Native American spirituality was 'socialised'.)

Although not in the same category of research, two other studies are worth reporting here. Shuler *et al.* (Shuler *et al.*, 1994) studied 50 homeless women; they found that 48 per cent reported using prayer as a coping strategy. Significantly fewer of those who used prayer to cope reported drinking in the last 6 months (41.7 per cent versus 69.2 per cent), although history of past drinking problems was similar in each group (25.0 per cent versus 26.9 per cent). This provides a helpful reminder that spirituality is not the exclusive domain of treatment programmes.

In a very different design, Walker *et al.* (1997) conducted a pilot study of intercessory prayer as a randomised adjunct to the treatment for alcohol abuse and dependence of 40 patients admitted to a public treatment facility. No difference between groups was found in alcohol consumption during follow-up. Such a study does not touch on the primary concern of this paper – that of the spirituality of those who receive treatment – but does touch on a whole other domain of research (concerning scientific studies of prayer). However, this rather suggests that spirituality as a component of treatment for alcohol dependence, if it is to be objectively beneficial, needs to be viewed as something requiring active participation, rather than as something that is passively received from others.

What may we observe in relation to these studies overall? First, sample sizes are often small, study designs are often cross-sectional, and the instruments used for measuring spirituality vary widely (see also Cook, 2004). The need for more high-quality studies, of the kind that Humphreys and Gifford identify, is clearly great. Second, even if the findings are somewhat mixed, there is at least sufficient evidence to suggest that further research is warranted and that, perhaps, spirituality will prove to be an important independent and dependent variable in future outcome studies. Third, there would appear to be a bias towards research emanating from North America, especially that focusing on 12-step spirituality. More studies from other geographical regions, focusing on other spiritual traditions, are greatly needed. Fourth, this research is extremely unsophisticated from a theological viewpoint. Perhaps this is unsurprising, as it is published in scientific journals and has a clearly defined practical purpose in view – that of the provision of effective treatment for alcohol dependence. However, it does raise the question as to whether or not more in depth theological reflection, anchored within particular spiritual traditions, might not better inform future interdisciplinary studies.

Conclusions

Spirituality has become an important concern in academic and clinical discourse on the treatment of drinking problems for various historical and other reasons. While there is continuing debate as to exactly how spirituality should be defined, it touches on important issues that are relevant to the treatment of alcohol dependence: the relationships of the drinker with others and the world around them, their willingness (or otherwise) to recognise their need for help from resources beyond (or within) themselves, the interpretation and meaning which they place on their condition, and the relationship of their struggles with dependence to any pre-existing belief system that they may have adopted or come to own. Given also the growing body of research which suggests that spirituality may influence outcomes, this would appear to be an aspect of clinical care which is important both because it is of concern to service users and because it is associated with an emerging evidence base.

An awareness of the spirituality of Alcoholics Anonymous would appear to represent a fundamental starting point, if only because of the large numbers of alcohol-dependent people who receive help either in local Alcoholics Anonymous groups or else in a professionally led treatment programme based on 12-step principles. However, many people in treatment still have not had contact with Alcoholics Anonymous, or else come to their problems from the perspective of a particular religious tradition, and others engage with faith-based, or explicitly religious, programmes. A wider and positive awareness of the way in which alcohol-dependent people formulate, understand and struggle with the spiritual problems inherent in alcohol dependence is required.

References and further reading

Abdel-Mawgood, M., Fateem, L. and Al-Sharif, A.I. (1995). Development of a comprehensive treatment program for chemical dependency at Al Amal Hospital, Damman. *Journal of Substance Abuse Treatment,* **12**, 369–76.

Alcoholics Anonymous (1976). *Alcoholics Anonymous,* 3rd edn. New York: Alcoholics Anonymous World Services.

Alcoholics Anonymous (1977). *Twelve Steps and Twelve Traditions.* New York: Alcoholics Anonymous World Services.

Alexander, W. (1997. *Cool Water: Alcoholism, Mindfulness, and Ordinary Recovery.* Boston: Shambhala.

American Psychiatric Association (1994). *Diagnostic and Statistical Manual of Mental Disorders: DSM-IV,* 4th edn. Washington DC: American Psychiatric Association.

Barrett, M.E. (1997). *Wat Thamkrabok*: A Buddhist drug rehabilitation program in Thailand. *Substance Use and Misuse,* **32**, 435–59.

Berenson, D. (1990). A systemic view of spirituality. *Journal of Strategic and Systemic Therapies,* **9**, 59–70.

Bien, T. and Bien, B. (2002). *Mindful Recovery: A Spiritual Path to Healing from Addiction.* New York: Wiley.

Borman, P.D. and Dixon, D.N. (1998). Spirituality and the 12 steps of substance abuse recovery. *Journal of Psychology and Theology* **26**, 287–91.

Brown, H.P. and Peterson, J.H. (1991). Assessing spirituality in addiction treatment and follow-up: Development of the Brown–Peterson Recovery Progress Inventory (B-PRPI). *Alcoholism Treatment Quarterly,* **8**, 21–50.

Carroll, S. (1993). Spirituality and Purpose in Life in alcoholism recovery. *Journal of Studies on Alcohol,* **54**, 297–301.

Cook, C.C.H. (1988a). The Minnesota model in the management of drug and alcohol dependency: miracle method or myth? Part I. The philosophy and the programme. *British Journal of Addiction,* **83**, 625–34.

Cook, C.C.H. (1988b). The Minnesota model in the management of drug and alcohol dependency: miracle method or myth? Part II. Evidence and conclusions. *British Journal of Addiction,* **83**, 735–48.

Cook, C.C.H. (2004). Addiction and spirituality. *Addiction,* **99**, 539–51.

Cook, C.C.H. (2006). *Alcohol, Addiction and Christian Ethics.* Cambridge: Cambridge University Press.

Day, E., Gaston, R.L., Furlong, E., Murali, V. and Copello, A. (2005). United Kingdom substance misuse treatment workers' attitudes toward 12-step self-help groups. *Journal of Substance Abuse Treatment,* **29**, 321–27.

Dollard, J. (1983). *Toward Spirituality.* Minnesota: Hazelden.

Edwards, G. and Gross, M. (1976). Alcohol dependence: Provisional description of a clinical syndrome. *British Medical Journal* **1**,1058–61.

Fetzer Institute and National Institute on Aging Working Group (1999). *Multidimensional Measurement of Religiousness/Spirituality for Use in Health Research.* Kalamazoo: Fetzer Institute.

Forcehimes, A.A. (2004). *De profundis*: Spiritual transformations in Alcoholics Anonymous. *Journal of Clinical Psychology,* **60**, 503–17.

Garrett, M.T. and Carroll, J.J. (2000). Mending the broken circle: Treatment of substance dependence among Native Americans. *Journal of Counseling and Development,* **78**, 379–88.

Hill, P.C. and Hood, R.W. (eds) (1999). *Measures of Religiosity.* Birmingham AL: Religious Education Press.

Honderich, T. (ed.) (1995). *The Oxford Companion to Philosophy.* Oxford: Oxford University Press.

Humphreys, K. and Gifford, E. (2006). Religion, spirituality and the troublesome use of substances. In: W.R. Miller and K. Carroll (eds), *Rethinking Substance Abuse: What the Science Shows and What We Should Do About It.* New York: Guilford, pp. 257–74.

Humphreys, K. and Moos, R. (2001). Can encouraging substance abuse patients to participate in self-help groups reduce demand for health care? A quasi-experimental study. *Alcoholism: Clinical and Experimental Research,* **25**, 711–16.

Jackson, P. and Cook, C.C.H. (2005). Introduction of a spirituality group in a community service for people with drinking problems. *Journal of Substance Use,* **10**, 375–83.

James, W. (1985). *The Varieties of Religious Experience.* Harmondsworth: Penguin Classics.

Koenig, H.G. (2005). *Faith and Mental Health.* Philadelphia: Templeton Foundation Press.

Kubicek, K.R., Morgan, O.J. and Morrison, N.C. (2002). Pathways to long-term recovery from alcohol dependence: Comparison of spontaneous remitters and AA members. *Alcoholism Treatment Quarterly,* **20**, 71–81.

Kurtz, E. (1991. *Not-God: A History of Alcoholics Anonymous.* Center City: Hazelden.

Mariz, C.L. (1991). Pentecostalism and alcoholism among the Brazilian poor. *Alcoholism Treatment Quarterly,* **8**, 75–82.

May, G.G. (2000). The nature of addiction. *The Way,* **40**, 303–13.

Mental Health Foundation (2002). *Taken Seriously: The Somerset Spirituality Project.* London: Mental Health Foundation.

Mercadante, L.A. (1996). *Victims and Sinners.* Louisville: Westminster John Knox Press.

Miller, W.R. (1998). Researching the spiritual dimensions of alcohol and other drug problems. *Addiction,* **93**, 979–90.

Moos, R.H., Mehren, B. and Moos, B. (1978). Evaluation of a Salvation Army alcoholism treatment program. *Journal of Studies on Alcohol,* **39**, 1267–75.

Morgan, O.J. (2002). Alcohol problems, alcoholism and spirituality: An overview of measurement and scales. *Alcoholism Treatment Quarterly,* **20**, 1–18.

Moss, R., Cook, C.C.H. and Sandoz, J. (2007). Maintenance and relapse prevention. In: D. Capuzzi and M.D. Stauffer (eds), *Foundations of Addictions Counseling.* Boston: Pearson, pp. 268–282.

Poage, E.D., Ketzenberger, K.E. and Olson, J. (2004). Spirituality, contentment, and stress in recovering alcoholics. *Addictive Behaviors,* **29**, 1857–62.

Powell, A. and Cook, C.C.H. (2006). Spirituality and Psychiatry Special Interest Group of the Royal College of Psychiatrists. *Reaching the Spirit: Social Perspectives Network Study Day.* Paper 9, pp. 34–35.

Project MATCH Research Group (1997). Matching alcoholism treatments to client heterogeneity: Project MATCH post-treatment drinking outcomes. *Journal of Studies on Alcohol,* **58**, 7–29.

Project MATCH Research Group (1998). Matching alcoholism treatments to client heterogeneity: Project MATCH three-year drinking outcomes. *Alcoholism: Clinical and Experimental Research* **22**, 1300–11.

Ringwald, C.D. (2002). *The Soul of Recovery: Uncovering the Spiritual Dimension in the Treatment of Addictions.* Oxford: Oxford University Press.

Roland, E.J. and Kaskutas, L.A. (2002). Alcoholics Anonymous and church involvement as predictors of sobriety among three ethnic treatment populations. *Alcoholism Treatment Quarterly,* **20**, 61–77.

Rush, B. (1943). An inquiry into the effects of ardent spirits on the human body and mind with an account of the means of preventing and of the remedies for curing them. *Quarterly Journal of Studies on Alcohol,* **4**, 325–41.

Rush, M.M. (2000). Power, spirituality, and time from a feminist perspective: Correlates of sobriety in a study of sober female participants in Alcoholics Anonymous. *Journal of the American Psychiatric Nurses Association,* **6**, 196–202.

Sandoz, J. (2004). *Exploring the Spiritual Experience in the 12-step program of Alcoholics Anonymous: Spiritus Contra Spiritum* (Studies in Religion and Society, 67). Lewiston: Edwin Mellen Press.

Sheldrake, P. (ed.) (2005). *The New SCM Dictionary of Christian Spirituality.* London: SCM.

Shuler, P.A., Gelberg, L. and Brown, M. (1994). The effects of spiritual/religious practices on psychological well-being among inner city homeless women. *Nurse Practitioner Forum,* **5**, 106–13.

Stone, R.A., Whitbeck, L.B., Chen, X., Johnson, K. and Olson, D.M. (2006). Traditional practices, traditional spirituality, and alcohol cessation among American Indians. *Journal of Studies on Alcohol,* **67**, 236–44.

Trotter, T. (1988). *An Essay, Medical, Philosophical, and Chemical On Drunkenness and Its Effects On the Human Body.* London: Routledge.

Vaillant, G.E. (1983). *The Natural History of Alcoholism: Causes, Patterns, and Paths to Recovery.* Cambridge MA: Harvard.

Walker, S.R., Tonigan, J.S., Miller, W.R., Comer, S. and Kahlich, L. (1997). Intercessory prayer in the treatment of alcohol abuse and dependence: A pilot investigation. *Alternative Therapies in Health and Medicine,* **3**, 79–86.

White, J.M., Wampler, R.S. and Fischer, J.L. (2001). Indicators of spiritual development in recovery from alcohol and other drug problems. *Alcoholism Treatment Quarterly,* **19**, 19–35.

World Health Organization (1992). *The ICD-10 Classification of Mental and Behavioural Disorders: Clinical Descriptions and Diagnostic Guidelines.* Geneva: World Health Organization.

Zemore, S.E. and Kaskutas, L.A. (2004). Helping, spirituality and Alcoholics Anonymous in recovery. *Journal of Studies on Alcohol,* **65**, 383–91.

▪ Part Five ▪

Clients with Complex Needs

23 Alcohol and social exclusion

Adrian B. Bonner

Exclusion from society is experienced when a person has problems with one of a number of factors relating to health, wealth, accommodation and relationships with family and friends. Perhaps the most important needs contributing to a sense of inclusion are feeling useful, having a role and being treated with respect. Social exclusion is a wide-ranging concept used to describe a situation that might occur at any period during, or in some unfortunate people, throughout the whole life cycle. The origins of later life health and social problems are laid down prenatally, and childhood deprivation and abuse are frequently cited by excluded and homeless people as major components of their problematic life styles. Moving from childhood into adolescence provides many challenges and psychosocial changes, which can be more difficult for some people than others (Bonner, 2006).

People who are homeless have worse physical health and more severe alcohol problems than the general population. These problems significantly contribute to the proportion of deaths in homeless people. Additionally, alcohol abuse is a major risk factor for arrest among homeless people. And homeless alcohol abusers are more likely to have comorbid psychiatric problems (Bonner, 2006). Alcohol and drug use may increase the risk of criminal activity (activities like drug dealing, theft and prostitution) to maintain intake levels. The linkage between alcohol and drug use and homelessness includes financing an addictive habit, resulting in financial priority being directed to obtaining these substances. Association with other homeless people may increase the chances of obtaining drugs. These strategies to cope with a very challenging lifestyle are directly related, or share common causes, such as social disadvantage or exposure to a criminal subculture. Alcoholics frequently report having been brought up in dysfunctional families, and display conduct problems in younger age, drop out of school and possess limited occupational skills (Tyler *et al.*, 2004).

Developmental influences

The associated problems of social exclusion and alcohol and drug misuse are most likely to originate in the early years of childhood and may be exacerbated by relationship issues and developmental problems of self-image and self identity in the adolescent years. Approximately

30 per cent of currently homeless adults have multiple experiences of homelessness during their childhood (Bonner, 2007). Homeless children are confronted by serious threats to their ability to succeed and their future well-being. Of particular concern are health problems, hunger, poor nutrition, developmental delays, anxiety, depression, behavioural problems and educational under-achievement. The needs of these children have been identified in a number of studies directed at informing public policy.

Several factors have been identified that may mediate the observed outcomes; these include inadequate housing conditions, instability in accommodation, inadequate services and barriers to accessing available health and social care services (Rafferty and Shinn, 1991). The increasing housing shortage in the UK is attributed to the rise in single parent households. Lone mothers are increasing in number as marital stability declines (British National Survey of Psychiatric Morbidity). Targosz (2003) found that lone mothers had prevalence rates of depressive episodes of 7 per cent, approximately three times higher than any other group, with increased frequencies of less severe mixed anxiety/depression. Homelessness has been associated with levels of stress beyond the normal strain of living in poverty. For mothers who are homeless, support from their social networks may provide a buffer from some of the stresses associated with being homeless. The problems of a lone parent and her offspring are exacerbated when the mother is separated from her newborn baby. As might be expected, separating a mother and her baby during the first week of the child's life involves much emotional strain for the mother. Women's perceptions of despair, powerlessness, homelessness, disappointment and lack of control include emotional instability, threat, guilt and insecurity (Nystrom and Axelsson, 2002). These formative influences of stress-related and intrinsic factors including genetic vulnerability, mediate the process of child development and point to the greater vulnerability of some children for later life ill health, psychopathology and consequential problematic alcohol and drug use.

This scenario is supported by the work of Kalin and colleagues (1991) who explored the link between fearfulness in children and a high risk for later emotional distress with reference to naturally occurring systems in the brain. Opiate-using neural pathways in the brains of primates appear to regulate affiliative behaviours (e.g. stress induced by separation from the mother), and benzodiazepines seem to be primarily involved in response to direct threats such as those from predators. A reduction of activity in opiate-sensitive systems caused by mother–infant separation enables motor systems in the brain to elicit alarm signals and communication aimed at restoring the child–mother bond. Childhood events that involve disruption of this critical relationship have, for some time, been linked to increased vulnerability to later life alcohol and drug dependence. Additionally, poor parenting and economic deprivation are associated with teenage antisocial behaviour and adult social dysfunction. Farrington (1993) studied 411 males, in London, aged between 8 and 32 years. He found that childhood nervousness, antisocial family background and hyperactivity–impulsivity attention deficit were the most significant predictors of teenage antisocial behaviour and adult social dysfunction, including drinking behaviour.

Leaving home to find work, to study or to join the armed forces can be a very lonely and challenging experience, and the development of a positive social network is a critical stage of growing up. New recruits to the armed forces, in particular the infantry regiments, are predominantly from disadvantaged family backgrounds. In the initial training phases and in operational situations stress levels are high, and the availability of large quantities of alcohol leading to intensive binge drinking between operational duties, linked with family-related problems, is managed, to some extent, within the institutional setting. When the soldier leaves the services after contracts of 3, 6 or 12 years the lack of institutional support, with a possible underlying alcohol problem, and the experiences of warfare, there is a considerably increased possibility of exclusion from society. This is evidenced by ex-service personnel constituting approximately 10–20 per cent of Salvation Army homeless hostel populations (Luscombe and Brook, 2005). Some ex-servicemen have particular problems of post-traumatic stress disorder (PTSD) and other mental health problems comorbid with alcohol dependency.

Alcohol, health and social exclusion

The homeless population in the UK is increasing and consists of three main subpopulations:

- rough sleepers and hostel dwellers, mainly the single homeless
- homeless families
- people who involuntarily live in shared or inadequate accommodation.

While some data is available relating to accommodation and health status of the first two groups, information on the third group is sparse. Ill health is often considered to be a consequence of social exclusion, but it can also be the cause. Chronic illness can result in social exclusion. Diseases such as rheumatism, multiple sclerosis, pulmonary emphysema and the duration of these primary diseases and comorbidity have all been associated with increased social exclusion and alcohol problems. The extent of exclusion is related to educational level, whether or not the person was employed or engaged in volunteer work, and whether or not he or she lived together with a partner. Bosma *et al.* (2005) measured social exclusion by means of the 'Autonomy outside the home' subscale of the 'Impact on participation and autonomy' questionnaire. This study of social exclusion of chronically ill patients showed that exclusion was significantly linked to income and the inability of the people to organise their own care. Social status and the level of communication between the health-service providers are important components of the biopsychosocial approach to health care. The Royal College of Physicians (Connelly and Crown, 1994) reported that physical, mental health and obstetric problems are significantly higher in homeless families and in people in inadequate accommodation. These problems also have been found in single homeless people. All these groups have problems in accessing appropriate healthcare services. The Royal College of Physicians calls for a coordinated approach to community care and housing policy to prevent vulnerable people from becoming homeless. Particular attention is drawn to the need for primary care, accident and emergency services, community care and discharge services to become more aware and coordinated in their response to the homeless.

Health inequalities in the community have been found to be highly correlated with social class and poverty. Communities in Europe were still characterised by the existence of social classes and social stratification; a predominance of high levels of unemployment and precarious jobs were found in the lower classes; where poverty was endemic, social problems were much worse than the EU average (Benach and Amable, 2004). Poverty and health status are inversely correlated. In Europe 15 per cent of people live in poverty; however estimates for the number of elderly people who live in poverty are much greater (Del Rey Calero, 2004). Social capital is the social structure that promotes the activities of people, stimulates production and allows for success. Social exclusion does not allow people to participate in society and poverty results in a wide range of basic and unmet needs relating to food, health and independence, and leads to reduced social cohesion. Macintyre and Ellaway (2000) found that health problems were more common in deprived areas in Scotland, where poorer mental health in the community was associated with low levels of social cohesion.

It is generally acknowledged that social cohesion will be improved by the promotion of social participation, empowerment, self-esteem and personal achievement. However, a very significant factor in social participation is the involvement of community members in both voluntary and paid work.

Health, employment and community development

In the UK, social deprivation and concurrent health problems are often found in regions of economic decline, due to the reduced availability of jobs. Some of the most deprived areas are found in Scotland and Wales (Pritchard and Puzey, 2004) where large-scale industrial areas have been run down, with resulting high levels of unemployment in local areas. In these areas increased numbers of people become homeless, with the resulting health needs related to poor living conditions. Links between accommodation problems and mental and physical ill health are well established. Regrettably a vicious cycle of unemployment, homelessness and poor health is found in these economically deprived areas. Communities in these areas are characterised by a high drinking culture. There have been many studies on these individuals and the psychological consequences of unemployment; consistent relationships are found between unemployment and minor psychological disorders. A more limited number of studies have included the pathological effects of unemployment but there is some evidence that increased physiological illness does occur, especially among unemployed girls.

Unemployment appears to be a risk indicator for increasing alcohol consumption, particularly in young men, with increased tobacco consumption and increased use of illicit drugs. These negative health behaviours result in deteriorating health giving mortality rates that are significantly higher among unemployed young men and women, especially in suicides and accidents. Social support and high employment rates have been found to have a protective effect on health (Hammarstrom, 1994).

Employment, mental health and problematic alcohol and drug use

The Department of Works and Pensions reported that 35 per cent of the population are unable to work due to 'mental health issues'. Other issues related to poisoning, accidents mitigating against engaging in employment also have a mental health dimension. These issues are currently being addressed by the development of Department of Works and Pensions/NHS Condition Management Programmes (Barnes and Hudson, 2006). High rates of mental health and substance use disorder have been reported in the homeless. A study of homeless men newly arriving at New York shelters found one-third to be in extreme distress, with 7 per cent reporting suicidal thoughts. In this study, 17 per cent of homeless men had a definite or probable history of psychosis, while a history of alcohol or drug abuse was evident in 58 per cent. A longitudinal study conducted between 1980 and 2000 in three homeless populations in St. Louis (Missouri) reported a prevalence rate of psychiatric disorders of 88 per cent in males and 69 per cent in females, and alcohol use disorder of 84 per cent in males and 54 per cent in females in 2000 (North *et al.*, 2004). Rates of bipolar and panic disorder, major depression, and substance use disorder were found to have increased considerably during the last 20 years. In a pilot study of mental health issues in Salvation Army Homeless centres in the UK, high levels of previous suicide attempts have been found in men (43 per cent) and high levels in women (45 per cent) (Bonner, 2007). These levels are comparable with those found in offending institutions (Taylor, 2007).

For those who need help in integration into the community, addressing their basic skills for employment, their criminal behaviour or problematic alcohol or drug misuse is important. A range of learning strategies and psychosocial interventions can be helpful. Such interventions should take account of the developmental issues in the person's life cycle, which will influence their response to the intervention. This chapter provides a developmental perspective on inclusion in or exclusion from social groups. The UK Office of Population Censuses and Surveys (OPCS) (Gill *et al.*, 1996) collected data from a range of people who did not have adequate shelter, including residents in hostels and people sleeping rough. The results of this survey showed that around 38 per cent of hostel residents displayed symptoms of neurotic disorders and 8 per cent displayed psychotic symptoms. Of hostel residents, 16 per cent were found to be alcohol dependent and 6 per cent were dependent on other drugs. Previous surveys undertaken by the Centre for Housing Policy and the 1991 British Household Survey reviewed by Bines (1994) highlighted the health problems of homeless people. These surveys found that mental health problems were higher among single homeless people compared to the general population: 28 per cent of hostel and bed-and-breakfast residents reported mental health problems; 36 per cent of day-centre users; and 40 per cent of soup-run users; this compares with just 5 per cent of the general population. In accounting for the effects of age and gender, mental health problems were found to be eight times higher among people in hostels and bed-and-breakfast hotels and eleven times higher among people sleeping rough compared to the general population. A high proportion of single homeless people also reported heavy drinking or alcohol-related problems and many homeless people had multiple issues of mental health and alcohol-related problems (30 per cent of those in hostels and almost 50 per cent of those sleeping rough). Physical health problems were also reported to be more prevalent in the single homeless population.

The link between post-traumatic stress disorder and alcohol misuse has been explained by the self-medication hypothesis (Khantzian, 1990). Early substance misuse increases the likelihood of exposure to potentially traumatising events, and hence the likelihood of developing post-traumatic stress disorder. People who begin using alcohol at an early stage are at particular risk because they have relied on alcohol as a way of combating stress and failed to develop more effective stress-reduction strategies. There is a high association between post-traumatic stress disorder and alcohol misuse in this group, associated with higher incidence of childhood physical and sexual abuse. A history of childhood sexual abuse has been shown to increase the risk of later alcohol problems by a factor of three (Winfield, 1990). Women are at a greater risk of developing post-traumatic stress disorder following dramatic events if they had early experiences of physical and sexual abuse (Breslau *et al.*, 1999). Farley and Barkan (1998) interviewed 130 women working as prostitutes in San Francisco. They found that 50 per cent had been sexually assaulted as children and 49 per cent reported being physically assaulted as children. As adults working as prostitutes, 82 per cent had been physically assaulted, 83 per cent had been threatened with a weapon, 68 per cent had been raped, and 84 per cent reported current or past homelessness. Of the 130 interviewed, 68 per cent met DSM-III-R criteria for a diagnosis of post-traumatic stress disorder. Around 88 per cent stated that they wanted to leave prostitution.

In a population of 600 homeless men and 300 homeless women in St Louis, the onset of post-traumatic stress disorder had preceded the onset of homelessness. The disorder was estimated using a revised Diagnostic Interview Schedule that includes a module for assessment of post-traumatic stress disorder. In both sexes, childhood histories of abuse and family fighting were predictive of both traumatic events and post-traumatic stress disorder. Symptomology of the disorder appeared long before the onset of homelessness (North and Smith, 1992). In a later report, the same authors highlighted the role of substance misuse and major depression in the episodes of violence in the lives of those diagnosed with the disorder. The violence was often received through victimisation and was expressed by specific violent traumatic events. The majority of men – and a substantial proportion of women – also had a history of physically aggressive behaviours, often beginning in childhood. These studies reflect the level of violence in the lives of the homeless, a major risk factor experienced by the homeless (North *et al.*, 1994).

War veterans are frequently identified in homeless populations, or presenting as socially excluded people in community homeless services. A significant number of war veterans have significant alcohol abuse problems and associated post-traumatic stress disorder as a result of experience in war situations or because of traumatic events occurring before they joined the armed services. Vulnerability to and the severity of post-traumatic stress disorder have been linked to childhood experiences underlying mental instability and social exclusion (Kasprow and Rosenheck, 2000). Post-combat stress has a significant impact on quality of life (Clark and Kirisci, 1996) and it has been estimated that more than 50 per cent of people suffering from post-traumatic stress disorder have drinking problems that relate to pre-war and combat experiences (Gruden *et al.*, 1999). Stress can result in long-term damage to specific brain areas such as the hippocampus, the area involved in learning and memory, with associated memory deficits. In combat veterans, the size of the hippocampus has been shown to correlate with deficits in verbal memory on neuropsychological testing (Bremner, 1999). These structural problems are accompanied by functional problems in information processing that relate to specific brain neurochemical systems, particularly those involving the neuromodulator serotonin (5-hydroxytryptamine; 5-HT). An understanding of these mechanisms in the prefrontal cortex provides an explanation for the link between post-traumatic stress disorder and alcohol abuse (Bonin *et al.*, 2000).

Nutrition and the homeless

Only a few studies have considered the nutritional status of socially excluded people. These have mainly focused on the street homeless, paying less attention to other groups of homeless people and those who are socially marginalised. A UK Government report in 2004 (Office of the Deputy Prime Minister, 2004) reported that 95,060 households were homeless and living in temporary accommodation including hostels, women's refuges, bed and breakfast hotels and other forms of temporary housing. However it has been estimated that there are as many as two million 'unofficial homeless' in the UK.

The lack of nutritional studies in this significant group of people in the UK is partly due to the transient and heterogeneous nature of socially marginalised people and also to the lack of funding for such work. The observable tip of this demographic iceberg can be seen on the streets – attendance at day centres and soup runs (Carillo *et al.*, 1990). However engaging with these people is difficult and obtaining valid information about their nutritional status is virtually impossible. This heterogeneous group consists of people who have been recently made homeless and long-term homeless people presenting with a range of mental health and substance abuse problems. An example in the literature where 'the homeless' was regarded – inappropriately – as a homogeneous group is Luder *et al.* (1989) in the US. Luder and colleagues collected nutritional data from users of two drop-in centres, bed-and-breakfast accommodation and two long-term accommodation units for previously homeless and psychiatrically ill people. The data were aggregated and the whole data set was analysed as one homogeneous group, preventing any investigation of the many confounding factors likely to affect the link between nutrition and successful rehabilitation.

Homeless people obtain food from community and voluntary-funded shelters, fast-food restaurants, delicatessens and refuse bins. In a survey of the adequacy of their dietary intake, namely the quality of shelter meals, Luder (1990) measured a range of objective clinical parameters of nutritional status in a heterogeneous group of urban homeless people. The group comprised mentally ill persons, alcohol users and illicit drug users and temporarily unemployed persons. Although 90 per cent in this study reported that they obtained enough to eat, dietary adequacy scores based on the basic four food groups were low, indicating that the quality of their diets was inadequate. Shelter meals and diet records showed high levels of saturated fat and cholesterol. Serum cholesterol levels over the desirable limit of 5.17 mmol/L (200 mg) were observed in 79 subjects (82 per cent). In addition to a prevalence of hypertension and obesity (observed in 37 subjects; 39 per cent) these homeless people were at high risk for developing or worsening of cardiovascular disease. The study concluded that homeless people obtaining meals at shelters are getting enough to eat, but the shelter meals should be modified to meet the nutritional needs and dietary prescriptions of the large number of clients suffering from various health disorders.

Homeless women

Pregnant homeless women present a number of challenges to healthcare and social care providers. They are at risk of a variety of illnesses that could affect their pregnancies, including sexually transmitted diseases and substance abuse. Poor access to health care, inadequate prenatal care, poor nutrition and poor housing cause these women to suffer poor birth outcomes. They are more likely to deliver low birthweight infants and have higher rates of infant mortality. This heterogeneous group often includes pregnant adolescents and women in homeless families (Beal and Redlener, 1995).

Excessive alcohol intake can result in reduced nutritional status, whereby calorific needs are derived mainly from this source. This may cause impaired folic acid metabolism and thus megaloblastic anaemia. Other drugs (such as barbiturates, including anticonvulsant and antipsychotic medications) cause malnutrition. A combination of primary and secondary factors combine in a complex way to provide a wide range of individual vulnerabilities. Frequently these factors are interrelated; for example, elderly people who experience limited mobility, loneliness, social isolation and depression are particularly vulnerable to malnutrition. Physical signs of nutritional deficiency may or may not be linked to some underlying disease process. A person's general and physical appearance, e.g. being excessively underweight or overweight, may indicate obesity or starvation, while muscle wasting or tenderness suggests thiamine deficiency or lack of protein. Skeletal deformities point to vitamin D deficiency, whereas depletion of vitamins C, K or A could account for bruised or dry, rough, inflamed skin. Thiamine deficiency or other vitamin B complexes might also be expressed as sensory losses, detected by an examination of the central nervous system.

Alcohol and nutrition

There is substantial evidence that Wernicke's encephalopathy is due to thiamine deficiency, the clinical features of which include diplopia and nystagmus, progressing to ophthalmoplegia and the cognitive changes of Korsakoff's psychosis, which include loss of memory, disorientation, confabulation and hallucinations. In the UK, US, Australia and other parts of the western world this progressive condition is associated with alcohol abuse. However, Wernicke's encephalopathy has also been described in elderly people with accidental hypothermia (Philip and Smith, 1973). Thiamine deficiency associated with confusional states in elderly orthopaedic patients has been reported (Older and Dickerson, 1982). In a study of 107 homeless men in Sydney, Darnton-Hill and Truswell (1990) concluded that the incidence and prevalence of Wernicke–Korsakoff syndrome in Australia may be the highest in the world. In their study a high prevalence of signs consistent with thiamine deficiency were found. Of their subjects, 24 per cent showed three or more signs of Wernicke–Korsakoff syndrome (ophthalmoplegia, nystagmus, ataxia, peripheral neuropathy and global confusion). These homeless men showed a high prevalence of dietary, biochemical and clinical features indicative of subclinical or early clinical thiamine deficiency. About half of the sample reported taking vitamin supplements (with varying duration and regularity), usually with a regimen consisting of thiamine, vitamin C, folic acid and a multivitamin B complex capsule. In this cross-sectional study, little effect was seen on clinical health between those reporting taking vitamin supplementation and those not doing so. However, biochemical measurements showed significant differences. The number of men classified as deficient were about 20 per cent more than those who reported not taking vitamins. On the basis of biochemically assayed vitamin status, the supplemented group had better health outcomes.

Chronic alcohol problems are one major cause of malnutrition in countries in the northern hemisphere. Nutritional status of chronic problematic alcohol users is not as severe as thought previously, however it should be anticipated that at-risk groups including the socially excluded and the elderly might not receive nutrition adequate for maintaining physiological homeostasis. Early studies reported grossly deficient nutrition in people with poor dietary intake and with alcohol-related diseases, in particular liver dysfunction. More recent studies of problem alcohol users without major complicating diseases have reported mean daily intakes of carbohydrates, proteins and fats that are similar to those of control populations. However, people from lower socioeconomic classes and those with alcohol-related disease do have significantly lower calorific intakes; in these cases alcohol may be a secondary cause of malnutrition. Mendenhall *et al.* (1986) concluded that 100 per cent of patients with alcoholic hepatitis and 60 per cent of chronic alcoholics with cirrhosis were malnourished. Treating malnutrition in people with alcohol dependency is essential before starting a programme of recovery and rehabilitation. However, this is complicated by linked problems of liver disease and neurological disorders.

The percentage of chronic alcoholics with a reduction in essential nutrients including B1, B2, B6, A, C, and E has been reported from 6 to 80 per cent). Cook and colleagues (Cook *et al.*, 1991) analysed 20 heavy drinkers admitted to hospital for detoxification, and found that only serum levels of vitamin E were significantly reduced compared with controls. Sgourus *et al.* (2004) found that 53.4 per cent of patients admitted to a community substance misuse department for detoxification in Stoke-on-Trent (UK) were deficient in vitamin B1 before treatment, in contrast to only 13.8 per cent of patients classified as 'underweight' on the basis of having a body mass index (BMI) of less than 20. The normal range for BMI is 20–24.

Vitamin B1 concentration has been found to be lower in alcoholic women than in alcoholic men (Mancinelli *et al.*, 2005). This observation was reflected in liver function tests that showed strikingly significant and severe problems that were considerably greater in women than in men. In this study, women started drinking heavily later but for a shorter time than men, yet more severe damage occurred in the women – confirming the so-called 'telescoping effect'. This highlights the need for prevention programmes that especially target women, paying particular attention to nutritional status, because alcohol abuse and nutritional deficits appear to have a detrimental effect on the health of women and their children. Special consideration should be paid to alcohol and diet in pregnancy in view of the well-known fetal alcohol spectrum disorder (FASD) and perhaps less-pronounced developmental effects.

Health services for the homeless and socially excluded

The *Black Report* on inequalities in health (Department of Health and Social Security, 1980) suggested a number of recommendations to reduce social class inequalities, including improving housing conditions and increasing child benefits. No action was taken to implement the *Black Report*. However, the spread of HIV/AIDS led to an increasing community focus that aimed to encourage people to change their behaviours and lifestyles. The White Paper (Department of Health, 1992) set targets for health improvement in coronary heart disease and stroke, cancer, mental health, HIV/AIDS and sexual health and accidents.

During recent years a number of significant policy developments are having, and will have, an impact on homeless and socially excluded people. *The Health of the Nation* (Department of Health, 1992) promoted a fairly narrow biomedical approach that did not particularly address the needs of the homeless, who were already seen as undeserving and were held responsible for their own health problems. In *Our Healthier Nation* (Department of Health, 1998) the key aim was to 'improve health of the population as a whole by increasing the length of people's lives and the number of years people spend free of disease'. In 2005 the life expectancy of 'rough sleepers' was still only 42 years, compared with the general population who live to an average age of 80 years. The Acheson Report (Stationery Office, 1998) noted that health inequalities had increased since the Black Report. In addition to responding to this, in *Our Healthier Nation* the UK Government focused action on tobacco in a white paper *Smoking Kills: A White Paper on Tobacco* (Department of Health, 1998) and a strategic planning process that addressed problematic drug use in the community.

Anti-substance-misuse strategies

Substance misuse is a major contributing factor in homelessness and social exclusion. Although consumption of alcohol and other drugs presents significant threats to health, there has been an increasing tendency to deal with these issues within a criminal justice agenda. The current UK Government's concern with antisocial behaviour is linked with the evolving strategies to address problematic alcohol and drug use in the community.

The first joined-up approach was initiated in 1995 by the appointment of a US-styled national anti-drugs coordinator (or 'Drugs Czar'). Keith Hellawell's task was to coordinate anti-drug-related activities across government departments, by means of a number of targets as set out in the 10-year strategy *Tackling Drugs Together* in 1995. This strategy was relaunched in 1998 with the publication of *Tackling Drugs: To Build a Better Britain* (The Stationery Office, 1998). This was updated in 2002 (*Tackling Drugs: Updated Strategy*).

The initial strategies in the 1980s focused on helping young people to resist drug misuse, and protecting communities from drug-related antisocial and criminal behaviour. They also targeted treatment of people with drug problems to enable them to overcome their problems and live healthy, crime-free lives. Availability was also targeted, by stifling illegal drugs on our streets. The updated strategy (Department of Health, 2002) used a more robust approach to class A drugs, placing more emphasis on education, prevention, enforcement and treatment. A measure of the Government's concern over drug misuse in the community was shown by the increasing budget allocated for these initiatives. The UK Government spends £1.5 billion annually on tackling drugs. The strategy initiated by joint action between the Home Office and the Department of Health is presently managed by the Criminal Justice Intervention Programme (CJIP) and the National Treatment Agency (NTA). The NTA is a Special Health Authority which is empowered to manage the delivery of the treatment services in England. By means of regional management teams, it works with the Drugs Prevention Advisory Service (DPAS), which is integrated into regional government offices. The NTA and DPAS are responsible for the development and quality control of services and for the workforce delivering treatment services. Despite these well-funded approaches for tackling the drug problems, the National Alcohol Strategy is still in an early stage and appears to lack political motivation, as in the case of the UK Drugs Strategy. This is regrettable in view of the potential harm likely to be caused to young people who engage in the high levels of drinking seen today.

Conclusions

Homelessness is associated with social exclusion, with negative educational experiences and outcomes, and with economic deprivation, as well as an array of physical and mental health consequences. The impact of being homeless on psychopathology, social identity and connectedness with a community not only has negative consequences for the individual but also for society. Alcohol misuse is common in these vulnerable people, many of whom are disengaged from employment and other dimensions of society. Antisocial behaviour associated with alcohol and misuse of other drugs increases their isolation from mainstream society, which intensifies their mental ill health, and leads to severe and enduring mental problems – and perpetuation of such problems.

References and further reading

Barnes H., and Hudson, M. (2006). *Pathways to Work: Qualitative research on the Condition Management Programme. Research Report No. 346*. London: Department of Work and Pensions.

Beal, A.C. and Redlener, I. (1995). Enhancing perinatal outcome in homeless women: the challenge of providing comprehensive health care. *Seminars in Perinatology*, **19**(4), 307–13.

Benach, J. and Amable, M. (2004). Social classes and poverty. *Gaceta Sanitaria*, **18**(Suppl.1), 16–23.

Bines, W. (1994). *The Health of Single Homeless People. Centre for Housing Policy Discussion Paper 9*. York: Joseph Rowntree Foundation.

Bonin, M.F., Norton, G.R., Asmundson, G.J., Dicurzio, S. and Pidlubney, S. (2000). Drinking away the hurt: the nature and prevalence of PTSD in substance abuse patients attending a community-based treatment program. *Journal of Behavior Therapy and Experimental Psychiatry*, **31**(1), 55–66.

Bonner, A.B. (2006). *Social Exclusion and the Way Out: An Individual and Community Response to Human Social Dysfunction*. Chichester: John Wiley.

Bonner, A.B. (2007). *Offending behaviour and mental health in socially excluded populations: A UK wide study of clients using Salvation Army Homeless Services*. Working Together: Interdisciplinarity in Forensic Mental Health, Montreal, Canada. International Association of Forensic Mental Health Services.

Bosma, H., Diederiks, J.P., van Santen, H.M. and van Eijk, J.T. (2005). More social exclusion of chronically ill patients with lower incomes. *Nederlans Tijdschrift Geneeskundd*, **149**(34), 1898–1902.

Bremner, J.D. (1999). Does stress damage the brain? *Biological Psychiatry*, **45**(7), 797–805.

Breslau, N., Chilcoat, H.D., Kessler, R.C. and Davis, Q.C. (1999). Previous exposure to trauma and PTSD effects of subsequent trauma: results from the Detroit Area Survey of Trauma. *American Journal of Psychiatry*, **156**(6), 902–07.

Carillo, T.E., Gilbride J.A. and Chan, M.M. (1990). Soup kitchen meals: an observation and nutrient analysis. *Journal of the American Dietetic Association*, **90**(7), 989–91.

Clark, D.B. and Kirisci, L. (1996). Posttraumatic stress disorder, depression, alcohol use disorders and quality of life in adolescents. *Anxiety*, **2**(5), 226–33.

Connelly, J. and Crown, J. (1994). *Homelessness and Ill Health: Report of a Working Party of the Royal College of Physicians*. London: Royal College of Physicians.

Cook, C.C.H., Walden, R.J., Graham, B.R., Gillham, C., Davies, S. and Prichard, B.N.C. (1991). Trace element and vitamin deficiency in alcoholic and control subjects. *Alcohol and Alcoholism*, **26**(5–6), 541–48.

Darnton-Hill, I. and Truswell, A.S. (1990). Thiamine status of a sample of homeless clinic attenders in Sydney. *Medical Journal of Australia*, **152**(1), 5–9.

Del Rey Calero, J. (2004). Poverty, social exclusion, social capital and health. *Annals of Real Academia Nacional de Medinicina (Madrid)*, **121**(1), 57–72.

Department of Health (1992). *The Health of the Nation*. London: The Stationery Office.

Department of Health (1998). *Our Healthier Nation*. London: The Stationery Office.

Department of Health and Social Security (1980). *Inequalities in Health: Report of a Research Working Group (Black Report)*. London: DHSS.

Estruch, R., Nicolas, J.M., Villegas, E., Junque, A. and Urbano-Marquez, A. (1993). Relationship between ethanol-related diseases and nutritional status in chronically alcoholic men. *Alcohol and Alcoholism*, **28**(5), 543–50.

Farley, M. and Barkan, H. (1998). Prostitution, violence, and posttraumatic stress disorder. *Women and Health*, **27**(3), 37–49.

Farrington, D.P. (1993). Childhood origins of teenage antisocial behaviour and adult social dysfunction. *Journal of the Royal Society of Medicine*, **86**(1), 13–17.

Gill, B., Meltzer, Hinds, H. and Pettigrew, M. (1996). *Psychiatric Morbidity Among Homeless People*. London: Office For National Statistics Social Survey Division.

Goldsmith, R.H., Iber, F.L. and Miller P.A. (1983). Nutritional status of alcoholics of different socioeconomic class. *Journal of the American College of Nutrition*, **2**(3), 215–20.

Gruden, V., Gruden, V. Jr and Gruden, Z. (1999). PTSD and alcoholism. *Collegium Antropologicum*, **23**(2), 607–10.

Hammarstrom, A. (1994). Health consequences of youth unemployment – review from a gender perspective. *Social Science and Medicine*, **38**(5), 699–709.

Her Majesty's Stationery Office (1995). *Tackling Drugs Together*. London: HMSO.

Kalin, N.H., Shelton, S.E. and Takahashi, L.K. (1991). Defensive behaviours in infant rhesus monkeys: ontogeny and context-dependent selective expression. *Child Development*, **62**(5), 1175–83.

Kasprow, W.J. and Rosenheck, R. (2000). Mortality among homeless and non-homeless mentally ill veterans. *Journal of Nervous and Mental Disease*, **188**(3), 141–47.

Khantzian, E.J. (1990). Self-regulation and self-medication factors in alcoholism and the addictions. Similarities and differences. *Recent Developments in Alcoholism*, **8**, 255–71.

Luder, E. (1989). Assessment of the nutritional status of urban homeless adults. *Public Health Reports*, **104**(5), 451–57.

Luder, E. (1990). Health and nutrition survey in a group of urban homeless adults. *Journal of the American Dietetic Association*, **90**(10), 1387–92.

Luscombe, C. and Brook, A. (2005). Prevalence of alcohol abuse in homeless populations: The use of holistic assessments in the non-statutory sector. *Alcohol and Alcoholism*, **40**(Suppl.1), S02–04.

Macintyre, S. and Ellaway, A. (2000). Neighbourhood cohesion and health in socially contrasting neighbourhoods: implications for the social exclusion and public health agendas. *Health Bulletin (Edinburgh)*, **58**(6), 450–56.

Mancinelli, R., Attilia, M.L., Spagnolo, P.A., Romeo, M., Rotondo, C. and Ceccanti, M. (2005). Female alcoholism and biomarkers: Gender differences in vitamin B1 (thiamine) levels. *Alcohol and Alcoholism*, **40**(Suppl.1), i45-46

Mendenhall, C.L. (1986). VA cooperative study on alcoholic hepatitis. II: Prognostic significance of protein–calorie malnutrition. *American Journal of Clinical Nutrition*, **43**(2), 213–18.

North, C.S. (2004). Are rates of psychiatric disorders in the homeless population changing? *American Journal of Public Health*, **94**(1), 103–08.

North, C.S. and Smith, E.M. (1992). Post-traumatic stress disorder among homeless men and women. *Hospital Community Psychiatry*, **43**(10), 1010–16.

North, C.S., Smith, E.M. and Spitznagel, E.L. (1994). Violence and the homeless: an epidemiologic study of victimization and aggression. *Journal of Trauma Stress*, **7**(1), 95–110.

Nystrom, K. and Axelsson, K. (2002). Mothers' experience of being separated from their newborns. *Journal of Obstetrics and Gynecological Neonatal Nursing*, **31**(3), 275–82.

Older, M.W. and Dickerson, J.W. (1982). Thiamine and the elderly orthopaedic patient. *Age and Ageing*, **11**(2): 101–07.

Office of the Deputy Prime Minister. (2004). *Achieving Positive Shared Outcomes in Health and Homelessness*. London: Homelessness and Housing Support Directorate.

Philip, G. and Smith, J.F. (1973). Hypothermia and Wernicke's encephalopathy. *Lancet*, **2**(7821), 122–24.

Pritchard, J.W. and Puzey, J.W. (2004). Homelessness – on the health agenda in Wales? *Reviews of Environmental Health*, **19**(3/4), 363–79.

Rafferty, Y. and Shinn, M. (1991). The impact of homelessness on children. *American Psychologist*, **46**(11), 1170–79.

Sgouros, X., Baines, M., Bloor, R.N., McAuley, R., Ogundipe, L.O. and Willmott, S. (2004). Evaluation of a clinical screening instrument to identify states of thiamine deficiency in inpatients with severe alcohol dependence syndrome. *Alcohol and Alcoholism*, **39**(3), 227–32.

Stationery Office (1998a). *Acheson Report: Report of the independent inquiry into inequalities in health.* London: The Stationery Office.

Stationery Office (1998b). *Smoking Kills: A White Paper on Tobacco.* London: The Stationery Office.

Stationery Office (1998c). *Tackling Drugs to Build a Better Britain.* London: The Stationery Office.

Stationery Office. (2002). *Tackling Drugs: Updated Strategy.* London: Home Office, ODPM/DES/DH/DWP/FCMO/HM Customs and Excise.

Targosz, S. (2003). Lone mothers, social exclusion and depression. *Psychological Medicine*, **33**(4), 715–22.

Taylor, P. (2007). *Suicide behaviour among offenders and offender-patients in institutions.* Working Together: Interdisciplinarity in Forensic Mental Health, Montreal, Canada. International Association of Forensic Mental Health Services.

Tyler, K.A., Cauce, A.M. and Whitbeck, L. (2004). Family risk factors and prevalence of dissociative symptoms among homeless and runaway youth. *Child Abuse and Neglect*, **28**(3), 355–66.

Winfield, I. (1990). Sexual assault and psychiatric disorders among a community sample of women. *American Journal of Psychiatry*, **147**(3), 335–41.

24 Clients involved with the criminal justice system

Jeanette Garwood and Terry Thomas

The link between alcohol and crime has been recognised for many years. The Victorians often saw the early police officer in quasi-religious terms, as a 'missionary' shining his light into those dark corners of society that had been morally corrupted by the excessive consumption of alcohol (Storch, 1976). Later, temperance societies would organise court 'missionaries' to 'save' people from the effects of drink; later still these court missionaries would evolve into our present day probation officers (McWilliams, 1983). In this chapter we outline the contemporary criminal justice system and the way in which practitioners, at various points in that system, offer interventions to offenders with alcohol problems. Alcohol – directly or indirectly – underpins crimes of violence, crimes of being drunk and disorderly – 'binge drinking' – and antisocial behaviour (Home Office, 2003b, para 3.31ff; Portman Group, 2002; Shepherd and Briskly, 1996).

For some young people a fight under the influence of alcohol is just part of a good night out (Benson and Archer, 2002; Tomsen, 1997). Our major cities are often said to have become 'no-go' areas for many older people after sunset. It is in this context that:

> Alcohol impairs cognitive skills... people may misread social cues, take bad judgements about risk or respond inappropriately in social situations. They may also respond aggressively when they believe they are being provoked leading to escalations of situations which would without the presence of alcohol be defused or calmed down fairly easily.
> (Alcohol Concern, 2004, para. 5)

Violence against women in the home from their spouses or partners is often referred to comfortingly as 'domestic violence' as though it is somehow 'different' to violence in the streets. The reality is that this violence is often just as cruel and vicious and it is often facilitated by alcohol. The Home Office estimate 100 homicides a year fall into this category (Home Office, 2003b; McMurran, 2003). Alcohol contributes to sexual assaults and rapes by influencing the behaviour of both the offenders and the victims (Horvath and Brown, 2006) and alcohol contributes to levels of homicide. Brookman found that alcohol had been consumed by either the victim or the offender (often to excess) in over half (actually 52 per cent) of all cases of masculine (male-on-male) homicides analysed in her study (Brookman, 2005, p. 44). Other serious crimes are committed under the influence of alcohol, such as burglary where alcohol has provided some 'Dutch courage' (removal of inhibition), or driving dangerously while drunk, or the commission of acquisitive crimes in order to get money to purchase alcohol. Some of these offenders will be more dependent or addicted to alcohol than others. Overall, recent UK government estimates put the annual cost of alcohol-related crime at some £7.3 billion (Cabinet Office, 2004, p. 44; *see also* Deehan, 1999).

In this chapter we identify the points in the criminal justice system at which help may be offered to the person with alcohol problems, but in doing so we should not forget that much of the activity of the criminal justice system is not about helping but about law enforcement and punishment. This tension between what we might call a 'welfare' approach as opposed to a 'justice' approach is ever present within the system.

The criminal justice system

What is the criminal justice system? The word 'system' relates to engineering terminologies whereby organised activities are based around a form of input, conversion, and output. In its simplest form, the 'system' consists of:

INPUT → CONVERSION → OUTPUT.

This model of a system sees the process of 'conversion' as being one of 'change'. A system that has people (offenders or alleged offenders) as its input at one end seeks to 'change' them and provide a different person (non-offender) as its output. Whether the criminal justice system actually achieves this is a debateable point, and to some extent it is beyond the scope of this chapter. What we can do is elaborate our model of a system to show that the criminal justice system is in fact a series of sub-systems that are linked together. These sub-systems are different agencies and together they make decisions (the 'conversion') on the offender as he or she passes through the criminal justice system (Box 24.1). Not every person entering the criminal justice system passes completely through all the different sub-systems and there are various exit points along the way. Some people never enter the system in the first place, because of under-reporting of crime to the police or because no-one was detected as being responsible. What we can do is identify the various points in the system where practitioners can make contact with offenders, where there is an underlying alcohol problem, and offer help where appropriate. These points of contact might be at the policing stage, prosecution stage, court sentencing stage or punishment stage.

Box 24.1   The sub-systems of the criminal justice system

- o   Commission of the crime
- o   The police
- o   Prosecution
- o   The courts
- o   Punishments (custodial, community, fines)
- o   End of the punishment

Policing

The police are invariably the first point of contact with offenders with alcohol problems at the start of an investigation or on arrest. In some of our bigger cities the police can avoid having to arrest a known, habitual drunkard by simply taking them to a designated 'treatment' centre. These arrangements have been available since the early 1970s (Criminal Justice Act, 1972, s.34). The advantage to the individual is that they are not arrested and not likely to be appearing before magistrates; it is also the potential start of a treatment programme. The advantage to the police is that their detention cells at the station are not filled with semiconscious drunks.

These 'treatment' or 'detoxification' centres have always been thin on the ground and have often struggled for funding. More recently they have been joined with a new version of the centre established under the same 1972 Criminal Justice Act. This version takes the form of a temporary provision – usually at weekends – taking medical care on to the streets to pick up the victims of 'binge drinking' (for example, see Home Office, 2004a). The custody suite area of police stations has been identified as a prime site for access to 'problem' drinkers, particularly so on Friday and Saturday nights (Deehan *et al.*, 2002; Man *et al.*, 2002). Custody suites are where arrestees are first detained on arrival at a police station. A code of practice guides the police on how all detainees should be treated in custody suites and this includes specific advice on how to treat people who are intoxicated by alcohol on arrival (Home Office, 2003c: para. C9ff and Annex H). Detainees should:

- be visited and aroused at least every half hour
- have their condition assessed
- have clinical treatment arranged if appropriate.

There have also been experiments in bringing alcohol treatment workers into custody suites in much the same way as drug specialists have been brought in as part of 'arrest–referral' schemes. Techniques such as 'brief interventions' have been made available, sometimes facilitated by forensic medical examiners or nurses in police stations. The UK Government admits 'there is no standard definition of a brief intervention' (Cabinet Office, 2004, p. 37) and sees it as being a range of interventions from a short conversation with a doctor or nurse to a series of sessions of motivational interviewing. Common features include:

- the giving of information and advice
- encouragement to consider the positives and negatives of their drinking behaviour
- support if a person decides they want further help (*ibid.*).

These brief interventions in custody suites appear promising. They are cheap to run and need few sessions, limited training and minimal administration (Sharp and Atherton, 2006). When forensic medical examiners (FMEs – once known as police surgeons) have been used to facilitate help to arrestees under the influence of drink the results are also good, although inevitably some FMEs are more committed to them than others (Deehan *et al.*, 2002; Noble *et al*, 2001). Evidence that brief interventions do impact on 'problem' drinkers has been forthcoming. Evaluation of a scheme in Nottinghamshire that judged success on the number of re-arrests claimed a 'modest degree of success' (Hopkins and Sparrow, 2006). Further, organisations such as Alcohol Concern have called for the extension of alcohol arrest referral schemes in all custody suites where monitoring indicates high levels of alcohol-related arrests (Alcohol Concern, 2006, p. 19).

Brief Interventions for alcohol use reduction have been evaluated within the wider population in the UK. Brief Interventions, with far less exposure than some more intensive interventions, were as effective as the 'relatively intensive treatment modalities' and 'the most favourable results tend to contain at least a strong social, or, at least interpersonal element' (UK Alcohol Treatment Trial, 2005, p. 12). This evaluation found that even seriously dependent alcohol users were effectively treated by this method, even if the mechanism by which this intervention 'works' is not clearly understood (Heather, 2003) – an issue that Hopkins and Sparrow (2006) are clearly sensitive to.

There is one very clear benefit of brief interventions – they are brief! People with a seriously chaotic lifestyles are much more likely to make two sessions than eight sessions, with little 'home work' or other commitments often required of other methods, such as the 12-step programmes, and cognitive–behavioural therapy. A second benefit is that workers from a variety of backgrounds can be trained to implement such programmes, freeing up forensic medical examiners and nurses for other, more technical, work. Brief interventions include motivational methods of intervention which originate in Prochaska and DiClemente's Trans-theoretical Model of Change (Prochaska and DiClemente, 1982). This model can be viewed as a wheel, with pre-contemplation of behaviour change as a rim enclosing the five stages of change; these are contemplation, determination, action, maintenance and relapse. As change is seen as cyclical, relapse in only a phase, and people who relapse are able to rejoin the cycle of behaviour change again within the spirit of self-efficacy and renewal (Bandura, 1977).

The Trans-theoretical Model of Change, however, is an approach, and not (in itself) a treatment. It tends to use the principles of the acronym FRAMES (Box 24.2).

Box 24.2	The FRAMES acronym (Miller and Sanchez, 1993)

F eedback of personal risk
R esponsibility of the patient/client
A dvice to change
M enu of ways to reduce drinking
E mpathetic counselling style
S elf-efficacy or optimism of the patient/client

The goal of FRAMES style interventions is to reduce, and not cease, alcohol consumption. A good example is given in Sharp and Atherton (2006). The brief intervention documented by Sharp and Atherton comprises two 1-hour long sessions, the completion of a drinking diary, and an action plan for altering drinking behaviours. It is designed to address information issues on the effects of alcohol, assessment of current drinking, discussion of strategies for avoiding those situations which makes people drink excessively, allowing them to explore the links between alcohol use and offending, and to their own health. The packages were delivered by staff specialising in alcohol reduction, unlike the programme evaluated in Hopkins and Sparrow (2006) where the intervention was delivered by custody nurses in Nottinghamshire.

The police may administer a formal caution to an offender as a way of diverting them from court and a caution may take into account the fact of their alcohol abuse. The Criminal Justice Act 2003 (Part 3) introduced the concept of 'conditional cautioning' whereby the offender takes on a commitment to certain conditions which might include attending for treatment for an alcohol problem. In order to administer a 'conditional caution' the offender must be aged 18 or over, must admit to the offence and the police must have sufficient evidence to charge and prosecute, should they wish to. The Code of Practice on 'conditional cautioning' specifically mentions the possibility of 'taking part in treatment for…alcohol dependency' (Home Office *et al.*, 2004, para. 5.2) as a condition that might be attached. Once the 'conditional caution' has been agreed and administered, compliance is duly monitored. If the conditions are not adhered to the offender may be brought back to court for the original offence.

Other options available to the police are more concerned with the enforcement side of things rather than the welfare side. These include such interventions as the fixed penalty notice – or 'on the spot fine' – for being drunk and disorderly, drunk on a highway, or for drinking in a designated public area (Criminal Justice and Police Act 2001 s.1 (1). The Violent Crime Reduction Act 2006 (ss1–14) introduces such provisions as drinking banning orders (DBOs). The police will be able to apply for these in much the same way as they do for antisocial behaviour orders (ASBOs). The application is made in a civil court for an order (the DBO) that places negative requirements on anyone concerned; breach of these requirements would bring that person before the criminal courts. Positive requirements such as attendance at a treatment centre cannot be added, given the civil nature of the Order.

Prosecuting

Once the police have arrested a person and decided that a caution is not appropriate, they will liaise with their local Crown Prosecution Service (CPS) officers concerning a possible prosecution. In reaching a decision the CPS will consider the evidence and the public interest in prosecuting, and will be guided by their own Code for Crown Prosecutors.

This Code makes no specific reference to alcohol problems as a factor to weigh in the deliberations of the CPS but it does suggest that a prosecution is less likely to be needed if 'a prosecution is likely to have a bad effect on the victim's physical or mental health' or if the defendant 'was at the time of the offence, suffering from significant mental or physical ill health' (CPS, 2004, paras 5.10f–g). Presumably this might include a consideration of alcohol dependency or addiction and this would need bringing to the attention of the CPS.

Sentencing

In general terms there has been a swing in the philosophies of sentencing from a position of 'rehabilitation' to one of 'retribution'. In the 1960s and early 1970s 'rehabilitation' ideals and attempts to treat or help the offender were attempted. In the 1990s this ideal was replaced by that of 'retribution' where the offender was seen as not requiring help and being able to take the consequences of their actions. This 'retribution' or 'just deserts' model now takes precedence, although in practice both elements – 'rehabilitation' and 'retribution' – are still present in sentencing offenders. In deciding a particular sentence the commission of an offence while under the influence of alcohol is considered an 'aggravating factor' and evidence of greater culpability on the part of the offender (Sentencing Guidelines Council, 2004, paras 1.20–1.22).

The remnants of the rehabilitative ideal can be found when it comes to sentencing offenders who have problems with alcohol. Community sentences may include a requirement of treatment and custodial sentences may include attempts in prison to address alcohol problems (for more on both, see below). Background information that actually guides the sentencer (the judge or magistrate) on the needs of an alcohol abuser is contained in the Pre-Sentence Report (PSR) written by the probation service or a social worker. The sentencer reads the PSR before making the sentencing decision and all the evidence about any alcohol problems is made available in the report. Guidance on how to write PSRs has been made available and has been updated over the years by the Home Office. In 1992, National Standards were produced and PSR writers were advised to record relevant personal or social information about the offender and their offending, and how this might impact on a possible sentence decision. The National Standards have been regularly updated since (Home Office, 2002).

Community orders

The Criminal Justice Act 2003 consolidated the law on community sentences available to the Courts. Community sentences are – by definition – punishments carried out while the convicted offender remains in the community rather than being taken into a custodial setting. The 2003 Act refers to all community sentences as Community Orders, thereby replacing the earlier terminologies of probation orders, community service orders and community rehabilitation orders, etc. The all-purpose Community Order is now the mainstay of punishment in the community and each order may have requirements or conditions attached to it, to 'customise' the order to each offender. In the case of offenders with alcohol problems, the Community Order may contain an Alcohol Treatment Requirement so that courts are able to specifically respond to those offenders who are dependent on alcohol and whose dependency requires and may be susceptible to treatment. The offender must agree in court to go along with this requirement (Criminal Justice Act 2003, s212).

Interestingly, the evaluation of brief intervention by Sharp and Atherton (2006) showed that those who believe themselves to be forced to take part in an intervention are not likely to follow the advice given, and fail to show any benefit compared with those who do not feel forced into compliance. A Community Order may just have the requirement that an offender is subject to supervision by a probation officer (what we used to call being on *probation*). This supervision may well pick up unaddressed alcohol problems and it would be part of the probation officer's role to suggest avenues of treatment and intervention to the offender; indeed to suggest anything that promotes the offender's rehabilitation. The National Probation Service (now part of the National Offender Management Service or NOMS) produced its own *Alcohol Strategy* in 2006 to try to coordinate levels of provisions in this area across the country (National Prison Service, 2006).

In treating alcohol dependency, the presence of other drug use has sometimes been overlooked and the need to broaden the treatment approach has been identified. Gossop (2005) points out that alcohol is a common adjunct to drug misuse but the focus of treatment tends to be on the drugs, rather than the alcohol. It is neither appropriate nor effective to separate out alcohol abuse from other substance abuse; it is better to keep programmes integrated.

Psychology-based interventions

Psychology-based interventions in this field are theoretically driven and usually premised on a relationship between the person delivering the programme – the therapist – and the person receiving treatment – the client. The goals of the treatment vary but normally involve increasing the client's self insight and understanding, with a view to alcohol or drug reduction. Methods incorporate a strong cognitive flavour, changing behaviour by forms of reasoning, and assuming that most behaviour is the product of intention.

Psychosocial interventions

Psychosocial interventions involve attempts to address deeply seated problems such as childhood abuse and neglect issues, and additional mental health problems such as anxiety and depression. Such interventions are not covered in any detail in this chapter as the need is to focus on alcohol-targeted approaches.

Cognitive-behavioural therapy (CBT) and coping skills-oriented interventions

CBT and coping skills-oriented interventions focus on the identification of cognitive factors and environmental influences which (in the widest sense) may facilitate or even control certain problem behaviours. Their origins are within clinical psychology, treating psychological problems such as depression (Beck, 1976). The method of treatment is didactic, giving clients strategies for overcoming negative thought processes, which are construed as self-disabling and self-destructive. In the case of alcohol consumption, clients are encouraged to think about what their trigger points for excessive consumption tend to be, and how these trigger points might be overcome in other ways. CBT interventions involve clients being given homework and tasks to undertake when they might be put under pressure to behave in the ways that they wish to change; that is, resisting temptation to drink excessively under certain conditions. If there are not opportunities to practise the skills discussed and developed in 'training' sessions, then it is difficult for clients to develop and sustain the skills that the therapist is trying to foster. CBT may not be very effective in a custodial setting for this reason.

Some alcohol users and drug users are able to stop using drugs on their own; people make their own decisions to change regardless of any therapeutic interventions (McMurran and Whitman 1990; Walters, 2005). This phenomenon leads us to question just what it is that makes people change and make decisions like this by themselves; can anything be done to facilitate this? If self-help groups can be used in both community and custodial settings (see below) then offenders might improve their own sense of self-efficacy.

Custodial orders

The Prison Service is responsible for all custodial sentences and has its own alcohol strategy (Her Majesty's Prison Service, 2004) which tackles the problem of the offender sentenced to custody who has problems with alcohol. This strategy recognises a number of interventions:

- Detoxification services: these are available on reception to all local and remand prisons (Her Majesty's Prison Service, 2004).
- Alcohol awareness courses.
- Alcoholics Anonymous: they have a presence in 50 per cent of prisons.

- Offending behaviour programmes in prisons: these may look at alcohol as a criminogenic factor.
- Good practice guide on treatment and intervention in custodial settings (produced by the Department of Health/HM Prison Service, 2004; *ibid.* 63).

On entering prison, each new prisoner is given a 'needs' assessment, that includes the degree of alcohol dependency. A self-report technique is deployed: the prisoner is asked how much alcohol they consume on a daily basis, and when they last had an alcoholic drink. If the physical level of dependence is deemed as high, then the prisoner enters a detoxification programme (Prison Service Order (PSO) 3550) which tackles the physical side effects of the withdrawal from alcohol (Department of Health/HM Prison Service, 2004). If, however, the physical level is low, then the prisoner is assessed by a psychometric test – the Alcohol Use Disorders Identification Test (AUDIT); Saunders *et al.*, 1993). This uses such statements as 'I often feel guilty after taking a drink?' and uses a Likert scale that rates answers from 'Strongly disagree' to 'Strongly agree.' Singleton, Farrell and Meltzer (1999) found that 63 per cent of male prisoners and 39 per cent of female prisoners were classifiable as hazardous drinkers using this scale. With the consent of the prisoner, a Substance Misuse Triage Assessment (SMTA) is carried out.

The SMTA has been validated to identify the prisoner's immediate requirements in terms of treatment for their alcohol withdrawal, and is constrained by the length of their sentence. Where available, the SMTA results may also help to set in motion any treatment required to combat adverse psychological effects. Any therapy or treatment programme prescribed should follow a care-plan, the objectives of which should be agreed with the prisoner, and adhered to and reviewed on a regular basis (Department of Health/HM Prison Service, 2004). Unfortunately, this depends on the availability of local funds – they are not in any way earmarked for this group (McMurran, 2006).

If the prisoner's use of alcohol has been assessed as hazardous and psychological problems connected to the withdrawal of alcohol have been raised, a prisoner may be put on a F2052SH document (Department of Health, HM Prison Service, 2004). This document alerts the prison staff to the possibility that this particular prisoner may be at high risk of self-harm and/or suicide. The prisoner can be closely monitored by the prison staff, who can observe and record his or her behaviour and mood, and so on. Even with the CARAT programme (Counselling Assessment Referral Advice and Through-care) it is very difficult to establish just how effective this through-care is (McMurran, 2006).

Even if it has been established that there is a severe alcohol problem, there is no guarantee of treatment within prison (it is difficult to establish how often this actually happens). The Prison Reform Trust (2004) identified only one out of 138 prisons in England and Wales that had a recognised alcohol-reduction programme; and in 2007 only five publicly run prisons directly mentioned alcohol-related programmes on their web sites (www.hmprisonservices.gov.uk/information/) and most services that are in place seem to focus on drug use, rather than problem drinking. Prison governors also have a discretionary power to test prisoners for alcohol consumption; this recognises the production of alcohol in prison or the smuggling of it into the prison. This discretion was provided for in the new Prison Rule number 50B (*The Prison (Amendment) Rules 2005*, SI 2005, no. 869 Schedule One). Although it is important that interventions of all kinds that are offered to offenders are effective (and appropriate) it is also important that they are appropriate in their criteria for success. McMurran (2006) is concerned that alcohol reduction programmes might be subject to the same criteria for success as illegal drug interventions – that of total cessation of use. A successful alcohol-reduction programme *reduces* alcohol consumption. It must be remembered that alcohol is not an illegal substance, and therefore people's human rights could be violated with programmes that are designed to eliminate legal behaviours. What the criminal justice system is involved in doing is reducing illegal behaviour, so it is the negative effects of excessive drinking, such as violent behaviour, which it needs to control. Therefore programmes associated with alcohol harm-reduction probably need some other elements, such as anger management training.

McMurran (2006) points out that within HM Prison Service, where resources are very stretched, there are few safeguards for effective treatments when treatment is not directly noted as a priority for a particular offender. Further, there are good psychopharmacological arguments for linking alcohol to aggressive and violent behaviour (Pihl and Hoaken, 1997; cited in McMurran, 2006). Alcohol reduction programmes alone may not be sufficient. McMurran and Cusens (2003) have, for example, developed a programmed called COVAID (Control of Violence for Angry and Impulsive Drinkers). This has been developed as a community-based programme, with those subject to the pilot study on probation or released on licence from prison, and therefore in a position to consume alcohol (something which cannot occur within a prison setting). They observed that alcohol consumption was definitely reduced, but given the brief follow-up period it was difficult to discern whether violent behaviour was also reduced. This is not a Brief Intervention, but an individual programme made up of ten 2-hour sessions, using cognitive–behavioural therapy methods. This level of intensity may not be easy to sustain in a community setting, but requires practise elements in a real-world setting as noted above in the context of CBT in general.

Conclusions

The UK Government's overall strategy for dealing with alcohol misuse (Cabinet Office, 2004) generally sets the parameters for agencies of the criminal justice system to make appropriate interventions with offenders. The prison service and the probation service both now have their own strategy statements to work within.

The dilemma for the Government has always been to balance the positives and the negatives of alcohol consumption. On the one hand, drinking alcohol has a positive and pleasurable side, and the industry that produces it (as well as the retailers that sell it) are important parts of the UK economy – not least the 'night-time economy'. On the other hand, there is a high social cost of alcohol misuse and its link with crime. Here are the sentiments of one junior Home Office minister:

> We're ... aiming to kick start a culture change where it will be less accepted by society for young men and women to go out and drink until they can't remember who they are, to start fighting in taxi queues and cause violent drink-fuelled scenes.
>
> (Home Office, 2004b)

In direct work with offenders the balance has been between law enforcement and providing help for the problem drinker ('Tough on crime – tough on the causes of crime'). But once again the dilemma has been between the need to promote the 'night-time economy' (seen with such innovations as 24-hour drinking) and the need to accept that making city centres 'no go' areas at night because of 'binge drinking' gangs in public spaces should actually be part of the antisocial behaviour agenda (see e.g. Richardson and Budd, 2004); up to press it has not been part of that agenda. The Prime Minister at that time was placed firmly on the horns of this dilemma when his own 16-year-old son was found collapsed in a drunken state by police in central London (*The Guardian*, 2000).

References and further reading

Alcohol Concern (2004). *Memorandum of Evidence to the House of Commons Home Affairs Committee, Anti Social Behaviour, 5th Report of Session 2004–05, Vol. 2 HC 80-ii*. London: Alcohol Concern.

Alcohol Concern (2006). *Wasted Lives Lost to Alcohol*. London: Alcohol Concern.

Bandura, A. (1977). *Social Learning Analysis*. Englewood Cliffs, NJ: Prentice Hall.

Beck, A.T. (1976). *Cognitive Therapy and the Emotional Disorders*. New York: International Universities Press.

Benson, D. and Archer, J. (2002). An ethnographic study of sources of conflict between young men in the context of the night out. *Psychology, Evolution and Gender, 4*(1), 3, 30.

Brookman, F. (2005). *Understanding Homicide*. London: Sage.

Cabinet Office. (2004). *Alcohol Harm Reduction Strategy for England*. London. Prime Minister's Strategy Unit.

Crown Prosecution Service. (2004). *The Code for Crown Prosecutors*. London: CPS.

Deehan, A. (1999). *Alcohol and crime: taking stock. Crime Reduction Series, Paper No.3*. London: The Home Office.

Deehan, A., Marshall, E. and Saville, E,. (2002). *Drunks and disorder: Processing intoxicated arrestees in two city centre custody suites. Police Research Series, Paper No.150*. London: The Home Office.

Department of Health/Her Majesty's Prison Service. (2004). *Alcohol Treatment/Intervention: Good Practice Guide*. London: HMSO.

Gossop M. (2005). *Treatment Outcomes: What We Know and What We Need to Know*. London: National Treatment Agency for Substance Misuse, NHS.

Heather, N. (2003). Brief alcohol interventions have expanded in range but how they work is still mysterious. *Addiction, 98*(8), 1025–26.

Her Majesty's Prison Service (2004). *Addressing Alcohol Misuse: A Prison Service Alcohol Strategy for Prisoners*. London: HM Prison Service.

Home Office (2002). *National Standards for the Supervision of Offenders in the Community*. London: The Home Office.

Home Office (2003a). *Respect and Responsibility: Taking a Stand Against Antisocial Behaviour*, Cm 5778. London: The Stationery Office.

Home Office (2003b). *Safety and Justice; the Government's Proposals on Domestic Violence*, Cm 5847. London: The Stationery Office.

Home Office (2003c). *Police and Criminal Evidence Act 1984. s60(1a) and s 66(1). Codes of Practice A–E. Revised Edition*. London: The Stationery Office.

Home Office (2004). *Conditional Cautioning: Criminal Justice Act 2003, ss. 22–27. Code of Practice*. London: The Home Office Crown Prosecution/Department of Constitutional Affairs Service.

Home Office (2004a). *Alcohol centre to save police time*. Press release, 23 January. London: The Home Office.

Home Office (2004b). *Police begin blitz on alcohol crime hotspots*. Press release, 8 July. London: The Home Office.

Hopkins, M. and Sparrow, P. (2006). Sobering up: arrest referral and brief intervention for alcohol users in the custody suite. *Criminology and Criminal Justice, 6* (4), 389–410.

Horvath, M. and Brown, J. (2006). The role of drugs and alcohol in rape. *Medicine, Science and Law, 46* (3), 219–28.

Man, L., Marshall, J., Godfrey, C. and Budd, T. (2002). *Dealing with Alcohol-Related Detainees in the Custody Suite: Research Findings 178*. London: The Home Office.

McMurran, M. (2003). *Alcohol and crime. Alcohol Concern Research Forum Papers (September)*. London: Alcohol Concern.

McMurran, M. (2006). Controlled drinking goals for offenders. *Addiction Research and Theory*, **14**(1), 59–65.

McMurran, M. and Cusens, B. (2003). Controlling alcohol-related violence: A treatment programme. *Criminal Behaviour and Mental Health*, **13**(1), 59–76.

McMurran, M. and Whitman, J. (1990). Strategies of self-control in male young offenders who have reduced their alcohol consumption without formal intervention. *Journal of Adolescence*, **13,** 115–28.

McWilliams, W. (1983). The mission to the English courts: 1876–1936. *Howard Journal of Criminal Justice,* **25**, 241–64.

Miller, W.R. and Sanchez, V.C. (1993). Motivating young adults for treatment and lifestyle change. In: G. Howard (ed.) *Issues in Alcohol Use and Misuse by Young Adults*. Notre Dame, IN: University of Notre Dame Press, pp. 55–81.

National Probation Service. (2006). *Working with Alcohol Misusing Offenders – A Strategy for Delivery*. London: National Probation Service.

Noble, A., Best, D., Stark, M. and Marshall, E.J. (2001). The role of the forensic medical examiner with 'drunken detainees' in police custody. *Police Research Series Paper 146*. London: Home Office, Crown Publications. Available at: http://rds. homeoffice.gov.uk/rds/prgpdfs/prs146.pdf July 2nd 2008 (last accessed August 2008).

Pihl, R.O. and Hoaken, P.N.S. (1997). Clinical correlates and predictors of violence in patients with substance use disorders. *Psychiatric Annals*, **27**(11), 735–40.

Portman Group. (2002). *Counting the Cost: The Measurement and Recording of Alcohol-related Violence and Disorder*. London: The Portman Group.

Prison Reform Trust. (2004). *Alcohol and reoffending – who cares?* Available at: http://www.prisonreformtrust.org.uk/ subsection.asp?id=253/ (last accessed August 2008).

Prochaska, J. and DiClemente, C. (1982). Trans-theoretical Therapy: towards a more integrative model of change. *Psychotherapy,* **19**, 276–88.

Richardson, A. and Budd, T. (2003). *Alcohol, crime and disorder: A study of young adults. Home Office Research Study 263*. London: The Home Office.

Saunders, J.B., Aasland, O.G., Babor, T.F., de la Fuente, J.R. and Grant, M. (1993). Development of the Alcohol Use Disorders Identification Test (AUDIT): WHO collaborative project on early detection of persons with harmful alcohol consumption. II. *Addiction*, **88**, 791–804.

Sentencing Guidelines Council (2004). *Overarching Principles: Seriousness*. London: SGC 2004.

Sharp, D. and Atherton, R.S. (2006). Out on the town: an evaluation of brief motivational interventions to address the risks associated with problematic alcohol use. *International Journal of Offender Therapy and Comparative Criminology,* **50**(10), 540–58.

Shepherd, J. and Briskly, M. (1996). The relationship between alcohol intoxication, stresses and injury in urban violence. *British Journal of Criminology*, **36**(4), 546–66.

Singleton, N., Farrell, M. and Meltzer, H. (1999). *Substance Misuse Among Prisoners in England and Wales*. London: Office for National Statistics.

Storch, R. (1976). The policeman as domestic missionary. *Journal of Social History*, **IX**(4), 481–509.

The Guardian (2000). Blair's son says sorry after 'drunk and incapable' arrest. 6 July, 2000.

Tomsen, S. (1997). A Top Night: Social protest, masculinity and the culture of drinking violence. *British Journal of Criminology,* **37**(1), 90–102.

UK Alcohol Treatment Trial. (2005). Effectiveness of treatment for alcohol problems: Findings of the randomised UK Alcohol Treatment Trial (UKATT). *British Medical Journal*, **331**, 541–44.

Walters, G. (2005). Spontaneous remission from alcohol, tobacco and other drug use: seeking quantitative answers to qualitative questions, *American Journal of Drug and Alcohol Abuse*, **26**(3), 443–54.

25 Eating disorders and substance abuse

Helen Fawkner

Clinicians working with people who have eating disorders need to be aware of a variety of comorbid diagnoses that can complicate case conceptualisation and consequently the potential treatment of their clients (O'Brien and Vincent, 2003). One of the most common comorbid diagnoses for people with eating disorders is substance abuse (Bushnell *et al.*, 1994; Mitchell *et al.*, 1985; Newman and Gold, 1992; O'Brien and Vincent, 2003). Therefore, the aims of this chapter are two-fold. First, it will outline the characteristics of eating disorders and examine the evidence of an association between eating disorders and substance use, specifically, by focusing on the relation between anorexia nervosa and bulimia nervosa and their association with substance use, in particular to binge drinking and alcohol abuse. Second, this chapter will critically review the hypotheses that have been proposed to explain the aetiology underpinning both eating disorders and alcohol abuse. In doing so, where feasible the clinical implications of these findings will be considered, and directions for future research will be suggested.

This book is primarily aimed at health professionals who work with people with alcohol problems, but in the majority who have comorbid eating and alcohol abuse problems, the eating disorder typically develops first (Franko *et al.*, 2005; Krahn, Kurth, Demitrack and Drewnowski, 1992). Thus, this chapter is written from the perspective that individuals may primarily present with an eating disorder, and the substance abuse is the comorbid (secondary) problem.

Characteristics of eating disorders

Eating disorders are complex and chronic illnesses. They generally relate to psychological disorders involving gross abnormalities in eating behaviour (Rosen, 1990). Currently, four distinct eating disorders are recognised by DSM-IV – anorexia nervosa, bulimia nervosa, binge-eating disorder, and eating disorder not otherwise specified (EDNOS). Obesity is not considered an eating disorder because there is no compelling evidence to suggest that obesity results from, or is characterised by, abnormal eating behaviour (Rosen, 1990). A comprehensive review of the diagnostic criteria for eating disorders is given in the DSM-IV (American Psychological Association, 1994).

Anorexia nervosa

In brief, this is characterised by a refusal to maintain a body weight that is appropriate for an individual's age and height (less than 15 per cent below the appropriate standard). Despite being severely underweight, people with anorexia nervosa display extreme anxiety about weight gain or becoming 'fat'. They also have a distorted self-perception, placing undue emphasis on their weight or shape in self-evaluation, and/or denying the seriousness of their own weight loss and/or demonstrate a distorted perception of their own body shape or weight. Another characteristic in females is the presence of amenorrhoea (American Psychological Association, 1994). Typically weight loss is achieved by self-starvation or extreme food restriction, but some people use self-induced vomiting or purging (misuse of laxatives, diuretics or enemas) as a form of weight reduction (Rosen, 1990). Therefore a distinction is made between anorexia nervosa (restricting type) and anorexia nervosa (binge-eating/purging type) (American Psychological Association, 1994). Between 0.5 and 3.7 per cent of women per year suffer from anorexia (American Psychiatric Association Work Group on Eating Disorders, 2000) compared with as few as 0.2 per cent of men (Lucas *et al*, 1991).

Bulimia nervosa

This is characterised by habitual cycles of self-induced vomiting and purging behaviour following binge-eating (American Psychological Association, 1994) or consumption of even small amounts of 'forbidden' foods (Rosen, 1990). A binge can be defined as the consumption of much more food than most people would eat in similar circumstances and in a similar period of time, and it is often accompanied by a feeling that the eating is out of control. Unlike people with anorexia nervosa, those with bulimia nervosa often maintain a normal body weight (Rosen, 1990); however, like people with anorexia nervosa, they have distorted self-perceptions, showing a persistent degree of over-concern with their weight and body shape (Russell, 1979). These symptoms are present independently of a diagnosis of anorexia nervosa. Note that the diagnosis may depend on when an individual presents for treatment; many display the symptoms of both anorexia nervosa and bulimia nervosa at different times, and it also is estimated that as many as half of those meeting the criteria for anorexia nervosa will later develop bulimia nervosa (American Psychological Association, 1994). Most people with bulimia nervosa are of the purging type, however, some present with the non-purging type of bulimia whereby they do not vomit or abuse laxatives or diuretics, but instead fast or exercise excessively in order to redress their binges and generally control their weight (American Psychological Association, 1994). Reports of the prevalence of bulimia nervosa vary. Estimates for women among the general population are between 1 per cent and 4 per cent (American Psychological Association, 1994; Johnson and Connors, 1987), though it may be much higher in certain populations. For example, it is estimated that 13–20 per cent of college-aged women meet the criteria for bulimia nervosa (Halmi *et al.*, 1981). Estimates for men range between 1 per cent and 5 per cent (Drewnowski *et al.*, 1988; Schotte and Stunkard, 1987; Striegel-Moore *et al.*, 1989).

Binge-eating disorder (BED)

Although there is still debate in the research literature about the exact clinical features and prevalence of binge-eating disorder, it has been recognised that some people experience recurrent episodes of binge-eating, accompanied by feelings of loss of control, and psychological distress (e.g. shame, guilt or embarrassment) regarding the binge (Wilson and Walsh, 1991). This includes anyone who does not meet the criteria for bulimia nervosa, that is they do not vomit, purge or abuse medication in an attempt to avoid weight gain (American Psychological Association, 1994; Wilson and Walsh, 1991). The prevalence of this disorder appears to be greater than for bulimia nervosa (Wilson and Walsh, 1991). It has been estimated that 2–5 per cent of community samples have it (American Psychiatric Association Work Group on Eating Disorders, 2000; Bruce and Agras, 1992; Spitzer *et al.*, 1993). Not all binge eaters are overweight, however there does appear to be some association between the degree of overweightness and binge-eating (Telch *et al.*, 1988).

Eating disorder not otherwise specified (EDNOS)

EDNOS is characterised by the presence of an eating disorder in someone who does not meet the strict criteria of any of the previously mentioned disorders (American Psychiatric Association Work Group on Eating Disorders, 2000; American Psychological Association, 1994).

Other psychological conditions affecting eating and weight

In essence, it is the disturbance of body image that distinguishes the above disorders from other psychological conditions that sometimes involve eating abnormalities and weight loss. Among these other conditions are pica (in which non-nutritive substances such as dirt or paper are eaten), ruminating disorder (characterised by repeated regurgitation and re-chewing of food) and feeding disorder (which is a failure to eat adequately as reflected by weight loss or a failure to gain weight) (American Psychological Association, 1994).

Gender and eating disorders

As is suggested by the prevalence rates already cited, all eating disorders (with the probable exception of binge-eating disorder) are more common in women than men. Studies examining people with eating disorders indicate that men constitute between 5 per cent and 10 per cent of anorexic patients (Dally *et al.* 1979; Jones *et al.*, 1980; Oyebode *et al.*, 1988a,b) and between 0.4 per cent and 20 per cent of bulimic patients (Carlat and Camargo, 1991; Drewnowski *et al.*, 1988; Halmi *et al.*, 1981; Pope *et al.*, 1984; Schotte and Stunkard, 1987; Striegel-Moore *et al.*, 1986, 1989). These may seem to be small percentages, but the rate of eating disorders may be increasing among men (Braun *et al.*, 1999). Furthermore, it is not clear whether these sex differences in the rates of diagnosis are due to biological, sociocultural, or psychodynamic factors, or if the rate is erroneously low due to the general reluctance of men to seek treatment (Margo, 1987) or because of the bias that favours diagnosis in women.

Men and women with eating disorders generally display similar phenomenology (Mitchell and Goff, 1984; Sharp *et al.*, 1994). Nevertheless, some sex differences have been reported (Herzog *et al.*, 1990). For example, male patients (as compared with female patients) were more likely to have divorced parents (35.1 per cent versus 13.5 per cent) (Braun *et al.*, 1999) and a higher age of onset (Braun *et al.*, 1999; Carlat *et al.*, 1997) and were less likely to seek therapeutic intervention (Olivardia *et al.*, 1995) or to have a good outcome (Oyebode *et al.*, 1988a,b). In addition, some studies have shown sex differences with respect to preferred methods of weight control. There is some evidence that women are more likely to use diet pills and laxatives (Braun *et al.*, 1999;

Johnson *et al.*, 1999) whereas men are more likely to use saunas, steam baths (Johnson *et al.*, 1999) and exercise to control their weight (Davis and Cowles, 1991a,b; Drewnowski and Yee, 1987). In fact, Braun *et al.*, reported that men diagnosed with eating disorders were more likely (than women with eating disorders) to be engaged in some occupation or athletic team in which control of weight was important for a good performance (36.7 per cent versus 13 per cent). Finally, a higher rate of homosexuality and gender identity disturbance is reported among men, as compared with women, with eating disorders (Kearney Cooke and Steichen Asch, 1990; Schneider and Agras, 1987). Higher rates of eating disorders are reported among homosexual men compared with heterosexual men by Herzog *et al.* (1984) and Yager *et al.* (1988).

Evidence of comorbidity for eating disorders and substance use

On the basis of both clinical and empirical evidence, it has been noted that there is a relationship between eating disorders (specifically, anorexia nervosa and bulimia nervosa) and several axis II and axis I disorders (O'Brien and Vincent, 2003). Clinicians have long posited a strong relationship between bulimia nervosa and cluster B personality disorder – specifically, borderline personality disorder (Carroll 1996; O'Brien and Vincent, 2003) – and empirical evidence supports this relationship (Carroll *et al.*, 1996; Herzog *et al.*, 1992a; Schmidt and Telch, 1990). In contrast, a higher prevalence of cluster C disorders (such as obsessive–compulsive personality disorder) has been associated with anorexia nervosa (O'Brien and Vincent, 2003); and this finding has been noted cross-culturally (Matsunaga *et al.*, 1998; Rastam, 1992; Wonderlich *et al.*, 1990). It should be noted that the comorbidity between borderline personality disorder and bulimia nervosa may be an artefact of the diagnostic system; Wolfe and Maisto (2000) described considerable overlap in the diagnostic criteria for borderline personality disorder, bulimia nervosa and substance use. Further longitudinal research would shed more light on the nature of this relationship.

For both anorexia nervosa and bulimia nervosa, the most common comorbid disorder is an axis I disorder – major depression (Braun *et al.*, 1994; Dansky *et al.*, 2000; Herzog *et al.*, 1992b; Rastam, 1992). In addition, anorexia nervosa and bulimia nervosa are commonly comorbid with obsessive–compulsive disorder (Bulik *et al.*, 1997; Halmi *et al.*, 1991) and other anxiety disorders including over-anxious disorder, simple phobia, avoidant disorder, separation-anxiety disorder and post-traumatic stress disorder (Geist *et al.*, 1998).

Finally, there is evidence of a strong relationship between eating disorders and substance use. People who receive treatment for eating disorders frequently report high rates of alcohol and other drug use; in fact, many often fulfil the criteria for comorbid substance use disorder (Bushnell *et al.*, 1994; Franko *et al.*, 2005; Mitchell *et al.*, 1985; Newman and Gold, 1992; Wolfe and Maisto, 2000). For example, between 18 per cent and 50 per cent of women with bulimia nervosa report current or past history of alcohol abuse or alcohol dependence (Holderness *et al.* 1994). Equally, high rates of eating disorders have been identified in people presenting for treatment for alcohol and substance-use problems (Higuchi *et al.*, 1993; Hudson *et al.* 1992; Jonas *et al.*, 1987; Peveler and Fairburn, 1990; Walfish *et al.*, 1992; Wilson, 1992). As many as 40 per cent of women who present for treatment of alcohol abuse report a current or past history of disordered eating (Holderness *et al.*, 1994). For more details on the comorbidity of eating disorders and substance use, and for specific rates of comorbidity, see the review articles by Holderness *et al.* (1994) and Krahn (1991). It is has been suggested that Berkson's bias (Berkson, 1946) partially explains the high rate of comorbidity (Telch and Stice, 1998). (Berkson's bias states that an individual with multiple diagnoses is more likely to seek treatment than an individual with a single diagnosis.) However, similar comorbidity findings have been found in research with non-clinical adult samples (Anderson *et al.*, 2005; Bulik, 1987; Cooley and Toray, 2001; Kendler *et al.*, 1991; Striegel-Moore and Huydic, 1993) and people who display subthreshold eating disorder symptomatology (Killen *et al.*, 1987; Krahn *et al.*, 1992; Striegel-Moore and Huydic, 1993; Timmerman *et al.*, 1990). In fact, even studies that do not directly support a link between eating disorders and alcohol abuse show that alcohol use is still a risk for an person with an eating disorder (Dunn *et al.*, 2002; Patton *et al.*, 2003). For example, Dunn *et al.*, reported that although their sample of college women who met the criteria for bulimia nervosa did not drink significantly more than women without eating disorders, they did report significantly more negative consequences related to alcohol and illicit drug use.

Much of the data on comorbidity comes from studies of women with bulimia nervosa (Goebel *et al.*, 1995) and it has been noted that this relationship appears to be strongest for bulimia nervosa and anorexia nervosa (bingeing subtype) (Stock *et al.*, 2002) and observed less – or not at all – in people with anorexia nervosa (restricting type) (Braun *et al.*, 1994; Stock *et al.*, 2002; Wolfe and Maisto, 2000; Wonderlich and Mitchell, 1997) nor BED (Telch *et al.*, 1988). Therefore for the remainder of this chapter, eating disorders will refer specifically to bulimia nervosa and bingeing/purging anorexia nervosa. Although it is important to recognise the frequent comorbidity of these disorders from a research perspective, and more importantly from a clinical perspective, it is more important and beneficial for clients if the nature of the relationship is understood (Wolfe and Maisto, 2000). Therefore now we will turn to a critical exploration of the hypotheses that have been postulated to explain the comorbidity of eating disorders and alcohol abuse. Essentially, these hypotheses either propose a shared aetiology (a common factor that predisposes an individual to both eating disorders and alcohol abuse) or a causal aetiology (whereby experiencing either eating disorder or alcohol abuse places an individual at risk for the other). Each of these approaches will be considered in turn.

Hypotheses based on a shared aetiology

There are four major hypotheses that posit that the comorbidity of eating disorders and alcohol abuse can be explained by a shared aetiology. These are the personality hypothesis, the endogenous opioid hypothesis, the family history hypothesis, and the developmental hypothesis.

The personality hypothesis

It has been proposed that an addictive personality may leave an individual vulnerable to a wide range of addictive substances and behaviours (Lang, 1983). Research illustrating that some people are often addicted to multiple substances is taken as evidence for the notion of an addictive personality (Miller, 1987). Holderness *et al.* (1994) proposed that an addictive personality might explain the comorbidity of eating disorders and substance use; that is, some people have personality traits that make them vulnerable to both behaviours. But what are these personality traits? There is some evidence that 'impulsivity' may underpin binge-eating and drinking in both clinical (Kane *et al.*, 2004) and non-clinical samples (Fischer *et al.*, 2004). Kane *et al.*, examined impulsivity in women with bulimia nervosa, in women with comorbid bulimia nervosa and alcohol abuse, and in women with neither condition (controls). They assessed their impulsivity, state anxiety and a behavioural measure of reward responsiveness (a behavioural analogue of impulsivity). As hypothesised, the women with bulimia nervosa scored higher on all measures compared with the control sample. Additionally, the women who were comorbid for bulimia nervosa and alcohol abuse scored significantly higher on impulsivity than women with bulimia nervosa. Similarly, Fischer *et al.* examined the role of trait urgency (a form of impulsivity) in binge drinking, binge-eating, and purging behaviour. In their sample of undergraduate college women, 22.2 per cent reported getting drunk at least once per week (which could considered a form of binge drinking), 4.7 per cent reported binge-eating, and 6.5 per cent reported purging in the previous 4 weeks. As predicted, levels of trait urgency were associated with levels of alcohol use, binge-eating, and purging. It is possible that the differences in individual levels of impulsivity may underpin eating disorders and alcohol abuse. That said, the personality hypothesis has come under much criticism.

At least three major criticisms can be levelled at the personality hypothesis. First, although people with alcohol abuse and/or eating disorders may share personality traits, an 'association' should not be confused with 'causality'. In fact many researchers and clinicians have cast doubt on the notion of an addictive personality (Chiauzzi and Liljegren, 1993; Wolfe and Maisto, 2000). Further, if there were such a thing as an addictive personality, then people with eating disorders should be equally likely to develop a dependence on any addictive substance. Nevertheless, it appears that people with eating disorders are more likely to report use of alcohol and stimulants such amphetamines and cocaine, as opposed to addictive substances like opiates (Hudson *et al.*, 1992; Walfish *et al.*, 1992). Second, although the research examining impulsivity in people with eating disorders and alcohol abuse provides some evidence of similar personality traits among them, other research has revealed personality differences (Hatsukami *et al.*, 1982). For example, Hatsukami *et al.*, reported that women being treated for bulimia nervosa and women being treated for alcohol abuse shared similar personality profiles (as measured by the Minnesota Multiphasic Personality Inventory, MMPI) but there were also significant differences, in that the women with alcohol abuse scored significantly higher than the women with bulimia nervosa on the majority of traits measured by the MMPI and the MacAndrew Alcoholism Scale, which is considered to assess traits associated with addiction. Third, but perhaps most importantly, it is debatable whether eating disorders should be conceptualised as addictive behaviours in the way that alcohol abuse is (Fairburn, 1995; Wilson, 1993). Specifically, Fairburn questions whether food can be considered an addictive substance (like alcohol or drugs) and notes that the behaviours of people with eating disorders and alcohol abuse are almost diametrically opposed. That is, many people with eating disorders strive to avoid food intake, however people who abuse alcohol actively seek to consume alcohol.

The endogenous opioid hypothesis

It has been suggested that people with eating disorders and substance-use problems may share a physiological predisposition for addiction (Wolfe and Maisto, 2000). Indirect evidence for this hypothesis comes from two sources. First, bingeing and purging produces elevations in beta-endorphin levels (the endogenous opioids) (Drewnowski, 1989). It is suggested that some people may become addicted to these (Goldbloom *et al.*, 1991; Jonas and Gold, 1988) and therefore the comorbidity of eating disorders and substance use may be explained by a shared vulnerability for addiction to both endogenous and exogenous substances. Second, naltrexone has been used successfully to treat both opiate addiction and binge-eating in women with bulimia nervosa (Jonas and Gold, 1988); again this provides indirect evidence of a shared physiological vulnerability to both disorders. In addition, more recent research suggests that naltrexone may be a useful treatment for binge drinking. For example, it has been shown to dampen the rewarding effects of alcohol consumption in heavy drinkers (Armeli *et al.*, 2006; Kranzler *et al.*, 2004). Even though these avenues of investigation are promising, as Wolfe and Maisto (2000) noted, the theory requires further elaboration and more research is required to discover the specific psychological, behavioural and biological factors that may underpin this physiological vulnerability to addiction.

The family history hypothesis

A familial link has also been proposed to underpin the relationship between eating disorders and substance use. One interpretation of the role of family history suggests that a common genetic component may underpin vulnerability to both disorders. Three different strands of evidence can be considered in testing this hypothesis (underpinned by common genetic factors) – prevalence among first-degree relatives, prevalence among parents and offspring, and prevalence among twins. A review of this research suggests that the empirical findings are equivocal.

In support of the familial link, research that compares the prevalence of alcohol abuse in first-degree relatives of people with and without bulimia nervosa shows a significantly higher prevalence among those with bulimia nervosa (Kassett *et al.*, 1989), even if they do not present with comorbid bulimia nervosa and alcohol abuse (Bulik, 1987). Also, high rates of eating disorders are found in people whose parents have alcohol abuse problems (Jonas and Gold, 1988).

Other research fails to confirm these findings. In contrast to the findings of Kassett *et al.* (1989), a study examining the rate of eating disorders among the relatives of people with and without alcohol abuse problems found no difference between these groups (Schuckit *et al.*, 1996). And in contrast to Jonas and Gold (1988), Mintz and colleagues found no difference in the rates of eating disorders when they compared non-clinical samples of people whose parents did or did not have alcohol abuse problems (Mintz *et al.*, 1995; Stout and Mintz, 1996). Moreover, a comparison of women with and without a familial history of alcohol abuse revealed no difference in their eating disorders scores (Meyer, 1997).

The evidence from large-scale twin studies is also not clearcut. Although research suggests that genetic factors contribute to the development of eating disorders (up to 83 per cent of the variance in anorexia nervosa and bulimia nervosa can be attributed to genetic factors), non-shared environmental factors such as differential treatment by parents, siblings and peers, and unique life events are also important (Bulik *et al.*, 1998; Klump *et al.*, 2000). The contribution made by genetic and environmental factors also appears to differ as a function of age (for example, there is evidence of a stronger genetic effect in adolescents than in pre-adolescent female twins) (Klump *et al.*, 2000). Studies examining the contribution of genetic factors in substance use, especially alcohol abuse, suggest a more complex aetiology than can be explained by genetic factors alone. Although some research suggests that genetics play a role in the aetiology of alcohol abuse, it appears that genetic factors might be more important in the aetiology of early-onset male alcoholism (King *et al.*, 2005; McGue *et al.*, 1992).

Little research has addressed the genetic contribution in the aetiology of both alcohol abuse and eating disorders. Nevertheless this research also challenges the notion of a shared genetic aetiology; for example, the work of Kendler *et al.*, suggests that the genetic influence on alcohol abuse was not related to the genetic factors associated with eating disorders (or mood or anxiety) (Kendler *et al.*, 1995).

A more promising line of enquiry with respect to the family history hypothesis is the role of family environment – family history may contribute to the development of eating disorders through non-genetic familial transmission. For example, there is a higher prevalence of pre-occupation about weight and disordered eating among adolescent girls whose mothers also report 'like' behaviour than among girls whose mothers report lower pre-occupation with weight and disordered eating (Francis and Birch, 2005; Pike and Rodin, 1991; von Ranson *et al.*, 2003).

So, rather than a genetic predisposition underpinning vulnerability to eating disorders and alcohol abuse, it has been suggested that disruption to the family environment, as a consequence of parental alcohol abuse, may leave an individual more vulnerable to the development of an eating disorder. The majority of research suggests that many people with eating disorders experience disturbed familial relationships (Grisset and Norvell, 1992; Humphrey, 1989; Johnson and Connors, 1987; Ratti *et al.*, 1996; Strober and Humphrey, 1987; Wonderlich *et al.*, 1996). In particular, people with eating disorders often self-report their family environment to be less supportive and more conflicted than the family environment of controls. Further, objective measures confirm that there are differences in the style of interactions between families with an adolescent with eating disorders and normal controls (Humphrey, 1989). Again even this research is equivocal; some studies do not support role of family relationship in development of eating disorders in adolescent girls (Attie and Brooks-Gunn, 1989) and other research has shown no differences in family disturbance in a non-clinical sample of women with bulimia nervosa and alcohol abuse, compared with women with bulimia nervosa and women controls (Bulik and Sullivan, 1993).

In conclusion, there is a lack of firm evidence for a familial predisposition as an explanation for comorbid eating disorders and alcohol abuse. Further research, especially longitudinal research, is required before such a relationship can be said to have been clearly demonstrated.

The developmental hypothesis

The final shared aetiology hypothesis suggests that the comorbidity of eating disorders and substance use might be a negative carry-on effect of normal adolescent development and experimentation (Krahn *et al.*, 1992). Adolescence is a time of heightened concern about appearance (Levine and Smolak, 2002; Tiggemann, 2002, 2005) and for adolescent girls there is social pressure to conform to the 'thin' ideal (Stice, 1994; Tiggemann, 2002, 2005). Equally, experimentation with a variety of substances including alcohol, cigarettes, marijuana and other recreational drugs is common during adolescence (Alcohol and Other Drugs Council of Australia, 2000; Hawthorne, 1997; Laure *et al.*, 2004; Wadsworth *et al.*, 2004). Therefore, adolescents may develop a problem with both eating behaviour and substance use. Evidence to support this hypothesis comes from research that illustrates an association between increased weight or body dissatisfaction, eating disorder symptomology, and substance use or initiation in adolescent girls (Fisher *et al.*, 19991; Stice and Shaw, 2003).

That said, although some adolescent girls who are pre-occupied with their weight and appearance may engage in substance use this hypothesis has at least three limitations. First, the developmental hypothesis fails to explain the specific mechanisms underpinning the comorbidity of eating disorders and substance use. Second, it fails to account for the large number of adolescent girls who diet and/or experiment with recreational drugs and alcohol, but do not develop an eating disorder or substance-use problem (Wolfe and Maisto, 2000). For example, it is estimated that as many as 70 per cent of adolescent girls are dissatisfied with two or more aspects of their bodies, up to 80 per cent would like to be thinner, and as many as 60 per cent engage in self-reported dieting behaviour (Levine and Smolak, 2002). In fact, body dissatisfaction is considered to be 'normative' for adolescent girls (Levine and Smolak, 2002). Third, the hypothesis fails to account for the comorbidity in non-adolescent females.

Hypotheses based on a causal aetiology

Three major hypotheses explain the comorbidity of eating disorders and alcohol abuse/substance use by a causal aetiology, whereby experiencing either an eating disorder or alcohol abuse places an individual at risk for the other. These are the self-medication hypothesis, the anxiety/tension-reduction hypothesis, and the food deprivation hypothesis. Here is a critical evaluation of each of these hypotheses.

The self-medication hypothesis

The self-medication hypothesis proposes that people use alcohol (or other substances) to reduce negative affective symptoms such as dysphoria or depression (Peveler and Fairburn, 1990). It was suggested that self-medication may underpin the eating disorder–alcohol abuse relationship because (as noted previously in this chapter) of the high prevalence of depression among people with both clinical eating disorders (Braun *et al.*, 1994; Bulik, 1987; Dansky *et al.*, 2000; Herzog, Keller, Sacks *et al.*, 1992; Kendler *et al.*, 1991; Killen *et al.*, 1987; Rastam, 1992) and community samples of people with sub-threshold eating disorders (Bulik, 1987; Kendler *et al.*, 1991; Killen *et al.*, 1987). Despite the intuitive appeal of this hypothesis, there is little confirmatory evidence. Krahn *et al.* (1992) found no association between depression and alcohol consumption in college-aged women with subthreshold eating disorders, and Weiss, Griffin, and Mirin (1992) reported no differences in the degree of self-medication in women with and without major depression. Moreover, Killen *et al.*, reported higher rates of substance use (of alcohol and marijuana) among bulimic women without depression as compared with controls.

The anxiety/tension-reduction hypothesis

Closely connected to the self-medication hypothesis is the anxiety/tension-reduction hypothesis. This proposes that alcohol and other drugs are used to reduce tension and anxiety that arises as a result of premorbid anxiety disorder and/or the presence of an eating disorder (Wolfe and Maisto, 2000). Again (as noted earlier) eating disorders are commonly comorbid with anxiety disorders (Geist *et al.*, 1998), and there is a high level of generalised anxiety, phobia and panic disorder in community samples (Kendler *et al.*, 1991) and in clinical samples (Schwalberg *et al.*,

1992) of individuals with bulimia nervosa; these findings indirectly support this hypothesis. An association does not equate with causality, however, and at present there is no direct evidence of a causal relationship (Wolfe and Maisto, 2000). Although there is evidence that food itself improves mood and decreases tension in people exhibiting bulimic attitudes and behaviours (McCormack and Carman, 1989) further research is required to establish that alcohol and other drugs act in a similar fashion (Wolfe and Maisto, 2000).

The food deprivation hypothesis

The final shared-aetiology hypothesis is the food deprivation hypothesis. This theory is underpinned by a learning-behaviourist framework and suggests that the removal of a primary reinforcer (food, in this case) results in increased reinforcement value for other substances that can provide reinforcement, such as alcohol and drugs (Krahn, 1993; Wolfe and Maisto, 2000). Animal studies provide evidence that support this hypothesis (Carroll *et al.*, 1979; Krahn, 1993), but the evidence from studies in humans is equivocal at best. For example, Keys and coworkers (1950) noted that men who were deprived of food increased their consumption of tobacco and coffee (the only drugs that were available to them) during the period of semi-starvation. In contrast, there was no difference in alcohol consumption when bulimic and control participants who had been food-deprived for 19 hours were compared (Bulik and Brinded, 1993). Although the researchers suggested that an increased deprivation period might result in greater alcohol consumption, ethical considerations make the testing of this suggestion untenable.

Conclusions

None of the theories postulated here have been sufficiently or unequivocally supported by the research to date. Additionally, some of the hypotheses need further elaboration in order to be empirically tested. There are still many research questions to be addressed (more detailed suggestions are discussed by Wolfe and Maisto, 2000) but two main suggestions can be highlighted here: first, there is a need for longitudinal field research that may increase our knowledge of the complex inter-relationships and patterns between eating disorders, substance use, and even other comorbid disorders like anxiety and depression; second, there is a need for empirical research that incorporates behavioural assessments (Wolfe and Maisto, 2000). Although this research will not clarify the mechanisms that underpin the eating disorder–substance use relationship, they will increase our knowledge about the complexity of the relationship between eating disorders and substance use. This knowledge would be of great value to clinicians who provide treatment to such people.

References and further reading

American Psychiatric Association Work Group on Eating Disorders. (2000). Practice guideline for the treatment of patients with eating disorders (revision). *American Journal of Psychiatry*, **157**(Suppl.1), 1–39.

American Psychological Association (1994). *Diagnostic and Statistical Manual of Mental Disorders*, 4th edn. Washington, DC: American Psychological Association.

Anderson, D.A., Martens, M.P. and Cimini, M.D. (2005). Do female college students who purge report greater alcohol use and negative alcohol-related consequences? *International Journal of Eating Disorders*, **37**, 65–68.

Armeli, S., Feinn, R., Tennen, H. and Kranzler, H.R. (2006). The effects of naltrexone on alcohol consumption and affect reactivity to daily interpersonal events among heavy drinkers. *Experimental and Clinical Psychopharmacology*, **14**, 199–208.

Attie, I. and Brooks-Gunn, J. (1989). Development of eating problems in adolescent girls: A longitudinal study. *Developmental Psychology*, **25**, 70–79.

Berkson, J. (1946). Limitations of the application of fourfold table analysis to hospital data. *Biometrics Bulletin*, **2**, 47–53.

Braun, D.L., Sunday, S.R. and Halmi, K.A. (1994). Psychiatric comorbidity in patients with eating disorders. *Psychological Medicine*, **24**, 857–67.

Braun, D.L., Sunday, S.R., Huang, A. and Halmi, K. (1999). More males seek treatment for eating disorders. *International Journal of Eating Disorders*, **26**, 413–24.

Bruce, B. and Agras, W.S. (1992). Binge-eating in females: A population-based investigation. *International Journal of Eating Disorders*, **12**, 365–73.

Bulik, C.M. (1987). Drug and alcohol abuse by bulimic women and their families. *American Journal of Psychiatry*, **144**, 1604–06.

Bulik, C.M. and Brinded, E.C. (1993). The effects of food deprivation on alcohol consumption in bulimic and control women. *Addiction,* **88**, 1545–51.

Bulik, C.M. and Sullivan, P.F. (1993). Comorbidity of bulimia and substance abuse: Perceptions of family of origin. *International Journal of Eating Disorders*, **13**, 49–56.

Bulik, C.M., Sullivan, D.F., Fear, J.L. and Joyce, P.R. (1997). Eating disorders and antecedent anxiety disorders: A controlled study. *Acta Psychiatrica Scandinavica*, **96**, 101–07.

Bulik, C.M., Sullivan, P.F. and Kendler, K.S. (1998). Heritability of binge-eating and broadly-defined bulimia nervosa. *Biological Psychiatry*, **44**, 1210–18.

Bushnell, J.A., Wells, J.E., McKenzie, J.M., Hornblow, A.R., Oakley-Browne, M.A. and Joyce, P.R. (1994). Bulimia comorbidity in the general population and in the clinic. *Psychological Medicine*, **24**, 605–11.

Carlat, D.J. and Camargo, C.A. (1991). Review of bulimia nervosa in males. *American Journal of Psychiatry*, **148**, 831–43.

Carlat, D.J., Camargo, C.A. and Herzog, D.B. (1997). Eating disorders in males: A report on 135 patients. *American Journal of Psychiatry*, **154**, 1127–32.

Carroll, J.M., Touyz, S.W. and Beaumont, P.J.V. (1996). Specific comorbidity between bulimia nervosa and personality disorders. *International Journal of Eating Disorders*, **19**, 159–170.

Carroll, M.E., France, C.P. and Meisch, R.A. (1979). Food deprivation increases oral and intravenous drug intake in rates. *Science,* **205**, 319–21.

Chiauzzi, E.J. and Liljegren, S. (1993). Taboo topics in addiction treatment: An empirical review of clinical folklore. *Journal of Substance Abuse Treatment*, **10**, 303–16.

Cooley, E. and Toray, T. (2001). Disordered eating in college freshman women: A prospective study. *Journal of American College Health*, **49**, 229–35.

Dally, P., Gomez, J. and Isaacs, A. (1979). *Anorexia Nervosa*. London: William Heinemann.

Dansky, B.S., Brewerton, T.D. and Kilpatrick, D.G. (2000). Comorbidity of bulimia nervosa and alcohol use disorders: Results from the National Women's Study. *International Journal of Eating Disorders*, **27**, 180–90.

Davis, C. and Cowles, M. (1991a). Body image and exercise: A study of relationships and comparisons between physically active men and women. *Sex Roles*, **25**, 33–44.

Davis, C. and Cowles, M. (1991b). Body image and exercise: A study of relationships and comparisons between physically active men and women. *Sex Roles*, **25**(1–2), 33–44.

Drewnowski, A. (1989). Taste responsiveness in eating disorders. *Annals New York Academy of Sciences,* **575**, 399–409.

Drewnowski, A. and Yee, D.K. (1987). Men and body image: Are males satisfied with their body weight? *Psychosomatic Medicine*, **49**(6), 626–34.

Drewnowski, A., Hopkins, S.A. and Kessler, R.C. (1988). The prevalence of bulimia nervosa in the US college student population. *American Journal of Public Health*, **78**, 1322–25.

Dunn, E.C., Larimer, M.E. and Neighbors, C. (2002). Alcohol and drug-related negative consequences in college students with bulimia nervosa and binge-eating disorder. *International Journal of Eating Disorders*, **32**, 171–78.

Fairburn, C.G. (1995). *Overcoming Binge Eating*. New York: Guilford Press.

Fischer, S., Anderson, K.G. and Smith, G.T. (2004). Coping with distress by eating or drinking: Role of trait urgency and expectancies. *Psychology of Addictive Behaviors*, **18**, 269–74.

Fisher, M., Schneider, M., Pegler, C. and Napolitano, B. (1991). Eating attitudes, health-risk behaviours, self-esteem, and anxiety among adolescent females in a suburban high school. *Journal of Adolescent Health*, **12**, 377–84.

Francis, L.A. and Birch, L.L. (2005). Maternal influences on daughters' restrained eating behaviour. *Health Psychology*, **24**, 548–54.

Franko, D.L., Dorer, D.J., Keel, P.K., Jackson, S., Manzo, I.P. and Herzog, D.B. (2005). How do eating disorders and alcohol use influence each other? *International Journal of Eating Disorders*, **28**, 200–07.

Geist, R., Davis, R. and Heinman, M. (1998). Binge/purge symptoms and comorbidity in adolescents with eating disorders. *Canadian Journal of Psychiatry*, **43**, 507–12.

Goebel, A.E., Scheibe, K.E., Grahling, S.C. and Striegel-Moore, R.H. (1995). Disordered eating in female alcohol dependent inpatients: Prevalence and associated psychopathology. *Eating Disorders: The Journal of Treatment and Prevention*, **3**, 37–46.

Goldbloom, D.S., Garfinkel, P.E. and Shaw, B.F. (1991). Biochemical aspects of bulimia nervosa. *Journal of Psychosomatic Research*, **35**(Suppl.1), 11–22.

Grisset, N.I. and Norvell, N.K. (1992). Perceived social support, social skills, and quality of relationships in bulimic women. *Journal of Consulting and Clinical Psychology*, **60**, 293–99.

Halmi, K.A., Eckert, E.M., P., Sampugnaro, V., Apple, R. and Cohen, J. (1991). Comorbidity of psychiatric diagnoses in anorexia nervosa. *Archives of General Psychiatry*, **48**, 712–18.

Halmi, K.A., Falk, J.R. and Swartz, E. (1981). Binge-eating and vomiting: A survey of a college population. *Psychological Medicine*, **11**, 697–706.

Hatsukami, D., Owen, P., Pyle, R. and Mitchell, J. (1982). Similarities and differences on the MMPI between women with bulimia and women with drug or alcohol abuse problems. *Addictive Behaviors*, **7**, 435–439.

Hawthorne, G. (1997). Pre-teenage drug use in Australia: The key predictors and school-based drug education. *Journal of Adolescent Health*, **20**, 384–95.

Herzog, D.B., Bradburn, I.S. and Newman, K. (1990). *Sexuality in Males with Eating Disorders*. In: A.E. Andersen (ed.) *Males with Eating Disorders*, pp. 40–53.

Herzog, D.B., Keller, M.B., Sacks, N.R., Yeh, C.J. and Lavori, P.W. (1992). Psychiatric comorbidity in treatment-seeking anorexics and bulimics. *Journal of the American Academy of Child and Adolescent Psychiatry*, **31**, 810–17.

Herzog, D.B., Keller, M.C., Lavori, P.W., Kenny, G.M. and Sacks, N.R. (1992). The prevalence of personality disorders in 210 women with eating disorders. *Journal of Clinical Psychiatry*, **53**, 147–52.

Herzog, D.B., Norman, D.K., Gordon, C. and Pepose, M. (1984). Sexual conflict and eating disorders in 27 males. *American Journal of Psychiatry*, **141**, 989–90.

Higuchi, S., Suzuki, K., Yamada, K., Parrish, K. and Kono, H. (1993). Alcoholics with eating disorders: Prevalence and clinical course (a study from Japan). *British Journal of Psychiatry*, **162**, 403–06.

Holderness, C.C., Brooks-Gunn, J. and Warren, M.P. (1994). Comorbidity of eating disorders and substance abuse: Review of the literature. *International Journal of Eating Disorders*, **16**, 1–34.

Hudson, J.I., Weiss, R.D., Pope, H.G., McElroy, S.K. and Mirin, S.M. (1992). Eating disorders in hospitalized substance abusers. *American Journal of Drug and Alcohol Abuse*, **18**, 75–85.

Humphrey, L.L. (1989). Observed family interactions among subtypes of eating disorders using structural analysis of social behaviour. *Journal of Consulting and Clinical Psychology*, **57**, 206–14.

Johnson, C. and Connors, M.E. (1987). *The Aetiology and Treatment of Bulimia Nervosa: A Biopsychosocial Perspective*. New York: Basic Books.

Johnson, C., Powers, P.S. and Dick, R. (1999). Athletes and eating disorders: The National Collegiate Athletic Association study. *International Journal of Eating Disorders*, **26**, 179–88.

Jonas, J.M. and Gold, M.S. (1988). Naltrexone treatment of bulimia: Clinical and theoretical findings linking eating disorders and substance abuse. *Advances in Alcoholism and Substance Abuse*, **7**, 29–37.

Jonas, J.M., Gold, M.S., Sweeney, D. and Pottash, A.L.C. (1987). Eating disorders and cocaine abuse: A survey of 259 cocaine abusers. *Journal of Clinical Psychiatry*, **48**, 47–50.

Jones, D.J., Fox, M.M., Babigan, H.M. and Hutton, H.E. (1980). Epidemiology of anorexia nervosa in Munroe County, New York: 1960–1976. *Psychosomatic Medicine*, **42**, 551–58.

Kane, T.A., Loxton, N.J., Staiger, P.K. and Dawe, S. (2004). Does the tendency to act impulsively underlie binge-eating and alcohol use problems? An empirical investigation. *Personality and Individual Differences*, **36**, 83–94.

Kassett, J.A., Gershon, E.S., Maxwell, M.E., *et al.* (1989). Psychiatric disorders in the first-degree relatives of probands with bulimia nervosa. *American Journal of Psychiatry* **146**, 1468–71.

Kearney Cooke, A. and Steichen Asch, P. (1990). Men, body image, and eating disorders. In: A.E. Andersen (ed.) *Males with Eating Disorders*, New York: Brunner Mazel, pp. 54–74.

Kendler, K.S., MacLean, C., Neale, M., Kessler, R., Heath, A. and Eaves, L. (1991). The genetic epidemiology of bulimia nervosa. *American Journal of Psychiatry*, **148**, 1627–37.

Kendler, K.S., Walters, E.E., Neale, M.C., Kessler, R.C., Heath, A.C. and Eaves, L.J. (1995). The structure of the genetic and environmental risk factors for six major psychiatric disorders in women: Phobia, generalised anxiety disorder, panic disorder, bulimia, major depression, and alcoholism. *Archives of General Psychiatry,* **52**, 374–83.

Keys, A., Brozek, J., Henschel, A., Mickelsen, O. and Taylor, H.L. (1950). *The Biology of Human Starvation*. Minneapolis, MN: University of Minnesota Press.

Killen, J.D., Taylor, C.B., Telch, M.J., Robinson, T.N., Maron, D.J. and Saylor, K.E. (1987). Depressive symptoms and substance use among adolescent binge eaters and purgers: A defined population study. *American Journal of Public Health*, **77**, 239–53.

King, S.M., Burt, S.A., Malone, S.M., McGue, M. and Iacono, W.G. (2005). Etiological contributions to heavy drinking from late adolescence to young adulthood. *Journal of Abnormal Psychology*, **114**, 587–98.

Klump, K.L., McGue, M. and Iacono, W.G. (2000). Age differences in genetic and environmental influences on eating attitudes and behaviours in preadolescent and adolescent female twins. *Journal of Abnormal Psychology*, **109**, 239–51.

Krahn, D.D. (1991). The relationship of eating disorders and substance abuse. *Journal of Substance Abuse*, **3**, 239–25.

Krahn, D.D. (1993). The relationship of eating disorders and substance abuse. In: E.S.L. Gomberg and T.D. Nirenberg (eds). *Women and Substance Abuse*. Stamford, CT: Ablex Publishing.

Krahn, D.D., Kurth, C., Demitrack, M. and Drewnowski, A. (1992). The relationship of dieting severity and bulimic behaviours to alcohol and other drug use in young women. *Journal of Substance Abuse*, **4**, 341–53.

Kranzler, H.R., Armeli, S., Feinn, R. and Tennen, H. (2004). Targeted naltrexone treatment moderates the relations between mood and drinking behaviour among problem drinkers. *Journal of Consulting and Clinical Psychology*, **72**, 317–27.

Lang, A.R. (1983). Addictive personality: A viable construct? In: P.K. Levison, D.R. Gerstein and D.R. Maloff (eds). *Commonalities in Substance Abuse and Habitual Behaviour.* Laxington, MA: D.C. Heath and Company, pp. 157–235.

Laure, P., Lecerf, T., Friser, A. and Binsinger, C. (2004). Drugs: Recreational drug use and attitudes towards doping of high school athletes. *International Journal of Sports Medicine*, **25**, 133–38.

Levine, M.P. and Smolak, L. (2002). Body image development in adolescence. In: T.F. Cash and T. Pruzinsky (eds). *Body Image. A Handbook of Theory, Research, and Clinical Practice*. Philadelphia: The Guilford Press. pp. 74–82.

Lucas, A.R., Beard, C.M., O'Fallon, W.M. and Kurland, L.T. (1991). 50-year trends in the incidence of anorexia nervosa in Rochester, Minnesota: A population-based study. *American Journal of Psychiatry*, **148**, 917–922.

Margo, J.L. (1987). Anorexia nervosa in males: A comparison with female patients. *British Journal of Psychiatry*, **151**, 80–83.

Matsunaga, H., Kririike, N., Nagata, T. and Yamagami, S. (1998). Personality disorders in patients with eating disorders in Japan. *International Journal of Eating Disorders*, **23**, 399–408.

McCormack, S. and Carman, R.S. (1989). Eating motivations and bulimic behaviour among college women. *Psychological Reports*, **64**, 1163–66.

McGue, M., Pickens, R.W. and Svikis, D.S. (1992). Sex and age effects on the inheritance of alcohol problems: A twin study.

Journal of Abnormal Psychology, **101**, 3–17.

Meyer, D.F. (1997). Codependency as a mediator between stressful events and eating disorders. *Journal of Clinical Psychology*, **53**, 107–16.

Miller, P.M. (1987). Commonalities of addictive behaviours. In: T.D. Nirenberg and S.A. Maisto (eds). *Developments in the Assessment and Treatment of Addictive Behaviours*. Norwood, NJ: Ablex Publishing, pp. 9–30.

Mintz, L.B., Kashubeck, S. and Tracy, L.S. (1995). Relations among parental alcoholism, eating disorders, and substance abuse in nonclinical college women: Additional evidence against the uniformity myth. *Journal of Counseling Psychology*, **42**, 65–70.

Mitchell, J.E. and Goff, G. (1984). Bulimia in male patients. *Psychosomatics*, **25**, 909–13.

Mitchell, J.E., Hatsukami, D., Eckert, E.D. and Pyle, R.L. (1985). Characteristics of 275 patients with bulimia. *American Journal of Psychiatry*, **142**, 482–85.

Newman, M.M. and Gold, M.S. (1992). Preliminary findings of patterns of substance abuse in eating disorder patients. *American Journal of Drug and Alcohol Abuse*, **18**, 207–11.

O'Brien, K.M. and Vincent, N.K. (2003). Psychiatric comorbidity in anorexia and bulimia nervosa: Nature, prevalence, and causal relationships. *Clinical Psychology Review*, **23**, 57–74.

Olivardia, R., Pope, H.G. Jr, Mangweth, B. and Hudson, J.J. (1995). Eating disorders in college men. *American Journal of Psychiatry*, **152**, 1279–85.

Oyebode, F., Boodhoo, J.A. and Schapira, K. (1988b). Anorexia nervosa in males: Clinical features and outcome. *International Journal of Eating Disorders*, **7**(1), 121–24.

Patton, G.C., Coffey, C. and Sawyer, S.M. (2003). The outcome of adolescent disorders: Findings from the Victorian Adolescent Health Cohort study. *European Child and Adolescent Psychiatry*, **12**, 25–29.

Peveler, R. and Fairburn, C. (1990). Eating disorders in women who abuse alcohol. *British Journal of Addiction*, **85**, 1633–38.

Pike, K.M. and Rodin, J. (1991). Mothers, daughters, and disordered eating. *Journal of Abnormal Psychology*, **100**, 198–204.

Pope, H.G. Jr, Hudson, J.I., Yurgelun-Todd, D. and Hudson, M.S. (1984). Prevalence of anorexia nervosa and bulimia in three student populations. *International Journal of Eating Disorders*, **3**, 45–51.

Rastam, M. (1992). Anorexia in 52 Swedish adolescents: Premorbid problems and comorbidity. *Journal of the American Academy of Child and Adolescent Psychiatry*, **31**, 819–29.

Ratti, L.A., Humphrey, L.L. and Lyons, J.S. (1996). Structural analysis of families with a polydrug-dependent, bulimic, or normal adolescent daughter. *Journal of Consulting and Clinical Psychology*, **64**, 1255–62.

Rosen, J.C. (1990). Body-image disturbance in eating disorders. In: T.F. Cash and T. Pruzinsky (eds). *Body Images: Development, Deviance, and Change*. New York: Guilford Press, pp. 190–214.

Russell, G.F.M. (1979). Bulimia nervosa: An ominous variant of anorexia nervosa. *Psychological Medicine*, **9**, 429–48.

Schmidt, N.B. and Telch, M.J. (1990). Prevalence of personality disorders among bulimics, nonbulimic binge eaters, and normal controls. *Journal of Psychopathology and Behavioral Assessment*, **12**, 169–185.

Schneider, J.A. and Agras, W.S. (1987). Bulimia in males: A matched comparison with females. *International Journal of Eating Disorders*, **6**, 235–42.

Schotte, D.E. and Stunkard, A.J. (1987). Bulimia versus bulimic behaviours on a college campus. *Journal of the American Medical Association*, **258**, 1213–15.

Schuckit, M.A., Tipp, J.E., Anthenelli, R.M., Bucholz, K.K., Hesselbrock, V.M. and Nurnberger, J.I. (1996). Anorexia nervosa and bulimia nervosa in alcohol-dependent men and women and their relatives. *American Journal of Psychiatry*, **153**, 74–82.

Schwalberg, M.D., Barlow, D.H., Alger, S.A. and Howard, L.J. (1992). Comparison of bulimics, obese binge eaters, social phobics, and individuals with panic disorder on comorbidity across DSM-III-R anxiety disorders. *Journal of Abnormal Psychology*, **101**, 675–81.

Sharp, C.W., Clark, S.A., Dunan, J.R., Blackwod, D.H.R. and Shapiro, C.M. (1994). Clinical presentation of anorexia nervosa in males: 24 new cases. *International Journal of Eating Disorders*, **15**, 125–34.

Spitzer, R.L., Yanovski, S.Z., Wadden, T., *et al.* (1993). Binge-eating disorder: Its further validation in a multisite study. *International Journal of Eating Disorders*, **13**, 137–53.

Stice, E. (1994). Review of the evidence for a socio-cultural model of bulimia nervosa and an exploration of the mechanisms of action. *Clinical Psychology Review*, **14**, 633–71.

Stice, E. and Shaw, H. (2003). Prospective relations of body image, eating, and affective disturbances to smoking onset in adolescent girls: How Virginia slims. *Journal of Consulting and Clinical Psychology*, **71**, 129–35.

Stock, S.L., Goldberg, E., Corbett, S. and Katzman, D.K. (2002). Substance use in female adolescents with eating disorders. *Journal of Adolescent Health*, **31**, 176–82.

Stout, M.L. and Mintz, L.B. (1996). Differences among nonclinical college women with alcoholic mothers, alcoholic fathers, and nonalcoholic parents. *Journal of Counseling Psychology*, **43**, 466–72.

Striegel-Moore, R.H. and Huydic, E.S. (1993). Problem drinking and symptoms of disordered eating in female high school students. *International Journal of Eating Disorders*, **14**, 417–25.

Striegel-Moore, R.H., Silberstein, L.R. and Rodin, J. (1986). Towards an understanding of risk factors for bulimia. *American Psychologist*, **41**, 246–63.

Striegel-Moore, R.H., Silberstein, L.R., French, P. and Rodin, J. (1989). A prospective study of disordered eating among college students. *International Journal of Eating Disorders*, **8**, 499–509.

Strober, M. and Humphrey, L.L. (1987). Familial contributions to the aetiology and course of anorexia nervosa and bulimia. *Journal of Consulting and Clinical Psychology*, **55**, 654–59.

Telch, C.F. and Stice, E. (1998). Psychiatric morbidity in women with binge-eating disorder: Prevalence rates from a non-treatment-seeking sample. *Journal of Consulting and Clinical Psychology*, **66**, 768–76.

Telch, C.F., Agras, W.S. and Rossiter, E. (1988). Binge-eating increases with increasing adiposity. *International Journal of Eating Disorders*, **7**, 115–19.

Tiggemann, M. (2002). Media influences on body image development. In: T.F. Cash and T. Pruzinsky (eds). *Body Image. A Handbook of Theory, Research, and Clinical Practice*. New York: The Guilford Press, pp. 91 – 98.

Tiggemann, M. (2005). Body dissatisfaction and adolescent self-esteem: Prospective findings. *Body Image. An International Journal of Research*, **2**, 129–35.

Timmerman, M.G., Wells, L.A. and Chen, S. (1990). Bulimia nervosa and associated alcohol abuse among secondary school students. *Journal of the American Academy of Child and Adolescent Psychiatry*, **29**, 118–22.

von Ranson, K.M., McGue, M. and Iacono, W.G. (2003). Disordered eating and substance use in an epidemiological sample: II. Associations within families. *Psychology of Addictive Behaviors*, **17**, 193–201.

Wadsworth, E.J.K., Moss, S.C., Simpson, S.A. and Smith, A.P. (2004). Factors associated with recreational drug use. *Journal of Psychopharmacology*, **18**, 238–48.

Walfish, S., Stenmark, D.E., Sarco, D., Shealy, J.S. and Krone, A.M. (1992). Incidence of bulimia in substance misusing women in residential treatment. *The International Journal of the Addictions*, **27**, 425–33.

Weiss, R.D., Griffin, M.L. and Mirin, S.M. (1992). Drug abuse as self-medication for depression: An empirical study. *American Journal of Drug and Alcohol Abuse*, **18**, 121–29.

Wilson, G.T. (1993). Binge-eating and addictive disorders. In: C.G. Fairburn and G.T. Wilson (eds). *Binge-eating: Nature, Assessment, and Treatment*. New York: Guilford Press, pp. 97–120.

Wilson, G.T. and Walsh, B.T. (1991). Eating disorders in the DSM-IV. *Journal of Abnormal Psychology*, **100**, 362–65.

Wilson, J.R. (1992). Bulimia nervosa: Occurrence with psychoactive substance use disorders. *Addictive Behaviors*, **17**, 603–07.

Wolfe, W.L. and Maisto, S.A. (2000). The relationship between eating disorders and substance use: Moving beyond co-prevalence research. *Clinical Psychology Review*, **20**, 617–31.

Wonderlich, S.A. and Mitchell, J.E. (1997). Eating disorders and comorbidity: Empirical, conceptual, and clinical implications. *Psychopharmacology Bulletin*, **33**, 381–90.

Wonderlich, S.A., Klein, M.H. and Council, J.R. (1996). Relationship of social perceptions and self-concept in bulimia nervosa. *Journal of Consulting and Clinical Psychology*, **64**, 1231–37.

Wonderlich, S.A., Swift, W.J., Slotnick, H.B. and Goodman, S. (1990). DSM-III-R personality disorders in eating-disorders subtypes. *International Journal of Eating Disorders*, **9**, 607–16.

Yager, J., Kurtzman, F., Landsverk, J. and Wiesmeier, E. (1988). Behaviors and attitudes related to eating disorders in homosexual male college students. *American Journal of Psychology*, **145**, 495–97.

■ Part Six ■

Reproductive and Developmental Concerns

26 Alcohol and fertility

Olga B.A. van den Akker

The effects of alcohol on fertility have been investigated in many different ways – neuroendocrinologically and morphologically, in relation to alcohol-related reproductive diseases such as cancers, as well as before conception, during pregnancy and in the perinatal period. However, because alcohol consumption does not occur in a vacuum, but takes place in a lifestyle context, research is hampered by many unforeseen and possibly confounding variables such as the comorbid effects of smoking, diet and age. The relationship between alcohol and fertility is further compounded for women because they face the additional consequences of pregnancy or nurture-related health effects on the offspring.

It is often assumed that fertility is either something which happens, or which doesn't happen, and when it doesn't happen it is largely due to physiological or neuroendocrine or hormonal factors. However, controllable and less easily controllable lifestyle factors can also favourably (or adversely) affect fertility; these include such things as maintaining a regular healthy diet, exercising, limiting alcohol and caffeine consumption, not engaging in risky sex, not smoking and not taking drugs. Even stress has been implicated in impaired fertility (Boivin and Schmidt, 2005; Demyttenaere *et al.*, 1989; Greil, 1997). A significant decline in sperm quality during recent decades (Auger *et al.*, 1995; Swan *et al.*, 2000) and changes in women's roles in general as well as their position within society have been implicated in the decline in fertility (Sundby and Schei, 1996), despite earlier reports (Gunnell and Ewings, 1994) and more recent reports (Kold Jensen *et al.* 2005) that show trends remained stable over time. Some of the increase in impaired fertility has been explained by the higher levels of education and alcohol consumption reported in a study of nearly 10,000 European women (Rostad *et al.*, 2006).

This chapter will provide an overview of the research carried out into the relationship between fertility and alcohol. It will demonstrate that the relationship between alcohol and fertility is inconclusive (Repromed *et al.*, 2007) but that even the equivocal evidence points to a need to promote the development of policy that focuses on health behaviours before conception, thereby alleviating some of the burden on fertility treatments. Specific healthy-lifestyle (alcohol) policies should be developed for women (and men) who are trying to become pregnant, or who are likely to become pregnant at some point in the future, as well as those who are already pregnant, to encourage healthy reproductive functioning and healthy offspring.

Smoking, like alcohol consumption, is one of the 'controllable' lifestyle choices that has received a huge amount of scientific and media attention alerting the public to the dangers of smoking for themselves, their fertility, their unborn fetuses and any offspring affected by passive smoking within their environment. Smoking can also change the balance of some hormonal functioning (oestrogen, progesterone and testosterone) and well as follicle development (Younglai *et al.*, 2005) and lead to the development of a thicker zona pellucida (Shiloh *et al.*, 2004) that affects sperm penetration. These factors can affect a couple's chances of conception (Kunzle *et al.*, 2003; Zenzes *et al.*, 1999).

Smoking during pregnancy may damage chromosomes leading to abnormalities in the fetus, or miscarriage. In the pregnant woman, smoking can lead to hypertensive vascular disease or metabolic disorders such as diabetes or thyroid dysfunctioning. There are many other effects of smoking on fertility, and effects of other toxins on fertility. Alcohol is one of those toxins, and has been identified as having significant effects on fertility in both men and women, although the mechanisms are less well described.

There is also good evidence to suggest that smoking and alcohol use (Breslau *et al.*, 1996) and other risky behaviours tend to cluster or co-occur together (Small and Luster, 1994; van den Akker and Lees, 2001; WHO, 1989; Young, 2003), thus making it even more difficult to be certain that any observed effects are due to one or several lifestyle factors. This chapter will show that the effect of alcohol on fertility is a public health issue, as listed below:

- Alcohol consumption is widespread and increasing in many countries.
- Women with higher alcohol consumption take longer to conceive (Hakim *et al.*, 1998).
- In women, alcohol may influence the timing of onset of menopause (Torgeson *et al.*, 1994, 1997).
- In men, alcohol is known to be present in sperm following alcohol ingestion and may be responsible for failures to conceive or implant (Asher *et al.*, 1979).
- It is possible that the effects of alcohol are cumulative; older women are less likely to conceive (Hull *et al.*, 1996; Templeton *et al.*, 1996) and the risks of miscarriage, genetic abnormalities (Lansac, 1995; Tarin, 1998) and delayed conception (Ford *et al.*, 2000) also increase with increasing age of the man.
- Specific alcoholic drinks can predispose to specific reproductive cancers (Goodman and Tung, 2003).
- It is equally important to warn women who do know and those who do not know they are pregnant about the possible threat that alcohol poses to the viability of their pregnancy, and the fetus, particularly in the early weeks (Collier *et al.*, 2002; Day *et al.*, 1989).
- It is essential to inform women that significant alcohol intake during pregnancy is likely to harm their baby (Harlap and Shiono, 1980; Wilsnack *et al.*, 1984).
- Alcohol leads to a higher incidence of miscarriages (Windham *et al.*, 1992; Henriksen *et al.*, 2004), placental abruption, preterm deliveries and stillbirth (Hadi *et al.*, 1987).

Fig. 26.1 shows how lifestyle factors, sociodemographc factors and individual differences interact in fertility. Lifestyle factors include alcohol use, smoking, sexual behaviour and drug taking. Sociodemographic factors include ethnicity, age, gender, educational and occupational situations. Individual differences include processing and metabolising toxins and weight.

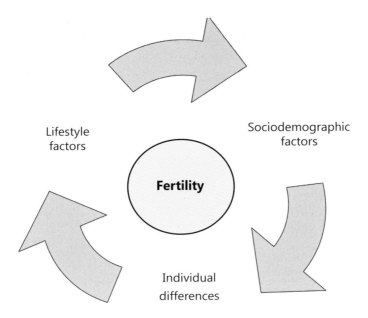

Figure 26.1 Lifestyle factors, sociodemographc factors and individual differences are three global factors that interact in fertility and determine the response to toxins. Adapted from Ebrahim *et al.*, 2000.

Descriptions and measurement of alcohol

Alcohol is a common term used to describe ethanol or grain alcohol, which is a colourless, mildly toxic and flammable chemical compound found in alcoholic drinks such as wine, beer and spirits. Alcohol is referred to as a psychoactive drug because of its depressant effects. Across the world, societies manufacture their own alcoholic beverages and many of them regulate alcohol consumption to adults or restrict its sale and consumption to some sections of the population. The concentration of alcohol in beverages is usually specified as the percentage of alcohol by volume (ABV), or as 'proof' which roughly consists of a 2 to 1 ratio to the percentage of alcoholic content by volume (so 40 per cent proof is the same as 20 per cent ABV). The international community adheres to similar descriptions of alcohol in 'units'. For example, 1 unit is the same as 10 mL of pure (ethanol) alcohol. In terms of actual consumption of different alcoholic drinks per glass, a simple formula used in the UK is:

$$\frac{\text{ABV} \times \text{volume in mL}}{1000}$$

So that:

- One 25 mL glass of spirits = 40 per cent ABV (1 unit).
- One 125 mL glass of weak wine = 8 per cent ABV (1 unit).
- One 125 mL glass of normal wine = 12 per cent ABV (1.5 units).
- One 284 mL half pint of weak beer = 3.5 per cent ABV (1 unit).

Awareness of over-consumption, using the UK unitary guidelines, is therefore important in relation to impaired functioning. Public health campaigns have ensured that information about the differential risks of alcohol intakes in men and women are acknowledged and adhered to, particularly when operating machinery or driving. This chapter will only refer to the generic common term 'alcohol'. Since alcohol is universally manufactured and used, albeit differentially, it has a number of societal uses – it has been used as part of a normal daily diet, for medical or hygienic reasons, specifically for relaxation, as an aphrodisiac, and so on.

Effects of alcohol on health

There are reports of the contribution of alcohol to longevity and other health benefits, provided that it is consumed in moderation (Cabot 1904; Truelsen *et al.*, 1998). However, not everyone is able to control the amount of alcohol they consume. Current health fears that are widely reported in the media and documented in the scientific literature concern the effects of binge drinking in young people (Bray, 1999), which can lead to liver damage or death in some (albeit a minority) who drink excessively. Nevertheless, although the actual amounts drunk by 'binge' drinkers tends to be over-estimated, addiction to alcohol is not uncommon and the effects of that addiction on the individual and those around them can be devastating; alcohol-addicted people lose all functions in society because of their inability to perform their roles, such as parenting, partner relationships, employment and education. In health terms, cirrhosis of the liver and serious withdrawal symptoms are among the most devastating problems. In reproductive health terms, alcohol consumption during pregnancy can lead to permanent impaired mental and physical defects in the child. These are referred to as 'fetal alcohol spectrum disorder' (FASD).

Alcohol's mechanism of action

Alcohol is absorbed into the bloodstream and because it is a small molecule it can cross the blood–brain barrier quite easily. Therefore it reaches the brain quickly and its effects are rapid. Since alcohol has a depressant effect on the central nervous system, it is unsurprising there are numerous side effects associated with its consumption, which depend to some extent on the circumstances of its use. For example, alcohol following a large meal has less intoxicating effects than if it consumed on an empty stomach. Its effects are also varied, ranging from initial relaxed disinhibitory feelings to difficulties in motor coordination. Alcohol can diffuse into most tissues in the body, and if highly concentrated can have fatal consequences.

Early studies of the effects of alcohol on fertility were speculative because the underlying mechanisms could not be established. Many early models of the possible effects of alcohol on fertility were based on animal studies, which will not be discussed here. Other reports came from observations of impotent alcoholic men, feminised alcoholic men and chronic alcohol abusers with hypogonadism (reduced or completely absent secretion of hormones from the gonads – the testes in men and the ovaries in women) or who were sterile (unable to reproduce) (van Thiel and Lester, 1974; Lemere and Smith, 1973). The research did not develop much beyond animal studies because, understandably, many alcohol-related problems were attributed to alcoholic cirrhosis, not reproductive failure, which was assumed to be secondary or comorbid (Morrione, 1944). However, advances in neuroendocrine measurement techniques allowed research to develop considerably. It was found that hepatic enzymes (important in the metabolism of male steroid sex hormones) are affected by long-term alcohol use (Gordon *et al.*, 1979; van Thiel, 1979). Decreased activity of 5-alpha-reductase (an enzyme that converts testosterone into dihydrotestosterone) affects normal male reproductive functioning. Increased activity of aromatases (hepatic and adrenal) that convert androgens to oestrogens may account for observations of increased oestrone levels in alcoholic men. Alcoholic men also demonstrate lower plasma testosterone levels, perhaps because they have increased sensitivity to oestrogen receptors (Lester and van Thiel, 1979; see Table 26.1).

Table 26.1 Some effects of alcohol on male hormones

Substance	Change due to alcohol	Overall effect in men
Active androgens	Decreased formation	Feminisation
Oestrogens (peripheral)	Increased formation	Feminisation
Oestreogen receptors	Increased sensitivity	Feminisation
Testosterone (circulating)	Decreased levels	Feminisation

It must be pointed out that hepatic function ranges from normal to impaired in alcoholic people with fertility problems (Boiesen *et al.*, 1979; Farnsworth *et al.*, 1978; van Thiel *et al.*, 1974) and that correlations between male fertility problems and the amount of liver damage are not always found (Lindholm *et al.*, 1978a,b). Nevertheless, it is clear that chronic and excessive alcohol use affects both male and female fertility in some way, and is teratogenic (that is, it leads to structural and/or functional birth defects). A classic example of the teratogenic consequences of parental alcohol abuse is demonstrated in offspring with fetal alcohol syndrome, which is discussed in more detail in Chapter 27.

The potential risks identified by early research in relation to alcohol consumption and (ethanol) toxicity need further elaboration, so that effective treatments for alcohol-related reproductive disorders can be developed. There is some evidence to suggest that there may be anti-promotional (chemopreventive) effects of alcohol in women (see Table 26.2) which reduce the risk of developing ovarian cancer. Alcohol could downregulate oestrogen production by interfering with circulating levels of gonadotropins, intra-ovarian concentrations of growth factor-1 and nitric oxide inhibiting ovulation (Dees *et al.*, 2001). Alcohol is likely to decrease concentrations of progesterone and dehydroepiandrosterone (Valimaki *et al.*, 1995) and irregular cycles evident in alcoholic women (Becker *et al.*, 1989) may decrease the risk of ovarian cancer (Risch, 1998).

Table 26.2 Some effects of alcohol on female hormones

Substance (proc	Change due to alcohol	Overall effect in women
Oestrogens	Downregulated	Irregular menstrual cycle
Progesterone (circulating)	Decreased levels	Irregular menstrual cycle
Dihydroepiandosterone	Decreased concentration	Irregular menstrual cycle

There have also been suggestions that alcohol can induce a rise in oestrogen, reducing secretion of follicle-stimulating hormone and suppressing ovulation (see Gill 2000 for a detailed overview of pre- and post-menopausal women). Even a direct effect of alcohol on the maturation of the ovum, ovulation and blastocyst behaviour has been described (Eggert *et al.*, 2004). Clearly both rising and falling oestrogen levels are involved in impaired fertility. However, overall the data are equivocal, probably because a number of critical variables have not been constant across studies, including the type of alcoholic drinks used and chronic or short-term use of alcohol, and insufficient consideration has been given to the half-life of plasma oestrogen levels (Purohit, 1996).

Alcohol and reproductive cancers

Research examining the relationship between dietary or lifestyle factors and ovarian cancer spans several decades (Byers *et al.*, 1983; Gwinn *et al.*, 1986; Kato *et al.*, 1989; Whittmore *et al.*, 1988). In general, the results have been negative in relation to alcohol, or have reported that people drinking around 10 g of alcohol or more were less likely to develop ovarian cancer than non-drinkers (Kushi *et al.*, 1999), whereas the opposite is true in relation to breast cancer, in which a moderate relationship with alcohol has been reported (Singletary and Gapstur, 2001). Goodman and Tung (2003) investigated the link between ovarian cancer and alcohol in a large mixed-race population-based study. Over 500 women with ovarian cancer (mostly malignant) and over 600 controls were interviewed and given a questionnaire that included items on food, alcohol (over their lifetime) and tobacco use during the year before they received their diagnosis. Women who consumed alcohol during the study time (but not former drinkers) were less likely to have ovarian cancer than 'never' drinkers. The type of alcohol consumed also affected likelihood estimates, inasmuch as women who drank red wine had reduced odds ratios for ovarian cancer than 'never' drinkers, whereas spirit drinking was associated with an increased risk of borderline serious tumours, and beer drinking was associated with a reduced risk of endometrioid carcinoma compared with 'never' drinkers. These results confirm earlier population studies by Gwinn *et al.* (1986) and Kushi *et al.* (1999) which showed that current rather than lifetime consumption is related to ovarian cancer. However, Wise *et al.* (2004) reported on a large population-based study from the Black Women's Health Study, and noted that the risk of uterine leiomyomata (fibroids) was positively associated both with the number of years of and current alcohol (beer) consumption.

Alcohol and fertility

High alcohol intake has sometimes been reported to have no effect on fertility (Curtis *et al.*, 1997; Florack *et al.*, 1994) and other times to have a detrimental effect on fertility (Olsen *et al.*, 1982, 1997). A lack of effect of moderate alcohol consumption on conception has been observed in couples undergoing donor insemination (Zaadstra *et al.*, 1994). Zaadstra *et al.* also reported that women with high alcohol intake were more fertile than women who did not drink at all. However, it is possible that these women changed their alcohol intake during the study period, and recall of alcohol intake at the end of the study period was not the same as that during the study periods (particularly when the pregnant women were asked to report their intake retrospectively, as in Olsen's studies of 1997 and 1982). Because these data are inconsistent, it is possible that different amounts of alcohol consumption have variable effects, depending on the particular stage around conception, and this has not always been controlled for in previous research. Animal research on biological models of the effects of alcohol on female reproductive functioning suggests this could be the case.

The first human prospective longitudinal study followed 423 couples over a cumulative total of 1596 cycles (Jensen *et al.*, 1998). Investigators assessed the impact of alcohol intake in both partners on fertility, directly taking into account the stage of questioning (around the ovulatory period). All couples enrolled in this study had stopped taking contraceptives with the intention to become pregnant, and all the men provided a sperm sample. During follow-up, the women recorded their vaginal bleeding and sexual activity on a daily rating scale. All couples also completed monthly questionnaires that included questions on lifestyle factors, such as the amount and type of alcohol consumed and diseases affecting fecundability (ovarian cysts and gonorrhoea). Sixty-four per cent of women who reported low alcohol intake (less than 5 drinks per week) became pregnant within 6 cycles compared to 55 per cent of women who reported a high intake of alcohol. The type of alcohol consumed was not as important a contributing factor to conception as the amount of alcohol consumed. However, Jensen *et al.*, reported that a number of other male and female factors contributed to the effect of alcohol consumption and conception in the women (see Table 26.3).

Table 26.3 **Demographic and lifestyle factors and their effects on fertility in men and women**

Factors relevent to fertility	In women	In men
Age	Yes	No
Age at menarche	No	—
Smoking	Yes	Yes
Smoking exposure	Yes	Yes
Caffeine intake	No	No
Diseases related to reproduction	Yes	Yes
Sperm concentration	—	Yes
Duration of menstrual cycle	Yes	—
Last method was oral contraceptive	Yes	—
Body mass index (BMI)	Yes	No

These results provided a major contribution to research, as this was a prospective evaluation of couples intending to conceive. Nevertheless, a number of other confounding variables which were not controlled for could have affected the results of this study. For example, it is possible that social class (Grenbaek *et al.*, 1995) or diet (Colditz *et al.*, 1991) should have been incorporated.

The fact that men's alcohol use is not a contributing factor to fecundity has been reported by some researchers (Curtis *et al.*, 1997; Florack *et al.*, 1994; Olsen, 1997) and supports research that shows a lack of relationship between sperm quality and alcohol intake (Dunphy *et al.*, 1991; Goverde *et al.*, 1995; Oldereid *et al.*, 1992). Research has also demonstrated no relationship between a man's alcohol intake and spontaneous abortions of pregnancy (Halmesmaki *et al.*, 1989; Parazzini *et al.*, 1990; Windham *et al.*, 1992).

However, in 2004 researchers reported the analysis of early biochemically detected and clinically detectable pregnancies in the same prospective sample (Henriksen *et al.*, 2004; Jensen *et al.* 1998). They found that of the 186 pregnancies, 131 were successful, and 30 per cent were spontaneously aborted. A high proportion of the clinically recognised pregnancies were aborted spontaneously between 6 and 15 weeks. The spontaneous abortions were significantly associated with high alcohol intake by women and men in the week that conception took place. These results are important because they include a male contribution of risk to the pregnancy, which had not been acknowledged previously because men had not been included in these studies. Other research supports the relationship of maternal alcohol intake and early pregnancy loss (Kesmodel *et al.*, 2002; Windham *et al.*, 1997). Since these data came from a prospective cohort, the results are noteworthy.

Three more recent studies also report significant male effects on fertility. Two of them evaluated the effects of chronic alcoholism on fertility hormones and the quality of semen; importantly they removed smoking as a covariate and found a significant effect of chronic alcohol consumption on follicle-stimulating hormone, luteinising hormone and oestradiol levels (they were significantly increased) and testosterone, progesterone and sperm quality (they were significantly decreased) (Muthusami and Chinnaswamy, 2005). Decreases in plasma testosterone, follicle-stimulating hormone and luteinising hormone were reported by Maneesh *et al.* (2006). Agarwal and Prabakaran (2005) obtained convincing evidence for the notion that smoking and alcohol enhances the generation of reactive oxygen species (ROS), causing destructive effects on mitochondria, sperm and DNA.

Alcohol and subfertility

Eggert and colleagues (2004) reported a dose–response relationship between attendance at a Swedish infertility clinic and reports of higher alcohol intakes. Much research has confirmed an effect for alcohol and problems with conception. Rostad *et al.* (2006) in a population-based questionnaire study of 9983 menopausal women reported a 4.8 per cent subfertility rate, 4.1 per cent voluntary childlessness, and 1.8 per cent involuntary childlessness. The lifestyle variables smoking and alcohol consumption were classified as follows: 'excessive' alcohol intake was based on affirmative responses from women reporting 'they were probably drinking too much'; women who did not think they drank too much, but did drink alcohol, were classified as 'moderate drinkers' and abstainers were rated as 'non-drinkers'. They found that subfertile and involuntarily childless women were more often 'excessive' alcohol drinkers. Impaired fertility was also associated with higher educational achievements.

An association of fertility and higher educational levels has been previously reported by Meyer (1999), and associations between alcohol and fertility by Tolstrup *et al.* (2003) and Juhl *et al.* (2001). However, these data were not all derived from population-based surveys, which seriously affects interpretation of the data. Previous studies utilising clinic-based samples may have provided underestimates of lifestyle-related unhealthy behaviours, thereby maximising the patient's chances of being accepted for treatment of infertility. Rostad's study was an exception, not only because it was based on a representative cross-section of the population, but also because huge numbers of responses were used in their analyses. Nevertheless, this study also had limitations in that it relied entirely on recall and diagnoses provided by the women, which are not necessarily the same as any medical diagnosis of infertility they may have had. Most importantly, it is impossible to know from these data if the women drank excessive levels of alcohol during the time they were trying to conceive. So although the subfertile and involuntarily childless women reported themselves more often as being excessive drinkers, this could only impair their fertility if they were excessive drinkers at the time they were trying to conceive. The authors themselves cautiously propose an alternative interpretation – that the higher alcohol consumption was the result of the distress of not conceiving!

Juhl *et al.* (2002) studied the time it took a large national cohort of pregnant Danish women to conceive between 1997 and 2000. They reported that in nulliparous women, moderate and high alcohol intakes were not associated with time to pregnancy; but in parous women, high alcohol intake was associated with the time taken to get pregnant. Interestingly, non-drinkers waited the longest time to get pregnant, suggesting alcohol intake is not adversely associated with fertility. In 2003 Juhl *et al.*, reported that wine drinkers had the shortest waiting time to conception (although one cannot exclude the possibility that other characteristics of wine drinkers could be responsible for these effects). In the study by Olsen *et al.* (1997) a relationship between high alcohol intake and delayed time to pregnancy was reported. Other research in normal populations indicates a relationship even with moderate intake of alcohol and delayed fertility (Hakim *et al.*, 1998).

In another study, this effect was seen only in infertile populations (Grodstein *et al.*, 1994). Jensen *et al.* (1998) found more than a 50 per cent reduction in fecundity in women taking any amount of alcohol compared to non-drinkers. Juhl *et al.* (2002) incorporated body mass index, smoking and parity as potentially associated factors. They used the Danish National Birth Cohort, which is a nationwide study of pregnant women and their children. Over 15,000 pregnant women completed the first telephone interview. Unlike Rostad *et al.* Juhl asked their study population to comment on their drinking habits before pregnancy (so that these habits would not be the result of a lack of fertility, as was possible in Rostad's study).

Alcohol and pregnancy

Population estimates of alcohol consumption in women of reproductive age, between 1988 and 1992, showed a decrease from 56 per cent to 51 per cent in line with a concomitant decrease in smoking in the target group (Ebrahim *et al.*, 1999). In 2000, Ebrahim and coworkers (Ebrahim *et al.*, 2000) examined national trends in alcohol and tobacco use among pregnant and non-pregnant women aged 18–44 years (two-thirds of them were white) who took part in the Behavioural Risk Factor Surveillance System survey (an ongoing state-based telephone survey of US civilians aged 18 and over). The estimates were retrospective because no information about these lifestyle factors was available before these women became pregnant. They reported a decreasing trend in smoking and drinking alcohol during pregnancy between 1987 and 1997. There was a significant decrease in smoking and drinking in pregnant women between 1987 (5.4 per cent) and 1990 (3.0 per cent) and in non-pregnant women (17.6 per cent and 14.2 per cent respectively). These figures failed to decrease further in 1997, particularly in younger women, although usage in older women decreased more dramatically, as shown in Fig. 26.2. Ebrahim *et*

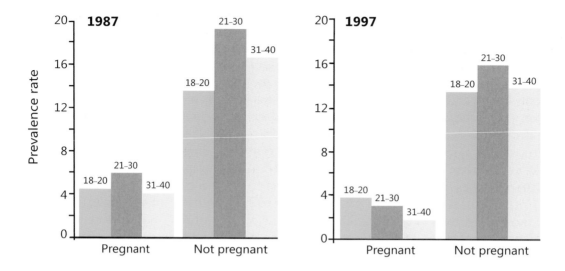

Figure 26.2   Prevalence rates of combined alcohol and tobacco use in pregnant and non-pregnant women aged 18–20, 21–30 and 31–40 years in 1987 (*left*) and 1997 (*right*). Adapted from Ebrahim *et al.* 2006.

al. (2000) also reported a higher prevalence of alcohol and tobacco use in unmarried women, which, when placed in context, might indicate comorbidity. According to Ebrahim *et al.*, this could include risky sexual behaviour and equally high rates among their male peers.

Effects on the fetus

Research has reported that about half of all women conceiving spontaneously are unaware they are pregnant until after the 4th week of gestation (Bar-Oz *et al.*, 1999; Floyd *et al.*, 1999). This means they are unlikely to have changed their lifestyle during the early stages of embryonic development. Many of the substances ingested during pregnancy enter the fetal circulation via the placenta from as early as the 5th week of gestation (Briggs *et al.*, 1994), hence they can affect the fetus directly (Morgan, 1977). The organs and tissues of an embryo develop during the first 2 months or so of gestation, and organ maturation and growth occurs from 2–9 months of gestation (Sastry, 1991). Research has shown that most teratogenic events occur during the embryonic period when the placenta is also still developing and is not fully functional and the embryo is still differentiating (Collier *et al.*, 2002). It is therefore problematic that during this critical period of development, maternal and environmental factors can alter the activity of constitutive metabolising enzymes. These maternal factors, coupled with research showing sperm chromosome or intergenerational effects (Robbins *et al.*, 2005), provide further evidence for the seriousness of the effects of alcohol on reproductively active populations. Public health calls to reduce the intake of noxious stimulants prior to conception and in the early stages of pregnancy are less well known about than those relating to the effects of chronic alcohol addiction on pregnancy and fetal alcohol spectrum disorders (FASD). This oversight needs to be addressed universally.

The main characteristic of FASD is brain damage in the child or children of women who drank alcohol during their pregnancy. The amount and timing of alcohol consumption is not important, as damage occurs at all stages of fetal brain development, from the first trimester through to the final trimester. Children with FASD or fetal alcohol syndrome can be recognised by their distinctive facial characteristics, namely a smooth upper philtrum and thin upper lip (Abel, 1996). Later on, diagnosis may include stunted physical and emotional development, impulsive behaviours, lack of remorse, and so on. These children are known to develop secondary disabilities such as drug addiction or mental illness. It has been reported that alcohol exposure during pregnancy is the leading cause of mental retardation in the population in the western world (Abel and Sokel, 1987). The cost of the health care of these children is huge and, in public healthcare terms, largely preventable.

Conclusions

The interplay between hormones, hypothalamus, pituitary gland, gonads and lifestyle factors all combine to make assessments of intra- and inter-individual differences a complex task. Any shift in levels of any one of the variables can have greater or lesser effects on individual people, or even no effects at all. It is likely, given the evidence presented, that greater or lesser amounts of alcohol consumption in men and women have differential effects depending on the age and reproductive stage they are at in life. Unfortunately, the data are ambiguous, probably because they are limited by multiple (and possibly inevitable) confounders, as well as problematic methodologies and inappropriate endpoints. The evidence, although equivocal, indicates it may be best to err on the side of caution. Long-term public health efforts aimed at helping people to protect their reproductive capacity and maintain a healthy lifestyle before conception and during pregnancy are to be encouraged. Across the world, alcohol is used as a recreational substance, and only a few people have learned from research how alcohol consumption can affect fertility. A modification of lifestyle factors (from uninformed to informed) at an early age would do much to prevent the numerous fertility and associated conditions (such as reproductive cancers) that plague large sections of the population. This chapter has demonstrated that prevention of inappropriate alcohol use is likely to result in savings in human suffering and health and welfare costs.

References and further reading

Abel, E. (ed.) (1996). *Fetal Alcohol Syndrome: From Mechanism to Prevention*. New York: CRC Press.

Abel, E. and Sokel, R. (1987). Incidence of fetal alcohol syndrome and economic impact of FAS-related anomalies: Drug alcohol syndrome and economic impact of FAS-related anomalies. *Drug and Alcohol Dependence*, **19** (1), 51–70.

Agarwal, A. and Prabakaran, S. (2005). Mechanism, measurement and prevention of oxidative stress in male reproductive physiology. *Indian Journal of Experimental Biology*, **43** (11), 963–74.

Akker, van den, O.B.A. and Lees, S. (2001). Leisure activities and adolescent sexual behaviour. *Sex Education*, **1** (2), 137–47.

Asher, I., Kraicer, P., Paz, G., *et al.* (1979). Ethanol and sulfamethoxazole for functional evaluation of male accessory glands. *Archives of Andrology*, **2**, 31–34.

Auger, J., Kunstmann, J., Czyglik, F. and Jouannet, P. (1995). Decline in semen quality among fertile men in Paris during the past 20, years. *New England Journal of Medicine*, **332**, 281–85.

Bar-Oz, B., Moretti, M., Maureels, G., *et al.* (1999). Reporting bias in retrospective ascertainment of drug induced embryopathy. *Lancet,* **354**, 1700–01.

Becker, U., Tonnesen, H., Kaas-Claesson, N., *et al.* (1989). Menstrual disturbances. and fertility in chronic alcoholic women. *Drug and Alcohol Dependence*, **24**, 75–82.

Boiesen, P., Lindholm, J., Hagen, C., *et al.* (1979). Histological changes in testicular biopsies from chronic alcoholics with and without liver disease. *Acta Pathologica et Microbiologica Scandinavica*, **87**, 139–42.

Boivin, J. and Schmidt, L. (2005). Infertility-related stress in men and women predicts treatment outcome 1 year later. *Fertility and Sterility*, **83**(6), 1745–52.

Bray, R.M. (1999) Prevention in the military. In: R.T. Ammerman (ed.) *Prevention. and Societal Impact of Drug and Alcohol Abuse.* Mahwah, NJ: Lawrence Erlbaum, pp. 345–67.

Breslau, N., Peterson, E., Schultz, L., *et al.* (1996). Are smokers with alcohol disorders less likely to quit? *American Journal of Public Health,* **86**, 985–90.

Briggs, G., Freeman, R. and Yaffe, S. (1994). *Drugs in Pregnancy and Lactation*, 4th edn. Williams and Wilkins: Baltimore, pp. xi–xvii.

Byers, T., Marshall, J., Graham, S., *et al.* (1983). A case control study of dietary and non dietary factors in ovarian cancer. *Journal of the National Cancer Institute*, **71**, 681–86.

Cabot, R.C. (1904). The relation of alcohol to arteriosclerosis, *Journal of the American Medical Association*, **43**, 774–75.

Colditz, G., Giovannuci, E., Rimm, E., *et al.* (1991). Alcohol intake in relation to diet and obesity in women. and men. *American Journal of Clinical Nutrition*, **54**, 49–55.

Collier, A., Tingle, M., Paxton, J., *et al.* (2002). Metabolizing enzyme localization and activities in the first trimester human placenta: the effect of maternal and gestational age, smoking and alcohol consumption. *Human Reproduction*, **17**, 2564–72.

Curtis, K., Savitz, D. and Arbuckle, T. (1997). Effects of cigarette smoking, caffeine consumption and alcohol intake on fecundability. *American Journal of Epidemiology*, **146**, 32–41.

Day, N., Jasperse, D., Richardson, G., *et al.* (1989). Prenatal exposure to alcohol: effect on infant growth and morphologic characteristics. *Paediatrics,* **84**, 536–41.

Dees, W., Srivastavada, V. and Hiney, J. (2001). Alcohol and female puberty: The role of intraovarian systems. *Alcohol Research and Health*, **25**, 271–75.

Demyttenaere, K., Nijs, P., Evers-Kiebooms, G. and Koninckx, P. (1989). The effect of a specific emotional stressor on prolactin cortisol and testosterone concentrations in women varies with their trait anxiety. *Fertility and Sterility*, **52**, 942–48.

Dunphy, B., Barratt, C. and Cooke, I. (1991). Male alcohol consumption and fecundity in couples attending an infertility clinic. *Andrologia*, **23**, 219–21.

Ebrahim, S., Decoufle, P. and Palakathodi, A. (2000) Combined tobacco and alcohol use by pregnant and reproductive aged women in the United States. *Obstetrics and Gynecology*, 96, (5), 767–71.

Ebrahim, S., Diekman, S., Decoufle, P., *et al.* (1999). Pregnancy related alcohol use among women in the United States, 1988–95. *Prenatal and Neonatal Medicine*, **4**, 39–46.

Eggert, J., Theobald, H. and Engfeldt, P. (2004). Effects of alcohol consumption on female fertility during an 18-year period. *Fertility and Sterility*, **81**, 379–83.

Farnsworth, W., Cavanaugh, A., Brown, J., *et al.* (1978). Factors underlying infertility in the alcoholic. *Archives of Andrology*, **1**, 193–95.

Florack, E., Zielhuis, G. and Rolland, R. (1994). Cigarette smoking, alcohol consumption and caffeine intake and fecundability. *Preventive Medicine*, **23**, 175–80.

Floyd, R., Decoufle, P. and Hungerford, D. (1999). Alcohol use prior to pregnancy recognition. *American Journal of Preventive Medicine*, **17**, 101–07.

Ford, W., North, K., Taylor, H., Farrow, A., Hull, M., Golding, J. and the ALSPAC Study Team (2000). Increasing paternal age is associated with delayed conception in a large population of fertile couples: evidence for declining fecundity in older men.

Human Reproduction, **15** (8), 1703–08.

Gill, J. (2000). The effects of moderate alcohol consumption on female hormone levels and reproductive function. *Alcohol*, **35**, 417–23.

Goodman, M. and Tung, K. (2003). Alcohol consumption and the risk of borderline and invasive ovarian cancer. *Obstetrics and Gynecology*, **101**, 6, 1221–28.

Gordon, G., Southern, A., Vittek, J. and Lieber, C. (1979). The effect of alcohol ingestion on hepatic aromatase activity and plasma steroid hormones in the rat. *Metabolism,* **28**, 20–24.

Goverde, H., Dekker, H., Janssen, H., *et al.* (1995). Semen quality and frequency of smoking and alcohol consumption – an explorative study. *International Journal of Fertility*, **40**, 135–38.

Greil, A. (1997). Infertility and psychological distress: A critical review of the literature. *Social Science and Medicine*, **45**, 1679–1704.

Grenbaek, M., Deis, A., Soresen, T., *et al.* (1995). Mortality associated with moderate intakes of wine, beer or spirits. *British Medical Journal*, **310**, 1165–69.

Grodstein, F., Goldman, M. and Cramer, D. (1994). Infertility in women and moderate alcohol use. *American Journal of Public Health*, **84**, 1429–32.

Gunnell, D. and Ewings, P. (1994). Infertility prevalence, needs assessment and purchasing. *Journal of Public Health Medicine*, **16**, 29–35.

Gwinn, M., Webster, L., Lee, N., *et al.* (1986). Alcohol consumption and ovarian cancer risk. *American Journal of Epidemiology*, **123**, 759–66.

Hadi, H., Hill, J. and Castillo, R. (1987). Alcohol and reproductive function: a review. *Obstetrics and Gynecology* Survey, **42**, 69–74.

Hakim, R., Gray, R. and Zacur, H. (1998). Alcohol and caffeine consumption and decreased fertility. *Fertility and Sterility*, **70**, 632–7.

Halmesmaki, E., Valimaki, M., Roine, R., *et al.* (1989). Maternal and paternal alcohol consumption and miscarriage. *British Journal of Obstetrics and Gynecology*, **96**, 188–91.

Harlap, S. and Shiono, P. (1980). Alcohol, smoking and incidence of spontaneous abortions in the first and second trimester. *Lancet,* ii, 173–76.

Henriksen, T., Hjollund, N., Jensen, T., *et al.* (2004). Alcohol consumption at the time of conception and spontaneous abortion. *American Journal of Epidemiology*, **160** (7), 661–67.

Hull, M., Fleming, C., Hughes, C. and McDermott, A. (1996). The age-related decline in female fecundity – a quantitative controlled study of implanting capacity and survival of individual embryos after *in vivo* fertilization. *Fertility and Sterility*, **65**, 783–90.

Jensen, T., Hjollund, N., Henriksen, T., *et al.* (1998). Does moderate alcohol consumption affect fertility? Follow-up study among couples planning first pregnancy. *British Medical Journal*, **317**, 505–10.

Juhl, M., Nyboe Andersen, A., Gronbaek, M. and Olsen, J. (2001). Moderate alcohol consumption and waiting time to pregnancy. *Human Reproduction*, **16**, 2705–09.

Juhl, M., Olsen, J., Nybo Andersen, A. and Gronbaek, M. (2003). Intake of wine, beer and spirits and waiting time to pregnancy. *Human Reproduction*, **18** (9), 1967–71.

Juhl, M., Andersen, A.M., Gronbaek, M. and Olsen, J. (2002). Moderate alcohol consumption and waiting time to pregnancy. *Human Reproduction*, **16** (12), 2705–09.

Kato, I., Tominaga, S. and Terao, C. (1989). Alcohol consumption and cancers of hormone-related organs in females. *Japanese Journal of Clinical Oncology*, **19**, 202–07.

Kesmodel, U., Wisborg, K., Olsen, S., *et al.* (2002). Moderate alcohol intake in pregnancy and the risk of spontaneous abortion. *Alcohol*, **37**, 87–92.

Kold Jensen, T., Joffe, M., Scheike, T., *et al.* (2005). Time trends in waiting time to pregnancy among Danish twins. *Human Reproduction*, **20**, 4, 955–64.

Kunzle, R., Mueller, M., Hanggi, W., *et al.* (2003). Semen quality of male smokers and non smokers in infertile couples. *Fertility and Sterility*, **79**, 287–91.

Kushi, L., Mink, P., Folsom, A., *et al.* (1999). Prospective study of diet and ovarian cancer. *American Journal of Epidemiology*, **149**, 21–31.

Lansac, J. (1995). Is delayed childbearing a good thing? *Human Reproduction*, **10**, 1033–35.

Lemere, F. and Smith, J. (1973). Alcohol induced sexual impotence. *American Journal of Psychiatry*, **130**, 212–13.

Lester, R. and van Thiel, D. (1979). Feminization of the alcoholic: The oestrogen/testosterone ratio (E/T). *Gastroenterology*, **76**, 415–17.

Lindholm, J., Fabricius-Bjerre, N., Bahsen, M., *et al.* (1978a) Sex steroids and sex hormone binding globulin in males with chronic alcoholism. *European Journal of Clinical Investigation*, **8**, 273–76.

Lindholm, J., Fabricius-Bjerre, N., Bahsen, M., *et al.* (1978b) Pituitary–testicular function in patients with chronic alcoholism. *European Journal of Clinical Investigation*, **8**, 269–72.

Maneesh, M., Dutta, S., Chakrabarti, A. and Vasudevan, D. (2006). Alcohol abuse duration dependent decrease in plasma testosterone and antioxidants in males. *Indian Journal of Physiology and Pharmacology*, **50** (3), 291–96.

Meyer, C. (1999). Family focus or career focus: Controlling for infertility. *Social Science and Medicine*, **49**, 1615–22.

Morgan, D. (1997). Drug disposition in mother and fetus. *Clinical and Experimental Pharmacology and Physiology*, **24**, 869–73.

Morrione, T. (1944). Effects of oestrogens on the testis in hepatic insufficiency. *Archives of Pathology*, **34**, 39–48.

Muthusami, K. and Chinnaswamy, P. (2005). Effects of chronic alcoholism on male fertility hormones and semen quality. *Fertility and Sterility*, **84** (4), 919–24.

Oldereid, N., Rui, H., and Purvis, K. (1992). Lifestyles of men in barren couples and their relationship to sperm quality. *International Journal of Fertility*, **37**, 343–49.

Olsen, J., Bolumar, F., Boldsen, J., *et al.* (1997). The European study group of infertility and subfecundity. Does moderate alcohol intake reduce fecundability? A European multicenter study on infertility and subfecundity. *Alcoholism: Clinical and Experimental Research*, **21**, 206–12.

Olsen, J., Rachootin, P., Schicdt, A., *et al.* (1982). Tobacco use, alcohol consumption and infertility. *International Journal of Epidemiology*, **12**, 179–84.

Parazzini, F., Bocciolone, L., La Vecchia, C., *et al.* (1990). Maternal and paternal moderate daily alcohol consumption and unexplained miscarriages. *British Journal of Obstetrics and Gynaecology*, **97**, 618–22.

Purohit, V. (1998). Moderate alcohol consumption and oestrogen levels in post-menopausal women: a review. *Alcoholism: Clinical and Experimental Research*, **22**, 994–97.

Repromed, G., Davies, M. and Norman, R. (2007). The impact of lifestyle factors on reproductive performance in the general population and those undergoing infertility treatment: a review. *Human Reproduction Update*. Advanced Access, 5th January 2007; doi:10.1093/humupd/dml056, pp. 1–15.

Risch, H. (1998). Hormonal aetiology of epithelial ovarian cancer, with a hypothesis concerning the role of androgens and progesterone. *Journal of the National Cancer Institute*, **90**, M1774–86.

Robbins, W., Elashoff, D., Xun, L., *et al.* (2005). Effects of lifestyle exposures on sperm aneuploidy. *Cytogenic and Genome Research*, **111** (3/4), 371–77.

Rostad, B., Schei, B. and Sundby, J. (2006). Fertility in Norwegian women: Results from a population-based health survey. *Scandinavian Journal of Public Health*, **34**, 5–10.

Sastry, B. (1991). Placental toxicology: tobacco smoke, abused drugs, multiple chemical interactions and placental function. *Reproduction, Fertility, and Development*, **3**, 355–72.

Shiloh, H., Lahav-Baratz, S., Koifman, M., *et al.* (2004). The impact of cigarette smoking on zona pellucida thickness of oocytes and embryos prior to transfer into the uterine cavity. *Human Reproduction*, **19**, 157–59.

Singletary, K. and Gapstur, S. (2001). Alcohol and breast cancer: Review of epidemiologic and experimental evidence and potential mechanisms. *Journal of the American Medical Association*, **286**, 2143–51.

Small, S.A. and Luster, T. (1994). Adolescent sexual activity: An ecological, risk-factor approach. *Journal of Marriage and the Family*, **56**, 181–92.

Sundby, J. and Schei, B. (1996). Infertility and subfertility in Norwegian women aged 40–42. *Acta Obstetrica et Gynecologica Scandinavica*, **75**, 832–37.

Swan, S., Elkin, E. and Fenster, L. (2000). The question of declining sperm density revisited: an analysis of 101 studies published in 1931–1996. *Environmental Health Perspectives*, **108**, 961–66.

Tarin, J. (1998). Long-term effects of delayed parenthood. *Human Reproduction*, **13**, 2371–76.

Templeton, A., Morris, J. and Parslow, W. (1996). Factors that affect outcome of in vitro fertilization treatment. *Lancet*, **348**, 1402–06.

Tolstrup, J., Kjaer, S., Holst, C., *et al.* (2003). Alcohol use as a predictor for infertility in a representative population of Danish women. *Acta Obstetrica et Gynecologica Scandinavica*, **82**, 744–49.

Torgeson, D., Avenall, A., Russell, I. and Reid, D. (1994). Factors associated with the onset of menopause in women aged 45–49. *Maturitas*, **9**, 83–92.

Torgeson, F., Thomas, R., Campbell, M. and Reid, D. (1997). Alcohol consumption and age of maternal menopause are associated with menopause onset. *Maturitas*, **26**, 21–25.

Truelsen, T., Gronbaek, M., Schnohr, P., *et al.* (1998). Intake of beer, wine and spirits and risk of stroke: the Copenhagen city heart study. *Stroke*, **29** (12), 2468–72.

Valimaki, M., Laitinen, K., Tiitinen, A., *et al.* (1995). Gonadal function and morphology in non-cirrhotic female alcoholics: A controlled study with hormone measurements and ultrasonography. *Acta Obstetrica et Gynecologica Scandinavica*, **74**, 462–66.

van Thiel, D. (1979). Feminization of chronic alcoholic men: a formulation. *Yale Journal of Biology and Medicine*, **52**, 219–25.

van Thiel, D. and Lester, R. (1974). Sex and alcohol. *New England Journal of Medicine*, **291**, 251–53.

van Thiel, D., Lester, R. and Sherins, R. (1974). Hypogonadism in alcoholic liver disease: Evidence of a double effect. *Gastroenterology*, **67**, 1188–99.

Whittmore, A., Wu, M., Paffenbarger, R. Jr, *et al.* (1988). Personal and environmental characteristics related to epithelial ovarian cancer II Exposures to talcum powder, tobacco, alcohol and coffee. *American Journal of Epidemiology*, **128**, 1228–40.

Wilsnack, S., Klassen, A. and Wilsnack, R. (1984). Drinking and reproductive dysfunction among women in a 1981 national survey. *Alcoholism: Clinical and Experimental Research*, **8**, 451–58.

Windham, G., Fenster, L. and Swan, S. (1992). Moderate maternal and paternal alcohol consumption and the risk of spontaneous abortion. *Epidemiology*, **3**, 364–70.

Windham, G., von Behren, J., Fenster, L., *et al.* (1997). Moderate maternal alcohol consumption and risk of spontaneous abortion. *Epidemiology*, **8**, 509–14.

Wise, L., Palmer, J., Harlow, B., *et al.* (2004). Risk of uterine leiomyomata in relation to tobacco, alcohol and caffeine consumption in the Black Women's Health Study. *Human Reproduction*, **19** (8), 1746–54.

World Health Organization (1989). *The Health of Youth*. Geneva: WHO.

Young, K.A. (2003). The effects of resilience factors on risk taking behaviours and academic achievement among urban adolescents. *Dissertation Abstracts International: Humanities and Social Sciences*, **63** (8A March), 2795.

Younglai, E., Holloway, A. and Foster, W. (2005). Environmental and occupational factors affecting fertility and IVF success. *Human Reproduction Update*, **11**, 43–57.

Zaadstra, B., Habbema, J., Looman, C., *et al.* (1994). Moderate drinking: no impact on female fecundity. *Fertility and Sterility*, **62**, 948–54.

Zenzes, M., Bielecki, R. and Reed, T. (1999). Detection of benzo(a)pyrene diol epoxide-DNA adducts in sperm of men exposed to cigarette smoke. *Fertility and Sterility*, **72**, 330–35.

27 Clinical presentation and prevention of fetal alcohol syndrome

Colin R. Martin

The goal of this chapter is to examine the salient clinical and screening issues regarding fetal alcohol syndrome (FAS). It focuses on several key areas that highlight the role of reliable, valid and easily administered screening tools for identifying women at risk of producing a baby with FAS. The review is designed to facilitate and emphasise the role that health professionals, particularly nurses and midwives, have in helping to reduce the incidence of this debilitating and preventable neurodevelopmental disorder. A central focus of the discussion are the issues surrounding effective screening practice, but other salient aspects of clinical management, including the pregnant woman who may require detoxification from alcohol, are also discussed.

The consequences of drug abuse and drug dependency are often seen as particular to the person with a drug problem. However, two discrete syndromes that can seriously affect the outcome of pregnancy have been established as diagnostic entities for many years, these being neonatal abstinence syndrome (NAS) and fetal alcohol syndrome (FAS). In NAS the negative consequences for the newborn are variable and diverse (de Cubas and Field 1993; Franck *et al.*, 2004) and may often be relatively short in duration and lead to non-problematic outcomes (Gustavsson 1992; Johnson *et al.*, 1990; Little *et al.*, 2003).

In contrast, FAS arguably represents a far more serious clinical presentation in that a diagnosis represents an irreversible neurodevelopmental disorder with long-term and lifelong consequences (Bearer, 2001; Berman and Hannigan, 2000). One pressing concern for both these syndromes is the relative salience given to them in terms of prevention. While NAS results from opiate use by the mother (Beauman, 2005), FAS results exclusively from alcohol use (Abel, 2006; Floyd *et al.*, 2005). In the United Kingdom, government funding for illicit drug treatment and prevention is actually increasing, but central funding for the treatment and prevention of problematic and dependent drinking is falling. A possible concern is that these trends may lead to differential treatment and prevention strategies for NAS and FAS. Given the severe and enduring clinical issues associated with FAS, this chapter will focus on this syndrome in relation to aetiological, screening, identification and treatment issues. Raising awareness of the issues of FAS will help facilitate the identification and treatment of pregnant women who may be drinking heavily and who may be at risk of delivering a baby with FAS.

What is fetal alcohol syndrome?

Fetal alcohol syndrome (FAS) is a diagnostic classification associated with a range of discrete developmental disorders as a consequence of the mother's alcohol consumption during pregnancy (Jones, 1986; Jones and Smith, 1973). FAS is the largest non-genetic and completely preventable neurodevelopmental disorder. It has a prevalence of up to 2 per 1000 births (Abel, 1995; May and Gossage, 2001) in western countries. Approximately 1 per cent of births are estimated to have some of the enduring neurodevelopmental deficits associated with FAS, but which do not satisfy the stringent diagnostic criteria for this disorder (May and Gossage, 2001). FAS was first described in terms of a characteristic set of clinical features constituting a diagnostic entity over 30 years ago (Jones, 1975; Jones and Smith, 1973; Jones, et al., 1973). Research into FAS has continued since then.

Now a number of clinical classifications are established that describe specific sets of symptoms characteristic of developmental abnormalities resulting from maternal drinking (Abel and Sokol, 1987; Sokol et al., 2003). All of these classifications are overarched by the broader classification of fetal alcohol effects (FAE) and often these more discrete classifications may be used interchangeably with FAS or FAE.

A diagnosis of FAS is based on three criteria (National Center on Birth Defects and Developmental Disabilities, 2004) as follows:

1. Growth retardation.
2. Facial characteristics.
3. Central nervous system abnormalities.

Before looking at these more closely, note that prenatal alcohol exposure may not necessarily be confirmed. Growth retardation is defined as less than the 10th percentile in body weight or body length (National Center on Birth Defects and Developmental Disabilities, 2004).

The facial abnormalities include a variety of distinct features which, taken together, indicate a typical and readily recognisable pattern of FAS; for diagnostic purposes they must include a smooth philtrum (University of Washington Lip–Philtrum Guide rank 4 or 5), a thin vermilion (University of Washington Lip–Philtrum Guide rank 4 or 5) and small palpebral fissures (below the 10th percentile). Other associated features include a hypoplastic or flat midface, a short nose, micrognathia (small lower jaw) and minor ear abnormalities.

The neurodevelopment abnormalities must demonstrate tacit examples of structural, neurological or functional deficits for a diagnosis of FAS to be made (National Center on Birth Defects and Developmental Disabilities, 2004). These include a head circumference equal to or less than the 10th percentile, adjusted for age and sex, neurological deficits not associated with other causes (e.g. traumatic head injury) and neurocognitive function significantly below that expected based on age (National Center on Birth Defects and Developmental Disabilities, 2004). These functional deficits must cover at least three specific domains such as cognition, motor function, attention problems, memory problems and language problems for a diagnosis to be made (National Center on Birth Defects and Developmental Disabilities, 2004). In this respect FAS represents a diagnostic entity, however fetal alcohol exposure may lead to a number of developmental abnormalities that will not satisfy the extensive diagnostic criteria for FAS.

More recently, the term fetal alcohol spectrum disorder (FASD) has been used to describe offspring with impairments related to prenatal alcohol exposure, but not all the characteristic features of FAS. FAS is a diagnostic classification, but FASD is not. There are a number of other classifications that relate to fetal alcohol exposure in which the characteristic features and diagnostic facial dysmorphia of FAS are not present, for example alcohol-related neurodevelopmental disorder (ARND) and alcohol-related birth defects (ARBD). Further, a partial FAS (PFAS) has been described, in which some of the facial dysmorphic features of FAS are present. It should be remembered that FASD covers all categories arising from prenatal alcohol exposure, including FAS.

Consequences of fetal alcohol syndrome

The neurodevelopmental consequences of FAS have been described extensively (Burden *et al.*, 2005; Coles *et al.*, 1991, 2002; Greene *et al.*, 1990, 1991; Harris *et al.*, 1993; Jacobson *et al.*, 1994). An important point to be made is that anyone with the diagnosis of FAS will face lifelong deficits in the areas of neurological function, including cognitive function, impulse control, attention and memory, in addition to often profound impairment in social function. Typically, a child with FAS will be unable to attend mainstream schooling, will need special educational provision (Streissguth *et al.*, 1996) and will often require supervision from teachers who are specially trained in working with the behavioural disturbances common with children with FAS. Children with FAS often experience a range of mental health problems, develop drug and alcohol problems, sexual behaviour problems, criminality and, as adults, encounter difficulties in independent and unsupported living (Streissguth *et al.*, 1996).

Children with FASD, but not formally diagnosed with FAS, also require special educational provision, often to the same degree as those with FAS. In many cases they face the same life-long challenges as children formally diagnosed with FAS. It should not be assumed that children with FASD (but not FAS) have fewer clinical, behavioural or social problems to contend with; for example they may still have a similar level of neurodevelopmental impairment as those with FAS (Mattson *et al.*, 1997, 1998).

Consuming safe amounts of alcohol while pregnant

Alcohol or more accurately, ethyl alcohol or ethanol, is a naturally toxic substance when ingested. Indeed, the toxic effects of alcohol are the effects often sought by those enjoying a drink. This broad spectrum of effects relating to the toxic effects of alcohol on the central nervous system, ranging from feeling relaxed and disinhibited through to physical incapacity and unconsciousness, have been experienced and enjoyed (even suffered) by drinkers for centuries. Importantly, during pregnancy any alcohol consumed will also be 'consumed' by the fetus, since from conception the developing fetus is completely dependent on the mother's liver to metabolise alcohol.

Alcohol can cause extensive damage to the central nervous system and the teratogenic effects of this substance have been extensively described (Chernoff, 1979; Gartner *et al.*, 1982; Little and Streissguth, 1981; Sampson *et al.*, 2000). More recent comparative experimental research has shown, interestingly, that the toxic effects of alcohol on cellular function seem to manifest through a variety of mechanisms, revealing that no cellular types, structures or bodily systems are immune from its effects (Adachi *et al.*, 2006; Hunter *et al.*, 2003; Nakahara *et al.*,

2002, 2003). The established teratogenic mechanisms have been extensively described and the interested reader might wish to consult other sources of information. Work on prenatal alcohol exposure confirms that there is no confirmed safe level of drinking during pregnancy (Pollock, 2004). Health advice should focus on the idea of abstinence from alcohol for the duration of pregnancy (Medical Council on Alcohol and Fetal Alcohol Syndrome Trust, 2006; US Department of Health and Human Sciences, 2005), though for comprehensiveness it should be mentioned that there have been suggestions for a central educational focus on alcohol abuse (Abel, 1998). The teratogenic effects of alcohol are by no means dose-dependent or predictable, and although common sense suggests that heavy drinkers may be a greater risk of FAS than lighter drinkers, any alcohol consumption promotes a risk of FAS or FASD or some central nervous system abnormality (Hepper *et al.*, 2005; Little *et al.*, 2002). Research in recent years shows that comparatively modest levels of alcohol consumption during pregnancy are associated with the occurrence of these conditions, (Hepper *et al.*, 2005; Little *et al.*, 2002). It has also been suggested that women who are thinking about becoming pregnant and are trying for a baby should abstain from alcohol (Medical Council on Alcohol and Fetal Alcohol Syndrome Trust, 2006; US Department of Health and Human Sciences, 2005).

Alcohol abusing or chemically dependent pregnant women

The issue of FAS is complicated when pregnant women present at clinical services (irrespective of service type) when currently abusing alcohol. Obviously this is a high-risk group, particularly women who are binge drinking, which is an additional risk according to data from both human and comparative studies (Gladstone *et al.*, 1996; Goodlett *et al.*, 1997; Livy *et al.*,2001, 2003; Maier *et al.*, 1997, 1999; Nanson, 1997). These women are likely to require extensive support and monitoring and possibly shared care or specialist referral to alcohol and drug agencies (with the woman's consent) and careful and thorough monitoring by maternity professionals, to facilitate achievement of abstinence for the remainder of the pregnancy. This goal may not be achieved, of course, but stopping drinking at any stage of pregnancy will be associated with a reduced risk of FAS or FASD, so this is an important clinical goal.

The issue of chemical dependency on alcohol (as distinct from non-dependent alcohol abuse) raises a number of clinical dilemmas. The goal again is to achieve abstinence for the duration of the remainder of the pregnancy (Medical Council on Alcohol and Fetal Alcohol Syndrome Trust, 2006; National Center on Birth Defects and Developmental Disabilities, 2004; US Department of Health and Human Sciences, 2005). However, because of the nature of the tolerance associated with chemical dependency (de Bruijn *et al.*, 2005; Heinz *et al.*, 2003; Kumar *et al.*, 2005; Pandey *et al.*, 2001) and the well-documented and life-threatening dangers of alcohol withdrawal associated in people with chemical dependency (Maser, 1977; Mayo-Smith and Bernard, 1995; Olbrich, 1979; Saitz, 1995; Thompson, 1978), alternative clinical management strategies need to be considered.

First among these is the issue of detoxification. Detoxification involves the substitution of alcohol with (typically) a benzodiazepine (in particular chlordiazepoxide), the dose of which is reduced over typically 5–7 days, to achieve a safe, systematic and well-controlled abstinent state. Thiamine is also prescribed throughout the detoxification. The process requires careful and comprehensive management, with extensive monitoring of withdrawal symptoms that may require modifying the tailored protocol (Keaney *et al.*, 2001; Saitz 1995; Wiseman *et al.*, 1998).

Benzodiazepines are meant to reduce the incidence of withdrawal symptoms, withdrawal seizures and delirium tremens (Department of Health, 2007). However, no detoxification procedure can be guaranteed to be without risk of these complications. What is worrying for evidence-based practitioners is the fact there is little research on the management of withdrawal from alcohol using benzodiazepines in pregnant women. This gap in the literature is even more concerning because there is some evidence that benzodiazepines are associated with birth defects (Bergman *et al.*, 1992; Cates 1999; Dolovich *et al.*, 1998; Game and Bergman, 1999; Iqbal *et al.*, 2002; Khan *et al.*, 1999). Withdrawal management using benzodiazepines is therefore recommended at the lowest dose possible to alleviate withdrawal symptoms.

Pregnancy is a key indicator for the desirability of inpatient detoxification. It is no understatement to say that uncontrolled alcohol withdrawal can be fatal to the pregnant woman and her fetus. Clinicians are in the unenviable position of having to balance treatments involving risks against non-intervention which is likely to be accompanied by significantly more deleterious health concerns. The clinical guidelines in this area (Department of Health, 2007) are extensive and worthy of consultation (extensive in relation to substance misuse and pregnancy; less so with respect to FAS) . The issue of maintaining abstinence following detoxification is highly problematic, since relapse rates following treatment for alcohol withdrawal are traditionally high (Chick *et al.*, 2000; Driessen *et al.*, 2001; Foster *et al.*, 2000; Shaw *et al.*, 1994; note that most research on relapse following detoxification has been conducted on males). Further support and monitoring is required by clinical staff and specialist colleagues, although yet again this offers no guarantee against relapse. Finally, pharmacological treatments developed to maintain abstinence, such as acamprosate (Scott *et al.*, 2005; Verheul *et al.*, 2005; Williams, 2005), have not been demonstrated to be safe in pregnancy.

Risk factors for fetal alcohol syndrome

Risk factors for FAS and FASD have been established by epidemiological and clinical research over recent years. The key risk factor is obviously fetal alcohol exposure (FAE). Determining the risk factors for an individual case requires taking as complete a history as possible. However, since alcohol use, alcohol abuse and alcohol dependence may all be associated with negative attributional biases and censure, it is entirely conceivable that pregnant women may not be entirely honest about their previous level of drinking or their current drinking status. Alternative measures may be available to detect drinking status; routine blood tests include liver function tests (LFTs) and full blood count (FBC). Classic markers from the LFT battery are alanine aminotransferase (ALT), aspartate aminotransferase (AST) and gamma glutamyltranspeptidase (GGT) (Aalto and Seppa, 2005; Dolman and Hawkes, 2005). These enzymes vary in their specificity as they can be raised by a number of other medical conditions. GGT, however, is particularly sensitive to the effects of alcohol and is a primary marker within the LFT battery (Banciu *et al.*, 1983). The value of liver function tests in determining alcohol abuse or dependency may be limited if the woman is also using other drugs, particularly opiates (Shaw *et al.*, 1982). The relative size of the red blood cell is estimated by the mean corpuscular volume (MCV) test, which is part of the FBC battery. MCV is often found to be raised with increasing alcohol consumption and is a widely used indicator of problematic drinking when used in association with LFTs (Aertgeerts *et al.*, 2001; Sillanaukee, 1996).

There are newer tests that detect recent alcohol consumption such as carbohydrate-deficient transferrin (CDT) (Bell *et al.*, 1994; Lesch and Walter, 1996; Lesch *et al.*, 1996; Sillanaukee *et al.*, 1998) but these special tests are not routinely used to screen for alcohol abuse or dependence. The established blood tests – FBC and LFTs – provide a useful confirmatory indicator of alcohol abuse or dependence when there is a positive self-report of (excessive) alcohol intake. Positive test results but negative self-report from a woman may provide a useful basis for discussing the inconsistency between findings. In relation to blood biochemistry screening, moderate alcohol consumption may reveal no blood test abnormalities whatsoever (Aertgeerts *et al.*, 2001; Limin *et al.*, 1999; Vanclay *et al.*, 1991). Conversely, a background permissive to alcohol abuse is a risk factor for FAS and/or FASD (May *et al.*, 2005), although the circumstances by which this risk factor may be recorded can only be speculated about should the information not be forthcoming from the woman concerned. A visit to an accident and emergency department may mean that other warning signs of alcohol abuse may already have been identified during an examination, which could help identify a woman at risk.

There are a plethora of other risk factors for FAS and/or FASD. Age has been observed to be a risk factor; specifically, older women are at elevated risk (Jacobson *et al.*, 2004; May *et al.*, 2004). The social circumstances of pregnant women also provide potent indications of elevated risks of FAS/FASD, in particular living with a partner with an alcohol problem, having a low socioeconomic classification (Abel and Hannigan 1995; Abel, 1995; May *et al.*, 2005) and being single (May *et al.*, 2005). Risk factors for alcohol use during pregnancy and, consequently, risk of FAS/FASD, include unemployment, smoking tobacco, using other drugs of abuse and living with a substance abuser (Leonardson and Loudenburg, 2003). A more tacit risk factor is already having a child with FAS (Abel, 1988). Since any alcohol consumption may lead to FAS or FASD, and there is currently no antenatal test for these disorders, the goal of assessment and identification of risk factors is to determine accurately prenatal exposure to alcohol.

It also makes good clinical sense to explore areas of comorbidity in relation to problematic drinking in order to get a more comprehensive picture of risk identifiers. For example, it is common for people using illegal drugs (class A, B and C) to be heavy drinkers too (Pedersen and Skrondal, 1999; Staines *et al.*, 2001). Therefore, evidence of illegal drug use may be an indicator of excessive alcohol consumption. Any discussion around this issue would be legitimate and helpful. Anxiety and depression are also comorbid with alcohol dependence and abuse (Burns *et al.*, 2005; Conway *et al.*, 2006; Grothues *et al.*, 2005; Kushner *et al.*, 2005; Martin and Bonner, 2000; Sher, 2006) and a history of these psychiatric disorders should prompt discussion around the issue of alcohol consumption. Surprisingly, there is a paucity of research into any relationship between FAS and FASD and these common psychiatric presentations despite the impressive and extensive body of evidence linking them to alcohol consumption. This gap in the literature is a cause for concern and an obvious and pressing direction for future research.

The role of the health professional

Nurses, midwives and medical staff can play instrumental parts in identifying women at risk of delivering a baby with FAS and/or FASD and in reducing or eliminating such risks completely. The vehicle by which this can be achieved is effective screening. It may take place at an antenatal booking clinic, in primary or (a range of) secondary care settings, in a health promotion setting, at any time before conception or during pregnancy. There are therefore widespread opportunities for screening beyond those that may be expected within the realm of the maternity services. Screening using validated measures that have established properties of validity and reliability is highly desirable. A number of suitable measures have been developed, some specifically for use during pregnancy and others for generic screening use for problematic alcohol consumption.

The two most widely used measures developed for use during pregnancy are the T-ACE (Sokol *et al.*, 1989; see Box 27.1) and the TWEAK (see Box 27.2) (Chan *et al.*, 1993; Chang *et al.*, 1999).

Box 27.1 The T-ACE acronym

T olerance
A nnoyed
C ut down
E ye-opener

These tools have the highly desirable characteristic of being short (only 4 or 5 questions), easily administered and easily scored. They both ask questions that relate to retrospective reports of problematic drinking, therefore even though the woman may have stopped drinking following the discovery of her pregnancy, the instrument will still reflect the possibility of a problematic drinking history. The T-ACE and TWEAK are both highly discriminating between problematic and non-problematic drinking in general populations (Chan *et al.*, 1993; Cherpitel, 1999) and at identifying high and problematic alcohol consumption in pregnant women (Dawson *et al.*, 2001; Moraes *et al.*, 2005). The 4-item T-ACE has recently been shown to be more effective than either medical records or clinician assessment for identifying women who consume alcohol during pregnancy (McNamara *et al.*, 2005). The case identification properties of both the TWEAK and the T-ACE are very good during pregnancy (Russell *et al.*, 1994, 1996). The small number of items in the T-ACE and the TWEAK mean the component items are readily available to link with the context of a clinical interview, as well as having a standard self-report format. However, adaptation and modification of any screening instrument in this way may impact on its accuracy.

Box 27.2 The TWEAK test

T olerance (How many drinks does it take to make you feel high?)

W orried (Have close friends or relatives worried or complained about your drinking in the past year?)

E ye-opener (Do you sometimes take a drink in the morning when you first get up?)

A mnesia (Has a friend or family member ever told you about things you said or did while you were drinking that you could not remember?)

K (c)ut down (Do you sometimes feel the need to cut down on your drinking?)

There are various other generic instruments that are also short and accurate and have been used extensively and internationally for several years. The most widely known are the

CAGE (Mayfield *et al.*, 1974) and the MAST test (Michigan Alcohol Screening Test; Pokorny *et al.*, 1972; Selzer 1968), both of which comprise just four items. Some variability has been noted between the MAST, CAGE and T-ACE in case detection during pregnancy (Gupman *et al.*, 2002). In fact, a recent study has found some evidence that supports the use of the T-ACE and TWEAK in preference to the CAGE during pregnancy (Moraes *et al.*, 2005). The T-ACE and TWEAK are therefore deemed the screening instruments of choice in this group. However, instruments with an impressive screening heritage (such as the MAST and CAGE) should not be discounted until more extensive and conclusive evidence is furnished that these pregnancy-specific instruments actually perform better than the widely used generic tools.

An instrument which has been developed more recently and may be of value in these women is the Paddington Alcohol Test (PAT) (Patton and Touquet, 2002). The PAT (see Chapter 3) was originally developed for screening for alcohol misuse in busy accident and emergency department settings. More contemporary research has shown the value of this accurate instrument in expediting referral to appropriate professional support for people who screen positive (Barrett *et al.*, 2006). The PAT is currently specific to the United Kingdom since it asks about units of alcohol consumed; consequently UK-based practitioners may wish to evaluate this instrument against the TWEAK or T-ACE in pregnant women to determine whether there is any screening advantage of this innovative new tool.

Self-report of alcohol history and screening are essential, and a choice of one of the above instruments could be invaluable in identifying high-risk individuals.

Conclusions

FAS is a devastating and entirely preventable neurodevelopmental disorder with lifelong implications for any child receiving the diagnosis. The implications for children with FASD can be of a similar magnitude to those with a formal diagnosis of FAS.

There is no safe level of alcohol consumption during pregnancy. Health professionals are in a unique and valuable position for not only offering advice and information about the potential effects of alcohol on the developing fetus, but also for offering appropriate information about the dangers of alcohol to women who are planning a pregnancy. Health professionals encounter pregnant women in a broad range of clinical settings and the availability of valid and reliable screening measures provides important opportunities for identifying those at high risk of producing a child with FAS or FASD. Those who screen positive should receive fast-track referral to appropriate sources of clinical support and help reduce the risk of a child being born with this devastating disorder.

It is important that practitioners are aware of the issues surrounding FAS and FASD and implementation of effective screening practice can make a valuable contribution to minimising the incidence of FAS and FASD as much as possible. Nurses and midwives are undoubtedly in a position to offer opportunistic and systematic screening of pregnant women with many risk factors for a FAS or FASD child. Evaluation of screening practice in this area is important for determining the effect of such an intervention on clinical outcome and risk modification and will provide an important contribution to the evidence base about this distressing and entirely preventable disorder.

References and further reading

Aalto, M. and Seppa, K. (2005). Use of laboratory markers and the audit questionnaire by primary care physicians to detect alcohol abuse by patients. *Alcohol and Alcoholism*, **40**, 520–23.

Abel, E.L. (1995). An update on incidence of FAS: FAS is not an equal opportunity birth defect. *Neurotoxicology and Teratology*, **17**, 437–43.

Abel, E.L. (1988). Fetal alcohol syndrome in families. *Neurotoxicology and Teratology*, **10**, 1–2.

Abel, E.L. (1998). Prevention of alcohol abuse-related birth effects – I. Public education efforts. *Alcohol and Alcoholism*, **33**, 411–16.

Abel, E.L. (2006). Fetal alcohol syndrome: a cautionary note. *Current Pharmaceutical Design*, **12**, 1521–29.

Abel, E.L. and Hannigan, J.H. (1995). Maternal risk factors in fetal alcohol syndrome: provocative and permissive influences. *Neurotoxicology and Teratology*, **17**, 445–62.

Abel, E.L. and Sokol, R.J. (1987). Incidence of fetal alcohol syndrome and economic impact of FAS-related anomalies. *Drug and Alcohol Dependence*, **19**, 51–70.

Adachi, J., Kudo, R., Asano, M., *et al.* (2006). Skeletal muscle and liver oxysterols during fasting and alcohol exposure. *Metabolism*, **55**, 119–27.

Aertgeerts, B., Buntinx, F., Ansoms, S. and Fevery, J. (2001). Screening properties of questionnaires and laboratory tests for the detection of alcohol abuse or dependence in a general practice population. *British Journal of General Practice*, **51**, 206–17.

Banciu, T., Weidenfeld, H., Marcoane, E. and Berinde, L. (1983). Serum gamma-glutamyl transpeptidase assay in the detection of alcohol consumers and in the early and stadial diagnosis of alcoholic liver disease. *Medicine Interne*, **21**, 23–29.

Barrett, B., Byford, S., Crawford, M.J., *et al.* (2006). Cost-effectiveness of screening and referral to an alcohol health worker in alcohol misusing patients attending an accident and emergency department: a decision-making approach. *Drug and Alcohol Dependence*, **81**, 47–54.

Bearer, C.F. (2001). Mechanisms of brain injury: L1 cell adhesion molecule as a target for ethanol-induced prenatal brain injury. *Seminars in Pediatric Neurology*, **8**, 100–07.

Beauman, S.S. (2005). Identification and management of neonatal abstinence syndrome. *Journal of Infusion Nursing*, **28**, 159–67.

Bell, H., Tallaksen, C.M., Try, K. and Haug, E. (1994). Carbohydrate-deficient transferrin and other markers of high alcohol consumption: a study of 502 patients admitted consecutively to a medical department. *Alcoholism: Clinical and Experimental Research*, **18**, 1103–08.

Bergman, U., Rosa, F.W., Baum, C., Wiholm, B.E. and Faich, G.A. (1992). Effects of exposure to benzodiazepine during fetal life. *Lancet*, **340**, 694–96.

Berman, R.F. and Hannigan, J.H. (2000). Effects of prenatal alcohol exposure on the hippocampus: spatial behaviour, electrophysiology, and neuroanatomy. *Hippocampus*, **10**, 94–110.

Burden, M.J., Jacobson, S.W., Sokol, R.J. and Jacobson, J.L. (2005). Effects of prenatal alcohol exposure on attention and working memory at 7.5 years of age. *Alcoholism: Clinical and Experimental Research*, **29**, 443–52.

Burns, L., Teesson, M. and O'Neill, K. (2005). The impact of comorbid anxiety and depression on alcohol treatment outcomes. *Addiction*, **100**, 787–96.

Cates, C. (1999). Benzodiazepine use in pregnancy and major malformations or oral clefts. Pooled results are sensitive to zero transformation used. *British Medical Journal*, **319**, 918–19.

Chan, A.W., Pristach. E.A., Welte, J.W. and Russell, M. (1993). Use of the TWEAK test in screening for alcoholism/heavy drinking in three populations. *Alcoholism: Clinical and Experimental Research*, **17**, 1188–92.

Chang, G., Wilkins-Haug, L., Berman, S. and Goetz, M.A. (1999). The TWEAK: application in a prenatal setting. *Journal of Studies on Alcohol,* **60**, 306–09.

Chernoff, G.F. (1979). Introduction: a teratologist's view of the fetal alcohol syndrome. *Current Alcohol*, **7**, 7–13.

Cherpitel, C.J. (1999). Screening for alcohol problems in the U.S. general population: a comparison of the CAGE and TWEAK by gender, ethnicity, and services utilisation. *Journal of Studies on Alcohol*, **60**, 705–11.

Chick, J., Howlett, H., Morgan, M.Y. and Ritson, B. (2000). United Kingdom Multicentre Acamprosate Study (UKMAS): a 6-month prospective study of acamprosate versus placebo in preventing relapse after withdrawal from alcohol. *Alcohol and Alcoholism*, **35**, 176–87.

Coles, C.D., Brown, R.T., Smith, I.E., Platzman, K.A., Erickson, S. and Falek, A. (1991). Effects of prenatal alcohol exposure at school age. I. Physical and cognitive development. *Neurotoxicology and Teratology*, **13**, 357–67.

Coles, C.D., Platzman, K.A., Lynch, M.E. and Freides, D. (2002). Auditory and visual sustained attention in adolescents prenatally exposed to alcohol. *Alcoholism: Clinical and Experimental Research*, **26**, 263–71.

Conway, K.P., Compton, W., Stinson, F.S. and Grant, B.F. (2006). Lifetime comorbidity of DSM-IV mood and anxiety disorders and specific drug use disorders: results from the National Epidemiologic Survey on Alcohol and Related Conditions. *Journal of Clinical Psychiatry*, **67**, 247–57.

Dawson, D.A., Das, A., Faden, V.B., Bhaskar, B., Krulewitch, C.J. and Wesley, B. (2001). Screening for high- and moderate-risk drinking during pregnancy: a comparison of several TWEAK-based screeners. *Alcoholism: Clinical and Experimental Research*, **25**, 1342–49.

de Cubas, M.M. and Field, T. (1993). Children of methadone-dependent women: developmental outcomes. *American Journal of Orthopsychiatry*, **63**, 266–76.

de Bruijn, C., vanden Brink, W., de Graaf, R., Vollebergh, W.A.M. (2005). Alcohol abuse and dependence criteria as predictors of a chronic course of alcohol use disorders in the general population. *Alcohol and Alcoholism*, **40**, 441–46.

Department of Health (2007). *Drug Misuse and Dependence: Guidelines on Clinical Management*. London: Her Majesty's Stationery Office.

Dolman, J.M. and Hawkes, N.D. (2005). Combining the audit questionnaire and biochemical markers to assess alcohol use and risk of alcohol withdrawal in medical inpatients. *Alcohol and Alcoholism*, **40**, 515–19.

Dolovich, L.R., Addis, A., Vaillancourt, J.M., Power, J.D., Koren, G. and Einarson, T.R. (1998). Benzodiazepine use in pregnancy and major malformations or oral cleft: meta-analysis of cohort and case-control studies. *British Medical Journal*, **317**, 839–43.

Driessen, M., Meier, S., Hill, A., Wetterling, T., Lange, W. and Junghanns, K. (2001). The course of anxiety, depression and drinking behaviours after completed detoxification in alcoholics with and without comorbid anxiety and depressive disorders. *Alcohol and Alcoholism*, **36**, 249–55.

Floyd, R.L., O'Connor, M.J., Sokol, R.J., Bertrand, J. and Cordero, J.F. (2005). Recognition and prevention of fetal alcohol syndrome. *Obstetrics and Gynecology*, **106**, 1059–64.

Foster, J.H., Peters, T.J. and Marshall, E.J. (2000). Quality of life measures and outcome in alcohol-dependent men and women. *Alcohol*, **22**, 45–52.

Franck, L.S., Naughton, I. and Winter, I. (2004). Opioid and benzodiazepine withdrawal symptoms in paediatric intensive care patients. *Intensive and Critical Care Nursing*, **20**, 344–51.

Game, E. and Bergman, U. (1999). Benzodiazepine use in pregnancy and major malformations or oral clefts. Induced abortions should be included. *British Medical Journal*, **319**, 918.

Gartner, L.P., Beauchemin, R.R. Jr. and Provenza, V. (1982). The teratogenic effects of alcohol. A selected literature review. *Journal of the Baltimore College of Dental Surgery*, **35**, 14–20.

Gladstone, J., Nulman, I. and Koren, G. (1996). Reproductive risks of binge drinking during pregnancy. *Reproductive Toxicology*, **10**, 3–13.

Goodlett, C.R., Peterson, S.D., Lundahl, K.R. and Pearlman, A.D. (1997). Binge-like alcohol exposure of neonatal rats via intragastric intubation induces both Purkinje cell loss and cortical astrogliosis. *Alcoholism: Clinical and Experimental Research*, **21**, 1010–17.

Greene, T., Ernhart, C.B., Ager, J., Sokol, R., Martier, S. and Boyd, T. (1991). Prenatal alcohol exposure and cognitive development in the preschool years. *Neurotoxicology and Teratology*, **13**, 57–68.

Greene, T., Ernhart, C.B., Martier, S., Sokol, R. and Ager, J. (1990). Prenatal alcohol exposure and language development. *Alcoholism: Clinical and Experimental Research*, **14**, 937–45.

Grothues, J., Bischof, G., Reinhardt, S., *et al.* (2005). Intention to change drinking behaviour in general practice patients with problematic drinking and comorbid depression or anxiety. *Alcohol and Alcoholism*, **40**, 394–400.

Gupman, A.E., Svikis, D., McCaul, M.E., Anderson, J. and Santora, P.B. (2002). Detection of alcohol and drug problems in an urban gynecology clinic. *Journal of Reproductive Medicine*, **47**, 404–10.

Gustavsson, NS. (1992). Drug exposed infants and their mothers: facts, myths, and needs. *Social Work and Health Care*, **16**, 87–100.

Harris, S.R., Osborn, J.A., Weinberg, J., Loock, C. and Junaid, K. (1993). Effects of prenatal alcohol exposure on neuromotor and cognitive development during early childhood: a series of case reports. *Physical Therapy*, **73**, 608–17.

Heinz, A., Schafer, M., Higley, J.D., Krystal, J.H. and Goldman, D. (2003). Neurobiological correlates of the disposition and maintenance of alcoholism. *Pharmacopsychiatry*, **36**(Suppl.3), S255–58.

Hepper, P.G., Dornan, J.C. and Little, J.F. (2005). Maternal alcohol consumption during pregnancy may delay the development of spontaneous fetal startle behaviour. *Physiology and Behavior*, **83**, 711–14.

Hunter, R.J., Neagoe, C., Jarvelainen, H.A., *et al.* (2003). Alcohol affects the skeletal muscle proteins, titin and nebulin in male and female rats. *Journal of Nutrition*, **133**, 1154–57.

Iqbal, M.M., Sobhan, T. and Ryals, T. (2002). Effects of commonly used benzodiazepines on the fetus, the neonate, and the nursing infant. *Psychiatric Services*, **53**, 39–49.

Jacobson, S.W., Jacobson, J.L. and Sokol, R.J. (1994). Effects of fetal alcohol exposure on infant reaction time. *Alcoholism: Clinical and Experimental Research*, **18**, 1125–32.

Jacobson, S.W., Jacobson, J.L., Sokol, R.J., Chiodo, L.M. and Corobana, R. (2004). Maternal age, alcohol abuse history, and quality of parenting as moderators of the effects of prenatal alcohol exposure on 7.5-year intellectual function. *Alcoholism: Clinical and Experimental Research*, **28**, 1732–45.

Johnson, H.L., Glassman, M.B., Fiks, K.B. and Rosen, T.S. (1990). Resilient children: individual differences in developmental outcome of children born to drug abusers. *Journal of Genetic Psychology*, **151**, 523–39.

Jones, K.L. (1975). The fetal alcohol syndrome. *Addictive Diseases*, **2**, 79–88.

Jones, K.L. (1986). Fetal alcohol syndrome. *Pediatrics in Review*, **8**, 122–26.

Jones, K.L. and Smith, D.W. (1973). Recognition of the fetal alcohol syndrome in early infancy. *Lancet* 2, 999–1001.

Jones, K.L., Smith, D.W., Ulleland, C.N. and Streissguth, P. (1973). Pattern of malformation in offspring of chronic alcoholic mothers. *Lancet*, **1**, 1267–71.

Keaney, F., Strang, J., Gossop, M., *et al.* (2001). A double-blind randomised placebo-controlled trial of lofexidine in alcohol withdrawal: lofexidine is not a useful adjunct to chlordiazepoxide. *Alcohol and Alcoholism*, **36**, 426–30.

Khan, K.S., Wykes, C. and Gee, H. (1999). Benzodiazepine use in pregnancy and major malformations or oral clefts. Quality of primary studies must influence inferences made from meta-analyses. *British Medical Journal*, **319**, 919.

Kumar, S., Singh, R.K., Goswami, U. and Khastgir, U. (2005). A study of the temporal course of phenomenology of alcohol dependence. *American Journal of Addiction*, **14**, 213–22.

Kushner, M.G., Abrams, K., Thuras, P., Hanson, K.L., Brekke, M. and Sletten, S. (2005). Follow-up study of anxiety disorder and alcohol dependence in comorbid alcoholism treatment patients. *Alcoholism: Clinical and Experimental Research*, **29**, 1432–43.

Leonardson, G.R. and Loudenburg, R. (2003). Risk factors for alcohol use during pregnancy in a multistate area. *Neurotoxicology and Teratology*, **25**, 651–58.

Lesch, O.M. and Walter, H. (1996). New 'state' markers for the detection of alcoholism. *Alcohol and Alcoholism*, **Suppl.1**, 59–62.

Lesch, O.M., Walter, H., Freitag, H., *et al.* (1996). Carbohydrate-deficient transferrin as a screening marker for drinking in a general hospital population. *Alcohol and Alcoholism*, **31**, 249–56.

Limin, S., Jarvie, D.R., Chick, J. and Simpson, D. (1999). Limitations of CDT and GGT in detecting relapses in patients attending an alcohol problems clinic. *Scottish Medical Journal*, **44**, 140–42.

Little, B.B., Snell, L.M., van Beveren, T.T., Crowell, R.B., Trayler, S. and Johnston, W.L. (2003). Treatment of substance abuse during pregnancy and infant outcome. *American Journal of Perinatology*, **20**, 255–62.

Little, J.F., Hepper, P.G. and Dornan, J.C. (2002). Maternal alcohol consumption during pregnancy and fetal startle behaviour. *Physiology and Behavior*, **76**, 691–94.

Little, R.E. and Streissguth, A.P. (1981). Effects of alcohol on the fetus: impact and prevention. *Canadian Medical Association Journal*, **125**, 159–64.

Livy, D.J., Maier, S.E. and West, J.R. (2001). Fetal alcohol exposure and temporal vulnerability: effects of binge-like alcohol exposure on the ventrolateral nucleus of the thalamus. *Alcoholism: Clinical and Experimental Research*, **25**, 774–80.

Livy, D.J., Miller, E.K., Maier, S.E. and West, J.R. (2003). Fetal alcohol exposure and temporal vulnerability: effects of binge-like alcohol exposure on the developing rat hippocampus. *Neurotoxicology and Teratology*, **25**, 447–58.

Maier, S.E., Chen, W.J., Miller, J.A. and West, J.R. (1997). Fetal alcohol exposure and temporal vulnerability regional differences in alcohol-induced microencephaly as a function of the timing of binge-like alcohol exposure during rat brain development. *Alcoholism: Clinical and Experimental Research*, **21**, 1418–28.

Maier, S.E., Miller, J.A. and West, J.R. (1999). Prenatal binge-like alcohol exposure in the rat results in region-specific deficits in brain growth. *Neurotoxicology and Teratology*, **21**, 285–91.

Martin, C.R. and Bonner, A.B. (2000). A pilot investigation of the effect of tryptophan manipulation on the affective state of male chronic alcoholics. *Alcohol and Alcoholism*, **35**, 49–51.

Maser, G.R. (1977). Drug abuse. Alcoholic convulsions and delirium tremens. *Journal of the Kansas Medical Society*, **78**, 228–29.

Mattson, S.N., Riley, E.P., Gramling, L., Delis, D.C. and Jones, K.L. (1997). Heavy prenatal alcohol exposure with or without physical features of fetal alcohol syndrome leads to IQ deficits. *Journal of Pediatrics*, **131**, 718–21.

Mattson, S.N., Riley, E.P., Gramling, L., Delis, D.C. and Jones, K.L. (1998). Neuropsychological comparison of alcohol-exposed children with or without physical features of fetal alcohol syndrome. *Neuropsychology*, **12**, 146–53.

May, P.A. and Gossage, J.P. (2001). Estimating the prevalence of fetal alcohol syndrome. A summary. *Alcohol Research and Health*, **25**, 159–67.

May, P.A., Gossage, J.P., Brooke, L.E., *et al.* (2005). Maternal risk factors for fetal alcohol syndrome in the Western cape province of South Africa: a population-based study. *American Journal of Public Health*, **95**, 1190–99.

May, P.A., Gossage, J.P., White-Country, M., *et al.* (2004). Alcohol consumption and other maternal risk factors for fetal alcohol syndrome among three distinct samples of women before, during, and after pregnancy: the risk is relative. *American Journal of Medical Genetics College Seminars in Medical Genetics*, **127**, 10–20.

Mayfield, D., McLeod, G. and Hall, P. (1974). The CAGE questionnaire: validation of a new alcoholism screening instrument. *American Journal of Psychiatry*, **131**, 1121–23.

Mayo-Smith, M.F. and Bernard, D. (1995). Late-onset seizures in alcohol withdrawal. *Alcoholism: Clinical and Experimental Research*, **19**, 656–59.

McNamara, T.K., Orav, E.J., Wilkins-Haug, L. and Chang, G. (2005). Risk during pregnancy – self-report versus medical record. *American Journal of Obstetrics and Gynecology*, **193**, 1981–85.

Medical Council on Alcohol (2006). *A few drinks can last a lifetime. If you are pregnant. DON'T DRINK*. Liverpool: Fetal Alcohol Syndrome Trust.

Moraes, C.L., Viellas, E.F. and Reichenheim, M.E. (2005). Assessing alcohol misuse during pregnancy: evaluating psychometric properties of the CAGE, T-ACE and TWEAK in a Brazilian setting. *Journal of Studies on Alcohol,* **66**, 165–73.

Nakahara, T., Hashimoto, K., Hirano, M., Koll, M., Martin, C.R. and Preedy, V.R. (2003). Acute and chronic effects of alcohol exposure on skeletal muscle *c-myc*, *p53*, and *Bcl-2* mRNA expression. *American Journal of Physiology, Endocrinology and Metabolism*, **285**, E1273–81.

Nakahara, T., Hirano, M., Uchimura, H., *et al.* (2002). Chronic alcohol feeding and its influence on *c-Fos* and *heat shock protein-70* gene expression in different brain regions of male and female rats. *Metabolism*, **51**, 1562–68.

Nanson, J.L. (1997). Binge drinking during pregnancy: who are the women at risk? *Canadian Medical Association Journal*, **156**, 807–08.

National Center on Birth Defects and Developmental Disabilities (2004). *Fetal Alcohol Syndrome: Guidelines for Referral and Diagnosis*. National Center on Birth Defects and Developmental Disabilities and National Task Force on Fetal Alcohol Syndrome and Fetal Alcohol Effect. Available at: http://www.guideline.gov/summary/summary.aspx?doc_id=5960 (last accessed August 2008).

Olbrich, R. (1979). Alcohol withdrawal states and the need for treatment. *British Journal of Psychiatry*, **134**, 466–69.

Pandey, S.C., Saito, T., Yoshimura, M., Sohma, H. and Gotz, M.E. (2001). cAmp signaling cascade: a promising role in ethanol tolerance and dependence. *Alcoholism: Clinical and Experimental Research*, **25**, 46S–48S.

Patton, R. and Touquet, R. (2002). The Paddington Alcohol Test. *British Journal of General Practice*, **52**, 59.

Pedersen, W. and Skrondal, A. (1999). Ecstasy and new patterns of drug use: a normal population study. *Addiction*, **94**, 1695–1706.

Pokorny, A.D., Miller, B.A. and Kaplan, H.B. (1972). The brief MAST: a shortened version of the Michigan Alcoholism Screening Test. *American Journal of Psychiatry*, **129**, 342–45.

Pollock, L. (2004). Is one glass one too many? Experts cannot agree. *Royal College of Midwives*, **7**, 460.

Russell, M., Martier, S.S., Sokol, R.J., *et al. (1994)*. Screening for pregnancy risk-drinking. *Alcoholism: Clinical and Experimental Research*, **18**, 1156–61.

Russell, M., Martier, S.S., Sokol, R.J., Mudar, P., Jacobson, S. and Jacobson, J. (1996). Detecting risk drinking during pregnancy: a comparison of four screening questionnaires. *American Journal of Public Health*, **86**, 1435–39.

Saitz, R. (1995). Recognition and management of occult alcohol withdrawal. *Hospital Practice (Minneapolis)*, **30**, 49.

Sampson, P.D., Streissguth, A.P., Bookstein, F.L. and Barr HM. (2000). On categorizations in analyses of alcohol teratogenesis. *Environmental Health Perspectives*, **108**(Suppl.3), 421–28.

Scott, L.J., Figgitt, D.P., Keam, S.J. and Waugh, J. (2005). Acamprosate: a review of its use in the maintenance of abstinence in patients with alcohol dependence. *CNS Drugs*, **19**, 445–64.

Selzer, M.L. (1968). Michigan Alcoholism Screening Test (MAST): Preliminary report. *University of Michigan Medical Center Journal*, **34**, 143–45.

Shaw, G.K., Waller, S., Majumdar, S.K., Alberts, J.L., Latham, C.J. and Dunn, G. (1994). Tiapride in the prevention of relapse in recently detoxified alcoholics. *British Journal of Psychiatry*, **165**, 515–23.

Shaw, S., Korts, D. and Stimmel, B. (1982). Abnormal liver function tests as biological markers for alcoholism in narcotic addicts. *American Journal of Drug and Alcohol Abuse*, **9**, 345–54.

Sher, L. (2006). Alcoholism and suicidal behaviour: a clinical overview. *Acta Psychiatrica Scandinavica*, **113**, 13–22.

Sillanaukee, P. (1996). Laboratory markers of alcohol abuse. *Alcohol and Alcoholism*, **31**, 613–16.

Sillanaukee, P., Aalto, M. and Seppa, K. (1998). Carbohydrate-deficient transferrin and conventional alcohol markers as indicators for brief intervention among heavy drinkers in primary health care. *Alcoholism: Clinical and Experimental Research*, **22**, 892–96.

Sokol, R.J., Aney-Black, V. and Nordstrom, B. (2003). Fetal alcohol spectrum disorder. *Journal of the American Medical Association*, **290**, 2996–99.

Sokol, R.J., Martier, S.S. and Ager, J.W. (1989). The T-ACE questions: practical prenatal detection of risk-drinking. *American Journal of Obstetrics and Gynecology*, **160**, 863–68.

Staines, G.L., Magura, S., Foote, J., Deluca A, and Kosanke, N. (2001). Polysubstance use among alcoholics. *Journal of Addictive Diseases*, **20**, 53–69.

Streissguth, A.P., Barr, H.M., Kogan, J. and Bookstein, F.L. (1996). *Understanding the Occurrence of Secondary Disabilities in Clients with Fetal Alcohol Syndrome (FAS) and Fetal Alcohol Effects (FAE)*. Final Report to the Centers for Disease Control and Prevention, Technical Report 96–06. Seattle: University of Washington.

Thompson, W.L. (1978). Management of alcohol withdrawal syndromes. *Archives of Internal Medicine*, **138**, 278–83.

US Department of Health and Human Sciences (2005). US Surgeon General Releases Advisory on Alcohol Use in Pregnancy. Available at: http://www.surgeongeneral.gov/pressreleases/sg02222005.html (last accessed August 2008).

Vanclay, F., Raphael, B., Dunne, M., Whitfield, J., Lewin, T. and Singh, B. (1991). A community screening test for high alcohol consumption using biochemical and haematological measures. *Alcohol and Alcoholism*, **26**, 337–46.

Verheul, R., Lehert, P., Geerlings, P.J., *et al.* (2005). Predictors of acamprosate efficacy: results from a pooled analysis of seven European trials including 1485 alcohol-dependent patients. *Psychopharmacology (Berlin)*, **178**, 167–73.

Williams, S.H. (2005). Medications for treating alcohol dependence. *American Family Physician*, **72**, 1775–80.

Wiseman, E.J., Henderson, K.L. and Briggs, M.J. (1998). Individualized treatment for outpatients withdrawing from alcohol. *Journal of Clinical Psychiatry*, **59**, 289–93.

28 Children's cognitive development between the ages of 8 and 12 and alcohol consumption

Susan Atkinson

There is growing concern about levels of drinking and particularly about binge drinking among teenagers and young adults (Alcohol Concern, 2007). There is also some evidence that younger children between the ages of 8 and 12 may be drinking more often and more heavily than before (Erens, 2002). This chapter looks at this evidence, specifically the pattern of normal cognitive development in this age group and the possible effects of regular or heavy alcohol consumption on cognitive development.

Evidence for levels of alcohol consumption among children aged 8 to 12 years old

Questionnaire surveys of children in this age group and evidence from hospital admissions suggest that a small proportion of these children are drinking alcohol more often (Erens, 2002), and when they do, they are drinking more heavily than previous surveys indicated (Erens and Hedges, 1997; Erens, 2002). The charity Alcohol Concern (2007) recently expressed concern about this, arguing that the legal age at which children are allowed to drink alcohol in the home should be raised from 5 to 15 years. Concerns relate to the likely physical effects of alcohol on children during a stage of rapid growth, to the risks of alcohol poisoning through accidental over-consumption relative to body size and weight, and to the documented links between age of the first drink and later problems with alcohol dependency. Very little evidence exists on the effects of alcohol consumption at this stage on cognitive development.

The experience of drinking in the age range 8–15 years is probably under-reported in home-based interviews (Erens, 2002) despite assurances of anonymity. According to Erens, at age 8, 14 per cent of boys and 8 per cent of girls claimed to have had an alcoholic drink at some point. By age 15, these proportions had risen to 87 per cent of boys and 86 per cent of girls. The frequency of consumption increases after age 13 with 26 per cent of boys and 22 per cent of girls saying they drink at least once a week.

The frequency of drinking does not appear to be linked to the socioeconomic status of their household (Erens, 2002). The proportion of children claiming to drink alcohol at least once a week has not changed between the Health Surveys for England in 1997 (Erens and Hedges,

1997) and 2002 (Erens, 2002) up until age 15. Among 11–13-year-olds who drink, consumption has doubled: teenagers are drinking more frequently and more heavily (Erens, 2002). As a result, Alcohol Concern is calling for it to be made illegal for children to drink at home before they are 15 (Diment *et al.*, 2007).

This suggests that the proportion of children drinking alcohol in this age bracket has not changed greatly over 5 years, though those in the sample appear to be drinking more when they do. Therefore, this chapter will discuss normal cognitive development and the likely effects of alcohol consumption on cognitive development in this age group.

Cognitive development in children aged 8 to 12 years

By the age of 8, most children have developed basic academic skills, particularly in literacy and mathematics and, over this period, automaticity develops in many skills. Cognitive development is characterised by increases in processing speed, efficiency and automaticity. This is enabled by spurts in brain growth (particularly in the frontal lobes) and myelinisation, affecting logical thought, spatial and attentional skills (Boyd and Bee, 2006). Automaticity is the ability to recall information directly from the long-term memory; it frees up the short-term memory for more complex processing. For example, motor skills like riding a bicycle become automatic, resulting in attention being available for coping with riding in traffic; cognitive skills like reading (word decoding) and spelling become automatic at these ages, allowing more attention to be paid to understanding the meaning (comprehension) of text or to conveying meaning (in writing). Automaticity, as well as metacognitive skills (knowing what one knows and how and when to learn and apply strategies to a situation) develop from changes in memory functioning.

Although there is evidence that the structure of children's memory is akin to that of adults from the age of 4 years (Alloway, Gathercole, Willis and Adams, 2004), their capacity and rehearsal strategies mature to adult levels over the course of the primary school years by about the age of 12. These changes in functioning are linked closely to developmental changes in attention and skill automaticity. Memory capacity, as shown by increases in recall of digit, letter or word spans, increases throughout middle childhood, due to development of processing efficiency and speed (Kail and Hall, 1994) and verbal articulation rates (Hulme *et al.*, 1984; Nicolson, 1981). There are also changes in rehearsal strategies and recoding, and the ability to apply these spontaneously and to effect. Spontaneous rehearsal in working memory, enabling the retention of information for longer and delaying decay, develops at about 7 years of age (Baddeley *et al.*, 1998; Gathercole *et al.*, 1994). Many children able to use articulatory rehearsal to support performance in some memory tasks by the age of 8 (Henry and Millar, 1993). Developmental changes in the rehearsal process can be identified, from the use of no strategy or simple labelling to remember stimuli in children aged between 4 and 6, with the more mature strategies of chunking and cumulative rehearsal appearing at about the age of 8 as verbal recoding of stimuli becomes more efficient (Palmer, 2000; Pickering, 2001). Between 8 and 12, children begin to use these strategies spontaneously to benefit recall (Pickering, 2001).

Memory skills have also been implicated as a factor in reading and literacy difficulties (de Jong, 1998; Siegel and Ryan, 1989; Swanson, 1994) in the acquisition of arithmetic skills (Bull and Scerif, 2001; Passolunghi and Siegel, 2001), in science (Gathercole *et al.*, 2004; Jarvis and

Gathercole, 2003), in college entrance scores (Daneman and Carpenter, 1980; Jurden, 1995) and in occupational success (Kyllonen and Chrystal, 1990).

At this stage, language skills also continue to develop: children learn how to employ a variety of ways to talk about the past, maintaining the topic of a conversation, creating unambiguous sentences, and how to sway their audience. New vocabulary is learned at the rate of several thousand words per year (Boyd and Bee, 2006). According to Anglin (1993; in Boyd and Bee, 2006), at age 8 or 9, there is a shift to a new level of understanding of the structure of language, realising the relationships between categories of words such as adjectives and adverbs or adjectives and nouns. The school curriculum also becomes increasingly dependent on literacy skills, and reading level and amount of reading affect the development of knowledge, vocabulary and intelligence (Stanovich, 1986). Children need to learn to read words quickly, fluently and automatically in order to develop effective reading comprehension skills and to apply these skills to other areas of learning. According to Stanovich (1986), 8 years of age is the crucial time when differences between competent readers and those falling behind become obvious and widen. Reading skill at this age impacts on later cognitive skills and knowledge (Cunningham and Stanovich, 1991), such as vocabulary development (Stanovich, 1986), comprehension ability (Stanovich and Cunningham, 1992) and declarative knowledge (Stanovich *et al.*, 1995).

Between the ages of 8 and 12, many children develop high levels of expertise and knowledge in areas of particular interest to them. Domain-specific knowledge can enable children to show memory capacity and use of strategies equivalent to or beyond that of older people. Chi (1978) demonstrated that expert chess players remember arrangements of chess pieces more quickly and accurately than novice players, even when the experts are children with adult novices. Schneider (1993) argues that domain-specific knowledge does not only allow children to process and remember domain-related information more efficiently, but also enables them to use strategies and new information more effectively in that domain than in areas where they lack specialist knowledge. In effect, specialist knowledge can scaffold and support memory capacity, strategies and metamemory. Domain-specific specialist knowledge, however, may not generalise more widely in children of this age. According to Johnson, Scott and Mervis (2004) specialist expertise about dinosaurs and their features may not generalise to other biological groupings and knowledge or theories, or indeed, beyond familiar dinosaurs.

Children's cognitive development at this stage, then, can be seen to be characterised by increasingly mature memory, language and metacognitive skills, by wider automaticity of both motor and academic skills, and deepening knowledge and expertise in areas of special interest which can support performance in that area, even though it may not be generalisable.

The effects of alcohol consumption on cognitive development in children aged 8 to 12 years old

There is little direct research evidence on the effects of alcohol consumption on cognitive development in this age group. This may be because most children of this age who drink any alcohol probably drink too little or too infrequently for the effects to be grossly apparent or to cause measurable brain damage. Lack of evidence may also result from the difficulties inherent in collecting reliable information on levels of alcohol consumption (Erens, 2002). Although serious physical problems seem to be rare in children who drink alcohol (Paton, 1999), they are more vulnerable to its effects than adults: a lower blood alcohol concentration causes more significant clinical effects, including more rapid development of coma (Lamminpaa, 1995). Ethanol may, however, be eliminated twice as quickly in children up to 13 years of age compared with adults (Lamminpaa, 1995).

Alcohol consumption also puts children at greater risk of accidents and assaults (Newburn and Shiner, 2001), but deaths directly from alcohol are rare. Long-term health effects for adolescents of heavy drinking (Alcohol Concern, 2006) include raised liver enzymes indicating damage; lowered hormone levels; lower bone mineral density in adolescent boys; reduced hippocampal volume in the brain (affecting memory and learning); and changes in the structure of white matter in the corpus callosum. Alcohol in any quantity acts as a depressant on the central nervous system, leading to dulling and slowing of the brain's responses, including reaction times, thought processes and coordination, as well as slurred speech, loss of self-control, blackouts, and memory failure when taken in large amounts (Alcohol Concern, 2006). As yet we do not know at what level of alcohol consumption damage occurs in children and adolescents (depending both on body weight and liver enzyme levels), or whether alcohol-induced changes are incremental and cumulative (building up over time), or whether changes may be caused following each exposure to alcohol. Even though even mild to moderate drinking can adversely affect cognitive functioning, research has shown that adolescent alcohol abusers (aged 10 years or more) show poorer language function than non-alcohol abusers, but they do not show neuropsychological signs of brain damage (Moss *et al.*, 1994, in Chassin and DeLucia, 1996).

An important question relates to whether the differences in cognitive functioning between children who drink alcohol and those who do not may predate alcohol consumption: does failure to achieve academically, and therefore disengagement and disaffection with education, lead to drinking problems?

Concerns have been expressed (by Alcohol Concern, 2007, among others) that the age at which children begin to drink is related to later problems with alcohol. The age at which children first drink is dependent on the society or culture within which they live and the norms within it, such as the patterns of drinking. Societies with an expectation of social drinking around meal times, such as France, Italy and Spain, report fewer problems with this than societies with binge-drinking cultures where alcohol may be seen as a youth-related problem, such as in the UK and Scandinavia and possibly Eastern Europe. The onset of drinking in early adolescence before the age of 16 has been related to level of alcohol use in adulthood (Pitkanen *et al.*, 2005), but in Pitkanen's longitudinal study socioemotional behaviour and school success at age 8 did not predict the age of onset of drinking. Drinking at an early age has been associated with later alcoholism in some western societies, but this relationship may not be causal: according to Prescott and Kendler (1999), children who begin to drink at a young age show high rates of disinhibited behaviour and psychopathology beforehand. So alcohol use may be a symptom of lack of behavioural control rather than the other way round. Fergusson *et al.* (1995), in a longitudinal study of 953 children, examined factors predicting problem drinking at 16. Significant predictors of abusive or hazardous drinking included: gender (males were more likely to develop problem drinking), the amount of alcohol consumed at age 14, and the number of friendships with substance-using peers at age 15. Family social background, changes of parents, levels of parental alcohol consumption, age of first drink and early conduct problems were not directly related to later drinking behaviour, but were associated with heavy alcohol use at 14 and affiliations with alcohol-using peers at 15.

It has also been suggested that a childhood diagnosis of attention deficit hyperactivity disorder (ADHD) may be a causal factor in alcohol-related problems, and that the rate of ADHD may be as high as 50 per cent in populations at high risk of drinking problems (Smith *et al.*, 2002). Under-achievement in school is a consequence of ADHD due to attentional and behavioural problems.

According to evidence from a longitudinal study (Wong, 2004) sleep problems in early childhood (ages 3–5) predict the early onset of use of alcohol, cigarettes and illicit drugs. Sleep problems in themselves can cause cognitive deficits. Mitchell (2005) argues that sleep-disordered breathing (SDB) causes reduced attention and memory, lower verbal and global IQ scores, and poorer problem-solving ability. Beebe and Gozal (2002) support this – childhood obstructive sleep apnoea (OSA) is associated with school failure and executive system dysfunction (disorganisation, rigid thinking, problems with judgement, attention, motivation, memory, planning, mood swings, impulsivity).

Evidence, then, for the negative effects of alcohol consumption on cognitive development in this age group is limited. A lack of finances and opportunity to buy alcohol may restrict most children's opportunities to consume large amounts with any regularity. For a small number of children, even small amounts could affect their functioning in the short-term and perhaps hinder optimum development, preventing them from achieving their potential in terms of academic attainment. Alcohol may interfere with the development of brain structures and with myelinisation processes at this stage, therefore hampering later cognitive skills.

Alcohol intake may also affect cognitive development in other ways; if the child is unwell as a result of alcohol he or she may miss school, or he or she may not have had adequate sleep or nutrition. If alcohol also interferes with attention, then their time at school may not be utilised well. In the absence of reliable research in this age group, it would be difficult to reliably identify the children whose cognitive development is suffering as a result of alcohol intake, as opposed to (or separately from) other indices of deprivation or at-risk status such as family background, socioeconomic status and previously existing conditions affecting cognitive development.

Conclusions

Many questions could usefully be addressed by future research on children in this age range. These include determining whether it is possible to identify any negative effects on their cognitive development as a result of mild to moderate sporadic exposure to alcohol. It may be possible to identify which of these children are most at risk from alcohol consumption.

The effectiveness of interventions targeted at specific populations should be investigated, including whole-population approaches like those advocated by groups such as Alcohol Concern – how well do they tackle the problems of this age group? Should the effects of alcohol consumption on cognitive development be the primary concern at this age, or is it more constructive to consider the whole child and their family circumstances? More work is needed to establish guidelines for parents to use regarding safe quantities of alcohol for children of this age group to drink, as well as advice on frequency of drinking.

References and further reading

Alcohol Concern (2006). *Acquire – Alcohol Concern's Quarterly Information and Research Bulletin: Young People's Drinking.* Available at: www.alcoholconcern.org/files/20070315_153945 (last accessed August 2008).

Alcohol Concern (2007). *Alcohol consumption amongst children reaches new heights.* Press release. Available at: www.alcoholconcern.org.uk/servlets/doc/1189 (last accessed August 2008).

Alloway, T.P., Gethercole, S., Willis, C.S. and Adams, A.M. ((2004). A structural analysis of working memory and related cognitive skills in young children. *Journal of Experimental Child Psychology*, **87**(2), 85–106.

Baddeley, A., Gathercole, S.E. and Papagno, C. (1998). The phonological loop as a language learning device. *Psychological Review*, **105**, 158–73.

Beebe, D.W. and Gozal, D. (2002). Obstructive sleep apnea and the prefrontal cortex: towards a comprehensive model linking nocturnal upper airway obstruction to daytime cognitive and behavioural deficits. *Journal of Sleep Research*, **11**(1), 1–16.

Boyd, D. and Bee, H. (2006). *Lifespan Development.* Boston, MA: Pearson Education.

Bull, R. and Scerif, G. (2001). Executive functioning as a predictor of children's mathematics ability: Inhibition, switching, and working memory. *Developmental Neuropsychology*, **19**, 273–93.

Chassin, L. and DeLucia, C. (1996). Drinking during adolescence. *Alcohol Health and Research World*, **20** (3), 175–81.

Chi, M. (1978). Knowledge structure and memory development. In: R.S. Siegler (ed.) *Children's Thinking: What Develops?* Hillsdale, NJ: Erlbaum.

Cunningham, A.E. and Stanovich, K.E. (1991). Tracking the unique effects of print exposure in children: Associations with vocabulary, general knowledge, and spelling. *Journal of Educational Psychology*, **83**, 264–74.

Daneman, M. and Carpenter, P.A. (1980). Individual differences in working memory and reading. *Journal of Verbal Learning and Verbal Behavior*, **19**, 450–66.

de Jong, P.F. (1998). Working memory deficits of reading-disabled children. *Journal of Experimental Child Psychology*, **70**, 75–96.

Diment, E., Shenker, D. and Sen, S. (2007). *A Glass Half Empty?* London: Alcohol Concern.

Erens, B. (2002). Alcohol consumption. In: K. Sproston and P. Primatesta (eds). *Health Survey for England 2002: The Health of Children and Young People.* London: The Stationery Office.

Erens, B. and Hedges, B. (1997). Alcohol consumption. In: P. Prescott-Clarke and P. Primatesta (eds). *Health Survey for England: The Health of Young People 1995–97.* London: The Stationery Office.

Fergusson, D.M., Horwood, L.J. and Lynskey, M.T. (1995). The prevalence and risk factors associated with abusive or hazardous alcohol consumption in 16-year-olds. *Addiction*, **90**, 935–46.

Gathercole, S.E., Adams, A-M. and Hitch, G.J. (1994). Do young children rehearse? An individual differences approach. *Memory and Cognition*, **22**, 201–07.

Gathercole, S.E., Pickering, S.J., Knight, C. and Stegmann, Z. (2004). Working memory skills and educational attainment: evidence from National Curriculum assessments at 7 and 14 years of age. *Applied Cognitive Psychology*, **18**, 1–16.

Henry, L.A. and Millar, S. (1993). Why does memory span increase with age? A review of the evidence for two current hypotheses. *European Journal of Cognitive Psychology*, **5**, 241–87.

Hulme, C., Thomson, N., Muir, C. and Lawrence, A. (1984). Speech rate and the development of short-term memory span. *Journal of Experimental Child Psychology*, **38**, 241–53.

Jarvis, H.L. and Gathercole, S.E. (2003). Verbal and nonverbal working memory and achievements on national curriculum tests at 11 and 14 years of age. *Educational and Child Psychology*, **20**, 123–40.

Johnson, K.E., Scott, P. and Mervis, C.B. (2004). What are theories for? Concept use throughout the continuum of dinosaur expertise. *Journal of Experimental Child Psychology*, **87**(3), 171–200.

Jurden, F.H. (1995). Individual differences in working memory and complex cognition. *Journal of Educational Psychology*, **87**, 93–102.

Kail, R. and Hall, L.K. (1994). Processing speed, naming speed, and reading. *Developmental Psychology*, **30**, 949–54.

Kyllonen, P.C. and Chrystal, R.E. (1990). Reasoning ability is (little more than) working memory capacity. *Intelligence*, **14**, 389–433.

Lamminpaa, A. (1995). Alcohol intoxication in childhood and adolescence. *Alcohol and Alcoholism*, **30**(1), 5–12.

Mitchell, R.B. (2005). Sleep-disordered breathing in children. *European Respiratory Journal*, **25**, 216–17.

Newburn, T. and Shiner, M. (2001). *Teenage Kicks? Young People and Alcohol: A Review of the Literature*. Joseph Rowntree Foundation: York.

Nicolson, R. (1981). The relationship between memory span and processing speed. In: M. Friedman, J.P. Dass and N. O'Connor (eds). *Intelligence and Learning*. New York: Plenum Press.

Palmer, S. (2000). Working memory: a developmental study of phonological recoding. *Memory*, **8**, 3. 179–93.

Passolunghi, M.C. and Siegel, L.S. (2001). Short-term memory, working memory, and inhibitory control in children with difficulties in arithmetic problem solving. *Journal of Experimental Child Psychology*, **80**(1), 44–57.

Paton, A. (1999). Reflections on alcohol and the young. *Alcohol and Alcoholism*, **34**(4), 502–05.

Pickering, S. (2001). The development of visuo-spatial working memory. *Memory*, **9**. 423–32.

Pitkanen, T., Lyyra, A. and Pulkkinen, L. (2005). Age of onset of drinking and the use of alcohol on adulthood: a follow-up study from age 8–42 for females and males. *Addiction*, **100**, 652–61.

Prescott, C.A. and Kendler, K.S. (1999). Age at first drink and risk for alcoholism: A noncausal association. *Alcoholism: Clinical and Experimental Research*, **23**(1), 101–07.

Schneider, W. (1993). Domain-specific knowledge and memory performance in children. *Educational Psychology Reviews*, **5**(3), 257–73.

Siegel, L.S. and Ryan, E.B. (1989). The development of working memory in normally achieving and subtypes of learning disabled children. *Child Development*, **60**, 973–80.

Smith, B.H., Molina, B.S.G. and Pelham, W.E. (2002). The clinically meaningful link between alcohol use and attention deficit hyperactivity disorder. *Alcohol Research and Health*, **26**(2), 122–29.

Stanovich, K.E. (1986). Matthew effects in reading: some consequences of individual differences in the acquisition of literacy. *Reading Research Quarterly*, **21**, 360–406.

Stanovich, K.E. and Cunningham, A.E. (1992). Studying the consequences of literacy within a literate society: The cognitive correlates of print exposure. *Memory and Cognition*, **20**, 51–68.

Stanovich, K.E., West, R.E. and Harrison, M. (1995). Knowledge growth and maintenance across the life-span: The role of print exposure. *Developmental Psychology*, **31**, 811–26.

Swanson, H.L. (1994). Short-term memory and working memory – Do both contribute to our understanding of academic achievement in children and adults with learning disabilities? *Journal of Learning Disabilities*, **27**, 34–50.

Wong, M.M. (2004). Sleep problems in early childhood and early onset of alcohol and other drug use in adolescence. *Alcoholism: Clinical and Experimental Research*, **28**(1), 578–87.

Concluding comments

Colin R. Martin

A review of the structure of this volume reveals a constellation of chapters covering topics as diverse as liver disease to spirituality within the context of alcohol dependency. The concept of alcohol dependency, its identification and its treatment, remains an area surrounded by controversy and often poorly informed opinion, although there is impressive progress in developing a coherent and integrated evidence base for approaching this enigmatic clinical presentation with confidence and optimism. There are many debates in the area of alcohol dependency that remain that, debates with a dominance of opinion and no robust conclusion. An example of this is the aetiological debate on the development of alcohol dependency, since at one extreme it can be considered purely a behavioural problem with roots in classical conditioning to another extreme where it may be perceived as essentially a disease in itself requiring medical management within a medical model. There are advocates for both perspectives and indeed, there is a whole spectrum of opinion somewhere between. However, health professionals must act within strict clinical guidelines which are, of course, subject to change and review, following the emergence of new contributions to the research literature within the field. Major advances in our understanding of alcohol dependency are being made apace, and keeping abreast of such developments not only contributes to the clinicians and academics continuing professional development but also helps optimise the client experience as recipient of expert care.

It is hoped that the rich tapestry of information contained within the chapters of this book will promote insight and good practice, in addition to facilitating discussion of the important issues central to the understanding of alcohol dependency at every level. If this book can help in these ways, then it has done what I intended.

Useful websites

Alcohol Concern
http://www.alcoholconcern.org

British Medical Association
http://www.bma.org

Department of Health
http://www.dh.gov.uk

European Medicines Agency (EMEA)
http://www.emea.europa.eu

Information Services Division of NHS National Services Scotland
http://www.alcoholinformation.isdscotland.org

National Association for Children of Alcoholics (NACOA)
http://www.nacoa.org.uk

National Institute for Health and Clinical Excellence
http://www.nice.org.uk

National Institute of Drug Abuse
http://www.nida.nih.gov

NHS Direct
http://www.nhsdirect.nhs.uk

NHS Quality Improvement Scotland
http://www.nhshealthquality.org

Oxford Bottled Beer database
http://www.bottledbeer.co.uk

Project MATCH (Matching Alcoholism Treatments to Client Heterogeneity)
http://www.pmatch.org

Scottish Intercollegiate Guidelines Network (SIGN)
http://www.sign.ac.uk

World Health Organization
http://www.who.int/nmh/WHA58.26en.pdf